FORERUNNERS AND RIVALS OF CHRISTIANITY

FORERUNNERS AND RIVALS OF CHRISTIANITY

FROM 330 B.C. TO 330 A.D.

FRANCIS LEGGE

IN TWO VOLUMES
BOUND AS ONE

Volume I

UNIVERSITY BOOKS New Hyde Park, New York

Thanks are due to the Libraries of the Union Theological Seminary
and the General Theological Seminary for providing
copies of this book for reproduction purposes

INTRODUCTION

THE EASIEST PART OF THIS BOOK to read, and the most obviously interesting, are the first chapters. These are largely great historical narrative. They tell us how the world empire created by Alexander survived
him as a world culture, Greek its common tongue, and how the local
gods and rites gave way to (more accurately, blended into) trans-
continental religions. In this grand arena the Gnostic "forerunners"
became the rivals of Christianity; Mithraism became the principal
religion of the Roman Legions; Manes founded the Manichean religion. It takes some seven centuries for one of these religions to become
dominant.

Beyond the first chapters of quite brilliant narrative the going
becomes harder. For now it is no longer narrative, but a full description of the religious beliefs and practices of the time. And these are so
strange, so outlandish, so unfamiliar, that the reader is hard-put to
relate to them. If the lay reader is reasonably well informed, by
today's standards, he will bring to these ensuing chapters some famili-
arity with the doctrines and the tales of the Old Testament and the
New. But what this reader will be confronted with appears, at least on
the first reading, to bear very little resemblance to what he knows.
What is bewildering about it is that many of the names are familiar,
but in utterly strange contexts. The later Gnostic literature, for
example, abounds in references to Jesus, Mary, Joseph, St. Paul,
Jerusalem, but it is as though these familiar names had been written
over the names in a Hindu pantheon or an African cosmogony. The
chapters on Mithra are a respite, for there are no familiar names tied
to unfamiliar tales. Then comes the long section on the Manicheans
and, unless the reader has learned elsewhere about the later Manicheans
of the Middle Ages, the victims of the Albigensian Crusade, once
again the reader is plunged into a bewildering literature which uses
familiar names but tied to alien doctrines and stories. Here is Adam,

but not the Adam of Genesis; Eve is not the mother of mankind but a she-fiend; the God of the Old Testament creates only evil; Jesus is eternal but never walked this earth; baptism usually takes place at death; Christianity is anti-Christ.

To grasp any substantial part of this the reader must be able to keep two ideas in mind.

The first is that he is reading about the forerunners and rivals of *ancient* Christianity. All of this is no more outlandish than was ancient Christianity itself. One must be able to put aside the modern versions and rationalizations of Christianity: not only the latest soothing sermons, but also the honest and resolute grappling of ministers and priests in the age of reconciliation between religion and science, the belated adaptation of Roman Catholicism begun by Pope John, and so on. One must be able to read afresh the New Testament and grasp to the full that its Jesus is a wonder-working rabbi. It is helpful to read, in order to get into the right frame of mind, the literature that actually belongs with the New Testament, but which fell by the wayside: the Apocrypha and the Pseudepigrapha. If the reader can thus get himself back in the state of mind and emotion of ancient Christianity, he will then be able to read in the same spirit the otherwise outlandish and fantastic myths of the Gnostics, the Mithraites and the Manicheans.

The second idea that the reader must hold in mind is the quite abrupt and decisive change which came when the Roman state adopted the Christian religion. Major force thereafter intervened in the competition among the religions. To this day we know, at bottom, quite little about the rivals of Christianity, for the good and sufficient reason that their history was written by the victors, who burned the books of their rivals, destroyed their churches, broke into pieces their stone monuments. As our author says elsewhere in his Introduction to one of the Gnostic fragments that escaped destruction, the *Pistis Sophia,* "We know from Eusebius that it was the policy of the triumphant Church after the pact with Constantine to destroy all the writings of the heretics, and that this policy was continuous is shown by the advice given by St. Augustine to burn, without regard for their volume or beauty, all the manuscripts of the Manicheans." Our author wrote the present book fifty years ago. New finds have been made since then of literary fragments belonging to the rivals of Christianity, but not enough to make a great difference. The plain fact is that Christian destruction of the ancient records and literature, sometimes dramatic as when bishops led mobs to burn libraries as at Alexandria, in the main not dramatic but routine clerical activity of destruction going on for centuries, did succeed in preventing humanity from ever successfully reconstructing what the others were like.

If the reader will keep these two ideas in mind, difficulties with this book will cease to deter him.

Francis Legge, who died in 1922 (his birthday, curiously enough, is not recorded in the obituaries but he had been a prominent scholar in Biblical archeology and related subjects for more than thirty years) is best understood as one of the immediate successors to the founders of comparative religion. This book appeared in 1915. Forlong's *Faiths of Man* had appeared in 1904, Frazer's *Golden Bough* in 1900. None of this work was welcomed by the powers that be, for England and Europe remained Christendom, and all this work was necessarily inimical to Christianity's claim to uniqueness. But by the time Legge wrote there was no longer great public controversy over these matters. He spent his life in fairly high posts as a permanent civil servant and wrote at no risk, or no great one. But this was because he stood on the shoulders of those who had won toleration for him. As he himself tells in his Introduction to later editions of Wynwood Reade's *Martyrdom of Man*, which was one of the first works (1872) prepared under the influence of the doctrine of organic evolution, and which showed the human origin of religion and waged war on clerical power, a veritable storm broke out about the head and person of the author, and Legge makes quite plain that he attributes to the abuse of this controversy the early death of Wynwood Reade in 1875. Reade's last work, published in the year of his death, is a novel called *The Outcasts* — the outcasts being those who dared to describe the human origin of religion. Legge was a grateful heir to the victories of the free-thought struggles of 1860-1910. Within the space of his own adult lifetime, when he himself was already writing on the Gnostics, Legge had witnessed such a spectacle as Balliol College at Oxford refusing to provide a room in which the Hibbert Lectures could be given (1893) by the distinguished Belgian scholar, Count Goblet d'Alviella. The principal scholarly societies to which Legge devoted his life, the Society of Biblical Archeology, and the Royal Asiatic Society, were created by laymen and functioned outside the academic pale. Because archeology and comparative religion remained unpalatable to the Establishment, when the author of *Faiths of Man,* Forlong, died in 1904, he left money to the Royal Asiatic Society and the Rationalist Press Association for the publication of works in this field.

The reader may today comfort himself with the thought that all these battles have been won and that now most of this scholarly work has been taken under the wing of the great universities. So it seems, for biblical archeology, to take one example, is under the aegis of the universities, and there are no longer laymen to be found like Legge. But is it really so? Were it so, why is it that this book has never been reprinted since 1915? Why is it that it is reprinted now, not under

INTRODUCTION

academic auspices, but outside? This is true not only of this book, but of the main body of the books written by the generation which founded comparative religion, and especially the books which seriously set out to tell the history of Christianity without fear or favor. The comparative religion, biblical archeology, critical study of Christianity which have found their place in the universities remain, to a quite considerable extent, emasculated. For, let the occasion of this book's reappearance remind us, we still live in Christendom.

June 15, 1964
JOHN C. WILSON

PREFACE

THE following pages are a modest attempt to bring before the public certain documents of great importance for the understanding of the growth and development of the Christian religion. They are not new, almost all of them having been translated at one time or another into English, French, German, or Italian: but they are all practically unknown save to scholars, are all fragmentary, and with hardly an exception, are difficult to understand without a running commentary. In these circumstances, I have ventured to follow, not for the first time, the advice given by Sir Gaston Maspero to his pupils in one of his luminous lectures at the Collège de France. "If" said in effect that great master of archaeology, "you find yourselves in the presence of scattered and diverse examples of any monument you cannot understand —funerary cones, amulets of unusual form, hypocephali, or anything else—make a collection of them. Search museums, journals of Egyptology, proceedings of learned societies, until you think they have no more novelties of the kind to offer you. Then put those you have collected side by side and study them. The features they have in common will then readily appear and in a little time you will find that you will perceive not only the use of the objects in question, but also the history of their development, their connexion with each other, and their relative dates." This has been the end aimed at in this book; and although, like most aims in this world, it has not been perfectly achieved, it may, I think, be said with confidence that these documents explain and supplement one another in a remarkable degree, and that in the majority of cases sense can now be read into what at first sight seemed to be nonsense. As more fragments of the same kind come to light, also, one has fair reason to hope that those points which are still obscure may be made clear.

The system of references adopted perhaps calls for some explanation. As I have no right to expect my readers to take what I say for gospel, I should have preferred to give my authority for every statement made by me in the text. But there are often many authorities supporting the same statement, and some discrimination between them was necessary unless these two volumes were to be swollen to an intolerable length. The same consideration for brevity, too, has often led me to quote at second or third hand rather than at first. References to well-known passages in the more widely read classical writers and Christian Fathers are not needed by scholarly readers, while to others they are difficult to check or verify. I have therefore deliberately and of choice preferred the less recondite sources to the more recondite, and have never hesitated to refer the reader to encyclopaedias, popular lectures, and the works avowedly addressed to the general public of writers like Renan and Mahaffy, rather than to the sources from which they have themselves drawn their information. In so doing, however, I have never consciously failed to check the statement quoted with the original source, and to see, so far as in me lay, that it correctly represents its purport. A fairly long experience has convinced me that to many readers the "Apoll. Rhod. ac Nigid. Schuster, p. 41" and the "Clemens de div. serv. Su 20" dear to certain German professors and their English admirers mean very little, and to the greater public nothing at all. For the translations which appear in the text or notes I have gleaned from all sources, but, except where expressly mentioned, I must personally accept all responsibility for them, and in cases in which any doubt seemed possible I have generally added the words of the original document.

Finally, I have not attempted to impress my own opinion on my readers, but merely to give them the material on which they can form their own; and where I have found myself in doubt as to what the facts of the case really were, I have never scrupled to say so. This is not a counsel of perfection, but the one which on the whole seemed to me best. If by doing so I have succeeded in sending to the documents themselves a few readers hitherto ignorant of them, I shall think I have not wasted my time.

F. LEGGE

6 GRAY'S INN SQUARE
July 1914

P.S. The outbreak of the war has caused the publication of this book to be postponed. I regret the delay the less that it has enabled me to make use of several works and studies which have appeared during the last twelve months.

F. L.

CONTENTS

CONTENTS

CONTENTS

CHAPTER IV

PRE-CHRISTIAN GNOSTICS: THE ORPHICI

CHAPTER V

PRE-CHRISTIAN GNOSTICS: THE ESSENES

CHAPTER VI

PRE-CHRISTIAN GNOSTICS: SIMON MAGUS

CONTENTS

AUTHOR'S
INTRODUCTION

THE worships, beliefs, and religious practices of the age which saw the birth and infancy of Christianity must always be the most interesting of all subjects to the student of history, nor are there many more deserving the attention of the general reader. The opponent, quite as much as the adherent of Christianity, must admit that the early struggles of the faith which is professed by nearly a third of the human race, which for fifteen centuries wielded unchallenged sway over the whole of Europe, and which has grown with the growth of European colonization until it now has a firm settlement in every quarter of the inhabited world, must ever possess surpassing interest for humanity. Yet the popular ideas on the subject are not only vague but erroneous. A general notion that, shortly before the coming of Christ, the Pagans had tired of their old gods, and, lost to all sense of decency, had given themselves up to an unbridled immorality founded on atheistic ideas, is probably about as far as the man who has given no special study to the subject would venture to go. Such a view, founded perhaps on somewhat misty recollections of the Roman satirists and a little secondhand knowledge of the denunciations of the early Christian writers, is almost the reverse of the truth. There has probably been no time in the history of mankind when all classes were more given up to thoughts of religion, or when they strained more fervently after high ethical ideals, than in the six centuries which have been taken for the subject of this book[1].

[1] For the pre-Christian centuries, the rise of ethical religions like that of the Greek Isis (see Chap. II *infra*) and of Mithras (see Chap. XII) is perhaps sufficient proof of this. For the post-Christian, see Tertullian's remarks as to the interest excited among the heathens by problems like the origin of evil (*de Praescript.* c. VII.). As to their striving after morality, see Eugène de Faye, " Formation d'une Doctrine de Dieu au IIme Siècle," *Rev. Hist. Rel.* t. LXIII. (Jan.–Fev. 1911) pp. 1, 2, for authorities. See, too, Hatch, *Hibbert Lectures*, 1890, pp. 291, 292 and Harnack as there quoted.

The cause of this misconception is, however, clear enough. Half a century ago, the general public was without guide or leader in such matters, nor had they any materials on which to form opinions of their own. The classical education which was all that the majority of men then got, carefully left all such matters as the origins of Christianity on one side. The treatises of the Fathers of the Church, for the most part written in late and inelegant Greek, were held to be too corrupting to the style of scholars reared on the texts of the purest period to be attempted by any but professional theologians, by whom indeed they were often very imperfectly understood. Nor was much to be gathered from the profane historians of the early Christian centuries, who maintained such an obstinate silence with regard to Christianity as to give rise to the theory that they must have conspired to ignore the new religion of the lower classes as something too barbarous for ears polite[1]. Moreover, the ruling maxim of education, especially of English education until the end of the XIXth century, was that it was better to know one thing thoroughly than to acquire a smattering of a great many, and that a scholar was better served by an intimate knowledge of second aorists than by any wide extent of reading; while the comparative method of study was still confined to sciences of analysis like anatomy and philology[2]. Above all, what has been called the catastrophic view of the Christian religion was still in fashion. Although our spiritual pastors and masters were never tired of reminding us that God's ways were not as our ways, they invariably talked and wrote on the assumption that they were, and thought an Omnipotent Creator with eternity before Him must needs behave like a schoolboy in control of gunpowder for the first time. Hence " the remarkable victory " which, in the words of Gibbon, the Christian faith obtained over " the established religions

---

[1] W. M. Ramsay, *The Church in the Roman Empire*, 1893, pp. 263, 264.

[2] Tiele, in his Gifford Lectures delivered in 1895, remarks on the ridicule with which the learned Hellenists of his youth received the efforts of those whom they called the *comparativi*. See *Elements of the Science of Religion*, 1897, vol. I. p. 7.

of the earth" was in the view of the orthodox chiefly due
to the miraculous powers placed at the disposal of the primitive
Church, and it was considered impious to look further for the
cause of the despotic rule which in a comparatively brief space
of time it succeeded in establishing over the minds of men.

From this state of things, the foundation of what is known
as the science of religions did much to deliver us. When
non-Christian faiths, such as Hinduism, Buddhism, Zoroastrianism, and Mohammedanism, came to be systematically
studied without preconceived hostility or desire to jeer at
their absurdities, it was seen that the same atmosphere of
miracle and legend had gathered round their infancy as round
that of the Christian Church. Outside the regular or canonical
scriptures—if the phrase may be used—of all of these faiths,
there had evidently grown up a vast literature of uncertain
date and authorship in which the same stories were repeated
and the same episodes introduced as in the Christian Apocryphal Gospels, Acts, and Lives of the Saints. It began to
dawn upon us that, as the human mind under the same conditions generally works in the same way, it was possible that
all religions, whether true or false, might have gone through
the same or similar stages of development[1].

That this view of the case was in itself a great step in
advance, everyone will readily admit who can remember the
horror with which any proposal to equate or even compare
Christianity with any other religion was once received. It
was much helped, however, by another novel hypothesis which
about that time had got over its period of obloquy and was
rapidly coming to the front, namely, the theory of evolution.
When Darwin in his *Origin of Species* enunciated the truth
that as more animals and plants than the earth can support
come into existence every year, it is only those varieties
which are best fitted to their environment which survive the

---

[1] No better proof can be given of the change in public opinion in such
matters than the comparison of Gibbon's words with regard to "the
miraculous powers ascribed to the primitive Church" (*Decline and Fall*,
Bury's edition, vol. II. p. 2) and the way the subject is treated in the article
"Wonders" in Cheyne's *Encyclopedia Biblica*, 1903.

consequent struggle for existence, he practically gave us a new standpoint from which to contemplate Nature.   Herbert Spencer, quickly grasping this principle and carrying its application much further than Darwin had ventured to do, showed that it governed the development not only of animal forms but of the intellectual and moral faculties of man, of political and social institutions, and even of what he called "ecclesiastical institutions," which included religions themselves. With the general acceptance of this view, it followed that the success in point of popularity of any creed at any period of the world's history was not due to any sudden or capricious exercise of the Divine will, but to the normal working of a universal and irresistible law.

But, at this point, we must stop a little to define what is meant by the science of religions.   Science, in this sense, has so far departed from its strict and etymological signification of knowledge, as to connote exact knowledge based upon ascertained fact, while a science is generally held to mean an organized system in which the largest possible number of related facts are gathered together with reference to one common subject of study.   At first sight, it appears that nothing can be more rigidly excluded by this definition than religion, which has been defined as "the effective desire to be in right relation to the power manifesting itself in the universe[1]."   This, which in some quarters would be called the religion "of the heart," can never form the subject of study based upon exact knowledge, because the relations between any human being and the power manifesting itself in the universe can be known only, so far as we can see, to that being and to that power. But in the science under consideration, there is no question of religion generally, but of religions, which is a very different thing.   By a religion, we generally mean the assembly of beliefs, traditions, and forms of worship which go to make up a faith or cult, and this, as it must, according to the experience of all history, have come into being through the agency of some man or men, should go through the same evolutionary

---

[1] The definition is that of Ira W. Howerth, *International Journal of Ethics*, 1903, p. 205.

process as all other human institutions. Hence there is at first sight a considerable probability that all religions whatever will be found on examination to follow the same law of development by the survival of those best fitted to their environment that we have seen operative in the case of animal forms.

Here, however, the Christian—or for that matter, the adherent of any faith which claims to have been founded by a special revelation—finds himself in the presence of a dilemma. His own faith, whether it be Christianity or another, is in his eyes true, as being not the work of man, but of God, and all others are false. How therefore are they to be compared ? Is the Jew, who believes the Law to have been delivered to his people "among the thunders of Sinai," the Parsi who is taught the special inspiration of Zoroaster by the "Omniscient Lord" Ahura Mazda, or the Mohammedan who thinks that Mohammed received the Koran from Allah himself, to be told that his faith has developed according to the same laws as that of the Christian, who is convinced that his has no other source than the teaching of the Divine Founder of Christianity?

To this it may be said that the dilemma is more apparent than real, and is due to a like confusion of thought with that which seized upon many when the evolutionary theory was first promulgated. No argument was then more common than that the Divine creation of the animals, including man, was authoritatively revealed once for all in the first chapter of Genesis, and that the bare formulation of the idea that man's bodily form had developed by a long process of evolution and selection from those of the lower animals was therefore a blasphemy that could only be uttered by atheistic men of science[1]. There is no occasion to go here into the tissue of sophistries and misconceptions with which Mr Gladstone, when confronted with this argument in controversy with M. Albert Réville, one of the founders of the science of religions, and with M. Réville's champion Prof. Huxley, tried to prove that the

---

[1] See Tiele, *op. cit.* vol. I. pp. 5 *sqq.* The controversies raging round Darwin's theory when first put forward are well summarized by F. W. Hutton in his *Darwinism and Lamarckism*, 1899, *passim.* Cf. Delage and Goldsmith, *Les Théories de l'Évolution*, Paris, 1909, pp. 28, 29.

assertion of the doctrine of evolution was to be found in the Book of Genesis. It is sufficient to say that Darwin never affirmed that natural selection or the survival of the fittest was the cause of the variation of animal forms, but simply that it was the mode in which that variation, however caused, operated[1]. In like manner, it may be said that the science of religions by no means attempts to discuss the causes which lead to the institution of any particular religion, but deals merely with the laws underlying its development when once instituted. The Christian religion, like those of Moses, Zoroaster, and Mohammed, however Divine its origin, was, like them, propagated by men who founded the Church, handed on the traditions, and gave form to the ceremonies. Is there, therefore, any reason why the same law of development should not apply to this as well as to its rivals ?

That the answer to this must be in the negative is at last beginning to be generally admitted. Prof. Tiele, writing in 1897, was obliged to confess that " the new science of religions was in many quarters regarded with suspicion[2]," but Dr Jevons, when lecturing at Hartford in 1908, was able to say that " the time has happily gone by when the mere idea of comparing Christianity with any other religion would have been rejected with horror as treasonous and treacherous[3]." Yet it may be doubted whether the clouds have rolled completely away, and it is fairly certain that the many learned and able Catholic priests who have done so much to elucidate the origins and tendencies of ancient religions other than their own have until lately avoided the discussion of their relations with the earliest forms of Christianity. This is the more to be regretted, because they are in many cases peculiarly fitted for the investigation, and their acquaintance with the extra-Canonical Christian writers before Constantine, hitherto much neglected by Protestant theologians, would make their conclusions upon it especially valuable. Yet it is along these lines that future

---

[1] See Hutton, *op. cit.* p. 111.

[2] Tiele, *op. cit.* vol. I. p. 11.

[3] F. B. Jevons, *Introduction to the Study of Comparative Religion*, 1908, p. 18.

inquiry will probably advance ; and if, as most of us believe, the Christian religion has outdistanced and survived all its early competitors because it was better fitted than they to its environment, it is of great importance even from the point of view of the most rigid orthodoxy, that we should have a clear conception of what that environment was. Fortunately the gaps in our knowledge have been in great measure filled by the work of Continental scholars outside the pale of the Catholic Church, who have been indefatigable of late years in discovering documents, editing texts, and publishing monuments which throw great light on the history of the religions which at the outset competed with Christianity for the favour of the Graeco-Roman world. A summary of these labours is one of the objects aimed at in the following pages.

If, now, we attempt to examine what these competitors were, we find at the outset that a good number of those which we once thought formidable may be eliminated from the list. Judaism, for instance, although the matrix in which Christianity was formed, was never at any time in effective rivalry with it. The words of the Gospel as to the Pharisees compassing sea and land to make one proselyte have misled the unwary into supposing that the number of Jewish proselytes was at one time or another large[1] ; but it must be remembered that it was the Sadducees and not the Pharisees who were the dominant party in the Jewish State, and that these last formed but a very small part of the total population of Judaea[2]. The Sadducees from their Hellenizing tendencies were much more likely to go over to the faith of the Gentiles than to make any great effort for their conversion, and both they and the Essenes, who formed in Josephus' day the third party among the Jews,

---

[1] Like the late Dean Stanley, who in his Lectures on the *History of the Jewish Church*, talked about the synagogue of the Jewish settlement in Rome under the first Emperors " fascinating the proud Roman nobles by the glimpse it gave of a better world " (vol. III. p. 410).

[2] According to Josephus (*Antiq.* XVIII. i. 3, 4) they did not amount to more than 6000 men distributed throughout the whole of Palestine. Morrison thinks that " the Pharisaic party had no attraction for the great bulk of the population," *The Jews under Roman Rule*, 1890, p. 307.

were too much set on procuring, by different means, the temporal supremacy of Israel, to care much about admitting any proselyte to share in it[1]. Although a few undistinguished persons of Gentile blood may have become converts to Judaism between the birth of Christ and the fall of the Temple, their number can never have been at any time important; and after 69 A.D., the furious hostility that arose between Jew and Gentile made any further conversions to the Jewish faith practically impossible. Never, so far as we know, did Judaism aim at becoming, and certainly never had the slightest chance of appearing as, a world-religion.

Not less hopeless, in this respect, was the case of the Graeco-Roman pantheon. The late Mr Long's picture of "Diana or Christ," representing a young woman called upon by a sympathetic Roman magistrate to choose between sacrificing to the statue of the many-breasted Artemis of Ephesus and condemnation to death as a Christian, attained great popularity in its day, and shows with fair clearness the view of the relations between Paganism and early Christianity supposed at the end of the last century to have been current in the first. Yet hardly anything could give a falser idea of the religious history of the period. The officials of the Roman Empire in time of persecution sought to force the Christians to sacrifice, not to any of the heathen gods, but to the Genius of the Emperor and the Fortune of the City of Rome; and at all times the Christians' refusal was looked upon not as a religious but as a political offence[2]. For the rest, the worship of the Olympian gods had, when Christianity came to the surface, almost entirely died out, and both Greek and Latin writers bear witness to the contempt with which it was regarded by both races at the beginning of our era. Cicero, while admitting that the world is governed by the providence of the gods, rejects all the myths attached to them as impious, and declares that the "Deity who is diffused in every part of Nature" appears as the earth under the name of Ceres,

---

[1] See Chap. V *infra*.

[2] See Neander, *General Hist. of the Christian Religion and Church*, Eng. ed. 1853, vol. I. p. 126.

as the sea under that of Neptune, and so on[1]. Plutarch, too, is plainly a monotheist, who worships "the one eternal, passionless Spirit far removed from the world of chance and change and earthly soilure" of Greek philosophy[2]; and, while lamenting the decay of faith which has led to the cessation of oracles, thinks that all the manifestations of the Divine providence are the work of no great deity, but of a crowd of inferior powers or demons who are hardly in a greater superiority of position to man than the fairies of our childhood[3]. Whatever rivalry the Christian Church had to face in its infancy, it had none to fear from the deities of Olympus.

It has been said, however, and to a certain extent accepted, that the first efforts of Christianity were sorely hindered by the followers of the great Greek philosophers. In this there is a certain amount of truth, for the Neo-Platonic school did indeed enter into an alliance with the few remaining worshippers of the Pagan gods which forced them into an attitude of opposition to Christianity. But this was at a date some time after the compact with Constantine, and consequently later than that within the scope of this book. Nor is it likely that at an earlier date philosophy and Christianity appealed to the same class of minds, and that they thus entered into serious competition with each other. As the late Dr Hatch has said, "the earliest forms of Christianity were not only outside the sphere of Greek philosophy, but they also appealed on the one hand, mainly to the classes which philosophy did not reach, and on the other hand, to a standard which philosophy did not recognize[4]." Faith, not reason, was the quality that the Apostles and their immediate successors sought in their hearers, and Celsus was probably not far wrong when he said

---

[1] *De Natura Deorum*, c. XXVIII. The statement is put into the mouth of Balbus whose arguments Cicero declares to have in his opinion "the greater probability." See also Athenagoras, *Legatio*, c. XXII. and Minucius Felix, c. XIX. With such interpretations or mythoplasms, Philo of Alexandria was familiar. Cf. F. C. Conybeare, *Apology of Apollonius*, 1894, p. 9.

[2] Dill, *Roman Society from Nero to Marcus Aurelius*, 1904, p. 419.

[3] *De Iside et Osiride*, c. XXV.

[4] Hatch, *Hibbert Lectures*, p. 124.

that the rule of admission into the infant Church was "Let no educated man enter, no wise man, no prudent man, for such things we deem evil; but whoever is ignorant, whoever is unintelligent, whoever is simple, let him come and be welcome[1]." To this state of mind the password of the early Christian communities, *Maran atha*, is a sufficient key. The confident expectation of the nearness of the Parusia or Second Advent for the primitive Christian overwhelmed all other considerations. "The Lord is at hand and His reward" was the one fact that he wished to keep before him. What need to trouble about the Highest Good or the hundred other questions that vexed the souls of the philosophers?

The religions competing with Christianity which are left after this elimination may be classed in three categories. First come the Oriental religions native to countries lying to the south and east of the Mediterranean and therefore mainly outside the sphere of Hellenic culture until after the conquests of Alexander. These religions, born or nurtured in Asia Minor, Persia, and Egypt, so soon as Alexander had carried out his project of the marriage of Europe and Asia, poured westward in a flood which a Roman satirist compared to the Orontes emptying itself into the Tiber, and gained, according to a well-known law in the history of religions, a far greater influence over the minds of men than they had exercised in their native home. The second category comprises the many strange sects which the first Fathers of the Church grouped together under the generic name of Gnostics. The faith which these professed was not, as it is sought to show later, one founded on religion at all but rather on magic, and had long been present in germ as a sort of heresy or alternative belief underlying the worship of the gods of Olympus. Finally, there arose the ambitious religion of Manes, which aimed at sweeping into one vast synthesis or eclectic church the three religions of Zoroaster, Buddha, and Christ, which at the time of its institution divided between them the allegiance of the civilized world.

Each of these categories shall be dealt with in turn; but

---

[1] Origen, *contra Celsus*, t. III. c. 44.   Cf. Hatch, where last quoted.

before doing so, it may be well to say something upon the state of our knowledge concerning them. Until lately, it was a commonplace of religious history that the Catholic Church had destroyed as far as possible all traces of the religions that she had supplanted, which was picturesquely expressed in the phrase that in her victory she had burned the enemy's camp. That this was her conscious policy may be gathered from the advice given by a Pope of the viith century, to " break the idols and consecrate the temples " of the heathen[1]; but of late many relics of the ancient faiths which had before escaped us have been disinterred by the care of scholars. During the last century, the lost heresiology of Hippolytus and considerable fragments of works by Gnostic authors were brought to light in circumstances to be described in their place[2], while the present decade has not only added to our stock of Gnostic fragments, but has revealed to us on the western frontier of China a hoard of Manichaean documents rich beyond our hopes[3]. These are not only valuable by reason of the information they afford, but give us ground for the belief that, as the interest in such matters becomes more widely spread, many more documents throwing light upon the subject will appear.

One word may be said in conclusion as to the relations of these rival religions between themselves. Whoever studies the documents here described cannot fail to be struck by the fact that certain ideas, phrases, and even words, seem common to them all. At the time that these documents were written this similarity excited no remark from the orthodox, as it was at once disposed of by the theory that these religions were one and all the invention of the Devil, and therefore naturally bore traces of their common origin. This explanation, however convenient, does not satisfy the demands of

---

[1] Cf. Dill, *Roman Society in the Last Century of the Western Empire*, 1899, p. 38, n. 4. See also the edict of Constantine quoted in the concluding chapter, *infra*. The steps which led up to the policy are well summarized by Walter Johnson, *Byways of British Archaeology*, 1912, p. 25.

[2] See Chap. VII *infra*.

[3] See Chap. XIII *infra*.

modern criticism, and it is therefore necessary to look further.
One way of accounting for the phenomenon is to suppose that
many if not all of the analogies noticed are due to the mistakes
of scribes and translators, who, when dealing with expressions
unfamiliar to them, were naturally inclined to repeat the same
phrases over and over again. This, as all know who have
had to do with ancient manuscripts, is accountable for much,
and it is extremely likely that a monk of the vth or vith century transcribing an account of the opinions of, for instance,
the Ophites who flourished in Phrygia before the birth of Christ
at the same time with those of the Manichaeans found in Rome
three centuries later, would not hesitate to express views
essentially different by the same phrases and even the same
words. Add to this the jumble that persons untrained in
philology naturally make between names in a foreign language
and those of similar sound in their own tongue, coupled with
the fixed idea of finding in the traditions of the heathen a
confirmation of the historical truth of the Hebrew Scriptures,
and you have some explanation of the cause which makes
many proper names recur unexpectedly in otherwise unrelated
documents. Thus the Armenian bishop, Moses of Chorene, in
narrating the story which he says he obtained from Berossus,
the Chaldaean historian who wrote at the beginning of our
era, says that " Before the building of the Tower of Babel and
the multiplication of tongues among the human race, after
the navigation of Xisuthros [*i.e.* Hasis-adra, the Babylonian
Noah] in Armenia, Zervan, Titan, and Japhet were princes of
the land. These persons," he adds, " seem to be Shem, Ham,
and Japhet[1]." Zervan is the name given by a late sect of
Zoroastrians to the " Boundless Time " whom they placed at
the origin of all things, while Titan belongs to the Hellenic
mythology, and Japhet may either be Saturn's brother Iapetus,
or the patriarch of the Book of Genesis. It is to be conjectured
that Berossus did not use these three names in the apposition
quoted or probably at all, and we can only guess vainly at
the real names which are concealed under those which Moses
of Chorene here gives.

[1] Langlois, *Collection des Historiens de l'Arménie*, Paris, 1868, t. I. p. 388.

But when all allowance is made for mistakes like these, there remains a fund of ideas common to all or many of the religions hereafter treated of, which cannot be explained away by any theory of verbal inaccuracy[1]. As an instance of this, let us take the notion of an archetypal or heavenly man created ages before the appearance upon earth of terrestrial man, who was nevertheless made in the image and after the likeness of his predecessor. This idea, as will be shown later, is met with among the Phrygian Ophites, where "a Man and a Son of Man" were said to be the origin of all subsequent things, as in the Avestic literature of Persia where Gayômort, the son, according to one story, of the Supreme God Ahura Mazda by his daughter Spenta-armaiti, is made at once the pattern and the source of the whole human race. The borrowings of Zoroastrianism from Babylonia were not few, and we might conceive this to be the survival of some old Babylonian tradition, such as that which modern critics believe to have been the origin of the Creation and Flood stories of Genesis; and this theory is strengthened by the predominant part which this "First Man" plays in Manichaeism, itself a Babylonian faith, where the Turkestan MSS. show him as a sort of intermediary between the gods of light and this earth. But how shall we account for the fact that in one of the earliest documents of the *Pistis Sophia*, the collection of Gnostic writings hereafter described[2], a great angel named Jeû, who is spoken of many times as the "overseer of the light" and the arranger of the Cosmos, is also alluded to as the "First Man," in a way which shows that the writer did not doubt that the allusion would be comprehended by his readers without further explanation[3]? The

[1] The late Dr Salmon's theory that writers like Hippolytus may have been taken in by a forger who made one document do duty for many different sects is given in Chap. VII *infra*, but the arguments in its favour are not conclusive.

[2] See Chap. X *infra*.

[3] Sir Gaston Maspero, "Sur l'Ennéade," *R.H.R.* Jan.–Fev. 1892, p. 8, says that the Egyptians regarded Osiris as the First Man, and Jéquier repeats the statement in his *Livre de ce qu'il y a dans l'Hadès*, Paris, 1894, pp. 9–10. Yet there seems no evidence that the Egyptians ever knew him under that name.

Pistis Sophia, although doubtless written in Greek in the first instance, comes to us in a Coptic dress, and the documents therein contained show more affinities with the Egyptian than with the Persian religion. How therefore can we account for the same idea appearing at almost the same time in countries between the peoples of which there was always bitter hostility, and which were separated moreover by the Arabian Desert and the whole breadth of Asia Minor ?

It seems to the present writer that no solution of this and of the numerous other difficulties of which this is but one example can be profitably suggested, until we know more than we do at present about the origin and dates of Zoroastrianism. Although this religion is still with us in the beliefs of the modern Parsis, there is none about the origin of which we know less, or concerning the antiquity of which there is greater discrepancy between ancient and modern writers. Thus, while Plutarch, quoting as is generally supposed Theopompos of Chios who flourished in the ivth century B.C., declares that Zoroaster himself wrote 5000 years before the Trojan War[1], modern writers of authority, like Prof. Williams Jackson and Mdlle Menant, are inclined to bring down the date of the eponymous prophet or reformer of the Persian religion to 700 B.C.[2] The discrepancy is too great to be bridged over by any compromise, and the question has been further complicated by the discovery a few years ago of inscriptions which show that Mithras, the Persian god whose worship formed the most dangerous rival to that of the Christian Church immediately before its alliance with Constantine, was one of the most exalted deities of the presumably Aryan Hittites or Mitannians at a date not later than 1272 B.C.[3] Signs are

[1] *De Is. et Os.* c. XLVI.

[2] See (Mdlle) D. Menant, "Parsis et Parsisme," *Conférences au Musée Guimet*, 1904, and Prof. Williams Jackson as there quoted. The same date is accepted with some hesitation by Prof. Hope Moulton in his *Early Zoroastrianism* (Hibbert Lectures), 1913, pp. 17 *sqq.*

[3] See H. G. Jacobi, "The Antiquity of Vedic Culture," *Journal of the Royal Asiatic Society*, 1909, pp. 720 *sqq.*, where the texts relied upon are given and discussed. The correspondence which followed upon this paper (see *J.R.A.S.* 1909, 1910) is full of interest. Fossey, "Les Fouilles

CHAPTER I

THE CONQUESTS OF ALEXANDER

A GLANCE at the map of Asia at the coming of Alexander will
convince us that all but a corner of the world known to the
ancients was then ruled by a single power.   The Persian Empire,
sprawling like a huge octopus over the centre of the continent,
dominated it from its four capitals at the head of the Persian
Gulf, and stretched without a break from the Caspian Sea to
the Indian Ocean.   In its eastern provinces were comprised
what is now Russian Turkestan from Krasnovodsk to Kashgar,
with the Khanates and the Pamirs, all Afghanistan, Seistan,
Baluchistan, the North-West Province, and part of the Punjab.
On the western side of the Great Central Desert came the countries which we now call Persia and Turkey in Asia containing
in themselves a territory half the size of the Continent of Europe,
together with the rich province to the south of the Caucasus
which has lately passed into the grip of Russia.   From here one
long tentacle had stretched across the Sinaitic Peninsula and had
seized Egypt ; and, although another had shrunk back hurt from
its attack on Greece, it yet held positions on the Bosphorus and
the Hellespont which formed a standing menace that the raid
might be repeated.   Apart from the Greek States which, as has
been well said, the Great King found easier to control through
their own venal orators than to conquer by his soldiers, there
remained outside his sway only the trading republic of Carthage
and the Italian cities just rising into prominence.   Travellers'
tales, more than usually improbable and untrustworthy, were,
indeed, told of great countries swarming with men and fabulous
monsters lying beyond the African and Indian deserts on the

1

southern, and the great ranges of mountains on the eastern, frontier of the Empire[1]; but these gave as little concern to its rulers as did the fringe of barbarian tribes, Cimmerians, Hyperboreans, Gauls, and Scyths, who filled up the space between the civilized world and the imaginary ring of waters which was called the Outer Ocean.

That this vast dominion should be loosely compacted was of the nature of things. The twenty or more provinces into which it was divided enjoyed a large measure of self-government, and had preserved, for the most part, their native laws and customs unaltered. Each of these divisions was ruled by a satrap who, like a Chinese viceroy, was allowed to maintain armies and even fleets of his own. But a check, imperfect no doubt but still existent, was exercised over his proceedings by the presence of a Royal Secretary in each satrapy, whose business it was to supervise the accounts, and to send up regular reports to the capital of the doings, of his coadjutor[2], while the troops were under the command of a general appointed directly by the Crown. From time to time, also, a Royal Commissioner called the King's Eye visited the province with a strong guard to hear complaints and to see that all was in order[3]. The satrap, too, only held his post during his master's pleasure, and was liable at any moment to be removed to another province, degraded, or put to death, on the strength of a simple letter bearing the Royal Seal; and the tribute which each satrapy had to pay to the Great King being settled at a fixed and known amount, there was less chance than under some similar systems of devolution that the satrap might squeeze out of his subjects a sum

[1] Such as the Arimaspi or one-eyed inhabitants of Russia, about whom Herodotus (Bk III. c. 116) quotes the legend that they stole gold from its griffin guardians, and those *myrmeces* or great ants whom Megasthenes (Strabo, Bk xv. c. 1, § 44) and other writers describe as digging for gold on the Thibetan frontier—a story of which more than one rationalistic explanation has been suggested.

[2] Rawlinson's *Herodotus* (1862 edition), II. p. 462 for authorities.

[3] Maspero, *Histoire ancienne des Peuples de l'Orient,* Paris, 1904, p. 706. Rawlinson, *op. cit.* p. 463, thinks this practice lapsed early, but Xenophon seems clear that it was in force in his time (*Cyropaedia,* Bk VIII. c. 6).

far greater than that which he transmitted to the Treasury[1]. Above all, the Persians were of Aryan stock, and early showed signs of the talent for governing older races which seems to have stuck to the Aryans throughout their history. They made excellent roads, and established swift running posts that did much to make communication easy between the most important parts of their empire; while, as the satraps' standing armies were composed either of native Persians or hired mercenaries, the subject populations had an opportunity, rare enough in the ancient world, of peacefully developing their internal resources without constant fear of disturbance by foreign enemies, or forced participation in wars of aggression[2]. It was only when the word went forth from Babylon or Susa, Ecbatana or Persepolis, for the calling-out of the Ban of the whole Empire that the other than Persian subject of Artaxerxes or Darius had to join the levy of his satrapy, and, on orders given to him through an interpreter, to assist the Great King in crushing some rebellious satrap or repelling foreign invasion. At other times, he must have known him only as a kind of divinity, having power to throw down and to set up, to whom he might cry, not always in vain, against the oppression of his own immediate ruler. Those writers are no doubt justified who say that the government of the Persian Empire was to the humbler classes of Asiatics a great improvement upon any that had preceded it[3], and that the rule of the Great King never awoke the fierce resentment in its subjects aroused by the tyranny of the Semitic Assyrians, or of the Chaldeans who were, in great part, of Mongoloid blood[4].

[1] He was probably allowed a reasonable sum for the maintenance of his court and government; but if he exceeded this, was liable to severe punishment. This appears from the execution by Alexander, on his return from India, of the satraps who had been guilty of extortion. He seems to have purposely preserved the Persian laws and customs on this point unaltered.

[2] This is the opinion of Rawlinson, *op. cit.* pp. 460 *sqq.*

[3] Rawlinson, *op. cit.* p. 464; Winwood Reade, *Martyrdom of Man*, 1910, p. 56; Sayce, *Ancient Empires of the East*, 1884, pp. 250, 251; Maspero, *op. cit.* p. 721.

[4] Oppert, *Le Peuple et la Langue des Mèdes*, Paris, pp. 17 *sqq.*; Maspero, *op. cit.* p. 559, n. 11.

It was doubtless the memory of this golden age, glorified as remembrances generally are by the lapse of centuries, that brought about the reaction to the Persian form of government and culture which we shall have to discuss later in the countries bled white by the Roman proconsuls.

Throughout this vast realm, Alexander's coming brought about a change such as the civilized world has never seen before or since. Among the world-conquerors who have been hailed as heroes in after times, Alexander—surely the greatest individual known to history—stands distinguished by the loftiness of his aims and the swiftness with which they were attained. It is wonderful that a boy of twenty with an army that cannot have exceeded 50,000 men all told should succeed in overcoming practically the whole of Asia in less time than it took the British Empire with the third of a million to break down the armed resistance of a few thousand Boers. More wonderful is it that he should a little later contrive to transport a force of about 100,000, comprising infantry, cavalry and artillery, over the three thousand miles that separate Macedonia from Karachi, at the same time preserving such perfect communication with his base that he seems never to have remained for long without letters from Europe, while the stream of recruits that reached him from the same source must have been continuous and unchecked[1]. Such a feat which, with all the aid which steam and electricity can give us, would still tax to the utmost the powers of our greatest modern generals, becomes almost miraculous when we think that the greater part of his line of communications must have lain through recently subjugated lands, and that his own

[1] Sir Thomas Holdich, in his excellent book *The Gates of India* (p. 104), says that when he defeated the Aspasians or Yusufzai in the Kuner Valley he sent the pick of their cattle back to Macedonia to improve the native breed. Arrian, *Anabasis*, Bk IV. c. 25, however, in quoting the story from Ptolemy, says only that Alexander " wished to send them " to till the soil. It seems impossible that they could have survived the journey before the days of steamships. Still more incredible is the story in Plutarch, *Life of Alexander*, c. L. that when Alexander was at Prophthasia (probably Farrah in Seistan), he received some grapes grown on the coast of Greece. But such stories, although coloured by age, may serve to show how perfect his communications were always thought to have been.

advance led him into countries unmapped and known only to him by the half fabulous tales of his enemies[1]. But the most astonishing thing about these exploits is that they were all performed with the conscious aim of making Asia Greek[2], and in this respect, as in all others, they were both original and successful. Everywhere that Alexander passed, he left behind him cities peopled by a mixture of his own veterans, of those camp followers which, then as now, have always stuck to a European army on the march, and of natives of the country either found on the spot or drawn from some other part of Asia ; and the permanence of these foundations still bears witness to the foreseeing eye of their founder. Alexandria in Egypt, Candahar, Secunderabad, all preserve to this day the memory of his royal name, and the continued importance of Khojend, Samarcand, Herat, Merv, and Cabul out of the many other Alexandrias that he established on his conquering way show that his statesmanlike perception of the chief markets of the East was as sure as his strategical insight[3]. Nor did he neglect other means of carrying out the great design that he had at heart. In the great feast at Susa, which he celebrated on his return from India, the " marriage of Europe and Asia," which had always formed his guiding idea, took visible shape. He had already wedded—it is said for love—the beautiful Roxana, a princess from Bactria in the Eastern (or Upper) Provinces

---

[1] Holdich, *op. cit. passim*, says that he must have had information from Persian sources, and that his route must have been laid beforehand. Sir Thomas' opinion, as that of a soldier as well as a student, is entitled to much respect. Yet the instances of Genghiz Khan and other Oriental invaders are perhaps against any such necessity.

[2] Freeman, *Historical Essays*, 1873, second series, pp. 192, 193.

[3] Khojend was probably Alexandria *eschata* or the furthest (East). Samarcand, of which the ancient name was Maracanda, is said by Baber to be a foundation of Alexander's. Herat was Alexandria Ariana, and Merv probably Alexandria Margiana, while Cabul seems to have been Ortospana. Among the other Alexandrias which have retained their old importance are Alexandria Arachosiana or Candahar, Alexandria Caucasiana or Begram, and Alexandria Sogdiana or Hyderabad. See J. W. McCrindle, *Invasion of India by Alexander the Great*, 1896, pp. 36 *sqq.*, and Droysen, *Histoire de l'Hellénisme*, (French edition), Paris, 1883, I. pp. 408 *sqq.*

of his new Empire[1], and now he took as a second consort Statira, the daughter of Darius, who, as the scion of the last native king of Persia, may be taken as the representative of its western centre. Nearly a hundred of his superior officers and some ten thousand of his humbler followers hastened to follow his example and to receive Asiatic brides with the rich dowries assigned them by the Conqueror[2]. Moreover the thirty thousand youthful recruits from his new conquests, whom he had ordered five years before to be trained in the Macedonian discipline and the Greek language, now arrived[3], and Alexander set to work with his usual energy to diffuse through his European army strong drafts of his Asiatic subjects in order to cement still further the alliance between the two Continents. Had he lived, it would have been a mixed army of Asiatics and Europeans that he would have led the following year to the conquest of the western world[4].

Destiny, however, is, as men would have said in those days, stronger than the immortal gods, and Alexander's early death put an instant stop to all ideas of further conquest. It is idle, until we know the causes of things, to speculate on what might have been ; but it seems probable that if Nearchus' expedition had sailed, the Conqueror's warlike plans would once again have proved to have been perfectly laid, that he would have crushed Carthage as easily as Thebes and Tyre, and that the Italian States would have received the same master as the Bactrians and Indians[5]. Yet so far as our immediate purpose is concerned, Alexander's work was done once for all, and the policy typified

---

[1] Droysen, *op. cit.* p. 481.

[2] See last note. The second marriage is dramatically described by Droysen, *op. cit.* I. pp. 638, 639. Cf. Arrian, *Anabasis*, Bk VII. c. 4; Plutarch, *Alexander*, c. LXX.

[3] Arrian, *op. cit.* Bk VII. c. 6; Plutarch, *Alexander*, c. LXXI. Cf. Droysen, *op. cit.* I. p. 646.

[4] Droysen, *op. cit.* I. p. 660. It was probably the fear of this mixture that caused the quarrel between him and his Macedonians at Opis. See Arrian, *op. cit.* Bk VII. c. 8; Plutarch, *Alexander*, c. LXXI.

[5] Droysen, *op. cit.* II. p. 34. Mahaffy, *Alexander's Empire*, 1887, p. 38, thinks that the Romans could never have withstood Alexander's cavalry and siege artillery, although he notes that Livy patriotically decided otherwise.

as the marriage of Europe and Asia was perhaps as well served
by his death as by his life.   During Persian times, the Court of
the Great King had always proved a magnet drawing to itself
with irresistible force the ever-restless Greeks, and the road to
Susa was trodden in turn by politicians like Alcibiades, leaders
of mercenaries like Xenophon, and Greek philosophers, artists,
and courtezans innumerable.   The traffic in mercenaries alone
must have been enormous when we find Greek troops forming
the stiffening of those huge armies of Darius which Alexander
overthrew at the Granicus, Issus, and Arbela[1]; while as for
the other sex, Themistocles, when turning his back on his own
country, could find no better or safer mode of approaching the
Persian Court than in a closed litter supposed to be conveying
a Greek woman to the harem of the Great King[2].   But when the
century-long wars for the succession to Alexander broke out
upon his death, there straightway appeared five courts where
before there had been but one, and these were now ruled over by
Greek and not by Persian kings.   Mercenaries of all kinds were
in urgent demand in every one of them, while the setting free
of the millions in bullion and specie found by Alexander in the
Persian capitals caused an outbreak of luxury like that which
followed in Germany the payment of the French milliards.
Soon every Greek who had strength, beauty, or talents to sell
was on foot to seek his or her fortune in Asia, and with them
went everywhere the petty Greek trader, as enterprising and
as fearless in pursuit of gain as those countrymen of his whose
booths Lord Kitchener saw set up on the field of Omdurman
before the rout of the Mahdists was complete, and whose
locandas still greet one in the smallest villages on the Nile.
The stream of fortune-hunters, now in full flood, quickly over-
flowed from the ancient capitals to the numerous Antigonias,
Antiochias, Lysimachias, Nicomedias, and Seleucias which the
new kings everywhere founded in imitation of their dead master,
and even the most distant provinces began to receive their

---

[1] Droysen, *op. cit.* I, pp. 186, 240, 333.   There were 30,000 Greek
mercenaries fighting on the side of Darius at Issus, and 4000 of these
remained faithful till his death.   *Ibid.* I. p. 368.

[2] Plutarch, *Themistocles*, c. XXVI.

quota of Greek citizens and Greek culture.   As has happened
more than once in history, Asia woke suddenly from her sleep,
and acquired a veneer of foreign manners in hardly longer time
than it has taken Japan in our own days to adopt European
armaments, teaching and dress.   When the Parthians overcame
Crassus, the Roman captives found the barbarian victors
amusing themselves with the plays of Euripides[1]; while the
Bactrian and Indian provinces, which the rise of the Parthian
power cut off from the western part of Alexander's Empire,
conceived such a taste for Greek art that the statues of Buddha
with which their capitals were afterwards decorated were carved
according to Greek instead of Hindu canons[2].   The so-called
Indo-Greek kings of these parts, the Euthydemi, Diodoti, and
Eucratidae, of whom we know hardly more than the names,
no more thought of using other than Greek designs and inscriptions for their coins than did the rulers of Pergamum or
Antioch[3].   The generation that had seen Alexander face to
face was hardly in its grave before the marriage of Europe and
Asia had become a very real and pregnant fact.

The importance of this for the history of religions can
hardly be exaggerated.   Greek was spoken everywhere throughout Asia, and for the first time in the world's history the
inhabitants of the civilized part of the earth had a common
tongue in which they could communicate their ideas to each
other.   No doubt the language spoken by the offspring of

[1] Plutarch, *Crassus*, c. XXXIII.   The play acted was the *Bacchae*, and
a Greek tragic actor, one Jason of Tralles, had been imported for the
principal part.   In the essay *De Alex. fortitudine*, I. c. 5, Plutarch says
that no sooner had Alexander subdued Asia than Homer became a favourite
reading-book, and Persian, Susianan, and Gedrosian boys learned to chant
the tragedies of Sophocles and Euripides.

[2] Droysen, *op. cit.* III. pp. 244, 255.

[3] Sylvain Lévi, " Bouddhisme et les Grecs," *Revue de l'Histoire des
Religions*, 1891, p. 2 ; Percy Gardner, *Catalogue of Bactrian and Indian
Coins in British Museum*.   Arts other than the plastic also received
attention.   Amitrochates, son of the famous Chandragupta or Sandracottus, wrote to Antiochus (Soter ?) to buy him some sweet wine,
dried figs, and a sophist.   He received the other commodities, but was
told that it was not lawful to sell sophists in Greece.   See Athenaeus,
Deipnosophistae, Bk XIV. c. 67 quoting Hegesander.

Greek colonists and their native spouses was not the tongue
of Sophocles or of Demosthenes any more than it was " the
strong-winged music of Homer " ; but it was a better medium
for the transmission of metaphysical theories than the founder
of any world-religion has ever had at his disposal before or
since. The missionaries whom modern nations send into the
distant parts of the earth for the propagation of the Christian
faith find one of their worst difficulties in the impossibility of
rendering its doctrines into the languages of peoples at another
stage of culture from themselves ; but no such barrier between
teacher and taught existed in the empire created by Alexander's
genius. The result of this possibility of intercommunication of
ideas was at once apparent. Anxious to show that they too
had a pedigree, the older nations of the world seized the
opportunity to inform their new masters of their own history
and traditions ; and, as all history was in those days sacred
history, they thus introduced to the Greeks their gods and
their beliefs as to the divine governance of the world. The
sacred books of the Chaldeans, of the Egyptians, of the
Jews, and no doubt of many other peoples whose records
are now lost to us, were translated into Greek ; and thus the
science of the history of religions was born. Writers like
Diodorus Siculus and Plutarch are still our chief guides for the
religions of the earliest populated parts of the ancient world ;
but how could these compilers have handed down to us the
traditions they have preserved save for writers like Berossus,
Manetho, and Philo of Byblus, who themselves wrote in Greek ?
Plutarch tells us that when he spent a year in Rome during the
reign of Trajan, he did not find it necessary to learn Latin, his
native tongue being apparently understood by everybody. One
may wonder how much of the sayings and doings of the Founder
of Christianity would have come down to us, had they not been
first recorded in the κοινή or *lingua franca* of the whole East[1].

There were, however, other ways in which Alexander's conquests prepared the way for a religion which could make appeal

---

[1] Droysen, *op. cit.* ɪɪɪ. p. 66. Cf. the *Omnis Oriens loquitur* of St Jerome
Prol. ad Epist. ad Galatas ; and Deissmann, *New Light on the New Testament*
(English edition), 1907, p. 30.

to men of every nation and language.   Nothing is more difficult
for those brought up in a monotheistic faith, with its inbred
contempt for the worshippers of many gods, than to realize how
the ancients regarded the Divine.   The peoples of classical antiquity seem to have everywhere believed in the gods of their
neighbours as absolutely as they did in their own, for they
imagined that their deities had, like men, only a limited sphere
of action, or, to put it scientifically, were subject to the same
conditions of space as their worshippers.   Thus, the Syrians
thought that Yahweh of Israel was a mountain god, who could
not help his people when fighting in the plains[1], and the Philistines believed that the ark in which he lived would bring
prosperity or disaster to the place in which it happened to be
for the time being[2].   This is almost an exact parallel to the
tale of the prince of Bactria, whose daughter was freed from
demoniacal possession by an image of the Egyptian god Khonsu
sent into Asia *ad hoc*, whereupon he decided that it would be
wise to keep so powerful a god in his own country, and did so
until frightened by a dream into sending the statue back[3].
But such ideas, however natural they may be to isolated or
backward peoples, soon lost their hold upon the acute and
logical Greeks, when they came into contact with civilized
nations having pantheons differing widely from their own.
The philosophers, indeed, by dint of hard reasoning on the
subject, had formed before the time of Alexander a conception
of the Supreme Being which does not differ materially from
that of the educated Christian of the present day.   " Loyal,"
says Pater, " to the ancient beliefs, the ancient usages, of the
religions of many gods which he had found all around him,
Socrates pierces through it to one unmistakable Person, of
perfect intelligence, power, and goodness who takes note of
him[4] "; and the same thing might be said with even greater
certainty of the deductions of Aristotle[5], whose declared

[1] 1 Kings xx. 23.   [2] 1 Sam. iv. 6, 7.

[3] Maspero, "La Fille du Prince de Bakhtan" in *Contes Populaires de
l'Ancienne Égypte*, Paris, p. 159.

[4] Pater, *Plato and Platonism*, 1901, pp. 85, 86.

[5] Aristotle, *Metaphysica*, Bk XI. c. 6.

monotheism caused him to be adopted in the Middle Ages as one of the Doctors of the Church. But there is no reason to believe that such lofty conceptions ever influenced in the slightest the beliefs of the common people, who alone count for anything in the evolution of the organized body of beliefs and practices which we call a religion. Socrates so successfully concealed his opinions in this respect from everybody but Plato, that the clear and practical mind of Xenophon seems to have never seen in him anything but a polytheist[1]: and that Aristotle's monotheistic teachings were not intended for the common herd may be judged from the correspondence, whether actual or imaginary, between him and Alexander himself, in which the hero reproaches his former tutor for having published doctrines which should only be taught by word of mouth, and learns in reply that his metaphysical theories would be unintelligible save to those whom he had himself instructed in philosophy[2].

It is evident, therefore, that the great mass of Alexander's subjects, whether Asiatics, Egyptians or Greeks, would require something more than the sublime theorizing of the philosophers before their religious ideas could be turned in the direction of monotheism. Nine hundred years before, Amenhotep IV of Egypt had indeed been led by his adoration of the material sun to put forward a religious reform which had as its principal feature the proclaiming abroad that there was only one God, in whose sight all mankind was equal; but the sole effect of this premature attempt to elevate the religion of his people was the loss of the external possessions of Egypt, and the posthumous branding of his own memory as that of a criminal. Possibly, too, the Hebrew Psalmists and Prophets had formed a like conception of the Deity when they asserted that among the gods there was none like unto Yahweh[3]; but that this

[1] Xenophon, *Memorabilia*, Bk I. c. 1, § 1–5.

[2] Plutarch, *Alexander*, c. VII.

[3] So F. H. Woods, *The Hope of Israel*, Edinburgh, 1896, p. 205, where he speaks of the religion of the Prophets and Psalmists, as "giving, on the whole, by far the most perfect and, as compared with other ancient literature, practically a unique example of monotheism." Yet as Winwood

idea seldom penetrated to their hearers is plain from their
incessant denunciation of these last for " whoring after " other
gods.   The mere announcement of the unity of God had therefore in itself an insufficient attraction for the masses, and for
the doctrine to be popular they had to be led to it by other
ways than those of argument or authority.   Now Aristotle
noted with his usual shrewdness of observation that the form
of religion in a state generally follows with fair closeness that
of its temporal government[1], so that men will be more inclined
to believe in what the Greeks called " monarchy," or the active
rule of One First Cause, if they live under a despot or absolute
king than if they are members of a democracy.   But when
did the world either before or after his time see such a beneficent and godlike despot as Alexander ?   The robber-kings
of Assyria had been accustomed to sweep across Western Asia
leaving behind them, as they boasted in their inscriptions, a
trail of vassal rulers impaled or flayed alive, of burnt cities,
and of plundered peoples.   The Persians, as has been said,
had more idea of the rights of their inferiors, and did not regard their subject territories as mere fields for exploitation ;
but the life of sensual luxury into which their kings sooner
or later subsided had its natural outcome in harem intrigues
and assassinations which deprived the central power of a great
part of its otherwise effective control over its satraps.   But
Alexander was in this, as in all other respects, the perfect type
of the benevolent master who thinks more of his servants'
welfare than of his own personal gratification.   Neither his
mother Olympias, domineering and masterful as she was, nor
his first mistress Barsine the widow of Memnon, nor his wife
Roxana of whom he is said to have been enamoured, nor the
Persian princess Statira to whom he gave his hand out of policy,
could boast that they ever influenced by one hairsbreadth the
direction of his sovereign will.   As for his justice, the swift

Reade points out, Solomon must have thought there were other gods than
Yahweh, because he worshipped other gods ; *op. cit. supra*, p. 201.
    [1] Aristotle, *Politica*, Bk I. c. 2, § 7.   Cf. Max Müller, *Religions of India*
(Hibbert Lectures), 1880, p. 292.

punishment that he measured out on his return from India to those of his officers whom he found guilty of oppression and malversation showed that under his far-seeing eye there would be none of those abuses of delegated power from which the satrapial system had suffered under his predecessors[1]. Modern historians have sometimes called him cruel; but in political matters severity is often the truest mercy, and the blood that he shed at Thebes and in Bactria probably saved a hundred times the number of lives which unchecked rebellion would have made it necessary to sacrifice; while the accidental and unpremeditated death of Clitus may well be pardoned to one who found not only his dignity as man but his royal authority wantonly outraged by a friend whom he had distinguished by exceptional marks of kindness. In every other respect his record is stainless. Although opposed at every step of his short career by orators and demagogues who saw in him the only obstacle to their unrestrained plunder of the fatherland, no legend has survived to his dishonour. On the contrary, all that we hear of him shows us for the first time in the world's history a conqueror who was at the same time a just and wise ruler, merciful to his fallen foe, scorning even in war to take mean advantage[2], and chivalrous to the weak to a degree that his age could neither understand nor imitate[3]. And with all this, he united in his own person those superficial advantages which have always been quick to win for their possessor the devotion of the mob. To a talent for generalship which neither Hannibal, Caesar, nor any modern general has equalled, he joined a personal bravery which often reached the level of recklessness and was always to be found in the forefront of the hottest battle. Whether we see him charging at the head of the Companion cavalry in the three great battles with Darius, pursuing with a handful of his guard the routed Persian army after Arbela, or first over the wall at Mooltan, Alexander is

---

[1] Arrian, *op. cit.* Bk VI. c. 27.

[2] See his repudiation of the night attack advised at Arbela: οὐ κλέπτω τὴν νίκην, "I steal no victory!" Plutarch, *Alexander*, c. XXXI.

[3] Plutarch, *op. cit.* c. XXI. and c. XXX.

always performing these feats of hardihood which in a leader strike more than anything the imagination of his soldiers. Add to this a generosity which made him willing to strip himself of his possessions to enrich his friends, a personal delight in that pomp and pageantry which forms the most direct road to the hearts of the proletariat, and a form, face and figure so distinguished that their one defect was for centuries after imitated by all who wished to be thought models of manly beauty[1], and we can no longer wonder that his contemporaries looked upon him as more than human. This wise and provident ruler of the world that he had conquered was at the same time a youth beautiful as Apollo, chivalrous as Bayard, clean as Galahad. Is it surprising that his name alone of all the conquerors of the East has endured through all changes of creed and culture, that the fierce chiefs of the Central Asian tableland still boast of him as their progenitor, and that the whole Mahommedan world still hold him the king of the believing Genii ? No Caesar, Attila, or Genghiz Khan has ever thus impressed the imagination of future ages[2].

Thus Alexander's coming gave an enormous impulse to that monarchical principle of government which from his time onward was to reign supreme for nearly two thousand years. Philosophers and sophists hastened to declare that democracy —as was indeed the fact—had proved itself incapable of governing, and that in the rule of one man was to be found the natural order of things and the only security for a well-ordered State[3]. Every one of the Diadochi or Successors of Alexander

---

[1] The wry neck or, in Mr Hogarth's words, " the famous inclination of his beautiful head towards the left shoulder " was imitated by dandies as late as the time of Severus. For authorities see Hogarth, *Philip and Alexander of Macedon,* 1897, p. 278, n. 2.

[2] Droysen, *op. cit.* I. p. 218 and p. 479, n. 1.   Major P. H. Sykes lately found an inscription in Khorassan to Sulayman Shah who reigned from 1667–1694 A.D., containing the words " His audience-chamber is the Sun ; his Army the Stars ; his authority is like Alexander's," *Journal of the Royal Asiatic Society,* 1910, pp. 1152, 1153.

[3] Bouché-Leclercq, *Hist. des Lagides,* Paris, t. I. p. 130, n. 2, points out that there was hardly a philosopher during the next three centuries who did not write a treatise Περὶ τῆς βασιλείας.

hurried in turn to assume the diadem, and Rome had no sooner contrived to crush her rival republic of Carthage than she too fell under the sway, first of dictators whose power was admittedly despotic, and then of emperors whose constitutional limitations were about the same as those of Alexander. That this was certain in time to react upon the universal conception of the Divine, followed directly from the law underlying religious phenomena which had been enunciated by Aristotle: but, before this could make way among the Greeks, thus suddenly promoted to the position of the ruling race, it was necessary that their own gods should be assimilated to those of their eastern fellow-subjects, or in other words, should be shown to be the same divinities under different names. Now, a movement with this object, even before Alexander's coming, had been set on foot in Greece itself, and was in fact the natural outcome of the ideas as to the origin and governance of the universe brought there by the philosophers of Ionia[1]. It was all very well for the masses—then as now, much given to pragmatism or the reduction of every abstract idea to its most material and practical expression—to believe that the power of every god was limited to an area of so many square feet surrounding his image or sanctuary; but how could such a notion be held by philosophers who had sought out the causes of things, by travellers who had visited neighbouring countries in pursuit of knowledge, or by soldiers who had fought there, and had found it necessary to pay reverence to gods other than their own? It is said that in naturalistic religions like those of Greece, there is always a tendency to consider as identical divinities with the same or like characteristics—to consider for instance all gods with solar attributes as but different forms of the sun-god—and the Greeks of the fourth century B.C. had thus taken many foreign gods into their pantheon. It was, as Socrates found out to his cost, an offence to bring the worship of new gods into the city; but the difficulty was got

[1] A parallel movement seems to have taken place in Babylonia, where all the gods were at one period identified with Marduk or Merodach. See Pinches, "Religious Ideas of the Babylonians," *Transactions of the Victoria Institute* 1893, p. 10.

over by the theory that the foreign divinity was only another form of some god already worshipped by the citizens[1], and by keeping his cult as private as possible. Later, when the popularity of the new deity seemed to be assured, an oracle of Delphi was generally secured authorizing the adoption of his worship under the name of his nearest Greek analogue, and in this way many foreign worships were brought into Athens itself[2]. Bendis, the moon-goddess of Thrace, had there from early times a temple or Bendideion[3], and the Syrian Adonis was publicly wailed for in the city when Alcibiades was setting out for Sicily[4]. This, too, was the more natural because the Greeks always acknowledged that their older divinities originally came to them from foreign parts. The myths in which the traditions of their origins were preserved gave Crete or Asia Minor as the birthplace of Zeus, an island in the Aegean as that of Apollo and Artemis, and the whole scene of the earthly trials of Demeter and Persephone was laid partly in Eleusis and partly in Asia[5]. As for Africa, Herodotus boldly asserts that the "names" of almost all the gods worshipped by the Greeks came from Egypt[6], and, although this is certainly not literally true, it gave him an excuse for identifying all the Egyptian deities of whom he had any knowledge with the Greek divinities whom he thought they resembled. But when Alexander's conquests had made the different subject nations really acquainted with each other's religion, the process of *theocrasia* or the fusion of one god with another received an impulse that carried it beyond all bounds[7]. The divinities of Asia Minor were naturally the first to be taken into the Greek pantheon, especially by the Athenians, always mindful of their Ionian

[1] Maury, *Histoire des Religions de la Grèce Antique*, Paris, 1857, III. p. 73.

[2] Demosthenes, *v. Midias*, p. 53; Herodotus, Bk VII. c. 189. Such gods were called by the peculiar epithet of πυθόχρηστοι. See inscription from Smyrna quoted by Rayet, *Revue Archéologique*, 1877, pp. 115–128.

[3] Xenophon, *Hellenica*, Bk II. c. 4.

[4] Plutarch, *Alcibiades*, c. CXVIII. Cf. Aristophanes, *Lysistrata*, ll. 387 *sqq.*

[5] Homeric *Hymn to Demeter, passim.*

[6] Herodotus, Bk II. c. 50.

[7] Droysen, *op. cit.* I. p. 698.

kinship; and the many-breasted goddess of Ephesus, Cybele of Pessinus with her consort Atys or Attis, and the Sidonian Astarte, were all worshipped in Greece after identification with different Greek deities in the manner that had served to naturalize the "Thracian" or Thessalian Dionysos, and the (probably) Egyptian Hermes[1]. As we shall see later, the Phrygian Sabazius and the Cretan Zagreus had already preceded them in secret, and Persian, Jewish, and perhaps Indian gods were to follow. From Greece, the passion for *theocrasia* spread both eastward and westward. The Greek kings of Upper India found it necessary to identify on their monuments the gods of their native subjects with the divinities of Homer[2], and those of the Central Provinces and of Asia Minor did the same with such effect that it is almost impossible for us to distinguish their many Artemises, Aphrodites, and different forms of Zeus from the gods worshipped under similar names in ancient Greece[3]. As for the West, the Romans, even before they became the masters of the world, took over the Greek pantheon *en bloc* by the simple process of calling their own Italian deities by Greek names; and if we still speak of Zeus as Jupiter, Athena as Minerva, Ares as Mars, and Hermes as Mercury, it is by reason of the syncretism brought into fashion by Alexander's conquests.

Neither must we forget that the deification of Alexander during his lifetime brought an entirely new conception of the Divine into the European world. The divinization of the king was indeed no new thing in Egypt, where the Pharaoh from

[1] See Maury, *Rel. de la Grèce*, t. III. cc. 15, 16. Aristophanes, *Horae* fragment 1 of Didot, and *Aves*, l. 874, is practically the earliest witness for their introduction into Athens. Cf. the Scholiast upon the last passage quoted, for their identification with Greek deities. M. Paul Foucart, *Les Associations Religieuses chez les Grecs*, Paris, 1873, pp. 57 and 85, shows the great rush of foreign gods into Attica after the Persian War and the mode in which their worship was propagated.

[2] Percy Gardner, *Catalogue of Coins*, etc., *passim*. Goblet d'Alviella, *Ce que l'Inde doit à la Grèce*, Paris, 1897, p. 73, notes that these coins reproduce "the usual type of the classical divinities Hercules, Dionysos, Poseidon, Helios, Pallas, Artemis, Niké."

[3] Droysen, *op. cit.* III. p. 73.

the earliest times was looked upon after his enthronement as the living form of the sun-god Horus ; but to the religious ideas of the Greeks it was evidently a surprising shock. The distinguishing attribute of a Greek god was his deathlessness or incorruptibility ; and although heroes like Theseus and Heracles were fabled to have become immortal and therefore fit subjects for worship, this was only because they were in the natural way the progeny of the gods themselves, and as such were taken into heaven by their fathers after death and the purging away of their mortal nature[1]. Alexander, on the other hand, demanded from the Greeks as from his other subjects divine honours during his life, and these were accorded to him with servile readiness by the governments of Athens and other Greek city-states, the Spartans not excepted[2]. What he meant exactly by this demand it would be hard to say, because his supposed sonship to Amen on which it was ostensibly based, was, as Sir Gaston Maspero has shown, merely the form by which, on a change of dynasty, the priests of Amen were accustomed to legitimize the accession to the throne of a king who could show no right. thereto but force[3]. It is evident, too, that Alexander did not himself take his deification very seriously, since he allowed its propriety to be discussed before him at a wine-party[4] ; and his apologists, Arrian and Plutarch, are possibly well-founded when they declare that it was a mere political device to secure the grudging obedience of his Macedonian countrymen[5]. But his successors in this matter went far beyond him. Ptolemy and Arsinoe, without any pretence of divine descent, were proclaimed " Saviour-gods " for their Greek as well as for their Egyptian subjects quite apart from any

[1] Callisthenes appears to have used this argument against the deification of Alexander during his lifetime, Arrian, *Anabasis*, Bk IV. c. 11. Cf. Budge, *Pseudo Callisthenes' History of Alexander the Great*, Cambridge, 1889, Bk III. c. 19, p. 135 ; Plutarch, *Pelopidas*, c. XVI.

[2] Droysen, *op. cit.* I. p. 668.

[3] Maspero, "Comment Alexandre devenait Dieu." *Annuaire de l'École des Hautes Études*, Paris, 1897 ; *id. Ét. Égyptol.* t. VI. pp. 286 *sqq.*

[4] Mr Hogarth, *Philip and Alexander*, pp. 197 *sqq.*. rightly points out that he never instituted any cult of himself, as did Demetrius Poliorcetes.

[5] Plutarch, *Alexander*, c. XXVIII ; Arrian, *Anabasis*, Bk VII. c. 29.

identification of themselves with Horus or any other native deity. Antigonus, when claiming to be the *strategos* or generalissimo of the whole Empire, was hailed as a god, which drew from the rough old king a repartee more pointed than decent[1]. So, too, was his son, Demetrius the City Taker, although at the time of his deification he had not even an independent kingdom of his own, but was merely ruling Greece as the viceroy of his father. And the barriers between the Divine and the human being thus broken down, men's minds soon became so familiar with the idea that they not only thought men might become gods, but declared that the gods were only deified men. The Athenians in the hymns that they sang to Demetrius declared that he was the only true god, and that the others were either asleep or too far off to be taken into account, or were not really gods at all[2]. But it is not with impunity that the religious ideas of a people can be thus suddenly and violently affronted. Within a few years from Alexander's death, Cassander's friend and envoy Euhemerus put forward, with the aid of a literary fraud something like that of Psalmanazar, the theory that all the gods worshipped by the Greeks had once been kings or at least distinguished men and women upon earth[3]—a doctrine that was received with as much enthusiasm in the Rome of the Republic as it once evoked in our own days among the followers of Herbert Spencer[4]. Later, the Epicurean philosophy, with its happy gods neither interfering with nor caring about the doings of mankind, came to the assistance of this rather crude atheism. Although the Stoic philosophers in their turn tried to introduce a more lofty idea of the Deity, it was probably not until late Roman times that they ever obtained anything like a grip on the people. Whether for good or ill, it is certain that the Greeks after Alexander's death never returned to the simple

[1] Plutarch, *de Is. et Os.* c. XXIV; *id. Apophthegmata Antigon.* 7. Cf. Droysen, *op. cit.* II. p. 295. Mr Tarn in his *Antigonos Gonatas*, Oxford, 1913, p. 251, would transfer the story to his grandson, but his reasoning is not convincing.

[2] Athenaeus, *Deipnosoph.* Bk VI. c. 62.

[3] Droysen, *op. cit.* III. p. 22 and note 2.

[4] Euhemerus' work was one of the first Greek books to be translated into Latin. See Cicero, *De Nat. Deor.* c. 42.

faith in their national gods which had sufficed for their fore-fathers.

This is a point that it is important to remember, because without it, it is hard to understand the passion for innovation in religious matters which seems for the next three centuries to possess unchecked sway over mankind. It appeared as if Alexander, who indeed had made all things new, had set free the gods of the ancient world to wander from one end of his Empire to the other, and the desire to proselytize appears for the first time in the world's history. Buddhism must have been prevalent in India for nearly a century before Alexander; but when it became the religion of the state in the reign of Asoka, grandson of that Chandragupta or Sandracottus who had talked with Alexander face to face, the Indian king boasted that he had sent out missionaries for the propagation of his new faith to the courts of Antiochus of Syria, Ptolemy of Egypt, Antigonus of Macedonia, Magas of Cyrene and Alexander of Epirus[1]. Whether the Indian missionaries ever reached the kings to whom they were sent may be doubted, and it is certain that these last did not pay the attention to them that Asoka claims; but it is quite possible that to the impulse given by such missions may be attributed some of the practices of the Jewish sect of the Essenes, and perhaps the monastic seclusion affected by certain worshippers of the Alexandrian god Serapis[2]. But if Buddhism could thus find its way westward from so distant a country as India, how much more must this have been the case with the other Oriental religions with which the Greeks had already some slight acquaintance, and which, as we shall see in the sequel, poured into Europe in such a flood that Juvenal compared it to the Orontes emptying itself into the Tiber. That the Greeks, ever eager for some new thing, were quick to avail themselves of the new ideas thus thrust upon them was only to be expected. But this rage for novelty was

[1] Droysen, *op. cit.* III. p. 341, n. 3. Rhys Davids, *Buddhist India*, 1903, p. 298, thinks it possible that the missions although duly recorded on stone were never sent.

[2] See Chapter II *infra*.

too violent to be content to follow the slow process of assimilation or *theocrasia* which was prevalent before Alexander. Religious associations for the worship of foreign gods were formed in which we may, if we like, see the first germs of the Christian Church[1]. In these each member had to pay a subscription towards the expenses of the cult, and the office-bearers instead of being appointed by the State were either taken from the members in rotation or chosen by lot. That these confraternities, as we should now call them, were at first composed of natives of countries other than Greece is shown by their clustering in the port of the Piraeus as the quarter where foreigners naturally congregated[2]; and their male members for the most part consisted of slaves, freedmen, and stranger merchants, who thus found a meeting-place in what was to them a foreign country. Their worship too was secret or rather was confined to members of the confraternity only, while its correctness of form was preserved by means of written books or rituals, thereby presenting many points of resemblance to that of the later Gnostics. But the superstitious, and especially the women who were always in Greece much addicted to *theoxenia* or the reception of strange gods, were early attracted by them, and they soon spread to every great city in the Empire. Thus we see for the first time in history bodies of men and women banded together, irrespective of nationality and social rank, for the purpose of religious observances, and religion becoming recognized as the affair of the individual rather than of the state, while each member of the association was directly interested in its extension. In this way, the Greeks became worshippers not only of their own sufficiently numerous deities but of those of well nigh the whole East as well. Their inscriptions show that Persian, Phrygian, and Lydian gods were worshipped by these associations, together with a whole crowd of Semitic deities among whom,

---

[1] Foucart, *Les Associations Religieuses*, etc., pp. 66–84. Cf. Maury, *Rel. de la Grèce*, II. p. 427. The composition of hymns was peculiarly the care of these associations; Foucart, *op. cit.* p. 114.

[2] Foucart, *op. cit.* p. 85.

if M. Cumont is right, there may even have been included the God of Israel[1].

The influence that these confraternities exercised in familiarizing the minds of the Greek citizens with the religious practices and tenets of foreign countries must have been very great. Every such association had a temple of its own, in which it offered sacrifices to its own particular god. But, after providing for this, the greater part of the subscriptions went in providing a periodical banquet at which its members could meet for social intercourse, and to which they were no doubt sometimes allowed to bring guests. But at these gatherings, as apparently at all others of the confraternity, all were equal, and there were no distinctions of rank. Moreover, in addition to the foreign members for whom the institution was originally designed, they must early have begun to admit Greeks ; and these were generally, though not always, persons who were in the first instance led to them by a leaning to foreign superstitions, and particularly to that orgiastic ritual with which the worship of the Asiatic gods was generally associated in Greek minds. It is noteworthy that among the Greek names inscribed upon the stelae containing the lists of members that have come down to us, those of women are far more numerous than those of men. Yet they seldom seem to have been of the highest class in their own community, and it is difficult to conceive of a Greek matron leaving her gynaeceum to take part with slaves and freedmen in nocturnal feasts or orgies. Among those whom we know otherwise as belonging to these confraternities are Phryne the celebrated courtezan, Tryphera and Aristion, who followed the same manner of life[2], and Glaucothea the mother of Æschines and a perfume-seller, a trade then considered as disreputable as in the reign of Louis XIV[3]. On the other hand, it seems to follow from what Plutarch says, that King Philip of Macedon first saw

---

[1] Franz Cumont, "Hypsistos," *Revue de l'Instruction publique en Belgique*, 1897, pp. 5–6 ; *id. Les Religions Orientales dans le Paganisme Romain*, Paris, 1906, p. 155 and note.

[2] Foucart, *Ass. Rel.* pp. 135, 136, 158.

[3] See Chapter IV *infra*.

and loved Olympias, mother of Alexander, at a meeting of one of these confraternities[1], and it is possible that outside Greece proper they lost something of their disreputable associations.

It must not be supposed, however, that these associations concerned themselves entirely with what we now call religion. The state, in cities like Athens, regarded them with great jealousy, and did its best to prevent them from forming a hierarchy by stipulating that their officers should only hold office for a year. This naturally prevented any continuity of policy such as a corporation like the priesthood of Amen could pursue, and set their chiefs upon making hay while the sun shone. Ignorant and degraded as most of their members were, and generally engaged in the pursuit of gain, it is not astonishing that they should thus have lent themselves to the worst and most dangerous because most profitable superstitions. The priests and especially the priestesses of the confraternities were always ready to lend themselves to the practices of divination and magic, to the sale of love-philtres and poisons[2], the interpretations of dreams and miraculous cures. To these charlatans came everyone who wanted his or her fortune told, or who wished to get rid of a rival, or to obtain the favour of a disdainful lover, or was simply tormented with idle fears or by some bodily disease incurable by regular means.

"The set of charlatans and market-men who hang about and wait round the altars of the Great Mother and Serapis; and who manufacture oracles either out of their own heads or by haphazard out of certain books for the benefit of house-slaves and silly women"

is the contemptuous way in which Plutarch describes these impostors[3]. Yet even in this way much was doubtless done to spread the knowledge of foreign religions; for many must have resorted to the foreign temples for magic or divination who would never have thought of joining the association by which they were maintained, and in magic it is

[1] Plutarch, *Alexander*, c. II.

[2] See Foucart, *op. cit.* p. 158, for the cases of Ninos and Theoris, priestesses who were condemned for such traffic.

[3] Plutarch, *Pythian Responses*, c. XXV.

always the least known gods and those worshipped by the races of lowest culture who are thought to be the most powerful. Moreover, many of these associations in time purified themselves by a sort of process of elimination from these undesirable accessories, and, so soon as they succeeded in attracting the adhesion of a sufficient number of respectable people, managed to get the god they were formed to worship enrolled among the native deities of the state or city. It was in this way that foreign gods like Serapis and Mithras, from being the divinities of a handful of foreign slaves, merchants or hostages, came, as we shall see, to occupy the highest places in the national worship of the Roman Empire. Thus Lucian tells us the story of the impostor Alexander of Abonoteichos, who with the help of a tame serpent with a cardboard mask gave himself out as the priest of an incarnation of Asklepios the Greek god of healing, and founded an association for its worship in Nicomedia in Bithynia. Later, he persuaded one Rutilianus, a man of consular rank who seems to have had influence at the Court of Marcus Aurelius, to join him in the propagation of his new cult and even to marry his daughter[1]. But the worship that he thus set up must have afterwards been recognized by the city of Nicomedia, for we find the representation of its god Glycon upon a Nicomedian coin of the time of the Emperor Gordian, the husband of Tranquillina[2].

It was apparently in these associations that the new spirit now manifest in the religion of the ancient world began to take organized shape. Among the Persians and Egyptians the priests were officers of state living on the property of their several corporations, and therefore with a natural leaning, except in the rare cases where their privileges or property were threatened by the Crown, against all innovations and interference with the established order of things. Among the Greeks, both in Hellas itself and in her colonies oversea, the priests with a very few exceptions were chosen from the

[1] Lucian, *Alexander or Pseudomantis, passim.* The story is well summarized by Sir Samuel Dill, in *Nero to Marcus*, pp. 473 *sqq.*

[2] Léon Fivel, "Le Dieu Glycon à Nicomédie," *Gazette Archéol.* 1879, p. 186.

native-born citizens at large either for their personal beauty, or for the wealth which enabled them to give in honour of the gods magnificent pageants and other festivals[1]. In no case did they regard themselves as having any teaching or pastoral mission, and were in no way interested in increasing the number of the worshippers of the god to whose service they were elected for a short term. Hence, their chief preoccupation was to keep strictly to precedent in the celebration of the public acts of worship entrusted to them, and they would have looked with horror on any alteration of the traditional rites. But in the associations founded for the worship of foreign gods, affairs were conducted on utterly different lines. There seems to have been a healthy spirit of emulation among the successive holders of the priestly office, for the vote of thanks inscribed on marble and displayed in the temple for the admiration of the confraternity was the distinction most sought after by them, and the deprivation of it was the most serious penalty exacted for dereliction of duty[2]. In order to obtain these rewards, it is plain that the officers had to carry out to the full the Apostolic injunction to be all things to all men, and there is actually a case on record where a priestess is praised because during her term of office she has offended nobody. This complaisance seems to have extended itself from the officials to the deities worshipped, who seem often to have been quite willing to fulfil a double office, and to appear as Aphrodite or Astarte to the Syrian and as Cybele to the Phrygian members of the association[3]. By these means, they made it possible for several nationalities to belong to the same association.

There was probably, however, a more intellectual side to this spirit of accommodation. All, or nearly all, of these associations celebrated mysteries or sacred dramas based on the same lines as the Eleusinian and setting forth, it would seem, the passion, death, and resurrection of some god. These plays, when we consider the relatively slender number of the

---

[1] Maury, *Rel. de la Grèce*, II. pp. 418 *sqq.*   Cf. Döllinger, *Judenthum und Heidenthum* (English edition), I. p. 214.

[2] Foucart, *Ass. Rel.* pp. 33–35.

[3] *Id. op. cit.* pp. 150, 151.

initiates and the limited means at their disposal, must generally have been acted with maimed and abbreviated rites in which a good deal was left to the imagination of the beholder. But this very fact must have set the always curious and inquisitive Greeks upon enquiry into the nature and origin of the scenes thus indicated rather than acted, and this in its turn must have led to many discussions and explanations of the gods there portrayed. For such conversations, too, there must have been far greater opportunities in the case of those *thiasi*, *orgeones*, or *erani* (as these associations were called), where members were few and in the habit of meeting each other daily than with the Eleusinian rites which were celebrated only once or twice a year and then in the presence of a huge crowd dispersed immediately after to the different parts of the Hellenic world. It is hardly putting it too strongly to say that anything like propagandism must have been confined to the smaller societies.

To sum up, then, Alexander united the whole civilized world for the first time under a single head and gave to it a common language and culture. By the natural gifts of his extraordinary personality, he at the same time set before it a perfect model of kingship and thus ensured the persistence of the monarchical principle for two millenia. This, his conscious work, had a direct effect on the evolution of monotheism, while in other respects his conquests proved the turning point in the history of religions. By breaking down the barriers which racial and lingual divisions had hitherto set up between different nations of the earth, these conquests led to a great fusion of the religions hitherto professed by them, and thus opened the door to the world-religions which were afterwards to share between them his vast Empire. Before his coming we see the ancient world divided into separate communities each with its own pantheon and forms of worship and neither knowing nor caring greatly about those of its neighbours. But immediately after, all this is changed. The interchange of ideas between East and West has thrown the different religions of the world as it were into a melting-pot, in which the germs of a different grouping of the human race are dimly visible. The

spirit of proselytism is abroad, and man now wants to impress
his own ideas of the Divine upon his fellows.   Above all, we
see the beginning of those great associations of mankind for
religious purposes which are henceforth to be the principal
factors in the world's history, and whose evolution has continued unchecked down to the present day.   All those that
followed Alexander were in this respect nothing more than his
conscious or unconscious imitators.   The great princes and
generals who after his death parted his Empire among them,
and the Romans who gradually ate up the fragments left to
these princes' effete descendants, could but carry on the work
set on foot by the Great Conqueror.   As Mr Hogarth has said,
very little that he did was ever undone, and for good or
ill, he has taken his place among the immortals[1].   Thus, from
the scientific point of view, there is none among the forerunners
of Christianity who did more to prepare and make ready its
way than Alexander.

[1] Hogarth, *Philip and Alexander*, pp. 277, 282.   Cf. Bouché-Leclercq
in Droysen, *op. cit.* I. p. vii.

CHAPTER II

THE ALEXANDRIAN DIVINITIES

WHEN Alexander's marshals began immediately after his death to divide his Empire among them, and Ptolemy the son of Lagos claimed and received for his share the province of Egypt, his more ambitious fellows must have smiled at his moderation. Egypt was an acquisition that had never been properly assimilated by the Persians, and although subjugated by Cambyses very early in their history, had more than once broken out into successful rebellion. Its inhabitants, then as now, were a race separated from the rest of the world by peculiarities of climate, devotedly attached to their own traditional institutions, and bitterly and obstinately hostile to the foreigner. Moreover, the enormous resources of the country were undeveloped, the importance of its new capital of Alexandria as the natural entrepôt of trade between East and West[1] had not then been made manifest, and the agricultural wealth which was afterwards to make Egypt the granary of Europe had been ruined by civil commotions and foreign invasions. Although Alexander was hailed by the Egyptians as a deliverer, and, like other conquerors before and after him, found little difficulty in coming to terms with the colleges of greedy and unpatriotic priests who were ready to welcome any foreign master so long as their own position was assured[2], he seems to have felt less interest in the unwarlike and servile *fellahin* than in the free warriors of Bactria and India who had fought so gallantly against him. Hence, he paid little

[1] Bouché-Leclercq, *Histoire des Lagides*, Paris, 1903 etc. t. I. p. 121. Dr Mahaffy, *Empire of the Ptolemies*, 1895, p. 11, thinks differently, but the importance of the city to the present day is against him.

[2] Bouché-Leclercq, *op. cit.* t. I. p. 104. Cf. Mahaffy, *E.P.* p. 4.

attention to their government, and Cleomenes, the ruler he had set over Egypt, thus found himself free to practise extortion on a scale which would certainly have brought down upon him the condign vengeance of his master had it taken place further east[1]. Or perhaps the Great Conqueror, among whose gifts the habit of attending to everything in its turn must certainly be reckoned, thought it well to let all things grow together till the harvest, in the consciousness that the campaign in Arabia, on which he was bent when struck down by the fatal fever, would bring him close to the confines of Egypt and therefore in a position to investigate on the spot the complaints against Cleomenes which had already come to his ears. Be this as it may, one of Ptolemy's first acts on reaching his satrapy was to seize Cleomenes and to put him to death, a proceeding which had, we learn, the full approval of his new subjects. This was but the earliest of a long list of benefits which his rule was to confer upon them, and which under his successors were to raise Egypt to a greater height of prosperity than she had ever enjoyed under her native Pharaohs.

It soon became evident also, that in choosing Egypt for his portion Ptolemy knew very well what he was about. While its western frontier was the Libyan desert and its southern was guarded by the cataracts, its northern coast was so badly off for harbours as to make it difficult to attack by sea, and it was practically unassailable from the east save at the Pelusiac or Port Said mouth of the Nile, and then only by an enemy marching through Syria[2]. Ptolemy, therefore, had ample time to consolidate his power by annexing Cyrene, making friends in his turn with the Egyptian priesthoods, and spending the money raised by Cleomenes' exactions in the enlistment of an army of mercenaries[3]. He also waylaid the body of Alexander on its way to the tombs of the Macedonian kings at Aegae, and installed it in a splendid sepulchre called the Sema at

---

[1] Droysen, *Hist. de l'Hellénisme*, t. II. p. 96; Bouché-Leclercq, *op. cit.* t. I. pp. 13, 14; Mahaffy, *E. P.* p. 25.

[2] As Demetrius the City-Taker, found to his cost. Cf. Mahaffy, *E.P.* p. 57.

[3] Droysen, *op. cit.* I. p. 14; Bouché-Leclercq, *op. cit.* I. p. 15.

Alexandria, thereby securing to himself, in the opinion of the time, a talisman of great power[1]. It was not long before the wisdom of these preparations was put to the proof; for, two years after Alexander's death, Perdiccas, the Regent of the Empire, had the new satrap tried in his absence for treason, and led a great army out of Asia Minor by way of Damascus to attack him. He found Ptolemy waiting for him in force at Pelusium, and after some of the royal troops had gone over to the enemy, and those under Perdiccas in person had suffered a severe repulse near Bubastis, Perdiccas was deposed and murdered[2]. The new settlement of the Empire which followed at Triparadeisos confirmed Ptolemy in the possession of Egypt, and left him in comparative peace to organize a kingdom which only ended three centuries later with Cleopatra[3].

Of the able and statesmanlike measures which Ptolemy took towards this end, only one need concern us here. The plan may have been Alexander's own, for no one was more likely to know Alexander's later mind than Ptolemy, who had been his master's companion from his youth, had shared his exile when banished by Philip, and had distinguished himself in India as one of his most trusted lieutenants. It is not impossible that among Alexander's plans for the government of his Empire, a religion common to both Greek and barbarian may have been included; for it is difficult otherwise to explain the active part that he took in the different religious observances of all his subjects, while the constant inquisitiveness concerning them which he showed can hardly have been merely archaeological[4]. At all events, soon after Ptolemy found himself secure in the possession of Egypt, he set himself to work to found a religion that should unite both his Greek and his Egyptian subjects in the bonds of a common faith. At first sight, no two things can seem more dissimilar than the religions of the two nations; but there was one point where they drew very near to each other, and it was to this that Ptolemy addressed himself.

[1] Droysen, *op. cit.* II. p. 103.
[2] Bouché-Leclercq, *Hist. des Lag.* I. pp. 24, 25.   [3] *Ibid.* I. p. 26.
[4] Droysen, *op. cit.* I. pp. 346, 699, 670. Cf. D. G. Hogarth, *Philip and Alexander*, p. 144.

Now religion in Egypt had always been very much in the hands of a professional priesthood who here, as elsewhere in Africa, formed organized corporations greedy for political sway, and sometimes proved more powerful than the king himself[1]. So far as the monuments show, the first of these corporations in point of time was that of the worshippers of the sun-god Ra, the chief seat of whose worship was Annu, On, or Heliopolis in the Delta. Its members were apparently the religious advisers of the vth or Pyramid-building Dynasty, and to them must be attributed the earliest or Heliopolitan recension of the *Book of the Dead* engraved on the walls of the chambers in the Saqqarah Pyramids. This corporation seems to have flourished unchecked until the Hyksos conquest, but was succeeded, when the invaders were cast out, by that of the priests of Amen of Thebes who, after crushing the " heresy " or religious revolt of King Amenhotep IV, gradually became the supreme power in the state, and established the theocracy or rule of the priest-kings, under which Egypt went rapidly down the hill. The decadence was stayed for a time by an uprising of the Libyan mercenaries, who placed their leader Sheshonq or Shishak, Solomon's suzerain, upon the throne, and thus founded the xxiind Dynasty. The deposed corporation of Amen thereupon transferred themselves to Ethiopia or Nubia, where they established a theocracy on the model of that at Thebes, and whence they returned later with an army of Sudanese to again enslave their native country. But Piankhi and his Ethiopians found themselves unable to rule Egypt from Napata, and when they finally retired behind the Cataracts, there was a brief but brilliant revival of old Egyptian ideas under the Saite or Philhellene kings of the Delta, who called in Greek and Carian mercenaries to the support of their throne. It was in their time that Herodotus visited the country, and Egypt began

[1] As when they seized the throne of Egypt at the close of the xxth Dynasty. So in Nubia in the time of the Ptolemies, the king was a mere puppet in the hands of the priests, who used to send him word when they thought that he had reigned long enough. For the story of Ergamenes (Ark-amen), who put an end to their rule, see Diodorus Siculus, III. 6. 3, or Budge, *History of Egypt*, 1899, vol. VIII. pp. 166 *sqq.*

again to play its part in the stirring events then fast coming upon Western Asia. It seems probable also that under them, the religious corporations, among whom the priests of Ptah of Memphis, one of the oldest of the gods of Egypt, for the first time take a prominent place, regained the influence which they had never wholly lost. Then came the Persian invasion, and although Egypt made more than one successful attempt to shake off the yoke of the foreigners, it was at last riveted firmly on her neck. After the flight of Nectanebo, the last king of the xxxth Dynasty, she was never again ruled by a prince of Egyptian blood[1].

During this long period—which is often quoted, not without reason, as the classic instance of the evils attending the Priest in Power—the mass of the Egyptian people had clung firmly to the worship of one god whose vogue goes back to very early times. While the rich and powerful were raising temples to Ra and Amen and showering wealth upon their priesthoods, the poorer classes remained faithful to Osiris and the gods of his cycle with such effect that most of the other divinities found it necessary to include him in their own cults. In the very earliest recension of the *Book of the Dead*, we find Osiris invoked together with Ra in a way that gives no hint that one has any superiority over the other[2]; in the great recension of the xviiith Dynasty, Osiris and Ra, already made into the "king of the gods" by his union with Amen, are said to have "joined souls" and become one[3]; and in the Saitic period, Osiris became united with Ptah and a very ancient divinity called Seker, in a triune deity called Ptah-Seker-Osiris to whom everyone looked for happiness after death[4]. So, when the bull Apis came to be

---

[1] See Breasted, *History of Egypt*, New York, 1909, *passim*; cf. Budge, *op. cit.*

[2] Wiedemann, *The Ancient Egyptian Doctrine of the Immortality of the Soul*, 1895, p. viii; Maspero, *Ét. Égyptol.* I. pp. 123, 167; *ibid.* II. p. 196, n. 1.

[3] Budge, *Gods of the Egyptians*, 1904, I. pp. 148, 149; Erman, *Handbook of Egyptian Religion*, 1906, p. 81.

[4] Erman, *op. cit.* p. 188. The fusion of Osiris with Ptah and Seker was a good deal older than the Saites. Cf. Wiedemann, *Religion of the Ancient Egyptians*, 1897, pp. 134, 135; Budge, *Osiris and the Egyptian Resurrection*, New York, 1911, I. p. 45.

adored, he was said to be the " life of Osiris," meaning probably
his earthly incarnation[1], and there is fairly good evidence that
Osiris had long before absorbed into himself the personality
of several older deities, such as Khent-Amentit "Lord of
Amenti," and Apuat "the opener of the ways[2]." It is plain,
therefore, that the practice of *theocrasia* which we have seen
rife among the Greeks was known to the Egyptians from the
very earliest times[3]. Yet, all this was effected without there
ever having been a special priesthood or college of priests of
Osiris such as undoubtedly existed in the case of Ra, Amen,
and probably Ptah. It seems really a case of the survival of
the fittest, or, in other words, of the choice by the Egyptian
people of the worship of the god best suited to their wants, in
spite of the well-meant attempts of their rulers to draw their
attention to other deities.

The reason for this obstinacy of choice is perhaps to be found
in the legend or myth of Osiris, which was at once more consistent and more direct in its appeal to human sympathies than
those handed down concerning the other gods of Egypt. We are
told that Osiris was the first-born of Nut the sky-goddess by
Geb the earth-god, that he appeared upon earth as a man among
men, and became king of Egypt, which he ruled wisely and well,
teaching the Egyptians the art of agriculture, giving them just
laws, and instructing them in the proper worship of the gods.
Later, he travelled over the whole earth, civilizing and subduing
the nations not by force of arms but by persuasion and especially
by the art of music which he took with him. On his return,
he was entrapped and murdered by his jealous brother Set or
Typhon who, with the aid of seventy-two conspirators and an
Ethiopian queen called Aso, shut him up in a coffin and threw
him into the Nile, by which his body was carried out to sea.

[1] Budge, *Gods of the Egyptians*, II. p. 196.

[2] Budge, *G.E.* II. pp. 118, 156, 264. So Naville, *Journal of Egyptian
Archaeology*, 1914, pp. 7, 8. M. Maspero thinks Apuat was originally god
of Siut and only a temple-companion of Osiris at Abydos, *Rev. Critique*,
1904, pt 2, pp. 194, 195.

[3] Steindorff, *Religion of the Ancient Egyptians*, New York, 1905,
p. 53; Erman, *H.E.R.* pp. 56, 57; Naville, *The Old Egyptian Faith*,
1906, pp. 146, 147.

We further learn that his sister-wife Isis, who had reigned in his stead during his absence, mourned greatly for his loss and wandered far and wide seeking and lamenting him, until she heard from some children that the coffin containing his remains had been carried away by the Tanitic mouth of the Nile. Following this, she found that it had been washed ashore at Byblus in Phoenicia and had been overgrown by a magnificent tamarisk, which the king of the country had had cut down and made into the roof-tree or pillar supporting his house. Then Isis disguised herself as a servant and became the nurse of the king's son, whom she would have made immortal but for the timidity of his mother, who cried out when she saw the child surrounded by the flames which were to burn away his mortality. On this, the goddess revealed herself, took away the pillar containing the coffin, and attempted to revive the corpse that it contained by her embrace. Afterwards, she gave birth to her son Horus, whom she destined from his cradle to be the avenger of his father. Meanwhile, the murderer Set had seized the throne of Egypt, and while hunting by moonlight came across the corpse of Osiris, which he tore into fourteen pieces, and scattered them throughout the land. Consequently Isis, who was at the time visiting Horus at nurse in her city of Buto, had to begin again her wanderings, sailing over the swamps in a boat of papyrus, and burying the fragments of the body of Osiris wherever she found them. One part, however, she could not find, this having been thrown into the Nile and devoured by fishes; and henceforth Osiris became king of the Underworld, where he rules for ever over the dead, welcoming those who successfully win through the ordeal of the judgment that all must undergo, and providing for them a happy life like that which the rich live on earth, in which agriculture plays a prominent part. Then Horus grew up to man's estate, and having provided himself with horse, fought three desperate battles with Set, many of whose followers came over to him. But, although he defeated his foe, he did not put an end to his existence, and Set still lives, haunting the deserts and wild places, and even, according to one variant of the story, ruling for a time over the south of Egypt (or perhaps only a part of it), while the sway of

Horus over the north remained unchallenged. As for the other gods of the cycle, Nephthys, the twin sister and reflection of Isis, was the wife of Set, but preferred to throw in her lot with Osiris, by whom she had a son, Anubis the jackal, the messenger of Osiris, who possessed many of the attributes of the Greek Hermes. So, too, Thoth, the ibis, was the judge who pronounced, or perhaps merely recorded, the final partition or arrangement between Horus and Set, and most of the other members of the Egyptian Pantheon were brought into the cycle one way or the other.

This is the legend of Osiris, as we find it in the tract *de Iside et Osiride*, which is generally attributed to Plutarch and was certainly written in the first century A.D. It has not been met with earlier in a connected form; but its main incidents are sufficiently corroborated by the monuments of the time to convince us that it fairly represents the popular belief of the Egyptians during the Ptolemaic period[1]. Plutarch, or the writer who assumed his name, gives us more than one explanation of it coupled with analogies drawn from other mythologies, which exhibit considerable archaeological knowledge and show us how far the comparative study of religions had proceeded even in his time. When he fails, it is generally from lack of acquaintance with the earlier forms of the religions of Egypt, which had evidently become in those days as much a mystery to the priests as to their flocks, and which the labours of modern Egyptologists have but recently begun to recover for us. Looked at by their light, and stripped of its many transparent inconsistencies and anachronisms, it seems plain that the story is not simple but compound, and represents an attempt to fuse together the religious ideas either of different peoples or of the same people at different stages of culture[2]. In the first place,

---

[1] Amélineau, *Essai sur le Gnosticisme Égyptien*, Paris, 1887, p. 144; Budge, "Papyrus of Nesi-Amsu," in *Archaeologia*, 1890, pt 2, p. 404; Maspero, *The Dawn of Civilization*, 1894, pp. 172–174; Erman, *H.E.R.* p. 32; Budge, *G.E.* II. p. 150. Manifest allusions to the legend are to be found in the Pyramid Texts. Cf. Maspero, *Les Inscriptions des Pyramides de Saqqarah*, Paris, 1894, pp. 105 *sqq.*

[2] This idea is treated at length in "The Legend of Osiris" in the *Proceedings of the Society of Biblical Archaeology*, 1911, pp. 139–154. See also "The Greek Worship of Serapis and Isis," *P.S.B.A.* 1914, pp. 79 *sqq.*

we see in it the animal gods of Egypt—Horus the falcon, Set the unknown animal or *scha* sacred to him, Anubis the jackal, and Thoth the ibis—whom we now know to have been the totems or rallying-signs of the different tribes who invaded Egypt, probably from other parts of Africa, in predynastic times. The *Sches-Hor* or Followers of Horus are so often alluded to in early dynastic texts that there can be no doubt that the tribe who had the falcon for their banner were originally the royal or leading tribe of these invaders. The memory of this fact was preserved in the custom, going back to the beginning of the ıst Dynasty, which assigned to the ruler of Egypt on his coronation a special name differing from that by which he was usually known, and borne in a rectangle representing the façade or front of a palace surmounted by a hawk[1]. Recent excavations at Abydos in Upper Egypt have shown that this custom was only once broken in the long course of Egyptian history, when a king of the ıınd or ııırd Dynasty, whose name is read Perabsen, cast out the falcon from above the *srekh* or rectangle containing his " hawk " or Horus name, and crowned it instead with the animal representing Set. This breach of conventional usage—whether significant of a political or a religious revolution or of some predominating foreign influence cannot be exactly determined—was healed by his immediate successor Khasekhmui, who bore both the falcon and the Set-animal above his *srekh* with an inscription proclaiming himself " He who has caused the two gods to be at peace " ; after which the rulers of Egypt returned to the hawk-crowned *srekh*, which was never again abandoned down to the last-known example under the Roman emperors. We may assume then that the fundamental stratum of the Osiris legend was a tradition more or less historical which preserved the memory of a struggle for supremacy occurring in the earliest historical times between the tribes represented by Horus and Set respectively. As the horse was a late comer into Egypt, and seems to have been introduced there by the Bedouins of the Sinaitic peninsula, where Perabsen's predecessors left their

[1] See " The Titles of the Thinite Kings " in *P.S.B.A.* 1908, pp. 86–94, 121–128, 163–177.

inscriptions, we may even read into it the statement that, while the Horus or falcon tribe were helped in the war by Bedouin cavalry, the followers of Set sought aid from the Nubian or " Ethiopian " tribes above the Cataracts[1].

To this foundation, however, there must have been added a myth conceived by a race in possession of a much higher degree of culture and greater imaginative powers than any with which the predynastic or protodynastic Egyptians can be credited. The earliest gods of Egypt of whom we have any record were, as we have seen, either animals or inanimate objects, a fact which is sufficiently explained by their totemic origin[2]. But spread throughout the basin of the Mediterranean, we find from the earliest times the worship of a god who was from his birth never anything but a man and a man who suffered a veritable death and passion before his resurrection and deification. Thus, in Crete we have the legend of the infant Zagreus, son of Zeus and Persephone, who was treacherously seized by the earth-born Titans, torn in pieces, and devoured, but was afterwards reborn as Dionysos to reign over gods and men[3]. So, too, in Cyprus, Syria, and Phoenicia, we hear of Adonis, the lover of Aphrodite, done to death by the boar's tusk, but returning yearly from the shades to spend part of the year with his mistress. In Asia Minor, again, was told the story of Atys, lover of Cybele, mother of the gods, who fatally mutilated himself in a fit of madness, but after death was resuscitated, and thereafter reigned with Cybele over all Nature. All these three legends bear too close a resemblance to that of Osiris for the four to have grown up independently, and although the point is not free from doubt, it is improbable that Egypt was

---

[1] In Plutarch's time the Ethiopians had a queen called Candace as in Acts viii. 27. Cf. Strabo, Bk XVII. c. 1, § 54. One wonders whether Plutarch in speaking of Aso did not confuse this title with an epithet of Thueris, the hippopotamus-goddess and wife of Set, who is called in a late magical text "Thueris, the great of sorcery, cat of Ethiopia." See Griffith and Thompson, *Stories of the High Priests of Memphis*, Oxford, 1900, p. 91.

[2] This is most clearly shown by M. Victor Loret in *L'Égypte au Temps du Totémisme*, Paris, 1906, *passim*. Cf. the same author's articles in *Rev. Égyptol.* 1902 and 1904.   [3] See Chapter IV, *infra*.

the source from which the others were derived[1]. No direct connection in ancient times can be traced between Egypt and the inland country of Phrygia, which seems to be the birthplace of the majority of these legends ; while it is of great importance to remember that Isis, Osiris' queen and sister, is represented in the early Egyptian myths as merely a magician or witch cunning in spells[2], whereas in the Phrygian and Syrian legends the consort of the dying god is the " mother of all living " or in other words Nature herself. It seems therefore probable that the legend of Osiris, like so many other things in Egypt, was African as to its body, but Asiatic or European as to its head.

It was therefore natural that in this legend of Osiris, Ptolemy should find the desired point of contact between the religions of the Egyptians and the Greeks. The religious institution which commanded the most respect among the Greeks of his time was undoubtedly the Mysteries of Eleusis[3], which were yearly celebrated with a circumstance that drew upon them the attention of the whole Hellenic world. Messengers went forth every year from Eleusis to all countries where Athenians could be found, to proclaim the Sacred Truce that was to ensure peace during the celebration of the Mysteries. Then on the appointed day in September, enormous numbers of Greeks from all parts of the world gathered together in Athens for a festival that lasted for nearly two weeks. First came the assembly of the worshippers and the proclamation of the hierophant that none but those unpolluted by crime and of intelligible speech (*i.e.* not barbarians) might take part in the Mysteries. Then

---

[1] See "The Greek Worship of Serapis and Isis," *P.S.B.A.* 1914, pp. 94–98, for this culture god of the Eastern Mediterranean. The original home of the myth was, possibly, Babylonia. Cf. " Legend of Osiris " in *P.S.B.A.* 1911, quoted above.

[2] See the story of Ra and Isis, Budge, *G.E.* pp. 360 *sqq.*

[3] By far the best and most consistent account of the Eleusinian Mysteries is that given by M. Paul Foucart in his three memoirs, *Recherches sur l'origine et la nature des Mystères d'Éleusis*, *Les Grands Mystères d'Éleusis*, and *Le Culte de Dionysos en Attique*. All these appeared in the *Mémoires* of the Académie des Inscriptions, tt. XXXV. (1895), XXXVII. (1900), and XXXVIII. (1904) respectively.

followed the solemn procession when the sacred objects, upon
which none but the initiated might look, were brought from
Eleusis under strong guard and lodged in the Eleusinion at the
foot of the Acropolis, their arrival being formally notified to
the priestess of Athena, the tutelary deity of the city.　Next
was made the proclamation of " To the sea, the initiates ! "
when all who were to take part in the ceremonies descended
to the harbour of Phalerum[1] to wash themselves and the
animals intended for sacrifice in the salt water, in the belief
that, as Euripides said, " Sea-waves wash away all sin."　After
a time spent in sacrificing and austerities very proper for
bringing the worshippers into a receptive state of mind, there
was formed the long procession which paced the Sacred Way,
twelve miles long, from Athens to Eleusis, beguiling the road
with hymns and choruses addressed to Iacchos, the infant
Dionysos[2], who was supposed to lead the procession from his
Athenian temple, the Iaccheion, with a pause at the bridge
over the Cephisus, where the crowd exchanged coarse jokes and
sarcasms in a manner peculiarly Attic.　Then came the arrival
by night of the procession at the Telesterion or Hall of Initiations
at Eleusis, the sky above which was made light by the glare of
the torches[3].　There, after more sacrifices, a sacred banquet,
in which it is not impossible that the mystic *cyceon* or consecrated drink was partaken of, and sacrifices in the temples of
Demeter, of Hades, and of Persephone with which the Hall was
surrounded, the initiates were shown a sacred drama, like the
mystery-plays of the Middle Ages, acted by the priests of the
cult, whose office, contrary to the custom of Greek cults generally,
was confined to two families in which it was hereditary and
highly paid.　This drama, the details of which were kept strictly
secret and can only be gathered from hints appearing in writers

[1] Foucart, *Les Grands Mystères*, p. 113.

[2] Iacchos was identified with Dionysos at least as early as the time of
Sophocles.　Cf. *Antigone*, ll. 1130 *sqq.*, and Dyer, *The Gods in Greece*, 1891,
p. 133.　Very likely, as M. Foucart suggests, he was originally the
personification of the cry repeated by the procession of the initiated.　See
Grds. Myst. p. 122.

[3] It had an opening in the roof for this purpose.　Foucart, *Grds. Myst.*
p. 137.

of a comparatively late date, seems to have set forth the Rape of Persephone, daughter of Demeter the earth-goddess, who was known and worshipped throughout Greece and her colonies as the teacher of agriculture and giver of laws to mortals. The initiates saw " with their own eyes " the capture of Persephone, when playing with her companions in the sunny fields of Eleusis[1], by Hades or Pluto the king of the dead, who takes her to his own gloomy abode beneath the earth, and the wanderings of Demeter in search of her lost child. Then they were shown how Demeter came to the house of Celeus, king of Eleusis, how she became nurse to the king's child Demophoon, and was detected by his mother attempting to burn away his mortal part in the way which the Egyptian legend attributed to Isis[2]. The next act, probably reserved for epopts or initiates of the second year only, exhibited the union of Zeus with Demeter[3], and the birth from the latter of a mysterious child in whom some see the Iacchos who conducted the procession from Athens to Eleusis, but who was certainly Dionysos in one or other of his forms[4]. We know also that the initiates took part in

[1] So Clement of Alexandria, *Protrepticus*, c. II. The scene of the Rape is laid in many different places. The Homeric *Hymn to Demeter* calls it " the Mysian plain," meaning probably Mysia in Asia Minor. A scholiast on Hesiod puts it in Sicily, Bacchylides in Crete, Orpheus in " the parts about Ocean," Phanodemus in Attica, Demades in " woodland glades." See Abel, *Orphica*, Fragm. 212, p. 239. Cf. Maury, *Religions de la Grèce Antique*, t. I. p. 479.

[2] Homeric *Hymn to Demeter*.

[3] Foucart, *Myst. d'Él.* p. 49 ; *id. Grds. Myst.* pp. 68, 69.

[4] M. Foucart, *Culte de Dion.* pp. 55–60, will not allow that Iacchos was ever identified with Dionysos and believes him to have been only the genius that led the procession. Dyer, on the other hand (*op. cit.* p. 128), makes Iacchos the young or second Dionysos born of Semele. But Aristophanes, *Frogs*, l. 321, and Strabo, Bk x. c. 10 (p. 402 Didot), both give him a higher position in the Mysteries than M. Foucart would assign to him, and the older opinion that he was the child whose birth was there shown seems to hold good. Cf. Maury, *Rel. de G. A.* t. II. p. 341, and Arrian, *Anabasis*, Bk II. c. 16, § 3 (p. 50, Didot). So Stephani, *Compte Rendu de la Commission Imperiale Archéologique*, 1859 (St Petersburg), p. 37, where monumental evidence is given in its support. Cf. Daremberg and Saglio, *Dict. des Antiquités, s.v.* Eleusinia (by F. Lenormant) ; Clem. Alex. *Protrept.* c. II. ; Libanius, ὑπὲρ Ἀριστοφάνους, vol. I. pp. 447, 448 (Reiske).

wanderings in dark passages and over obstacles and difficulties, which were supposed to give them an idea of the sufferings of the uninitiated dead in the next world, and that they were then restored to upper air in a blaze of brilliant light, were shown the mysterious objects brought with such care from Eleusis to Athens and back again, were given a glimpse of the beatitudes awaiting the dead who had been initiated in their lifetime, and were at the same time instructed in certain mysterious phrases or formulas which it seems fair to conclude they were to treasure as passwords through the realms of Hades[1]. It seems probable from this that the initiates were supposed to accompany Hermes the Psychopomp or "leader of souls" as the messenger of Zeus to the underworld, there to accomplish the deliverance of Persephone and to witness her restoration to the heavenly regions where she was again united to her sorrowing mother. Finally, there appeared Triptolemus, Celeus' son and Demeter's pupil, setting out in his car drawn by serpents to spread the knowledge of agriculture throughout the world, "an ear of corn reaped in silence" being, as we learn from a Christian writer, the "mighty and wonderful and most perfect mystery" exhibited to the highest degree of initiates[2].

It will be noticed that we have spoken hitherto of initiates; for none might enter the Telesterion unless they had previously been initiated, and two young Acarnanians who unwittingly did so were formally tried for sacrilege and put to death[3]. This initiation, or entry into the ranks of those privileged to behold these wonderful sights, began at the Little Mysteries, which were celebrated six or seven months before the Great or Eleusinian Mysteries properly so called, at Agra on the left bank of the Ilissus. These mysteries of Agra were under the control of the same sacred families as the Mysteries of Eleusis, for which

---

[1] Foucart, *Myst. d'Él.* p. 66.

[2] Hippolytus, *Philosophumena*, Bk v. c. 1, p. 171, Cruice. The whole drama is described by Foucart, *Myst. d'Él.* pp. 43–74 *q.v.*

[3] Livy, XXXI. 14. Cf. Foucart, *Grds. Myst.* p. 94. They betrayed themselves by asking questions which showed they had not been initiated. Hence the ἱερά or sacred objects could hardly have been statues, as some have thought.

they formed a necessary preparation. They were kept, if possible, even more strictly secret than the Great Mysteries, and the only direct evidence that has come down to us as to their nature tells us that they also took the form of a sacred drama, and that the scenes there enacted were taken from the legend of Dionysos[1]. This Dionysos, however, was not in the first instance the Theban god of wine born from Semele and celebrated by the poets, but his Cretan namesake Dionysos Zagreus or " the hunter," who was said to have been begotten by Zeus in the form of a serpent upon his own daughter Persephone, and while still a child was, as has been mentioned above, torn in pieces by the earth-born Titans from jealousy at hearing that the child was to be made the ruler of the world. It was also said that the scattered members of the baby-god were collected by Demeter, put together and revivified, a myth which late researches seem to show was alluded to in the Anthesteria, a festival celebrated in the Dionysion at Athens in the same Anthesterion or " flower month " as the Little Mysteries. There is much reason to think that the Anthesteria showed forth in a manner unintelligible to the beholders unless otherwise acquainted with the details of the legend, the putting-together of the different members—said to be fourteen in number—of the infant Dionysos, his subsequent resurrection, and his marriage with a priestess called "the Queen" who doubtless represented Demeter or Persephone. The inference seems unavoidable that it was some part of this legend that was acted in a manner impossible to misunderstand or mistake before the eyes of those admitted to the Little Mysteries[2].

[1] Foucart, *Culte de Dion.* p. 68; Stephen of Byzantium in Hesychius, *Etymologium Magnum, s.v.* Ἄγραι. Cf. Maury, *Rel. de la Grèce Ant.* II. p. 324. All that Stephen says is that here was acted a pantomime (μίμημα) of the things that happened to Dionysos.

[2] All these ceremonies of the Anthesteria are reconstructed and described by M. Foucart, *Culte de Dion.* pp. 107–163. That the tearing in pieces of Dionysos and the consequent origin of man was taught in the Little Mysteries seems to follow from Pindar's words (*Threnoi* Frag. x. 7, p. 102, Cod. Bö.) that those who have been initiated have seen " the God-given beginning of life." Transmigration seems to have been also

We see then that between the legend of Osiris as told by Plutarch and the legend of Eleusis as set forth in the Mysteries there were resemblances so close as to make it almost impossible that one should not be derived from the other, unless we are prepared to consider them as having a common origin. As Osiris was torn into fourteen pieces, so was Dionysos, the difference in the agents of this "diaspasm," as it was called, being due to the exigencies of Egyptian traditional history. The wanderings of Isis, again, find an exact parallel in those of Demeter, the object of the search differing slightly in the two cases, while the mysterious birth of Horus, the successor of Osiris, corresponds point for point with that of Dionysos in his second form of Iacchos. That both stories may have had their source in the folk-lore explaining the phenomena of the annual decay and rebirth of vegetation, Dr Frazer has shown with great attention to detail in *The Golden Bough* and elsewhere[1] to be possible; but this was too philosophical an idea for the sixth century B.C., when the Mysteries of Eleusis were founded or reduced to order[2]. Herodotus, a century later, no doubt expressed the views of the learned of his day when he asserted that the worship of Dionysos was brought into Greece from Egypt[3], and among modern scholars M. Foucart, who has done more than anyone to collate the few relics that remain to us of the Eleusinian worship, fully supports him in this. It

taught in them (see Plutarch, *Consolatory Letter*, § x.). There were therefore three degrees of initiation at Eleusis: (1) The Little Mysteries showing the history of Dionysos, (2) The Great Mysteries with the Rape of Persephone and the Wanderings of Demeter, and (3) The Epopsy (open to initiates of the second year only), showing the marriage of Zeus and Demeter and the birth of the new Dionysos.

[1] Frazer, *The Golden Bough* (third edition), Part IV, c. 5; Part V, vol. i, pp. 12, 263.

[2] The end of the Athenian monarchy and flight of the Pisistratids took place about 500 B.C. (see Chapter IV, *infra*). The Eleusinia were probably reformed not long before.

[3] Herodotus, Bk II. c. 49; Diod. Sic. Bk I. c. 96, § 4 *sqq.* It may, on the other hand, have been introduced from Asia Minor or the Mediterranean Islands, where it was certainly prevalent at a very early date. See articles in *P.S.B.A.* for 1911 and 1914 above quoted.

is therefore plain that the resemblances between the Diony-siae and the Egyptian worship were many and salient. Hence Ptolemy found his way clear when he invited Timotheos the Eumolpid, a member of one of the sacred families in which the Eleusinian priesthood was, as has been said, hereditary, and associated with him the Egyptian priest Manetho in the task of founding a religion which should be common to Egyptians and Greeks alike[1].

In framing this new religion, the first care of the king and his advisers was evidently to avoid shocking the religious and artistic feelings of the Greeks. Ptolemy Soter's position seems to have been much like that of a modern Governor-General of India; for, while he was not only tolerant but careful of the religious susceptibilities of the native Egyptians, his own Court remained in everything predominantly or exclusively Greek. In Alexandria, the site of which under the native Pharaohs had been the small fishing village of Rhacotis, he had practically virgin soil, in which it is doubtful whether any Egyptian temple existed, and it was consequently, as Alexander intended it should be, in all respects a Greek city. Greek was the language there spoken, and it was to the care taken by Alexandrian scholars to preserve the language and literature of Hellas in its native purity, that we are indebted for most of what we know of the classic tongue at its best. Its large garrison consisted almost entirely of Greek soldiers drilled and armed in the Mace-donian fashion, and to the great University or Museum, which Ptolemy's munificence founded for the sustentation of scholars, there flocked learned men from every part of the Hellenic world[2]. Here, indeed, was the first instance of the endowment

[1] Plutarch, *de Is. et Os.* c. XXVIII; Tacitus, *Hist.* IV. cap. 83, 84. Plutarch calls Timotheos the " exegete," *i.e.* the interpreter or dragoman; so that his being a Eumolpid would seem to rest on the testimony of Tacitus only; but there were " exegetes " attached to the Eumolpids at Eleusis, see Foucart, *Grds. Myst.* pp. 79 *sqq.* Bouché-Leclercq, *Hist. des Lagides*, I. p. 118, thinks the names Timotheos and Manetho only cover the fact that the new religion was compounded from the Eleusinian and the Osirian cults.

[2] Bouché-Leclercq (*Hist. des Lagides*, I. p. 129, n. 2) thinks the tradition that the Museum was founded by Ptolemy II Philadelphus erroneous. The

of research ; and the experiment had important results for most
of the modern sciences, not excluding that transmutation of
metals which made such wild work among some of the best
brains of the Middle Ages and Renaissance, but which Sir
William Ramsay has lately shown to be more capable of accomplishment than could have been expected from an alchemist's
dream.   At the Museum, Eratosthenes, "the Inspector of the
Earth," first set on foot the serious study of geography,
Hipparchus laid the sure foundations of the modern science
of astronomy, and Hero invented the first steam engine.   The
investigation of those secondary laws by which their insight
perceived nature to be governed was indeed the constant
occupation of King Ptolemy's "stuffed capons," as Timon of
Phlya contemptuously called them[1].   But these philosophers
would have been the first to receive with scorn the proposition
that anyone should be asked to worship the "brutish gods"
of Egypt under those animal forms in which they had long been
known to the more simple minded Egyptians.   Osiris, the
"bull of Amenti," as he is called in the early texts, was
worshipped under the actual form of the bull Apis at Memphis
and as a ram or goat at Mendes.   Isis was often portrayed with
the cow's head which commemorated one of the incidents of
her myth as set forth by Plutarch.   Horus, who was in fact
an older god than either of them, was, as the totem of the royal
tribe of the first invaders, worshipped at Edfu and elsewhere
as a hawk, and although the Egyptian priests kept up as long
as possible the distinction between this "Horus the elder"
and Horus the son of Isis, it is certain that their Greek worshippers saw no difference between the two.   While Timotheos
was doubtless willing to recognize the Eleusinian deities, of
whose worship his family were the traditional guardians, in the
Egyptian triad of Osiris, Isis, and Horus, he must have been
sure that he could not ask his art-loving countrymen to do
them homage in the guise of beasts or birds.

date of Demetrius of Phalerum's leaving Athens to take charge of it
marks it as the foundation of Ptolemy Soter. Cf. Mahaffy, *Empire of
Ptolemies*, pp. 91, 92.

[1] See Mahaffy, *op. cit.* p. 98.

The difficulty was got over in a way that was characteristic enough. The *theocrasia* or fusion of one god with another which we have seen playing such a prominent part in the religion of both Egyptians and Greeks, was of the very essence of the religion of Eleusis. At no time from the earliest mention of the Eleusinian worship onwards, is it possible to draw any sharp dividing line between Demeter and her daughter Persephone, or as Mr Louis Dyer rather flamboyantly puts it, Demeter and Persephone were at Eleusis " regarded as one, being so filled with mutual love that all barriers between them melted away[1]." " Excepting," he says again, " in her days of thoughtless youth, Demeter's Persephone is Demeter's self twice told," and the same dogma seems to have been prematurely revealed by Xenophanes of Colophon, who was exiled for his declaration that all the gods of his fellow-countrymen were but varying forms of the one deity. This identity of the goddesses of Eleusis must have been constantly present to the mind of the Greeks, who hardly ever spoke of Demeter and Persephone save as " the Goddesses Twain " or as the Mother-and-Daughter. But this was only the first step in what was called without circumlocution the " mystic *theocrasia*[2]," which went so far as to include in the persons of the Eleusinian deities nearly all the gods of the Hellenic pantheon. In the original Cretan legend, the infant Dionysos is the son of Zeus, whom he is destined to succeed upon his throne, as Zeus had succeeded in the Homeric myths his father Kronos, and this last, *his* father Ouranos. But the Zeus of Eleusis was by no means the Zeus of Olympos whom Homer hails as " father of gods and men," but who had to yield the empire of the seas to his brother Poseidon and that of the netherworld to his brother Hades. Originally known at Eleusis

[1] Dyer, *Gods in Greece*, pp. 178, 179, and pp. 73, 74. An inscription making the identification has been found at Smyrna. See O. Rayet in the *Rev. Archéologique* for 1877, pp. 175–178, where its date is put at the middle of the third century B.C., and the vases of Gerhard there quoted. Cf. Maury, *Rel. de la Grèce*, II. p. 362; F. Lenormant in Daremberg and Saglio's *Dict. des Antiquités*, *s.v.* Eleusinia, p. 549, and authorities there quoted.

[2] Damascius, *Vit. Isidor*, § 106. For definition of term, see *ibid.* §§ 3, 5.

as " the God " only, as Demeter with or without her daughter
was called " the Goddess," the Eleusinian god was also invoked
as Zeus Chthonios or the infernal Zeus, called by euphemism
Zeus Eubuleus (Zeus of Good Counsel), Pluto (Bringer of Riches)
and other similar names[1]. But by whatever name he was called,
he was always the king of the dead, and was thus again brought
near to Dionysos, whom Heraclitus of Ephesus, two centuries
before Alexander, had declared to be the same god as Hades,
lord of the netherworld[2]. In this double capacity, Dionysos
was therefore the brother, father, and spouse of his consort
Demeter, of whom he was also the child. He might therefore
be considered one of the first instances known in the history
of religions as a god who was, according to the way in which
he was regarded, either father or son[3]. Nor did the *theocrasia*
stop here. The Asiatic forms of Dionysos, whether we call
them Atys, Adonis or by any other name, were often represented as of both sexes, a doctrine which is also denoted by
Dionysos' Orphic epithet of Mise, and led to his being portrayed
in effeminate shape[4]. Hence, Dionysos and Demeter or Persephone might be regarded as the God under both the male and
female aspect. Moreover, Zeus was said to have ordered the
corpse of Dionysos to be buried at Delphi, where secret ceremonies were celebrated in connection with it by five priests
called Hosioi ; and this seems to have led to the idea common

---

[1] Foucart, *Myst. d'Él.* p. 34. He suggests that the real names were
" ineffable," *i.e.* only revealed to initiates. Xenocrates, whose date may
be put at 396–314 B.C., seems to have known of a supernal and infernal
Zeus (Clem. Alex. *Strom.* Bk v. c. 11), and a fragment attributed to
Euripides identifies Zeus with Hades (*id. loc. cit.*).

[2] Plutarch, *de Is. et Os.* c. XXVIII. ; Clem. Alex. *Protrept.* c. II.

[3] This was noticed by Clement of Alexandria, who (*Strom.* Bk v. c. 14)
says that Homer and Orpheus both " show forth " the Christian doctrine
in this respect. The verse he quotes from Orpheus makes Dionysos both
the father and son of Zeus. Cf. Abel's *Orphica*, Frag. 237.

[4] As in the Orphic verse : " Zeus is a male, Zeus is an immortal virgin,"
Abel, *Orphica*, Fr. 46. Hatch, *Hibbert Lectures*, p. 140, points out that
Xenocrates and the Stoics both made the same assertion. Cf. authorities
quoted by him and Euripides, *Bacchae*, ll. 330–350. A statue from
Smyrna showing a markedly effeminate type of Dionysos is to be seen at
the Ashmolean Museum.

to the classic poets Pindar, Aeschylus, and Euripides, that
Dionysos and Apollo were different forms of the same god, a
theory which is expressly confirmed by Plutarch[1]. But Apollo
"the Far-Darter" was always to the Greeks a sun-god, and
Horus from the first had the same character among the Egyptians, the emblem of the sun-disk being often added to the Horus-
hawk of their protocol by the Pharaohs of the New Empire.
Thus the identification of the gods of the Osiris cycle with their
Greek analogues was complete. It was agreed that Osiris was
to be represented as the Greek Hades, Isis as Demeter, and the
child Horus as Apollo. Herodotus and probably other Greek
writers had long before made the same identifications[2].

This settled, the question of the material forms under which
the triad was to be worshipped by Ptolemy's new subjects
became easy. A convenient dream, so runs the story told in
Roman times, revealed to the king the existence of a statue of
Hades or Pluto at Sinope in Pontus that was exactly fitted to
his purpose[3]. It is said to have been of colossal size, the work
of Bryaxis, the fellow-worker of Scopas, and to have been
composed of a mixture of the most precious metals with fragments of gems, the whole being coloured with a dark varnish.
This statue was given up by—or according to another version
was stolen from—the city of Sinope, and was installed with great
pomp in the magnificent temple or Serapeum built for it at
Alexandria, which for centuries formed one of the wonders of

[1] Macrobius, *Saturnalia*, lib. I. c. 18, for authorities; also Pindar,
Threnoi, x. 8, p. 116 (Bergk); Plutarch, *On the E at Delphi*, c. IX.

[2] Lafaye, *Culte des Divinités d'Alexandrie*, Paris, 1884, pp. 6–12, and
authorities there quoted. Cf. Foucart, *Culte de Dion.* pp. 66, 67.

[3] So Plutarch and Tacitus where before quoted. The conflicting traditions on the subject have been reconciled by Krall, *Tacitus und der
Orient*, Th. I. Bd iv. 83, 84. Cf. Bouché-Leclercq, *Hist. de la Divination*,
t. III. p. 378, n. 1; *id. Hist. de Lagides*, t. I. p. 118; Lafaye, *Culte*, etc.
pp. 16, 17. There is little doubt that the statue of Bryaxis represented
Asklepios as Bouché-Leclercq (*Rev. Hist. Rel.* 1902, pp. 26, 27) surmises.
Isidore Lévy sums up the whole question in the *Revue* last quoted, 1911,
pp. 146, 147, and 1913, pp. 308 *sqq.* So Ad. Reinach, *Rev. cit.* pt 2, p. 69.
The statue is described by Rufinus Aquilensis, *Hist. Eccl.* Bk II. c. 23.
Cf. Dionysius, *Periegetes*, ll. 254, 256 (Didot, *Geogr. Gr. mi.* t. II. p. 116);
Amelung, *Rev. Archéol.* 1903, pt 2, pp. 187–204.

the Hellenistic world. It doubtless formed the model for all the later representations of the new god called henceforth Serapis (in Egyptian, Asar-hapi or Osiris in his manifestation as Apis), which resemble each other in all important particulars. They show a bearded man of mature age, whose features have much of the majesty and dignity of the Phidian Zeus. On his head he wears the *modius*, a crown of basket-work on which are sometimes represented olive trees and which is said to be a reproduction of the *calathos* or consecrated basket carried in the sacred procession to Eleusis, and doubtless possessed for the initiated some mystical or symbolical meaning[1]. He is generally represented with an eagle at his feet, and by the side of him appears a triple monster which may perhaps represent the classical Cerberus with a serpent twisted round its body and equipped with the heads of a lion, a dog, and a wolf. It seems, therefore, that in choosing this statue the founders of the Alexandrian religion had quite turned their backs on the lighter and more joyous aspects of the mystic Dionysos, and intended to regard him as the god of the dead merely[2]. The same was not the case with his consort Isis, who is generally represented as a young matron of stately appearance having sometimes the crescent moon on her head, and sometimes a crown of lotus flowers interspersed with ears of corn. She is dressed in a fringed tunic reaching to her feet, having over her shoulders a mantle tied by its ends between the breasts in a peculiar knot. In one hand she bears the *sistrum* or rattle used in her worship, and in the other a horn of abundance or other emblem, while the head is frequently covered by a long veil. Both the attitude and the dress are always of the strictest modesty, and the features wear an expression of gentle

[1] Probably it had some reference to his character as god of vegetation, as shown by his epithet of "Frugifer." The explanation of Macrobius, *Saturnalia*, I. c. 20, which refers it to the sun, is absurd. Perhaps it may be connected with his epithet of πολυδέγμων "receiver of many." So Æl. Aristides speaks of him as the receiver of souls. See p. 60 *infra*.

[2] See last note. The eagle was adopted as a kind of family crest by the Ptolemies and appears on all their coins. See examples in Mahaffy, *Emp. of the Ptolemies, passim*. What is probably a reproduction of Bryaxis' statue is now at Naples and is described by Lafaye, *op. cit.* p. 274.

benevolence, in which it is possible to see a trace of melancholy. The Alexandrian Horus is seldom represented otherwise than in child form, the type being taken from the Egyptian Horus known as Har--pa-khrat (Horus the Child) of which the Alexandrians made Harpocrates. In this form he was represented with his finger in his mouth in accordance with the usual Egyptian ideogram for childhood, and this gave rise to the story among the Greeks that he was the god of silence. Sometimes he is shown with wings like the classical Eros, frequently seated on the lotus or with the lotus flower on his head, and very often with the hawk which formed his proper emblem[1]. He was seldom represented in a group containing Serapis, although bas-reliefs and statues showing Serapis and Isis together are common ; but groups representing Isis suckling Horus have been found in some numbers. Generally it may be said that the *modius* on the head is the distinguishing mark of the figure of Serapis, the peculiar breast-knot that of Isis, while Horus can seldom be recognized with certainty save by the gesture of the forefinger in the mouth or, as the Greek artists preferred to represent it, on the lips. From this time forward, the Alexandrian Greeks could worship the chief deities of their native fellow-citizens under forms which they felt to be worthy of the Divine.

Thus, the worship of the great Egyptian triad under their Greek forms was inaugurated, as was our own English Reformation in the sixteenth century, as a measure of statecraft, by a king who hardly cared to conceal that in doing so he had only his own interest to serve. Yet it may be said at once, that so far as its political purpose was concerned, the Alexandrian religion was from the outset foredoomed to failure. The Egyptians of Philhellenic times were of all the nations of the earth at once the most superstitious and the most fanatically attached to their traditional modes of worship. Although until the rise of the theocracy, the importation of foreign gods was not unknown, under the Ethiopians, the Persians, and Alexander, the Egyptians had not scrupled to sacrifice their nationality to their religion, and to accept a foreign governor

---

[1] See Lafaye, pp. 259, 260. Except in amulets, representations of Harpocrates are not very common. Cf. *P.S.B.A.* 1914, p. 92.

so long as the worship of their native gods under types that had been observed by them for more than four millenia remained untouched. How then could they be expected to recognize their native deities in forms beautified and dignified by Greek art indeed, but so foreign to all their traditional ideas that nothing distinctly Egyptian about them remained ?

To this question there could be but one answer, and it is not extraordinary that the native Egyptians proved as recalcitrant to their new king's endeavour to unite them in a common worship with their Greek masters as the Jews did under the somewhat similar attempt of Antiochus Epiphanes. The Egyptian priests allowed Ptolemy to set up at Memphis, which had become since the ruin of Thebes the religious capital of the country, a Serapeum, doubtless modelled on that of Alexandria, by the side of the native temple established for the delectation of the living Apis and for the solemn burial of his predecessors : but they took care that it should be separated from the Egyptian Serapeum by a long avenue of sphinxes, and that no Greek prayers should ever be allowed to defile the purity of the native Egyptian sanctuary[1]. Moreover, Egypt, resembling in this perhaps all countries with strongly marked geographical characteristics, has exhibited through all ages a wonderful power of conquering her conquerors, or, in other words, of forcing her foreign rulers to accept the ideas that they found there, instead of adopting at their instance innovations on customs consecrated by centuries of usage. Hence the Ptolemies, as time went on, found it necessary to pay ever more and more attention to the native Egyptian religion, and Ptolemy V Epiphanes was crowned at Memphis, as is recorded on the Rosetta Stone, with all the religious ceremonies that made him in the eyes of the Egyptians the living Horus, son of the sun-god, the beloved of Ptah and the rest, as fully as any of the ancient Pharaohs[2]. All the Ptolemies, too, seem to have spent

[1] Maury in *Revue des Deux Mondes*, Sept. 1855, p. 1073 ; Mariette, *Le Sérapeum de Memphis*, ed. Maspero, Paris, 1882, I. pp. 114, 115, 124.

[2] Bouché-Leclercq, *Hist. des Lagides*, I. pp. 232, 233. Cf. Mahaffy, *Empire of Ptolemies*, pp. 204 *sqq.* The Egyptianizing tendencies of the later Ptolemies shown by the decrees of the priests on the Rosetta and

very considerable sums on the restoration and keeping-up of
the temples in Egypt dedicated to such thoroughly native gods
as Amon of Thebes and Horus of Edfu, besides those at Philae
and elsewhere raised not to the Alexandrian but to the Egyptian
Osiris and his cycle. What truth there is in the statement
of Macrobius that Ptolemy Soter compelled by " tyranny "
the Egyptians to take Serapis into their temples, it is impossible
to say ; but as his image in Greek form has never been found
in any of them, it is plain that the priests must have found some
way of evading the royal order, if it were really given[1].

Ptolemy, however, was building better than he knew, and
the hybrid cult which the provident old soldier had fashioned
as an instrument of government turned out to be the first, and
not the least successful, of the world-religions for which Alexander's conquests left clear the way. During the wars of the
Diadochi, all the powers who at any time found themselves
Ptolemy's pawns in the mighty war game then played on a
board stretching from India to Thrace, thought to curry favour
with their rich ally by giving countenance to his new religion.
An association of Sarapiasts or worshippers of Serapis held
their meetings in the Piraeus not long after the institution of
the Alexandrian cult[2] ; and before the death of Ptolemy Soter,
a Serapeum was built in Athens over against the Acropolis
itself[3]. Cyprus, Rhodes, Antioch, Smyrna, and Halicarnassus
were not long in following suit, and before the end of the century
several of the islands of the Ægean together with Boeotia, which
was said by some to be the native country of Dionysos, had
adopted the new worship. In the second century B.C., the
temples of the Alexandrian gods were to be found in Delos,
Tenedos, Thessaly, Macedonia and the Thracian Bosphorus
in Europe, and in Ephesus, Cyzicus and Termessus among

Canopus Stones were first pointed out by Revillout in the *Revue Archéologique*, 1877, pp. 331 *sqq.* A new decree of the same kind under Epiphanes
has been published by M. Daressy, *Recueil de Travaux* etc., 1911, pp. 1 *sqq.*

[1] Macrobius, *Saturn.* Bk I. c. 7.

[2] Foucart, *Les Associations Religieuses*, p. 207, Inscr. 24 ; *C.I.G.* No. 120.
The tablet is now in the British Museum.

[3] Lafaye, *Culte*, etc. p. 35 ; Pausanias, Bk I. c. 18, 4.

other places in Asia Minor[1]. But their greatest triumph was awaiting them further west. Invited by Hiero II into Sicily, they were not long in working their way up the coast, and a hundred years before our era a temple to Serapis was in existence at Puteoli[2]. It was evidently no new foundation and had probably been built some fifty years earlier, at which date perhaps the first Isium at Pompeii was also in existence[3]. Somewhere about 80 B.C., the Alexandrian worship was introduced into Rome itself, and thereafter no action of the authorities was able to expel it[4]. Its temples were more than once thrown down by order of the consuls; but they were always rebuilt, and in 43 B.C., the aedile Marcus Volusius, who had been proscribed by the triumvirs, found the linen robe and the dog's head mask of a priest of Isis the most efficient disguise in which to escape Sulla's bravos[5]. Under the Empire, the temple of Isis in the Campus Martius became one of the fashionable resorts of the Roman youth; and, although Tiberius seized the occasion of a real or pretended scandal in connection with it to exile a large number of the faithful to Sardinia, his successors were themselves initiated into the faith; while under Nero the worship of the Alexandrian gods was formally recognized by the state[6]. From that time, it followed the Roman arms into every quarter of the ancient world, and its monuments have been found in Morocco, Spain, France, Great Britain, Germany, and the Danube provinces. Ridicule was as powerless to stop its march as persecution, and the satire of Juvenal and Martial had no more effect on it than the banter of the New Comedy, which was quick to observe that even in

[1] Lafaye, *op. cit.* pp. 35–38; *id. Dictionnaire des Antiquités* of Daremberg and Saglio, *s.v.* Isis; Drexler in Roscher's *Lexikon der Mythologie, s.v.* Isis, esp. p. 379.

[2] Lafaye, *op. cit.* p. 40; *C.I.L.* I. 577.

[3] Lafaye, see last note.

[4] Lafaye, *op. cit.* pp. 44 *sqq.*

[5] Lafaye, *op. cit.* pp. 44–47. For the story of Marcus Volusius see Appian, *de Bello Civili*, Bk IV. c. 6, § 47.

[6] Tibullus, *Elegiacs*, I. iii. .23; *ibid.* I. vii. 27; Ovid, *Am.* II. xiii. 7; *id. op. cit.* II. xiv. The story of the expulsion is told by Josephus, *Antiquities*, XVIII. c. 3. Cf. Lafaye, *op. cit.* chap. III *passim.*

Menander's day the gilded youth of Athens swore " by Isis " or
" by Horus[1]." Under the Antonines, it probably reached its
apogee, when the Emperor Commodus appeared in the pro-
cessions of the cult among the bearers of the sacred images,
and few Romans seem to have been aware that the Alexandrian
gods were not Roman from the beginning. Like Ptolemy's
master, Ptolemy's gods might have boasted that they commanded the allegiance of the whole civilized world[2].

The causes of this astonishing success must be looked for
within the religion itself. No name has come down to us of
any prophet or priest of the Alexandrian religion possessing
a commanding personality like St Paul, Mohammed, Luther,
or Calvin ; and we must therefore conclude that it was its own
intrinsic merits which thus commended it to so many widely-
differing peoples[3]. Foremost among these was, it would seem,
its extraordinary timeliness. Alexander's conquests had broken
down the barriers that speech and race had set up between
neighbouring peoples, and had at the same time united many
hundreds of jealous and discordant states under a single head.
In the many royal courts which had been set up as a result
of the partition of Alexander's Empire, philosophers of every
school were chanting the political advantages of an enlightened
monarchy over the greedy scramble for place and power inseparable from democracy, and the doctrine was bound sooner
or later to be applied to religion[4]. We have seen how far both
Egyptians and Greeks had before then carried the practice of
theocrasia, but the founders of the Alexandrian religion were
not slow in pushing it to its only legitimate conclusion. Serapis,
unlike the Greek Zeus, from the first declined to brook any
partition of his empire over nature. " Wouldst thou know

---

[1] *Comicor. Graecor. Fragmenta* of Didot, pp. 517 and 629, and Lafaye,
op. cit. p. 31.

[2] Lafaye, *op. et loc. cit.* and especially p. 62.

[3] So Parisotti, *Ricerche sul culto de Iside e Serapide*, Roma, 1888,
p. 52 *sqq.* ; and Dill, *Nero to Marcus*, pp. 564, 565: "The history of
the Isiac cult at Rome from Sulla to Nero is really the history of a great
popular religious movement......."

[4] See Chapter I, *supra*, pp. 12, 14. Cf. Droysen, *op. cit.* II. p. 471.

what god I am," said his oracle at the Alexandrian Serapeum to Nicocreon, the Cypriote king. "I myself will tell thee. The heavenly cosmos is my head; the sea my belly. My feet are the earth; my ears are in the aether. My far-beaming eye is the radiant light of the sun[1]." In other words, Serapis is himself the universe, which is probably the meaning to be attached to the name given to Osiris in the *Book of the Dead* which Egyptologists translate "Lord of Totality." But Aeschylus had already said the same thing about Zeus[2], and as the gods of the Greeks were never anything else than the powers of nature, Serapis thus comprised in his single person the whole Greek pantheon. Hence "Serapis alone is Zeus" came to be a sort of watchword in the Alexandrian religion to be endlessly repeated on statues, gems, and all the other material relics of the cult[3]. A little later and we find Serapis drawing to himself the worship of all the Mediterranean gods who had a common origin with Osiris and Dionysos. Adonis, as appears from the beautiful idyll of Theocritus, in the reign of Ptolemy Soter's successor was worshipped as another form of Osiris in the royal palace itself[4]. Atys, Cybele's lover, was also identified with him[5]; and, as the Stoic philosophy, which taught that all the gods were but different forms of the one Divine energy,

[1] Macrobius, *Saturn.* Bk I. c. 20. Bouché-Leclercq (*R.H.R.* 1902, t. XLVI. p. 19, n. 1) says these lines are a forgery of late date. Krall, *Tacitus*, etc. Th. I, Bk iv., is of the contrary opinion. Nicocreon of Cyprus was certainly a contemporary of Ptolemy Soter, and helped him against Perdiccas.

[2] Clem. Alex. *Strom.* Bk v. c. 14. So Ælius Aristides, *in Serapidem*, p. 91 (Dindorf), says that Serapis "is present in all things and fills the universe."

[3] Lafaye, *Culte*, etc., pp. 306, 307, 324, 325, for examples. Cf. Inscription from Kios in Bithynia given by Robiou in *Mélanges Graux*, Paris, 1884, pp. 601, 602; Parisotti, *op. cit.* p. 55.

[4] Theocritus, *Idyll*, xv.; Damascius, *Vit. Isidor.* 106; Socrates, *Hist. Eccl.* Bk III. c. 23. In *Le Culte d'Adonis-Thammuz*, Paris, 1901 (pp. 51–54, 69, 109), M. Ch. Vellay has shown the fusion in early Christian times of the legends of Adonis, Atys and Osiris.

[5] Frazer, *Golden Bough*, Part IV, p. 357 and n. 1; cf. Stephen of Byzantium, *s.v.* 'Αμαθοῦς; Döllinger, *Jud. und Heid.* I. p. 145; Decharme in Daremberg and Saglio, *s.v.* Cybele for authorities.

came into fashion, Serapis was equated with the numerous sun-gods whose worship poured in from the Semitic east. "The eternal sun" came to be one of his most-used epithets, and he is often invoked as the equivalent of the Greek Helios and of the Persian sun-god Mithras[1]. Nor did his consort long remain behind him. "I, the parent of the works of nature" is the style in which Isis announces herself to her votary Lucius in Apuleius' romance,

"queen of all the elements, earliest offspring of the ages, highest of godheads, sovereign of the Manes, first of the heavenly ones, one-formed type of gods and goddesses. The luminous heights of heaven, the health-giving breezes of the sea, the sad silences of the lower world, I govern by my nod. I am she whose godhead, single in essence, but of many forms, with varied rites and under many names, the whole earth reveres. Hence the Phrygians, first born of men, call me Pessinuntica, Mother of the Gods; here the first inhabitants of Attica, Cecropian Minerva, there the wave-rocked Cypriotes, Paphian Venus; the arrow-bearing Cretans, Diana Dictynna; the three-tongued Sicilians, Stygian Proserpine; the Eleusinians, the ancient goddess Ceres;—others Juno, others Bellona, these Hecate, those Rhamnusia; and they who are lighted by the first rays of the sun-god on his rising, the Ethiopians, the Africans, and the Egyptians skilled in the ancient teaching, worshipping me with ceremonies peculiarly my own, call me by my true name, Queen Isis[2]."

As we shall see later (p. 64, *infra*) her spouse Osiris claimed also to be the highest of godheads; and the final unity of the Divine essence to which the μυστικὴ θεοκρασία was logically bound to lead could hardly be stated in clearer language[3].

[1] Julian, *ad Reg. Sol.* Orat. IV. cc. 135, 136; Eusebius, *Praep. Ev.* Bk III. c. 15; Kenyon, *Greek Papyri in British Museum*, 1893, p. 65; Wessely, *Griechische Zauberpapyri von Paris*, etc., Wien, 1888, pp. 61 *sqq.*; Leemans, *Papyri Graeci Mus. Ant. Pub. Lugduni-Batavi*, Leyden, 1885, II. pp. 26, 27; Parthey, *Zwei griech. Zauberpapyri*, Berlin, 1866, p. 127.

[2] Apuleius, *Metamorphoses*, Bk XI. c. 5.

[3] So Ramsay, *Cities and Bishoprics of Phrygia*, Oxford, 1895, I. p. 92, says that "the essential idea" of the mysteries was that all the gods there worshipped were but different forms of the one. In the "Greek Worship of Serapis and Isis," I have endeavoured to show how this idea was elaborated in the cult of the Alexandrian divinities.

Thus, we see that what has been called a monotheistic pantheism instead of an incoherent mass of local worships was one of the advantages of the Alexandrian cult. But in the religion of the crowd, feeling plays a more important part than reason, and the idea which it first gave mankind of what would be now called the " fatherhood of God " was probably by far its most alluring feature. It has frequently been said that the Greeks although they feared, did not love their gods, and so far as the Homeric deities are concerned, it is difficult to see why they should. Apollo openly expresses his contempt for " pitiful mortals, who like unto leaves now live in glowing life, consuming the fruit of the earth, and now again pine unto death[1]," Hera does not hide her scorn for " the creatures of a day," and the help that Athena gives the Greeks in their war against Troy is expressly said to be due to no kindlier feeling than rage at the slight which Paris had put upon her beauty[2]. As for the Egyptian religion, if it ever exhibited the lofty conceptions and sublime ideas with which the earlier Egyptologists were inclined to credit it, it had long before Ptolemy's time lost all trace of them, and had degenerated into " a systematized sorcery " in which the gods were compelled to grant merely material benefits directly they were demanded with the proper ritual[3]. But when we turn from the Greek and Egyptian creeds to the new faith which was compounded from the two, we are at once struck by the complete change which seems to have come over the worshippers' conception of the Divine. Isis, from the wily magician of Pharaonic Egypt, has now become " the haven of peace and the altar of pity[4]."

" O thou holy and eternal protectress of the race of men " are the terms with which Lucius addresses her,

" thou who ever givest good gifts to comfort-needing mortals, thou dost bestow upon the lot of the wretched the sweet affection of a

---

[1] Homer, *Iliad*, XXI. 462 (translation by Lang, Leaf and Myers).

[2] Cf. Penelope's speech on the jealousy of the gods, *Odyssey*, XXIII. 208.

[3] Sayce, *Religions of Ancient Egypt and Babylonia* (Gifford Lectures), Edin. 1902, p. 201; Naville, *The Old Egyptian Faith*, pp. 308, 309; Maspero, *Ét. Égyptol.* I. p. 163 and II. p. 277.

[4] Apuleius, *Met.* Bk XI. c. 15.

mother. There is no day nor night nor smallest moment which is
not occupied with thy good deeds. Thou dost protect mankind by
sea and land, and scattering the storms of life dost stretch forth to
them thy saving hand, with which thou dost even spin anew the
hopelessly twisted web of the Fates, and dost temper the blasts of
fortune and restrain the hostile courses of the stars[1]."

So Ælius Aristides in his encomium of Serapis written after
having been saved from shipwreck, as he considered, by the
direct intervention of the god, tells us that Serapis is the god
who " purifies the soul with wisdom, and preserves the body
by giving it health[2]," that he alone

" is adored by kings as by private persons, by the wise as by the
foolish, by the great as by the small, and by those on whom he has
bestowed happiness as well as those who possess him alone as a
refuge from their trouble[3],"

that he is " the protector and saviour of all men[4]," " the most
loving of the gods towards men[5]," " greatly turned towards
mercy[6]," and " the light common to all men[7]." We hardly
want his elaborate demonstration that Serapis alone of all the
gods is ready to assist him who invokes him when in need, to
convince us that the reign of the warlike gods and goddesses
of Homer—always, as Renan says, brandishing a spear from
the top of an acropolis—is over, and that instead of them man
has at last found

......" Gods, the friends of man
Merciful gods, compassionate "

who would certainly " answer him again," as a father would
his children.

The providence and beneficence of the Alexandrian gods
towards man, moreover, extended beyond the grave. In Homer,
we find a conception of the next world which for dreariness and

---

[1] *Ibid.* c. 25.   [2] Aristides, *in Serapid.* p. 89.
[3] *Ibid. loc. cit.*   [4] *Ibid.* p. 90.
[5] *Ibid.* p. 97.   [6] *Ibid. loc. cit.*
[7] *Ibid.* p. 100.

hopelessness is only paralleled by the Jewish ideas concerning
Sheol. " Nay, speak not comfortably to me of death, great
Odysseus," says the shade of Achilles to the hero who has
called him up from Hades. " Rather would I live upon the soil
as the hireling of another, even with a landless man who had
no great livelihood, than bear sway among all the dead who
are no more[1]." But the Eleusinian Mysteries were hailed as
giving deliverance from these horrors, and as robbing death of
much of its terrors for those who had been initiated. " Blessed
is he," says Pindar in a passage in which commentators agree
to see a direct allusion to the Mysteries, " who has seen the
things that are under the earth. He has seen the end of life; he
has seen also the God-sent beginning[2]." " Thrice blessed," says
Sophocles, " are they among mortals, who after having beheld
these mysteries, go to the house of Hades : for it is theirs alone
there to live, but to the others there will arrive all ills[3]." The
Homeric *Hymn to Demeter*, which may be about a century
earlier than Pindar, is as emphatic as he as to the saving grace of
initiation. " Happy," it says, " is the man on earth who has
seen these things. But he who has not been initiated in these
holy rites, who has not shared in them, never has the same lot,
when he has utterly faded away in the dark gloom[4]." Those
who believe with M. Foucart in the Egyptian origin of the
Eleusinian rites will doubtless see in this a direct borrowing
from the Egyptian views regarding the beatitude awaiting the
justified or " triumphant " dead who in life had been worshippers of Osiris. How much or how little of the Osirian
faith as to the state of these worshippers in the next world
passed into the Alexandrian religion cannot now be said ; but
it is certain that the protection of Isis and Serapis was held to
be as powerful in the life beyond the tomb as in this.

---

[1] *Odyssey*, XI. 491 *sqq.* (Butcher and Lang's translation).

[2] Pindar, *Threnoi*, Frag. x. p. 102, Cod. Bö.

[3] Sophocles, *Triptolemus* (Plutarch, *de Audiendis Poetis*, 21 F), Frag.
348 of Didot.

[4] Homeric *Hymn to Demeter*, ll. 480 *sqq.* So an inscription on the
statue of a hierophant quoted by M. Foucart, *Myst. d'El.* p. 55, says that
death to the initiated is not an evil but a good.

"When the term of thy life is spent,"

says the apparition of the goddess to Apuleius' Lucius,

" and thou at length descendest to the lower regions, there also, even in the subterranean hemisphere, thou, dwelling in Elysian fields, will often adore me who art propitious to thee, and whom thou shalt see shining among the shades of Acheron and reigning over the secret places of Styx[1]."

So, too, Aristides says of Serapis, that he is " the Saviour and leader of souls, leading souls to the light and receiving them again[2]," that " he raises the dead, he shows forth the longed-for light of the sun to those who *see*, whose holy tombs contain endless numbers of sacred books[3]," and that " we can never escape from his sway, but he will save us, and even after death we shall be the objects of his providence[4]." We may imagine, if we please, although there is really no proof of any connection between the two, that in its assertion of the fatherhood of God as in earthly matters, the Alexandrian religion owed something to the Stoic philosophy ; but it is fairly certain that in the glimpses it afforded of the next world, its inspiration must have been drawn either from Eleusis or from Egypt.

What we know, too, of the actual worship of the Alexandrian triad shows that it was designed to attract the devotion of the multitude with a skill that argues the existence behind it of many centuries of priestcraft. It is still a moot point whether Herodotus was well-founded when he asserted the existence of " mysteries " in the Egyptian religion[5]; and it is quite clear that the scenes in the earthly life of Osiris and the gods of his cycle which in the case of their Greek counterparts were carefully concealed from all but initiates, were in Egypt openly

[1] Apuleius, *Met.* Bk XI. c. 6.
[2] Aristides, *in Serapid.* p. 93.
[3] *Ibid.* p. 95.   [4] *Ibid.* p. 96.
[5] Maspero says ("Les Hypogées Royaux de Thebes," *Ét. Égyptol.* II. p. 178) that " if ever there were in Pharaonic Egypt mysteries and initiates, as there were in Greece and Greek Egypt," it was in the time of decay evidenced by the rare books preserved in the tombs of the kings of the xxth and later Dynasties. Later, *ibid.* p. 180, he says that they must have been confined to a very small class. Cf. *ibid.* p. 278.

portrayed on the walls of the temples[1]. But Timotheos and Manetho must have been too well aware of the prestige attaching throughout the Hellenic world to the secret worships of such centres of religion as Eleusis and Samothrace to forgo its advantage for their new religion ; and the Alexandrian gods too had a system of initiation which seems to have been modelled upon that of the " Goddesses Twain." Thanks to Apuleius we can, up to a certain point, follow the Alexandrian course of initiation step by step. Those whom Isis singled out as fitted for her service[2]—which we may without uncharitableness interpret as meaning those whom the priests thought likely to be of use to the religion—were assigned a " mystagogue " who no doubt gave them such instructions as he thought fit in the meaning of the rites which he saw performed in the temple, and the incidents in the life of the gods to which they were attached. When after a course of such instruction, which was of varying length, the mystagogue was convinced of the soundness of the aspirant's vocation, the formal initiation began. In strict accordance with a ritual which Apuleius assures us was written down in Egyptian characters and carefully preserved in the secret places of the sanctuary (*opertis adyti*), the aspirant underwent a solemn lustration with water or baptism at the hands of the priest, and was ordered to abstain from all food which had had life, from wine and from the company of the other sex for a space of ten days[3]. This period was doubtless spent as far as possible within the temple precincts, much importance being attached to the prolonged contemplation of the statue of the goddess, which was, as we have seen, fashioned in a manner worthy of Greek art, and was further adorned with

[1] *E.g.* the mystic marriage of Zeus or Dionysos with Demeter, which according to Hippolytus, *Philosophumena*, Bk v. c. 1, § 8, p. 171, Cruice, and Clement of Alexandria, *Protrept.* c. II., formed the crowning scene of the Eleusinian Mysteries. At Dendera, the corresponding union of Osiris and Isis, from which, according to M. Foucart, the Eleusinian legend was derived, was depicted in the most realistic way on the temple walls. See Mariette, *Dendérah*, Paris, 1875, t. IV. pl. 65 *sqq.*, or Budge, *G.E.* pp. 132–137.

[2] Apuleius, *Met.* Bk XI. c. 21, *queis tamen tuto possint magna religionis committi silentia, numen deae soleat elicere.* [3] *Ibid.* cc. 22, 23.

rich robes and jewels after the manner of the Catholic images of the Virgin. At the expiration of the ten days' retreat, the candidate was clothed in a linen garment and was exhibited to the general body or congregation of the faithful who presented him with gifts. The secret ceremonies were then performed before him, the nature of which are only revealed to us in the guarded words of Apuleius' hero :

"I approached the bounds of death, and, borne through all the elements, returned again to the threshold of Proserpine which I had already trod. I saw at midnight the sun shining with pure light, I came before the Gods of the Upper and Lower World, and I worshipped them from anigh[1]."

Collating these hints—which Apuleius tells us are all that it is lawful for him to give—with what we know of the origin of the Alexandrian religion and with the scraps of information that have come down to us regarding other ceremonies of a like nature, we may gather from this that the candidate underwent a mock death, being probably made to enact in his own person the passion of Osiris and his shutting-up in a coffin[2], that he was shown the happy lot of the initiated and the correspondingly miserable fate of the uninitiated in the life after death, that he was subjected to certain " trials," or proofs of his courage and sincerity, by fire, water, earth, and air, and that he was finally shown in a brilliant light the glorious company of the gods represented either by their images, or by priests arrayed with their best-known attributes. Nothing seems to have been omitted that could impress the imagination of the neophyte, and when the night of initiation was at length over, he was again displayed before the congregation of worshippers clothed in what was known as the Olympian garment (*stola Olympiaca*) consisting of a dress of byssus or linen embroidered with flowers, over which was cast a rich mantle decorated with figures of fabulous animals, and bearing in his right hand a flaming torch,

---

[1] *Op. cit.* end of c. 23.

[2] Perhaps this is the meaning of the formula said by Clement of Alexandria, *Protrept.* c. II., to be repeated by the initiates at Eleusis: "I have fasted...I have drunk of the cyceon...I have entered into the chest (παστός)."

while on his head was a crown of palm-leaves with leaves pro-
jecting, as he says, "like rays of light." In this costume he
was placed in a wooden pulpit before the statue of the goddess
in the public portion of the temple, and was thus exhibited for the
adoration of the crowd, when the ceremony of opening took
place[1]. As the last stage of the secret rite seems to have been the
successive imposition upon the initiate of twelve robes, doubtless
typifying the twelve signs of the Zodiac, we hardly want the
rayed crown, and the explicit words of Apuleius to inform us that
in this costume he was intended to represent the material sun
(*exornatus instar Solis et in vicem simulacri constitutus*)[2]. The
sun-god, however, was in the later phases of the Egyptian
religion not Osiris but either Ra or Horus[3], and this last-named
god was in the Alexandrian triad equated with the Greek Apollo.
It therefore seems likely that the initiate represented here the
child of Isis begotten, as has been said, by Osiris after his
death and passion, and this corresponds with the statement
put into the mouth of Isis and preserved by Proclus: "I am
that which has been, is, and will be. My garment none has
lifted. The fruit which I bore has become the sun[4]." It is
significant that the later and especially the Christian writers
speak of Osiris and not Horus as the son of Isis; but the
distinction between father and son in the Egyptian triads was
never sharply defined, and there are many signs that Horus,
the son of Isis, was looked upon as Osiris re-born[5].

The initiation strictly so-called was concluded with a banquet

---

[1] Apuleius, *Met.* c. 24.

[2] See last note.

[3] Ra was always the material sun; while Horus was probably in
ancient times the god of the sky: Maspero, *Ét. Égyptol.* t. II. p. 229. With
the Middle Empire the emblem of Ra began to be added to that of Horus
as the "crest" of the Pharaoh's cognizance, showing that the king was
himself regarded as the representative of a composite divinity, Horus-Ra.
Cf. "Titles of Thinite Kings," *P.S.B.A.* 1908, p. 89.

[4] Proclus, *in Timaeum Platonis*, I. 30 D. (Schneidewin).

[5] Minucius Felix, *Octavius*, c. XXI.; Arnobius, *adv. Gentes*, Bk I. c. 36;
Athenagoras, *Presbeia*, c. XXII. Cf. also Griffith and Thompson, *Stories of
High Priests of Memphis*, pp. 107, 121; Maspero, *Ét. Égyptol.* II. p. 246,
and especially p. 361; *P.S.B.A.* 1914, pp. 92, 93.

provided by the initiate in which he celebrated what he was
henceforth to regard as his natal day, as his formal entry into
the religion was considered by him as a re-birth. Nor was this
all. Twelve months after his initiation into the first degree
or Mysteries of Isis, Apuleius' hero is summoned to undergo a
further initiation, this time into the mysteries " of the Great
God and highest progenitor of the Gods, the unconquered Osiris
(*magni dei deumque summi parentis, invicti Osiris*)," of which
we are only told that a further preparation of ten days was
necessary and that the aspirant was in addition " enlightened
by the nocturnal orgies of the princely god Serapis (*insuper
etiam Serapis principalis dei nocturnis orgiis illustratus*)[1]."
Very shortly after this a *third* initiation was prescribed to Lucius
and was backed up by a dream in which Osiris " the God of the
great Gods, or rather the Highest of the Greater Gods and the
Greatest of the Highest and the Ruler of the Greatest (*deus deum
magnorum potior et majorum summus et summorum maximus et
maximorum regnator Osiris*) " appears to him ; but we learn
nothing of the nature of this fresh initiation, save that it was
preceded like the two others by a ten-days' fast[2]. No other
text or monument that has yet come to light gives any hint
as to the revelations made in these two last degrees or initiations ;
but it seems likely from the words above quoted that they were
concerned with the true nature of Osiris[3], and that he must have
been finally proclaimed to the initiate as the one and only Source
of Being. The apparent inconsistency between this and Isis'
own statement given above that she is herself the " highest
of godheads...first of the heavenly ones, one-formed type of

---

[1] Apuleius, *Met.* Bk XI. c. 27.

[2] *Op. cit.* c. 28.

[3] Ælius Aristides (*in Serapid.* p. 88) refuses to discuss this ; but
Athenagoras (see note 5 p. 63, *supra*) says that when the members of the
body of Osiris were found, they were presented to Isis with the remark that
they were the fruits of the vine Dionysus and that Semele was the vine
itself. But see p. 65, *infra*. Plutarch, *de Is. et Os.* c. LXXIX. says that
" the priests of these days," meaning, as is evident from the context, the
priests of the Alexandrian divinities, " try to conceal " the fact that Osiris
rules over the dead. The old religion of Egypt never did ; but perhaps
this, too, was part of the secret teaching of the Alexandrian Mysteries.

gods and goddesses " can perhaps be got over by supposing that the Supreme Being was supposed to be at once the father and mother of the inferior gods, an idea of which there are many traces in the Egyptian myths of later Pharaonic times[1]. Some connection between Osiris in his Egyptian form and the Greek wine-god Bacchus may be implied by the dream which heralded the second initiation showing " one clothed in consecrated linen robes, and bearing thyrsi, ivy and certain things which I may not mention[2] "; but M. Baillet has found a bronze statue of the Ptolemaic period in which Osiris is represented with grapes and a vine-shoot[3], and it is therefore unlikely that any identification of the kind formed part of the secrets reserved for initiates[4].

This, therefore, seems to be all that can be usefully said about the secret part of the worship of the Alexandrian gods. But the founders of the cult must have always borne in mind that while in every religion there are a few devotees who are prepared to go all lengths in theology or enquiry into the nature of their gods, the majority are attracted to it more from a vague desire to enter into amicable relations with the spiritual world than from any other feeling. Even with the Mysteries of Eleusis, it is fairly certain that only a very small proportion of those who attended the ceremonies really grasped the full meaning of what they saw and heard. " Many are the thyrsus-bearers," quotes Plato in this connection, " but few are the mystes[5] "; and it is plain that, as the Telesterion at Eleusis could at the outside accommodate three thousand persons, the greater part of the huge crowd in the Iacchos procession must have come only to look on[6]. But even this more or less

---

[1] Maspero, *Ét. Égyptol.* II. pp. 254–255, 361, 446; *P.S.B.A.* 1914, p. 92.

[2] Apuleius, *Met.* c. 27.

[3] " Osiris-Bacchus " in *Ägypt. Zeitschr.* 1878, p. 106.

[4] Unless we suppose that the statue was one of those used in the mysteries, see note 3 p. 64, *supra*. Plutarch, however, in his address to Klea makes no secret of the identification. See *de Is. et Os.* c. xxxv.

[5] Plato, *Phaedr.* in Abel's *Orphica*, Fragm. 228. Olympiodorus says that the verse comes from Orpheus.

[6] Dyer, *Gods in Greece*, p. 209. He thinks the crowd sometimes numbered 30,000, relying upon the story in Herodotus, Bk VIII. c. 65,

careless multitude did much to spread the fame of the Eleusinian religion, while it was doubtless from their ranks in the first instance that the true initiates were drawn. With this in view, the Alexandrian priests laid themselves out to cater for the half-convinced crowd as well as for their real devotees, and did so with a success which put the Eleusinian Mysteries entirely in the shade. In this, they were much helped by the practice of the native Egyptian temples in Pharaonic times which has been clearly set forth by M. Moret. Every day in every temple in Egypt there seems to have been a solemn Service of Opening when the statue of the god was taken from its resting-place, purified with incense, dressed, and anointed before the doors were opened, and the public, or perhaps only the king as representing mankind in general, were admitted to adore the god[1]. This practice was copied with great fidelity in the worship of the Alexandrian gods, and " the morning opening of the temple " (*templi matutinas apertiones*) became an elaborate ceremony in which the white curtains which hid the statue of Isis from the gaze of the worshippers were drawn back (*velis candentibus reductis*), and it was displayed blazing with actual robes, gems, and ornaments, like a Madonna in Southern Europe at the present day[2]. We also learn from Apuleius that prayers to the goddess were offered at the same time, while one of the priests made the circuit of the different altars within the temple, pouring before each of them a libation of Nile water, and " the beginning of the First Hour " was solemnly proclaimed, with chants and shouts which have been compared to the muezzin of the Mahommedans, but which more probably resembled the choral singing of a morning hymn by the assembled congregation[3]. We know also from a casual allusion in one of Martial's Epigrams, that the eighth hour was also celebrated by

of the Spartan who before the battle of Marathon heard the Iacchos-song sung " as if by 30,000 persons." Cf. Foucart, *Les Gds. Myst.* p. 136.

[1] Moret, *Le Culte Divin Journalier en Égypte*, Paris, 1902, p. 9.

[2] Apuleius, *Met.* c. 20. Lafaye, *Culte*, etc. p. 136, gives the "trousseau" of a statue of Isis found in Spain including earrings, necklaces, etc.

[3] See the scene in the Herculaneum fresco described on p. 68, *infra*.

a chant of the priests, and it seems likely that this announced the closing of the temple to the profane, and was attended by similar solemnities to those of the opening[1]. But it is abundantly plain that between these hours the temple remained open for what may be called private worship, and that this took the form of meditation or silent adoration before the statue of Isis. Apuleius' Lucius repeatedly speaks of the pleasure that he derived even before his initiation from the prolonged contemplation of the goddess's image[2], and the Roman poets are full of allusions to the devout who passed much of their time seated before her statue on benches, the place of which is clearly marked out in Isiac temples like that of Pompeii[3]. That such " meditations " were thought to have in them a saving grace is apparent from a passage in Ovid, where he tells us that he had seen one who had offended " the divinity of the linen-clad Isis " sitting before her altar[4], and it also seems to have been part of the necessary preparation for those who sought initiation. When we consider that the Eleusinian festivals were celebrated at the most but twice a year, and then only in one part of Greece, we see how greatly the daily services and frequentation of the temples in nearly every large town in the West must have operated in drawing to the Alexandrian worship the devotion of the citizens.

In addition to these, however, there were far more elaborate ceremonies of which we obtain a passing glimpse. At Herculaneum, were found early in last century two mural frescoes portraying scenes in the worship of Isis, and of an Isis who, from the style of the paintings and the place where they were found, can be no other than the Alexandrian goddess. One of these, now in the Museum at Naples, shows a temple surrounded by trees, the porch of which is approached by a staircase and

---

[1] Martial, Bk x. Epig. 48. Apuleius, *Met.* c. 17, describes the ceremonies which included a solemn dismissal of the people, and the kissing by them of the feet of a silver statue of the goddess.

[2] Apuleius, *Met.* c. 19.

[3] Lafaye, *Culte*, etc. pp. 118, 119, and Plate facing p. 192. Cf. Ovid, Propertius and Tibullus, where quoted by Lafaye, *op. cit.* p. 120.

[4] Ovid, *Pontic. Epist.* Bk I. Ep. 1, v. 51.

is guarded by two sphinxes[1]. Before the door and at the head
of the stairs stands a priest with the shaven crown of the Alexandrian priesthood, holding with both hands an urn breast-high,
while behind him are two others, one of whom (probably a
woman) is completely clothed, wears long hair, and shakes
a sistrum, while the other is naked to the waist and has his
head shaved like the central figure. At the foot of the
staircase is another priest bearing a sistrum in his left hand
and a sort of pointed baton or hiltless sword in his right[2],
with which he seems to be commanding a body of persons of
both sexes, who from the shaven crowns of the men are evidently
a congregation or college of initiates, and are ranged in two
rows upon the steps. In the foreground are three altars, the
middle one with a fire burning on it, which an attendant is
fanning, while on the right of this is a flute-player seated on
the ground, having in front of him a priest with a wand like
that before described in either hand, and on the left a man and
a woman shaking sistra. The scene evidently represents a
religious service of some kind, and this may possibly be, as
M. Lafaye suggests, the Adoration of the Sacred Water or water
of the Nile, which as Plutarch and Apuleius both hint, was
considered the emblem of Osiris[3]. If so, we may further suppose
that the initiates are here singing antiphonally, or in two choirs,
the hymn to Serapis, a particular air on the flute being, as we
shall see, sacred to that god. The other fresco shows a temple
porch like its fellow, although the steps leading up to it are fewer
in number and the two sphinxes on either side of the opening
are here replaced by two Doric pillars ornamented with garlands.
The central figure is a bearded man of black complexion,

[1] The Baron von Bissing thinks this is a copy of the Serapeum of
Alexandria. See *Transactions* of the Third International Congress of
Religions, Oxford, 1908, i. pp. 225 *sqq.*

[2] Is this the *bacchos* or short rod carried by the faithful in the Iacchos-
procession at Eleusis? See Scholiast in *Knights* of Aristophanes, l. 408
(p. 48 of Didot).

[3] Hippolytus puts it quite plainly: "Now Osiris is water." See
Philosophumena, Bk v. c. 7, p. 149, Cruice. Cf. Lafaye, *Culte*, etc. p. 115.
So Origen, *c. Cels.* Bk v. c. 38, says that the fables of Osiris and Isis lead
men to worship cold water and the moon.

crowned with the lotus and a chaplet of leaves. One hand rests
on his hip, and the other is raised in the air, which attitude,
perhaps from its likeness to that of the statue known as the
Dancing Faun, has given rise to the idea that it is a sacred
dance which is here represented[1]. Behind this figure are two
women, one of whom plays a tympanum or tambourine, two
children, and a priest or initiate with shaven crown, sistrum
in hand, and naked to the waist. In the foreground is the altar
seen in the other fresco, with a flame rising from it, and standing
to the right of it a priest with a sistrum and another musical
instrument in his hands, a flute-player, a child, a kneeling man,
a woman clothed in a long garment and bearing, besides the
sistrum, a palm-branch, and other worshippers. On the left
is a priest with a sistrum, a child bearing in one hand a basket
and in the other a small urn, while a woman crowned with
leaves, with a sistrum and a dish filled with fruits, kneels at
the head of the steps. From the black complexion of the
principal figure, M. Lafaye considers that he may represent
Osiris himself and that he is here shown at the moment of
resurrection, a scene which he considers, not without reason,
may have formed the concluding act in one of the sacred dramas
or mystery-plays undoubtedly associated with the worship of
the god. If so, it is unlikely that it formed part of the initiation
into the Mysteries, the particulars of which were carefully
concealed from the profane and would hardly have been painted
on the walls of temples or dwelling-houses. It seems more
probable that the scene in question, whatever be its meaning,
was acted in pantomime in, or rather before, the temple at a
particular period of the year, that the uninitiated were allowed
to be present at it as well as at the Adoration of the Sacred
Water, and that these two therefore were familiar and attractive
objects to the populace throughout the Roman world.

That the Passion—as it was distinctly called—and Resurrection of Osiris were yearly and openly celebrated by the
worshippers of the Alexandrian gods with alternate demon-
strations of grief and joy, the classical poets have put beyond

---

[1] von Bissing in the paper quoted in note 1 p. 68, *supra*, suggests that
this is the dance of the god Bes.

doubt. The celebration took place in the month of November
and began with a ten-day fast on the part of all the faithful
which was often spent in the temples. Then followed the
representation of the passion of and the seeking for Osiris, and
its result, which a Christian writer of the IIIrd century A.D.[1]
thus sums up :

" You behold the swallow[2] and the cymbal of Isis, and the tomb of
your Serapis or Osiris empty, with his limbs scattered about.... Isis
bewails, laments and seeks after her lost son[3], with her Cynocephalus[4]
and her bald-headed priests ; and the wretched worshippers of Isis
beat their breasts, and imitate the grief of the most unhappy mother.
By and by, when the little boy is found, Isis rejoices, and the priests
exult. Cynocephalus the discoverer boasts, and they do not cease
year by year either to lose what they find, or to find what they lose."

" These," he says, " were formerly Egyptian rites, and now
are Roman ones " ; and it is plain that all the incidents of
which he speaks were perfectly familiar to the Roman people.
Juvenal[5] speaks of the bald-headed multitude uttering lamentations and running to and fro, and of their exultant cries when
Osiris is found ; and the banquets in the temples and great
festivals and public games which celebrated the " Finding of
Osiris " when the Alexandrian worship was recognized by the
state must have made the recurrence of this chief festival of
the Alexandrian religion familiar to every one[6].

How many lesser festivals than these formed part of its
public ceremonial we do not know, but they were probably
numerous enough. The Roman calendars tell us of a festival
of Isis Pharia, probably in her capacity of tutelary goddess of

[1] Minucius Felix, *Octavius*, c. 21.

[2] The swallow refers to the story that Isis changed herself into a
swallow who flitted round the pillar containing the coffin of Osiris. Plutarch, *de Is. et Os.* c. XVI.

[3] Evidently a confusion between Horus and Osiris which would have
been impossible had not the Isiacists looked upon Horus as Osiris re-born.
Cf. Lactantius, *Institutes*, Bk I. c. 21, where the same confusion occurs;
P.S.B.A. 1914, p. 93.

[4] The "dog-headed " Anubis.

[5] Juvenal, *Satir.* VI. l. 533 ; *ibid.* VIII. l. 30.

[6] Lafaye, *Culte*, etc. p. 128.

Alexandria, and of another of Serapis, both in the month of April, while Plutarch speaks of the Birth of Horus celebrated, as was natural with a sun-god, after the vernal equinox, when nature awakens and the sun begins to show forth his power. But there was another spring festival which took place on the 5th of March[1] to mark the reopening of navigation and commerce after the departure of winter, in which the faithful went in procession to the sea (or probably in its absence to the nearest water), and there set afloat a new ship filled with offerings which was known as the vessel of Isis. Apuleius has left us a description of this festival at once so lively and so imbued with the spirit of the devout Isiacist, that it may be pardonable to quote from it at some length. The procession, which in the case he is describing sets forth at dawn from the gates of Cenchreae the eastern port of Corinth, is heralded by a carnival in which burlesque representations of magistrates, gladiators, hunters, and fishermen jostle with caricatures of ancient Greek heroes and demigods like Bellerophon and Ganymede. After this had dispersed, " the procession proper of the Saviour Goddess," he says, set itself in motion, and may be described in his own words[2] :

" Women shining in white garments displayed their joy by divers gestures, and crowned with spring blossoms strewed from their laps flowers upon the road over which marched the holy throng. Others, with glittering mirrors held behind them, showed to the advancing Goddess their ready service. Others, who bore ivory combs, by the motion of their arms and the twining of their fingers represented the combing of her royal hair, while yet others sprinkled the ways with drops of sweet-smelling balsam and other unguents. A great crowd also of both sexes followed with lamps, torches, candles and other kinds of lights making propitious with light the source of the heavenly stars. Thereafter came gentle harmonies, and reeds and flutes sounded with sweetest modulations. A graceful choir of chosen youths followed, shining in snowy dresses of ceremony and singing a beautiful hymn which by grace of the Muses a skilful poet had set to music, although its theme recalled the prayers of our forefathers.

[1] Lafaye, *Culte*, etc. p. 120.
[2] Apuleius, *Met.* cc. 9, 10, 11.

Then came flute-players consecrated to the great Serapis, who on the slanted reed held under the right ear, repeated the air usual in the temple of the God, in order that everyone might be warned to make room for the passage of the holy things. Then pressed on the multitude of those who had been initiated into the divine mysteries, both men and women of every rank and age, shining in the pure whiteness of their linen robes, the women with hair moist with perfume and covered with a transparent veil, the men with closely shaven hair and glistening heads. Earthly stars of the great religion were these, who made a shrill tinkling with brazen silver or even gold sistra. Then came the priests of the holy things, those distinguished men who, tightly swathed in white linen from the breast-girdle to the feet, displayed to view the noble emblems of the most mighty God. The first held forth a lamp shining with clear light, not exactly resembling those which give light to nocturnal banquets, but in the form of a golden boat and emitting a broader flame through its central opening. The second, clothed in the same way as the first, carried in his two hands the little altars, *i.e.* the *auxilia* to which the helping foresight of the high Goddess has given a peculiar name. The third bore a palm-tree with tiny golden leaves, and likewise the *caduceus* of Mercury. The fourth exhibited the emblem of Equity, a left hand represented with outstretched palm, which from its inborn disinclination to work, and as being endowed with neither skill nor expertness, seems better suited to typify Equity than the right. He also bore a golden vase in the rounded shape of a female breast, from which he poured libations of milk. The fifth carried a winnowing-fan composed of golden wires, and yet another an amphora.

"Without interval, the Gods who have deigned to walk with the feet of men go forward. Here—dread sight!—is he who is the messenger between the supernal and the infernal deities. Upright, of a complexion black in some parts, golden in others, Anubis raises on high his dog's head, bearing in his left hand the *caduceus*, and shaking in his right the budding palm-branch[1]. Close upon his footsteps, follows a cow, held on high in an erect posture—the cow, fertile image of the Goddess who brings forth all things—which one of the blessed ministry with pantomimic steps bears seated on his shoulders. The chest containing the mysteries was carried by

[1] Is this the "golden bough" of initiation? Cf. Baillet, "Osiris-Bacchus," cited p. 65, *supra*.

another, thus wholly concealing the hidden things of the sublime religion[1]. Yet another bore within his happy bosom the revered likeness of the Supreme Divinity, resembling neither a domestic animal, nor bird, nor wild beast, nor even man himself; but yet to be revered in the highest degree alike for its skilful invention, and for its very novelty, and also as that unspeakable evidence of the religion which should be veiled in complete silence. As to its outward form, it was fashioned in glittering gold—an urn hollowed out with perfected art with a round base and carved externally with the marvellous images of the Egyptians. Its mouth was not much raised and jutted forth in an extended spout with a wide stream; while on the opposite side was attached the handle bent far out with a wide sweep, on which sate an asp in wreathed folds uplifting the swollen stripes of his scaly neck."

This description will leave little doubt on the mind of the reader as to the supreme importance in the religion of the urn which is being held up for the adoration of the faithful in the fresco from Herculaneum before described; and this is borne out by a bas-relief in the Vatican in which a similar urn to that described by Apuleius is represented as being carried in procession[2]. "They say," says Hippolytus speaking of the worshippers of Isis, "that Osiris is water," and Celsus, according to Origen, confirms him in this[3]. According to this last, Isis represented the earth, and the doctrine may therefore be an allegory representing the fertilization of the land by the Nile. It is more likely, however, that it is to be attributed to one of the older cosmogonies current in Egypt, wherein water, personified by the god Nu, is the origin of everything[4]. The main

---

[1] Probably the *pudendum* of Osiris. See Hippolytus, *Philosophumena*, Bk v. c. 7, p. 149, Cruice; Socrates, *Hist. Eccl.* Bk v. c. 16; Clem. Alex. *Protrept.* c. II., says the Corybantes did the same thing with that of Bacchus.

[2] Lafaye in Daremberg and Saglio's *Dict. des Antiq. s.v.* Isis.

[3] See note 3 p. 68, *supra*. Cf. Leemans, *Papyri Gr.* pp. 26, 27.

[4] Maspero, *Ét. Égyptol.* II. p. 345, says this Nu was "neither the primordial water, nor the sky, but a very ancient god, common to all humanity," whom he compares to the Thian of the Chinese, the Dyaus of the pre-Vedic, and the Uranos-Oceanos of the pre-Hellenic peoples. "At the beginning," he continues, "he is himself the Celestial Ocean."

point to note for our present purpose is that an urn or vase
containing liquid, was, in the public ceremonies of the Alexandrian religion, the recognized symbol of the Supreme Being.

Apuleius next describes the procession as having reached
the seashore where the images of the gods were arranged in
order [1] :

" Then the Chief Priest, pouring forth with chaste mouth the most
solemn prayers, consecrated and dedicated to the goddess, after having
thoroughly purified it with a lighted torch, an egg, and some sulphur,
a ship made with the highest art and painted all over with the
wonderful pictures of the Egyptians.   The shining sail of this blessed
bark had the words of a prayer woven in it ; and these words re-
iterated the petition that the navigation then commencing might
be prosperous.   And now the mast was stepped, a round piece of
pine, lofty and smooth, and conspicuous from the handsome appearance of its truck, and the poop with its twisted goose-neck shone
covered with gold-leaf, while the whole hulk was gay with polished
citron wood.   Then all the people, both the religious and the profane, heaped emulously together winnowing-fans laden with spices
and such like offerings, and poured upon them crumbled cakes
made with milk, until the ship, filled with magnificent gifts offered
in fulfilment of vows, was loosed from its moorings and put to sea
with a gentle breeze that seemed to spring up on purpose.   After
her course became indistinct to us by reason of the distance that
she was from our eyes, the bearers of the holy things again took up
each his own load, and joyfully returned to the fane in the same
solemn procession as before.   But when we arrived at the temple,
the Chief Priest and the bearers of the divine effigies, and those who
have been already initiated into the ever to be revered secrets,
entering into the chamber of the Goddess put away the breathing
images with due ceremony.   Then one of them, whom men call the
Scribe, standing before the doors and having called together as if
for a discourse the company of the Pastophori [2]—which is the name
of this sacrosanct college—forthwith recited from a lofty pulpit
prayers written in a book for the Great Prince, the Senate, the
Equestrian Order, and the whole Roman people, their sailors and

---

[1] Apuleius, *Met.* Bk xi. c. 16.

[2] The bearers of the sacred Pastos (box or coffin ?).   He says elsewhere
that this particular college dated from " the days of Sulla," *i.e.* 87–84 B.C.

ships, and all who are under the sway of our native land, and then closed the address according to the Greek rite thus : ' Let the people depart[1].' Which announcement was followed by a shout of the people showing that it was favourably received by all. Then the multitude, rejoicing exceedingly and bearing olive-branches, laurel-twigs, and chaplets, after having kissed the feet of a statue of the goddess fashioned in silver which stood on steps [within the porch ?], departed to their own homes."

What most strikes one in this account by an eye-witness, which must have been written about the year 170 A.D., is the entirely modern tone of it all. In the scene that passes under Lucius' eyes, there is hardly anything that might not be seen at an Italian *festa* at the present day. The joyous crowd, respectful rather than devout, and not above introducing a comic or rather a burlesque element into the day's rejoicing, the images and sacred vessels carried solemnly along, the crowd of tonsured priests, and the chants and hymns sung in chorus, the return to the temple, with its prayers for Church and State, and its dismissal of the people—all these are paralleled every day in countries where the Catholic Church is still dominant. Not less modern, too, is the way in which Lucius alludes to the faith of which all these things illustrate the power. For him, there is no other god than Isis—" thou who art all[2]," as one of her votaries calls her on his tombstone, in whom " single in essence, though with many names[3]," all other gods are contained. Hence, he can think of no other religion than her worship. It is always with him " the holy " or " the sublime religion," and the goddess is she whom the whole earth adores. It is she in whom one can trust not only for happiness beyond the tomb, but for present help in all the troubles of this life, and to devote oneself to her service, to thoroughly learn, to understand her nature, is the proudest lot which can befall man while upon earth. Hence all her initiates were " earthly stars," her priests were all happy or blessed in that they were allowed to be near

[1] The reading has been contested, but is well established. Cf. the concluding words of the Mass : "Ite, missa est."

[2] *"Una quae es omnia," C.I.N.* 3580. The stone was found at Capua.

[3] Apuleius, *Met.* Bk XI. c. 5.

and even to carry and handle the divine images, and the religion was a real bond which united people of all ranks and ages. We feel that we have here got a very long way from the time when the power of each god was supposed to be limited to the small space surrounding his sanctuary.

That this change had been brought about by the work of the Isiac priesthood, there can be little doubt. Between the foundation of the Alexandrian religion by Ptolemy and the date at which Apuleius wrote, a space of five centuries elapsed, and this must have seen many changes in the constitution of what may be called the Isiac Church. The Greeks always set their faces against anything like a priestly caste set apart from the rest of the community, and the priests of the Hellenic gods were for the most part elected, like modern mayors of towns, for a short term only, after which they fell back into the ranks of the laity with as little difficulty as do municipal officers at the present day. The Eleusinian Mysteries were indeed committed to certain families in whom their priesthood was hereditary ; but no professional barriers existed between these families and the rest of the citizens ; and we find Callias, the " torch-bearer " and one of the highest officials at the Mysteries, not only fighting in the ranks at Marathon, but distinguishing himself by his " cruelty and injustice " in retaining an unfair share of the plunder for himself[1]. The Eumolpidae and Lycomidae of Eleusis, also, were probably maintained not by any contribution from the state, but by the revenues of the temple lands and by the fee of a few obols levied from each initiate. But the Alexandrian Church in Egypt must from the first have been endowed and probably established as well. To judge from the analogous case of the dynastic cult or worship of the sovereign, which Ptolemy Soter set up, the " sublime religion " was in its native Egypt maintained by a tax on the revenues of those *wakf* or temple lands held in mortmain with which the native gods of Egypt were so richly provided from the earliest times. When the Alexandrian religion became a missionary faith and established itself in Athens and other parts of the Hellenic world, it no doubt depended in the

[1] Plutarch, *Aristides*, c. v.

first instance on the voluntary contributions of the associations of Sarapiasts or Isiaci founded for its maintenance. But we may be sure that politic princes like the first three Ptolemies, who were besides the richest and most opulent of all the Successors of Alexander, did not let these outposts of their empire languish for lack of funds, and we may guess that the subscriptions of their members were supplemented in case of need by large donations from the King of Egypt or from those who wished to stand well with him. When the faith passed into Western Europe and into territories directly under Roman sway, it had already attained such fame that a large entrance-fee could be demanded from the initiates, and Apuleius tells us more than once that the amount of this was in every case fixed by a special revelation of the goddess, and was no doubt only limited by the length of the aspirant's purse and the strength of his vocation[1]. Like other Greek priests of the time, also, the ministers of the Alexandrian religion found a way of adding to their income by the practice of divination or fore-telling the future, and the oracle of Serapis at Alexandria soon became as celebrated in the Hellenistic world as that of Delphi. There were probably more ways than one of consulting this; but the one which seems to have been specially its own, and which afterwards spread from Egypt into all the temples of the faith in other countries, was by the practice of *incubatio* which meant sleeping either personally or by deputy in the precinct of the god until the consultant had a dream in which the god's answer was declared. Such a practice seems to date from the dream sent to Ptolemy Soter at the foundation of the religion, and doubtless formed a great source of revenue to its priesthood[2]. The highest personages in the Roman Empire deigned to resort to it, and Vespasian was vouchsafed a divine vision in the temple of Serapis when he consulted the god about " the affairs

[1] Apuleius, *Met.* cc. 21, 28, 30.

[2] See p. 48, *supra*. Oracles given in dreams were, however, an old institution in Egypt. See the dream of Thothmes IV concerning the Sphinx, Breasted, *History of Egypt*, p. 325, and *Ancient Records*, Chicago 1906, vol. II. No. 815.

of the Empire[1]." Not unconnected with this were the miraculous cures with which Serapis, originally perhaps by confusion with Asklepios the Greek god of healing[2], was credited. The sick man was given a room in the temple precincts, where he doubtless lived the regular and orderly life of a modern hospital, and before long dreamed of a remedy for the malady on which his thoughts were concentrated. As the mind sometimes influences the body, and a belief in the healing power of the medicine is often of more importance than its nature, he very often recovered, and was no doubt expected to be generous in his offerings to the god who had intervened in his cure. Nor were worse means of raising money unknown to the Alexandrian priests, unless they have been greatly belied. They are said to have acted as panders and procurers for the rich, and it was the seduction of a noble Roman lady by a lover who assumed the garb of the god Anubis which led to their expulsion from the Pomoerium under Tiberius[3]. Astrology, too, which depended entirely on mathematical calculations and tables, was peculiarly an Alexandrian art, and the same Manetho who had been one of the persons consulted at the founding of the Alexandrian religion was said to have taught its principles to the Greeks. Whether this be so or not, it is certain that in Ovid's time the Alexandrian priests used to beg in the streets of Rome after the fashion of the Buddhist monks from whom they may have indirectly borrowed the practice, and that it was thought "unlucky" to reject their importunities[4].

It is plain, however, that, by the time Apuleius wrote, the

[1] Tacitus, *Hist.* Bk IV. cc. 81, 82.

[2] Asklepios or Esculapius was one of the gods absorbed by Serapis. It is most probable that the great statue by Bryaxis in the Alexandrian Serapeum was originally an Asklepios. See Bouché-Leclercq, *Rev. de l'Hist. des Rel.* 1902, pp. 26, 27, 28. There seems also to have been a chapel to him in the Greek Serapeum at Memphis. See Brunet de Presle, "Le Sérapéum de Memphis," Paris, 1865, pp. 261–263. Cf. Forshall, *Greek Papyri in the British Museum*, 1839, p. 33, and note 1 p. 80, *infra.*

[3] Josephus, *Antiquities*, Bk XVIII. cc. 3, 4.

[4] Lovatelli, *Il Culto d' Iside in Roma*, Roma, 1891, p. 174; Ovid, *Pontic. Epist.* Bk I. Ep. I.

necessity for any such shifts had passed away. The Alexandrian religion had then become a state religion, and was served by a fully organized and powerful priesthood. As there were not less than seven temples of Isis in Rome itself, the number of the Roman faithful must have been very considerable, and on their offerings and the gifts of the state, a large staff of priests was maintained. We hear not only of a high priest in each temple to whom all the lesser ministers of the cult were apparently subject[1], but of hierophants, scribes, stolists or ward-robe-keepers, singing-men and singing-women, and a host of subordinate functionaries down to the *neocoros* or temple-sweeper and the *cliduchos* or guardian of the keys. Women as well as men were eligible for some of these offices, and the inscriptions tell us of a female *oneirocrites* or interpreter of dreams and of several *canephorae* or carriers of the sacred basket, besides many priestesses whose functions are not defined[2]. The high priest and the more important officers lived in the temple and probably devoted their whole time to its service [3]; but the lesser offices seem to have been capable of being held concurrently with lay occupations, like that of the churchwardens at the present day. But one and all were devoted to the faith and its propagation, and formed in the words of Apuleius " a sacred soldiery " for its extension and defence. It is probable that they were all drawn in the first instance from the ranks of the initiates only.

These were what may be called the secular clergy of the Alexandrian Church ; but there was in addition a body of devotees attached to it whose mode of life singularly reminds us of that afterwards adopted by the Christian monks. A lucky chance has revealed to us some fragments of papyrus found on the site of the Serapeum at Memphis, which contain among other things the petitions of a Macedonian named Ptolemy the son of Glaucias to King Ptolemy VI Philometor

---

[1] As M. Lafaye (*Culte*, etc. p. 132) points out, the hierophant in Apuleius calls the other priests " his company," *suus numerus* (*Met.* c. 21).

[2] For all these, see Lafaye, *op. cit.* chap. VII : *Le Sacerdoce.*

[3] Lafaye, *op. cit.* p. 150.

about the year 166 B.C.[1] From these it is evident that there
were at that time a body of recluses lodged in the Serapeum
who were vowed to a seclusion so complete that they might not
stir forth from their cells under any pretence, and when the
king visited Memphis he had to speak with his namesake and
petitioner through the window of the latter's chamber. These
recluses were in some way devoted to the service of the god,
and their stay in the temple was to all appearance voluntary,
although in Ptolemy's case, it had at the time he wrote lasted
already fifteen years. He does not seem to have been driven to
this by poverty, as he speaks of a considerable property left him
by his father; and as the object of his petitions is to champion
the rights of two priestesses of Serapis who had been wrongfully
deprived of their dues of bread and oil by the officials of the
temple, he seems to have been in some sort given to the per-
formance of "good works." How he otherwise occupied his
time, and whether his title or description of κάτοχος implied
any connection with the oracle of Serapis is still a disputed
point. Yet the correspondence in which his name appears
shows clearly the existence within the Serapeum of a large
population of both men and women living at the expense of the
temple revenues, some of whom took part in the ritual of the
services there celebrated, while others were fixed by their own
vows in the strictest seclusion. Whichever way the controversy
alluded to above is decided, it seems plain that there is here a
parallel between the practice of the Catholic Church with its
division of the clergy into regular and secular and the Alexandrian

[1] These fragments are scattered among the different European
museums. Some are in the Vatican Library and were published by
Mgr. Angelo Mai in 1833 (Brunet de Presle, "Les Papyri Grecs du Louvre,"
Mém. de l'Acad. des Inscript. XVIII. pt 2 (1865), p. 16), others in the
Leyden Museum (Leemans, *Papyri Graeci*, I. pp. 6 *sqq.*), others in the
Louvre (Brunet de Presle, *op. cit.* p. 22), and the largest number in the
British Museum (Kenyon, *Greek Papyri*, p. 1). The whole story, so far as
it has been ascertained, is told by Brunet de Presle, *op. cit.* pp. 261–263,
and by Sir Frederic Kenyon, *op. cit.* pp. 1–5, and the questions arising out
of it are admirably summed up by M. Bouché-Leclercq in his article, "Les
Reclus du Sérapéum de Memphis" in *Mélanges Perrot*, Paris, 1903, p. 17.

religion, which until the discovery of the papyri some fifty years ago was entirely unsuspected.

It has been said above that the Alexandrian religion reached its apogee in the time of the Antonines. How it came to decline in power cannot be traced with great exactness, but it seems probable that it only lost its hold on the common people from the greater attractions presented by other religions competing with it for the popular favour. Other cults began to press in from the East, including the worship of Mithras, which in the time of Diocletian finally supplanted it in the favour of the state, and acquired perhaps a stronger hold on the army from reasons to be examined in detail when we come to deal with the Mithraic religion. But the rise of Christianity is in itself sufficient to account for its decline in popularity among the lower classes of the Empire. To them the Catholic Church, purged and strengthened by a sporadic and intermittent persecution, offered advantages that the Alexandrian religion could never give. In this last, the possession of wealth must always have assured its possessor a disproportionate rank in the religion, and without the expenditure of a large sum of money, it was impossible, as we have seen, to arrive at its most cherished secrets. Nor do we find in any of the few documents of the faith that have come down to us any parallel to that wide and all-embracing spirit of charity which in its early days made the Christian Church a kind of mutual benefit society for all who were willing to enter into her fold. To the poorest as to the wealthiest, the Catholic Church, too, always held out the promises of a faith to be understood by all and free from the mystery with which the cardinal doctrines of the Alexandrians were shrouded from all but the highest initiates. Its promises of happiness beyond the grave also were extended to even the most degraded, and the fulfilment of them was taught to be dependent on conduct within the reach of even the pauper or the repentant criminal rather than on the long, difficult and expensive course of instruction which its rival demanded. Nor were more material inducements neglected. The highest offices within the Church were open to the lowest of its members, and it was quite possible for a slave or a freedman to ascend the chair of Peter, there to negotiate on equal terms with emperors and proconsuls. Unlike the religions of the ancient world which were first converted by Alexander's conquests from national into universal cults, the Christian religion was from its foundation organized on the democratic lines laid down in the text : " He that is greatest among you shall be your servant[1]." Moreover, the predictions of the Christian missionaries as to the immediate coming of the Second Advent began to spread among the masses outside the Church, and found a soil ready to receive them in the minds of superstitious men trampled on by the rich, harried by the tax-gatherers, and torn this way and that by constant insurrections and civil wars stirred up, not by the Roman mob (kept quiet as it was with State doles) but by its too ambitious masters. Quite apart from the spiritual comfort that it brought to many, and from the greater unity and simplicity of its doctrines, we can hardly wonder that the proletariat everywhere turned eagerly to the new faith.

The effect of this upon the Alexandrian religion must have been fatal. Unfortunately the destruction of pagan literature has been so great that we know hardly anything about its decline from the mouths of its adherents[2]. What we are able to perceive is that the persons who adhered to the Alexandrian faith after the time of the Antonines generally practised many other religions as well. Alexander Severus had in his palace a *lararium* or private chapel in which, like most of the later Roman emperors, he placed statues of the gods whose worship he particularly affected. We find there Serapis and Isis, indeed, but surrounded with a great crowd of other divinities together with the images of philosophers like Socrates and Apollonius of Tyana, and—if the Augustan History is to be believed—that

---

[1] Matth. xxiii. 11. Cf. the Pope's title of " Servant of the Servants of God " (*Servus servorum Dei*).

[2] Julian in his letters (*Ep.* 52) speaks of Alexandria even in his time as being given up to the worship of Serapis. It is probable that in this, as in other matters, the philosophic Emperor believed what he wished to believe. Yet his contemporary, Ammianus Marcellinus, *Hist.* Bk XXII. c. 16, § 20, speaks of the elements of the sacred rites being still preserved there in secret books, by which he seems to be referring to the worship of the Alexandrian divinities.

of the Founder of Christianity Himself[1]. So, too, the funeral inscription of Ulpius Egnatius Faventinus, an augur of high rank who flourished in the reign of Valens and Valentinian, records that the dead nobleman was a priest of Isis, but a hierophant of Hecate, a hieroceryx of Mithras, and a " chief Herdsman " of Bacchus as well. So, again, Fabia Aeonia Paullina, wife of Vettius Praetextatus, a Prefect and Consul Designate of about the same period, describes herself on her tombstone as consecrated at Eleusis to Dionysos, Demeter, and Persephone, and a hierophantis of Hecate, but merely a worshipper of Isis[2]. We see here a great change from the exclusive fervour of Apuleius' Lucius, who thinks it only just that Isis should require him to devote his whole life to her service.

But a violent end was soon to be put even to the public exercise of the Alexandrian religion. The conversion of Constantine had left it unharmed, and we find Julian writing to the Alexandrians during his brief reign as if the supremacy of their religion in Egypt's capital at any rate was assured[3]. But under Theodosius, an order was obtained from the Emperor for the demolition of the " heathen " temples at Alexandria, and Theophilus, " the perpetual enemy of peace and virtue[4]," who was bishop of the city at the time, was not the man to allow the decree to remain a dead letter. According to the ecclesiastical historians[5], he began operations on the temple of Dionysos, which he converted into a Christian church. In the course of doing so, he professed to have discovered certain emblems of virility which seem to have been used in the Mysteries to illustrate the legend of the Diaspasm or tearing in pieces of the god, and these he had paraded through the city as evidence of what the heathens, according to him, worshipped in secret. The same emblems were also used in the worship of Isis, where

[1] See Renan, *Hibbert Lectures*, 1884, p. 197, for authorities.

[2] Orelli, *Inscript. Latin. select.* pp. 406–412. All these have now been transferred to the *Corp. Inscr. Latin. q.v.*

[3] See note 2 p. 82, *supra*.

[4] Gibbon, *Decline and Fall* (Bury's edition), III. p. 200.

[5] Theodoret, *Hist. Eccl.* Bk v. c. 23 ; Socrates, *Hist. Eccl.* Bk v. c. 16 Sozomen, *Hist. Eccl.* Bk VII. c. 15.

they probably were shown to initiates as explaining the loss of the generative power by Osiris after his death and passion[1]. Hence their profanation was in the highest degree offensive to the last adherents of the Alexandrian religion, who, few in number but formidable from their position and influence, threw themselves into the world-famed Serapeum and determined to resist the decree by force of arms. The Christian mob of Alexandria, hounded on by the bishop and his monks, assaulted the temple which the philosopher Olympius and his followers had converted into a temporary fortress, and many attacks were repulsed with loss of life to the besiegers. At length, a truce having been negotiated until the Emperor could be communicated with, a fresh decree was obtained in which the defenders of the temple were promised a pardon for their share in the riot, if the Serapeum were quietly given up to the authorities. This offer was accepted, and Theophilus had the pleasure of seeing Bryaxis' colossal statue of Serapis demolished under his own eyes without the event being followed by the predicted earthquake and other catastrophes which we are told the Christians as well as the heathens confidently expected. The magnificent Serapeum with all its wealth of statues and works of art was destroyed, and a church dedicated to the Emperor Arcadius was afterwards erected on its site.

Thus in the year 391, the chief seat and place of origin of the Alexandrian religion was laid waste, and the religion itself perished after a successful reign of seven centuries. Ecclesiastical writers say that this was followed by the conversion of several of the "Hellenists" or adherents of the worship of Serapis and Isis to Christianity[2], and there seems every likelihood that the story is founded on fact. Is this the reason why we find so many of the external usages of Isis-worship preserved in or revived by the Catholic Church? Macaulay, in speaking of the contest between Catholicism and Protestantism at the Reformation compares it to the fight between Hamlet and Laertes where the combatants change weapons. The comparative study of religions shows that the phenomenon is more widespread than he thought, and that when one religion finally

---

[1] See note 1 p. 73, *supra*.   [2] Socrates, *op. cit.* Bk v. c. 17.

supplants another, it generally takes over from its predecessor such of its usages as seem harmless or praiseworthy. The traditional policy of the Catholic Church in this respect was declared by Saint Gregory the Great, when he told the apostle to the Saxon heathens that such of their religious and traditional observances as could by any means be harmonized with orthodox Christianity were not to be interfered with[1], and this was probably the policy pursued with regard to the converts from the worship of Serapis. Gibbon[2] has painted for us in a celebrated passage the astonishment which "a Tertullian or a Lactantius" would have felt could he have been raised from the dead to witness the festival of some popular saint or martyr in a Christian church at the end of the fifth century. The incense, the flowers, the lights, and the adoration of the relics of the saint would all, we are told, have moved his indignation as the appanage of heathenism. Yet none of these things would have been found in a temple like that of Delphi, where probably no more than one worshipper or sacred embassy penetrated at a time, and where nothing like congregational worship was known. It was, however, the mode of worship to which the Hellenistic world had become daily accustomed during the seven centuries that the Alexandrian religion had endured, and it is not to be wondered at that the converts brought it with them into their new faith. The worship of the Virgin as the Theotokos or Mother of God which was introduced into the Catholic Church about the time of the destruction of the Serapeum, enabled the devotees of Isis to continue unchecked their worship of the mother goddess by merely changing the name of the object of their adoration, and Prof. Drexler gives a long list of the statues of Isis which thereafter were used, sometimes with unaltered attributes, as those of the Virgin Mary[3]. The general use of images, the suspension in the churches of *ex voto* representations of different parts of the human body in gratitude for miraculous

---

[1] Renan, *Marc Aurèle*, Paris, 1882, p. 630, for authority. Cf. Gibbon, *Decline and Fall* (Bury's edn.), IV. pp. 78, 79.

[2] Gibbon, *op. cit.* III.

[3] Drexler in *Roscher's Lexikon*, *s.v.* Isis. Cf. Maury, *Rel. de la Grèce*, t. II. p. 222.

cures of maladies[1], and the ceremonial burning of candles, may also be traced to the same source ; while the institution of monachism which had taken a great hold on Christian Egypt, is now generally attributed to St Pachomius, who had actually been in his youth a recluse of Serapis[2]. Prof. Bury, who thinks the action of the earlier faith upon the later in this respect undeniable, would also attribute the tonsure of the Catholic priesthood to a reminiscence of the shaven crowns of the initiates of Isis, to which we may perhaps add the covering of women's heads in churches[3].

These instances are for the most part fairly well known, and some have been made use of in controversy between Protestants and Catholics ; but it is probable that there were also many resemblances between the external usages of the two faiths which would, when they flourished side by side, strike even the superficial observer, but the traces of which are now well nigh lost[4]. "Those who worship Serapis are Christians, and those who call themselves bishops of Christ are vowed to Serapis," wrote the Emperor Hadrian[5] from Alexandria on his visit there in A.D. 124, and this would possibly explain the respectful and almost mournful tone in which, as Renan noted, the Christian Sibyl announces to Serapis and Isis the end of their reign[6]. It is not impossible that the resemblance which thus deceived the Emperor was connected with the celebration of

---

[1] Amm. Marcell. *op. cit.* Bk XXII. c. 13. According to Deubner, *De incubatione*, Leipzig, 1900, c. IV. Cyril of Alexandria had to establish the worship of two medical saints in the Egyptian hamlet of Menuthis near Canopus to induce the people to forget the miraculous cures formerly wrought there in the sanctuary of Isis.

[2] Bury in Gibbon, *op. cit.* vol. IV. Appendix 3, p. 527.

[3] Cf. Apuleius' description of the veiling of the women's heads in the Isis procession, p. 72, *supra.*

[4] A writer in Maspero's *Recueil de Travaux* for 1912, p. 75, mentions that the Isiac *sistrum* or rattle is still used by the Christians of Abyssinia.

[5] Vopiscus, *Saturninus* (*Hist. August. Scriptor.* VI. t. II. pp. 718–730). The authenticity of the letter has been defended by Lightfoot, *Apostolic Fathers*, 1891, I. p. 481. The date is fairly well fixed by the death of Antinous in 122 A.D., and Hadrian's visit to Syria a few years later. Ramsay (*Church in Roman Empire*, 1903, p. 336) makes it 134 A.D.

[6] Renan, *Marc Aur.* p. 433.

the Eucharist among certain sects of Christians[1]. The Adoration of the Sacred Water as the emblem of Osiris, which we have seen represented on the Herculaneum fresco, has many points in common with the exhibition of the Sacrament of the Mass to the people, and it is possible that the words of consecration were not altogether different in the two cases. " Thou art wine, yet thou art not wine, but the members of Osiris," says a magic papyrus in the British Museum in the midst of an address to " Asklepios of Memphis," the god Esculapius being one of the gods with whom Serapis in his day of power was most often confounded[2]. So, too, M. Revillout has published an *amatorium* or love-charm in which the magician says, "May this wine become the blood of Osiris[3]." It is true he sees in it a blasphemous adaptation of the Christian rite ; but this is very unlikely. It has been shown elsewhere[4] that many—perhaps all—of the words used in the ceremonial magic of the period are taken from the rituals of religions dying or extinct, and the papyrus, which dates somewhere about the IVth century A.D., may possibly

[1] In the Catholic Church at this period the Eucharist was celebrated, if we may judge from the *First Apology* of Justin Martyr (c. LVI), in a very simple manner, but apparently in the presence of all the faithful. In that part of the Apostolical Constitutions (Bk VIII. c. 66), which is probably later in date than Justin, the catechumens, heterodox, and unbelievers are directed to be excluded before consecration (see Hatch, *Hibbert Lectures*, p. 301). It does not follow that the ceremonial was as simple with the Gnostics. Marcus is said by Irenaeus (Bk I. c. 6, pp. 116, 117, Harvey) to have made the mixture of wine and water in the cup to appear purple and to overflow into a larger vessel ; while similar prodigies attend the celebration in the *Pistis Sophia* and the *Bruce Papyrus*, for which see Chap. X, *infra*. As such thaumaturgy was intended to astonish the onlookers, it is probable that the elements were displayed before the whole congregation. That the later form of the ritual of the Christian sacraments was taken from the Gnostics, see Hatch, *Hibbert Lectures*, pp. 295–305, and 307–309, and de Faye, *Introduction à l'Ét. du Gnosticisme*, Paris, 1903, pp. 106, 107.

[2] Kenyon, *Greek Papyri*, p. 105. Sir Frederick Kenyon questions the *theocrasia* of Serapis and Esculapius, but see Bouché-Leclercq, *Rev. Hist. Rel.* 1902, p. 30.

[3] Revillout, *Rev. Égyptol.* 1880, p. 172.

[4] " The Names of Demons in the Magic Papyri," *P.S.B.A.* 1901, pp. 41 *sqq.*

have here preserved for us a fragment of the ritual in use in the
Alexandrian temples. "Give him, O Osiris, the cooling water"
is the epitaph often written by the worshippers of Isis on the
tombs of the dead[1], and it may seem that we have here a hint
of mystic communion with the deity brought about by the
drinking of his emblem.

The resemblances between the Alexandrian and the Christian
religion thus sketched, refer, however, merely to matters which
are either external or superficial, or which, like the worship of
the Virgin, the use of images and relics, and the institution of
monachism, could be abandoned, as was the case at the German
Reformation, without necessarily drawing with them the
repudiation of the cardinal tenets of Christianity. That the
Christian Church owed at her inception any of her more fundamental doctrines to the Alexandrian religion is not only without
proof, but is in the highest degree unlikely. The Apostles and
missionaries of the Apostolic Age, living as they did in daily
expectation of the return of their Risen Lord, had no need to
go to an alien faith for the assertion of His divinity, of the truth
of His resurrection, or of His power of salvation ; nor do the
Fathers of the Ante-Nicene Church speak of Serapis and Isis
as entitled to any peculiar reverence or as differing in any
respect from the other gods of the heathen. Whether the
tenets of the Alexandrian religion may not have had some
influence on the discussions which raged round the definition
of the Divine nature and attributes at the earlier Ecumenical
and other Councils of the Church is another matter. The conception of the Supreme Being as a triune god was a very old
one in Egypt, and reappeared, as we have seen, unchanged in
the worship of Serapis, Isis, and Horus. "Thus from one god
I became three gods," says Osiris in his description of his self-
creation in a papyrus dated twelve years after the death of
Alexander[2]; and the dividing-line between the three persons
of the Alexandrian triad is so often overstepped that it is plain
that their more cultured worshippers at one time considered

[1] Lafaye, *Culte*, etc. p. 96, and inscriptions there quoted.
[2] Budge, "Papyrus of Nesi-Amsu," p. 442.

them as but varying forms of one godhead[1]. Hence, the Trinitarian formulas set out in the Creeds of Nicaea and of St Athanasius would be less of a novelty to those familiar with the Alexandrian religion than to those brought up in the uncompromising monotheism of the Jews. Too little is known of the steps by which the full assertion of the doctrine of the Trinity was reached for any discussion of the matter to be here profitable[2]. The deepest influence that the Alexandrian religion exercised upon the Church was probably not direct, but through those scattered and heretical sects which, although finally condemned and anathematized by her, yet ever acted as feeders by whom she obtained converts from among the heathen. To these we may now turn our attention.

[1] See "The Greek Worship of Serapis and Isis," *P.S.B.A.* 1914, pp. 93, 94.

[2] That the Trinitarian doctrine of the Creed of Nicaea evolved gradually will now, I suppose, be admitted by all. Mr Conybeare, *Apology of Apollonius*, 1894, p. 14, probably goes too far when he says that " the doctrine of the Trinity in Unity " is not met with till the end of the third century. So Guignebert, *L'Évolution des Dogmes*, Paris, 1910, pp. 293, 294, tells us how in his opinion the dogma followed " at some distance " the assertion of the Divinity of Christ. Harnack, *Expansion of Christianity*, Eng. ed. 1904, II. pp. 257, 258, seems to attribute the first formulation of the dogma to Tertullian who, according to him, owed something to the Gnostics. It is at any rate plain that neither Hermas, nor the Apologists, nor Irenaeus, nor Clement of Alexandria, nor Origen were in accord with later orthodoxy on the point. Monsignor Duchesne, *Early History of the Christian Church*, Eng. ed. 1909, p. 20, puts the matter very frankly when he suggests that the average Christian troubled himself very little about it. " This is the Christian doctrine of the Trinity," he says after defining it, " not certainly as it was formulated later in opposition to transient heresies, but as it appeared to the general conscience of the early Christians....The generality of Christians in the first century even in apostolic days stood here almost exactly at the same point as present-day Christians. Theologians knew, or at any rate said, far more about it."

CHAPTER III

THE ORIGIN OF GNOSTICISM

THE worship of the Alexandrian gods was in every sense a religion. Not only did it form a common bond between men and women of different rank and origin, but it had its roots in the idea of propitiating the spiritual world. In the belief of its votaries, the blessings of health, of riches, of long life, and of happiness in this world and the next, were the gifts of Serapis and Isis, which they might extend to or withhold from mortals as seemed to them good[1]. But now we approach beliefs and practices, for the most part formed into organized cults, which were founded on the opposite idea. Those treated of in this and the seven succeeding chapters all have as their common root the notion that it is possible instead of propitiating to compel the spiritual powers. If these beings, greater and stronger than man as they were thought to be, were once invoked by their real names and with the proper ceremonies, it was said that the benefits demanded of them would follow as a matter of course without regard to the state of mind of the applicant and without the volition of the invisible ones themselves entering into play. This idea appears so early in the history of religions that it is thought by some to be the very source and origin of them all. A number of able writers, of

---

[1] Thus an Orphic verse, preserved by a commentator on Plato, says that Dionysos " releases whom he wills from travail and suffering." See Abel's *Orphica*, Fr. 208, p. 237. Servius in his commentary on Virgil's First Georgic, after declaring that Dionysos or " Liber Pater " is identical with the Osiris torn in pieces by Typhon, says that he is called Liber because he liberates. Cf. fragment and page quoted.

whom Lord Avebury[1] was one of the earliest, and Dr Frazer[2] is one of the latest examples, contend that there was a time in the history of mankind when man trusted entirely to his supposed powers of compulsion in his dealings with the invisible world, and that the attempt to propitiate it only developed out of this at a later period. It may be so, and the supporters of this theory are certainly not wrong when they go on to say that the same idea probably inspired those earliest attempts at the conquest of Nature which formed the first gropings of man towards natural science[3]. Up till now, however, they have failed to produce any instance of a people in a low state of culture who practise magic—as this attempted compulsion of the spiritual world is generally called—to the exclusion of every form of religion ; and until they do so, their thesis cannot be considered as established. On the contrary, all researches into the matter lead to the conclusion that magic generally begins to show itself some time after the religious beliefs of a people have taken an organized shape, and most prominently when they have passed their period of greatest activity[4]. This is particularly noticeable in the case of Ancient Egypt, which affords, as M. George Foucart has lately shown with much skill[5], a far more lively and complete picture of the evolution of religious ideas than can be found in the beliefs of savages. Here

---

[1] Lubbock, *Origin of Civilisation*, 5th ed., pp. 332, 333, and 349.

[2] *The Golden Bough*, 3rd ed. pt I. vol. I. p. 226, n. 2. Cf. Hubert and Mauss, *Esquisse d'une Théorie générale de la Magie*, Paris, 1904, p. 8. Goblet d'Alviella, reviewing Dr Frazer's 2nd edition, *Rev. Hist. Rel.* t. XLVIII. (July–Aug. 1903), pp. 70, 79 rebuts his theory. Mr E. S. Hartland, at the British Association's Meeting in 1906, propounded the view that both magic and religion were based on the conception of a transmissible personality or *mana*. Cf. *id. Ritual and Belief*, 1914, pp. 49 *sqq*.

[3] Hubert and Mauss, *op. cit.* p. 7.

[4] Thus the German Reformation, which (whatever be its merits) was certainly accompanied by a general questioning of ideas till then considered the very basis of all religion, was followed by the terrible outbreak known as the Witch Mania of the XVIth century. See Mackay, *Extraordinary Popular Delusions*, 1869, pp. 101–191. Other authorities are quoted in "Witchcraft in Scotland," *Scottish Review*, 1891, pp. 257–288.

[5] *Histoire des Religions et Méthode Comparative*, Paris, 1912, pp. 21–61.

we see beliefs and practices, once religious in every sense of the term, gradually becoming stereotyped and petrified until all memory of their origin and reason is lost, and the religion itself lapses into the systematized sorcery before referred to.

This phenomenon appears with great regularity in history; and it is an observation very easily verified that the practice of magic generally spreads in places and times where the popular religion has become outworn[1]. As, moreover, enquiry shows us that words taken from the rituals of dead faiths play the chief part in all ceremonial magic[2], we might be led to conclude that magic was but an unhealthy growth from, or the actual corruption of, religion. But if this were the case, we should find magicians despoiling for their charms and spells the rituals of cults formerly practised in their own countries only; whereas it is more often from foreign faiths and languages that they borrow. The tendency of all peoples to look upon earlier and more primitive races than themselves as the depositaries of magical secrets is one of the best known phenomena[3]. Thus, in modern India, it is the aboriginal Bhils and Gonds who are resorted to as sorcerers by the Aryans who have supplanted them[4], while the Malays seem to draw their magic almost

---

[1] See note 4 on p. 91, *supra*. Cf. also the great increase of magical practices which followed the attempted overthrow of religion by the philosophers after Alexander.

[2] Some instances, such as "hocus-pocus" (*hoc est corpus meum*), are given in *P.S.B.A.* xx. (1898), p. 149. An excellent example is found in a spell to cause invisibility in a magic papyrus at Berlin where the magician is directed to say among other words *anok peusire penta set tako* " I am that Osiris whom Set murdered "—evidently a phrase from some Egyptian ritual extinct centuries before the papyrus was written. See Parthey, *Zwei griechische Zauberpapyri*, 1866, p. 127, l. 252. Cf. Erman, " Die Ägyptischer Beschwörungen " in *Ägyptische Zeitschrift*, 1883, p. 109, n. 1.

[3] Tylor, *Primitive Culture*, 1871, I. pp. 102–104. Cf. Crookes, *Popular Religion and Folklore of Northern India*, 1896, II. p. 283; Hubert and Mauss, *op. cit.* pp. 26, 27; A. Réville, *Religion des Peuples non-civilisés*, 1883, II. p. 173.

[4] Crookes, *op. cit.* II. p. 261, says that witchcraft in Northern India is at present almost specialized among the Dravidian, or aboriginal people—of which fact Mr Rudyard Kipling makes great use in his charming story " Letting in the Jungle."

entirely from the beliefs of their Arab conquerors[1]. So, too, in Egypt we find that the magicians of the xixth Dynasty made use in their spells of foreign words which seem to be taken from Central African languages[2], and those of early Christian times use Hebrew phrases with which they must for the first time have become acquainted not very long before[3].

At the same time there are many proofs that magic is something more than a by-product of religion. No people, however backward, who do not practise magic in some or other of its forms, have yet been discovered; while at the same time it has always persisted among those nations who consider themselves the most highly civilized. Thus, we find the Mincopies who inhabit the Andaman Islands and are thought by some to be the lowest of mankind, threatening with their arrows the spirit that is supposed to cause tempests, and lighting fires on the graves of their dead chiefs to drive him away[4]. At the other end of the scale we have the story of the Scottish Covenanter,

" John Scrimgeour, minister of Kinghorn, who, having a beloved child sick to death of the crewels, was free to expostulate with his Maker with such impatience of displeasure, and complaining so bitterly, that at length it was said unto him, that he was heard for that time, but that he was requested to use no such boldness in time coming ":

and a similar story is told of Ignatius Loyola, the founder of the

[1] W. W. Skeat, *Malay Magic*, 1900, pp. 533 *sqq.*
[2] Chabas, *Le Papyrus Magique Harris*, 1860, pp. 151, 162 *sq.* Erman, *Life in Ancient Egypt*, Eng. ed. p. 355, while admitting that the Egyptians thought the words in question belonged to a foreign tongue, says that they were " pure inventions." He is certainly wrong, for some of them can be identified.
[3] Leemans, *Papyri Graeci Mus. Antiq. Lugduni-Batavi*; Wessely, *Griechische Zauberpapyrus von Paris und London*, and *Neue Griechische Zauberpapyri*, Wien, 1893, *passim.* Cf. Kenyon, *Greek Papyri in the British Museum*, p. 62. So in mediaeval magic, the words in the spells unintelligible to the magician are generally Greek. See Reginald Scot, *Discovery of Witchcraft* (1651), p. 168.
[4] Réville, *Rel. des Peuples non-civilisés*, II. p. 164.

Jesuits[1]. It seems then that magic is so inextricably intertwined with religion that the history of one of them cannot be effectually separated from that of the other, and neither of them can be assigned any priority in time. This does not mean, however, that they are connected in origin, and it is probable that the late Sir Alfred Lyall was right when he said that magic and religion are in their essence antagonistic and correspond to two opposing tendencies of the human mind[2]. The same tendencies lead one man to ask for what he wants while another will prefer to take it by force, and it is even possible that the same alternative of choice is sometimes manifested in the lower animals[3].

Now it is evident that in the practice of cults where the idea of the compulsion of the invisible powers is prominent, the essential factor will be the *knowledge* of the proper means to be adopted to attain the end sought. But this does not at once strike the observer, because at first sight these appear to be the same as those used in the cults which rest on the idea of propitiation. Prayers and sacrifices indeed appear in magical quite as often as in the case of propitiatory rites, but the reason of them is entirely different. Prayer in a religion—could any such be found—entirely free from all admixture of magic or compulsion, would be based on the attempt to move the pity of the divinity invoked for the miserable and abased state of the suppliant, or by some other means. A striking example of this can be found in the Assyrian prayers from the palace of Assur-bani-pal, which might be, as the rubric informs us, made to any god[4]. Says the suppliant :

[1] Scott in the *Heart of Midlothian* quotes the first story, I think, from Peter Walker, but I have not been able to find the passage. For Ignatius Loyola, see Böhmer, *Les Jésuites*, French ed. 1910, p. 10. Cf. Alphandéry, *R.H.R.* 1911, p. 110.

[2] *Asiatic Studies*, 1882, p. 77.

[3] *E.g.* well-fed dogs who worry sheep, and cats who steal fish and other delicacies rather than have them given to them. The actions of the animals show in both cases that they know that what they are doing is displeasing to their owners.

[4] Sayce, *Gifford Lectures*, pp. 420 *sqq.* For these penitential psalms generally, see Jastrow, *The Religion of Babylonia and Assyria*, Boston, 1898, chap. XVIII.

"O my god my sins are many, my transgressions are great.
I sought for help, and none took my hand.
I wept, and none stood by my side ;
I cried aloud, and there was none that heard me.
I am in trouble and hiding, and dare not look up.
To my god, the merciful one, I turn myself, I utter my prayer.
The feet of my goddess I kiss and water with tears....
O Lord, cast not away thy servant...."

The same spirit may be noticed in the early religions of the Greeks, although here the worshipper uses, as his means of propitiation, flattery rather than entreaty, as when the Achilles of the *Iliad* tries to move Zeus by an enumeration of his different titles, addressing him as "Father Zeus, that rulest from Ida, most glorious, most great[1]," and Athena is appealed to by Nestor in the *Odyssey* as "Daughter of Zeus, driver of the spoil, the maiden of Triton[2]" and so on. As, however, magical ideas come to the front, we find these prayers giving way to others containing neither appeals for mercy nor flattery, but merely long strings of names and attributes, all designed to show an acquaintance with the antecedents and supposed natural disposition of the divinity addressed, and inspired by the fear that the one name which might exert a compelling effect upon his answer might accidentally have been omitted[3]. So, too, the sacrifices, which in early times were chosen on the sole principle of giving to the god what was best and costliest, came later to be regulated by the supposed knowledge of what was especially appropriate to him for reasons based on sympathetic magic or the association of ideas. Thus, swine were sacrificed to Demeter, he-goats to Dionysos, cattle and horses to Poseidon, and rams to Heracles[4], instead of the animals, chosen only for their youth and beauty and with or without gilded horns, that

[1] *Il.* III. ll. 280 *sqq.* (Lang, Leaf, and Myers trans. p. 57).
[2] *Odyss.* III. ll. 373 *sqq.* (Butcher and Lang trans. p. 43).
[3] According to Maspero, *Ét. Égyptol.* I. p. 163, this was always the case in Egypt, at least in historic times. "Prayer," he says, "was a formula of which the terms had an imperative value, and the exact enunciation of which obliged the god to concede what was asked of him."
[4] Maury, *Religions de la Grèce Antique*, II. pp. 97 *sqq.*

we read about in the *Iliad* and *Odyssey*[1]. Clearly such distinctions necessitate a much closer knowledge of the divine nature than where the answer to prayer or sacrifice depends merely on the benevolence of the deity.

It is also evident that such ideas will give rise to curiosity with regard to the nature and history of the gods, to their relations with one another, and to the extent and division of their rule over Nature, which would hardly affect those who think that all events depend simply upon the nod of the superhuman powers[2]. Hence it is evident that one of the first consequences of a large admixture of magic in a religion will be a great increase of myths and legends in which the actions of the gods will be recounted with more or less authority, and some observed natural phenomenon will be pointed to as evidence of the truth of the stories narrated[3]. Moreover, the means by which the consequence of any voluntary or involuntary transgression of the supposed commands of the gods can be averted will be eagerly sought after, and these, whether they take the form of purifications, lustrations, or other expiatory rites, will all be strictly magical in character, and will generally consist in the more or less detailed representation of some episode in their history, on the well-known principle of magic that any desired effect can be produced by imitating it[4]. In all these cases it is knowledge and not conduct which is required, and thus it is that *gnosticism* or a belief in the importance of acquaintance with the divine world, its motives, and the influences to which it is subject, enters into religion. Then it comes about that man begins to trouble himself about the origin of the universe and its end, the cause of his own appearance upon the earth, and the position that he occupies in the scale of being. Hence theogonies or tales relating how the gods came into existence, and

---

[1] *Il.* x. l. 292 ; *Odyss.* xi. l. 30, and where before quoted.

[2] Perhaps it is to this last view that we should attribute the well-known indifference of the Semitic peoples to mythology and science.

[3] *E.g.* the Rainbow in Genesis ix. 12–16. Erman, in his *History of Egyptian Religion*, p. 31, points out that Egyptian mythology is found only in magical books.

[4] Frazer, *Golden Bough*, 3rd ed. pt I. vol. I. p. 52.

their kinship to one another, cosmogonies or accounts of the creation of the world, and apocalypses or stories professing to reveal the lot of man after death and the fate to which our universe is destined, take shape to an extent unknown to religions which remain merely or chiefly propitiatory.

There is, however, another and a less sublime kind of knowledge which is everywhere associated with the appearance of gnosticism. This is the knowledge of ceremonies and formulas, of acts to be done and of words to be said, which are thought to exercise a compelling effect on the supra-sensible world, and which we may class together under the generic name of ceremonial magic. Our acquaintance with these at the period under discussion has lately been much enlarged by the decipherment and publication of the so-called Magic Papyri found for the most part in Egypt and now scattered throughout the principal museums of Europe[1]. These turn out on investigation to be the manuals or handbooks of professional sorcerers or magicians, and to range in date from the IIIrd century before to the IVth or Vth after Christ. They contain, for the most part without any order or coherence, details of the different ceremonies used for the personal aggrandizement of the user, for gaining the love of women and (conversely) for putting hate between a man and his wife; for healing disease and casting out devils; for causing dreams, discovering thieves, and gaining knowledge of the thoughts of men and of things past and to come; and for obtaining, by other than direct means, success in athletic competitions. In others, we find directions for evoking gods or spirits who may thus be bound to the service of the magician, for raising the dead for necromantic purposes, and for the destruction of enemies, mingled with technical recipes for making ink and for the compounding of drugs. A feature common to nearly all these charms is their illustration by certain roughly-drawn pictures and formulas which seem at first to be mere strings of letters without sense.

A few specimens of these charms may help to make this

[1] The principal collections of these are indicated in note 3 on p. 93, *supra.* Cf. "The Names of Demons in the Magic Papyri," *P.S.B.A.* 1901,

description clearer.   In a papyrus now in the British Museum which is said from the writing to date from the ivth century A.D.[1], we find the following charms for obtaining an oracular response in a dream :

" Take of the inner leaves of the laurel and of virgin earth and wormwood seeds flour and of the herb cynocephalium (and I have heard from a certain man of Heracleopolis [now Ahnas el-Medineh] that he takes of the leaves of an olive-tree newly sprouted)....
It is carried by a virgin boy ground up with the materials aforesaid and the white of an ibis' egg is mixed with the whole compound.   There must also be an image of Hermes clad in the chlamys, and the moon must be rising in the sign of Aries or Leo or Sagittarius.   Now let Hermes hold the herald's wand, and do thou write the spell on hieratic paper.   And take a goose's windpipe, as I also learned from the Heracleopolite, and insert it into the figure so as to be able to blow into it.   When you wish for an oracular answer, write the spell and the matter in hand, and having cut a hair from your head, wrap it up in the paper and tie it with a Phoenician knot, and put it at the feet of the caduceus, or, as some say, place it upon it.   Let the figure be in a shrine of limewood, and when you wish for an oracular answer place the shrine with the god at your head, and make invocation, offering frankincense on an altar and some earth from a place where there is growing corn, and one lump of sal ammoniac.   Let this be placed at your head and lie down to sleep after first saying this, but giving no answer to anyone who may address you :

" Hermes, lord of the world, inner circle of the moon
Round and square, originator of the words of the tongue
Persuading to justice, wearer of the chlamys, with winged sandals
Rolling an ethereal course under the lower parts of the earth
Guide of spirits, greatest eye of the sun
Author of all manner of speech, rejoicing with lights
Those mortals whose life being finished are under the lower parts
    of the earth.

[1] Kenyon, *Gk. Pap. in Brit. Mus.* p. 77.   This is the date of the MS. The spells themselves are probably much older.

III]   *The Origin of Gnosticism*   99

Thou art called the foreknower of destinies, and the divine vision
Sending oracles both by day and by night.
Thou dost heal all the ills of mortals with thy medicines.
Come hither, blessed one, greatest son of perfect memory
Appear propitious in thy own shape, and send a propitious form
That by the excellence of thy divining art I, a hallowed man, may
    receive what I need.
O Lord grant my prayer, appear and grant me a true oracle !

" Make the adjuration at the risings of the sun and moon.

" (The inscription to be written on the paper wrappings of the figure.)

    " *Huesemigadôn, Orthô Baubô, noê odêre soire soire*
        Kanthara, Ereschchigal, sankistê, dodekakistê " etc.

In this charm we have nearly all the typical elements of
the magic of the period. The windpipe of a goose or other
long-necked animal was, we learn from Hippolytus, inserted
into the hollow head of the metal statue of the god, in order
that the priest might use it as a speaking tube, and thus cause
the statue to give forth oracular responses in a hollow voice[1].
Hence its use would be thought particularly appropriate when
an oracle was sought, although in circumstances where it would
be ineffective for purposes of deceit. The fragment of a hymn
in hexameter verse to a god whom it addresses as Hermes is
doubtless of great antiquity and taken from the ritual of some
half-Greek, half-Oriental worship such as we may imagine to
have been paid to the Cabiri, in which a god identified by
the Greeks with their own Hermes was particularly honoured.
The words of the spell to be written on the paper are by no means
the mere gibberish they seem, although they have been so
corrupted that it is almost impossible to recognise even the
language in which they are written. The word *Huesemigadôn*
is, however, an epithet or name of Pluto the ruler of Hades,

---

[1] *Philosophumena*, Bk IV. c. 28. Hippolytus is probably wrong in
thinking this a conscious imposture. The magician, like his clients, does
not connect cause and effect in such cases. Sir Alfred Lyall told Lord
Avebury that he had often seen Indian sorcerers openly mixing croton
oil with the ink in which their charms were written so as to produce
a purgative effect when the ink was washed off and swallowed. See
Lubbock, *Origin of Civilization*, p. 24.

and occurs in that connection, as has been shown elsewhere, in many of these magic spells[1]. The *Orthô Baubô* which follows it is generally found in the same context and seems to cover the name of that Baubo who plays a prominent part in the Mysteries of Eleusis and appears to have been confused in later times with Persephone, the spouse of Pluto[2]. *Ereshchigal* [Eres-ki-gal], again, is a word borrowed from the first or Sumerian inhabitants of Babylonia, and means in Sumerian "the Lady of the great (*i.e.* the nether) world," being a title frequently used for Allat the goddess of hell, who appears in the very old story of the Descent of Ishtar and is the Babylonian counterpart of Persephone[3]. Why she should have been called *dodekakistê* or the 12th cannot now be said; but it is possible that we have here a relic of the curious Babylonian habit of giving numbers as well as names to the gods, or rather of identifying certain numbers with certain divinities[4]. On the whole, therefore, it may be judged that the words of the spell once formed part of the ritual of a Sumerian worship long since forgotten and that they travelled across Western Asia and were translated as far as might be into Greek, when that language became the common tongue of the civilized world after Alexander's conquests.

This may be taken for a spell having its origin in, or at any rate depending for its efficacy upon, the relics of some Western

[1] *P.S.B.A.* xxii. (1900), pp. 121 *sqq.* An explanation of the name is attempted by Giraud, *Ophitae*, Paris, 1884, p. 91, n. 5.

[2] Daremberg and Saglio, *Dict. des Antiq. s.v.* Baubo. The name Ortho perhaps suggests that of the very ancient goddess later called Artemis Orthia, whose original name seems to have been Orthia only. Cf. M. S. Thompson's paper "The Asiatic or Winged Artemis" in *J.H.S.* vol. xxix. (1909), pp. 286 *sqq.*, esp. p. 307.

[3] *P.S.B.A.* xxii. (1900), p. 121, and see Griffith and Thompson, *Demotic Magical Papyrus of London and Leiden*, p. 61 and note.

[4] Probably, however, it refers to the number of letters in the name in some more or less fantastic spelling or cryptogram. When Hippolytus speaks of the Demiurge Ialdabaoth as "a fiery God, a fourth number" (*Philosophumena*, Bk v. c. 7, p. 153, Cruice), there can be little doubt that he is referring to the Tetragrammaton or four-lettered name of Jehovah. Cf. the "hundred-lettered" name of Typhon, p. 104, *infra*.

Asiatic faith.   The following taken from another papyrus now
in the Bibliothèque Nationale at Paris shows acquaintance
with the Egyptian religion—probably through the Alexandrian
or Isiacist form of it described in Chapter II—and is perhaps
a more salient example of the compulsive element common to
all magic, but particularly associated with the Egyptian magicians.   It is given in the shape of a letter purporting to be
addressed by a certain Nephotes to the Pharaoh Psamtik whom
the Greeks called Psammetichos, and who managed, as has been
said above, to drive out the Ethiopians and to rule Egypt by the
help of Greek mercenaries.   There is no reason to suppose that
this attribution is anything more than a charlatanic attempt to
assign to it a respectable origin; but it is probable from certain
indications that it was really taken from an earlier hieratic
or demotic MS. of pre-Christian times.   It has been published
by Dr Karl Wessely of Vienna[1] and is written in Greek characters
of apparently the IIIrd century A.D.

"Nephotes to Psammetichos king of Egypt, the ever living,
greeting. Since the great god [Serapis?] has restored to thee an
eternal kingdom, and Nature has made thee an excellent adept, and
I am also willing to show forth to thee the love of art which is mine—
I have sent to thee this ceremony, a holy rite made perfect with all
ease of working, which having tested, you will be amazed at the
unexpected nature of this arrangement. You will see with your
own eyes in the bowl in what day or night you will and in what
place you will. You will see the god in the water, receiving the word
from the god in what verses you will. [It will reach also?] the
world-ruler and if you ask a question of him he will speak even of
all the other things you seek. [A description of the ointment to be
used doubtless once followed, but has been omitted in the Paris MS.[2]]

---

[1] *Griechische Zauberpapyri von Paris und London*, pp. 24–26.

[2] The use of ointment for magical purposes is well known, and it was
the incautious use of an ointment of this kind which changed Lucius, the
hero of Apuleius' romance, into an ass. The use of ointments which had
the property of translating the user to the Witches' Sabbath frequently
occurs in the witch-trials of the Renaissance, and it has been suggested
that drugs producing hallucinations were thus applied. The word κοινή
often found in these spells seems to point to some ointment or preparation
used in *all* the magic ceremonies described.

Having thus anointed yourself and having put together before the rising of the sun in this form (?) what things you will, when the third day of the moon has come, go with the mystagogue upon the roof of the house, and spread upon the earth a clean linen cloth, and having crowned yourself with black ivy at the 5th hour after noon, lie down naked on the linen cloth, and order him [the mysta-gogue] to bind your eyes with a bandage of black linen ; and having laid yourself down like a corpse [or, on your back ?], close your eyes, making the sign of consecration towards the sun with these words :—

" O mighty Typhon of the sceptre on high, sceptred ruler, God of Gods. King *Aberamenthôu*[1], hill shaker, bringer of thunder, hurricane, who lightens by night, hot-natured one, rock shaker, destroyer of wells, dasher of waves, who disturbs the deep with movement. *Io erbêt autauimêni.* I am he who with thee has uprooted the whole inhabited world and seeks out the great Osiris who brought thee chains. I am he who with thee fights on the side of the gods (some say against the gods). I am he who has shut up the twin sides of heaven, and has lulled to sleep the invisible dragon. and who has established the sea [and ?] the red springs of rivers. Until thou shall no longer be lord of this dominion, I am thy soldier, I was conquered [and hurled] headlong by the gods. I was thrown down by [their] wrath in vain [or, because of the void]. Awake ! I come as a suppliant, I come as thy friend, and thou wilt not cast me out, O earth-caster. King of the gods. *aemonaebarôtherree-thôrabeaneïmea*[2]. Be strong, I entreat ! Grant me this grace that, when I shall command one of the gods themselves to come to my incantations, I may see them coming quickly ! *Naïne basanaptatou eaptou mênô phaesmê paptoumênôph aesimê trauapti peuchrê, trauara ptoumêph, mouraianchouchaphapta moursaaramei. Iaô aththaraui-mênoker boroptoumêth attaui mêni charchara ptoumai lalapsa trauei*

---

[1] *Aber-amenti :* " Lord (lit. Bull) or Conqueror of Amenti," the Egyp-tian Hades. The name is of frequent occurrence in all these spells. Jesus, in one of the later documents of the *Pistis Sophia*, is called *Aberamenthô*, in circumstances that would make the title peculiarly appropriate.

[2] A palindrome containing the same word or sentence written both forwards and backwards. The phrase here given (*aemonaebarôth*) is probably Hebrew, which the scribe may have known was written the reverse way to most European languages. It is noteworthy that a mistake in transcription is made when the phrase is written backwards.

trauei mamôphortoula[1] *aeêio iou oêôa eai aeêiôi iaô aêi ai iaô*[2]. On your repeating this three times, there will be this sign of the alliance[3]. But you having the soul of a magician will be prepared. Do not alarm yourself, for a sea-hawk hovering downwards will strike with his wings upon your body[4]. And do thou having stood upon thy feet clothe thyself in white garments, and in an earthen censer scatter drops of frankincense speaking thus : ' I exist in thy sacred form. I am strong in thy sacred name. I have lighted upon the flowing-forth of thy good things, O Lord, God of Gods, king demon. *Atthouin thouthoui tauanti laôaptatô.*' Having done this, you may descend like a god, and will command the [order ?][5] of Nature through this complete arrangement of autoptic [*i.e.* clairvoyant] lecanomancy. It is also a way of compelling the dead to become visible. For when you wish to enquire concerning [any] events, you must take a brazen jar or dish or pan, whichever you will, and fill it with water, which if you are invoking the celestial gods must be living [Qy. running or sparkling ?] ; but, if the terrestrial divinities, from the sea ; and if Osiris or Sarapis, from the river [Nile ?] ; and, if the dead, from a well. Take the vessel upon your knees, pour upon it oil made from unripe olives, then bending over the vessel repeat the following invocation and invoke what god you will and an answer will be given to you and he will speak to you concerning all things. But if and when he shall have spoken, dismiss

[1] This sentence was probably once Egyptian from the frequent recurrence of *p* and *t* as the initial letters of words. They are the masculine and feminine forms of the definite article in Coptic.

[2] These " boneless strings of vowels," as C. W. King calls them in his *Gnostics and their Remains*, 1887, p. 320, are thought by him to cover the name of Jehovah. Another theory is that they are a musical notation giving the tone in which the spell is to be pronounced.

[3] Σύστασις. The text gives the most usual meaning of the word : but it may here mean something like the " materialization " spoken of by spiritualists.

[4] The word used (πλάσμα) properly means image. But no image or idol has been mentioned. It is curious that in the Mithraic mysteries, we hear of the initiates, apparently during the reception of a candidate, " striking [him ?] with birds' wings." Cf. the text attributed (doubtfully) to St Augustine in Cumont, *Textes et Monuments relatifs aux Mystères de Mithra*, Bruxelles, 1896, t. II. p. 8.

[5] Some word like οἰκονομία seems to have been omitted by the scribe.

him with the dismissal which you will wonder at, using the same speech.

"Speech to be said over the vessel. *Amoun auantau laimoutau riptou mantaui imantau lantou laptoumi anchômach araptoumi.* Hither, such and such a god! Be visible to me this very day and do not appal my eyes. Hither to me such and such a god! giving ear to my race [?]. For this is what *anchôr anchôr achachach ptoumi chancho charachôch chaptoumê chôraharachôch aptoumi mêchôchaptou charach ptou chanchô charachô ptenachôcheu*, a name written in a hundred letters, wishes and commands. And do not thou, most mighty king, forget the magicians among us; because this is the earliest name of Typhon, at which tremble the earth, the abyss, Hades, heaven, the sun, the moon, the place of the stars and the whole phenomenal universe. When this name is spoken, it carries along with its force gods and demons. It is the hundred-lettered name, the same name as last written. And when thou hast uttered it, the god or the dead person who hears it will appear to thee and will answer concerning the things you ask. And when you have learned all things, dismiss the god only with the strong name, the one of the hundred letters, saying 'Begone, Lord, for thus wills and commands the great god!' Say the name and he will depart. Let this treatise, O mighty king, be kept to thyself alone, being guarded from being heard by any other. And this is the phylactery which you should wear. It should be arranged on a silver plate. Write the same name with a brazen pen and wear it attached with a strip of ass's skin[1]."

The purpose of the charm just given is, as will be seen, to produce apparitions in a bowl containing liquid after the fashion still common in the near East[2]. It amply bears out the remark of Iamblichus that the Egyptian magicians, differing therein from the Chaldaean, were accustomed in their spells to threaten the gods[3], and many other instances of this can

[1] Because the ass was considered a Typhonic animal.

[2] The form of hypnotism known as crystal-gazing. A full description is given in Lane's *Modern Egyptians*, 1896, pp. 276 *sqq.* Cf. "Divination in the xviith Century," *National Review*, 1899, pp. 93–104, for its practice in England.

[3] See the letter of Porphyry to Anebo quoting Chaeremon. That this practice was peculiar to the Egyptian magicians is stated by Iamblichus,

be found in other passages of the magic papyri. But it should be noticed that in this case the magician is dealing with a power thought to be hostile alike to man and to the beneficent gods. Typhon, who is, as Plutarch tells us, the Greek equivalent of the Egyptian Set, was looked upon in Hellenistic times as essentially a power of darkness and evil, who fights against the gods friendly to man with the idea of reducing their ordered world to chaos. Yet the magician avows himself on his side, and even speaks of his name as being able to compel the heavenly gods, to whom he must therefore be superior. Iamblichus tries to explain this, and to refine away the obvious meaning of such spells, but their existence certainly justifies the accusation of trafficking with devils brought by the early Christian Fathers against the practisers of magic.

Another charm may be quoted for the purpose of showing the acquaintance, superficial though it was, with the religions of all nations in the Hellenistic world and the indifference with regard to them which the practice of magic necessitated. It appears in the papyrus in the British Museum last quoted from and is directed to be spoken over " the lamp " which plays so great a part in all magical processes[1]. Of its real or supposed author, Alleius Craeonius, nothing is known :

" A spell of Allêius Craeonius spoken over the lamp. *Óchmarmachô*, the *nouraï chrêmillon* sleeping with eyes open, *nia*, Iaô equal-numbered[2] *soumpsênis siasias*, Iaô who shakes the whole inhabited world, come hither unto me and give answer concerning the work [*i.e.* the

---

de Mysteriis, Bk IV. c. 7. A good instance is given by Maspero, " Sur deux Tabellae Devotionis " in *Ét. Égyptol.* 1893, t. II. p. 297, where a magician threatens, if his prayer be not granted, to go down into the secret places of Osiris and destroy his shroud.

[1] Kenyon, *Greek Papyri in the British Museum*, pp. 79–81.

[2] Or isopsephic. *i.e.* composed of letters having an equal numerical value. One of the many forms of juggling with words and letters current in the early Christian centuries. The " number of the beast " in Revelation xiii. 18, where, as is now generally admitted, 666 covers the name of Nero Caesar which has that numerical value in Hebrew, is the most familiar instance. Other instances can be found in the Epistle of Barnabas, c. 9, Hilgenfeld, *N.T. extra Canonem receptum*, Lips. 1884, and Hippolytus, *Philosophumena*, Bk VI. c. 48, p. 318, Cruice.

matter in hand] *kototh phouphnoun nouebouê* in the place prepared
for thy reception [?]. Take an inscription[1] with on the obverse
Sarapis seated holding the royal sceptre of Egypt and upon the
sceptre an ibis. On the reverse of the stone, carve the name and
shut it up and keep it for use. Take the ring in your left hand,
and a branch of olive and laurel in your right, shaking it over the
lamp[2], at the same time uttering the spell seven times. And, having
put it (the ring) upon the Idaean finger[3] of your left hand, facing
and turning inwards [Qy. away from the door of the chamber ?]
and having fastened the stone to your left ear, lie down to sleep
returning no answer to any who may speak to you :

"'I invoke thee who created the earth and the rocks [*lit.* the
bones] and all flesh and spirit and established the sea, and shakes
the heavens and did divide the light from the darkness, the great
ordering mind, who disposes all, the everlasting eye, Demon of
Demons, God of Gods, the Lord of Spirits, the unwandering Æon.
Iao ouêi [Jehovah ?] hearken unto my voice. I invoke thee the
ruler of the gods, high-thundering Zeus, O king Zeus Adonai, O Lord
Jehovah [?]. I am he who invokes thee in the Syrian tongue as the
great god *Zaalaêr iphphou*[4] and do thou not disregard the sound in
Hebrew *ablanathanalba*[5] *abrasilôa*. For I am *silthachôouch lailam
blasalôth* Iaô ieô *nebuth sabiothar bôth arbath iaô* Iaôth Sabaoth *patourê
zagourê Baruch adonai elôai iabraam*[6] *barbarauô nausiph*, lofty-
minded, everliving, having the diadem of the whole ordered world,
siepê saktietê of life (twice) *sphê nousi* (twice) *sietho* (twice). *Chthe-
thônirinch ôêaêêol aôê Iaô asial Sarapêolsô ethmourêsini sem lau lou
lurinch.*'

[1] The context shows that a scarab set in a ring is indicated.

[2] A rude drawing representing the magician in this attitude often
appears in the margin of papyri such as that quoted in the text. See Wessely,
Griech. Zauberp. p. 118.

[3] Doubtless the index, because the Idaean Dactyli were said to be the
first of men.

[4] This seems to be a corruption of some name like Baal-zephon. The
confusion of ζ for β in these papyri is very common.

[5] A Hebrew name meaning "Thou art our father." It was thought
especially valuable because it could be read either way.

[6] Of these words, *Iaoth Sabaoth* is "Jehovah of hosts"; *patoure zagoure*,
"who openeth and shutteth" (cf. Revelation i. 8); *Baruch adonai eloai
iabraam*, "Blessed be the Lord God of Abraham." All are fairly good
Hebrew not very much corrupted.

" This spell loosens chains, blinds, brings dreams, causes favours, and may be used for any purposes you wish."

In this spell, we have Zeus and Yahweh associated with Serapis in the apparent belief that all three were the same god. Although the magician parades his learning by using the name of one of the Syrian Baals, and it is possible that some of the unintelligible words of the invocation may be much corrupted Egyptian, he is evidently well acquainted with Hebrew, and one of the phrases used seems to be taken from some Hebrew ritual. It is hardly likely that he would have done this unless he were himself of Jewish blood ; and we have therefore the fact that a Jewish magician was content to address his national god as Zeus and to make use of a " graven image " of him under the figure of the Graeco-Egyptian Serapis in direct contravention of the most stringent clauses in the Law of Moses. A more striking instance of the way in which magicians of the time borrowed from all religions could hardly be imagined.

The uncertain date of the charms under discussion prevent any very cogent argument as to their authorship being drawn from them ; but there are other grounds for supposing that the use of magic was never so wide-spread as in the last three centuries before and the first three centuries after the birth of Christ, and that this was mainly due to the influx of Orientals into the West. One of the indirect effects of Alexander's conquests was, by substituting Greek kings for the native rulers who had till then governed the countries lying round the Nile and the Euphrates, to break up the priestly colleges there established, and thus to set free a great quantity of the lower class of priests and temple-servants who seem to have wandered through the Hellenistic world, selling their knowledge of curious arts, and seeking from the credulity of their fellows the toilless livelihood that they had till then enjoyed at the expense of the state. The names given to the most famous of these charlatans in the early Roman Empire—Petosiris, Nechepso, Astrampsuchos[1],

---

[1] Astrampsuchos appears, oddly enough, as the name of one of the celestial guardians of a heaven in one of the documents of the Bodleian Bruce Papyrus which is described in Chap. X, *infra*. See Amélineau, *Le*

and Ostanes[1]—are in themselves sufficient to show their origin; and " Chaldaicus " passed into the common language of the time as the recognized expression for the professional exponent of curious arts. Even in the time of Sulla there seems to have been no lack of persons who, if not magicians, were at all events professional diviners capable of interpreting the Dictator's dreams[2], and the writers of the Augustan age allude frequently to magic, such as that taught by the papyri just quoted, as being generally the pursuit of foreigners. The Thessalian magicians are as celebrated in the Roman times which Apuleius describes as in those of Theocritus. The Canidia or Gratidia of Horace had also a Thessalian who assisted her in her incantations[3]. But these, like the Chaldaean and Egyptian sorcerers just mentioned, were at the head of their profession, and in many cases made large sums out of the sale of their services. The taste for magic of the poorer classes, slaves, and freedmen, was catered for by the crowd of itinerant magicians, among whom the Jews (and Jewesses) seem to have been the most numerous, who used to hang about the Circus Maximus[4]. Renan is doubtless perfectly right when he says that never were the Mathematici, the Chaldaei, and the Goetae of all kinds so abundant as in the Rome of Nero[5]. Their prevalence in the great cities of the eastern provinces of the Empire may be judged from the frequency of their mention in the New Testament[6].

It would, of course, be very easy to consider all such practices as the result of deliberate and conscious imposture. This is

Papyrus Gnostique Bruce, Paris, p. 109, who transcribes it Etrempsuchos, while Schmidt (*Koptisch-gnostische Schriften*, Leipzig, 1905, Bd. I. p. 345) writes Strempsuchos. Hippolytus gives the name as that of one of the Powers worshipped by the Peratae, *v. Philosophumena*, Bk v. c. 14, p. 196, Cruice.

[1] M. Maspero contends that this name is a corruption of an epithet of Thoth. See *Ét. Égyptol.* v. p. 259.

[2] See Plutarch, *Sulla, passim*, especially cc. IX. XXVIII. and XXXVII. from which last it appears that he consulted " the Chaldaeans."

[3] Horace, *Epode*, v.

[4] Juvenal, *Sat.* VI.

[5] Renan, *L'Antéchrist*, Paris, 1873, p. 28, n. 4, for authorities.

[6] Acts xiii. 8 ; *ibid.* xix. 13–19. Cf. Renan, *op. cit.* p. 421.

the course taken by Hippolytus in the *Philosophumena*, in which the heresiologist bishop gives a description of the tricks of the conjurors of the IIIrd century accompanied by rationalistic explanations which sometimes make a greater demand on the credulity of the readers than the wonders narrated[1]. These tricks he accuses the leaders of the Gnostics of his time of learning and imitating, and the accusation is therefore plainly dictated by the theological habit of attempting by any means to discredit the morals of those who dissent from the writer's own religious opinions[2]. But a study of the magic papyri themselves by no means supports this theory of conscious imposture. The spells therein given were evidently written for the use of a professional magician, and seem to have been in constant employment. Many of them bear after them the note written in the hand of the scribe that he has tested them and found them efficacious. The pains, too, which the author takes to give variations of the process recommended in them—as for example in the quotations from a " man of Heracleopolis " in the first of the spells given above— all show that he had a more or less honest belief in the efficacy of the spells he is transcribing. The recording in the same papyri of what would be now called "trade secrets" such as recipes for the manufacture of ink all point the same way, and go to confirm the view that the magicians who made use of them, although willing to sell their supposed powers over the supernatural world for money, yet believed that they really possessed them.

This is the more likely to be true because many of the phenomena which these spells are intended to produce are what would now be called hypnotic. The gods and demons invoked are supposed to appear sometimes in dreams, but more generally to a virgin boy gazing fixedly either at a lamp or at the shining

---

[1] Book IV. c. 4, *passim*, especially the device for making sheep cut off their own heads by rubbing their necks against a sword, or for producing an earthquake by burning upon coals the dung of an ichneumon mixed with magnetic ore (pp. 99, 111, Cruice). Tertullian, *de Praescript.* c. 43, accuses the Gnostics of frequenting magicians and astrologers.

[2] *Philosophumena*, Bk IV. c. 15, pp. 112, 113, Cruice.

surface of a liquid. This is, of course, the form of " crystal-
gazing " or divination by the ink-pool still used throughout
the East, a graphic description of which is given in Lane's
Modern Egyptians[1]. In this case as in the charms for the healing
of disease—especially of epilepsy and other nervous maladies—
given in the same papyri, the active agent seems to be the
power of suggestion, consciously or unconsciously exercised
by the operator or magician. A full but popular explanation
of these phenomena from the standpoint of modern science
will be found in the lectures on " Hypnotisme et Spiritisme "
delivered at Geneva by Dr Émile Yung in 1890[2], while the subject
has been treated more learnedly and at greater length by a great
number of writers, among whom may be specially mentioned
M. Pierre Janet[3], the successor and continuator of the researches
of the celebrated Charcot at the Salpêtrière.

The influence that such practices exercised upon the
development of the post-Christian sects or schools generally
classed together under the name of Gnostic is not very clearly
defined. It may, indeed, be said that the great diffusion of
the magical rites that took place during the centuries immediately preceding, as in those immediately following, the birth
of Christ, predisposed men's minds to the search for a cosmogony
or theory of the universe which should account for its evolution
as part of an orderly and well-devised system rather than as the
capricious and, as it were, incoherent creation of the gods.
That some such force was at work may be gathered from the
fact that magical beliefs and practices seem to have crept into
the religion of the whole civilized world at this period. But
that the schools calling themselves Gnostic owed their development directly or exclusively to them is an idea that must be
repudiated. Hippolytus, as has been said, does, indeed, make
some such charge, but only in general terms and without any
evidence in its support. When later he goes through the sects
seriatim, he only reiterates it in the cases of Simon Magus, of

[1] Paisley, 1896, pp. 277–284.
[2] *Hypnotisme et Spiritisme*, Genève, 1890, *passim*.
[3] *L'Automatisme Psychologique*, Paris, 1899, *passim*.

his successor Menander, and of Carpocrates of Antioch ; and it is probable from the context that in all these cases he is only referring to what seemed to him the superstitious attention paid by the " heretics " in question to the externals of worship, such as the use of pictures and statues, lights and incense, which seem in many cases to have been borrowed directly from paganism.

This attention to the details of ritual, however, did in itself contain the germ of a danger to the survival of any organized cult in which it was present in excess, which was to receive full illustration in the later forms of Egyptian Gnosticism properly so-called. As will be shown in its place, the seed of Gnosticism fell in Egypt upon soil encumbered with the débris of many older faiths which had long since passed into the stage of decay. Nor could the earnestness or the philosophic insight of the great Gnostics of Hadrian's time, who started their propaganda from Alexandria, contend for long with the inherited preconceptions of a degraded and stubborn peasantry who had learned for millennia to regard all religion as sorcery. Here Gnosticism degenerated quickly into magic of the least enlightened and basest kind, and thus lost all right to be considered in any sense a religion[1]. The case was different in other parts of the Roman Empire, where a better intellectual equipment and the practical syncretism or fusion of worships offered more favourable ground for the development of new faiths not appealing to the members of one nationality only.

That this idea of Gnosticism or of the importance of knowledge—were it only the knowledge of charms and spells—in dealing with the spiritual and invisible world was bound to play a prominent part in the evolution of the world-religions which Alexander's conquests had rendered possible is therefore evident. Some writers have gone further and have declared that Christianity itself may be " only an episode—though a very important episode—in the history of Gnosticism[2]." But

---

[1] This is treated more fully in Chap. X, *infra*.

[2] Cf. "Cerinthus and the Gnostics" in the *London Quarterly*, Oct. 1886, p. 132.

to say this, as will presently be shown, is to go too far, and Christianity, although she obtained many converts from those Gnostic sects with which the Church of the Apostolic and sub-Apostolic ages found itself in competition[1], yet proved in the long run to be the most bitter enemy of Gnosticism. From the first, the Catholic Church seems to have recognized that the ideas which lay at the root of Gnosticism—to which word I have ventured here to give a meaning more extended than that which it connotes in heresiological writers—were opposed to religion altogether ; and if allowed to triumph would have had their end in the development of a science, which, if not absolutely atheistic, would at least reduce the necessary action of the spiritual world upon this to the vanishing point[2]. It would indeed be quite possible to argue that such ideas must always appear when a people of inferior culture, but of vigorous intellect, come into frequent contact for the first time with a material civilization higher than their own. It is sufficient for the present purpose to have shown that they were widely spread during the centuries which immediately preceded the appearance of Christianity, and that they count for something in the evolution of the many heretical sects who came to trouble most seriously the peace of the Catholic Church in the early centuries of our era. The same causes, however, must have been at work some time before, and it is impossible to explain some of the features of Gnosticism in its more extended sense without going back to an early period of Greek history. For it was in Greece that the Orphic teaching first appeared, and it is to this that most of the post-Christian Gnostic heresies or sects attributed, not untruly, their own origin.

Connected in practice with, yet entirely different in origin

---

[1] Thus Epiphanius had been a Nicolaitan, St Ambrose of Milan a Valentinian, and St Augustine a Manichaean before joining the Catholic Church.

[2] So Hippolytus objects not only to the astrology of his time, but to the arithmetical calculations on which it was professedly based. The estimates attributed to Archimedes of the relative distances of the earth from the sun, moon and planets are marked out by him for special condemnation. Cf. *Philosophumena*, Bk IV. c. 1, pp. 67–76, Cruice.

from, this magic was the astrology or star-lore which after the conquest of the Euphrates valley by the Persians began to make its way westwards. It would seem that its birthplace was the plains of Chaldaea, where the clear air brings the starry expanse of the sky nearer, as it were, to the observer than in the denser and more cloudy atmosphere of Europe, while the absence of rising ground not only enables him to take in the whole heaven at a glance, but gives him a more lively idea of the importance of the heavenly bodies. There the careful and patient observation of the Sumerian priests at a period which was certainly earlier than Sargon of Akkad (*i.e.* 2750 B.C.) established the fact that certain groups of stars appeared and disappeared at regular intervals, that others moved more swiftly than their fellows, and that the places of both with reference to the apparent path of the sun varied in a way which corresponded with the recurrence of the seasons. Primitive man, however, does not distinguish between *post hoc* and *propter hoc*, or rather he assumes unhesitatingly that, if any natural phenomenon occurs with anything like regularity after another, the first is the cause of the second. Hence the swifter stars soon came to be clothed in the minds of the early astronomers with attributes varying with the phenomena of which they were supposed to be the cause. Thus, the planet or " wandering " star which we call Jupiter came to be known as the " god of good winds," the Hyades and Pleiades were looked upon as the bringers of rain, and the stars whose appearance ushered in the cold and darkness of winter were considered as hostile to man[1]. As time progressed, however, these observations accumulated—largely, one would think, because of the imperishable material on which they were recorded—and it then began to be perceived that the movement of the heavenly bodies were not due to their individual caprice or will, but were dictated by an inexorable and unchangeable law. In the drawing of this conclusion, the patient and logical mind of the Mongoloid inhabitants of Sumer, ever mindful at once of the past and the future of the race, no doubt played its full part.

---

[1] P. Jensen, *Die Kosmologie der Babylonier*, Strassburg, 1890, pp. 140 *sqq.* and especially p. 295.

The effect of this change in the mental attitude of man towards the universe was to introduce an entirely new conception into religion. At first the Babylonians, pushing, as man generally does, the application of their last discovery further than the facts would warrant, declared that all events happened in a regular and prearranged order; and that man could therefore predict the happening of any event directly he knew its place in the series. Thus in the "astrological" tablets preserved in the palace of Assur-banipal at Nineveh, some of which certainly go back to the reign of Sargon of Akkad[1], we read:

"In the month of Nisan 2nd day, Venus appeared at sunrise. There will be distress in the land....An eclipse happening on the 15th day, the king of Dilmun is slain, and someone seizes his throne....An eclipse happening on the 15th day of the month Ab the king dies, and rains descend from heaven, and floods fill the canals....An eclipse happening on the 20th day, the king of the Hittites in person seizes the throne....For the 5th month an eclipse on the 14th day portends rains and the flooding of canals. The crops will be good, and king will send peace to king. An eclipse on the 15th day portends destructive war. The land will be filled with corpses. An eclipse on the 16th day indicates that pregnant women will be happily delivered of their offspring. An eclipse on the 20th day portends that lions will cause terror and that reptiles will appear; an eclipse on the 21st day that destruction will overtake the riches of the sea[2]."

---

[1] See the tablets made for this king and published by Sir Henry Rawlinson in the *Cuneiform Inscriptions of Western Asia*, vol. III. Many of these are translated by Sayce in "The Astronomy and Astrology of the Babylonians," *Trans. Soc. Bibl. Arch.* vol. III. (1874), pp. 145–339. I have taken the lowest date for Sargon, on the authority of Mr King, *Chronicles of Early Babylonian Kings*, 1907, I. p. 17, although the well-known text of Nabonidus would make him a thousand years earlier. The origin of Babylonian astronomy is discussed by Jastrow, *Religion of Babylonia and Assyria*, chap. XXIII. The immense antiquity attributed to the Babylonian observations by the classical authorities quoted in Sayce's paper may be considerably reduced if we substitute lunar for solar years; yet there seems little doubt that the star worship which arose from them went back to the "oldest period of Babylonia." Cf. Sayce, *Gifford Lectures*, 1902, p. 480.

[2] Jastrow, *op. cit.* pp. 365 *sqq.*

These events are evidently predicted from a knowledge of what happened immediately after the occurrence of former eclipses and other celestial phenomena, and it is perhaps characteristic of the lot of man that most of them are unfavourable and that the disasters greatly outnumber the good things. But it is plain that as time went on, the observers of the stars would begin to perceive that even such unusual celestial phenomena as eclipses occurred at intervals which, although long compared with the lifetime of a man, could yet be estimated, and that the element of chance or caprice could therefore be in great measure eliminated from their calculation. Then came about the construction of the calendar, and the formation of tables extending over a long series of years, by which the recurrence of eclipses and the like could be predicted a long time in advance. All this tended to the formation of different ideas of the laws which, it was now seen, governed man's life, and the shape which these now took were equally erroneous, although at first sight more rational than those held by the first observers.

This new idea was in effect that system of " correspondences " which occupied a prominent place in nearly all religious systems from the time of Assyria's apogee to the triumph of Christianity, and which through the mediaeval Cabala may be said to retain to the present day some shadow of its former power over the minds of the superstitious. This was the notion that the earth in effect is only a copy of the heavens, and that the events which happen here below are nothing but a copy of those which are taking place above[1]. If any great catastrophe such as the fall of an empire like that of Assyria or the sudden death of a man distinguished above his fellows like Alexander occurs, it is because of some conjunction or meeting of hostile stars ;

[1] Among modern German archaeologists Winckler and Jeremias have pushed the effect of this " astral theory " of the universe beyond all limits. Their position is at once exposed and refuted by Rogers in *The Religion of Babylonia and Assyria*, 1908, pp. 212 to end. Yet such a view of the universe as is given in the text was undoubtedly held by many during the six centuries here treated of, and can be seen as it were underlying most of the religions of the time. That it had its origin in Babylonia seems most probable. See Cumont, *Astrology and Religion among the Greeks and Romans*, 1912, pp. 1–26, and authorities there quoted.

and if some great and unexpected benefit such as universal peace or an abundant harvest smiles upon mankind, it is because those stars most generally favourable to him have recovered temporary sway. The result was a sort of mapping-out of the heavens into regions corresponding to those of the earth, and the assigning of a terrestrial " sphere of influence " to each[1]. But as the predictions made from these alone would have been too speedily and too evidently falsified in most cases by the march of events, it became necessary to attribute a predominant influence to the planets, whose swifter and more irregular movements introduced new factors into the situation. These planets were decided to be seven in number, Uranus and Neptune not having yet been discovered, and the Sun and Moon being included in the list because they were thought like the others to move round the earth. Hence all terrestrial things were assumed to be divided into seven categories corresponding to the seven planets, the Moon, Mercury, Venus, Mars, the Sun, Jupiter, and Saturn, and to be in an especial way under the influence of the heavenly bodies of which they were the earthly representatives.

Into the details of the so-called science of astrology thus founded, it is not our purpose to enter. To do so would occupy a greater space than is at our disposal, and would involve besides the discussion of a great many documents only just beginning to come to light, and the exact meaning of which is still uncertain[2]. But it may be mentioned here that astrology entirely changed its character when it came into contact with the dawning science of mathematics, which is perhaps the most enduring monument which bears witness to the fertility and inventiveness of the Greek mind. So soon as the observations of the Babylonians were placed at their disposal, the Greek

[1] Cumont (work last quoted), p. 18. The idea appears plainly enough in astrological works like Ptolemy's *Tetrabiblos*. It was not confined to Babylonia, for the Egyptians thought the earthly Nile corresponded to a heavenly one.

[2] Cumont's *Catalogus Codicum Astrologorum Graecorum* of which 10 volumes have been published will be of great use in this respect. See also Kroll's *Vettii Valentis Anthologiarum Libri*, 1908.

mathematicians set to work in real earnest to discover the laws
of the universe and established the science of astronomy pretty
much on the basis on which it stands at the present day.   The
discovery of the Metonic cycle, of the trigonometrical method
of measuring the celestial sphere, and of the precession of the
equinoxes all followed in succession, and the prediction of
eclipses, conjunctions of stars, and other celestial phenomena
which had before been more or less a matter of guesswork, now
became a matter of calculation presenting no mystery to anyone
versed in mathematics.   The heavens were mapped out, the
stars catalogued, and tables were produced which enabled the
place of any particular star to be found at a given moment
without the actual inspection of the heavens[1].

The result of this improved state of things was not long in
reacting both upon religion, and its congener, magic.   On the
first of these, the effect was much the same as that produced
by the discoveries of Copernicus in the xvith century and those
of Darwin in the xixth.   We do not know enough of the history
of thought at the time to be aware if the Greek additions to the
ascertained laws of Nature aroused the same resentment in
priestly minds as did those of the Prussian and the English
philosophers ; but it is evident that if they did so, the quarrel
was speedily made up.   Every religion in the Graeco-Roman
world which sought the popular favour after the discoveries
of Hipparchus, took note of the seven planetary spheres which
the geocentric theory of the universe supposed to surround
the earth, and even those known before his time, like Zoroastrianism and Judaism, hastened to adopt the same view of
the universe, and to modify the details of their teaching to accord
with it.   The seven stoles of Isis are as significant in this respect
as the seven-stepped ladder or the seven altars in the mysteries
of Mithras, while the seven Amshaspands of the Avesta and the
attention paid to the seven days of the week by the Jews go to
show how even the most firmly held national traditions had to
bow before it.   As for magic, the sevenfold division of things

---

[1] Cumont, *Astrology and Rel.* pp. 12, 13.   Cf. Theon of Alexandria's
Commentary on the IIIrd book of the Almagest (Abbé Halma's ed.), 1813,
t. I. p. 1.

which implied that each planet had its own special metal, precious stone, animal, and plant, placed at the disposal of the magicians an entirely new mode of compulsion which lent itself to endless combinations; while, for the same reason, special conjurations were supposed, as we have seen, only to exercise their full influence under certain positions of the stars. Perhaps the climax of this state of things is reached in one of the Gnostic documents described later, where the salvation of Christian souls in the next world is said to be determined by the entry of one of the beneficent planets into one or other of the signs of the Zodiac[1].

One of the most important results of this impulse was the sudden importance thus given to the worship of the material sun, which henceforth forms the centre of adoration in all non-Christian religions. As we have seen, in the worship of Isis, the newly-made initiate was made to personify the daystar in the public, as no doubt he had done in the secret, ceremonies of the cult. All the post-Alexandrian legends of the gods were turned the same way, and Serapis, Mithras, Attis were all identified with the sun, whom philosophers like Pliny and Macrobius declared to be the one supreme god concealed behind the innumerable lesser deities of the Graeco-Roman pantheon[2]. Even the Christians could not long hold out against the flood, and the marks of the compromise to which the Catholic Church came in the matter may perhaps be seen in the coincidence of the Lord's Day with Sunday and the Church's adoption of the 25th day of December, the birthday of the Unconquered Sun-God, as the anniversary of the birth of Christ[3]. It is certainly by no accident that the emperors whose reigns immediately preceded the establishment of Christianity all turned towards the worship of the sun-god who was looked upon as

[1] In the *Pistis Sophia* (for which see Chapter X, *infra*) the soul of a sinless man who has not found the mysteries has to wait until the planets Jupiter and Venus come into a certain aspect with the sun, "Saturn and Mars being behind them." It is then reincarnated and wins for itself life eternal, pp. 387, 389 (Copt.).

[2] Pliny, *N.H.* Bk II. c. 4. Macrobius, *Saturnalia*, Bk I. cc. 18–23.

[3] Goblet d'Alviella in *Rev. Hist. Rel.* LXV. (May–June, 1912), p. 381.

the peculiar divinity of the family to which Constantine belonged[1].

To Gnosticism, whether we use the word in the sense in
which it has been used in this chapter, or in its more restricted
connotation as the generic name of the earlier heresies which
afflicted the nascent Church, the development of astrology came
as a source of new life. Henceforth to the knowledge of the
history of the personal dispositions and of the designs of the
gods, had to be added that of the laws governing the movements
of the stars. Moreover, the new theory introduced into Gnosticism an element which had hitherto been foreign to it, which
was the idea of destiny or of predetermined fate[2]. If all things,
as the astrologers said, happened in a certain regular order of
which the movements of the stars were at once the cause and the
symbol, it follows that their course is determined beforehand,
and may possibly be capable of being ascertained by man.
Hence came in all the ideas as to the predestination of certain
souls to happiness and of others to misery both in this world and
the next, which play such an important part in the religions of
the centuries under consideration, and the influence of which
is by no means extinct at the present day. It is true that, as
M. Cumont has recently pointed out, man is never rigidly true
to his beliefs, and has generally invented some compromise by
which either the favour of the gods or his own conduct is
supposed to free him from the worst effects of a predetermined
fate. Such compromises appear furtively here and there in
Christian Gnosticism, but without sufficient prominence to take
away the effect of the general notion that man's fate in the
next world is determined before his birth in this.

The general effect of these considerations is, it is thought,
that the Gnosticism which came to trouble the peace of the
Christian Church during its infancy and adolescence had its

---

[1] Aurelian and Diocletian each instituted a worship of the sun-god,
the deity of the second Flavian family.

[2] Cumont, *Astrology and Rel.* pp. 28, 29. He is probably right when
he points out that irregular phenomena like comets and shooting stars
gave a loophole for the opponents of a rigid predestinarianism of which
they were not slow to avail themselves.

roots, first in the decay of the earlier faith, which showed itself
in the popular taste for cosmogonical and other myths, until
then wholly or partly absent from the ideas of the more civilized
nations of the Persian Empire. On the top of this, came the
great spread of ceremonial magic which seems to have followed
the first introduction of something like upright and just government by the Aryan conquerors of the East ; and then the idea
of a universe ruled not by the unchecked will of capricious
gods, but by the regular and ordered movement of the stars.
The predestinarian view of the fate of the individual which
naturally follows from this last conception, as has just been said,
was subject to exceptions and compromises, but yet appears
as a kind of background or framework to all the religions
(orthodox Christianity excepted) which came into prominence
during the six centuries to which our survey is limited. But
before dealing with those hitherto unnoticed, it is necessary
that we should glance at those pre-Christian forms of Gnosticism, the earliest of which was perhaps that which appeared
simultaneously in most parts of the Greek world at the beginning of the vth century before Christ and is generally known
as Orphism.

CHAPTER IV

PRE-CHRISTIAN GNOSTICS : THE ORPHICI

ALL scholars seem now agreed that the legendary Orpheus never really existed[1], and that the many verses and poems attributed to him were the work of various hands, one of the earliest of their authors being Onomacritos of Athens, who fled with the Pisistratids to the court of Darius at Susa in the first decade of the vth century B.C.[2] Yet there is little doubt that the peculiar myths alluded to in these poems were known at an early date in Crete, whence they probably found their way into Athens with Epimenides, the Cretan wizard or wise man who was sent for to purify the city from the guilt incurred by the murder of Cylon[3]. This event evidently marks a turning on the part of the Greeks towards purifications and other magical rites unknown in Homer's time[4]; but the tendency,

[1] Lobeck in his *Aglaophamus*, Königsberg, 1829, vol. I. pp. 233–1104, makes this clear. It was also the opinion of Aristotle according to Cicero (*de Nat. Deor.* Bk I. c. 38). Other authorities are collected by Purser in his article "Orphica" in Smith's *Dict. of Greek and Roman Antiquities*, 1890, vol. II. who quotes with approval Preller's remark that Orpheus was "eine litterarische Collectivperson." See also Paul Monceaux in Daremberg and Saglio's *Dict. des Antiq. s.v.* Orphica.

[2] Herodotus, Bk VII. c. 6. Tatian, *adv. Graecos*, c. XLI. ; Clem. Alex. *Strom.* Bk I. c. 21; Sext. Emp. *Pyrrh. Hypotyp.* III. p. 115 B. Cf. Purser, *art. cit.*

[3] K. O. Müller, *Hist. of the Literature of Ancient Greece*, Eng. ed. vol. I. pp. 308, 309 ; and authorities quoted by O. Kern, *de Orphei, Epimenidis Pherecydis Theogoniis*, Berlin, 1888, p. 6.

[4] The first mention of such rites is said to have been made by Arctinus of Miletus in his *Æthiopis*, where he describes Ulysses as purifying Achilles for the murder of Thersites. See Grote's *History of Greece*, 4th ed. vol. I. pp. 23, 24.

to whomever due in the first instance, undoubtedly received a
great impulse from the break-up of the Pythagorean school in
Italy about 500 B.C.[1] This event, which in its effects may be
compared to the dispersion of the priestly corporations of
Babylon and Egypt which followed Alexander's conquests,
sent wandering a great number of speculative philosophers
trained in the formation of associations for political and other
purposes, and they probably joined forces with a previously
existing Orphic sect, nearly all the early Orphic poems being
ascribed, with more or less likelihood, to Pythagoreans[2]. There
are certain features in these poems which, if we met with them
after the reform of the Zoroastrian religion by the Sassanian
kings, we should certainly attribute to Persian influence; but
this can hardly be done so long as we remain ignorant of what
the Persian religion was in the time of the Achaemenides. The
most probable account of the matter is that the religious
teaching attributed to Orpheus was of Asiatic and particularly
of Phrygian provenance, that it had long been current in Crete
and the other islands of the Mediterranean, that a part of it
came into Greece through Thrace in the time of the Pisistratids,
and that it was finally put into an organized and consistent
shape by those Pythagorean philosophers who made their way
back to Greece after the overthrow of their political power in
Magna Graecia[3]. It found in Pindar a warm adherent, and was
well known to and spoken of with reverence by the three great

---

[1] K. O. Müller, *op. cit.* I. pp. 310, 311.

[2] Clem. Alex. *Strom.* Bk I. c. 21.

[3] The search for its original home seems hopeless at present. It might
easily be connected with Babylonian beliefs, and the Orphic Dionysos has
too many features in common with Tammuz, the lover of Ishtar, for the
resemblance to be entirely accidental. But other elements in the story, such
as the mundane egg, are found in the Vedas, and may point to an Indian
origin. The discovery a few years ago at Boghaz Keui in Cilicia of inscriptions showing that the Vedic gods were worshipped in Asia Minor at least
as early as 1270 B.C., makes it very difficult to say whether the Vedic gods
may not have reached India from Asia Minor or *vice versa*. In this case,
it is possible that Onomacritos may have learned some of the legends at
the Court of the Great King at Susa.

tragic poets Aeschylus, Sophocles, and Euripides[1]. Its greatest
influence, however, was probably exerted through the Eleusinian
and other mysteries which it captured and transformed. It
continued to dominate them from before the time of Herodotus
down to the prohibition of these secret rites by the Christian
emperors, and Orpheus was thus said by everyone to be their
founder[2].

The whole of this teaching centred round the legend of
Dionysos who is described by Herodotus as the youngest—that
is to say the last-adopted—of the great gods of Greece[3]. This
Orphic Dionysos was the Cretan form of the god worshipped
all round the Mediterranean, who was always represented in
human form, and as suffering a violent death and then rising
again from the dead. But to this nucleus, the Orphic poets
added at different times and by degrees a great quantity of
other myths which together formed a complete body of doctrine
setting forth the origin of the world, and of man, and his life
after death. First, they said, existed Chronos or Time " who
grows not old," from whom sprang Aether and the formless
Chaos. From these was formed a silver egg which, bursting
in due time, disclosed Eros, or Phanes the first born, a shining
god, with wings upon his shoulders, at once male and female, and
having within himself the seeds of all creatures. Phanes creates
the Sun and Moon and also Night, and from Night begets
Uranos and Gaea (Heaven and Earth). These two give birth
to the Titans, among whom is Kronos, who emasculates his
father Uranos and succeeds to his throne. He is in turn
deposed by Zeus, who swallows Phanes, and thus becomes the
father of gods and men[4].

---

[1] Pindar, *Isthm.* VI. i. 3 ; Aeschyl. *Sisyphus Drapetes*, fr. 242 of Didot ;
Sophocles, *Antigone*, ll. 1121 *sqq.*; Euripides, *Rhesus*, ll. 942 *sqq.* Cf.
Döllinger, *Jud. und Heid.* Eng. ed. vol. I. p. 259.

[2] Demosthenes, *adv. Aristog.* I. p. 773. Cf. Maury, *Rel. de la Grèce*, II.
p. 320 ; Daremberg and Saglio, *Dict. des Antiq. s.v.* Orphica and Eleusinia,
for other authorities.

[3] Herodotus, Bk II. cc. 145, 146.

[4] This is the " Theogony of the Rhapsodists," which seems to have been
the most popular of all the Orphic theogonies. The different texts in which

This part of the Orphic story comes to us almost entirely from Neo-Platonic sources, and possesses several variants. It is so manifestly an attempt to reconcile the popular theology of Greece found in Homer and Hesiod with different Oriental ideas of the origin of the world that we might consider it to have been concocted in post-Christian times, were it not that Aristophanes had evidently heard about Chaos and the mundane egg, and its production of Eros and Night, which confused genealogy he burlesques in *The Birds*[1]. It is probable also, as Alfred Maury pointed out, that this legend was first taken by the Orphics from the philosophers of Ionia, and especially from that Pherecydes of Syros who is said to have been Pythagoras' master[2]. Attempts have been made to derive it from Indian, Egyptian, Chaldaean, and even Jewish sources; but its resemblances to parallel beliefs among some or all of these nations are too few and sparse for any useful conclusion to be drawn from them. One of its most marked features is its succession of divine rulers of the universe, which the Orphics made use of to exalt their own god Dionysos to the highest rank. The story they told of this Dionysos was that he was originally the Phanes whom Zeus swallowed, but that at his second birth he became the offspring of Zeus by Persephone, the daughter whom Zeus had himself begotten on one of the earth-goddesses who is sometimes called Rhea, sometimes Cybele, and sometimes Demeter. Persephone, described by the Orphics as the "especial" or "single" daughter of Zeus[3], was seduced by her father in

it is preserved have been collected by Abel, *Orphica,* Lips. 1885, pp. 48–140. It is well summarized by Purser in Smith's *Dict. of Antiq.* where before quoted. Cf. Daremberg and Saglio, *s.v.* Orpheus.

[1] Aristoph. *Aves,* ll. 691–706.

[2] *Religions de la Grèce,* t. III. p. 310.

[3] Μουνογένεια. See Orphic Hymn on p. 142, *infra.* Persephone has also Zeus for her father in the Homeric *Hymn to Demeter,* l. 396. The epithet cannot imply that she was his only daughter, as he had other daughters among the Homeric gods, such as Athena and Aphrodite, but rather that she was "unique," or one of a kind. The mistaking of the word Μονογενής for μονογέννητος by Christian and Jewish writers has led to much confusion; and Renan (*L'Église Chrétienne,* Paris, 1879, p. 200, n. 2) notes that George the Syncellus calls Bar Coziba, the Jewish Messiah,

the form of a serpent, and in due course brought to light Dionysos, sometimes called Zagreus or "the Hunter." This god, who had the horns of a bull[1], became the darling of his father, who destined him for his successor and allowed him, while yet a child, to sit on his throne and to wield the thunder-bolts[2]. But the Titans, the monstrous sons of Earth, either spurred on by jealousy at the child being given the sovereignty of the world, or incited thereto by Hera, laid a plot for his destruction. Beguiling him with childish toys such as a top, a hoop, and a mirror, they stole upon him unawares with blackened faces, and, in spite of his struggles and his transformation into many shapes, tore him limb from limb, cooked his several members in a cauldron, and ate them. The heart, however, was saved from them by Pallas Athene, who bore it to Zeus, who swallowed it, and it thus passed into the Theban Dionysos, son of Zeus and Semele, who was in turn Zagreus re-born. Zeus also blasted the Titans with his lightning, while he ordered Apollo to collect the uneaten members of the little god and to bury them at Delphi. A variant or perhaps a continuation of the story makes Demeter, having, as the earth goddess, received the members of the little god, put them together and revivify them, and join herself in marriage with the resuscitated corpse, whence the infant Iacchos is born[3].

Μονογενής. See the story of the begettal of Persephone which Maury, *op. cit.* III. pp. 321, 322, quotes from Clement of Alexandria and Arnobius. Both authors derive from it the name of Brimo given to Demeter in the Mysteries. Cf. Chap. VIII, *infra*.

[1] Orphic Hymn XXX in Abel's *Orphica*, where he is called "First-begotten, of a double nature, thrice-born, Bacchic king, Hunter, Ineffable One, Hidden One, two horned, and of double form." Cf. his epithet "bull-faced" in Orphic Hymn XLV. So Clement of Alexandria quotes a verse from some unnamed poet that "the bull has begotten a serpent, the serpent a bull," *Protrept.* c. II.

[2] As in the statue at Megalopolis in Arcadia described by Pausanias, Bk VIII. c. 31, where Polycleitos portrayed the young god with a cup and a *thyrsos*, besides wearing *cothurni*, but with the eagle and the name of Zeus Φιλίος. Ael. Aristides, *in Dionysum*, says that Dionysos is Zeus himself, a doctrine which Justin Martyr, *Cohort.* c. XV, attributes to Orpheus.

[3] The story with full references to authorities is given by Maury, *Rel. de la Grèce Antique*, t. III. pp. 342 *sqq.*; Purser in Smith's *Dict. of Greek and*

In this part of the story, also, the desire of the authors to fit it in with the existing mythology is manifest. At Eleusis from very early times there had been worshipped with mysterious rites a divine couple who were known only as " the God " and " the Goddess[1]." This pair were, as we may guess from an allusion in Hesiod, otherwise called Zeus Chthonios or the infernal Zeus, god of the underworld, and Demeter[2], the ancient earth-goddess, who was worshipped with her lover under the various names of Ma, Cybele, Astarte, Rhea and Isis throughout Asia Minor, Syria, Phoenicia and Egypt. As the lover of the earth-goddess in all these cases suffered death and resurrection, the Orphics had to work these episodes into the history of their Dionysos Zagreus. But they carried the idea further than any of their predecessors by connecting this death and re-birth with the origin of man and his survival after death[3]. Man,

Roman Antiquities, 1890, *s.v.* Orphica; Cecil Smith, " Orphic Myths on Attic Vases," *J.H.S.* 1890, pp. 343–351; Dyer, *The Gods in Greece*, 1891, p. 128; Paul Monceaux in Daremberg and Saglio's *Dict. des Antiq. s.v.* Orphica. The eating of a god or other being in order to obtain possession of the victim's qualities is a common idea among primitive peoples, as is set forth at length in Frazer, *Golden Bough*, 3rd ed. pt v, vol. II. ch. 10. It was familiar to the Egyptians, as is seen in the Pyramid Texts of the VIth Dynasty, where the glorified King Unas is represented as chasing, catching, cooking, and eating the gods in the next world in order to assimilate their powers. See Maspero, *Les Pyramides de Saqqarah*, pp. 67 *sqq.* So in a magic papyrus now at Leyden, the magician threatens the god Set whom he is invoking, that if he is not obedient, he will speak to " the Great God " (Serapis ?) who will tear Set " limb from limb and give his powers to a mangy dog sitting on a dung-hill to eat." See Leemans, *Papyri Graeci*, vol. II. pp. 18, 19.

[1] Foucart, *Myst. d'Él.* pp. 27, 28.

[2] Foucart, where last quoted; Hesiod, *Works and Days*, l. 465 (p. 39, Didot).

[3] Such ideas may, however, have been current in the religions of the Eastern Mediterranean long before Orphic times. Dr Budge in his book *Osiris and the Egyptian Resurrection*, I. p. 28, reiterates what he has before stated elsewhere, *i.e.* that Osiris was to his worshippers " the god-man, the first of those who rose from the dead," and that his death and resurrection were therefore supposed to be in some way beneficial to mankind. This is very likely, but I know of no Egyptian text that in any way connects the creation of man with the death of Osiris. On the contrary, a text which

they said, was made out of the ashes of the Titans, and was therefore born to sorrow, his soul being buried in his body as in a charnel-house[1]. But he also had within him a spark of the life of Zagreus, the infant ruler of the universe[2], and this enables him to purify himself from the guilt of the earthborn Titans, and so to leave the circle of existence and cease from wickedness. For that the soul of man after leaving his body went, unless purified, to inhabit the bodies of other men and even animals, passing from one to the other as in a wheel or endless chain, was a dogma which the Orphics had taken over from the Pythagoreans[3]. How now was this purification to be obtained?

The answer that the earlier Orphics gave to this question must have astonished the pleasure-loving and artistic Greeks. The true Orphic, they were told, must make his whole earthly

Dr Budge has himself published makes men and women to come into being from the tears which came forth from the eye of the god Khepera, here probably to be identified with Nu, the primaeval Ocean or Deep. See Budge, *The Gods of the Egyptians*, vol. I. p. 299. The Zoroastrian religion, in the late form in which we have it in the *Bundahish* (see West, *S.B.E.* Oxford, 1880, *Pahlavi Texts*, pt I.), does indeed make man spring from the death of Gayomort, the First or Primaeval Man, slain by Ahriman. If we choose to suppose that this conception went back to the times of Zoroaster himself, that is to say, about 700 B.C., Onomacritos might easily have found this part of the story at the Court of Susa. Cf. Bousset, *Hauptprobleme der Gnosis*, Göttingen, 1907, pp. 215–223. It is significant that, according to Pausanias, Bk VIII. c. 37, it was Onomacritos who first made the Titans evil powers, or as he says "contributing to the sufferings of Dionysos."

[1] Clement of Alexandria, *Strom.* Bk III. c. 3, quotes this expression from "Philolaos the Pythagorean." Athenaeus, *Deipnosophistae*, Bk IV. p. 157 c (Teubner) from "Euxitheus the Pythagoric." It evidently went back to the earliest Orphic teaching reduced to writing.

[2] See Lobeck, *Aglaophamus*, I. p. 566, for authorities.

[3] κύκλου τ' ἀλλῦσαι καὶ ἀναψῦξαι κακότητος. The line is attributed to Orpheus by Simplicius in his Commentary on Aristotle, *de Caelo*, II. p. 168 (ed. Karsten). According to Proclus, *in Plat. Tim.* v. 330 A, B, it was part of a prayer which Orphics used when being initiated in the mysteries of "Demeter and Cora." The Pythagorean doctrine of transmigration and its adoption by the Orphics are well set out by Luebbert in his *Commentatio de Pindaro dogmatis de migratione animarum cultore*, Bonn, 1887, *q.v.*

life a preparation for the next. He must partake at least once of a mystic sacrifice, in which a living animal was, in memory of the fate of Zagreus, torn in pieces and eaten raw ; but thereafter he must never again eat any food that has had life nor even eggs, and he must observe perfect chastity[1], and wear only linen garments even at his burial, nor must he go near a sepulchre.

" We aim at a holy life, whence I am become a mystes of Idaean [*i.e.* Cretan] Zeus," says the Orphic in a surviving fragment of Euripides' *Cretenses*, " and having completed the life of night-wandering Zagreus and the raw flesh-devouring feasts, I uplifted the torches of the mountain mother, and having been purified by expiatory offerings, I was hailed as Bacchus by the Curetes.... But now clothed in white garments, I fly the generation of mortals, and to a corpse I draw not nigh, and I shun the eating of things which have had life[2]."

The meaning of this is fairly plain and is in everything a great deal more magical than religious. By a well-known rule common to nearly all people in a low state of culture, the victim sacrificed to a god becomes a god himself[3] ; and, as the eating of the victim makes him part of the eater, it has the same effect on the votary as the swallowing of Phanes by Zeus had upon this last, the Dionysiac soul in the participant of the sacrifice is thereby strengthened, and he becomes so far identified with the god as to bear his name. Henceforth, however, he must have no further dealings with Titanic matter, and in particular must shun the corpse which represents the Titanic part of man without the Dionysiac, and must do nothing which can start

[1] All these prohibitions persisted, and we meet with them in nearly all the religions hereafter described including the Manichaean. The filiation may well be direct, as such sects as the Valentinians grew up in an atmosphere of Orphic teaching. If, however, it should appear that the Orphic notions on this subject were derived from some Western Asiatic source, it is plain that the Ophites and Manichaeans may have drawn theirs from the same fount and independently.

[2] Euripides, *Cretenses*, p. 733 (Didot). The fragment is found in Porphyry, *de Abstinentia*, Bk IV. c. 19. Cf. Euripides, *Hippolytus*, l. 952.

[3] See Frazer and Maspero as quoted in note 3 p. 125, *supra*.

another being on " the ceaseless round of changing existences[1]."
If he were successful in observing these austerities to the end,
he might hope that, when his soul was released from its prison
house, it would be reunited to Dionysos, and rest for ever free
from the stains of matter. This was in effect the formal teaching
of Pythagoras with regard to the transmigration of souls, and
depended on the view that the soul, or incorporeal part of man,
had once formed part of the soul of the universe diffused throughout Nature. "I have heard," says Cicero, "that Pythagoras
and the Pythagoreans...never doubted but that we possess
minds plucked from the universal divine mind"; a phrase
that he explains in discussing the nature of the gods by saying
that Pythagoras "thought there was a mind spread through
and pervading the whole nature of things whence our minds
are plucked[2]." A similar doctrine of transmigration appears
clearly in Pindar[3], who was one of the first to give voice to the
Orphic teaching, which his lays did much to diffuse. The
addition that the Orphic poets made to the doctrine was doubtless the attribution to Dionysos and the Eleusinian goddess
of the task of presiding over and arranging these rebirths.

Yet the austerities prescribed by the Orphic life, however
fitted to a philosophic school, could hardly be practised by
people engaged in the business of the world. It was impossible, as
the Pythagoreans had probably found, for people to devote themselves entirely to the welfare of their souls, and yet to live among
their fellows. Hence some other means by which man could be
assured a happy lot after death had to be devised, and there seems

[1] That this was the regular Orphic phrase is plain from the verse quoted
above, note 3 p. 127. Cf. the gold plates of Naples, p. 133, *infra*.

[2] Cf. Luebbert, *op. cit.* p. v. The confusion in Cicero between *animus*
and *anima*, or mind and soul, is curious. Cf. Olympiodorus, *Comment. ad
Plat. Phaed.* as given in Fr. 225 of Abel's *Orphica* (p. 245).

[3] Orpheus is mentioned in the ivth Pythian ode as the "father of songs,"
and in fragments of the *Threnoi* as "the golden-sworded son of Oiagreus,"
p. 116 (Bergk). In the vith Isthmian ode, Dionysos is made the temple-
companion or assessor (πάρεδρος) of Demeter. The delights of the blessed
dead are set forth in fragments of the *Threnoi* (see Fragment x. 1, 2, 3, 4 of
Teubner, pp. 95, 96, Cod. Boeckh); their reincarnation as heroes in a fragment from the same poem : *ibid.* Frag. x. 4, p. 98, Cod. Bö.

no doubt that the post-Pythagorean Orphics taught that this
was to be found in participation in the mysteries or secret
rites already in existence in Greece before the commencement
of their teaching. Whether the Eleusinian Mysteries were in
their inception anything more than the worship of the Chthonian
or infernal deities, as the gods presiding over agriculture and
vegetation considered as a symbol of generation and death,
is still undecided[1]; but there can be no doubt that under
Orphic influence they underwent a complete change. Dionysos,
identified with Hades or Zeus Chthonios, begins, after the
break-up of the Pythagorean school, to take part in them by
the side of Demeter and Persephone, and the story of his
mysterious birth from the goddess, and his identification as
Zagreus with Iacchos, the child-god leading the procession,
seems from this period onwards to have been told in them[2].
But the mode in which the Mysteries were regarded by the
Greeks in general materially altered after the introduction of
the Orphic teaching, and this also can hardly be attributed to
anything else than the direct influence of its professors. We
are told on all sides that no religious teaching formed part of
the Mysteries of Eleusis, and that on the contrary the initiates
were simply shown certain scenes and objects, and heard certain
mysterious words on which they were left to put their own

---

[1] The earlier idea espoused by Creuzer and others (see Guigniaut,
Religions de l'Antiquité, vol. III. *passim*, and especially pp. 1207, 1208) that
the Chthonian gods were worshipped as the symbols of generation and death
seems a good deal nearer the truth than the " Corn-spirit " theory set on
foot by the *Golden Bough* that they were the gods of agriculture and vegetation. Of course both explanations can be read into what we know of the
Mysteries. Why these last should have been kept secret even before the
rise of Orphism is hard to see. M. Paul Foucart's view that they came
originally from a foreign country (according to him from Egypt) offers one
explanation of this ; but see n. 2 p. 139, *infra*.

[2] So F. Lenormant in Daremberg and Saglio's *Dict. des Ant. s.v.*
Eleusinia. See, too, his article on Dionysos Zagreus in the *Gazette Archéologique*, 1879. So Purser in Smith's *Dict. of Antiq.* as last quoted (cf.
article "Eleusinia"). Aeschylus, *Sisyphus Drapetes*, frag. 242, p. 238, Didot,
and Alcmaeonis, in *Etymologicum Magnum, s.h.v.* both know of Zagreus,
and Sophocles, *Antigone*, ll. 1140–1154 identifies Dionysos and Iacchos.

interpretation[1]. But the Orphics discovered in them a sacramental or purifying grace which was thought to have a kind of magical effect on the lot alike in this life and after death of those who took part in them. It was enough to have *seen* these mysteries, as the poets aver[2], for man's place in the next world to be changed for the better, and thus it is the knowledge thus obtained, and not conduct or favour, which is thought to influence his destiny. The doctrine thus baldly stated moved to indignation Diogenes the Cynic, who pointed out that Patecion the brigand, who had been initiated, had earned for himself by this one act happiness after death, while Epaminondas, best of patriots, by the fact that he had not been initiated, was condemned to be plunged in mud and to undergo other tortures[3].

The very important part in Orphic practice played by this belief in the magical power of initiation has lately been put beyond doubt by the discovery of certain inscriptions in the tombs of worshippers of the Orphic deities at places so far apart as Petelia in Magna Graccia, Calabria, Eleutherna in Crete, Naples, and Rome. On palaeographic grounds their dates are said to range over at least three centuries, the earliest having apparently been made in the IVth or IIIrd century B.C., and the latest in the Ist or IInd century of our era. They are all engraved on thin gold plates, are in Greek hexameter verse, and in the opinion of scholars are all taken from the same ritual, and therefore afford evidence of the permanence and fixity as well as of the wide spread of the Orphic teaching[4]. They contain instructions

---

[1] Synesius (Ptol. Episcop.), *Dion* (Migne, *Script. Gr.* t. 66, pp. 1153–1156), says so plainly. Cf. Galen, *de Usu Partium* (Kuhn's *Medici Graeci*, Claudius Galenus, vol. IV. pp. 702, 703), and Plutarch, *de Defect. Orac.* p. 422 (*Moralia*, vol. I. p. 514, Didot).

[2] Sophocles, *Triptolemus* (Frag. 348, Didot). Homeric *Hymn to Demeter*, ll. 480 *sqq.* (p. 565, Didot). See also Chap. II, *supra*.

[3] Plutarch, *de audiend. Poet.* IV. 76 (Reisk); Diogenes Laertius, *Vit. Phil.* c. VI.

[4] They have been many times described, especially by Kaibel and Comparetti (for references see Monceaux in Daremberg and Saglio's *Dict. des Antiq. s.v.* Orphica). The translations in the text are by Prof. Gilbert

to the dead as to the things to be done and avoided by him or her in the next world and also the formulas to be repeated to the powers there met with, which will have the effect of magically procuring for the deceased an exalted rank among its inhabitants. One of the earliest in date, found at Petelia and now in the British Museum, runs thus:

" Thou shalt find to the left of the House of Hades a well-spring
And by the side thereof standing a white cypress.
To the well-spring approach not near;
But thou shalt find another by the Lake of Memory.
Cold water flowing forth, and there are guardians before it.
Say: I am a child of Earth and of Starry Heaven[1]
But my race is of Heaven (above). This you know yourselves.
And lo! I am parched with thirst and I perish, Give me quickly
The cold water flowing forth from the Lake of Memory[2].
And of themselves they will give me to drink from the Holy Well-
    Spring."

Another set of plates from tombs at Eleutherna, now in the National Museum at Athens, is to this effect:

' I am parched with thirst and I perish.—Nay, drink of Me
The well-spring flowing for ever on the right where the cypress is
Who art thou ?...
Whence art thou ?   I am the son of Earth and of Starry Heaven."

The magical and gnostical purport of this is plain. As in the Egyptian *Book of the Dead*, to which these plates bear a great resemblance, their aim was to give the deceased person in whose tomb the inscription was buried[3], the *knowledge* of the infernal or subterranean regions which was to make his entry into them safe and profitable. That his soul or immaterial

Murray and are taken from his Appendix to Miss Jane Harrison's *Prolegomena to Study of Greek Religion*, 1903, *q.v.*

[1] The same phrase is used in the Orphic Hymn XIII. with regard to Kronos, Abel, *Orphica*, p. 66.

[2] This idea reappears in one of the documents of the *Pistis Sophia*. See Chap. X, *infra*.

[3] So Aelius Aristides (*in Serapidem*, p. 98) speaks of the light of the sun being restored by Serapis " to those whose tombs contain holy books."

part was a part of Dionysos, the descendant of Uranos and Gê[1], and more directly the offspring of Demeter the earth-goddess by Zeus, the god of the sky, had already been shown to the dead on his initiation.   But it was necessary that he should prove to the gods of death and generation that he *knew* this, when they would have no alternative but to admit him to all the privileges attached to his high descent and the rank he had attained in the scale of being by initiation.   This is made plainer still by the statements put into the mouth of the dead by the gold plates from Naples, now in the Naples Museum, which read thus :

" Out of the Pure I come, Pure Queen of those Below,
And Eukles and Eubouleus[2] and other Gods and Demons ;
For I also avow that I am of blessed race.
And I have paid the penalty for deeds unrighteous
Whether it is that Fate laid me low, or the Gods Immortal,
Or [that Zeus has struck me ?] with star-flung thunderbolt
I have flown out of the sorrowful weary Wheel ;
I have passed with eager feet to the Circle desired ;
I have sunk beneath the bosom of Despoena[3], Queen of the Under-
    world
I have passed with eager feet to [*or* from] the Circle desired ;
And now I come a suppliant to Holy Persephone
That of her grace she receive me to the seats of the Hallowed."

    Then comes Persephone's answer

" Happy and Blessed One, Thou shalt be God instead of Mortal,"

---

[1] As Foucart, *Culte de Dionysos*, p. 34, n. 3, has pointed out, this cannot refer to the Titanic part of man, which he was enjoined by the Orphics to mortify as far as possible.   There is something to be said for M. Foucart's view that the dead is here shown as another Osiris, son of the earth-god Geb and the sky-goddess Nut.   It is curious that this last is always portrayed on Egyptian monuments with a star-spangled body, while I know of no Greek representation of Uranos which connects him with the stars.

[2] " Of good counsel."   A name of Dionysos, as appears from the Orphic Hymns given later in this chapter.

[3] A name of Demeter, Persephone, and some other Chthonian goddesses. See Aristophanes, *Thesmophoriazusae*, l. 286.   It probably means merely " mistress."

while a prose formula " A kid I have fallen into milk " which
seems to have been a password among the Orphics is written
in the midst of the verses and appears upon this and several
of the other plates[1].

In the Naples plate, we have the teaching, more or less dimly
indicated in the quotations from the Orphic poems which occur
in classical and patristic writers, brought to a focus.   The dead
has during his earthly life taken part in the mystic rites which
have told him whence life comes and whither it is tending.   He
now has the right to demand from the deities who preside over
the death and rebirth of mortals that he be relieved from the
endless round of incarnations ; and he backs up this request
by proof of the knowledge he possesses of their nature and his
own origin, at the same time uttering passwords which he has
received on his initiation.   The effect of this, although out of
reverence represented as an act of grace on the part of the
divinities addressed, is in fact magical or automatic.   The
powers addressed perforce grant the request of the dead and he
becomes like them a god[2], freed from the necessity for any
further deaths and rebirths.   The same idea is traceable
throughout the whole of the Egyptian *Book of the Dead* from
which it may have been directly derived[3], and also in other

---

[1] It has been suggested that this is a figure for the initiated dead
receiving all that they wish.   It should be noted, however, that in the
Zoroastrian religion the flood of molten metal which is to burn the wicked
is to feel to the faithful like warm milk.   So N. Söderblom, *La Vie Future
d'après la Mazdéisme*, Paris, 1901, p. 266, quoting the *Dinkard* and the
Bundahish.   The phrase is discussed by M. Salomon Reinach in *Revue
Archéol.* 1901, II. pp. 202–213, and *Cultes, Mythes et Religions*, Paris,
1909, t. II. pp. 123–134.   M. Alline, in *Xenia*, Athens, 1912, connects it
with the supposed Orphic idea that blessed souls inhabit the Milky Way.

[2] Perhaps not directly.   There is some reason for thinking that the soul
of the true Orphic was supposed to pass through the intermediate stages of
hero and demon: see Hild, *Étude sur les Démons*, Paris, 1881, p. 144, where
the subject is excellently treated.   Cf. Pindar, *Threnoi*, Frag. x. 4, p. 98,
Cod. Bö.   The deification of the dead was also a Pythagorean doctrine,
as appears in the *Aurea Carmina*, ll. 70, 71, ed. Gaisford.

[3] This is the suggestion of Foucart, *Myst. d'Él.* p. 72.   That the
Egyptian dead was supposed to become one with Osiris himself is an idea
that appears as early as the Pyramid Texts, cf. Maspero, *Les Pyramides de*

religions with which it would seem the Orphic teaching can
have had no connection[1]. But the point to remember at
present is that it appears henceforward in all the cults or sects
to which we have given the generic name of Gnostic[2].

How this idea was propagated in Greece and her colonies
is a question over which still hangs a great deal of obscurity.
There exist a great number of quotations from poems attributed
to Orpheus, which were clearly the composition of the Orphic
school, and all these are, like the gold plates, in hexameter verse.
These, as Damascius implies, were recited by professional
declaimers called Rhapsodists[3] at the different games and
festivals held in honour of the gods, as were once the so-called
Homeric Hymns and the poems of Pindar, which they perhaps
succeeded and displaced. In this way they doubtless became
familiar to many thousands who would otherwise never have
heard of the Orphic teaching, and our conviction on this point
is strengthened when we see how very numerous the festivals
in which the Chthonian gods were celebrated really were.
Besides Eleusis, we hear of the worship of Dionysos, Demeter
and Persephone as infernal deities in Achaea, in the Argolid,
in Arcadia, in Messenia, in Sparta, and in other parts of the
Peloponnesus[4]. It also spread through Boeotia, where the
national cult of Dionysos no doubt ensured it a good reception,
and thence early passed into the islands of the Aegean. Crete
had, as we have seen, practised it even before it came to
Athens; and Demeter and Persephone were not only worshipped
in Sicily, but were taken to be the tutelary gods of the island.
The Ionian colonists also took the worship of the Eleusinian
triad with them into Asia and they were adored in parts of

Saqqarah, passim, where the dead kings are each in turn hailed as " this
Osiris."

    [1] Buddhism, for instance, which can hardly have reached the West
before the death of Onomacritos.

    [2] As in the *Pistis Sophia,* where Jesus says to his disciples, " Know ye
not that ye are all gods...", p. 247 (Copt.).

    [3] For Damascius, *Quaest. de primis principiis,* see Abel's *Orphica,* Frag.
48. Cf. as to Rhapsodists, Maury, *Rel. de la Grèce,* I. pp. 240, 345, 346.

    [4] See Maury, *op. cit.* II. pp. 370 *sqq.*

Asia Minor as far distant from Greece as Cyzicus[1]. At all, or nearly all, these places, mysteries were celebrated having more or less likeness to those of Eleusis, and were followed by games and festivals like the Eleusinia, at which the songs of the Rhapsodists would be heard[2]. The frequent Dionysia. or festivals of Dionysos, scattered all over the Greek-speaking world, but especially in its Northern or Balkan provinces, no doubt offered an even better opportunity for making known these poems.

The Orphic poets, also, by no means confined their songs to the worship of the deities adored at Eleusis. The Thracians, including in that name the inhabitants of Macedonia and Thessaly, always had extraordinary ideas about the future life, and Herodotus describes how they used to gather weeping round the new-born child, bewailing his entry into this miserable world, while they rejoiced over the death of any of their fellows, declaring that he had thus obtained a happy deliverance from his troubles[3]. These, however, were the very doctrines of the Orphics, who declared that the body was the grave of the soul, and that the life of the world to come was the only one worth living. Hence the mythical Orpheus was said to have been a Thracian, and the worship of Bacchus or the Theban Dionysos as the god of wine to have come into Attica from Thrace by way of Boeotia, a theory which derives some colour from the orgiastic dances and ravings of the Maenads and Bacchanals, who seem therein to have reproduced the rites of the savage Thracians[4]. When the Phrygian divinities—Cybele the Mother of the Gods, and her consort Attis—were brought into Greece, the Orphics seized hold of their legends also, and so transformed them that it is now impossible for us to tell how much of them is Asiatic,

---

[1] Maury, *op. cit.* II. p. 374.

[2] Such as the Mysteries of Samothrace, held in honour, according to one account, of Pluto, Demeter, and Persephone, together with Hermes. See Maury, *op. cit.* II. pp. 306 *sqq.* for authorities. It was at these mysteries that Philip of Macedon was said to have first seen and loved Olympias (Plutarch, *Alexander*, c. 2).

[3] Herodotus, Bk v. c. 4.

[4] See Maury, *Rel. de la Grèce*, II. p. 203, for authorities.

and how much is the result of Orphic interpolation[1]. The same thing may be said of the worship of the Syrian Adonis, whose mystic death turned him into the spouse of Persephone, and enabled the Orphics to identify him with Eubuleus or the infernal Zeus or Dionysos, and of that of the Thracian moon-goddess Bendis, early worshipped in Athens, whom an Orphic verse preserved by Proclus declares to be Persephone herself[2].

The foreign god, however, in whose worship the Orphic doctrine is most plainly visible was Sabazius, who also seems originally to have come from Phrygia. He is described in an early Greek inscription as " Lord of all[3] " and said later to be the son of Cybele. The Greeks, however, quickly identified him with Dionysos Zagreus[4], and an orgiastic worship of him penetrated into Athens some time before Alexander's conquests. This seems to have been well known to Aristophanes, who declaims in the *Lysistrata* against the " wantonness " of the Athenian women, who gave themselves up to the pursuit of this god and the Syrian Adonis[5]. But the associations formed for the worship of these divinities seem to have been recruited almost entirely from among the courtezans of the Piraeus and the trades dependent on them, and more than one of its priestesses were put to death for " impiety " or interference with the religion of the State. The low estimation in which it was generally held may be judged from the invective of Demosthenes against

[1] As in the Orphic Hymn to Mise given on p. 143, *infra*, where the Eleusinian Dionysos, called also Eubuleus and Iacchos, is identified with Cybele, the Cyprian Aphrodite, and the Egyptian Isis. See, too, the Hymn " of the Great Mysteries " given in the *Philosophumena* of Hippolytus, where Dionysos is equated with Adonis, Osiris, the god of Samothrace, Attis, and others. See n. 1 p. 139, and Chap. VIII, *infra*.

[2] See last note ; Proclus, *in Plat. Polit.* p. 353 (Abel's *Orphica*, Frag. 184).

[3] πανκοίρανος. *C.I.G.* t. II. No. 3791 (Bö.). Cf. the Aeschylean description of Zagreus as the " Highest of All " (πανυπέρτατε πάντων) quoted by Gaisford in his notes to *Etymologicum Magnum* (see *Cycli Fragmenta* of Didot, *s.v.* Epigoni vel Alcmaeonis).

[4] Cf. the Σαβάζιε...ὃς Βάκχον Διόνυσον of Hymn XLVIII. Abel's *Orphica*.

[5] *Lysistrata*, ll. 386-390. Cf. Foucart, *Les Ass. Rel.* pp. 61-64, who quotes nearly all the available authorities in his notes. See also Monceaux in Daremberg and Saglio's *Dict. des Antiq. s.v.* Sabazios.

his rival Aeschines, whose mother Glaucothea was a priestess
of Sabazius, and who had himself in his youth assisted her in
her duties[1] :

"When you became a man, you knew by heart the books of your
mother and helped her to make up others ; and you nightly gave
the initiated the *nebride* (fawn-skin) and baptized them and purified
them, wiping off the clay and bran, and raising them after the
purifications, teaching them to say ' I have shunned evil. I have
found good.'...By day you led fine *thiasi* (confraternities)
through the streets crowned with leaves of fennel and poplar,
you heading the procession and squeezing the broad-jawed serpents,
waving them above your head while you shouted *Evoe Saboï* and
danced *Hyes Attis, Attis Hyes* ; and the old women hailed you
as leader of the dance, and chief, and chest-bearer, and sieve-bearer,
and with such like titles ; while you received from them as your
pay sops and twisted loaves and cakes. Who would not think himself lucky with such a life ! "

The whole of this tirade may be explained by reference to
the Orphic teaching about Dionysos Zagreus. The fawn-skin
or *nebride* was worn, as appears on thousands of vases, in the
Dionysiac rites as in those relating to the burial of Osiris. The
clay and bran are thought to refer to the disguise which the
Titans assumed when stealing upon the infant god, and the
speech about shunning evil apparently denotes the putting away
of the Titanic nature and the resolution in future to cultivate
the Dionysiac soul. The serpents are explained by a custom
peculiar to the Sabazian rites of putting a live serpent into the
bosom of the initiate's garment and taking it out at the foot
in memory of the shape in which Zeus begot Dionysos on his
daughter Persephone. The mystic cry of "Evoe" is a well
known feature of the orgiastic worship of Dionysos ; while
"Saboï" seems to cover some name or epithet of Sabazius[2],
and the phrase "Hyes Attis" shows the connection with Attis,

---

[1] Demosthenes, *de Corona*, pp. 259 *sqq.* Cf. Foucart, *Les Ass. Rel.* p. 67,
n. 1.

[2] In the Orphic Hymn to Hippa (Hymn XLIX. Abel's *Orphica*, p. 84),
the mysteries of the " pure Sabos ? " (ἁγνοῦ Σάβου) are alluded to in terms
which make it possible that the name was one of the epithets of the Iacchos
of Eleusis.

whose identity with Dionysos forms the subject of more than one Orphic Hymn[1]. In all this also it may be noticed that there is no pretence of considering conduct as influencing the destiny of the initiate or even of conciliating the divinity invoked. The whole of the rites described are entirely magical, and owe all their efficacy to the knowledge of the right means to be used to compel the spiritual world to perform the votaries' will. It is obvious that people with such ideas will be in no great hurry to extend the advantage of their discoveries to others less lucky than themselves and will on the contrary do much to keep them a secret confined to a few[2].

Did the Orphics, however, at any time form themselves into a church or brotherhood pledged to mutual support and the propagation of the faith ? Some writers of authority have thought so[3] ; but there seems to be no evidence available to

[1] In a hymn preserved for us by Hippolytus (*Philosophumena*, Bk v. c. 1, p. 176, Cruice) the " multiform Attis," who has just been declared " in a hymn of the Great Mysteries " to be the god who is called Adonis, Osiris, Adam (by the Samothracians), Corybas and Pappas, is thus addressed : " I will sing Attis, son of Rhea, not with the sound of trumpets, nor with the Idaean flutes in harmony with the songs of the Curetes. But I will mingle with my lay Phoebus' music of lutes. *Evoe Evan*, since thou art Pan, since thou art Bacchus, since thou art the shepherd of white stars." In the address to Musaeus with which the collection of Orphic Hymns begins, the Mother of the Gods, Attis, Men, Aphrodite Urania, and Adonis are invoked together. See Abel's *Orphica*, p. 58. In Roman times Attis and Sabazius seem to be identified, while Adonis is often confounded with them. See Maury, *Rel. de la Grèce*, III. p. 102 and n. 4.

[2] This is, perhaps, the only satisfactory reason that can be assigned for the secrecy with which the Mysteries of Eleusis, of the Great Mother, and the rest were surrounded. The notion put forward by the Fathers that the mystic rites were kept secret because of their obscenity has little weight when we consider the Phallophoria and the Terms, or street statues of Hermes, which were publicly exhibited. The existence of secret rites among primitive folk like the black races of Africa and the native Australians can be explained in the same way.

[3] Purser, *ubi cit. supra*, speaks of it as " an ascetic religious brotherhood," as did K. O. Müller, *Introduction to a Scientific System of Mythology* (Eng. ed.), p. 318, and *Litt. of Ant. Greece*, I. p. 307. Döllinger, *Jud. und Heid.* I. p. 161, says truly that there is no evidence that at any time there existed a regularly formed association of Orphici in Greece. So Monceaux in Daremberg and Saglio, *s.v.* Orpheus.

warrant the supposition. Although the worshippers of Cybele,
Attis, Adonis, Dionysos, the Eleusinian deities, and Sabazius,
were by no means averse from announcing the nature of their
faith on their tombstones, we nowhere find any funeral inscriptions declaring the dead to have belonged to any body of
worshippers calling themselves Orphici. A more likely theory
is that the Orphics were banded together in the small independent associations known as Thiasi, Erani, or Orgeones[1], like
those which we have seen founded at Athens and elsewhere for
the worship of foreign gods. It would seem probable enoug'\ ;
but as yet all documentary evidence is entirely lacking. Records,
generally in the shape of stelas or tablets containing the lists
of members and the regulations of the associations, have been
found in some numbers for the *thiasi* of nearly all the gods
honoured by the Orphic poets who were not the gods of the
Greek States ; but among them no association calling itself
Orphic has yet been discovered. What we do know is, that in
the days of Plato, there was a class of strolling charlatans
called Orpheotelestae who were accustomed to haunt the doors
of the rich with a heap of books said to have been written by
Orpheus, out of which they offered, in exchange for money,
to perform ceremonies of purification and initiation which they
affirmed would purge from the recipient all trace of personal
or inherited guilt and assure him a happy lot in the next world[2].
They also told fortunes, offered to dispose of enemies, and
sometimes gathered together in some numbers so as to make a
more vivid and imposing representation of the pains of the
uninitiated in Hades, and thus induce the superstitious to pay
the price of their charms[3]. They had a certain amount of
success, and Theophrastus in his *Characters* exhibits his *Deisi-
daemon* or Superstitious Man as going to them with his wife
and family to be purified once a month[4]. Such vagabonds
could hardly have made a living had there been any organized

---

[1] This was the opinion of Guigniaut, *Religions de l' Antiquité*, Paris, 1825,
t. III. p. 1203.

[2] Plato, *Republic*, Bk II. c. 7, is the classical passage. Cf. Döllinger,
op. cit. I. pp. 165–167, and references there given.

[3] See Döllinger as in last note.   [4] Theophrastus, *Characteres*, c. XVI.

body ready to render like services in a regular way, and the fact of their existence and the contempt with which they are spoken of by the writers of the period go some way to show that no more regular Orphic brotherhood or sect was ever known in Greece.

There have nevertheless come down to us upwards of eighty hymns attributed to Orpheus which all bear a certain likeness to each other and were evidently intended by the compiler for use in some religious or magical ceremony[1]. They are, like all the fragments of Orphic poems that we have, in hexameter verse, and most of them conclude with an invocation to the divinity to whom they are addressed to be present or to aid in the accomplishment of some " work," while this invocation often alludes to " mysteries " and " initiates." More than one text of these hymns exist, and the differences between them are so small that it is plain that their contents must for a long time have been known and settled. Much variety of opinion exists among the learned as to their date, the theory of their first modern commentator being that they were the actual hymns used in the Eleusinian Mysteries[2], while Petersen thought that they were composed in the ist or iind century of our era, although he admitted that some eight or nine of them were probably older[3]. One of the latest and best opinions seems to be that of Prof. Albrecht Dieterich, who thinks that the collection dates from the period between 200 B.C. and the birth of Christ, and that it was probably made on the sea-coast of Asia Minor and that of Egypt near Alexandria[4]. That the hymns were brought

[1] There are 88 in the text published by Abel (*Orphica*, pp. 55–102). This includes the Hymn to Ares generally classed among the Homeric Hymns.

[2] The celebrated Thomas Taylor the Platonist. Pausanias, Bk ix. cc. 27 and 30, says that the Hymns of Orpheus were short and few, and that the Lycomidae knew and sung them in the Mysteries.

[3] Abel, *Orphica*, p. 55, n. 1.

[4] Dieterich, *de Hymnis Orphicis*, Marp. Catt. 1891. Otto Kern in the *Festschrift* presented to Prof. Carl Robert. 1910, points out that there is no trace of the worship of the Emperor in the Hymns, and that these must therefore all be anterior to the Christian era; also that the Egyptian deities are so seldom named in them, that the collection cannot have been made in Egypt. He thinks it comes from Asia Minor.

together for some religious or magical use associated with the
Orphic teaching, is evident from the Preface, which purports
to be an address to Musaeus, the legendary son of Orpheus,
although it is really an invocation to all the gods worshipped
by the Orphics, including several who are not specially addressed
in the hymns which follow.   Of the 87 or 88 hymns common to
most of the codices, all but nine bear after their titles a specifica-
tion of the particular perfume—frankincense, myrrh, spices
and the like—to be burnt while they are sung or recited.   Most
of the texts bear also an endorsement in another hand reading
" Comrade ! use [it] with good fortune ! " and this has induced
Prof. Dieterich and others to conclude that the collection was
made for the liturgic use of some confraternity or *thiasus*
professing Orphic doctrines[1].   The following Hymn to Persephone will perhaps give a fair notion of the lines upon which
these hymns are framed :

HYMN TO PERSEPHONE[2]

" Persephone, daughter of great Zeus, come, thou beloved one,
Only-begotten[3] goddess, accept the offerings well pleasing to thee.
Much-honoured consort of Pluto, dear giver of life,
Praxidice, decked with love-locks, chaste offspring of Deo.
Giver of birth to the Eumenides, queen of those below the earth,
Virgin whom Zeus begot in unspeakable nuptials[4]
Mother of the loud-shouting, many-formed Eubuleus[5].

[1] The collection may have been used as an oracle or divining-book like
any other poems written in hexameters.   See a curious instance of this in
Kenyon, *Greek Papyri in British Museum*, pp. 83 *sqq.*

[2] This is numbered XXIX. in Abel's text.   This, and the hymns of
Hecate, Pluto, the Curetes, Dionysos Bassareus, the Ever-living Deliverer
(Bacchus), Aphrodite, Nemesis, Nomos, and the doubtful one to Ares are
the only hymns out of the original collection which have not the note
appended as to the perfume to be burnt.

[3] Μουνογένεια, " Unique," see n. 3 p. 124, *supra.*

[4] So Clement of Alexandria, *Protrept.* c. II. speaks of " the mysteries of
Demeter, and Zeus' wanton embraces of his mother and the wrath of
Demeter...also the entreaties of Zeus, and the drink of gall, the plucking-
out of the hearts of sacrifices and deeds we dare not name."   Arnobius, *adv.
Gentes*, Bk v. cc. 20, 21, tells substantially the same story.

[5] See n. 2 p. 133, *supra.*   In these hymns it is used always as an epithet
either of Bacchus or Hades with whom the mystic Bacchus was identified.

Playfellow of the Hours, light-bringer of glorious form,
Dread ruler of all, virgin teeming with fruit
Brilliant-rayed, horned-one, the sole desire of mortals.
Vernal one, who rejoicest in the breath of the meadows
Who dost bring to light the sacred shape of green fruit buds.
Who in autumn time wast wedded in a ravished bed :
Who art alone the life and death of much-enduring mortals.
Persephone ! For thou dost ever nourish and slay all things.
Hear, blessed goddess, and send up fruits from the earth
Granting us in abundance peace and gentle-handed health
And a life of happiness, such as leads old age untroubled
To thy realm, O queen, and to dread Pluto."

By the side of this we may perhaps put the Hymn to Dionysos
in the same collection. It is probably later than the other in
date, the syncretism which equates Persephone with Aphrodite,
Cybele, and Isis pointing to a post-Alexandrian origin.

[HYMN] OF MISE—PERFUME : STORAX[1]

" I invoke the law-giving, rod-bearing, Dionysos
The never-to-be-forgotten seed, Eubuleus of many names
Who art[2] sacred and sacrosanct Mise, ineffable queen !
Male and female, of double nature, the redeemer [*or* curse-loosing][3]
    Iacchos
Whether thou art delighting in the sweet-smelling temple of Eleusis
Or art solemnizing mysteries with the Mother in Phrygia,
Or art rejoicing in Cyprus with the fair-crowned Cytherea,
Or dost exult in the pure wheat-bearing plains
With thy mother divine, black-robed, august Isis
And thy busy nurses[4] near the Egyptian stream,
Be gracious and come thou benevolent to accomplish our tasks."

[1] No. XLII. in Abel's *Orphica*. Persephone was called Mise Kore at
Pergamum (C. Radet, *Revue des Études anciennes*, January–March, 1911,
p. 77), which shows how closely she had become identified with her consort.
Otherwise the word is only known, I believe, as a name of Dionysos.

[2] τε...τε.   [3] Λύσειος.

[4] Doubtless the bees, who throughout Asia Minor were said to be
the attendants of the Great Goddess. The priestesses of the Ephesian
Artemis were called Μέλισσαι or Bees, and there were Μέλισσαι at Eleusis.
See Foucart, *Grds. Myst.* pp. 66, 67. Cf. Aristophanes, *Frogs*, l. 1274. So
were those of Cybele : cf. Lactantius, *Div. Inst.* Bk I. c. 22. Cf. also, A. B.
Cook, " The Bee in Greek Mythology " in *J.H.S.* xv. (1895), pp. 17 *sqq.*

Whatever date be assigned to these hymns, it is at least admitted by all commentators that they were composed for the use of persons' professing Orphic doctrines, and we shall be on safe grounds if we assume that they represent the later state of the Orphic teaching. Collating them with the fragments of Orphic verses preserved in the quotations of writers during the late Pagan and early Christian centuries, we are able to reconstitute the whole Orphic creed, as it was known shortly before the triumph of Christianity. We see from this that the Orphics attributed the actual beginning of the universe to their god Dionysos, who first appeared from the egg formed from Night or Chaos. In that manifestation, he was bisexual[1], and thus mother, as well as father, of all the gods and goddesses of the popular pantheon, the swallowing of his heart by Zeus making him one with the Homeric " father of gods and men." His second birth was due to the ineffable, or mystic, union of Zeus and Demeter, and he was in infancy torn in pieces and eaten by the Titans as narrated above. From the ashes of these last, men were born, while Dionysos himself became Hades, the King of the Dead, over whom he rules with his consort Persephone, the daughter, as Dionysos is the son, of Zeus and Demeter, and perhaps known to the initiate as only the female form of her consort[2]. This pair preside over the life and death of mortals, the soul or Dionysiac spark within each man or woman having to pass repeatedly through the bodies of other human beings and animals until finally purified, when it will be united with Dionysos and thus become god[3]. But the process can be made easier and shorter by the saving grace of the Mysteries, which by the knowledge they confer on the initiate of the constitution and ramification of

---

[1] διφυῆ. See Orphic Hymn VI. in Abel's *Orphica*.

[2] As in the Orphic Hymn to Mise quoted above. Cf. Dyer, *op. cit.* pp. 178, 179.

[3] That this may have been thought to be the result of the mystic union of the initiate with Dionysos seems possible from the statement of Plutarch, that this last was born as a man, but by his merit was translated from this earthly and suffering body, *Life of Pelopidas*, c. XVI. Cf. Budge, *Pseudo-Callisthenes' Life of Alexander the Great*, p. 135.

the divine nature, of the geography, so to speak, of the next world, and of the magical words and formulas to be there repeated, give him a vast advantage over his less favoured fellows[1]. The third incarnation of Dionysos, god of wine, begotten by the father of gods and men on Semele, daughter of Cadmus, after the heart of the infant Zagreus had been sewn in his thigh, must be looked upon as a concession to the popular belief in a different mythology. To those initiated, whether in the Eleusinian or in other mysteries, the last incarnation of Dionysos was that brought about by the union of Zeus in serpent shape[2] with Persephone, and he must have been the child whose mystic birth was acted in the Mysteries of Eleusis where he was identified with Iacchos, the leader of the procession.

The effect of this creed, the real symbol of the greatest movement which ever took place within the religion of the pre-Christian Greeks, upon the religions that followed its appearance, remains to be considered. In the first place, Orphism went a great way towards weaning the minds of men from the idea of separate gods for different nations, and towards teaching them that all their national and local deities were but different forms of one great Power, who was himself the source of all being. There can be little doubt that the Orphics thus regarded their god Dionysos, whom they made one with his father Zeus, and hailed as being in himself female as well as male, and the common type of all goddesses as well as of all gods. By their readiness to identify him alike with the chthonian god of Eleusis, and with all the foreign gods—Adonis, Attis, Sabazius, and Osiris—with whom they were brought in contact, they showed how far they were willing to go in the path of syncretism ; and, but for the rise of Christianity and other religions, there can be little doubt but that the whole of the Graeco-Roman deities

---

[1] A sort of echo of this is perhaps to be found in the idea prevalent in the primitive Church that martyrs for the faith passed direct to a state of blessedness without waiting like the rest of the faithful for the Last Judgment. Cf. Revelation vi. 9–11 ; Neander, *Ch. Hist.* i. p. 463.

[2] Zeus Chthonios or the Zeus below the earth. The serpent was always to the Orphic poets a symbol or pictorial representation of earth.

would eventually have merged in Dionysos[1]. Yet although in this, as well as in their sanguine idea of the perfectibility of man's nature, the Orphics may seem to have done somewhat towards elevating and purifying religion, it seems plain that their influence was on the whole hostile to it, and had they ever aimed at and attained supreme power, would have ended in the negation of all religion whatever. Whether the Orphics originally demanded from their followers any moral as well as material purification cannot now be said; but the proceedings of the Orpheotelestae show us how very early in their teaching all such ideas were dropped, and the magical theory of the efficacy of the Mysteries as a means of salvation came to outweigh everything else in the eyes of their votaries. The compulsion of the gods, however, is an idea that, once rooted in the mind of man, is sure to bring forth most unwholesome fruit; and Orphism seems to have brought with it from the beginning all the worst practices of magic. The Orpheotelestae did not scruple, as has been said, to undertake to rid their initiates of an inconvenient adversary[2]; and although this may not at the outset have implied anything worse than idle curses, it was at any rate murder in intention, and in Greece, as everywhere else, early led to the calling-in of the aid of poison. Magical rites, too, generally bring with them a more or less pronounced worship of devils or evil beings as such, and there are many signs that the Orphics by no means confined their invocations to powers supposed to be friendly to man. Among the Orphic Hymns may be found an invocation to the Titans, who were the legendary enemies of Zeus Dionysos and all the celestial gods, and it is probable that this instance is not a solitary one[3]. The worship of gods given up to evil generally results in the depravation of the morals of their votaries, and the purposes for which they are invoked are seldom sublime. Most of this

[1] This seems to be the upshot of the remarks in Pseudo-Callisthenes (Budge, *op. cit. supra*), pp. 8, 12, 40–48, 127, 135. The same idea is specially marked in the writings of Proclus and other Neo-Platonists and by them attributed to Orpheus. Cf. Abel's *Orphica, s.v.* Teletai, *passim*.

[2] Plato, *Republ.* Bk II. c. 7.

[3] No. XXXVII. in Abel's *Orphica*, p. 78.

evil sorcery seems to have centred round the cult of Hecate, herself a mystery goddess revered at Eleusis and especially dear to the Orphics[1]. Down to the very end of paganism, and indeed, onward through the Middle Ages and the Renaissance, Hecate remained the mistress of magicians and the patron saint of sorcerers[2].

One other consequence of the Orphic teaching deserves to be noted. The syncretistic tendency, which led the true Orphic to regard Zeus, Apollo, Hades, and all the gods and goddesses of the popular pantheon as so many varying forms of his own Dionysos, must have always rendered him indifferent as to what deity received his public devotions. Secure in the sacramental grace bestowed upon him by the mere participation in the Mysteries, and fortified by the knowledge of the formulas which were by themselves sufficient to ensure him a happy lot in the next world, it is plain that he must always have held himself at liberty to adore any god or goddess worshipped by those among whom he found himself, and that he must have been ready to conform outwardly to any religion which seemed to offer him any personal advantage. Knowledge, not faith, was to him the one thing needful to the soul, and he would be as little likely to think of enduring persecution for opinion's sake as to approve of inflicting it. The secret rites and the secret formulas comprised the whole of his religion.

To sum up, then, the practical result of their speculations, the Orphics taught that the universe had passed through several stages of evolution since it was formed from chaos by its First God or Divine Workman. Each of these stages was described as the reign of a fresh ruler or supreme divinity, who was the " son " of the foregoing or, as it would seem, a new incarnation of him. Man came into being through the mystic death and dispersion throughout the universe of one of the last of these incarnations, and therefore contains within himself a spark

---

[1] See Maury, *La Magie et L'Astrologie dans l'Antiquité et en Moyen Âge*, Paris, 1860, pp. 54, 55, for authorities. The Orphic Hymns above quoted begin with an invocation to Hecate.

[2] As in Shakespeare's *Macbeth*.

of the Divine nature which is capable of purification from the contamination of soulless matter. This is effected in the ordinary way by a succession of deaths and rebirths in the course of which man's soul would pass into that of other animals and human beings. But the process was thought to be shortened by participation in certain mysteries or secret rites handed down by tradition, wherein the hidden constitution and purpose of Nature were disclosed to the initiate, and he was equipped with mysterious names and formulas thought to possess magical power. These, by their mere utterance, gave him the right to demand his release from the painful circle of rebirths which was the common lot of mankind, and in effect turned him into a being superior to man. The possession of this wonder-working knowledge or gnosis was not however granted indiscriminately to all, but remained a secret confined to a favoured few, who were pledged under sufficiently severe sanctions not to disclose it. That all religions professed by mankind were equal and indifferent in the eyes of the Orphic seems to follow logically from this, as does the position that he might himself profess any of them that seemed to him expedient. We shall find all these features present in the many sects of post-Christian Gnostics.

CHAPTER V

PRE-CHRISTIAN GNOSTICS : THE ESSENES

IT comes as rather a wrench to leave the graceful, if vain, speculations of the Greeks, with their joyous and free life and their passionate worship of beauty, which saw in every shifting aspect of nature the revelation of some Being more perfect and glorious than man, for the gloomy and misanthropic monotheism of the Palestinian Jews. Nor is the change made more pleasant when we consider the contrast between the ideas of the two nations as to the perfectibility of man's nature and his lot after death. While the Greeks under Orphic influence had come to look upon their gods as usually well-disposed to mankind[1] and even willing to share their power and place with, at any rate, a few highly-gifted or fortunate men, the fanatics among the Jews who returned from the Babylonian Captivity seem to have seen in their national Deity a jealous and uncompromising tyrant, possessed with a hatred for humanity in general, and only extending a modified favouritism to one small nation not distinguished by any specially attractive qualities[2].

[1] So Euripides makes Iphigenia (*I. in Taur.* l. 400) say, "I think not that any one of the gods is bad." Cf. J. A. Hild, *Ét. sur les Démons*, pp. 53, 136. In sharp contrast to the Jewish idea exemplified in Deuteronomy of a god whose "name is Jealous" is Plato's description of the Creator in the *Timæus* (40 c.), "He is not jealous, for he is good, and in him that is good no jealousy exists."

[2] It should be noted that what is said here of the Jews applies not to the Hebrew race in general, but only to those members of it who settled in Palestine after the return from the Captivity. Winwood Reade puts the matter with no less truth than point when he says (*Martyrdom of Man*, p. 203): "The people who did return were chiefly the fanatics, the clergy, and the paupers. The harvest...was worthy of the seed."

To this nation, Yahweh had, according to their own traditions, promised exclusive temporal advantages ; but in spite of this promise they had become in turn the slaves or tributaries of the Egyptians, the Philistines, the Assyrians, Chaldaeans, and Persians, and had been more than once forcibly removed by their masters from the land that they looked upon as their God-given inheritance.   Moreover, the grace, such as it was, of the Deity they worshipped was held by them to extend to this life only, after which they thought they would either perish like the beasts or would lead at the best a shadowy and colour-less existence in Sheol or Hades, like that which called forth the complaints of the Achilles of the *Odyssey*[1]. Hence the soil of Judaea at the coming of Alexander might have seemed to anyone to be as unlikely a field for the propagation of ideas resembling those of the Orphics as could well be imagined.   But the Jews, with all their pragmatism and narrowness of ideal, have always shown a power of assimilating the ideas of others and of adapting themselves to the usages of the peoples among whom they are cast by a sort of protective mimicry like that to which the preservation of certain insect types is said to be due.   This quality had already stood them in good stead during their different periods of captivity in Egypt and Chaldaea, where before Alexander's conquests they had contrived to get a good deal of the financial management of their captors' affairs into their own hands, and where they doubtless acted as spies and guides to the armies of the Great Conqueror[2]. For these services Alexander after his fashion royally rewarded them ; but the real crisis of the nation's fate approached when Alex-ander's work was done, and when the different nationalities which he had forced, as it were, into the melting-pot, became tired of acting as pieces in the war game played by his generals and successors, and began to look favourably upon the security offered by the Roman government.   In this new order of the world, Palestine, which had hitherto owed its autonomous

---

[1] R. H. Charles, *A Critical History of the Doctrine of a Future Life* (Jowett Lectures), 1899, pp. 33–50, and authorities there quoted.

[2] J. P. Mahaffy, *Empire of the Ptolemies*, pp. 85, 86.

existence to the fact that it formed a useful buffer state or neutral ground separating the two great powers Egypt and Syria and was not vehemently desired by any other nation, saw the reason for her *quasi*-independence vanishing. Ptolemy Soter, with his usual prescience, had early seen the advantage of getting this borderland into his own custody, and had captured Jerusalem, it is said, one Sabbath morning, when the superstition of the inhabitants deterred them from defending it effectually[1]. The story, as thus told, probably owes something to the necessity for flattering the national vanity; but it is evident that the politic Lagides knew how to reconcile the Jews to the easy yoke of their suzerainty, and under the early Ptolemies the Jews remained generally faithful to Egypt. When Egypt's sway became enfeebled after the reign of Ptolemy IV Philopator, Antiochus the Great seized upon Palestine, probably with the connivance of a part of its inhabitants[2]; and although it remained fairly contented with its new masters until Antiochus' death, in the reign of his successor, Antiochus Epiphanes, the Jews found themselves confronted with a very disagreeable dilemma. For Antiochus Epiphanes, after his successful attack upon Egypt had been frustrated by the Romans, saw plainly enough that only an empire united and homogeneous in faith and culture could resist for long the new power rising in the West[3], and resolved to force on the complete Hellenization of the Jews at all hazards. How he failed is told in the Books of the Maccabees, although his failure brought little good to his rebellious subjects, who soon passed with the rest of his empire into the hands of the victorious Romans.

To this end, the splitting-up of the chosen people into warring sects materially contributed. Josephus, writing somewhere about the year 70 A.D., tells us that there existed in his day three "philosophic" sects among the Jews[4]. The first two of these were the Pharisees and Sadducees familiar to everybody

---

[1] Droysen, *Hellénisme*, II. p. 155.
[2] Mahaffy, *op. cit.* p. 87 and n. 1; *ibid.* p. 293 and nn. 1 and 2.
[3] W. D. Morrison, *Jews under Roman Rule*, pp. 5, 6.
[4] Jos. *de Bell.* Bk II. c. 8, *passim.*

through their mention in the New Testament, and the third was the "Essenes." These Essenes—a name which by some has been thought to mean "the Pure[1]"—he describes as a small sect numbering not more than 4000 in all, and scattered throughout the villages of Palestine. They lived entirely by manual labour, such as agriculture, and were extraordinarily hospitable to other members of the same sect, so that an Essene never found it necessary to take anything with him on a journey, but could always obtain what he wanted from his fellow-sectaries, even though personally unknown to them. As to their doctrines, he tells us that though "Jews by birth" they abjured marriage[2], and only recruited their ranks by adoption. They practised, on the same authority, the fullest community of goods, and forbade conversation on worldly matters before the rising of the sun, at which they repeated certain traditional prayers, "as if they made supplication for his rising." Their meals were always eaten in common and in a sacramental manner, purification in cold water and the donning of white garments being a necessary preliminary[3]. Sobriety and restraint in speech were, he says, among their most marked characteristics, and they avoided the taking of judicial oaths, averring that "he who cannot be believed without swearing by God is already condemned." Initiation into the sect was both long and difficult. The novice on his first reception was presented with a hatchet, a girdle and a white garment, but was not allowed to associate with the rest of the order, it being held that they would be defiled if he did so. In spite of this, he was forced to observe the austerities of the order for a year before being allowed "the waters of purification," and for two years further before being admitted to full

---

[1] Or "the Pious." See Morrison, *op. cit.* p. 327 ; A. Jülicher in *Encyc. Bibl. s.v.* Essenes, col. 1397, n. 1.

[2] There was, says Josephus, *loc. cit.* § 13, another order of Essenes which married and had children. The reason given for the celibacy of the first order is not the Orphic one, *ibid.* § 2.

[3] Cf. the *Agapae* or love-feasts of the Greek *thiasi* and the Christian Church. There is no authority, however, for supposing that the meal was regarded by the Essenes as a sacrifice.

association with the other members and the common meal[1].
After this probation, he was sworn on

" the most tremendous oaths to be just towards all men and faithful
to the order, not discovering any of their doctrines to others, no,
not though he should be compelled to do so at the risk of his life."

Moreover, he had to swear

" to communicate their doctrines to no one in any other manner
than that in which he had received them himself; to abstain from
robbery[2] and that he would equally preserve the books belonging to
the sect and the names of the angels."

Their doctrine concerning the future life was:

" That bodies are corruptible and that the matter of which they are
made is not permanent; but that souls are immortal, and continue
for ever; and that they come out of the most subtle air, and are
united to their bodies as in prisons, into which they are drawn by
a certain natural enticement[3]; but that when they are set free from
the bonds of the flesh, they then, as released from a long bondage,
rejoice and mount upward[4]."

---

[1] The girdle has been thought to be identical with the *kosti* or sacred
thread of the Parsis.   The use of the hatchet or pick was to bury the *ejecta*,
perhaps for sanitary reasons.   The Essenes were said to be further divided
into four classes (Josephus, *loc. cit.* § 10), but Josephus does not say what
these classes were, and it is doubtful whether there is any foundation for
the statement.

[2] *Ibid.* § 7.   From the context, it would seem that " robbery " here
means the attempt to obtain possession of the secrets of the order by
stealth.   In an earlier part of the same section the neophyte is said to be
sworn to " keep his hands clear from theft, and his soul from unlawful
gains."

[3] *I.e.* by sexual desire.   The same idea is met with in the doctrines of
Simon Magus, see Chap. VI, *infra*, and in many other sects.   Cf. Cumont,
Recherches sur le Manichéisme, Bruxelles, 1908, pt I. Appx 1, "La Séduc-
tion des Archontes " for particulars.

[4] Dr Kohler, apparently a Rabbi of New York, gives other particulars
of the Essenic initiation, including a song describing Heaven and Hell.
This he takes from the *Testament of Job* described by him in the Festschrift
called Kohut's *Semitic Studies*, Berlin, 1897, pp. 265 *sqq.*   Among other
things, he thinks the initiate was told that Satan was the cosmocrator, or

Finally, Josephus tells us that the Essenes take great pains in "studying the writings of the ancients and choose out of them what is most for the advantage of their soul and body," that they were much given to the practice of medicine, and had those among them " who undertake to foretell things to come by reading the holy books and using several sorts of purifications, and being perpetually conversant in the discourses of the prophets,"—a statement which is explained by another passage[1] wherein he tells us that they believed " fate forms all things and nothing befalls men but according to it." From yet another passage[2] we learn that they were excluded from the Temple worship and offered their sacrifices for themselves instead of through the regular Jewish priesthood[3].

That Josephus' account of the Essenes is fairly accurate and well informed appears from the fact that Philo of Alexandria, writing some fifty years earlier than he, also asserts that they numbered "in his opinion about 4000," and explains their abstention from the Temple worship as being due to their objection to sacrificing living animals[4]. Philo further tells us that there were among them no makers of warlike weapons, that they refrained from trade and had no slaves ; but that their principal study was that of the Jewish Law and the " enquiry into the being of God and the creation of the universe."

ruler of the world, and that the sacred girdle was an amulet which would enable him both to defy Satan's snares, and to see the wonders of the world of angels.   But I do not see that he brings forward any proof that either this book or what he calls the whole Job literature is attributable to the Essenes.

[1] Joseph. *Antiq.* Bk XIII. c. 5, § 9.

[2] *Id. op. cit.* Bk XVIII. c. 1, § 5.

[3] Their supposed sun-worship seems to resolve itself into the usual Jewish prayer at dawn, see Cheyne, *Jewish Religious Life after Exile*, New York, 1898, note on p. 251, and Jülicher, *Encyc. Bibl. s.v.* Essenes.

[4] Philo Judaeus, *Quod Omnis Probus Liber*, c. XII. ; *id. Apologia* in Eusebius, *Praep. Evang.* Bk VIII. c. 13.   The authenticity of both works has been attacked (for the controversy *v.* Morrison, *op. cit.* p. 347, n. 2) with some success.   While therefore there can be no doubt that they are from the pen of some of Philo's school, it is not impossible that they may be later than Josephus and have copied his statements.

According to him, on the seventh or holy day when no work was done, they were accustomed to meet together, when one

" takes up the holy volume and reads it, and another of the men of the greatest experience [among them] comes forward and explains what is not very intelligible, for a great many precepts are delivered in enigmatical modes of expression and allegorically."

He at the same time confirms Josephus' statement as to their having all goods in common.

Pliny in his *Natural History* also speaks of the Essenes ; but adds little to our knowledge, except the remark that it was the irksomeness of this present life which in his opinion gave rise to the sect[1]. Of the Christian heresiologists, Hippolytus in his *Philosophumena* merely repeats the statements of Josephus with the doubtfully accurate addition that the Essenes believed in a final conflagration of the world[2] and the eternal punishment of the damned ; while Epiphanius in his *Panarion* shows plainly that he had no first-hand knowledge of the Essenes and did not understand the traditional accounts of the sect which must have been extinct a long time before he wrote[3]. Porphyry in his treatise *on Abstinence* avowedly quotes from Josephus only[4].

We see, then, that all we really know about the Essenes is contained in the accounts of Josephus and Philo ; but on this slender foundation there has been raised a vast superstructure of conjecture which the unprejudiced reader will probably consider too heavy for its base. The Essenes have been claimed by different writers as merely a strict order of Pharisees, as

---

[1] Pliny, *Hist. Nat.* Bk v. c. 15: *In diem ex aequo convenarum turba renascitur large frequentantibus, quos vita fessos ad mores eorum fortunae fluctus agitat.*

[2] Hippolytus, *Philosophumena*, Bk IX. c. 27, pp. 465, 466, of Cruice. Later, he attributes the same doctrine to the Pharisees. His desire to show that in both cases it was derived by the Jews from the Pythagoreans or the Stoics is manifest.

[3] Epiphanius, *Panar.* Bk I. t. I. Haer. x. c. 1 (pp. 75, 76 of Oehler, vol. II. pt 1). Epiphanius makes them a Samaritan sect.

[4] Porphyrius, *de Abstinentia*, Bk IV.

Zoroastrians, and as Buddhists. It has been argued that
St John Baptist was an Essene and even that Jesus Himself
belonged to the sect[1]. A more probable theory is that the
Essenes derived some of their tenets from the Orphics, whose
views were particularly prevalent at Alexandria in the time of
the early Ptolemies, as well as in Asia Minor under the Seleucids.
From the death of Alexander the Great until that of Antiochus
Epiphanes, Palestine was, as we have seen, successively under
the sway of these two rival dynasties, and it was the rapid
progress of the Jews towards Hellenization in culture, religion,
and morals that brought about the Maccabaean uprising, in
connection with which we first hear of the Essenes[2]. Hence
this is the time when, if ever, we should expect the Orphic
teaching to affect the Jews, and it is difficult to see whence the
Essenes derived their views of the pre-existence of the soul—if
that be indeed the construction to be placed upon the scanty
and obscure words of Josephus—except from Orphism[3]. Save
for this, however, there is no very cogent reason for attributing
to this Jewish sect an Orphic origin. The use of white garments
is in a hot climate too general a practice to be really characteristic, while the abstinence from the procreation of children
and from food that has had life, although common to the
Essenes and the Orphics[4], may easily have come to the Jews

[1] Jülicher in *Encyc. Bibl. ubi cit.* and Ritschl and Lucius there quoted;
J. B. Lightfoot, *Epistles to Colossians and to Philemon*, 1876, pp. 82–93,
348–419, and Hilgenfeld, *Die Ketzergeschichte des Urchristenthums*, Leipzig,
1884, p. 156; Arthur Lillie, *Buddhism in Christendom*, 1887, *passim*; *id.
Buddha and Buddhism*, Edinburgh, 1900, pp. 159 *sqq.* Buddhism is however
posterior in time to Orphism, as Buddha did not die till B.C. 483 (see Fleet in
J.R.A.S. 1909, p. 22), which was some years after the break-up of the
Pythagorean school.

[2] See note 1 p. 154, *supra.*

[3] There is no evidence of a belief in the pre-existence of the soul in
Persian religion until the rise of the worship of Mithras in the 1st century B.C.
See Chap. XII, *infra.* Marshall (Hastings' *Dict. of Bible, s.v.* Pre-existence)
would find proof of the doctrine among the Jews in the Book of Wisdom
and Philo. Both are much later than Orphism.

[4] But see note 2 p. 152, *supra.* Jewish priests after the Exile were forbidden to wear wool or to touch corpses, prohibitions which have an Orphic
twang. See Ezekiel xliv. 17, 23.

from more quarters than one. To the Essene refusal to take oaths and to engage in trade there is no parallel whatever in the Orphic teaching[1].

But, although there is thus little sign of a direct connection of the Essenes with the Orphics, there can hardly be any doubt that the Jewish sect were Gnostics in the larger sense in which the word is used above. The one distinguishing fact which stands out from Josephus' account of them is that they had secret doctrines of a kind differing from the beliefs of the rest of the Jews. This is shown by the great pains taken by them in the choice of neophytes, the " tremendous oaths " by which they, who forbade swearing in-general, enforced secrecy upon them, and the prohibition to confide their teaching to any save by a long and tedious process of initiation. The only hints we have as to the nature of these doctrines are contained in Philo's statement that they were given to the enquiry into the being of God and the creation of the universe, and in that of Josephus that the initiate into these secrets was sworn " to preserve the books of the sect and the names of the angels." Dr Kohler and other Jewish writers see in Philo's statement a reference to the speculations of the later Jewish Cabala upon what is there called " the Mystery of the Chariot " and " the Mystery of the Creation[2] "; or in other words how the universe came forth from God and how it is governed. Although the proof of this is slender, it seems probable from the tendency of the whole of the Apocryphal literature of the time which dealt principally with the same subjects. It is evident that the Essene interpretation of the Old Testament, then recently made familiar to the Jews by the Alexandrian translation into Greek known as the Septuagint, must have been different in some respects from that of the other Jews, and that it must have been in some way likely to shock those who held by the traditional interpretation, as otherwise there would have been no necessity for the Essenes

---

So far from despising wealth, many of the Orphic Hymns pray for riches. Cf. Hymns x. xiii. xiv. xix. xl. etc. in Abel's *Orphica*.

K. Kohler, *Testament of Job*, in Kohut's *Semitic Studies*, Berlin, 1897, pp. 281, 282 ; Isidore Loeb in *La Grande Encyclopédie*, Paris, *s.v.* La Cabbale Juive, p. 587.

to bind their neophytes to so strict a secrecy.   From Philo's
language on this point it would seem that they interpreted both
the Law and the Prophets in some non-natural manner, and it
is likely enough that this took the shape of the juggling with
the numerical values of the letters of which we find at least one
instance in the Revelation of St John, and to which we shall
have to return later[1].

What now can be said in explanation of Josephus' statement
that the Essenes were sworn to secrecy as to the "names of
the angels"?   The personal name of no angel appears in the
Old Testament except in the Book of Daniel, now generally admitted to have been written in the reign of Antiochus Epiphanes,
and there is on the face of it no reason why any Jew should
wish to keep those there given—Gabriel and Michael—secret.
But the knowledge of the name of an inhabitant of the spirit
world was at the time of which we are speaking held throughout
the East to give a magician full power over the being named,
and this belief was universal in the magic of all the nations
among whom the Jews had found themselves since the Captivity[2].
There is thus every likelihood that the Essenes used " the names
of the angels " for magical purposes, and this is borne out by
the tradition that it was as exorcists of demons and healers of
disease that they were afterwards celebrated[3].   The manner in
which these names were used may be judged from the tradition
among the Jews that each tribe or order of demons was governed
by an angel, and that his subjects were bound to obey upon
being addressed by his name[4].

[1] Rev. xiii. 18.   A. Hausrath, *History of New Testament Times* (Eng.
ed.), 1878, vol. I. pp. 113–117, gives all the different processes of what is
called the "Practical" Cabala with illustrations.   Cf. Ad. Franck, *La
Kabbale*, Paris, 1843, p. 167, n. 2.

[2] J. G. Frazer, *The Golden Bough*, 3rd ed. pt II. vol. I. pp. 318–334,
gives references to, I think, all the authorities for this belief, which even
at the present day is universal among primitive people.

[3] Morrison, *op. cit.* p. 338, for authorities.   Exorcism for the healing of
disease followed naturally from their demonology, which taught that
diseases were caused by demons.   See Hausrath, *Hist. of N. T. Times*
(Eng. ed.), I. p. 127.

[4] Hausrath, *op. cit.* I. pp. 124, 125 ; *Clementine Homilies*, Bk v. c. 5.

It was partly, and perhaps mainly, from this sect of the
Essenes that there came, according to the general opinion of
scholars, the apocryphal or secret literature which, from the
name of its principal book, may be described under the generic
name of Enochian[1]. In the *Book of Enoch* in its various forms
was set forth a vast system of teaching on matters which the
Canonical books of the Old Testament hardly touch. Here we
have a complete cosmogony in which the mundane egg[2] of the
Orphics plays its part ; and the duties of the innumerable orders
of angels and their connection with the heavenly bodies, the
rebellion of Satan and his host against God, the fall of the
Watchers, or angels set over the earth, through the beauty of
mortal women, and the arrangement of the different heavens
and hells all find a place in it[3]. But it also deals at great
length with that Messianic hope which had for two centuries
been dangled by the Prophets before Israel, and which, thanks
to the materialistic sense in which it was interpreted by the
vast majority of Jews, was to lead directly to their extermination as a nation[4]. The *Book of Enoch* and its many successors
and imitators are full of predictions of the coming of a Messiah,
who should lead the chosen race to the conquest of the world,
and, what was to them probably an even more alluring prospect,
to the overthrow and enslavement of all the other peoples in it[5].

---

[1] F. C. Porter in Hastings' *Dict. of Bible*, *s.v.* Apocrypha, and Well-
hausen as there quoted. A list of the books comprised in the expression
used in the text with conjectural dates and authorship is given by R. H.
Charles in the same work, *s.v.* Apocalyptical Literature. Cf. article
under same heading (also by Charles) in *Encyclopaedia Biblica*. Prof.
Charles is less inclined than earlier writers (*e.g.* Lightfoot and Kohler,
opp. cit.) to credit the Essenes with the composition of the whole of this
literature ; but he admits that part of the Book of Enoch, chap. cviii.
1–15, is by Essene hands. The other parts attributed to the Essenes by
Sieffert, Tideman, and Cheyne are indicated by him in *The Book of Enoch*,
Oxford, 1893, pp. 13, 14, 21.

[2] *The Book of the Secrets of Enoch* (Morfill and Charles trans.), Oxford,
1896, p. 32.

[3] Charles, *Book of Enoch, cit. sup.* pp. 24–33.

[4] *Id. op. cit.* chap. xc. 28–38 ; cf. *id. Crit. Hist.* p. 192.

[5] Charles, *Book of Enoch*, xc. 30.

In the earlier parts of the Ethiopic version—which is in itself, as Dr Charles has pointed out, but " a fragmentary survival of an entire literature that once circulated under the name of Enoch[1] "—it is described how

" the Holy and Great One will come forth from His dwelling, the God of the world, and going from thence He will tread on Mount Sinai and appear with His hosts, and in the strength of His might appear from heaven[2]."

The judgment and destruction of all but the elect is next described, and the hurling down of the sinning angels into " the abyss of fire," while the elect—that is, the Jews, or perhaps only the Essenes—are to live among millennial blessings of a material kind and in the enjoyment of universal peace[3]. This seems to represent fairly the earlier Essene teaching upon this point, and there is reason to suppose that it was written before the Maccabaean struggles, after which the decadence of the Syrian Empire under Antiochus Epiphanes—hard pressed as he was by the Romans on one side and the Parthians on the other—allowed the Jews to obtain a temporary independence, and to set up a kingdom of their own for the first and last time in their history[4]. But the wine of military success and political independence proved too strong for the heads of the race which had hitherto been the tributaries and subjects of the Persian, the Greek, the Egyptian, and the Syrian Empires in turn, and, like their kinsmen the Arabs of Mohammed's time and the Mahdists in our own, nothing less would now satisfy the fanatical among them than universal domination.   In the later parts of the same work, the aspirations of the writers become more bloodthirsty and less spiritual, and we hear of a time " When the congregation

---

[1] Charles, *Book of Enoch*, p. 24.

[2] *Id. op. cit.* chap. i. 4.   [3] *Id. op. cit.* chap. i. 8.

[4] David had the Philistines for suzerain, as Solomon had Egypt, cf. Stanley A. Cook, in *Encyc. Bibl. s.v.* David, and Maspero, *Hist. anc. des Peuples de l'Orient*, 1904, pp. 391, 422. Their successors, too, up to the Captivity seem to have always been tributaries to Assyria, Chaldaea, or Egypt. After that event, they were of course vassals to the Persian and Macedonian Empires.

of the righteous will appear[1]," a phrase which seems to cover the coming-forth of some sect or society till then kept in seclusion. "Then," it goes on to say, "will the kings and the mighty perish and be given into the hand of the righteous and holy[2]." In another part of the same book, we hear of angels being sent to

" the Parthians and Medes, to stir up the kings and provoke in them a spirit of unrest, and rouse them from their thrones, that they may break forth from their resting-places as lions and as hungry wolves among the flocks[3]."

These are to make one final assault upon Jerusalem, and

" to tread under foot the land of His elect ones and the land of His elect ones will be before them a threshing floor and a path. But the city of My righteous [*i.e.* Jerusalem] will be a hindrance to their horses, and they will begin to fight among themselves, and their right hand will be strong against themselves, and a man will not know his brother, nor a son his father or his mother, till the number of corpses through their slaughter is beyond count, and their punishment be no idle one. And in those days Sheol will open his jaws, and they will be swallowed up therein, and their destruction will be at an end. Sheol will devour the sinners in the presence of the elect[4]."

This, according to the author who has made the most exhaustive study of the Enochian literature yet attempted, must have been written after the spirit which had inspired the Maccabaean revolt had died away under the tyranny and luxury of the later

---

[1] Charles, *Book of Enoch*, chap. xxxviii. 1.

[2] *Op. cit.* chap. xxxviii. 5. Cf. xlvi. 4, " And this Son of Man whom thou hast seen will arouse the kings and the mighty ones from their thrones, and will loosen the reins of the strong and grind to powder the teeth of the sinners."

[3] *Op. cit.* chap. lvi. 5. This verse, which Dr Charles considers an interpolation, was evidently written in 40 B.C., when a Parthian army under Pacorus invaded Palestine and put a puppet of their own on the throne of Jerusalem, and before 39 B.C., when Publius Ventidius Bassus drove the Parthians back to their own country. Cf. Morrison, *Jews*, etc., pp. 58–61, and authorities there quoted.

[4] Charles, *Book of Enoch*, chap. lvi. 6–8.

Jewish kings[1]. It seems very difficult, in the face of the many interpolations that the documents have undergone at the hands of Jewish and even Christian writers, to decide how much of these prophecies can be attributed directly to the sect of the Essenes ; but there can be little doubt that they accurately represent the hope of supremacy over the nations which they shared with the Pharisees and the other fanatics among the Jewish nation. Only thus can we explain the community of goods and the very un-Jewish contempt for money-making which formed the most singular features of Essene practice[2]. To those who expected to be immediately put in possession of the whole earth all desire for worldly advancement must have been a matter of indifference. A similar conviction led to the maintenance of the same practice in the Christian Church so long as she continued to believe in the nearness of the Parusia or Second Coming of her Founder[3].

From this dream of universal dominion, nothing seemed able to arouse the poorer Jews. In vain did the Sadducees, who comprised those of the nation who had become rich either by trading with the Gentile or by dependence on the luxurious Jewish Court, try to persuade the people that they had better make the best of the Hellenist culture thrust upon them than try to arrest its progress by fighting against powers that would crush them like glass when once sufficiently provoked[4]. In vain did the Syrian Empire, warned by the mistakes of Antiochus

---

[1] Charles, *op. cit.* p. 108. He there puts the date of the Similitudes, as this portion of the Book of Enoch is called, about a quarter of a century before the Parthian invasion. In that case, the prediction in the text would be about the only instance of fulfilled political prophecy known. But the discrepancy is doubtless to be explained by the theory of interpolation after the event.

[2] As in the admittedly Essene portion of the *Book of Enoch* (Charles, *op. cit.* chap. cviii. 8) : " Who loved God and loved neither gold nor silver, nor any of the goods of the world."

[3] Compare with this the desire to rid themselves of this world's goods which seized upon the inhabitants of Western Europe in 1000 A.D., when it was believed that the Second Advent was at hand, and donations to the Church beginning " in view of the approaching end of the world " were common.

[4] Schürer, *Hist. of Jewish People* (Eng. ed.), II. pp. 157, 158.

Epiphanes in Hellenizing the Jews against their will, accord
them the largest possible religious liberty and even acknowledge
their right to self-government in exchange for tribute[1].   When
the Romans, whom, according to their own account, they had
called in to protect them against their Syrian overlords, destroyed
once for all their chance of remaining an independent state, they
not only gave the Jews the fullest liberty to practise their own
religion, but set over them first a vassal king and then tetrarchs
of Semitic blood, who might be supposed to moderate the too
pronouncedly Western ideas of the Roman governor of Syria[2].
But these concessions were no more effective in inducing the
Jews to settle down quietly as the peaceful tributaries of a great
empire than had been the severities of Antiochus.   They seized
every opportunity to revolt, every time with the accompani-
ment of horrible atrocities committed upon those unfortunate
Gentiles who for a moment fell into their power, until, some
sixty years after the Destruction of the Temple by Titus,
Hadrian had to wage against them the awful war of extermination which extinguished their nationality for ever.   At the
Fair of the Terebinth, when every able-bodied Jew left alive
in Palestine was sold into slavery, the nation must have realized
at last the vanity of its dream[3].

During this time, that is to say, between the years 168 B.C.
and 135 A.D., the flood of Apocalyptic literature never ceased to
pour forth.   All of it was what is called pseudepigraphical, that
is to say, the books of which it was composed were falsely
attributed to Enoch, the sons of Jacob, Moses, Job, Ezra,
Baruch, and other personages of the Old Testament.   Not all
of these have come down to us, but a considerable number of
books have survived.   The pre-Christian ones that we have,

---

[1] Josephus, *Antiq.* Bk XIII. cap. 2, 3, where the tributes and taxes are
set forth.   Morrison, *op. cit.* p. 360, notes that the Jews showed no hostility
to the tribute payable to the Greek kings, and that it was the Roman
system of taxation which most embittered their feelings against the Gentiles.

[2] Morrison, *op. cit.* pp. 41, 42.

[3] Renan, in *L'Église Chrétienne*, chap. XI, tells the story with as
much grace as truth.   His account is largely taken from the investigations
of Hartwig Derenbourg, himself of Jewish blood.   Cf. Morrison, *op. cit.*
pp. 198–206.

included, beside the Ethiopian *Book of Enoch* quoted above, the *Testaments of the XII Patriarchs*, the *Psalms of Solomon*, and part of the *Sibylline Oracles*. Later probably than the beginning of our era, appeared the *Book of the Secrets of Enoch*, which Dr Charles thinks was written in Egypt, the *Wisdom* literature, certainly having the same place of origin, the *Book of Jubilees* or little Genesis, the *Assumption of Moses*, the rest of the *Sibyllines*, the *Apocalypse of Baruch*, the later books of *Maccabees*, and the *Fourth Book of Esdras*[1]. One and all of these deal with the glories before the Jewish nation, when by supernatural help it will be able to turn the tables on its would-be civilizers, and one and all breathe the most virulent hatred against every body who is not a Jew[2]. They show no consensus of opinion as to the future lot of the Gentiles ; for, while some teach that the victories of the Messiah will end in their complete

[1] They are arranged in the text as near as possible in the order of their probable dates. As to these and on the question of authorship, see Charles, *Crit. Hist.* pp. 172–226. The Sibylline Oracles can now be consulted in the scholarly edition of Rzach (*Sibyllina Oracula*, 1891), and in Dr Charles' *Apocrypha of the O.T.* (see below). The Greek text of the Psalms of Solomon with a French translation and critical introduction has been published by Dr J. Viteau and M. François Martin (*Les Psaumes de Salomon*, Paris, 1911). (The Odes of Solomon recently recovered for us by Dr Rendel Harris are most probably Christian hymns.) The Latin text of the 4th Book of Esdras is given by Bensly and James in Cambridge *Texts and Studies*, vol. III. No. 2, and an English translation of part of it appears in the Apocrypha of the A. V. (see *Speaker's Commentary* for a good text and commentary by Lupton). The *Wisdom Literature*, *i.e.* the *Wisdom of Solomon* and *Ecclesiasticus*, also appears in the Apocrypha of the A.V., as do the Books of *Maccabees*. English versions of all the other books with critical notes and introductions have been published by Prof. Charles as follows : *Book of Enoch*, Oxford, 1893 ; *Book of the Secrets of Enoch*, Oxford, 1896 ; *Apocalypse of Baruch*, 1896; *Assumption of Moses*, 1897; *Book of Jubilees*, 1902 ; and *Testament of the XII Patriarchs*, 1908. All the above appear in English dress in Dr Charles' *Apocrypha and Pseudepigrapha of the O.T.*, Oxford, 1913.

[2] See note 2 p. 149, *supra*. The essentially Jewish tendency towards hyperbole and exaggeration in language must, however, be allowed for. As someone has said, " Jacob I have loved, and Esau I have hated," in the mouth of a Jew means little more than that on the whole the speaker prefers Jacob to Esau. See also note 1 p. 163, *supra*.

annihilation, others declare that they will be preserved to become, as Isaiah had prophesied, the servants and hand-maidens of the Jews, to build up the walls of Jerusalem, and to be the herdsmen, ploughmen, and vinedressers of Israel[1]. Others again, held that the Gentiles would be hurled into Gehenna with the sinning angels[2]—even those who were dead being raised again for that purpose—and would there be tormented for ever in the presence of the Jews, who were to find one of their chief pleasures in the sight of their sufferings[3].

" And I saw all the sheep that had been left, and all the beasts of the earth, and all the birds of the heaven,"

says the pseudo-Enoch in a vision wherein he describes under this figure the nations which had not been destroyed by the celestial hosts of the Messiah,

" falling down and doing homage to those sheep [*i.e.* the Jews] and making petition to and obeying them in every thing[4]."

For the world was made for the Jews and the perversity of the Gentiles was divinely ordained for the express purpose that their " punishment " might be great[5].

" All this I have spoken before thee, O Lord," says the Apocryphal Ezra, " because thou madest the world for our sakes. As for the other people which also came of Adam, thou hast said that they are nothing, but are like unto spittle, and hast likened the abundance of them unto a drop that falleth from a vessel[6]. And now O Lord behold, these heathen, which have ever been reputed as nothing, have begun to be lords over us, and to devour us......If the world now be made for our sakes, why do we not enter into possession of our world ? How long shall this endure ? " And then comes Yahweh's answer: " Behold I will call together all the kings of the earth to reverence me, which are from the rising of the Sun, from the South, from the East, and Libanus : to turn themselves one against

---

[1] Isaiah xiv. 2 ; lx. 10 ; lxi. 5. All these passages are now said to be post-Exilic by Charles, *Crit. Hist.* p. 115.

[2] Charles, *Apocalypse of Baruch*, chap. xxx. 4, 5 ; chap. xxxvi. 11 ; 4 Esdras vii. 87.

[3] Charles, *Book of Enoch*, chap. xlviii. 9 ; lxii. 9–12.

[4] *Op. cit.* chap. xc. 30.   [5] See note 3 p. 166, *infra*.

[6] Cf. Isaiah xl. 15.

another, and repay that they have done to thee. Like as they do yet this day unto my chosen, so will I do also, and recompense in their bosom[1]." " After the signs have come of which thou wast told before," says the *Apocalypse of Baruch*, " when the nations become turbulent, and the time of My Messiah is come, He shall both summon all the nations, and some of them He shall spare and some of them He shall slay. These things therefore shall come upon the nations which are to be spared by Him. Every nation which knows not Israel, and has not trodden down the seed of Jacob, shall indeed be spared. And this because some out of every nation shall be subjected to thy people. But all those who have ruled over you, or have known you, shall be given up to the sword[2]."

So in the *Book of Jubilees* we are told that God

" sanctified [Israel] and gathered it from amongst all the children of men ; for there are many nations and many peoples, and all are His and over all hath He placed spirits in authority to lead them astray from Him. But over Israel He did not appoint any angel or spirit[3]."

As for the delight in the sufferings of the damned Gentiles it is poetically expressed in the *Assumption of Moses* :

" For the Heavenly One will arise from His royal throne
And He will go forth from His holy habitation
And His wrath will burn on account of His sons
* * * * * * * *
And the horns of the Sun will be broken and he shall be turned into darkness ;
And the moon shall not give her light, and be turned wholly into blood
And the circle of the stars shall be disturbed
* * * * * * * *
For the Most High will arise, the Eternal God alone,
And He will appear to punish the Gentiles
And He will destroy all their idols
Then thou, O Israel, shalt be happy
And thou shalt mount upon the neck of the eagle[4]
And the days of thy mourning will be ended
* * * * * * * *

[1] 4 Esdras vi. 55–59 ; xv. 20, 21.

[2] Charles, *Apocalypse of Baruch*, chap. lxxii. 2–6.

[3] Charles, *Book of Jubilees*, chap. xv. 31, 32.

[4] *I.e.* the Roman Empire.

And thou shalt look from on.high and shalt see thy enemies in
   Gehenna,
And thou shalt recognize them and rejoice
And thou shalt give thanks and confess thy Creator[1]."

And in what has been called the Apocalypse of Salathiel, we
hear that the righteous Jews will " have joy in seven ways " :

" First of all they shall see with great joy the glory of him who
receives them up, for they shall rest in seven orders. The first
order because they have striven with great labour to overcome
' the innate evil thought[2] ' which was fashioned together with
them, that it might not lead them astray from life into death. The
second order, because they see the round in which the souls of the
ungodly wander and the punishment that awaits them.....[3]."

A comparison of the dates of these documents lends little
support to the view that this hatred of the Gentiles was wrung
from the Jews by oppression ; and there seems grounds for
supposing that it had been present to their minds ever since
their return from the Captivity[4]. Tacitus was certainly justified
when he speaks of the nation as animated by bitter enmity
against the rest of the human race[5].

How far the Essenes were responsible for the whole of this
later literature, it is now impossible to say. Nearly every one
of the books above quoted have been claimed as of Essene
origin by some scholar or another[6], and those who, like

---

[1] Charles, *Assumption of Moses*, chap. x. 3, 5, 7, 8, 10.

[2] Evidently a reminiscence of the Zoroastrian demon who is opposed to
the Amshaspand Vohu Mano or "Good Thought."   See Chapter VI,*infra*.

[3] 4 Esdras vii. 91–93.

[4] The earliest document quoted is the part of the *Book of Enoch* which
Prof. Charles considers was written between 166–161 B.C. ; the latest, the
Fourth Book of Esdras, which he puts at 90 A.D. Yet he shows that the
hatred of the Gentiles and the hope that they would be eternally destroyed
or made slaves to Israel were present many centuries earlier and are to be
found in the writings attributed to Ezekiel, Haggai, Joel, and Zachariah,
as well as in Isaiah. Cf. *Crit. Hist.* p. 160.

[5] Tacitus, *Historia*, Bk v. c. 5.

[6] Thus Jellinek, *Ueber das Buch der Jubilaen und das Noah-Buch*,
Leipzig, 1855, *passim*, says that the Book of Jubilees is of Essene origin,

Dr Charles, are inclined to reduce Essene influence upon them to a minimum, admit that considerable interpolations have been made in most of the documents by Essene hands. Moreover, all those books which do not purport to be by Enoch himself either mention his name with peculiar reverence, or give the same account of celestial physics and other matters as the Ethiopic Book of Enoch, or quote it directly[1]. There seems, therefore, little doubt that all this literature came forth from the same school, and that it was directly or indirectly the result of Essene teaching.

A point more difficult to determine is how the Essenes managed to reconcile their secret doctrines with the reverence for the Mosaic Law and its promulgator which they undoubtedly professed[2]. There is no direct evidence with regard to this save Philo's remark quoted above as to their allegorical interpretation of Scripture. This, too, may have had its origin in Orphic practice, for we know that the Orphics were accustomed to carry allegory so far as to both materialize their gods, as when they spoke of Bacchus as Wine, and to deify abstractions, as when they made hymns to Health, Peace and other abstract conceptions as if they were actual persons[3]. But besides this, the Essenes probably practised a mode of interpretation peculiar to themselves, which they kept secret or confined to members of the sect. Something of the kind was not unknown among the Greeks, for some of the Orphic gold plates found in Magna

and Schmidt and Merx, *Archiv für wissenschaftliche Erforschung des Alten Testaments*, I. II. (1868) pp. 111–152, make the same claim for the *Assumption of Moses* and so on. For the *Book of Enoch* itself see above.

[1] For the quotations from Enoch in the *Testament of the XII Patriarchs* see Charles, Introduction to that book, p. lix ; for those in the *Book of Jubilees* see *B. of J.* pp. 13, 36, 37, 53, 62–64, 102, 134, 146, 150, 212, 213 ; in the *Apocalypse of Baruch*, see *A. of B.* p. 101 and notes ; in the *Assumption of Moses*, see *A. of M.* x. 4, 9.

[2] Josephus, *ubi cit.* in note 4 p. 151, *supra*, says (§ 8) that they honoured the name of Moses next after that of God Himself ; and that any who blasphemed him was punished capitally.

[3] Cf. Abel's *Orphica*, Fr. 160, 161, 162, 202, 203, 204. From the Orphics the practice passed into the Mysteries and the writings of the post-Christian Gnostics. See Hatch, *Hibbert Lectures*, 1888, pp. 69, 74–75.

Graecia are intended to be read acrostically[1], and the Graeco-Egyptian magic papyri contain many instances of a similar use of the Homeric poems by which they could be converted into an oracle or fortune-telling book[2]. By such means any document can of course be made to mean anything, and the Essenes seem to have added to this the practice of isopsephism or regarding words as equivalent in sense which had the same numerical value. The most familiar instance of this is in the Revelation of St John where " the number of the Beast " is said to be " the number of a man ; and his number is six hundred threescore and six " ; or, in other words, Nero Caesar, whose name written in Hebrew letters is equivalent to the number given[3]. In like manner we read in the *Book of Enoch*, in the story of the sinning angels :

" This is the number of Kesbeêl, who showed the head of the oath to the holy ones when he dwelt high above in glory, and its name is Bêqâ. And this angel requested Michael to show him the hidden name, that they might mention it in the oath, so that those who revealed all that was hidden to the children of men might quake before that name and oath. And this is the power of that oath, for it is powerful and strong, and he placed this oath Akae in the hand of Michael[4]."

[1] Like the Gold Plate of Caecilia Secundina, Chapter IV, p. 133, *supra*. So the Sibylline Oracles contain the acrostic ΙΧΘΥΣ which covers the name and titles of Jesus, Renan, *L'Église Chrétienne*, p. 535 and note. The Greeks must have caught the taste for such devices, for an acrostic is found in a treatise on astronomy by Eudoxos of Cnidos copied in the second cent. B.C. Many other instances are given by Brunet de Presle, *Les Papyrus Grecs du Musée du Louvre*, Paris, 1865, pp. 43, 44. He says with some reason that the practice was borrowed by the Greeks from the Jews.

[2] Kenyon, *Gk. Pap. in B. M.*, Papyrus CXXI, pp. 83 *sqq.*

[3] Hausrath, *op. cit.* pp. 114–116, where many other instances are given. The explanation of " Nero(n) Caesar " as the Number of the Beast is in fact as old as Irenaeus, who remarks that the variant 616 given in some texts is due to the omission of the final *n* in Latin. It does not seem to be seriously disputed by any modern theologian. Isopsephism however was not the invention of the Essenes, but of the Babylonians, among whom it was in use, to judge from Berossos, in the time of Alexander. See Alexander Polyhistor in Cory, *Ancient Fragments*, 2nd ed. p. 25.

[4] Charles, *Book of Enoch*, chap. lxix. 13–15. Cf. *id.*, *The Apoc. etc. of the O.T.*, II. p. 234, where he has made some verbal alterations in the reading.

From the context, it would appear that the words Akâe and Bêqâ both cover the Tetragrammaton or four-lettered name of JHVH, by means of which omnific word it is said the heavens and earth were created[1]. The mysterious name of Taxo given in the *Assumption of Moses* as that of the protagonist against Antiochus is doubtless to be interpreted in some such fashion[2].

Of the history of the Essenes as an organized sect, we know hardly anything. If we accept Josephus' account of their numbers as relating to his own time[3], it would seem that they were flourishing at the date of the Destruction of the Temple under Titus. This event would probably affect them little directly, because, as we have seen, they took no part in the Temple worship; and, scattered as they were through the villages of Palestine, they may easily have escaped the punishment meted out by the Romans to those towns which were the strongholds of the rebellion. But it is extremely improbable that they can have survived the War of Extermination under Hadrian, when the partizans of the false Messiah kept up a futile resistance in the country as well as in the towns, and Hadrian's general, Severus, had in consequence to lay the land desolate[4]. Moreover, it is not improbable that the sect may have taken an active part in the Revolt, which they may easily have looked upon as the fulfilment of their Messianic hopes, and may thus have perished under the stern measures of repression which the fanaticism and barbarities of the rebels forced upon the conquerors. At any rate, we hear little more of the Essenes after this date. But the fantastic method of interpreting Scriptures which they practised and probably introduced, lingered long, and, after being used by the earliest

---

[1] Hausrath, *op. et loc. cit.*

[2] Charles, *A. of M.* chap. ix. 1, and the note beginning on p. 35, *op. cit.* Hausrath, *op. cit. sup.* pp. 116, 117, thinks the name is arrived at by the process called Atbash.

[3] If the authenticity of the Fragment quoted above from Philo could be established, it would seem probable that Josephus simply copied the figure from this last, and that 4000 was the number of the Essenes about 20 A.D.

[4] Renan, *L'Église Chrétienne*, p. 209.

Christian writers[1], was revived, as has been said, by the Cabalists of the Middle Ages, and has even survived into our own time. It was especially high in favour with those numerous bodies of heretics who in the first three centuries of our era asserted that knowledge was the one thing needful for salvation and were thus called, both by themselves and by their opponents the Fathers of the Church, by the generic and distinctive name of Gnostics[2].

[1] Hausrath, *op. cit.* pp. 116, 117, for examples. By the method called Temura he gets *Romah hagedôlah* for Armageddon in the Canonical Apocalypse. So Justin Martyr, *Cohort.* c. XXIV. says that Moses is unintelligible without mystic insight, and that the name of Christ contains a hidden meaning (*2nd Apol.* c. VI.).

[2] Thus Irenaeus, *Adv. Haer.* Bk I. c. XII. § 11, p. 146, Harvey, makes Marcus the heresiarch show that Alpha and Omega, the name given to Jesus [?] in Revelation, means the Dove which descended upon Him at His baptism, because it has the same numerical value ($\pi\epsilon\rho\iota\sigma\tau\epsilon\rho\acute{a}$) of 801.

CHAPTER VI

PRE-CHRISTIAN GNOSTICS : SIMON MAGUS

WE see, then, that the Essenes, in spite of the quietism and love of peace that they professed, became in the long run either the instigators of political revolt or, at best, the tools of those who thought to make use of the fanaticism excited by their teaching in order to throw off the yoke of the Gentiles. But these fanatics were almost exclusively the Jews of Judaea, whose adherence to their own institutions caused them to leave Babylon, where they were fairly well off, to be cooped up in a land which in no time can have yielded an easy subsistence to a large number of souls[1]. That people so circumstanced, confronted with a power vastly superior to their own, and resolutely bent on compelling its subjects to enter into its own system of orderly government, should have looked to rebellion and supernatural help as their sole means of escape, was only to be expected. But there were besides a great number of Jews dispersed among the heathen, who had succeeded in acquiring vast wealth together with the power which wealth brings with it ; and these were by no means inclined to upset the settled order of things which the rise of the Roman Empire had brought into the East. To the humble fisherman, vinedresser or husbandman of Judaea, daily vexed and harassed by the Roman tax-gatherer and Roman police measures, the Roman peace, the freedom from foreign conquest, and the higher standard of

---

[1] The fanaticism of the Palestinian Jews in time affected their co-religionists elsewhere, as when the Jews in Asia Minor rebelled and committed atrocities in the reign of Trajan. See Morrison, *Jews under Roman Rule*, p. 191, and Renan, *Les Évangiles*, Paris, 1877, p. 503. Probably such outbreaks were condemned by those of the nation who had anything to lose, as was certainly the case during the Revolt under Hadrian.

comfort that came in with the legions, must have appeared far less desirable than they did to the rich trader of Alexandria, Caesarea, or Damascus, whose aptness in taking advantage of the foibles of his rulers had enabled him to imitate their luxury and in some cases to share their power[1]. Yet, with the tenacity peculiar to their nation, even these rich Jews outside Palestine, while adopting gladly enough the material benefits of the Graeco-Roman civilization, clung firmly to the one exclusively national possession which remained to them, the Law of Moses with all its observances. They were, however, quite sharp enough to see that the rules laid down for the conduct of a loosely-compacted mass of nomad tribes suddenly flung among hostile neighbours were unfitted to a more settled civilization ; and the thinkers among them were put to much pains to discover some means by which they could claim their share of Hellenistic culture without ceasing to be Jews[2]. At first this generally took the form of pseudonymous writings bearing the name of some author respected by the Greeks, and designed to prove that all the Hellenistic arts, sciences, and doctrines were derived from the Hebrew patriarchs. Thus, verses were ascribed to Orpheus and the Sibyl, and historical works to Hecataeus of Abdera and a certain Aristaeus, having for their object the praise of the Jewish nation, which were certainly not written by the authors whose names were appended to them. So Artapanus' book " On the Jews " claimed that the Egyptians were indebted to the Hebrews for all they knew, including even the worship of their gods, and that this went back to the days of Abraham, who availed himself of his stay in Egypt to teach astrology to the Pharaoh of his time[3].

History, however, was at all times much less to the taste of the Jews than metaphysics, and the many teachers of philosophy

---

[1] Morrison, *op. cit.* p. 375 ; Mahaffy, *Greek Life and Thought*, 1887, pp. 468–482 ; *Greek World under Roman Sway*, 1890, p. 47.

[2] Schürer, *History of the Jewish People*, Eng. ed. II. pp. 157, 158. One of the best proofs of this tendency is the fashion among all classes of Jews at this period of giving their children Greek names. See Mahaffy, *Greek Life and Thought*, p. 480. Even among the Apostles we have Andrew and Philip.

[3] Schürer, *op. cit.* II. pp. 206, 306, 309 ; Morrison, *op. cit.* p. 395.

scattered through the Hellenistic world found in them eager
scholars, who were willing to listen respectfully to any doctrine,
so long as it could be shown to be not inconsistent with their
national religion and traditions. The most sincere attempt
thus to combine Hellenic and Jewish teaching that has come
down to us is that of Philo of Alexandria, who wrote probably
shortly after the Birth of Christ. In his system[1], God is undefinable and has no qualities that can be perceived by man. As
He is absolutely perfect, He cannot come into contact with
matter, and all His dealings with it must therefore be conducted
through intermediate beings. These intermediate beings are
the powers or attributes of God, inconsistently, as Zeller points
out, figured by Philo " as at once independent hypostases and
immanent determinations of the Divine existence[2]." All the
Divine Powers are summed up in the Logos or Word of God,
who is not only their chief but their source, and the great
intermediary between God and the universe. He is neither
unbegotten nor begotten after the manner of finite things, but
is the vicegerent and ambassador of God, who constantly makes
intercession for the world. As for man, his soul is itself nothing
but one of those powers of God which in another state of
existence are called angels or daemons, and it is his material
body which is the source of all evil, and the prison of the soul.
Man can only free himself from this by resisting the allurements
of the senses, which God puts it into his heart to do. By such
resistance, he can exceptionally and occasionally acquire such
virtue that, even in this life, he may attain to the Divine Vision,
when he will be " lifted above and out of himself," and the Spirit
of God will henceforth dwell in him and " stir him like the
strings of a musical instrument." In the ordinary way, however,

[1] Schürer, *op. cit.* II. pp. 369–380, following, as he tells us, Zeller, gives
an excellent and coherent account of Philo's system, which see. As Schürer
points out (*op. cit.* II. p. 368), Philo " hellenized " so thoroughly that
practically the only Judaic elements in his system are the assertion of
monotheism, a contempt for image-worship, and the claim that the Jews
possessed through the Mosaic revelation the highest religious knowledge.

[2] Schürer, *op. cit.* II. p. 372. For a definition of hypostasis in this
connection and its original equivalence to οὐσία and *substantia* (as in the
Quicunque vult), see Hatch, *Hibbert Lectures*, 1888, p. 275.

his emancipation will only take place when his soul returns to its original incorporeal condition, a reward which is bestowed on those who have kept themselves free from attachment to this sensuous body[1].

That people holding tenets so far removed from anything in the Law and the Prophets should form themselves into small sects or societies[2] and take other means for their propagation is only natural, and no doubt many such sects of which we have lost all trace existed in secret among the Hellenizing Jews at the beginning of the Christian era[3]. Such a sect were probably the Sethiani described by Hippolytus, whose " entire system," according to the author of the *Philosophumena*, was derived from " the ancient theologians Musaeus, Linus, and Orpheus, who elucidates especially the ceremonies of initiation as well as the Mysteries themselves[4]." So far as Hippolytus explains their system, which he appears to have very imperfectly understood, it set forth three principles, which he calls " Light, Darkness, and an intermediate one which is Spirit " ; but all the passages quoted from the " Paraphrase of Seth," which he declares to be the work of the sect in question, refer for their authority to the Old Testament, which it is evident the Sethiani received as a real revelation[5]. But the one of these half-Jewish

---

[1] Were those who did not attain to this height in Philo's opinion annihilated or re-incarnated ? His view that for the wicked this life is the real hell (*De congr. erud. grat.* § XI.) would suit either theory ; but in *de Cherub.* § I. it is plain that he contemplates the eternal punishment of the damned.

[2] Secret, not from the jealous motive of the Gnostics, but because if their opinions had become generally known they would have been cast out of the synagogue.

[3] So Renan, *Les Évangiles*, p. 452. It is quite possible that the sect of the Essenes may have included many divisions.

[4] Hippolytus, *Philosophumena*, Bk v. c. 3, p. 218, Cruice.

[5] M. de Faye is probably right in saying (*Étude Critique des Documents du Gnosticisme Chrétien*, Paris, 1913, pp. 352, 353) that the Sethiani were never a very important sect. Stähelin's theory (*Die Gnostischen Quellen Hippolyts*, Leipzig, 1890) that Hippolytus was deceived by a forger who drew all his " heresies " from one document (see Chapter VII, *infra*) is too fantastic to be correct, but it has done good service in calling attention to the family likeness between most of the systems which he sketches. Cf.

half-Gentile sects of which we have the most detailed account is that which passed under the name of Simon Magus, whom the Fathers of the Church were unanimous in describing as the parent and origin of all later Gnosticism[1].

This Simon, the New Testament describes as a man who had formerly " used sorcery, and bewitched the people of Samaria, giving out that himself was some great one : to whom all gave heed, from the least to the greatest, saying ' This man is the great power of God[2] '." The author of the Acts then goes on to say that Simon " believed " and was baptized by Philip, and that when Peter and John came from Jerusalem to Samaria, " he offered them money saying: Give me also this power, that on whomsoever I lay hands, he may receive the Holy Ghost." It is from this offer, which seems to betray a desire to set up a Church of his own, that his name, curiously enough, has since been associated in ecclesiastical law with the offence of buying and selling benefices or cures of souls[3]. Of Simon's future career, however, the Acts of the Apostles tell us nothing save that he left Peter with the request for the Apostle's prayers on his behalf. It is evident, from the text quoted above, that both Simon's sorceries and his acclamation by the people as " the great power of God " took place before his conversion to Christianity, whether this was real or feigned. Hence, Simon must have been at the time already the leader of a school or sect, and as the events narrated are in the same book set out before the Conversion of St Paul and his preaching to the Gentiles, this sect must have been a pre-Christian one[4].

E. de Faye, *Intro. à l'Ét. du Gnost.*, Paris, 1903, p. 68. We are not likely to reach any more definite conclusion unless some lucky discovery reveals to us the sources of Hippolytus' compilation.

[1] Irenaeus, Bk I. c. 16, p. 191, Harvey ; Hippolytus, *Philosophumena*, Bk VI. c. 20, p. 267, Cruice; Augustine, *de Haeres. lib.* cc. I., II., III.; Praedestinatus, *de Haer.* Bk I. c. 1 ; Pseudo-Tertullian, *adv. omn. Haer.* c. I. etc.

[2] Acts viii. 9, 10.

[3] From the story in Acts, it appears that what Simon tried to buy was the power of ordination. The offence in modern ecclesiastical jurisprudence seems to be the obtaining the priestly office by purchase rather than by merit or gift.

[4] Cf. Amélineau, *Gnosticisme Égyptien*, p. 51.

That this sect was also one of those which sought to reconcile Judaism with Hellenism seems antecedently probable. Samaria had been stripped of a great part of its former inhabitants by Alexander the Great and Ptolemy Soter, who had colonized it by " Macedonian " settlers, probably of Syrian blood[1]. These colonists had accepted without difficulty the religious reforms of Antiochus Epiphanes, and had offered that king, according to Josephus, to dedicate their temple on Mt Gerizim to Zeus Hellenios[2]. Later, on the death of Antiochus, John Hyrcanus, the ethnarch or high-priest of the Jews, on the same authority, "revolted from the Macedonians," invaded Samaria, besieged its chief city and, when he gained possession of it, entirely demolished it[3]. Gabinius, when proconsul of Syria, rebuilt this and other cities which had been destroyed by the Jews, and Herod the Great about 25 B.C. restored and beautified it while renaming it Sebaste in honour of Augustus[4]. These events had intensified the hatred already existing between the Jews and the Samaritans, and this was not diminished by the possession by the latter of the Mt Gerizim temple which was in some sort the rival of that of Jerusalem[5]. To judge from its later developments, the religion of the Samaritans at the beginning of the Christian era retained little of Judaism besides a reverence for the Pentateuch or Five Books of Moses[6], and its other elements were apparently Greek. We should therefore expect to find in Simon's teaching before his meeting with the Apostles, a leaning towards a mixed religion in which Greek elements played the chief part, although the sanction attached to it might be Jewish.

[1] Morrison, *op. cit.* p. 351.   Cowley in Cheyne's *Encyclopaedia Biblica*, *s.v.* Samaritans, omits this; but see Josephus, *Ant.* Bk XII. c. 2, § 1.

[2] Josephus, *op. cit.* Bk XII. c. 5, § 1.

[3] *Ibid. op. cit.* Bk XIII. c. 10, § 3.

[4] *Ibid. op. cit.* Bk XV. c. 9, § 5.

[5] "Neither at Jerusalem, nor on this mountain [Gerizim] shall men worship the Father," John iv. 21.

[6] Cowley in *Encyc. Bibl. s.v.* Samaritans, col. 4260.   According to Renan, *Les Évangiles*, p. 451, the Samaritans at the beginning of our era were divided into a great number of sects, all more or less attached to Simon.   The authorities he quotes are, however, too late to establish this satisfactorily.

Such an expectation is abundantly justified by the evidence of post-Apostolic writers. The documents known as the *Clementine Homilies* and *Recognitions* are now generally admitted to be a kind of religious novel or romance composed for edification, and no consensus of opinion exists as to their date, which has been taken by many learned critics as ranging from the ist to the ivth century A.D.[1] They set forth with much detail how Simon, after his first meeting with St Peter in Samaria, everywhere opposed the chief of the Apostles, and followed him about on many of his journeys, disputing with him at great length, until finally put to flight by the superior dialectic of Peter[2]. The Apocryphal *Acts of Peter and Paul*, which seem to be either wholly or in part earlier than 275 A.D., further narrate that Simon attempted to convert to his heresy the Emperor Nero, by flying over the Campus Martius at Rome in a car drawn by demons ; but was vanquished by St Peter, who by a solemn adjuration caused him to fall violently to the earth and thus to perish miserably[3]. This story became later the universal tradition of the Catholic Church. All the patristic writers agree that Simon Magus was accompanied in his missionary journeys by a woman of immoral life whom he called the Ennoia or Thought of God, and declared to be a reincarnation of Helen of Troy[4], while one of the Clementine documents makes her, together with Simon, to have been

[1] The question was discussed and resolved, as far as it could be in the then state of our information, by Salmon in Smith's *Dictionary of Christian Biography*, *s.v.* Clementines. Mgr. Duchesne, *Early History of the Christian Church*, Eng. ed. 1909, p. 96, n. 2, sums up in favour of their ultimate derivation from the *Preaching of Peter* composed at the end of the iind or beginning of iiird cent. He thinks the Clementines orthodox save for a slight Arian tendency.

[2] So Theodoret ; but this was a common form in the patristic accounts of such disputes. It is repeated in the dispute of Archelaus with Manes, mentioned in Chapter XIII, *infra*, which see.

[3] See Tischendorf's edition, *passim*. The age of the book may be guessed by its containing the *Quo Vadis* story quoted by Origen.

[4] Irenaeus, Bk i. c. 16, p. 191, Harvey; Hippolytus, Bk vi. c. 1, § 19, p. 264, Cruice ; Epiphanius, *Panar.* Bk i. ; *Haer.* xxi. c. 2 (p. 125 of Oehler's vol. ii. pt. 1).

among the followers of John the Baptist[1]. There is no external corroboration of either story; and such accusations of immorality were too frequently bandied about between the early Christians and their adversaries for any particular weight to be laid upon them[2]. Nor need the latest German theory, that Simon Magus is in the Clementine literature but a pseudonym for St Paul as the supposed opponent of St Peter, be discussed here[3].

The first writer who gives us any authoritative account of Simon's pre-Christian teaching is Hippolytus, who in his *Philosophumena* quotes freely from a book which he attributes to Simon and calls the *Great Announcement*[4]. Whether this be really Simon's work or no, its quotation in the *Philosophumena* at least proves that a sect bearing his name existed in the sub-Apostolic age, and that they held the doctrines set forth in Hippolytus' quotations from this document, which can hardly have been due to anyone else in the first instance than Simon himself[5]. In the *Great Announcement* the First Cause of

[1] *Clementine Homilies*, II. c. 23.

[2] Marcion and Marcus, both leaders of Gnostic sects, were both accused by the Catholics of seduction, while the Pagans naturally put the worst construction on the intimacy existing between confessors and martyrs and their converts, as is evidenced by the story of Paul and Thekla.

[3] This seems to have been first set on foot by Baur and the Tübingen school, and has lately been revived by Schmiedel in the *Encyc. Bibl. s.v.* Simon Magus. Even if we were to admit that it was well founded with regard to the *Clementines*, it would not get rid of the testimony of the Acts and of Justin Martyr that Simon Magus had an actual historical existence.

[4] Ἀπόφασις μεγάλη. "Declaration" would perhaps be a better translation of the word; but that given in the text is the one used by most writers on the subject.

[5] Simon's authorship of the book has been defended by Renan (*Les Apôtres*, Paris, 1866, p. 267 and note) and attacked by many other writers. Salmon, *op. cit.*, Schmiedel, *op. cit.*, and Stock in the *Encyclopaedia Britannica* (last edition), *s.v.* Simon Magus, aver that there were two Simons, one the personage of the Acts, and the other, a Gnostic leader of the IInd cent. to whom or to whose followers the *Great Announcement* is to be attributed. This theory, although attractive, would prove too much; for Justin Martyr, himself a Samaritan, has no doubt that Simon the heresiarch is the Simon of the Acts, and if he is wrong in this, a matter which may well have been within his own personal knowledge, Hippolytus is our best and earliest authority for Simon's doctrines.

all things is declared to be fire, on the strength of the statement
in Deuteronomy that " God is a burning and consuming fire[1]."
This Infinite or Boundless Power, as he calls it, Simon held to
be not simple but two-fold, having two natures, a hidden and a
manifold one, so intermingled that " the hidden one is concealed
in the manifest, and the manifest comes into being from the
hidden one," by which, as we shall see later, he meant male and
female. The manifest, again, can be perceived by the senses
like things with an actual existence, while the hidden nature
can only be apprehended by the mind, or in other words imagined.
In all this he seems at first sight to be echoing, as Hippolytus
points out[2], the notions of Plato upon the Intelligible ($\tau\grave{o}$
$\nu o\eta\tau\acute{o}\nu$) and the Sensible ($\tau\grave{o}$ $a\grave{\iota}\sigma\theta\eta\tau\acute{o}\nu$), those of Aristotle on
Power or Potentiality ($\delta\acute{\nu}\nu a\mu\iota\varsigma$) and Actual Existence ($\grave{\epsilon}\nu\acute{\epsilon}\rho\gamma\epsilon\iota a$),
and, as Hippolytus does *not* say, those of Philo upon the First
Cause and the Logos[3]. The Cosmos or ordered universe came
into being, Simon goes on to say, from the unbegotten or self-
existent fire, by means of six " Roots " called respectively
Mind ($No\hat{\nu}\varsigma$) and Thought (''$E\nu\nu o\iota a$)[4], Voice ($\Phi\omega\nu\acute{\eta}$) and Name
(''$O\nu o\mu a$), Reason ($\Lambda o\gamma\iota\sigma\mu\acute{o}\varsigma$) and Desire ('$E\nu\theta\acute{\upsilon}\mu\eta\sigma\iota\varsigma$). Although
it is not here formally stated, it is noteworthy that this is a
system of couples or pairs, the name of one of each of the above
pairs being masculine and the other feminine[5]. In these six,

[1] Deut. iv. 24.

[2] Hippolytus, *op. cit.* Bk VI. c. 1, § 9, p. 247, Cruice.

[3] As when he says that the Logos is not God, but his reflection. See
Philo, *de Somn.* I. 41 (p. 656 of Mangey). " Just as those who cannot gaze
upon the sun may yet gaze upon a reflection of it." Cf. Hatch, *H. L.* p. 248.

[4] Irenaeus and Epiphanius (where before quoted) both call this second
partner in the first pair of " Roots " ''$E\nu\nu o\iota a$. Hippolytus, *op. cit.* Bk VI.
c. 1, § 13, p. 251, Cruice, has '$E\pi\acute{\iota}\nu o\iota a$. Does this mean " after-thought "
or " second thought " as showing her posteriority to Nous ? At any rate
it is some indication that he is copying from a different source than that
of his predecessors. King (*Gnostics and their Remains*, 2nd ed. p. 61) would
translate '$E\nu\theta\acute{\upsilon}\mu\eta\sigma\iota\varsigma$ by " thought," while he calls ''$E\nu\nu o\iota a$ " Intelligence."
The Abbé Cruice translates '$E\nu\theta\acute{\upsilon}\mu\eta\sigma\iota\varsigma$ " Conceptio." It seems here to mean
Desire not in a fleshly but a mental sense.

[5] The names of ''$O\nu o\mu a$ and $\Phi\omega\nu\acute{\eta}$ are placed in the reverse order to the
others, inasmuch as in this pair the feminine comes first. This is curious
because in the same section they are compared to the Sun and Moon, the
sex of which is transposed in several mythologies.

Simon imagined that the Boundless Power existed potentially, but not actually, that is to say, that each of them represented one particular aspect or quality under which the Supreme Being might be considered, but had no existence apart from Him, while it required the addition together of all the six to make up His entire being. A similar conception seems to underlie the Zoroastrian idea of the six Amshaspands, from which it is likely enough that Simon copied this part of his system[1]. It is here that we meet for the first time in Gnosticism with the idea of emanation or the flowing-forth of the Divine nature, which differs entirely from that of creation, whether *e nihilo* or from pre-existing matter, inasmuch as the emanation still remains connected with the parent source and never forms an entity distinct from it[2].

We see, then, that in Simon's system, the primal world was a hebdomad or consisted of seven Powers, being the three pairs of Roots enumerated above together with a seventh, their source, in whom they were all summed up[3]. But after this, and apparently created by it, is a second or intermediate world, as to which the *Great Announcement* thus expresses itself :

[1] The names of the Amshaspands of Zoroaster are, *Vohu Mano*, or Good Mind, and *Asha Vahishta*, or Truth; *Kshathra Vairya*, or Right Law, and *Spenta Armaiti*, or Wisdom; *Haurvetat*, or Good Health, and *Ameretat* or Immortality. The likeness between this and Simon's system has been noticed by, among others, Harvey the editor of Irenaeus, in his Introduction to that author, pp. lxv *sqq.* For the resemblance between post-exilic Judaism and Zoroastrianism, see Cheyne, *Jewish Religious Life*, pp. 157, 210, 251, 257 *sqq.* But see p. 197, *infra.*

[2] Emanation is well defined by Mallet (*Culte de Neit à Saïs*, Paris, 1888, pp. 212, 213) as " a perpetual flowing-forth, which does not imply any effort, and which consequently neither exhausts nor even diminishes the productive principle." Emanations, however, he goes on to say, become weaker and less perfect the further they get from their first source. The first mention I can find of the word is in Plutarch (*de Is. et Os.* c. XLIX.) who says that the visible Cosmos is " the flowing forth (ἀπορροή) and displayed image of Osiris."

[3] Curiously enough, the author of the *Clementine Homilies* adopts this notion for orthodoxy, when he makes St Peter (XVII. c. 9) declare that God possesses six " extensions " having the nature of six infinites and that He with them makes up the " mystery of the hebdomad."

" Unto you therefore I say what I say, and write what I write. The writing is this. There are two stocks of all the Aeons put together, having neither beginning nor end, springing from one Root, the which is Power-Silence, invisible, incomprehensible (ἀκατάληπτος)[1]. Of which two stocks, one appears above, which is a great Power, the Mind of the universes, which pervades all things, and is male : the other [appears] below, a great Thought, is female, and gives birth to all things. Thus, these, corresponding to one another[2], form a pair (συζυγία), and show forth the Middle Space (διάστημα), an incomprehensible air having neither beginning nor end. In this is the Father who sustains (βαστάζων) all things and nourishes all those things which have a beginning and end[3]. This is he who standeth, hath stood, and shall stand[4], being both a male and female power after the likeness of the pre-existing Boundless Power[5], which has neither beginning nor end, but exists in Oneness (Μονότης). For the Thought which came forth from the power in Oneness became two[6]. And each of them was one. For he, when he contained her within himself, was alone, nor was he the first, although he existed before, but having appeared from himself, a second came into being. But he was not called Father before [Thought] had named him Father. Just as, then, he drawing forth himself from himself

---

[1] *I.e.* "which cannot be grasped," "intangible," as in the Athanasian Creed.

[2] ἀντιστοιχέω " set over against each other." It seems to be a term used in logic.

[3] This is *not* the Supreme Father, but the Logos or his representative in the world succeeding his. It is with this being that Simon according to the author of the Clementines (*Hom.* II. c. 24) identified himself.

[4] Ὁ ἐστώς, στάς, στησόμενος. This seems to be the expression which the author of the Canonical Apocalypse is trying to reach in his fearful solecism ἀπὸ ὁ ὢν καὶ ὁ ἦν καὶ ὁ ἐρχόμενος. See Revelation i. 4.

[5] So the Supreme Being of Simon is androgyne.

[6] The difficulty in deducing both male and female divinities from a male or sexless Supreme being has led to some strange mythology. The Egyptians cut the knot in an effective if coarse way. " Thus from one god I became three gods," says the Egyptian deity " the Lord of the Universe," in his account of the Creation. See Budge, " Papyrus of Nesi-Amsu," and *Egyptian Hieratic Papyri in the British Museum*, pp. xiii, xiv and 14, 15. Was the author of the *Apophasis* acquainted with this story ? The Clementines make Simon's associates Egyptians or rather Alexandrians. See *Clem. Hom.* Bk IV. c. 6.

manifested to himself his own Thought, so the same Thought when she appeared did not create him, but, beholding him, concealed the Father, that is to say, Power, within herself, and [thus] there exists a male-and-female (*i.e.* hermaphrodite) Power-and-Thought. For Power does not in any way differ from Thought, they being one. Without the things which are above is found Power ; without those which are below, Thought. Thus, there is that, also, which appeared from them, the which being one is found to be two, a male-and-female containing the female within itself. This one is Mind in Thought ; for they, being one when undivided (ἀχώριστος) from one another, are [yet] found to be Two[1]."

This statement seems at first to be merely an explanation and recitation of what has been previously said as to the emanation of the " Roots " from the Boundless Power, and by no means justifies the words of the *Great Announcement* in which it is magniloquently proclaimed to be " the Book of the Showing-forth of Voice and Name from the Thought of the Great Boundless Power. Wherefore it will be sealed up and hidden and veiled and will rest in the habitation wherein the root of the worlds is established (θεμελιόω)[2]." But when we examine the words just quoted by the light of the other systems said to be derived from Simon's, we see that they really indicate the belief of the author in a succession of worlds, wherein every later or lower one is a reflection, as in a glass, of that which was above it[3]. These lower worlds, like the primal one, should each contain three pairs of " Roots," emanating from one source like rays from a lamp or other source of light. It also seems that this source is, alike in the primal world and its successors, in itself potentially both male and female, that is to say, the female nature, which alone has the power of conception or producing new beings, was originally concealed within the other as a thought is concealed within the mind, and only becomes

---

[1] Hippolytus, *op. cit.* Bk VI. c. 1, § 18, pp. 261, 262, Cruice.

[2] *Op. cit.* Bk VI. c. 1, § 9, p. 246, Cruice.

[3] Amélineau, *Gnosticisme Égyptien*, p. 39, makes this perfectly clear. Cf. Ad. Franck, " Le Gnosticisme Égyptien " in *Journal des Savants*, Avril, 1888, pp. 212, 213. Hatch (*H.L.* p. 205) points out that it is the doctrine of " Philo and the Platonists."

comprehensible when utterance is given to it. Hence each of these Powers or, as Simon here calls them for the first time, aeons, like the Supreme Being, has a double aspect. Seen from below, that is to say, as it appears to the aeon which succeeds it, it is female, that is to say, a source of being. To that which is above it, or earlier in emanation, it is male, that is to say, it is the cause of conception, and also the sustainer and director at once of the conceiver and of that which she conceives[1].

Why now did Simon, or whoever wrote under his name, use such obscure and at first sight unintelligible terms for his speculations on the nature of the Supreme Being and the origin of the world ? Simply, it would seem, that he might reconcile two things which like certain chemicals found themselves in presence of each other without any affinity for combination. These were the Mosaic Law which, since the Captivity, both Jew and Samaritan held themselves bound to treat as divinely inspired[2], and the Greek " theological " ideas which then pervaded the whole civilized world and were at the time accepted by all educated men who thought about such subjects in much the same way as are in these days the conclusions of physical science[3]. This forced him and others who attempted to found a religion acceptable to both Jew and Greek, to use language which could be interpreted in their own sense by either. His Supreme Being is One, as Israel declared that her God was One, but, by a not immodest metaphor, he contains within himself

[1] As will be seen later, the post-Christian Gnostics of the IInd cent. generally attributed the existence of evil to the escape of one of the syzygies from the control of her spouse and her consequent fall into matter. See Chapter VIII, *infra*.

[2] The excessive reverence of the Samaritans for the Pentateuch is well brought out by Cowley in the *Encyc. Bibl. s.v.* Samaritans. He says it was the only part of the Jewish books which they took over and held sacred (col. 4260). Simon in the *Great Announcement* thought it necessary to " explain " each of the Five Books separately. See Hippolytus, *op. cit.* Bk VI. c. 1, §§ 15, 16, pp. 253–258, Cruice.

[3] Throughout all the philosophical and religious literature of the time, it seems to have been sufficient to quote " Orpheus and the other theologists " to command a hearing. See Clement of Alexandria, *passim*, for examples.

the power of becoming both male and female, as Adonis, or Attis, or Dionysos, or, to take the mythological person he most resembles, the Orphic Phanes, was both male and female[1]. Simon also goes out of his way to affirm that his first syzygy or pair, Mind and Thought, are in the second world called Heaven and Earth, and thus forms a pretty close parallel to the Orphic couple Uranos and Ge[2]. But he is careful to mix with this explanations which shall also accord with the account of creation given in the Book of Genesis. He who standeth, hath stood, and will stand, *i.e.* the Eternal Being who is not liable to fall or corruption, and is the " Father " of the " Middle Space " is no less the " I am that I am " of Exodus than the Father of gods and men of Homer. So, too, his companion from the beginning, called Silence, because she has no independent existence until he gives utterance to his thought, resembles the Nux or Night of Orpheus from whom Phanes begot Heaven and Earth ; but she is also, as Simon expressly says, the Spirit of God which moved over the face of the waters in the Mosaic account of the Creation[3]. If, again, Simon makes his first pair of " Roots " in the second world Heaven and Earth, his second pair, Voice and Name, he declares to be equivalent to the Sun and Moon, and his third, Reason and Desire, to Air and Water[4]. This, he expressly says, is because the Book of Genesis says that three clear days elapsed before the Sun and Moon came into being, and these three " days " are an allusion to the Boundless Power and the first pair Mind and Thought[5]. To a much greater extent than Philo, therefore, Simon uses the religious traditions of both Greeks and Hebrews to give sanction to his own speculations.

The use of the word aeon, which our English Testament translates " age " (*saeculum*) as the generic name of the six Roots or Powers reflected in the second universe, seems also to have peculiar signification in this connection. Among the

[1] See Chapter IV, p. 123, *supra*.
[2] See especially Fr. 239 in Abel's *Orphica*.
[3] Hippolytus, *op. cit.* Bk VI. c. 1, § 14, pp. 252, 253, Cruice.
[4] *Ibid.* Bk VI. c. 1, § 13, pp. 251, 252, Cruice.
[5] *Ibid. loc. cit.* Cf. Amélineau, *Gnost. Ég.* p. 39.

Greeks, Hesiod sang of a golden age, succeeded by others of silver, of brass, of one unnamed metal, and finally one of iron ; and the Orphics, working after their manner on older materials, assigned the first of these ages to their god Phanes, and the others to Night, Uranos, Kronos, and Zeus in succession, asserting that the last age would be that of Dionysos[1]. The use of the word by Simon seems to show that he conceived his emanations or " Roots " as succeeding one another and perhaps depending from one another like the links of a chain. But as he had already personified these emanations, we have the curious result that he considered them both as persons—or, to be more accurate, aspects of the Deity—and spaces of time. Nor was this all. The great spread given to the Chaldaean star-worship throughout the East by the events described in Chapter III above, had caused the stars to be accepted by every nation in the Hellenist world as the most convenient types of divinity[2]. The planets, including in that phrase the Sun and Moon, were all known by the names of the most important gods in the various pantheons of all the nations of antiquity, and were thought in some not very clearly defined way to be identified with the divinities whose names they bore[3]. Even before the time of Alexander, the Platonic cosmogony had made of the stars and planets habitations where the souls of men were supposed to rest on their way to mortal bodies[4] ; and Philo, while admitting that the stars were the rulers of earthly

---

[1] Abel's *Orphica*, pp. 186, 254, 255.

[2] " The visible and generated Gods." So Alcmaeon of Crotona and Xenocrates both call stars and planets gods. See Clem. Alex. *Protrept.* c. VI. ; Plato, *Timaeus*, c. XV. The prophets of the Jews, indeed, blamed their co-religionists for " worshipping the sun towards the east " as Ezekiel saw them doing in the Temple, or for " serving all the host of heaven " as Jeremiah says the inhabitants of Jerusalem did ; but their reproaches make it plain that the bulk of the nation were in this respect like their Gentile neighbours.

[3] So Clem. Alex. *Strom.* Bk VI. c. 13, says the worship of the sun, moon, and stars was instituted, so that the nations might not become utterly godless.

[4] See Bouché-Leclercq, *L'Astrologie grecque*, Paris, 1899, p. 21, for references.

things, could do no more than remind his readers that they were not independent rulers, but only viceroys of Yahweh[1]. Hence Simon, when he called three of his aeons by the names of Earth, Sun, and Moon, made them places or worlds as well as persons and periods of time. It was an extraordinary complication of ideas from which none of the Gnostics who followed him succeeded in entirely freeing themselves[2].

To return, however, to Simon's system of emanations. Have we any right to consider that the Heaven and Earth, Sun and Moon, and Water and Air, with which he peopled his second universe, were those which are perceptible by our senses, or did he regard them as existing above our ken and as merely the patterns which were in their turn reflected into our universe ? Hippolytus unfortunately breaks off his quotations from the *Great Announcement* at this point, and his own report of Simon's doctrines is neither lucid nor implicitly to be trusted. Irenaeus, however, writing half a century before Hippolytus, declares that it was the female aeon Thought, whom we have seen is equivalent in the second or intermediate world to Ge or Earth, " who, comprehending the wish of the Father, descended to the lower regions, and there produced angels and the lower authorities (αἱ κάτω ἐξουσίαι) who made the universe (κόσμος)[3]." If we believe, as seems most probable, that Simon carried his theory of the lower world being a reflection of the upper throughout all existing things, it follows that the second world, containing as we have seen Heaven and Earth, Sun and Moon, and

---

[1] Philo, *de Monarch.* Bk I. c. 1.

[2] Except perhaps Marcion. But we have so little literature remaining which can with any certainty be attributed to the Marcionites that we cannot speak with any certainty as to his phraseology. In his treatise against the Valentinians (c. xx.) Tertullian gibes at that sect for " thinking the different heavens intelligent, and for making angels of them."

[3] Irenaeus, Bk I. c. 16, § 2, p. 192, Harvey. Theodoret, *Haer. Fab.* Bk I. c. 5, echoes the statement, and Hippolytus, Bk VI. c. 1, § 19, p. 263, Cruice, gives what is probably the original Greek of Irenaeus. Hatch, *H. L.* pp. 185, 186, points out that Philo held not only that the angels were God's instruments in making the worlds, but the patterns after which they were made. Cf. Philo, *de Monarch.* Bk II. c. 6.

Air and Water together with "the Father" in whom the six were contained, was the pattern or paradigmatic world which was reflected in the lower universe to which we belong. In this case it is probable that the six "Roots" again changed their generic name, and after having been called powers (δυνάμεις) in the primal world, and aeons in the second, were now designated angels and authorities. If this conjecture is right, we have here a parallel to the chain of being fabled by the Orphics which, beginning with the gods, descended through demi-gods, heroes, and demons down to men. An accurate knowledge of the different ranks of this supramundane hierarchy was, as has been said, of great importance for magical purposes such as exorcism, and its description occupied a great part of the Enochian literature[1].

Simon, however, had still to account for the creation of man and the part which he played in the scheme of the universe. His reverence for Moses prevented him from directly contradicting the statement in Genesis that Yahweh "formed man out of the dust of the ground," and this he echoes in the words of the Septuagint, which speaks of God moulding (ἔπλασε) man by "taking dust (χοῦς) from the Earth (Γῆ)." The part here played by the Yahweh of Genesis he transfers to "the Father" of his second or intermediate world[2]; and as Genesis says that God made man in his own image, he is also compelled to say that man was originally made in the likeness of the Father. But "the Father" of Simon's intermediate world was, as we have seen, an hermaphrodite, or rather a male containing a female power within himself[3]. Hence man was originally both male and female, or in the words of the *Great Announcement*

---

[1] These "orders" of supernatural beings passed into orthodox Christianity. Cf. the εἴτε θρόνοι, εἴτε κυριότητες, εἴτε ἀρχαί, εἴτε ἐξουσίαι of Coloss. i. 16, whence the "Thrones, Dominations, Virtues, Princedoms, Powers" of Milton. The functions of all these different orders are set out by Dionysius the Areopagite so-called, and present a certain likeness to Simon's ideas as given in the text. See Lupton in *Dict. Christian Biog. s.v.* Dionysius.

[2] That is Zeus, "Father of Gods and Men"; not the Juppiter Optimus Maximus of later philosophy.

[3] Possibly an allusion to the "rib" story of Genesis.

" not simple, but double according to image and resemblance[1]."
But this was clearly not the man of this world as we know him,
but the Heavenly or Archetypal Man who remained in the world
above ours, and was, as Philo held, a man-woman[2]. How did
Simon account for the separation of the sexes, and its influence
upon subsequent humanity ?

The answer to this question involves Simon's ideas as to
the cause of evil in this world and the means by which man can
escape from it. Man was, as we have seen, formed out of dust,
but to make him, in the words of Genesis, " a living soul," it
was necessary that he should be animated by the breath
($\pi\nu\epsilon\hat{v}\mu a$) of the Divinity. So efficiently was this done that
everyone, as Simon said, has within him potentially but not
in act, " that which is blessed and incorruptible," that is to
say, " He who standeth, hath stood and will stand," or in
other words the " Father " of the intermediate world. " He
it is," he goes on to say, " who stood above in the Unbegotten
Power, who stands below, coming into being by reflection ($\dot{\epsilon}\nu$
$\epsilon\dot{\iota}\kappa\acute{o}\nu\iota$) in the rush of the waters, and will stand above by the
side of the blessed and Unbegotten Power if he should receive
reflection or image ($\dot{\epsilon}\grave{a}\nu$ $\dot{\epsilon}\xi\epsilon\iota\kappa\sigma\nu\iota\sigma\theta\hat{\eta}$)[3]." For " there are three
who stand, and unless there are three aeons that stand, the
unbegotten one, who according to them [Qy. the Hebrews ?]
was borne over the face of the water, is not in her proper place
in the universe ($o\dot{v}$ $\kappa\sigma\sigma\mu\epsilon\hat{\iota}\tau a\iota$)[4]. The which unbegotten one is
fashioned by resemblance as perfect and heavenly, but becomes,
in regard to Thought alone, inferior to the Unbegotten Power."
This Unbegotten Power, he goes on to say in words that remind
one of several different myths[5], is the "One power cloven in twain

---

[1] $o\dot{v}\chi$ $\dot{a}\pi\lambda o\hat{v}\nu$, $\dot{a}\lambda\lambda\grave{a}$ $\delta\iota\pi\lambda o\hat{v}\nu$ $\kappa a\tau$' $\epsilon\dot{\iota}\kappa\acute{o}\nu a$ $\kappa a\grave{\iota}$ $\kappa a\theta$' $\dot{o}\mu o\iota\acute{\omega}\sigma\iota\nu$. Hippolytus,
Bk VI. c. 1, § 14, p. 253, Cruice.

[2] So Philo, *Legg. Allegor.* III. p. 1089, Mangey; *Quis rer. divin.*
p. 503 *id.* Cf. Döllinger, *Jud. und Heid.* Eng. ed. II. p. 430.

[3] Hippolytus, Bk VI. c. 1, § 17, p. 259, Cruice.

[4] See last note.

[5] So Iacchos is at once the father, son, and spouse of Persephone.
Horus is by his identification with Osiris in like manner the son, spouse
and brother of Isis. The seeking and finding seems to be an allusion to
this last pair. Cf. *P.S.B.A.* 1914, p. 93.

above and below, who gives birth to itself, increases itself, seeks itself, finds itself, being its own mother, its own father, its own sister, its own spouse (σύζυγος), its own daughter, its own son, a mother-father [and is] *one*, being the root of all the universes[1]." It was the Thought of this Power who was charged with bringing the Divine Spark to this world ; but apparently, while she was brooding over the face of the waters, she was seized by the angels and authorities whom she had produced, " through motives of jealousy, because they were unwilling to be looked upon as the progeny of any other being[2]." These words are put into the mouth of Simon by Irenaeus, who goes on to say that Thought was thus prevented from returning to the Father and was shut up in a human body.   At this point, the account of Irenaeus agrees with that of the *Philosophumena* which narrates that (according to Simon) the world-making angels caused Thought (Ennoia) to enter one body after another, including that of Helen of Troy (*causa teterrima belli*), until she finally entered into the body of Simon's companion Helena whom he found in a brothel at Tyre[3].   Hippolytus says, however, that Simon made up this part of the story out of shame as regards his disciples[4] in order to explain his companying with Helena, and it may be noticed that he nowhere quotes the *Great Announcement* in its support[5].   Epiphanius, who seems

---

[1] Hippolytus, Bk VI. c. 1, § 17, p. 259, Cruice.   For the μήτηρ, πατήρ of the text it is necessary to read μητροπάτωρ unless we are to believe that the author is here repeating without rhyme or reason the statement already made in the same sentence that the power he is describing is its own mother and its own father.   The expression μητροπάτωρ is found in an address to Zeus attributed to Orpheus and quoted by Clement of Alexandria, *Strom.* Bk v. c. 14.   Cf. Frgs. 238, 239 of Abel's *Orphica.*   He remarks concerning it that, by this μητροπάτωρ, Orpheus meant not only birth from the Μὴ ὤν, but also " gave occasion to those who bring in the emanations and perhaps imagine a spouse of God,"—which gives some colour to the surmise that Clement may have been acquainted with Simon's writings.

[2] Irenaeus, Bk I. c. 16, § 2, p. 192, Harvey.   A similar motive was assigned by the Orphics for the murder of the infant Dionysos by the Titans.

[3] Hippolytus, Bk I. c. 16, § 19, pp. 263, 264, Cruice.

[4] τοὺς μαθητὰς αἰδούμενος τοῦτον τὸν μῦθον ἔπλασεν, *loc. cit.*

[5] See *ibid.*, p. 264, Cruice.

to have used the same documents as Irenaeus, gives a different reason for the conduct of the world-making angels from that of Irenaeus, and makes out that they were seduced by the beauty of "Epinoia," as he calls Ennoia or Thought, the female aeon who had come down, and detained her below out of sensual desire[1]. Both Irenaeus and Epiphanius are agreed that Simon in some way "redeemed" Helena, although they do not say in what way, and Hippolytus declares that Simon having purified Helena, in like manner brought salvation to men by his own discernment[2]. Why Simon should thus have power of salvation he does not explain directly, but he, Irenaeus, and Epiphanius alike tell us, by what seems to be a wilful or unconscious misinterpretation of the account in the New Testament[3], that Simon gave himself out as the Supreme God, who, seeing that the angels mismanaged this world from their desire for rule, came here to put it right and descended through the different worlds, changing his shape in each to accord with that of the rulers therein, until he appeared here as man, " although he was not a man[4]." Hippolytus further says, as does Irenaeus, that

[1] Epiphanius, *op. cit.* Bk I., *Haer.* XXI. c. 11 (p. 125 of vol. II. pt I. of Oehler). Probably this idea is a mere echo of the story in Genesis vi. 2, of the " sons of God " being captivated by the " daughters of men," which is much insisted on in the Enochian literature. Cf. Cumont, *Recherches sur le Manichéisme; La Séduction des Archontes* or Chapter XIII, *infra* for later elaborations of the legend.

[2] Τὴν δὲ Ἑλένην λυτρωσάμενος, οὕτως τοῖς ἀνθρώποις σωτηρίαν παρέσχε διὰ τῆς ἰδίας ἐπιγνώσεως. See note 3 p. 190, *supra.* The ἐπίγνωσις of the text seems to indicate that Simon discovered the way of salvation not by any revelation from a higher power, but by his own intelligence and examination. Cf. what he says (Hippolytus, *Phil.* Bk VI. c. 16, p. 256, Cruice) about the knowledge of Gentile writings being sufficient for the ἐπίγνωσις τῶν ὅλων.

[3] Acts viii. 9, 10, only says that Simon bewitched the people of Samaria, giving himself out to be some great one (λέγων εἶναί τινα ἑαυτὸν μέγαν); and that it was the people who said of him : " This man is the so-called great power of God " (Οὗτός ἐστιν ἡ δύναμις τοῦ θεοῦ ἡ καλουμένη μεγάλη). He was therefore only in the same position as Paul and Barnabas in Phrygia when they were hailed by the populace as Zeus and Hermes respectively. Cf. Acts xiv. 12.

[4] Irenaeus, Bk I. c. 16, § 2, p. 193, Harvey ; Epiphanius as in n. 1 *supra.* This episode of the Saviour changing his form so as not to be

Simon was alleged " to suffer in Judaea in the likeness of Jesus, although in appearance only, and to have appeared to the Jews as Son, to the Samaritans as Father, and to the other nations as the Holy Spirit[1]." His death he accounts for by the story, found nowhere else in post-Christian literature, that at some place, the name of which has slipped out of the text of the *Philosophumena*, Simon

" taught sitting under a plane-tree. Moreover, exposure being at hand through long delay, he said that if he were buried alive he would rise again the third day. And a grave having been dug by his orders by his disciples, he directed that he should be buried. His disciples did what he commanded, but he remained there to this day. For he was not Christ[2]."

In all this account, Hippolytus gives an entirely different account from that of the Clementines, with the manifest purpose of holding Simon up to obloquy as one of the " false Christs " predicted in the New Testament. It is obvious also that, so far from giving us Simon's pre-Christian teaching, he is here

recognized by the powers of the heavens through which he passes on his way to earth, is a favourite one in the post-Christian Apocryphal literature. Cf. R. H. Charles, *The Ascension of Isaiah*, p. 62. In the *Pistis Sophia* (for which see Chapter X, *infra*), Jesus in like manner changes His appearance in each heaven on His descent to earth. When He returns in His proper shape the spirits in every " place " into which He enters fling themselves on their faces and cry : " How did the Lord of the Universe change himself, so that we knew him not ? " : see p. 21 Copt. *et al.* The " Docetic " theory which made the earthly body of Jesus a phantasm or illusion appears again in the heresy of the Valentinians and elsewhere. See Chapter IX, *infra*.

[1] Hippolytus, *loc. cit.* p. 265, Cruice.

[2] *Ibid.* § 20, p. 267, Cruice. The story here told is in direct contradiction to the received tradition of the Church, that Simon met his death when attempting to fly heavenward before the Emperor Nero. That given in the text seems to be taken from the doings of some Indian Yogi, and the idea of Simon teaching " sitting under a plane tree " is distinctly Buddhistic. It is mentioned by no other writer than Hippolytus ; but Justin Martyr (*First Apolog.* c. 26) says that he persuaded his followers that he would never die, and that some in Justin's day still believed this. A sort of echo of it appears in the *Acts of Peter and Paul*, where it is said that the body of Simon after being dashed to pieces was kept by the Emperor Nero for three days " to see whether he would rise again."

handing down a garbled account of some tradition of the heresiarch's disciples after his death.

That the stories told by the Fathers, except when they are quoting immediately from the *Great Announcement*, are not a trustworthy account of Simon's doctrines is evident from their manifest inconsistency. If Simon's disciples believed, as Hippolytus says, in the lawfulness of promiscuous intercourse, why should he feel called upon to justify to them by an artifice his connection with Helena ? If, too, Simon, or the Supreme Being in his likeness, came down from the highest heaven to earth for the sake of redeeming his spouse Epinoia there held captive, why did he not return with her when recovered, and for what purpose did he simulate death in Judaea ? Nor is there any plausible reason assigned for the angels' detention of Epinoia on earth by Hippolytus, which he attributes, like Irenaeus before him, to jealousy and the desire for rule, any more than by Epiphanius, who will have it to be caused by their concupiscence—a story probably derived from the account of the Watchers in the *Book of Enoch*. Hippolytus makes Epinoia come to earth to establish, instead of taking away, the rule of the angels, who were by his account her own progeny ; and if the angels were, as Epiphanius says, inflamed with love for her, the last thing they would be likely to do would be to transform her out of her first and heavenly shape, and finally place her in a brothel—as they are said to have done with Helena, Simon's mistress.

The key to Simon's theory on the connexion between the salvation of mankind and its division into sexes is probably to be found in a paragraph in the *Philosophumena* in which Hippolytus seems to quote directly from the *Great Announcement* :

" And because," he says, " the beginning of the generation of things which are begotten[1] is from fire, he [Simon] devises (κατανόει) a certain similar figure. Generation of all such things exists, [and] the beginning of the desire of generation comes from fire. So, for example, to desire changeable generation is called being inflamed

---

[1] ἀπὸ πυρὸς ἡ ἀρχὴ τῆς γενέσεως ἐστι τῶν γεννωμένων.

with love.   But the fire, which is one, undergoes two changes.   In the man," he says, " the blood which is hot and yellow as typifying fire is changed into seed ; but in the woman, the self-same blood is changed into milk[1].   And the [result of the ?] change of the masculine blood is begetting ; but the [result of the ?] change of the feminine, the nourishment of that which is begotten[2].   This," he says, "is the flaming sword turning both ways to guard the way to the Tree of Life.   For the blood turns into seed and milk, and that power becomes [at once] mother and father of the things which are born, and the increase of those which are nursed, having no need of any external help and being sufficient unto itself.   The Tree of Life," he says, "is guarded by the flaming sword turning both ways, as we have said, [and] the seventh power which contains all things, and which is stored up in the six powers, [comes forth ?] from the sword.   For, if the flaming sword did not turn both ways, that beautiful tree would be corrupted and destroyed.   But if the Word which is stored up potentially in them (the six powers), being the lord of the proper place, is turned into seed and milk, within it is born the Word of souls, beginning from the smallest spark, which will be magnified and will increase and will become a boundless power, unchangeable in the unchanging aeon, and it is born no more until [it reaches ?] the boundless aeon[3]."

[1] Clement of Alexandria (*Paedagogus*, Bk I. c. 6) says practically the same thing.

[2] Καὶ γίνεται ἡ τοῦ ἄρρενος τροπή, γένεσις· ἡ δὲ τῆς θηλείας τροπή, τροφὴ τοῦ γεννωμένῳ.   Note the curious jingle between τροπή and τροφή, γένεσις and γεννωμένῳ.

[3] Hippolytus, Bk VI. c. 1, § 17, pp. 259, 260, Cruice.   That this refers to the conjunction of man with his twin-soul or affinity is certain from Hippolytus' former quotation from the *Apophasis*, that man was made by God οὐχ ἁπλοῦν, ἀλλὰ διπλοῦν κατ᾿ εἰκόνα καὶ καθ᾿ ὁμοίωσιν " not single, but two-fold according to copy and resemblance ": and that he will " perish with the world " unless he be made into the likeness of the Spirit who was borne upon the face of the waters, and who was, like that of which it was the reflection, androgyne (Hippolytus, *op. cit.* Bk VI. c. 1, p. 253, Cruice).   " But if he be made into this likeness," Hippolytus continues, " and is born from an indivisible point as it is written in the *Apophasis*, that which is small will become great.   And that which is great will exist in the boundless and incorruptible aeon, which will not be born again."   Besides the idea of the indivisible point, which we shall meet with again in the Bruce Papyrus (for which see Chapter X, *infra*), it seems

The meaning of this very complicated and confused imagery —which we may be sure Hippolytus has purposely made as obscure and ridiculous as possible—seems to be this. In the two superior or heavenly worlds which we have called the primal and the second, the " roots " are male and female after the model of the Supreme Being. But this only means that the female is the external manifestation of the male, *within* whom she has at one time been contained. No thought of sex, as we understand it, enters into their relations, and no progeny follows from their conjugation, the lower world coming into life after the pattern of the upper by an impulse which, although due in the first instance to the male, is translated into action by the female member of the first syzygy. But with our universe and the appearance of man, a change in the system takes place. Although our world, constituted after the heavenly model, contains the three pairs, Heaven and Earth, Sun and Moon, Air and Water, and is animated by the breath of life brought from above by Epinoia or Ennoia, man is formed from previously-existing matter and is therefore largely made up of an element hostile or repugnant to God. Lest the Divine spark within him should free itself from matter and return to the world above, each human soul has been divided, as Plato tells us in the *Symposium*[1], and the two parts placed in different bodies so that the male is imperfect without the female and the female without the male, and the soul can make no effort to raise itself in the world of being until it meets and is conjoined with its affinity. This is probably in Simon's view the device

evident that Simon was here teaching that those who find their twin-souls will rise in the scale of being and thus escape the cycle of changing existences dreaded by the Orphics (see Chapter IV, *supra*). An explanation of the metaphor of the flaming sword is suggested later. See note 3 on p. 67 of vol. II, *infra*.

[1] Plato, *Symposium*, cc. 17, 18. Diotima later on in the same Dialogue says that it is an old story that those who are in love are seeking their lost half. In one of the documents of the *Pistis Sophia*, it is said that " the servants of the Sphere of Destiny " after making the soul of man, divide it into two parts, and give one part to a man and another to a woman who are then bound to come together (no matter how far apart they may be) and to unite, when a new soul is the result (*Pistis Sophia*, p. 346. Copt.).

of the angels, who have brought it about, according to Hippolytus, in order that Epinoia, the mother of life, may remain longer in the world and therefore prolong their rule[1]. But they are defeated by the Divine arrangement, which compels the two parts of the soul, after having once entered upon the round of mutable generation (ἡ μεταβλητὴ γένεσις), to change into one body after another according to the Orphic theory of transmigration until each meets with its twin. Thus did the soul of Helen of Troy pass from one body into another until in the shape of Helena of Tyre it met with its own affinity in the body of Simon. Then it became again bisexual after the image of the boundless power to which it would again rise. Thus must it be with all mankind until all the souls are thus disentangled from matter[2]. According to Hippolytus, this event is to coincide with the deliverance (λύσις) of the world, which seems to mean that it is to be freed from the rule of the angels. Irenaeus and Epiphanius twist this into the assertion that it is to be dissolved, while one of the later Gnostic documents says that it is to be " caught up," that is to say, reabsorbed by the world of which it is the image. But Hippolytus expressly

---

[1] So in the *Pistis Sophia* (p. 37, Copt.), Jesus says that the angels bound in the stars were, until His coming, in the habit of turning about and devouring their own matter, from which the souls of men and other animals were made, in order that their rule might endure the longer.

[2] Probably this is the meaning of the well-known saying of Jesus, generally quoted as coming from the *Gospel according to the Egyptians*, in answer to Salome's enquiry as to the time of the coming of His kingdom: Ὅταν τὸ τῆς αἰσχύνης ἔνδυμα πατήσητε, καὶ ὅταν γένηται τὰ δύο ἕν, καὶ τὸ ἔξω ὡς τὸ ἔσω; καὶ τὸ ἄρρεν μετὰ τῆς θηλείας, οὔτε ἄρρεν οὔτε θῆλυ. "When ye tread under foot the garment of shame, and when the two shall be one, and the outside as the inside, and the male with the female, neither male nor female." See Hilgenfeld, *N. T. extra Canon. recept.*, Lipsiae, 1884, vol. IV. p. 44. "The outside as the inside" may refer to the body and the rib which was in the Genesis story taken out of it. So the *Pistis Sophia* (p. 378, Copt.) speaks of "the Light of Lights, the places of Truth and Goodness, the place of the Holy of Holies, the place of the Holy of all Holies, the place in which there is neither male nor female, nor shape, but Light everlasting, unspeakable." Hippolytus, *op. cit.* Bk v. c. 7, p. 146, Cruice, carrying this a step further, speaks of heaven as a place "where there is neither male nor female, but a new creature, a new man who is androgyne (ἀρρηνόθηλυς)."

includes this last doctrine among those invented by "those
who imitated the error" of Simon Magus, or in other words by
his successors[1], and it need not therefore be here discussed.

Whence Simon derived the doctrine of which we get glimpses
in the *Great Announcement* will probably remain in doubt until
we recover more fragments of that document. It appears
likely, however, that he drew from a number of sources. Even
in his day and after the wholesale depopulation of Samaria by
the Syrians, Egyptians, and Jews, there must have remained
many of the inhabitants who were lineal descendants of that
mixed Semitic and Persian stock who "feared the Lord and
served brazen images." Hence his speculations may well have
been influenced by the Persian religion of Zoroastrianism and
Mazdeism, and some have thought that they can see in them
traces of the primitive fire worship of the Magi[2]. Yet he
need not have gone so far, for, as we have seen, his idea of fire
as the origin of all things might well be taken from a too literal
interpretation of a passage in the Samaritan Pentateuch. So
with regard to the six "roots," although they may have been
mere copies of the Persian Amshaspands, they may also have
come from a Pythagorean or Orphic source, since Athamas the
Pythagorean is said to have taught that "there are four roots—
fire, water, air, earth; for from these is the genesis of what is
produced," and a verse of Empedocles is preserved which
makes the same assertion[3]. The likeness of Simon's system
to Egyptian and Alexandrian teaching is even closer. In
ancient Egypt there was, as M. Maspero thinks, a well-defined
system of correspondences including three worlds, each of which
was a likeness or reflection of the preceding. At Hermopolis,
too, there was worshipped an ogdoad or family of four pairs of
gods and goddesses who on the same authority were merely
attributes of one higher deity[4]. So in the tract *de Iside et
Osiride*[5], we are told that genesis or coming into being is the
image or reflection in matter of that which really exists, and

---

[1] Hippolytus, Bk VI. c. 1, § 19, p. 266, Cruice; Irenaeus, Bk I. c. 16,
§ 2, p. 194, Harvey; Epiphanius, *Haer.* XXI. c. 2, p. 124, Oehler.

[2] Franck, *Le Gnost. Ég.* p. 212.   [3] Clem. Alex. *Strom.* VI. c. 2.

[4] Maspero, *Ét. Égyptol.* II. pp. 187 and 385.

[5] *de Is. et Os.* cc. LIII. LIV. and LVI.

that Horus, who seems here to represent the perceptible world, is the εἰκών or image of the νοητὸς κόσμος or ideal world, and is the child of this last world and matter. After all, there is little more in this than an extension of Plato's theory of ideas which are the paradigms or patterns of perceptible things : but as Simon, according to the Clementines[1], had studied in Alexandria he may well have acquired such a notion either from Plato's writings direct, or, as is more likely, from the Alexandrian religion of Serapis and Isis as set forth in the tract in question.

Of the history of the Simonian sect, we know very little more than has been said. The Fathers accuse the Simonians of leading immoral lives, of teaching the advisability of promiscuous intercourse, and of being addicted to magic[2]. Irenaeus declares that they worshipped an image of Simon in the likeness of Jupiter, and another of Helena in the shape of Athena[3], to which Hippolytus adds that they were exceedingly angry if any one ventured to call these statues either Simon or Helena and instantly cast him forth of the sect as being ignorant of their mysteries[4]. Eusebius—a very late witness—adds to this that they worshipped these images with " prostrations and incense and sacrifices and libations[5]," which taken with the other statements seems to show that the Simonians, or perhaps only the pre-Christian followers of Simon, really took part in the worship of the Greek gods Zeus and Athena, possibly by way of complaisance with the Greek and Roman rulers of Samaria, and that the likening of their statues to Simon and Helena was only the patristic gloss on the fact. Epiphanius goes further and attributes to them " mysteries of iniquity " and secret and obscene rites, including the filthy parody of the Eucharist depicted by the late J. K. Huysmans in his novel of *Là-Bas*[6]. But this also was an accusation common to the adherents and opponents of Christianity at the time he wrote.

---

[1] Clem. *Hom.* II. c. 22.

[2] Irenaeus, Bk I. c. 16, § 3, p. 194, Harvey ; Hippolytus, *op. cit.* Bk VI. c. 1, § 20, p. 266, Cruice.

[3] Irenaeus and Hippolytus where last quoted.

[4] Hippolytus where last quoted.

[5] Eusebius, *Hist. Eccl.* Bk II. c. 13.

[6] Epiph. *Haer.* XXI. c. 4 (p. 125, vol. II. pt I., Oehler).

He also says that their sacrifices were offered to "the Father of the Universes" (τῶν ὅλων) through the rulers and authorities[1], and that they thought that the God of the Jews was one of the angels in this lower universe who created man and divided the nations among them by lot[2], an idea of which there is a trace in the Book of Daniel[3]. But it is plain that Epiphanius, in his desire to prove that Simon is the parent of all subsequent heresy, is here mixing together the opinions of different Gnostic sects with a result inconsistent even in his own eyes. That the later Simonians had secret rites after the manner of those described by Lucian in the case of Alexander of Abonoteichos[4] is likely enough, but rests on no real proof[5].

Of the extent and persistence of the religion set on foot by Simon we have some few indications, although these, too, hardly agree with one another. Irenaeus declares that he was succeeded in the leadership of the sect by Menander[6], another Samaritan, and this is confirmed by Epiphanius, Philaster, and all the lesser writers on heresy down to and including Eusebius[7]. Although there seems nothing new in the doctrine which they assign to Menander, it is very probable that, after Simon's death, the tenets of the sect underwent a good deal of modification. According to Theodoret, the Simonians spread chiefly in Syria, Phrygia, and Rome[8]. Justin Martyr, writing in the reign of Antoninus Pius, speaks of their school as still existing apparently in Rome[9]. Origen, in the following reign, says indeed

[1] See last note.

[2] Epiph. *Haer.* XXIV. c. 1, p. 145, Oehler. It is here attributed to Basilides, but Epiphanius has before said that this last borrowed his ideas from "Simon and Satornilus."

[3] Dan. x. 13.

[4] Lucian, *Pseudomantis, passim.*

[5] Epiphanius says that Simon taught none could be saved unless he learned [Simon's] system of initiation (μυσταγωγία). See Epiph. *Haer.* XXI. c. 4, p. 127, Oehler.

[6] Irenaeus, Bk I. c. 17, p. 195, Harvey.

[7] Epiph. *Haer.* XXII. p. 133, Oehler; Eusebius, *Hist. Eccl.* Bk III. c. 26. Cf. Justin Martyr, *First Apol.* c. 26. Schmiedel, *s.v.* Simon Magus in *Encyc. Bibl.*, says the exact contrary—a curious slip.

[8] Theodoret, *Haer. Fab.* I. 1.

[9] See note 7 *supra*.

in his tract against Celsus that there were no Simonians to be
found anywhere throughout the world[1] ; but he was probably
mistaken in this, as Eusebius in the reign of Constantine speaks
of them as still numerous, although forced to hide themselves[2].
After this, and so soon as the Church, now triumphant, began
in her turn to persecute, they no doubt either became converted
to Christianity or joined other sects.

In these matters, as in many others concerning the Gnostics,
the Fathers of the Church were badly informed. The Gnostic
indifference to outward forms of religion made it very easy for
any body of Gnostics to conceal themselves in time of persecution[3], and thus to resist in the most practical way any attempt
to estimate their true strength, or the relations of the different
sects to one another. Gnosticism was, as the Church was to find
out later, a hydra, the heads of which when cut off renewed
themselves with amazing rapidity. Moreover, the very essence
of Gnosticism was secrecy for all but the initiated, and if we may
judge from the words of the *Great Announcement* quoted above,
the Simonians took abundant care when they committed any of
their doctrines to writing that the result should be unintelligible
without a good deal of previous instruction. But if the fragments
quoted are, as seems fairly certain, the work either of Simon
Magus himself or of some prominent and early member of his
school, the Fathers were abundantly justified in regarding him
as the source of all subsequent Gnosticism. The syncretic
religion which they unfold seems to have been admirably
adapted to catch those " barbarian " enquirers, of whom there
were evidently many in the first years of our era, who were
trying by might and main to reconcile the traditions of Judaism
with the Greek learning and culture for the first time brought
within their reach. The system of terribly forced interpretation of the Jewish scriptures employed by the Simonians was

[1] Origen, *cont. Celsus*, Bk VI. c. 11.
[2] Eusebius, *Hist. eccl.* Bk II. c. 13.
[3] Tertullian, *Scorpiace*, c. 1.   Eusebius, *H. E.* Bk II. c. 1, says, speaking
of his own times, that those who follow Simon's most scoundrelly
(μιαρωτάτην) heresy were baptized into the Church, and kept their own
doctrines in secret till detected and expelled. Cf. Origen, *c. Cels.* Bk VI.
c. 11.

probably their own invention, and would certainly never have passed muster in a community possessed of a modicum of literary sense[1]; yet it enabled them, as has been said, to turn their backs upon the plain meaning of the books of the Old Testament. By their doctrine of emanation, whether derived from Persian sources or not, they contrived, perhaps for the first time, to bridge the huge gulf fixed by the philosophy and physics of the time between their Supreme Being and the gross matter which was thought to exist independently of and in opposition to him; while their scheme of redemption, like that of the Orphics from whom they apparently borrowed, went far, as they boasted, to rob death of its terrors.

These features we find reproduced in the teachings of nearly every later sect and school into which we shall have to enquire, and although our information as to their doctrines is not exact enough to enable us to determine the extent of the obligations of all of them to the teaching of Simon, the chances are that in every case there was a more or less conscious borrowing. Nor did the influence of the Samaritan *magus* cease with the suppression of the many heresies which the Fathers declared to be inspired by him. His speculations as to the succession of heavens and of orders of heavenly beings passed into the teaching of the Church[2] and obtained too firm a footing there to be dislodged until the German Reformation. The memory of them extended even beyond its pale, and while, in the VIIth century of our era, they came to inspire such cosmology as is taught in the Koran, the system of Sephiroth or successive

---

[1] It was of course quite different from the Cabalistic methods, ridiculous as those were, of the Essenes and other Jews, from the acrostics of the Orphics, and from the allegories of Philo. With a touching belief in the verbal inspiration of the Pentateuch, Simon and his followers claimed that every word of it must be true and a revelation even when transferred into another context. Thus they claimed to teach obstetrics from geographical phrases. The only modern parallel is to be found among the Puritans of our own Civil War, who, as Sir Walter Scott wrote, were accustomed to pervert the language of Scripture by adapting it to modern events, and kept a Bible lying on the Table of the House for reference as to the better conduct of its business.

[2] See J. Turmel, " L'Angélologie depuis le faux Denys l'Aréopagite," *Rev. d'Hist. et Litt. Rel.* Paris, t. IV. No. 3 (1898), pp. 219 *sqq.*

emanations of the Deity, which underlies the farrago of mystical nonsense called in the Middle Ages the Cabala of the Jews, is directly derived from them. It may even be said that the influence of Simon's doctrines is not even now extinct in Europe, for in the writings of Swedenborg, which still find exponents, many of his ideas seem to be revived.

That Simon's system as described in the *Great Announcement* was the result either of deep philosophic speculation or of original thought can hardly be said. Its one novel feature was the rather clumsy fusion of the Orphic cosmogony with the Mosaic account of creation, which reads like a parody on Philo's well-thought-out doctrine. Philo was born, apparently, about 25 B.C., and was therefore in all probability a few years older than Simon, so that such a parody is not altogether impossible. One of the main differences between the two systems is that to the asceticism of Philo and the Essenes Simon opposed, not perhaps a recommendation to licence, but a theory making the union of the sexes part of the scheme for the redemption of mankind. By so doing, he probably made a much stronger appeal to Samaritans and Jews alike than did the strict celibacy demanded by Orphics, Essenes, and the other pre-Christian Gnostics. It is probable also that he included in his propaganda some sort of thaumaturgy or wonder-working of the kind employed, according to Lucian, by Alexander of Abonoteichos and, according to Irenaeus, by the Jewish impostor Marcus. Although the stories about this in the Clementines are manifestly fiction, we cannot absolutely reject the universal testimony of the Fathers that Simon and his followers made use of incantations and magical arts, and these are probably the " sorceries " with which the writer of the Acts declares he bewitched the Samaritans. Charlatanism, or more or less conscious imposture of this kind, was rife, as will be presently shown, among the lower classes of Palestine in his day, and would agree well with the bombastic language of the extracts from the *Great Announcement* which Hippolytus has preserved for us.

FORERUNNERS AND RIVALS OF CHRISTIANITY

FROM 330 B.C. TO 330 A.D.

FRANCIS LEGGE

IN TWO VOLUMES
BOUND AS ONE

Volume II

UNIVERSITY BOOKS *New Hyde Park, New York*

COPYRIGHT 1964 BY UNIVERSITY BOOKS, INC.

MANUFACTURED IN THE UNITED STATES OF AMERICA
LIBRARY OF CONGRESS CATALOG CARD NUMBER: 64-24125

Thanks are due to the Libraries of the Union Theological Seminary
and the General Theological Seminary for providing
copies of this book for reproduction purposes

CONTENTS

iii

CONTENTS

CHAPTER IX

POST-CHRISTIAN GNOSTICS: VALENTINUS

CHAPTER X

THE SYSTEM OF THE PISTIS SOPHIA AND ITS RELATED TEXTS

CHAPTER XI

MARCION

CONTENTS

CHAPTER VII

POST-CHRISTIAN GNOSTICS

It will be seen, from what has been said in the first volume, that, even at the beginning of the Christian era, there was no lack of αἵρεσις or choice of creeds offered to those peoples of the Levant who had outgrown their national religions ; and it may be a surprise to many that more notice was not taken by the Christians of the Apostolic age of these early essays at a universal faith. Some writers, indeed, among whom Bishop Lightfoot is perhaps the most notable, have thought that they could detect allusions to them in the Canonical writings, and that by the "worshipping of angels, intruding into those things which man hath not seen, vainly puffed up by the understanding of his flesh[1]" which St Paul condemns in the Epistle to the Colossians, must be understood the teachings of Gnostic sects already in existence[2]. Others have gone further, and think that the Fourth Gospel was itself written under Gnostic influence[3], and that the Apocalypse attributed to the same author vituperates under the name of the Nicolaitans a Christian sect professing Gnostic tenets[4]. Even if this be so, however, the comparatively late date assigned to all these documents[5] must prevent their being received as

---

[1] Col. ii. 18.

[2] Lightfoot, *St Paul's Epistle to the Colossians*, pp. 90 *sqq.*

[3] So A. Jülicher in *Encyc. Bibl. s.v.* Gnosis.

[4] Irenaeus, *op. cit.* Bk I. c. 23, p. 214, Harvey. Salmon in *Dict. of Christian Biog. s.v.* Nicolaitans, thinks this an idea peculiar to Irenaeus alone and not to be found in the older source from which he drew his account of the other Gnostics.

[5] The Canonical Apocalypse was probably written after the siege of Jerusalem by Titus in 70 A.D., while the first unmistakable mention we have of St John's Gospel is by Theophilus of Antioch a hundred years later. Earlier quotations from it are anonymous, *i.e.* they give the words of the Gospel as in the A.V. but without referring them to any specified author. See Duchesne, *Early Christian Church*, Eng. ed. pp. 102, 192.

evidence of what happened in the earliest stage of the Christian Church ; and we find no proof that Gnosticism ever seriously competed for popular favour with orthodox Christianity until well into the IInd century[1].   That the first Christians would take little heed either of organized religions like that of the Alexandrian divinities, or of the speculations of the Orphic poets and of such sects as the Simonians is plain, when we consider the way in which their expectation of the Parusia or Second Coming dominated every moment of their lives[2].   They believed with the unquestioning faith of children that their dead Master would presently return to the earth, and that it would then be destroyed to make way for a new state of things in which, while the majority of mankind would be condemned to everlasting fire, His followers should taste all the joys of Paradise.   With this before their eyes, they turned, as has been said, their possessions into a common fund[3], they bound themselves together in a strict association for mutual help and comfort, and they set to work to sweep their fellows into the Christian fold with an earnestness and an energy that was the fiercer because the time for its exercise was thought to be so short. " The Lord is at hand and His reward," a saying which seems to have been a password among them[4], was an idea never absent from their minds, and the result was an outburst of proselytism such as the world till then had never seen.

" They saw," says a writer who was under no temptation to exaggerate the charity and zeal of the primitive Church, " their fathers and mothers, their sisters and their dearest friends, hurrying onward to that fearful pit, laughing and singing. lured on by the fiends whom they called the gods.   They felt as we should feel were we to see a blind man walking towards a river bank.... Who that could hope to save a soul by tears and supplications would remain quiescent

[1] Hegesippus, quoted by Eusebius, *Hist. Eccl.* Bk IV. c. 22, says that the Church was untroubled by heresy until the reign of Trajan.

[2] Hegesippus (see last note) in his account of the martyrdom of " James the Brother of the Lord," *op. cit.* Bk II. c. 23.

[3] See Schmiedel, *Encyc. Bibl. s.v.* Community of Goods. Cf. Lucian, *de Mort. Peregrini,* c. XIII, and Mozley's comments in *Dict. Christian Biog. s.v.* Lucianus.

[4] *Maran atha.* See *Epistle of Barnabas,* c. XXI.

as men do now ?....In that age every Christian was a missionary. The soldier sought to win recruits for the heavenly host ; the prisoner of war discoursed to his Persian jailer ; the slave girl whispered the gospel in the ears of her mistress as she built up the mass of towered hair ; there stood men in cloak and beard at street corners who, when the people, according to the manners of the day, invited them to speak, preached, not the doctrines of the Painted Porch, but the words of a new and strange philosophy ; the young wife threw her arms round her husband's neck and made him agree to be baptised, that their souls might not be parted after death[1]...."

How could people thus preoccupied be expected to concern themselves with theories of the origin of a world about to perish, or with the philosophic belief that all the gods of the nations were but varying forms of one supreme and kindly power ?

Before the end of the Ist century, however, this belief in the immediate nearness of the Second Coming had died away[2]. The promise that the second Gospel puts into the mouth of Jesus that some of His hearers should not taste of death until they saw the Son of Man come with power[3], had become incapable of fulfilment by the death of the last of those who had listened to Him. Nor were all the converts to the faith which His immediate disciples had left behind them possessed with the same simple faith and mental equipment as themselves[4]. To the poor fishermen and peasants of Judaea had succeeded the slaves and freedmen of great houses—including even Caesar's own,—some of them professionally versed in the philosophy of the time, and all with a greater or less acquaintance with the religious beliefs of the non-Jewish citizens of the great Roman Empire[5]. The preachings and journeys of St Paul and other missionaries had also brought into the Christian Church many believers of other than Jewish blood, together with the foreign

---

[1] Winwood Reade, *op. cit.* pp. 237 *sqq.*

[2] Eugène de Faye, " Formation d'un Doctrine de Dieu au IIme Siècle," *R.H.R.* t. LXIII. (1911), p. 9. He quotes Harnack in his support.

[3] Mark xi. 1.

[4] On the ignorance of the first Christian writers, see de Faye, *op. cit.* p. 4.

[5] Origen, *cont. Celsum*, Bk III. c. 12. Cf. Krüger, *La Grande Encyclopédie*, Paris, *s.v.* Gnosticisme.

merchants and members of the Jewish communities scattered throughout the Roman world, who were better able than the Jews of Palestine to appreciate the stability and the organized strength of the Roman Empire and to desire an alliance with it. To ask such men, deeply engaged as many of them were in the pursuit of wealth, to join in the temporary communism and other-worldliness practised by the first Christian Church would have been as futile as to expect the great Jewish banking-houses of the present day to sell all that they have and give it to the poor.

Another cause that profoundly altered the views of the early Christian communities must have been the catastrophe and final dispersion of the Jewish nation. Up to the time of the destruction of the Temple of Jerusalem under Titus, the Christians not only regarded themselves as Jews[1], but were looked upon by such of the other subjects of Rome as had happened to have heard of them, as merely one sect the more of a race always factious and given to internal dissensions. Yet even in St Paul's time, the Christians were exposed to a bitter persecution at the hands of those orthodox Jews who seemed to the Gentile world to be their co-religionists[2], and it is probable that in the outbreak of fanaticism attending the first Jewish war, they suffered severely at the hands of both combatants[3]. The burning of the Temple must also have been a crushing blow to all who looked for a literal and immediate fulfilment of the

[1] " Those which say they are Jews, but are not " ; Rev. ii. 9 ; *ibid.* iii. 9. The *Clementine Homilies,* though of much later date, never speak of the Christians otherwise than as Jews. Cf. Duchesne, *Early Christian Church,* p. 12.

[2] Acts viii. 1.

[3] Renan (*L'Antéchrist,* p. 511, and note 1) gives a passage, which he thinks is from Tacitus, showing that Titus aimed at the suppression of the Christians as well as the Jews. Doubtless many Christians perished in the punitive measures taken in the 1st century against the Jews in Antioch and elsewhere. Cf. Josephus, *Wars of the Jews,* Bk VII. c. 3 ; Eusebius, *H. E.* Bk III. cc. 12, 17, 19, 20. It was the persecution by the fanatical Jews that compelled the flight of the Christians to Pella shortly before the siege. See Eusebius, Bk III. c. 5 ; Epiph. *Haer.* XXIX. c. 7, p. 239, Oehler. The episode of the "Woman clothed with the Sun" of the Canonical Apocalypse is supposed by some to refer to this.

Messianic hope, and its result was to further accentuate the difference between the Christians and the Jews[1]. Moreover, the hatred and scorn felt by these last for all other members of the human race had now been recognized by the Gentiles[2], and the repeated insurrections attempted by the Jews between the time of Titus and the final war of extermination under Hadrian showed these feelings were shared by some Jewish communities outside Palestine[3]. It was therefore not at all the time which worldly-wise and prudent men, as many of the later Christian converts were, would choose for identifying themselves with a race which not only repudiated the relationship in the most practical way, but had lately exposed themselves on other grounds to the execration of the civilized world.

It is, then, by no means surprising that some of the new converts should have begun to look about them for some compromise between their recently acquired convictions and the religious beliefs of the Graeco-Roman world in which they had been brought up, and they found this ready to their hand in the pre-Christian sects which we have ventured above to class together under the generic name of Gnostic. In the Orphic poems, they found the doctrine of successive ages of the world, each with its different characteristics, which coincided well enough with the repeated declaration of the Christians that the old world was passing away,—as was indeed the fact

[1] So that the members of the little Church of Pella who retained the name of Jews gradually ceased to be regarded as orthodox by the other Christian communities and were called Ebionites. See Renan, *L'Anté-christ*, p. 548. Cf. Fuller in *Dict. Christian Biog. s.v.* Ebionites for authorities. The connection that Fuller would find between the Essenes and the Ebionites seems to rest on little proof.

[2] Thus Mgr Duchesne, *op. cit.* p. 14, says that " St Paul was a Jew by birth, imbued with the exclusiveness and disdainful spirit which inspired his race and influenced all their dealings with other nations."

[3] Many of the Sicarii and other fanatics managed to escape before the catastrophe of the First Jewish War to Egypt and the Cyrenaica, where they continued to commit outrages and make rebellion until they brought on themselves and their co-religionists the wrath of the Romans. See Josephus, *Wars*, Bk VII. cc. 10, 11. Cf. Renan, *L'Antéchrist*, p. 539 ; *id., Les Évangiles*, p. 369.

since the conquests of Alexander[1]. They found, too, both in the Orphic poems and in the mixed religions like that of the Alexandrian divinities which had sprung from the doctrines taught by these poems, the legend of a god dying and rising again for the salvation of mankind told in a way which had many analogies with the Gospel narratives of the Passion and Resurrection of Jesus[2]. Among the Essenes, too, who may have owed, as has been said above, some of their doctrines to Orphic inspiration, they found all the modest virtues of sobriety, chastity, and mutual help which had already distinguished the Christian Church above all the other religious associations of the time. And among both the Orphics and the Essenes was to be noticed the strained and fanciful system of interpretation by allegory and figure which enabled them to put their own construction upon the words not only of the books of the Jewish Canon, but of those writings which had begun to circulate among the scattered Christian communities as containing the authentic teaching of Jesus and His immediate disciples[3]. Add to this that the Simonians, and no doubt other pre-Christian Gnostic sects of which we have lost all trace, had already shown the mixed populations of the Levant how to reconcile the innovations of a teacher of impressive and commanding personality with their own ancestral traditions[4], and that the many mysteries then diffused throughout the ancient world

[1] Abel's *Orphica*, Frgs. 243–248, especially the quotation from Nigidius.

[2] See Chapter II, *supra*.

[3] So Renan, *L'Antéchrist*, p. 300, says that the Synoptic Gospels probably first took shape in the Church at Pella. Thus he explains the so-called "little Apocalypse" of Matthew xxiv., Mark xiii., and Luke xxi. Cf. *ibid.*, p. 296 and note. For the symbolic construction placed upon them by the Gnostics, see Hatch, *H. L.*, p. 75.

[4] Hegesippus, who probably wrote about 150 A.D., speaks of Thebuthis, Dositheus, and others as leaders of early sects. Eusebius, *Hist. Eccl.* Bk IV. c. 22, and Origen (*cont. Cels.* Bk VI. c. 11) make this last a contemporary of Simon Magus. The *Clementine Homilies* (Bk II. c. 24), from whom both authors may have derived their information, have a long story about Dositheus being with Simon a follower of John the Baptist, and disputing with Simon the headship of the sect. From presumably other sources, Hegesippus speaks of the Essenes, the Masbothoeans and the Hemero-baptists, for which last see Chapter XIII, *infra*, as pre-Christian sects.

offered a ready means of propagating new doctrines under cover of secrecy ; and it will be seen that most of the sources from which the founders of the great post-Christian sects afterwards drew their systems were then lying open and ready to hand.

The prize which awaited success was, moreover, no mean one. It is sometimes said that the only distinction that awaited a leader of the Church at this time was the distinction of being burned alive[1]. Yet the fear of impeachment to be followed by a still more horrible death never prevented English statesmen in the xviith century from struggling with each other for place and power ; while the State had not as yet made any serious attempt to suppress the propagation of Christianity by force. On the other hand, a Christian bishop, even at this early date, occupied a position which was really superior to that of most functionaries of the secular State. Gifted with almost complete power over his flock in temporal as well as in spiritual matters, he was at once their judge and their adviser ; and, so long as there were Pagan emperors on the throne, the faithful were forbidden to come to any tribunal but his[2]. His judgments, too, had a greater sanction than those of any temporal judge ; for while he could not indeed lawfully condemn any of his hearers to death, he had in the sentence of excommunication which he alone could pronounce, the power of cutting them off from eternal life. The adoration with which he was regarded by them also surpassed the respect paid to proconsul or legate[3] ; and the literature of the time is full of allusions to the way in which, when brought before the temporal rulers, he was attended

---

[1] Winwood Reade, *op. cit.* p. 244. Probably this is what is meant by Gibbon when he says (*Decline and Fall*, Bury's ed. III. p. 153, n. 54) that no future bishop of Avila is likely to imitate Priscillian by turning heretic, because the income of the see is 20,000 ducats a year.

[2] *Apostolical Constitutions*, Bk II. cc. 45, 46, 47. Harnack, *Expansion of Christianity*, Eng. ed. II. p. 98 n. 1, gives the date of this work as "middle of the 2nd century." Duchesne, *op. cit.* p. 109, thinks it is derived from the *Didache* which he puts not later than Trajan.

[3] *Apost. Const.* Bk II. c. 26 : "He (*i.e.* the bishop) is your ruler and governor ; he is your king and potentate ; he is next after God, your earthly divinity, who has a right to be honoured by you."

by weeping multitudes who crowded round him even in prison, imploring his blessing and kissing his fetters[1].   Hence it is not to be wondered at that such a position was eagerly sought after, that envy of the episcopate was the principal sin against which the Christian writers of the sub-Apostolic age warned their readers[2], and that it is to the disappointment at failing to attain the highest places in the orthodox Church that they ascribe the foundation of all the principal post-Christian sects[3]. Without taking this accusation as literally correct, it is plain that the chance of irresponsible power over those whom they could convince must have proved a most alluring bait to religious-minded persons who were also ambitious and intellectual men of the world[4].

Thus it came about that during the IInd and IIIrd centuries, there arose more than one teacher who set himself to construct a system which should enable its votaries to retain the Hellenistic culture which Alexander's conquests had spread throughout the whole civilized world with the religious and moral ideas which the enthusiasm and energy of the first Christians had begun to diffuse among the lower classes of citizens[5].   Alexandria, the natural meeting-place between the East and West, was no

---

[1] Lucian, *Proteus Peregrinus, passim* ; *Acts of Paul and Thekla* ; *Acts of Peter of Alexandria.*

[2] Clement of Rome, *First Epistle to the Corinthians*, c. 44.

[3] So Irenaeus, *op. cit.* Bk I. c. 26, pp. 219, 220, Harvey, says it was the desire to become a διδάσκαλος or teacher that drove Tatian, once a hearer of Justin Martyr's, into heresy.   Hegesippus, *ubi cit. supra*, says that Thebuthis first corrupted the Church, on account of his not being made a bishop.   For the same accusation in the cases of Valentinus and Marcion, see Chapters IX and XI, *infra.*

[4] Celsus *apud* Origen (*op. cit.* Bk III. cc. 10, 11) says : " Christians at first were few in number, and all held like opinions, but when they increased to a great multitude, they were divided and separated, each wishing to have his own individual party ; for this was their object from the beginning "—a contention which Origen rebuts.

[5] Thus in Egypt it was almost exclusively the lower classes which embraced Christianity at the outset.   See Amélineau, " Les Actes Coptes du martyre de St Polycarpe " in *P.S.B.A.* vol. x. (1888), p. 392.   Julian (*Cyr.* VI. p. 206) says that under Tiberius and Claudius there were no converts of rank.

doubt the scene of the first of these attempts, and the writings of Philo, fortunately still extant, had already shown the way in which the allegorical system of interpretation could be used to this end. That many of the founders of post-Christian Gnostic sects were Alexandrian Jews is the constant tradition of the Christian Church, and is antecedently probable enough[1]. But other Gnostic leaders were certainly not Alexandrians and came from centres sufficiently distant from Egypt to show that the phenomenon was very widely spread, and that the same causes produced the same results in the most distant places and entirely outside the Jewish community. Marcion, the founder of the Marcionite Church, was a native of Pontus. Saturnilus or Saturninus—the name is spelt differently by Irenaeus and Hippolytus—came from Antioch, Theodotus from Byzantium, others, such as Cerdo, and probably Prepon the Syrian, began teaching in Rome, while we hear of a certain Monoimus, who is said to have been an Arab[2]. Most of these are to us merely names, only very brief summaries of the different systems founded or professed by them having been preserved in the heresiologies compiled by the Fathers of the Church both before and immediately after the alliance of the Christian Church with the Roman State under Constantine.

[1] Thus Cerinthus, who is made by tradition the opponent of St John, is said to have been a Jew and to have been trained in the doctrines of Philo at Alexandria (Theodoret, *Haer. Fab.* Bk II. § 3). Cf. Neander, *Ch. Hist.* (Eng. ed.) vol. II. pp. 42–47. Neander says the same thing about Basilides (*op. cit.* p. 47 and note) and Valentinus (p. 71), although it is difficult to discover any authority for the statement other than the Jewish features in their doctrines. There is more evidence for the statement regarding Marcus, the heresiarch and magician whom Irenaeus (*op. cit.* Bk I. c. 7) accuses of the seduction of Christian women, apparently in his own time, since the words of Marcus' ritual, which the Bishop of Lyons quotes, are in much corrupted Hebrew, and the Jewish Cabala was used by him. Renan's view (*Marc Aurèle*, pp. 139 *sqq.*) that Christianity in Egypt never passed through the Judaeo-Christian stage may in part account for the desire of Jewish converts there to set up schools of their own.

[2] For Marcion, see Chapter XI, *infra*. Summary accounts of the doctrines of other Gnostics mentioned are given by Irenaeus and Hippolytus in the works quoted. See also the *Dict. of Christian Biog.*, under their respective names.

Of these treatises, the two, which, up to about sixty years ago, formed our main sources of information with regard to the Gnostics of the sub-Apostolic age[1], are the writings of St Irenaeus, Bishop of Lyons about the year 177 A.D., and of Epiphanius, Bishop of Constantia in Cyprus, who tells us he wrote in the seventh year of Gratian or 374 A.D. The first of these is considerably later in date than the heresiarchs in refutation of whose doctrines he wrote his five books "against Heresies"; and although he is most probably honest in his account of their tenets, it is evident that Irenaeus was incapable of distinguishing between the opinions of the founders of the sects which he controverts and those of their followers and successors. Epiphanius, on the other hand, wrote when the Catholic Church was already triumphant, and his principal object seems to have been to blacken the memory of those competitors whom she had already outdistanced in the race for popularity and power. Hence he spares no pains to rake together every story which theological hatred and unclean imagination had ever invented against her opponents and rivals; while his contempt for consistency and the rules of evidence show the intellectual depths to which the war which orthodox Christianity had from the first waged against Hellenistic culture had reduced the learning of the age. The language in which he and the other Catholic writers on heresy describe the Gnostics is, indeed, the first and most salient instance of that intolerance for any other opinions than their own, which a recent writer of great authority declares the Apostles and their successors derived from their Jewish nationality[2]. "The first-born of Satan," "seducers of women," "savage beasts," "scorpions," "ravening wolves," "demoniacs," "sorcerers," and "atheists" were the mildest terms in

---

[1] The lesser heresiologists, such as Philaster of Brescia, St Augustine, the writer who is known as Praedestinatus, the author of the tract *Adversus omnes Haereses* wrongly ascribed to Tertullian, and the other writers included in the first volume of Oehler's *Corpus Haereseologici*, Berlin, 1856, as well as writers like Eusebius, all copy from one or other of these sources. The *Excerpta Theodoti* appended to the works of Clement of Alexandria are on a different footing, but their effect at the time spoken of in the text was not appreciated. Cf. Salmon in *Dict. Christian Biog. s.v.* Valentinus.

[2] Bouché-Leclercq, *L'Intolérance Religieuse et Politique*, Paris, 1912, p. 140.

which Epiphanius and his fellow heresiologists can bring themselves to speak of the sectaries. They afford ample justification for the remark of the philosophic Emperor Julian that " no wild beasts are so hostile to men as Christian sects in general are to one another[1]."

From this lack of trustworthy evidence, the discovery in 1842 at a convent on Mt Athos of eight out of the ten books of the *Philosophumena* now generally attributed to Hippolytus, Bishop of " Portus Romana " in 230 A.D.[2], seemed likely to deliver us. The work thus recovered bore the title of the *Refutation of all Heresies*, and did succeed in giving us a fairly clear and coherent account of some twenty Gnostic sects, the very existence of many of which was previously unknown to us. Moreover, it went a good way beyond its predecessors in pointing out that the real origin of all the heretical sects then existing was to be found, not so much in the diabolic inspiration which other writers thought sufficient to account for it, as in the Pythagorean, Platonic, and other philosophies then in vogue, together with the practice of astrology and magic rites which had come to form an important part of all the Pagan religions then popular. It also showed a very extensive and apparently first-hand acquaintance with the works of the Gnostic leaders, and the lengthy quotations which it gives from their writings enable us to form a better idea than we had before been able to do both of what the Gnostic tenets really were and of the arguments by which they were propagated. Unfortunately the text of the *Philosophumena* has not been able to withstand the assaults of those textual critics who have already reduced the Book of Genesis to a patchwork of several authors writing at widely separate times and places, and writers like Dr Salmon and Prof. Stähelin have laboured to show that the author of the *Philosophumena* was taken in by a forger who had himself concocted all the documents which Hippolytus quotes as being

---

[1] Ammianus Marcellinus, Bk XXII. c. 5, § 4.

[2] An excellent and concise account of the discovery and the subsequent controversy as to the authorship of the book is given by Salmon in the *Dict. Christian Biog. s.v.* Hippolytus Romanus. For Mgr Duchesne's theory that Hippolytus was a schismatic Pope, see his *Hist. Christian Church*, pp. 227–233.

the work of different heresiarchs[1]. Their conclusions, although
they do not seem to put the matter entirely beyond doubt,
have been accepted by many theological writers, especially in
Germany, and in the course of the discussion the fact has
emerged that the documents quoted can hardly go back to an
earlier date than the year 200 A.D.[2] It is therefore unlikely that
Hippolytus had before him the actual words of the heresiarchs
whom he is endeavouring to refute; and if the *Philosophumena*
were all we had to depend upon, we might despair of knowing
what "the great Gnostics of Hadrian's time" really taught.

The reason for this paucity of documents is also plain
enough. "The antidote to the scorpion's bite," to use a patristic
figure of speech[3], was felt by the early Church to be the actual
cautery, and its leaders spared no pains to rout out and burn
the writings of the heretics pending the time when they could
apply the same treatment to their authors. Even before their
alliance with Constantine had put the resources of the State
at their disposal, they had contrived to use the secular arm
for this purpose. In several persecutions, notably that of
Diocletian, which was probably the most severe of them all,
the Christian scriptures were particularly sought for by the
Inquisitors of the State, and many of the orthodox boasted that
they had arranged that the police should find the writings of
the heretics in their stead[4]. Later, when it came to the turn
of the Christians to dictate imperial edicts, the possession of
heretical writings was made punishable with severe penalties[5].

[1] Salmon's position is set out by him in *Hermathena*, Dublin, 1885,
pp. 389 *sqq.* For Stähelin's, see his tractate *Die Gnostische Quellen Hippolyts*, Leipzig, 1890, in Harnack's *Texte und Untersuchungen*. Both are
skilfully summarized by de Faye in his *Introduction à l'Étude du Gnosticisme*,
Paris, 1903, pp. 25 *sqq.*

[2] De Faye does not accept Stähelin's contention as to the forgery, but
his conclusion as to the date is as stated in the text. See *Introduction*, etc.
pp. 68, 71.

[3] Tertullian, *Scorpiace*, c. 1.

[4] Neander, *Ch. Hist.* (Eng. ed.), I. p. 208, quotes a case from St Augustine
which I have not been able to verify.

[5] Gibbon, *Decline and Fall*, II. p. 110 and note 144 (Bury's ed.). For
the search which the Christian emperors directed to be made for the
heretics' books, see Eusebius, *Vita Constantini*, Bk III. cc. 64, 65.

Between orthodox Christian and Pagan it is a wonder that any have survived to us.

A lucky chance, however, has prevented us from being entirely ignorant of what the Gnostics had to say for themselves. In 1851, a MS. which had been known to be in the British Museum since 1778, was published with a translation into a curious mixture of Latin and Greek by the learned Petermann, and turned out to include a sort of Gospel coming from some early Gnostic sect[1]. From a note made on it by a writer who seems to have been nearly contemporary with its scribes, it is known as *Pistis Sophia* or " *Faith-Wisdom* "; and the same MS. also contains fragments of other works coming from a cognate source. In 1891, a papyrus in the Bodleian Library at Oxford, which had been brought into this country in 1769 by the traveller Bruce, was also published with a French translation by M. Amélineau, an ex-Abbé who has long made the later Egyptian language his peculiar study, and proved to contain two documents connected with the system disclosed in the *Pistis Sophia*[2]. Both MSS. are in Coptic of the dialect of the Sahid or Upper Egypt, to which fact they probably owe their escape from the notice of the Byzantine Inquisitors; and they purport to contain revelations as to the next world and the means of attaining salvation therein made by Jesus on His return to earth after the Resurrection. Although these several documents were evidently not all written at one time and place, and cannot be assigned to a single author, the notes and

[1] The actual transcription and translation were made by Maurice Schwartze, a young German who was sent over here to study the documents in the British Museum at the expense of the King of Prussia. He died after the completion of his task, and before the book could be printed.

[2] Amélineau's transcription and translation appeared in the *Notices et Extraits*, etc. of the Académie des Inscriptions, t. xxix. pt 2 (Paris, 1891). He has also published a translation into French without text of the *Pistis Sophia* (Paris, 1895). Dr Carl Schmidt, of the University of Berlin, has published translations into German of both works under the title *Koptisch-Gnostische Schriften*, Bd i., Leipzig, 1905. None of these versions are entirely satisfactory, and it is much to be wished that an authoritative edition of the two works could be put forward by English scholars. The present writer gave a short history and analysis of them in the *Scottish Review* for 1893 under the title " Some Heretic Gospels."

emendations appearing on the MSS. show that most of them must have been in the possession of members of the same school as their composers; and that therefore we have here for the first time direct and authentic evidence of the Gnostic tenets, as put forward by their adherents instead of by their opponents.

The collation of these documents with the excerpts from other Gnostic writings appearing in early writers like Clement of Alexandria who were not professed heresiologists[1], shows that the post-Christian Gnostic sects had more opinions in common than would be gathered from the statements of St Irenaeus, Hippolytus, and Epiphanius, and that they probably fulfilled a real want of the age[2]. All of them seem to have held that there was one Supreme Being, the source of all good, and that matter was inherently malignant and opposed to him. All of them, too, seem to have taught the perfectibility of man's nature, the salvation of at any rate the majority of mankind, and the possibility of their rising in the scale of being; and all of them held that this was to be effected mainly by means of certain mysteries or sacramental rites which were assumed to have a magical efficacy. All these fundamental character-istics find their origin in the beliefs of the pre-Christian religions and religious associations described above, and doubtless owed much to their influence. But with these, there was now combined for the first time the recognition of the divinity of One who, while appearing upon earth as a man among men,

[1] Clement was so far from being a heresiologist that he has not escaped the reproach of being himself a heretic. He repeatedly speaks in praise of the " true Gnostic," meaning thereby the perfect Christian, and although this is probably a mere matter of words, it seems to have induced Photius in the ixth century to examine his writings with a jealous eye. The result was that, as M. Courdaveaux points out (*R.H.R.* 1892, p. 293 and note), he found him guilty of teaching that matter was eternal, the Son a simple creature of the Father, the Incarnation only an appearance, that man's soul entered several bodies in succession, and that several worlds were created before that of Adam. All these are Gnostic opinions, and it may be that if we had all Clement's books in our hands, as had Photius, we might confirm M. Courdaveaux's judgment, as does apparently Mgr Duchesne. Cf. his *Hist. of Christian Ch.* pp. 244, 245.

[2] Cf. A. C. McGiffert, *Prolegomena to the Church History of Eusebius* (Schaff and Wace's Nicene Library), Oxford, 1890, vol. i. p. 179 and note.

was yet thought by all to be endowed with a greater share of the Divine nature than they. Orpheus, Moses, Homer, and the Jewish prophets had in turn been claimed as religious teachers who were divinely inspired ; but Jesus was asserted by every later Gnostic school of whose teachings we have any evidence to have been Himself of higher essence and substance than the rest of mankind[1]. How far this assertion was dictated by the necessity for finding a superhuman authority for the revelation which each Gnostic leader professed to make to his disciples may be open to question ; but in view of some contemporary controversies it is well to draw attention to the fact that the Divinity in some shape or other of Jesus, as well as what is now called His "historicity," was never for a moment called in question during the first three centuries by Gnostic or Catholic. Μονογενής or *Monogenes*[2]—a word which Catholic writers later confused with Μονογεννητός or "only-begotten," but which is best represented by the corresponding Latin expression *unicus* or "unique" (*i.e.* one of a kind)—is the word in which the Gnostics summed up their conceptions of the nature of Jesus[3].

This belief, however, led to consequences which do not at first sight seem to follow from it. The gods of classical antiquity were indeed supposed to be of like passions with ourselves, and the Greek of Homer's time never thought it shame to attribute to them jealousy or lust or fear or vanity or any other of the weaknesses which afflict us[4]. But the one feature besides their beauty that distinguished the Greek gods from humanity was

[1] Of the heresies mentioned in the *Philosophumena* only two, viz. that of Simon Magus and that of those whom Hippolytus calls the Sethiani, do not admit, either expressly or by implication, the divinity of Jesus. This may be accounted for by what has been said above as to both being pre-Christian in origin.

[2] *E.g.* Irenaeus, *op. cit.* Bk I. c. 1, I. p. 9, Harvey. Here he is called ὅμοιος τε καὶ ἴσος τῷ προβαλόντι, "like and equal to him who had sent him forth." There is certainly here no allusion to "begetting" in the ordinary sense of the word.

[3] As in the epithet of Persephone in the Orphic Hymn quoted above. See Chapter IV, *supra*. The unanimity with which all post-Christian Gnostics accepted the superhuman nature of Jesus seems to have struck Harnack. See his *What is Christianity?* Eng. ed. 1904, pp. 209, 210.

[4] *Iliad* I. ll. 560 *sqq.* ; IV. ll. 57, 330 ; XIV. ll. 320 *sqq.*

their immortality or freedom from death ; and if demigods like Heracles were said to have gone through the common experience of mortals, this was held as proof that their apotheosis or deification did not take place until they had left the earth[1]. So much was this the case that the Greeks are said to have been much amused when they first beheld the Egyptians wailing for the death of Osiris, declaring that if he were a god he could not be dead, while if he were not, his death was not to be lamented[2] ; and Plutarch, when repeating the story to his countrymen, thought it necessary to explain that in his view the protagonists in the Osiris and Set legend were neither gods nor men, but " great powers " or daemons not yet deified and in the meantime occupying a place between the two[3]. The same difficulty was, perhaps, less felt by the other Mediterranean peoples, among whom, as we have seen, the idea of a god who died and rose again was familiar enough[4] ; but the Gnostic leaders must always have had before their eyes the necessity of making Christianity acceptable to persons in possession of that Hellenistic culture which then dominated the world, and which still forms the root of all modern civilization. How, then, were they to account for the fact that their God Jesus, whether they considered Him as the Logos or Word of Philo, or the Monogenes or Unique Power of the Supreme Being, had suffered a shameful death by sentence of the Roman procurator in Judaea ?

The many different answers that they gave to this question showed more eloquently than anything else the difficulties with which it was surrounded. Simon, according to Hippolytus, said that Jesus only appeared on earth as a man, but was not really one, and seemed to have suffered in Judaea, although he had not really done so[5]. Basilides the Egyptian, the leader

---

[1] *Odyssey* XI. ll. 600 *sqq.* ; Plutarch, *Life of Pelopidas*, c. XVI.

[2] Plutarch, *de Is. et Os.* c. LXXI.

[3] *Ibid.* cc. XXV., XXVII., XXX.

[4] Probably this was one of the reasons why the Mysteries which showed the death of a god had in Greece to be celebrated in secret. See Diodorus' remark (Bk V. c. 77, § 3) that the things which the Greeks only handed down in secret were by the Cretans concealed from no one.

[5] Hippolytus, *op. cit.* Bk VI. c. 19, p. 265, Cruice.

of another sect, held, according to Irenaeus, that the body of Jesus was a phantasm and had no real existence, Simon of Cyrene having been crucified in his stead[1]; while Hippolytus, who seems to have drawn his account of Basilides' teaching from a different source from that used by his predecessor, makes him say that only the body of Jesus suffered and relapsed into "formlessness[2]," but that His soul returned into the different worlds whence it was drawn. Saturninus, another heresiarch, held, according to both authors, to the phantasmal theory of Jesus' body, which attained such popularity among other Gnostic sects that "Docetism," as the opinion was called, came to be looked upon by later writers as one of the marks of heresy[3], and Hippolytus imagines that there were in existence sects who attached such importance to this point that they called themselves simply Docetics[4]. Valentinus, from whose teaching, as we shall see, the principal system of the *Pistis Sophia* was probably derived, also adhered to this Docetic theory, and said that the body of Jesus was not made of human flesh, but was constructed "with unspeakable art" so as to resemble it, the dove-like form which had descended into it at His baptism leaving it before the Crucifixion[5]. According to Irenaeus, too, Valentinus held that the Passion of Jesus was not intended as an atonement or sacrifice for sin, as the Catholics taught, but merely as a symbol or reflection of something that was taking place in the bosom of the Godhead[6].

Another point in which the chief post-Christian Gnostic sects seem to have resembled one another is the secrecy with which their teachings were surrounded. Following strictly the practice of the various mysteries—the Eleusinian, the Isiac, Cabiric, and others—in which the Mediterranean god, whether called Dionysos, Osiris, Attis, Adonis, or by any other name, was worshipped, none were admitted to a knowledge of their doctrines without

---

[1] Irenaeus, *op. cit.* Bk I. c. 19, II. p. 200, Harvey.

[2] ἀμορφία. Hippolytus, *op. cit.* Bk VII. c. 27, p. 366, Cruice.

[3] Irenaeus, *op. cit.* Bk I. c. 18, p. 197, Harvey. Hippolytus, *op. cit.* Bk VII. c. 28, p. 368, Cruice.

[4] Hippolytus, *op. cit.* Bk VIII. c. 8.

[5] Irenaeus, *op. cit.* Bk I. c. 1, § 13, pp. cxli and 61, Harvey.

[6] *Ibid.* Bk I. c. 1, § 31, pp. cxli and 62, Harvey.

undergoing a long, arduous, and expensive course of initiation. More than one Gnostic teacher is said to have told his hearers to conceal from men what they were, or in other words not to let it be known that they were affiliated to the sect[1], and all the Fathers bear witness to the way in which in time of persecution the Gnostics escaped by professing any faith that would satisfy the Roman authorities. By doing so, they laid themselves open to the accusation hurled at them with great virulence by the Church, that their secret rites and doctrines were so filthy as to shock human nature if made public—an accusation which at the first appearance of Christianity had been brought against the Catholics, and which the Church has ever since made use of against any sect which has differed from her, repeating it even at the present day against the Jews and the Freemasons[2]. There is, however, no reason why the accusation should be better founded in one case than in the others; and it is plain in any event that the practice of secrecy when expedient followed directly from the magical ideas which have been shown above to be the foundation of the dogmas of all the pre-Christian Gnostics, besides permeating religions like that of the Alexandrian divinities. The willingness of the post-Christian Gnostics to subscribe to any public profession of faith that might be convenient was no doubt due to the same cause[3]. As has been well said, to the true Gnostic, Paganism, Christianity, and Mahommedanism are merely veils[4]. The secret words and formulas delivered, and the secret rites which the initiate alone knows, are all that is necessary to assure him a distinguished place in the next world; and, armed with these,

---

[1] Irenaeus, *op. cit.* Bk I. c. 19, § 3, p. 202, Harvey; Hippolytus, *op. cit.* Bk IV. c. 24, p. 225, Cruice; Tertullian, *Scorpiace*, c. I.

[2] For the accusation against the Christians, see Athenagoras, *Apologia*, cc. III., XXXI; Justin Martyr, *First Apol.* c. XXVI. For that against the Jews, Strack, *Le Sang et la fausse Accusation du Meurtre Rituel*, Paris, 1893. For that against the Freemasons, "Devil Worship and Freemasonry," *Contemporary Review* for 1896.

[3] See n. 1, *supra*. So Eusebius speaks of the Simonians receiving baptism and slipping into the Church without revealing their secret tenets, *Hist. Eccl.* Bk II. c. 1.

[4] Revillout, *Vie et Sentences de Secundus*, Paris, 1873, p. 3, n. 1.

he can contemplate with perfect indifference all outward forms of worship.

These and other points which the post-Christian Gnostic sects seem to have had in common[1] can therefore be accounted for by their common origin, without accepting the theory of the textual critics that the Fathers had been deceived by an impostor who had made one document do duty several times over. Yet until we have the writings of the heresiarchs actually in our hands, we must always be in doubt as to how far their opinions have been correctly recorded for us. The post-Christian Gnostic sects have been compared with great aptness to the Protestant bodies which have sprung up outside the Catholic Church since the German Reformation[2], and the analogy in most respects seems to be perfect. Yet it would probably be extremely difficult for a bishop of the Church of Rome or of that of England to give within the compass of an heresiology like those quoted above an account of the tenets of the different sects in England and America, without making grave and serious mistakes in points of detail. The difficulty would arise from want of first-hand knowledge, in spite of the invention of printing having made the dissemination of information on such subjects a thousand times more general than in sub-Apostolic times, and of the fact that the modern sects, unlike their predecessors, do not seek to keep their doctrines secret. But the analogy shows us another cause of error. The " Free Churches," as they are called in modern parlance, have from the outset shown themselves above all things fissiparous, and it is enough to mention the names of Luther, Zwingli, Calvin, Socinus, Wesley, and Chalmers to show how hopelessly at variance the teachings of the founders of sects at first sight are. But in spite of this, there seems to have been always a sort of fluidity of doctrine among them, and hardly any of

---

[1] Amélineau, *Le Gnosticisme Égyptien*, p. 75, thus enumerates them: the doctrine of emanation, an unknown [*i.e.* an inaccessible and incomprehensible] God, the resemblance of the three worlds, the aeonology of Simon, and a common cosmology. To this may be added the inherent malignity of matter and the belief in salvation by knowledge. See Krüger, *La Grande Encyclopédie*, *s.v.* Gnosticisme.

[2] Renan, *Marc Aurèle*, p. 114.

the Nonconformist sects now profess the dogmas with which they first came into existence. The changes in this respect, however, never involve the borrowing of new tenets from sources external to them all, but seem to be brought about by a sort of interfiltration between one sect and another. Thus, for example, for many centuries after the Reformation the majority of the dissident sects which rejected all connection with the Catholic Church were among the stoutest defenders of the Divinity of Jesus, and the Socinians who held the contrary opinion were in an entirely negligible minority. At the present day, however, the tendency seems to run the other way, and many Nonconformist bodies are leaning towards Unitarian doctrines, although few of them probably have ever heard the name of Socinus. A similar tendency to interpenetration of doctrines early showed itself among the Gnostics; and there can be little doubt that it sometimes led to a fusion or amalgamation between sects of widely differing origin. Hence it is not extraordinary that certain tenets are sometimes recorded by the Fathers as peculiar to one Gnostic leader and sometimes to another, and to trace accurately their descent, it would be necessary to know the exact point in the history of each sect at which such tenets appeared. But the Fathers seldom thought of distinguishing between the opinions of an heresiarch and those of his successors, and the literary habits of the time were not in favour of accurate quotation of documents or even of names[1]. This forms the chief difficulty in dealing with the history of the Gnostic teaching, and although the discovery of fresh documents contemporary with those we now possess would undoubtedly throw additional light upon the subject, it is probable that it will never be entirely overcome.

[1] Witness the confusion between Ennoia and Epinoia in Chapter VI, vol. I. p. 180, n. 4, *supra*, and between Saturnilus and Saturninus in this chapter, p. 9. So Irenaeus and others record the opinions of an associate of Marcus whom they call "*Colarbasus*," a name which modern criticism has shown to be a mistake for קול ארבע Kol-arba, "The Voice of the Four" or the Supreme Tetrad. See Renan, *Marc Aurèle*, p. 129; Hort in *Dict. Christian Biog. s.h.v.* So Clement of Alexandria, *Protrept.* c. II. mistakes Evoe, the mystic cry of the Bacchantes, for the Eve of Genesis.

Generally speaking, however, Gnosticism played a most important part in the history of Christianity. Renan's view that it was a disease which, like croup, went near to strangling the infant Church is often quoted[1]; but in the long run it is probable that Gnosticism was on the whole favourable to her development. In religion, sentiment often plays a larger part than reason ; and any faith which would enable men of weight and influence to continue the religious practices in which they had been brought up, with at the outset but slight modification, was sure of wide acceptance. There seems no doubt that the earlier Gnostics continued to attend the mysteries of the Chthonian deities in Greece and of their Oriental analogues, Osiris, Attis, Adonis, and the like elsewhere, while professing to place upon what they there saw a Christian interpretation[2]. Here they acted like the little leaven that leaveneth the whole lump, and this did much to spread the knowledge of the new faith among those spiritually-minded Gentiles, who would never have felt any interest in Christianity so long as it remained merely a branch of Judaism[3]. Most of them, moreover, sooner or later abandoned their Gnosticism, and became practising members of the Catholic Church, who sometimes went a long way to meet them. As Renan has said, none of them ever relapsed into Paganism[4], and in this way the so-called heresies became at once the feeders of orthodox Christianity and its richest recruiting-ground[5]. They offered in fact an easy road by which the wealthy, the learned, and the highly-placed could pass from Paganism to Christianity without suffering the inconvenience imposed upon the first followers of the Apostles.

[1] Renan, *L'Église Chrétienne*, p. 140.

[2] Hippolytus, *op. cit.* Bk v. c. 9, p. 177, Cruice.

[3] As in the case of Clement of Alexandria, who seems to have been initiated into most of the heathen mysteries then current. It is to be noted, too, that Origen, although he speaks of the Ophites as an insignificant sect (see Chapter VIII, *infra*), yet professes to know all about their secret opinions.

[4] Renan, *Marc Aurèle*, p. 139.

[5] Thus Ambrose of Milan had been before his conversion a Valentinian, Epiphanius a Nicolaitan. See Eusebius, *H.E.* Bk VI. c. 18 ; Epiph. *Haer.* XXVI. c. 17, p. 198, Oehler.

On the other hand, it may be argued that the Church in receiving such recruits lost much of that simplicity of doctrine and practice to which it had hitherto owed her rapid and unvarying success. The Gnostics brought with them into their new faith the use of pictures and statues, of incense, and of all the paraphernalia of the worship of the heathen gods. Baptism which, among the Jewish community in which Christianity was born, was an extremely simple rite, to be performed by anybody and entirely symbolical in its character[1], became an elaborate ceremony which borrowed the name as well as many of the adjuncts of initiation into the Mysteries. So, too, the Agape (love-feast) or common meal, which in pre-Christian times was, as we have seen, common to all Greek religious associations unconnected with the State, was transformed by the Gnostics into a rite surrounded by the same provisions for secrecy and symbolizing the same kind of sacrifice as those which formed the central point of the mystic drama at Eleusis and elsewhere. Both these sacraments, as they now came to be called, were thought to be invested with a magical efficacy, and to demand for their proper celebration a priesthood as exclusive as, and a great deal more ambitious than, that of Eleusis or Alexandria. The daring speculations of the Gnostics as to the nature of the godhead and the origin of the world also forced upon the Catholics the necessity of formulating her views on these points and making adhesion to them a test of membership[2]. To do so was possibly to choose the smaller of two evils, yet it can hardly be denied that the result of the differences of opinion thus aroused was to deluge the world

---

[1] It could be even self-administered, as in the *Acts of Paul and Thekla*, where Thekla baptizes herself in the arena. See Tischendorf's text. The *Clementine Homilies* (Bk XIV. c. 1) show that it could be immediately followed by the Eucharist without any intermediate rite or preparation. Contrast with this the elaborate ceremonies described by Cyril of Jerusalem, where the white-robed band of converts after a long catechumenate, including fasting and the communication of secret doctrines and passwords, approach on Easter Eve the doors of the church where the lights turned darkness into day. See Hatch, *H. L.* pp. 297, 299.

[2] Duchesne, *Hist. Christian Ch.* p. 32 ; Harnack, *What is Christianity?* Eng. ed. p. 210.

with blood and to stay the progress of human knowledge for more than a thousand years[1]. It is said that if Gnosticism had not been forcibly suppressed, as it was directly the Christian priesthood obtained a share in the government of the State, Christianity would have been nothing but a battle-ground for warring sects, and must have perished from its own internal dissensions. It may be so ; but it is at least as possible that, if left unmolested, many of the wilder sects would soon have withered away from their own absurdity, and that none of the others would have been able to endure for long. In this respect also, the history of the post-Reformation sects offers an interesting parallel.

Be that as it may, it is plain that the Catholic Church, in devoting her energies to the suppression of the Gnostic heresies, lost much of the missionary power which till then had seemed all-conquering. During the two centuries which elapsed between the siege of Jerusalem under Vespasian and the accession of Aurelian, the Church had raised herself from the position of a tiny Jewish sect to that of the foremost among the many religions of the Roman Empire. A brief but bloody persecution under Diocletian convinced the still Pagan Emperors of the impossibility of suppressing Christianity by force, and the alliance which they were thus driven to conclude with it enabled the Church to use successfully against the Gnostics the arm which had proved powerless against the Catholics[2]. Yet the

---

[1] As Hatch, *H. L.* pp. 274–279, has pointed out, the term ὁμοούσιος, which led to so much shedding of Christian blood, first occurs among the post-Christian Gnostics, and led in turn to most of the wranglings about " substance," " person," and the other metaphysical distinctions and their result in " strife and murder, the devastation of fair fields, the flame of fire and sword " (*ibid.* p. 279). For the possibilities of Greek science, had it not been opposed by the Church, see *ibid.* p. 26.

[2] See the edict of Constantine, which Eusebius (*Vit. Constantini*, cc. LXIV., LXV.) quotes with unholy glee, prohibiting the Gnostics from presuming to assemble together either publicly or privately, and commanding that their "houses of prayer" should be confiscated and handed over to the Catholic Church. Eusebius (*ibid.* c. LXVI.) says that the result of this was that the " savage beasts crept secretly into the Church," and continued to disseminate their doctrines by stealth. Perhaps such a result was to be expected.

triumph was a costly one, and was in its turn followed by a schism which rent the Church in twain more effectually than the Gnostic speculations could ever have done. In the West, indeed, the Latin Church was able to convert the barbarians who extinguished the Western half of the Roman Empire; but in the East, Christianity had to give way to a younger and more ardent faith. How far this was due to the means taken by the Church to suppress Gnosticism must still be a matter of speculation, but it is certain that after her first triumph over heresy she gained no more great victories.

CHAPTER VIII

POST-CHRISTIAN GNOSTICS: THE OPHITES

ALTHOUGH the Ophites were one of the most widely-spread and in some respects the most interesting of the heretical sects which came to light after the foundation of the Christian Church, we know nothing at first hand about their origin. Philastrius, or Philaster of Brescia, writing about 380 A.D., includes them among those "who taught heresies before the Coming of Christ[1]"; but the phrase does not perhaps bear its apparent meaning, and the late date at which he wrote makes it unlikely that he possessed any exclusive evidence on the point. A more plausible tradition, which is common to St Augustine[2], to the tractate *Against All Heresies* which passes under the name of Tertullian[3], and to the similar one attributed to St Jerome[4], is that the Ophites derived their doctrines from Nicolaus or Nicolas of Antioch, the deacon mentioned in the Acts[5], and that they are therefore alluded to under the name of Nicolaitans[6] in the address to the Church of Ephesus in the Canonical Apocalypse. Origen, on the other hand, in his *Discourse against Celsus* says that they boasted of one Euphrates

[1] "Eorum qui ante adventum Christi Haereseos arguuntur." Philastrius, Ep. Brixiensis, *de Haeresibus Liber*, c. i. vol. i. p. 5, Oehler.

[2] Augustinus, *de Haeresibus* (cf. *ad Quod vult deum*) *Liber*, c. XVII. i. p. 200, Oehler.

[3] Pseudo-Tertullianus, *Adversus omnes Haereses*, cc. v., vi. p. 273, Oehler. The writer was probably Victorinus of Pettau.

[4] Pseudo-Hieronymus, *Indiculus de Haeresibus*, c. III., vol. i. p. 285, Oehler.

[5] Acts vi. 5. It will be noted that Epiphanius, who himself belonged to the sect in his youth, interposes only the Basilidians between them and the followers of Saturninus, the "heresy" of which last he derives directly from that of Simon Magus.

[6] Rev. ii. 6, 15.

as their founder[1] ; while Hippolytus declares that their tenets
were said by themselves to be due to " the very numerous
discourses which were handed down by James the brother of
the Lord to Mariamne[2]." From which contradictory statements we may gather that the " heresy " of the Ophites was,
even as early as 230 A.D., a very old one, which may have
appeared even before Christianity began to show its power,
and that it was probably born in Asia Minor and owed much
to the Pagan religions there practised and little or nothing
to any dominant personality as did the systems of Simon Magus
and the heresies treated of in the succeeding chapters.

It is also probable that between the time when the Canonical
Apocalypse was written and that of Origen and Hippolytus[3],
the Ophites altered their doctrines more than once. We may
not be able to go so far as their historian, Father Giraud, who
thinks that he can distinguish between their earlier opinions,
which he would attribute to the Naassenes or Ophites[4] described
by Hippolytus, and those of a later school to which he would
assign the name of Ophites specially[5]. Yet many of the

[1] Origen, *cont. Celsum*, Bk VI. c. 28. Possibly the Euphrates called
" the Peratic " or Mede by Hippolytus (*op. cit.* Bk IV. c. 2, p. 54, Cruice).

[2] Hippolytus, *op. cit.* Bk V. c. 7, p. 141, Cruice. This Mariamne is
doubtless the sister of Philip mentioned in the Apocryphal *Acta Philippi*
(c. XXXII., Tischendorf), which have, as is said later, a strong Gnostic or
Manichaean tinge. Celsus knew a sect which took its name from her. See
Origen, *cont. Cels.* Bk v. c. 62.

[3] The Canonical Apocalypse is not earlier than 70 A.D., and was probably written soon after the fall of the Temple of Jerusalem. Hippolytus
and Origen wrote 130 years later.

[4] Naassene is evidently derived from the Hebrew or Aramaean נחש
" Serpent," cf. Hipp. *op. cit.* Bk v. c. 6, p. 139, Cruice, and exactly corresponds to the Greek ὀφίτης and the Latin *serpentinus* (Low Latin *serpen-
tarius*). " Worshipper of the Serpent " seems to be the patristic gloss on
the meaning of the word.

[5] Giraud, *Ophitae*, c. 4, § 65, p. 89. The question really depends upon
Hippolytus' sources, as to which see last chapter, pp. 11, 12. Cf. De Faye,
Introduction, etc., p. 41. Hippolytus' Naassene author cannot be much
earlier than 170 A.D. since he quotes from St John's Gospel, and probably
later than the work of Irenaeus written in 180–185. Yet the Ophite system
described by Irenaeus is evidently not a primitive one and has been added
to by his Latin translator. See n. 3, p. 47, *infra*.

Fathers confuse their doctrines with those of the Sethians, the Cainites, and other sects which seem to have had some distinguishing features[1]; while Hippolytus, who shows a more critical spirit than the other heresiologists, says expressly that the other heresies just named were little different in appearance from this one, being united by the same spirit of error[2]. The confusion is further increased by his statement that the Naassenes called themselves Gnostics, although Carpocrates' followers, who must have been later in time, are elsewhere said to be the first to adopt this name[3]. For there was at least one other sect of heretics who did the same thing, and to whom Epiphanius in his *Panarion* attributes, together with a theological and cosmological system not unlike that hereafter described, mysteries of unnameable obscenity with which the Ophites were never charged[4]. In this respect it may be as well to remember the words of Tertullian that the heretics

"know no respect even for their own leaders. Hence it is that schisms seldom happen among heretics because, even when they exist, they do not appear; for their very unity is schism. I am greatly in error," he continues, " if they do not amongst themselves even diverge from their own rules, since every man, as it suits his own temper, modifies the traditions he has received after the same fashion as did he who handed them down to him, when he moulded them according to his own free will.... What was allowed to Valentinus is allowable to the Valentinians, and that is lawful for the Marcionites which Marcion did, *i.e.* to innovate on the faith

---

[1] Irenaeus, Bk I. c. 27, § 1, p. 226, Harvey, says that the Ophites are the same as the Sethians; Hippolytus, *op. cit.* Bk V. c. 11, p. 184, Cruice, that they are connected with the Peratae, the Sethians, and the system of Justinus. Epiphanius, *Haer.* XXXVII. c. 1, p. 494, Oehler, while deriving them from Nicolaus the Deacon, gives them a common origin with those whom he calls Gnostics simply, and identifies these last with the Borboriani, Coddiani, Stratiotici, Phibionitae, Zacchaei, and Barbelitae (see *Haer.* XXVI. c. 3).

[2] Hippolytus, *op. cit.* Bk V. c. 11, p. 184, Cruice.

[3] ἑαυτοὺς γνωστικοὺς ὀνομάζοντες. Hippolytus, *loc. cit.* Eusebius, *H. E.* Bk IV. c. 7, says that Carpocrates was the father of the heresy of the Gnostics and contemporary with Basilides.

[4] Epiphanius, *Haer.* XXVI. c. 7, pp. 174, 176, Oehler.

according to his own judgment. In short, all heresies when in-
vestigated are found to be in many particulars disagreeing with
their own authors[1]."

If Tertullian was right, it is idle to expect that after the
lapse of nineteen centuries we can hope to distinguish between
the opinions of an heresiarch and those of his followers who
differed from or improved upon his teaching.

Of the country in which the Ophites first appeared, and
where to the last they had their strongest following, there can,
however, be little doubt. Phrygia, by which is meant the
entire central part of Asia Minor or, to use its modern name,
Anatolia, must from its situation have formed a great meeting-
place for different creeds, among which that of the Jews occupied
in the first centuries of our era a prominent place. Seleucus
Nicator had followed the example of Alexander in Egypt in
granting the Jews full rights of citizenship in all his cities,
and Antiochus the Great took even more practical steps towards
inducing them to settle there when he transported thither two
thousand Jewish families from Mesopotamia and Babylon[2].
These Jews of the Eastern Diaspora or Dispersion had, however,
by no means kept whole the faith of their forefathers, and there
seems in consequence to have been less racial hatred between
them and the earlier inhabitants of the country here than elsewhere[3].   In religious matters, these last, too, seem to have been
little affected by the Euhemerism that had destroyed the faith
of the more sophisticated Greeks, and the orgiastic worship of
Cybele, Attis, and Sabazius found in Phrygia its principal seat.
The tendency of the inhabitants towards religious hysteria was
not likely to be lessened by the settlement in the centre of
Asia Minor of the Celtic tribes known as the Galatae, who had
gradually passed under the Roman yoke in the time of Augustus,
but seem long to have retained their Celtic taste for innovations

---

[1] Tertullian, *de Praescript. Haer.* c. XLII.

[2] Josephus, *Antiq.* Bk XII. c. 3.

[3] Ramsay, *Cities and Bishoprics of Phrygia*, II. pp. 667 *sqq.* ; *St Paul*,
pp. 142 *sqq.*; *Commentary on Galatians*, pp. 189 *sqq.* The fact that Timothy,
the son of the Jewess Eunice by a Greek father, was not circumcised (see
Acts xvi. 1) is quoted in support.

in religious matters, and to have supplied from the outset an endless number of heresies to the Church[1]. Moreover, in the Wars of Succession which followed the death of Alexander, Phrygia had been bandied about like a shuttlecock between Antigonus and Lysimachus ; in the decadence of the Seleucid house, it had been repeatedly harried by the pretenders to the Syrian crown ; and it had, during the temporary supremacy of Mithridates and his son-in-law Tigranes, been subject to the tyranny of the Armenians[2]. Thanks to the policy of these barbarian kings, it had in great measure been denuded of its Greek-speaking inhabitants[3], the growth of its towns had been checked, and the country seems to have been practically divided among a crowd of dynasts or priest-kings, generally the high-priests of temples possessing vast landed estates and preserving their importance by the celebration of yearly festivals. Dr Mahaffy compares these potentates with the prince-bishops and lordly abbots produced by nearly the same conditions in mediaeval Europe[4], and Sir William Ramsay's and Mr Hogarth's researches of late years in Anatolia have shown how much truth there is in the comparison.

The religion practised by these priest-kings throughout the whole of Asia Minor differed slightly in form, but was one in substance[5]. It was in effect the worship of the bisexual and mortal gods whom we have already seen worshipped under varying names in the Eastern basin of the Mediterranean. These deities, whose alternate appearance as male and female, infant and adult, could only be explained to Western ears as the result of incestuous unions, could all on final analysis be reduced to one great divinity in whom all Nature was contained. The essence of the Anatolian religion, says Sir William Ramsay, when describing the state of things that existed in Phrygia immediately before the preaching of St Paul, was

---

[1] *E.g.* the Montanist, the most formidable of the heresies which attacked the primitive Church, apart from Gnosticism. Cf. also Galatians i. 6.

[2] Mahaffy, *Greek World under Roman Sway*, p. 168. For the tyranny of the Armenians, see Plutarch, *Lucullus*, cc. XIV., XXI.

[3] Mahaffy, *Gk. World*, p. 100.

[4] Mahaffy, *ibid.* p. 225.

[5] Ramsay, *Cities*, etc., I. p. 9.

" the adoration of the life of Nature—that life apparently subject to death, yet never dying, but reproducing itself in new forms, different and yet the same. This perpetual self-identity under varying forms, this annihilation of death through the power of self-reproduction, was the object of an enthusiastic worship, characterized by remarkable self-abandonment and immersion in the divine, by a mixture of obscene symbolism and sublime truths, by negation of the moral distinctions and family ties that exist in a more developed society, but do not exist in the free life of Nature. The mystery of self-reproduction, of eternal unity amid temporary diversity, is the key to explain all the repulsive legends and ceremonies that cluster round that worship, and all the manifold manifestations or diverse embodiments of the ultimate single divine life that are carved on the rocks of Asia Minor[1]."

Whether the Phrygians of Apostolic times actually saw all these sublime ideas underlying the religion of their country may be doubted ; but it is fairly certain that at the time in question there was worshipped throughout Anatolia a divine family comprising a goddess known as the Mother of the Gods, together with a male deity, who was at once her son, her spouse, her brother, and sometimes her father[2]. The worship of this pair, who were in the last resort considered as one bisexual being, was celebrated in the form of festivals and mystery-plays like those of the Middle Ages, in which the birth, nuptials, death, and resurrection of the divinities were acted in dramatic form. At these festivals, the worshippers gave themselves up to religious excitement alternating between continence sometimes carried to the extent of self-mutilation on the part of the men, and hysterical or religious prostitution on the part of the women[3]. The gathering of foreign merchants and slaves in the Anatolian cities, and the constant shifting of their

[1] Ramsay, *Cities*, etc., i. p. 87.
[2] Ramsay, *ibid.* i. p. 92.
[3] Ramsay, *ibid.* i. pp. 93, 94. The Galli or priests of Cybele, who mutilated themselves in religious ecstasy, seem to have been the feature of Anatolian religion which most struck the Romans, when the statue of the Mother of the Gods first appeared among them. Cf. next page. For the other side of the religion, see Lucian, *de Dea Syria*, cc. VI., XLIII., and Apuleius, *Metamorph.* Bk VIII. c. 29.

inhabitants by their successive masters, had forced on the votaries of these Phrygian deities a *theocrasia* of the most complete kind, and the Phrygian god and goddess were in turn identified with the deities of Eleusis, of whom indeed they may have been the prototypes, with the Syrian Aphrodite and Adonis, with the Egypto-Greek Serapis and Isis, and probably with many Oriental deities as well[1]. At the same time, their fame and their worship had spread far beyond Phrygia. The primitive statue of the goddess of Pessinus, a black stone or baetyl dignified by the name of the Mother of the Gods, was transported to Rome in the stress of the Second Punic War and there became the centre of a ritual served by eunuch priests supported by the State[2]; while, later, her analogue, the Syrian goddess, whose temple at Hierapolis, according to Lucian, required a *personnel* of over three hundred ministrants, became the object of the special devotion of the Emperor Nero[3]. As with the Alexandrian divinities, the respect paid to these stranger deities by the legions carried their worship into every part of the Roman world[4].

The element which the Jews of Asia contributed to Anatolian religion at this period was probably more important than has been generally supposed. M. Cumont's theory that the epithet of the "Highest" ($\Upsilon\psi\iota\sigma\tau\sigma$) often applied to the God of Anatolia and Syria really covers the personality of Yahweh of Israel rests upon little proof at present[5]. It may be conceded that the tendency to monotheism—or to speak strictly their hatred

---

[1] As in the hymn to Attis said to have been sung in the Great Mysteries, given in the *Philosophumena* (see p. 54, *infra*). Cf. Ramsay, *Cities*, etc., I. pp. 132, 263, 264, for other identifications. The Anatolian name of the *Dea Syria* to whose cult Nero was addicted, was Atargatis, which Prof. Garstang would derive from the Babylonian Ishtar (Strong, *Syrian Goddess*, 1913, p. vii); see Cumont, *Les Religions Orientales dans le Paganisme Romain*, Paris, 1906, p. 126. The whole of Cumont's chapters on Syria and Asia Minor (*op. cit.* pp. 57–89) can be consulted with advantage. The American edition, 1911, contains some additional notes. See, too, Decharme's article on Cybele in Daremberg and Saglio's *Dict. des Antiq.*

[2] Dill, *Nero to Marcus Aurelius*, pp. 548 *sqq.*

[3] See n. 1, *supra*; Suetonius, *Nero*, c. LVI.

[4] Dill, *loc. cit.*, and authorities there quoted.

[5] Cumont, *Rel. Or.* p. 77, and see index to American edition, 1911.

for the worshippers of many gods—rooted in the Jews from the Captivity onwards may at first have done much to hasten the progress of the *theocrasia* which was welding all the gods of the Mysteries into one great God of Nature. But the Babylonian or Oriental Jews, called in the Talmud and elsewhere the Ten Tribes, probably had some inborn sympathy with the more or less exalted divinities of the West. Even in the temple of Jerusalem, Ezekiel sees in his vision " women weeping for Tammuz[1]," while Jeremiah complains of the Jews making cakes to the Queen of Heaven, which seems to be another name for the Mother of the Gods[2]. The feminine side of the Anatolian worship can therefore have come to them as no new thing. Perhaps it was due to this that they so soon fell away from their ancestral faith, and that, in the words of the Talmud, " the baths and wines of Phrygia separated the Ten Tribes from their brethren[3]." That their collection of money for the Temple in Roman times was due not so much to any religious motive, as to some of the financial operations in which the Jews were always engaging, Cicero hints with fair plainness in his Oration in defence of Flaccus[4]. They seem, too, to have intermarried freely with the Greek citizens, while the sons of these mixed marriages did not undergo the circumcision which the Jews of the Western Dispersion demanded not only from native Jews but also from proselytes of alien blood[5].

The Jews also brought with them into Phrygia superstitions or side-beliefs to which they were probably much more firmly attached than to their national religion. The practice of magic had always been popular among the Chosen People as far back as the time of Saul, and the bowls inscribed with spells against enchantments and evil spirits form almost the only relics which

---

[1] Ezekiel viii. 14.

[2] Jeremiah vii. 18 ; lxiv. 17–19.

[3] Ramsay, *Cities*, etc., II. p. 674, quoting Neubauer, *Géographie du Talmud*.

[4] Cicero, *pro Flacc.* c. XXVIII. The Jews of the Dispersion in Egypt had temples of their own, in one at least of which Yahweh had for assessors a goddess Anat and a subordinate god Bethel. See René Dussaud, " Les Papyrus judéo-araméens d'Elephantiné," *R.H.R.* t. LXIV. (1911) p. 350.

[5] Acts xvi. 2, 3. See n. 3, p. 28, *supra*.

they have left in the mounds which mark their settlement at
Hilleh on the site of the ancient Babylon[1]. From this and
other evidence, it would seem that the Babylonian Jews had
borrowed from their Chaldaean captors many of their views as
to the importance of the Name in magic, especially when used
for the purposes of exorcism or of spells; that they thought
the name of their national god Yahweh particularly efficacious;
and that the different names of God used in the Old Testament
were supposed, according to a well-known rule in magic, to be
of greater efficiency as the memory of their meaning and actual
significance died out among them[2]. The Babylonian Jews,
moreover, as is evident from the Book of Daniel, no sooner
found themselves among the well-to-do citizens of a great city
than they turned to the professional practice of divination and
of those curious arts whereby they could make a living from
their Gentile neighbours[3].

Hence it is that Phrygia, like the rest of Asia
Minor during the Apostolic Age, was full of strolling
Jewish sorcerers who undertook for money to cast out devils,
to effect and destroy enchantments, to send and interpret
dreams, and to manufacture love philtres[4]. That in doing so
they made great use of the name of their national deity seems
plain from Origen's remark that "not only do those belonging
to the Jewish nation employ in their prayers to God and in the
exorcising of demons the words: God of Abraham and God of

---

[1] Layard, *Nineveh and Babylon*, 1853, pp. 509 *sqq*. Was this why Daniel
was called "Master of the Magicians"? Dan. iv. 9; v. 11.

[2] Thus, in a Coptic spell, the Words from the Cross: "Eli, eli, lama
sabachthani," are described as "the revered names of God." See Rossi,
"*Trattato gnostico*" in *Mem. della Real. Accad. di Torino*, Ser. B, XLII.
fol. 9. So in mediaeval magic the word "Eieazareie" or "Escherie"
is frequently used, apparently without any suspicion that it covers the
אהיה אשר אהיה 'Ehyeh 'asher 'ehyeh—"I am that I am" of Exodus.

[3] Hausrath, *Hist. of New Testament Times*, Eng. ed. 1878, I. pp. 126, 127,
and authorities there quoted.

[4] See last note. In the Acts, Bar-jesus or Elymas the sorcerer, the
seven sons of Sceva, and some of those who burned their magical books
at Ephesus, are said to be Jews. Harnack, *Expansion of Christianity*,
Eng. ed. I. pp. 156, 157, says the Jews were known as exorcisers of
demons throughout the Roman Empire.

Isaac and God of Jacob, but so also do most of those who occupy themselves with magical rites. For there is found in treatises on magic in many countries such an invocation of God and assumption of the divine name, as implies a familiar use of it by these men in their dealings with demons[1]." This is abundantly borne out by the spells preserved for us by the Magic Papyri before mentioned, where the expressions "God of Abraham," "God of Isaac," "God of Jacob" constantly occur. One spell given above contains, as we have seen, along with many unfamiliar expressions drawn from Greek, Persian, Egyptian, and even Sumerian sources, the words "Blessed be the Lord God of Abraham[2]," and in nearly every one do we find the Tetragrammaton or four-lettered name of God transliterated in the A.V. Jehovah, either with or without some of the other Divine names used in the Old Testament. The names of the angels Gabriel, Michael, and Raphael given in the Old Testament and the Apocrypha are also common in all this literature[3].

Did the Babylonian Jews bring with them into Phrygia any theory of the universe other than the direct and unfettered rule of Jehovah and the creation of the world from nothing, which they gathered from their sacred books? There is little evidence on the point, save some expressions of doubtful import in the Magic Papyri[4] and the statement of Origen that " the name Sabaoth, and Adonai and the other names treated with so much reverence among the Hebrews.... belong to a secret

---

[1] Origen, *cont. Cels.* Bk IV. c. 33. Cf. *ibid.* c. 34, and Bk I. c. 22. Also Justin Martyr's *Dial. c. Tryph.* c. LXXXV.

[2] See Chapter III, vol. I. n. 6, p. 106, *supra*.

[3] Karl Wessely, in *Expositor*, Series III, vol. IV. (1886), pp. 194 *sqq.*, gives many specimens of these spells. The papyri from which they are taken are printed in full in his *Griechische Zauberpapyrus von Paris und London*, Wien, 1888, and his *Neue Griechische Zauberpapyri*, Wien, 1893.. See also Parthey, *Zwei griechische Zauberpapyri des Berliner Museums*, Berlin, 1866 ; Leemans, *Papyri Graeci Mus. Ant. Publ. Lugduni Batavi*, t. II., Leyden, 1885, and Kenyon, *Gk. Papyri in B.M.* before quoted.

[4] They sometimes speak of certain expressions being used by the ἀρχιερεῖς " high priests," Leemans, *op. cit.* t. II. p. 29. Does this mean the adepts in magic or the heads of a sect ?

theology which refers to the Framer of all things[1]." It might
be possible to deduce from this that the elaborate system known
as the Cabala or secret tradition of the Jews was already in
existence[2]. This system, on its theoretical or speculative side,
attempts to explain the existence of the physical universe by
postulating a whole series of intermediate powers emanating
from the Supreme Being of whom they are the attributes or
names; while, on the other or "practical," it professes to perform
wonders and to reveal mysteries by a childish juggling with
letters in the shape of anagrams and acrostics or with their
numerical values[3]. As has been said above, follies of this last-
named kind were unknown neither to the later Orphics nor to
the primitive Church, and might well be thought to have been
acquired by the Jews during their stay in Babylon, where the
Semitic inhabitants seem from a very early date and for magical
reasons to have used numbers instead of letters in writing the
names of their gods[4]. It would not have been difficult for them
to have acquired at the same time from the Persian masters
of Babylon the doctrine of emanation instead of creation which
is to be found in the Zend Avesta as well as in all the post-Christian Gnostic systems. But there are other channels besides the
Anatolian religion through which these ideas might have come
into the West[5], and it will be better not to lay any stress upon
this. That the Cabala in the complete form in which it appears
in the books known as the *Sepher Jetzirah* and the *Sepher
Zohar* does not go further back than the VIth or VIIth century
of our era, seems to be the opinion of all those best qualified
to judge in the matter. M. Isidore Loeb, who has given the
most coherent and compact summary of Cabalistic teaching
that has appeared of late years, finds its germs in Babylonian
Judaism at about the same period which saw the blossoming of

---

[1] Origen, *cont. Cels.* Bk. I. c. 24.

[2] So Kuenen, *Religion of Israel* (Eng. ed.), III. p. 314, says that the
existence of the Cabala is indicated in the Talmud.

[3] See Chapter V, vol. I. pp. 169, 170, *supra*.

[4] The Sumerian moon-god, Nannar, was denoted by the number 30,
Marduk called 50 and so on. See King, *Seven Tablets of Creation*, 1902, I.
p. 66.

[5] See Chapter VII, *supra*.

the Christian Gnostic sects, without going so far as to derive
either of the later doctrines from the other[1].

However this may be, there is a fair consensus of opinion
among the Fathers of the Church as to the doctrines current
among those whom, for reasons to be presently seen, they called
the Ophites or worshippers of the Serpent. The aim of the
sect seems to have been to produce an eclectic system which
should reconcile the religious traditions current from time
immemorial in Western Asia with the worship of the Hellenized
gods of Asia Minor, and the teachings of the already powerful
Christian Church. With this view they went back to what is
probably the earliest philosophical theory of the origin of the
universe, and declared that before anything was, there existed
God, but God conceived as an infinite ocean of divinity, too
great and too remote to be apprehended by man's intelligence,
of whom and of whose attributes nothing could be known or
said, and who could only be likened to a boundless sea. Something like this was the view of the earliest inhabitants of Babylonia, who declared that before heaven or earth or the gods
came into being there was nothing but a vast waste of waters[2].
At some time or another, the same idea passed into Egypt,
when the Egyptians attributed the beginning of things to Nu
or the primaeval deep[3]; and it was probably the spread of
this tradition into Ionia which induced Thales of Miletus, the
earliest of the Ionian philosophers, to assert that water was
the first of all things[4]. This unknowable and inaccessible

---

[1] Isidore Loeb, *La Grande Encyclopédie, s.v.* La Cabbale juive; *ibid.*
F. Herman Krüger, *s.v.* Gnosticisme, and Franck, *La Kabbale*, Paris, 1843,
p. 203, both notice the likeness between Gnosticism and the Cabala and
say that they are derived from the same source.

[2] See the Sumerian Hymn of Creation translated by Sayce, *Religions
of Ancient Egypt and Babylonia* (Gifford Lectures), Edinburgh, 1902, p. 380;
Jastrow, *Religion of Babylonia and Assyria*, Boston, U.S.A. 1898, p. 490;
King, *Seven Tablets*, p. 3; Rogers, *Rel. of Bab.*, p. 108.

[3] "Au commencement était le Nun, l'océan primordial, dans les pro-
fondeurs infinies duquel flottaient les germes des choses. De toute éternité
Dieu s'engendra et s'enfanta lui-même au sein de cette masse liquide sans
forme encore et sans usage." Maspero, *Hist. Ancienne des Peuples de
l'Orient*, p. 326.

[4] Diogenes Laertius, *Vit. Philosoph.* Bk I. c. 6.

power, the Ophites declared to be ineffable or impossible to name, and he was only referred to by them as Bythos or the Deep. The same idea and the same name were adopted by most of the later Gnostics[1].

---

[1] Including in that name some who attained to high office in the Catholic Church. Thus Hatch, *H. L.* p. 255, says with apparent truth that Clement of Alexandria " anticipated Plotinus in conceiving of God as being ' beyond the One and higher than the Monad itself,' which was the highest abstraction of current philosophy." The passage he here relies on is in Clement's *Paedagogus*, Bk I. c. 8. Hatch goes on to say, " There is no name that can properly be named of Him : ' Neither the One nor the Good, nor Mind, nor Absolute Being, nor Father, nor Creator, nor Lord ' "—expressions to be found in Clement's *Stromata*, Bk v. c. 12. Clement's orthodoxy may be called in question ; but no fault has been found in that respect with Synesius, Bishop of Ptolemais and the friend of Hypatia. Yet in his Hymns he uses expressions which would have come naturally to the lips of any Ophite. Thus :

Σὺ δ' ἄρρην, σὺ δὲ θῆλυς,	"Male thou and female,
Σὺ δὲ φωνά, σὺ δὲ σιγά,	Voice thou and silence,
Φύσεως φύσις γονῶσα,	Nature engendered of Nature.
Σὺ δ' ἄναξ, αἰῶνος αἰών,	Thou King, Aeon of Aeons.
Τὸ μέν, ῇ θέμις βοᾶσαι ;	What is it lawful to call thee ?

and again

Πατέρων πάντων	Father of all Fathers,
Πάτερ, αὐτοπάτωρ,	Father of thyself,
Προπάτωρ, ἀπάτωρ,	Propator [Forefather] who hast no father,
Υἱὲ σεαυτοῦ	O Son of thyself
Μύστας δὲ νόος	But the initiated mind
Τά τε καὶ τὰ λέγει,	Says this and that,
Βυθὸν ἄρρητον	Celebrating with dances
'Αμφιχορεύων.	The Ineffable Bythos."

(Hymn III)

The ineffability of divine names was an old idea in Egypt, especially in the Osirian religion, where it forms the base of the story of Ra and Isis. So the name of Osiris himself was said to be ineffable. See Eug. Lefébure in *Sphinx*, Stockholm, vol. I. pp. 99–102. The name of Marduk of Babylon is in the same way declared ineffable in an inscription of Neri_glissar, *Trans. Roy. Soc. Litt.* 2nd series, vol. VIII. p. 276. The name of Yahweh became ineffable directly after Alexander. See Halévy, *Revue des Études juives*, t. ix. (1884), p. 172. In every case, the magical idea that the god might be compelled by utterance of his secret name seems to be at the root of the practice. Cf. Erman, *Life in Ancient Egypt*, Eng. ed. p. 354.

From this unknowable principle or Father (Πατὴρ ἄγνωστος) there shone forth, according to the Ophites, a Primordial Light, infinite and incorruptible, which is the Father of all things subsequent to him[1]. Here they may have been inspired, not by the Babylonian, but by its derivative, the Jewish tradition given in the Book of Genesis[2]. But this Light was in effect, though not in name, the chief god of their system, and in Asia Minor the gods had never perhaps been imagined as existing in any but human form. Accordingly they described this Light as the First Man, meaning thereby no terrestrial creature, but a heavenly or archetypal man in whose likeness mankind was afterwards made[3]. From him came forth a second Light sometimes called his Ennoia or Thought, which expression seems to cover the idea that this Second Man or Son of Man, by both which names he was known to the Ophites, was not begotten in the ordinary way of mortals, but was produced from the First Man as a thought or concept is formed in the brain[4]. Or we may, to take another metaphor, regard this Ennoia as the rays of light which emanate or flow forth from a lamp or other source of light, but which have no independent existence and still remain connected with their parent. Such was the Ophite idea with regard to the two great Lights or the

[1] The whole account of Ophite doctrine as to the origin of things is here taken from Irenaeus, Bk I. c. 28, pp. 226 *sqq.*, Harvey.

[2] Genesis i. 8.

[3] Philo explains that there is a vast difference between man as now made and the first man who was made according to the image of God, *De opificio mundi*, c. 46. This idea of an archetypal man was widely spread over Eastern Europe and Asia, and Bousset, *Hauptprobleme der Gnosis*, Göttingen, 1907, Kap. IV, " Der Urmensch," has collected all or nearly all the references to it in the literature of the period that could be produced up to that date. As to its origin, the issue is still very doubtful. While we should naturally expect to find it in the Babylonian legends, the Tablets of Creation contain no certain allusion to it, while it is certainly to be traced in the Zend Avesta and its related books. Until we are able to compare the dates of these two sources it seems idle to speculate as to which is the original one and which the derived. But see Introduction (pp. lxi–lxiii and note on last page quoted) *supra.*

[4] This is a less primitive and therefore probably later way of accounting for the birth of one spiritual or superhuman being from another, than that of Simon Magus who made his Supreme Being androgyne.

First and Second Man whom they refused to consider as separate, giving them both the name of Adamas, or the Unconquered, a classical epithet of the Hades already identified at Eleusis with Dionysos[1]. They also called them, as will be seen later, the Father-and-Son. In this, perhaps, they did not go outside the conception of the Anatolian religion, which always represented the Divine Son as the spouse of the goddess who gave him birth, and in this way eternally begetting himself. Thus, the Phrygian goddess Cybele under the name of Agdistis was said to be violently enamoured of Atys who was in effect her own son[2]. The same idea was familiar to the Egyptians, among whom more than one god is described as the "bull (*i.e.* male or husband) of his mother," and it may thus have passed into the Alexandrian religion, where Horus was, as we have seen, often given instead of Osiris as the lover of Isis[3]. At Eleusis it was more modestly concealed under the myth which made Dionysos or Hades at once the ravisher of Persephone and her son by Zeus in serpent form—a myth which is summed up in the mystic phrase preserved by Clement of Alexandria that " The bull is the father of the serpent, and the serpent the father of the bull[4]."

Thus the Ophites accounted for the divinity who was in effect their Supreme God, the still higher Bythos, as we have seen, being put in the background as too awful for human consideration[5]. But it was still necessary to make manifest

---

[1] Theocritus, *Idyll*, II. l. 34. For the identity of Hades and Dionysos see Chapter II. vol. I. *supra.*

[2] Pausanias, *Descpt. Graec.* Bk VIII. cc. 17, 20 ; Arnobius, *adv. Gentes*, Bk V. cc. 5, 7. Cf. Decharme in Daremberg and Saglio's *Dict. des Antiq. s.v.* Cybele.

[3] See Chapter II. vol. I. *supra.*

[4] Clem. Alex. *Protrept.* c. II.; Arnobius, *op. cit.* Bk VI. c. 21, calls it " the well-known senarian verse of a poet of Tarentum," and connects it with the Sabazian rites, whence it probably found its way to Eleusis.

[5] This relegation of the really Supreme God to an unregarded place in the pantheon is common enough in the history of religions. Thus the Shilluks of the Upper Nile take little notice of their great god Jôk, to whom they only sacrifice once a year, reserving all the rest of their worship for a being intermediate between God and man called Nyakang. See Gleichen, *The Anglo-Egyptian Soudan*, vol. I. pp. 162, 197, and *R.H.R.* 1911, Juillet-Août.

the feminine aspect of the deity which was always very prominent in Asia Minor. The Mother of the Gods, known as
Ma in Lydia, Cybele in Phrygia proper, Artemis at Ephesus,
the unnamed Syrian goddess at Hierapolis, and Aphrodite in
Cyprus and elsewhere[1], was in the early Christian centuries
the most prominent person in the Anatolian pantheon, a fact
which Sir William Ramsay would attribute to the matriarchate,
Mutterrecht, or custom of descent in the female line, which he
thinks indigenous to Asia Minor. In the earliest Phrygian
religion there seems little doubt that the supreme goddess was
originally considered to be bisexual, and capable of production
without male assistance, as is expressly stated in the legend of
Agdistis or Cybele preserved by Pausanias[2], and perhaps hinted
at in the stories of Amazons spread throughout the whole of
Asia Minor. But it is probable that, as Sir William Ramsay
himself says, this idea had become less prominent with the
immigration from Europe of tribes of male warriors without
female companions[3], while Semitic influence was always against
it. Hence the Ophites found themselves compelled to make
their female deity inferior or posterior to their male. " Below
these, again (*i.e.* below the First and Second Man or Father-and-
Son)," says Irenaeus in reporting their doctrines, " is the Holy
Spirit....whom they call the First Woman[4]." Neither he nor
Hippolytus gives us any direct evidence of the source whence
this feminine Power was thought by them to have issued. But
Hippolytus says without circumlocution that " this Man,"
i.e. Adamas or the Father-and-Son, " is both male and female[5],"
and he quotes the words of an Ophite hymn[6] addressed to him
that : " *From* thee is Father and *through* thee is Mother, two
names immortal, parents of Aeons, O thou citizen of heaven,

[1] See n. 1, p. 31, *supra.* The *Dea Syria* was otherwise called Atargatis,
of which Derketo was, *teste* Prof. Garstang, a homonym. See Strong, *The
Syrian Goddess,* p. 52 and n. 25.

[2] See n. 1, p. 31, *supra.*

[3] Ramsay, *Cities,* etc., I. p. 9.

[4] Irenaeus, *op. cit.* Bk I. c. 28, p. 227, Harvey.

[5] ἀρσενόθηλυς, Hippolytus, *op. cit.* Bk v. c. 1, p. 139, Cruice.

[6] See next note.

Man of mighty name[1] ! " Later, he puts in the mouth of the Naassene or Ophite writer from whom he repeatedly quotes, the phrase :

" The Spirit is where the Father and the Son are named, from whom and from the Father it is there born ; and this (that is, the Spirit) is the many-named, myriad-eyed Incomprehensible One for whom every nature in different ways yearns,"

or in other words the soul or animating principle of Nature[2]. It therefore seems that the first Ophites made their Supreme God a triad like the Eleusinian, the Alexandrian, and the Anatolian, consisting of three persons two of whom were males and the third a female, or a Father, Mother, and Son, of whom the Son was but another and renewed form of the Father, while the union of all three was necessary to express every aspect of the Deity, who was nevertheless one in essence[3].

---

[1] Ἀπὸ σοῦ πατὴρ καὶ διά σε μήτηρ, τὰ δύο ἀθάνατα ὀνόματα, Αἰώνων γονεῖς, πολῖτα οὐρανοῦ, μεγαλώνυμε ἄνθρωπε, Hippolytus, *op. cit.* Bk v. c. 1, p. 140, Cruice. Salmon points out that almost the same words occur in Hippolytus' account of the heresy of Monoimus the Arab, where he describes the monad as being among other things : Αὕτη μήτηρ, αὕτη πατήρ, τὰ δύο ἀθάνατα ὀνόματα, *op. cit.* Bk VIII. c. 12, p. 410, Cruice. He is inclined to attribute this to the real or supposed fact that both the Naassenes and Monoimus borrowed from the *Apophasis* of Simon. See Salmon in *Dict. Christian Biog. s.v.* Monoimus.

[2] Τὸ δὲ πνεῦμα ἐκεῖ [ἐστιν] ὅπου καὶ ὁ Πατὴρ ὀνομάζεται καὶ ὁ Υἱός, ἐκ τούτου [καὶ ἐκ] τοῦ Πατρὸς ἐκεῖ γεννώμενον, κ.τ.λ., Hippolytus, *op. cit.* Bk v. c. 9, pp. 174, 185, Cruice. The words in brackets are Cruice's emendation. Duncker and Schneidewin omit them and read γεννώμενος for γεννώμενον. Giraud, *op. cit.* pp. 92, 93, agrees with Cruice's reading, and points out that both the Spirit and the Son are here put forward as the masculine and feminine forms respectively of the great Adamas. It is evident, however, that among the earlier Ophites represented by Irenaeus' Greek text, the Spirit or First Woman was thought to come into being *after* the First Man and the Son of Man. See Irenaeus, Bk I. c. 28, p. 227, Harvey.

[3] Thus after saying that " he who says all things are composed (συνε-στάναι) from one (substance) errs, but that he who says they are framed from three speaks the truth," he goes on to say Μία γάρ ἐστι φησίν, ἡ μακαρία φύσις τοῦ μακαρίου ἀνθρώπου τοῦ ἄνω, τοῦ Ἀδάμαντος· μία δὲ ἡ θνητὴ κάτω· μία δὲ ἡ ἀβασίλευτος γενεὰ ἡ ἄνω γενομένη, κ.τ.λ., " For one is the blessed nature of the blessed Man above, viz. : Adamas, and one is the

This threefold division of things, said the Ophites, ran through all nature " there being three worlds or universes : the angelic (that sent directly from God), the psychic, and the earthly or material ; and three Churches : the Chosen, the Called, and the Captive[1]." The meaning of these names we shall see later when we consider the Ophite idea of the Apocatastasis[2] or return of the worlds to the Deity.

First, however, another Power had to be produced which should serve as an intermediary or ambassador from the Supreme Triad to the worlds below it. This necessity may have arisen from Plato's view, adopted by Philo of Alexandria, that God was too high and pure to be contaminated by any contact with matter[3]. But it may also owe something to the idea common to all Orientals that a king or great man can only communicate with his inferiors through a *wakil* or agent ; and that this idea was then current in Phrygia seems plain from the story in the Acts of the Apostles that in the Lycaonian province Barnabas, who was of majestic presence, was adored and nearly sacrificed to as Zeus, while Paul, who was the principal speaker, was only revered as Hermes[4]. The later Ophite account of the production of this intermediary power or messenger which we find in Irenaeus is that the Father-and-Son " delighting in the beauty of the Spirit "—that is of 'the First Woman—" shed their light upon her " and thus brought into existence " an incorruptible light, the third man, whom they call Christos[5]." With this last addition the

nature below which is subject to death, and one is the kingless race which is begotten above," etc. Hippolytus, *op. cit.* Bk v. c. 8, p. 157, Cruice.

[1] Hippolytus, *op. cit.* Bk v. c. 1, p. 140, Cruice.

[2] ἀποκατάστασις (see p. 57 *infra*). As Salmon has shown with great clearness, this, rather than the redemption of individual souls, is the aim of all post-Christian Gnostic systems,'*Dict. Christian Biog. s.v.* Gnosticism.

[3] Philo, *de Sacrificantibus*, c. 13 ; II. p. 261, Mangey.

[4] Acts xiv. 11–18.

[5] Postea, dicunt, exultante primo homine cum filio suo super formositate Spiritus, hoc est foeminae, et illuminante eam, generavit ex ea lumen incorruptibile, tertium masculum, quem Christum vocant. So the Latin version of Irenaeus, Bk I. c. 28, p. 227, Harvey. The Greek text, which should contain Irenaeus' own words, only says : Ἐρασθῆναι δέ φασι τὸν

Divine Family was considered complete, and the same author
tells us that Christos and his mother were " immediately drawn
up into the incorruptible aeon which they call the veritable
Church[1]." This seems to be the first appearance in Gnosticism
of the use of the word Church as signifying what was later
called the Pleroma or Fulness of the Godhead ; but it may be
compared to the " Great Council " apparently used in the same
sense by some unidentified prophet quoted by Origen, of which
Great Council Christ was said by the prophet to be the "Angel"
or messenger[2].

From this perfect Godhead, the Ophites had to show the
evolution of a less perfect universe, a problem which they
approached in a way differing but slightly from that of Simon
Magus. This last, as we have seen, interposed between God
and our own world three pairs of " Roots " or Powers together
with an intermediate world of aeons whose angels and authorities had brought our universe into existence. These angels
purposely fashioned it from existing matter, the substance most
removed from and hostile to God, in order that they might

πρῶτον Ἄνθρωπον, καὶ τὸν δεύτερον, τῆς ὥρας τοῦ Πνεύματος...καὶ παιδοποιῆ-
σαι φῶς...ὁ καλοῦσι Χριστόν. Something, however, has evidently been
expunged from the earlier version of the story, and it is possible that the
later interpolation is due to the desire of the translator to make the
teaching of the heretics as repulsive as possible. Theodoret merely copies
the Latin text of Irenaeus.

[1] εἰς τὸν ἄφθαρτον ἀνασπασθῆναι Αἰῶνα, ἣν καὶ ἀληθινὴν ἐκκλησίαν καλοῦσι.
Irenaeus, *loc. cit.* p. 228, Harvey.

[2] This Divine Family or Council must have been an old idea in post-
exilic Judaism. Justin Martyr, *Dial. c. Tryph.* c. 126, says that Christ
is called the " Angel of the Great Council " by Ezekiel, but the expression
is not to be found in the A.V. Origen, *cont. Cels.* Bk v. c. 53, also speaks
of a prophecy in which Jesus was described as the " Angel of the Great
Council, because he announced to men the great counsel of God "—a pun
which curiously enough is the same in Greek as in English. The Jews of
Elephantine worshipped in their temple a god and a goddess who were looked
upon as the assessors, if the inferiors, of Yahweh (see n. 4, p. 32, *supra*).
In the Talmud, it is said that God has an upper or celestial *familia* or
tribunal without consulting which he does nothing, and which is indicated
by the " holy ones " of Dan. iv. 17. See Taylor, *Pirke-Aboth*, Cambridge,
1877, II. p. 43, n. 7. The expression " Angel of the Great Council " recurs
in the Gnostic epitaph from the Via Latina given later (Chapter IX).

rule over it and thus possess a dominion of their own. But the Ophites went behind this conception, and made the first confusion of the Divine light with matter the result of an accident. The light, in Irenaeus' account of their doctrines, shed by the Father-and-Son upon the Holy Spirit was so abundant that she could not contain it all within herself, and some of it therefore, as it were, boiled over and fell down[1], when it was received by that matter which they, like Simon, looked upon as existing independently[2]. They described this last as separated into four elements, water, darkness, the abyss, and chaos, which we may suppose to be different strata of the same substance, the uppermost layer being apparently the waste of waters mentioned in Genesis. Falling upon these waters, the superfluity of light of the Holy Spirit stirred them, although before immovable, to their lowest depths, and took from them a body formed apparently from the envelope of waters surrounding it. Then, rising again by a supreme effort from this contact, it made out of this envelope the visible heaven which has ever since been stretched over the earth like a canopy[3]. This superfluity of

[1] Irenaeus, Bk I. c. 28, pp. 227, 228, Harvey.

[2] Giraud, *op. cit.* p. 95, thinks that in the Naassene teaching matter does not really exist, all things being contained in Adamas. The absolute antagonism of God and matter is, however, too strongly marked a feature of nearly all the sources from which the Ophites can have drawn their doctrine for his theory to be entertained. Berger, *Études des Documents nouveaux fournis sur les Ophites par les Philosophumena*, Nancy, 1873, p. 25, puts forward the same idea as a mere figure of speech and in order apparently to reconcile the Ophite doctrine with St John's statement that without the Word " nothing " was made. Later he (*ibid.* pp. 61, 104, 105) points out that the tendency of the Ophite like all other Gnostic doctrine is to widen rather than to narrow the abyss between Spirit and Matter.

[3] This is a variant, and an important one, of the Babylonian myth which makes Bel, after defeating Tiamat the Dragon of Chaos, cut her in two halves and make out of them the visible heaven and earth. See Rogers, *op. cit.* p. 126. The heaven which there is fashioned from the powers of evil, is here at any rate half divine. In later systems, such as one of those in the *Pistis Sophia* and especially that of the Manichaeans, the older Babylonian idea is returned to. It would therefore seem that for the modification here introduced, the Ophites were indebted to Jewish influence and forced it to agree with the story of Genesis. See Irenaeus, *op. cit.* Bk I. c. 28, p. 229, Harvey.

light which thus mingled with matter, the earlier Ophites called, like the authors of the Wisdom-literature, Sophia, and also Prunicos (meaning apparently the " substitute ") and described as bisexual[1].   Another and perhaps a later modification

[1] Irenaeus, *loc. cit.* p. 228, Harvey.   This is the first unmistakable allusion to the figure of the Sophia which is so prominent in most of the Gnostic systems and reappears in Manichaeism.   There can, I think, be no doubt that she is in effect the Great Goddess worshipped throughout Western Asia, who appears under different names in Lydia, Phrygia, Syria, Ionia, Crete, and Greece, and who is to be identified on etymological grounds, if Prof. Garstang (n. 1, p. 31, *supra*) is correct, with the Babylonian Ishtar.   That the Alexandrians saw her in their goddess Isis has already been shown in Chap. II.   Her most prominent characteristics show her to be a personification of the Earth, the mother of all living, ever bringing forth and ever a virgin, as is shown in the " Goddesses Twain," Demeter and Cora.   The dove was throughout Asia her symbol and perhaps her totem animal (Strong, *The Syrian Goddess*, pp. 22–24 for authority), as the serpent was that of her spouse or male counterpart (Justin Martyr, *First Apol.* c. xxvii.; Clem. Alex. *Protrept.* c. ii.).   In the Orphic cosmogonies she appears under her name of Gaia or Ge as the " first bride " (Abel's *Orphica*, fr. 91) spouse of Uranos, as well as under all her subsequent personifications.   She seems, too, to bear much analogy with the Persian Amshaspand, Spenta Armaiti, who is also identified with the earth, and is called Sophia or Wisdom (Tiele, *Religion of the Iranian Peoples*, Eng. ed. Bombay, 1912, pp. 130, 131).   Whether the Persians also drew this conception from the Babylonian Ishtar is a question which some years ago might have been answered in the affirmative.   Now, however, it has been complicated by the identification of this Spenta Armaiti with the Aramati of the Vedas—for which see M. Carnoy's article *Aramati-Armatay* in *Le Muséon*, Louvain, vol. xiii. (1912), pp. 127–146—and the discovery of Winckler that the Vedic gods were worshipped in Asia Minor before 1272 b.c. Her appearance in the cosmology of the Gnostics under the name of Sophia is, however, probably due to the necessity of effecting by hook or by crook a harmony between Gentile and Jewish ideas, and is doubtless due in the first instance to the passage in the Book of Proverbs viii., ix., where Wisdom חָכְמָה or ᾿Αχαμώθ (in both languages feminine) is described as existing from the beginning and the daily delight of Yahweh, rejoicing always before him and his instrument in making the universe (Clem. *Hom.* xvi. c. 12).   It is said that Simon Magus called his mistress Helena by the name of Sophia, but the story only occurs in Victorinus of Pettau and is probably due to a confusion with the Sophia of later sects like that of Valentinus.   In all these, with the single exception of that of Marcion, she plays a predominant part in the destiny of mankind.

of their doctrine fabled that it sprang from the left side of the First Woman while Christos emerged from her right. They therefore called it Sinistra and declared it to be feminine only[1]. Both traditions agreed that this Sophia or Prunicos put forth a son without male assistance, that this son in like manner gave birth to another power and so on, until at last seven powers at seven removes sprang from Sophia. Each of them fashioned from matter a habitation, and these are represented as heavens or hemispheres stretched out one under the other, every one becoming less perfect as it gets further from the Primordial Light[2]. Irenaeus and Hippolytus are agreed that the first or immediate son of Sophia was called Ialdabaoth, a name which Origen says, in speaking of the Ophites, is taken from the art of magic, and which surely enough appears in nearly all the earlier Magic Papyri[3]. Hippolytus says that this Ialdabaoth

---

[1] This appears in the Latin version of Irenaeus only.

[2] Ὑφ᾽ ἑκάστου δὲ τούτων ἕνα οὐρανὸν δημιουργηθῆναι, καὶ ἕκαστον οἰκεῖν τὸν οἰκεῖον. Irenaeus, *op. cit.* Bk I. c. 28, p. 230, Harvey.

[3] Origen, *cont. Cels.* Bk VI. c. 32. This Ialdabaoth or Jaldabaoth appears in the systems or heresies of the Nicolaitans and of those whom Epiphanius calls "Gnostics" *par excellence*. See Epiphanius, *op. cit.* Bk I. t. ii., *Haer.* 25, p. 160, and *Haer.* 26, p. 184. Theodoret, *Haer. Fab.* Bk V. c. 9, makes him belong also to the system of the Sethians. In all these he is the son of Sophia and presides over one or more of the super-terrestrial heavens, although the particular place assigned to him differs in the different sects. In the *Pistis Sophia* he is described (in the story of Pistis Sophia proper) as a power "half flame and half darkness" (cf. Ezekiel viii. 2) projected by one of the "triple-powered" gods of our universe and sent down into Chaos for the destruction of the heroine ; in one of the later documents of the book we see him as lord of a particular portion of Chaos, where he presides over the punishment of a certain class of sinning souls. His name offers many difficulties. Gieseler reads it ילדא בהות, "son of Chaos," and this Salmon, *Dict. Christian Biog.* s.h.v., considers the most probable derivation, although Harvey's reading of יה-אל-דאבהות "Lord (or Jah) God of the Fathers," is certainly more appropriate. In the great Magic Papyrus of Paris, the name appears as αλθαβωτ, which can hardly be anything else that Aldabôt or Adabôt, since we have αλθωναι for Adonai in the next line (Griffith, *The Old Coptic magical texts of Paris*, p. 3 ; extract from the *Zeitschrift für Ägyptische Sprache*, Bd. XXXVIII.). In Papyrus XLVI of the British Museum (Kenyon, *Gk. Pap.* p. 69), we find βαλβναβαωθ, probably a clerical error for Jaldabaoth, which is again followed as before

was the Demiurge and father of the visible universe or phenomenal world[1]. Irenaeus also gives the names of the later
" heavens, virtues, powers, angels, and builders " as being
respectively Iao, Sabaoth, Adonai, Eloaeus, Oreus, and Astaphaeus or Astanpheus, which agrees with the Ophite document
or Diagram to be presently mentioned[2]. The first four of these
names are too evidently the names given in the Old Testament
to Yahweh for us to doubt the assertion of the Fathers that
by Ialdabaoth the Ophites meant the God of the Jews[3]. The
last two names, Oreus and Astaphaeus, Origen also asserts to

by the name Αδωναι. In the Leyden Papyrus which calls itself
the " 8th Book of Moses," we have a god invoked as Aldabeim, which is
there said to be an Egyptian name, and to be the φυσικὸν ὄνομα
" natural name " of the sun and the boat in which he rises when he dawns
upon the world (Leemans, *op. cit.* pp. 87, 119, 127). It is not at all certain,
however, which of these is the right spelling, for the German editors of
Hippolytus read in one place Esaldaios for Ialdabaoth, and the Magic
Papyrus last quoted has a name Aldazaô which is said to be quoted from
a book of Moses called *Archangelicus* (Leemans, *op. cit.* p. 157). The name
Ialdazaô (" El Shaddai " ?) is used as that of the " God of Gods " in the
great Magic Papyrus of Paris, with whose name that of the aeon Sophia
is mentioned (Wessely, *Griech. Zauberpap.* p. 50). The most probable
conclusion is that Jaldabaoth represents some name or epithet of God current among the Semitic Babylonians which had fallen into disuse and had
been much corrupted by being turned into and out of demotic. So Revillout (*Revue Égyptologique*) gives an instance where the invocation ἐπίσχες
ἐπί με " Come unto me ! " by a like process became transmogrified into
" episkhesepimme " without being recognized by the scribe as Greek.

[1] εἰδικὸς κόσμος, Hippolytus, *op. cit.* Bk v. c. 7, p. 153, Cruice.
By the expression Demiurge he means that he fashioned it from pre-existent
matter, as a workman builds a house.

[2] Irenaeus, Bk I. c. 28, p. 230, Harvey.

[3] Thus Irenaeus, Bk I. c. 18, p. 198, Harvey, in summarizing the teaching
of Saturninus says that the god of the Jews was one of the (world-creating)
angels. That Saturninus' opinion was derived from or coincided with
that of the Ophites, see Salmon, *Dict. Christian Biog. s.v.* Saturninus.
Hippolytus Naassene also calls Jaldabaoth " a fiery god " and " a fourth
number," *op. cit.* Bk v. c. 7, p. 153, Cruice, in allusion to the text about God
being a consuming fire and to his Tetragrammaton or four-lettered name.
Epiphanius, *Haer.* XXXVII. c. 4, p. 500, Oehler, says Καὶ οὖτός ἐστι, φασίν,
ὁ θεὸς τῶν Ἰουδαίων ὁ Ἰαλδαβαώθ, " And this Ialdabaoth is, they [the
Ophites] say, the God of the Jews."

be taken from the art of magic, and may be supposed to have some connection with fire and water respectively[1]. It is probable that the later Ophites identified all these seven heavens with the seven astrological " planets," *i.e.* Saturn, Jupiter, Mars, the Sun, Venus, Mercury and the Moon in probably that order[2].

How now did the earth on which we live come into being ? The primitive Babylonians, whose ideas and culture were at a very early date spread over the whole of Asia Minor, conceived the earth not as a globe but as a circular boat like the ancient coracle, over which the heavens stretched like a canopy or hemisphere[3]. Hence we must regard these heavens of the planetary powers, Ialdabaoth and his progeny, as a series of covers fitting one within the other like, in the words of the Fathers, " juggling cups," or to take another simile, the successive skins of an onion. The earth stretched below these, but was at the stage of creation at which we have arrived really without form and void, being the formless waste of waters which covered the denser darkness and chaos. The ordered shape which it afterwards assumed and which we now see, was, in the Ophite story, the result of the fall of no deity, angel, or heavenly power, but of Man. Irenaeus' account of this Second Fall is that the six powers descended from Ialdabaoth began to quarrel with their progenitor for supremacy—an idea which perhaps is to be referred either to the Jewish tradition of the revolt of the angels or with more likelihood to the astrological ideas about the benefic and malefic planets[4]. This so enraged

---

[1] Origen, *cont. Cels.* Bk VI. c. 32.

[2] Hippolytus, *op. cit.* Bk IV. c. 11.

[3] See the picture by Faucher Gudin of the universe according to the Babylonians in Maspero, *Hist. Ancienne des Peuples de l'Orient Classique*, Paris, 1895, t. I. p. 543.

[4] Irenaeus, Bk I. c. 28, pp. 231, 232, Harvey. A sort of echo or perhaps a more detailed repetition of the story is found in one of the latest documents of the *Pistis Sophia*, where Jesus tells His disciples that the ἀρχοντες or rulers of Adamas once rebelled and persisted in begetting " archons and archangels and angels and serving spirits and decans " ; that the 12 aeons, who are evidently the Signs of the Zodiac, divided into two companies of six, half of them under the rule of one Jabraôth repenting and being translated into a higher sphere, while the others were " bound " in our

him that he glared in his wrath upon the underlying dregs of matter, and his thought (ἔννοια) implanted there took birth and shape[1]. This fresh son of his was possessed of a quality of the possession of which he himself had never given any evidence, and was called Nous or Intelligence like the male of Simon's first syzygy or pair of roots. But he was said to be of serpent form (ὀφιόμορφος) because, as says the Naassene or Ophite author quoted by Hippolytus, "the serpent is the personification of the watery element," and therefore, perhaps, the symbol of that external ocean which the ancients thought surrounded the inhabited world[2]. It seems more probable, however, that the Ophites were compelled to introduce this form because the serpent was worshipped everywhere in Asia Minor as the type of the paternal aspect of the earth-goddess' consort[3]. This is best shown, perhaps, in the Eleusinian legend of Zeus and Persephone; but Alexander himself was said to have been begotten by Zeus in the form of a serpent, and no Phrygian goddess seems ever to have been portrayed without one[4]. So

firmament under the rule of the five planets. Perhaps the origin of the whole story is the battle of the Gods and the serpent-footed giants, which appears on the Mithraic bas-reliefs, for which see *P.S.B.A.* 1912, p. 134, and Pl. XVI, 7. It is certainly of Asiatic or Anatolian origin, and seems to be connected with volcanic phenomena. Hippolytus, *op. cit.* Bk v. c. 13, p. 192, Cruice, says this rebellion is a "Chaldaean" doctrine.

[1] τὸν δὲ ἀθυμήσαντα, εἰς τὴν τρύγα τῆς ὕλης ἐρεῖσθαι τὴν ἔννοιαν, καὶ γεννῆσαι υἱὸν ὀφιόμορφον ἐξ αὐτῆς, "and [they say that] he being enraged, beheld his thought in the dregs of matter, and a serpent-formed son was born from it," Irenaeus, Bk ɪ. c. 28, p. 232, Harvey. Perhaps this explains how the Ennoia or Thought of God was supposed to take definite shape. Other editors wish to read ἐρείδεσθαι "fixed" for ἐρεῖσθαι.

[2] Hippolytus, Bk v. c. 9, p. 178, Cruice.

[3] See n. 1, p. 45, *supra*. So Hippolytus, *op. cit.* Bk v. c. 9, p. 178, Cruice, when speaking of the Ophites frequenting the mysteries of the Magna Mater, says that there is no temple anywhere [he means in Phrygia] without a serpent. See Ramsay, *Cities*, etc., ɪ. pp. 51, 87. As King, *Gnostics and their Remains*, p. 225, noted, all the principal cities of Asia Minor, Ephesus, Apamea and Pergamum depicted serpents on their coins. For the story of Alexander's birth, see Budge, *Alexander the Great* (Pseudo-Callisthenes), p. 8.

[4] See Ramsay in last note.

much was this the case that in the Apocryphal *Acta Philippi* it is said that sacred serpents were kept in all the heathen temples in Asia. Hierapolis is, in the same document, called Ophioryma or the serpent's stronghold, whence idolatry seems to be spoken of as the Echidna or Viper[1]. The connection of the serpent with the Sabazian rites has already been mentioned.

This Ophiomorphus, or god in serpent form, was in the later Ophite teaching the cause not only of man's soul but of his passions. The Latin text of Irenaeus says that from him came " the spirit and the soul and all earthly things, whence all forgetfulness, and malice, and jealousy, and envy, and death came into being[2]." This was evidently written under the influence of the Christian idea that the serpent of Genesis was Satan or the Devil. But Hippolytus tells us, no doubt truly, that the Ophiomorphus of the earlier Ophites was in the opinion of his votaries a benevolent and beneficent power. After saying that they worship

" nothing else than Naas, whence they are called Naassenes, and that they say that to this Naas (or serpent) alone is dedicated every temple, and that he is to be found in every mystery and initiatory rite," he continues, " They say that nothing of the things that are, whether deathless or mortal, with or without soul, could exist apart from him. And all things are set under him, and he is good and contains all things within himself, as in the horn of the unicorn, whence beauty and bloom are freely given to all things that exist according to their nature and relationship[3]."

It can hardly be doubted that the writer from whom Hippolytus here quotes is referring to the soul or animating principle of the world, whom he here and elsewhere identifies with the great God of the Greek mysteries[4]. Hence it was the casting-down to this earth of Ophiomorphus which gave it life and shape,

---

[1] *Acta Philippi* (ed. Tischendorf), *passim.*

[2] dehinc et Spiritum, et animam et omnia mundialia ; inde generatum omnem oblivionem, et malitiam, et zelum, et invidiam, et mortem. Irenaeus, Bk I. c. 28, p. 232, Harvey. So Dionysos, whose emblem (Clem. Alex. *Protrept.* c. II.) was the serpent, is identified with the soul of the world. Cf. Berger, *Études sur la Philosophumena*, Nancy, 1873, pp. 39 *sqq.*

[3] Hippolytus, *op. cit.* Bk v. c. 9, p. 178, Cruice.

[4] *Ibid.* Bk v. c. 7, pp. 144, 145, Cruice.

and thus stamped upon it the impress of the First Man[1]. As Ophiomorphus was also the child of Ialdabaoth son of Sophia, the Soul of the World might therefore properly be said to be drawn from all the three visible worlds[2].

We come to the creation of man which the Ophites attributed to the act of Ialdabaoth and the other planetary powers, and represented as taking place not on the earth, but in some one or other of the heavens under their sway[3]. According to Irenaeus—here our only authority—Ialdabaoth boasted that he was God and Father, and that there was none above him[4]. His mother Sophia or Prunicos, disgusted at this, cried out that he lied, inasmuch as there was above him " the Father of all, the First Man and the Son of Man[5] " ; and that Ialdabaoth was thereby led on the counsel of the serpent or Ophiomorphus to say, " Let us make man in our own image[6] ! "   Here the Greek or older text of Irenaeus ends, and our only remaining guide is the later Latin one, which bears many signs of having been added to from time to time by some person more zealous for orthodoxy than accuracy.   Such as it is, however, it narrates at a length which compares very unfavourably with the brevity and concision of the statements of the Greek text, that Ialdabaoth's six planetary powers on his command and at the instigation of Sophia formed an immense man who could only writhe along the ground until they carried him to Ialdabaoth who breathed into him the breath of life, thereby parting with some of the light that was in himself ; that man " having thereby become possessed of intelligence (Nous) and desire (Enthymesis) abandoned his makers and gave thanks to the First Man " ; that Ialdabaoth on this in order to deprive man of the light he had given him created Eve out of his own desire ; that the other planetary powers fell in love with her

---

[1] Is this the origin of the ideas on the Macrocosm and the Microcosm ? See Chapter XIII, *infra*.

[2] See n. 3, p. 41, *supra*.

[3] Cf. Charles, *Book of the Secrets of Enoch*, pp. 7, 57.

[4] Irenaeus, Bk I. c. 28, p. 232, Harvey.

[5] It is curious that she did not also mention herself or the First Woman.

[6] This is the story of the earliest or Greek text ; the Latin says that he said it to divert the minds of his rebellious sons.

beauty and begot from her sons who are called angels; and
finally, that the serpent induced Adam and Eve to transgress
Ialdabaoth's command not to eat of the fruit of the Tree of
Knowledge[1].   On their doing so, he cast them out of Paradise,
and threw them down to this world together with the serpent
or Ophiomorphus.   All this was done by the secret contrivance
of Sophia, whose object throughout was to win back the light
and return it to the highest world whence it had originally
come.   Her manner of doing so seems to have been somewhat roundabout, for it involved the further mingling of light
with matter, and even included the taking away by her of
light from Adam and Eve when turned out of Paradise and
the restoring it to them when they appeared on this earth—
a proceeding which gave them to understand that they had
become clothed with material bodies in which their stay would
be only temporary[2].   Cain's murder of Abel was brought about
by the same agency, as was the begettal of Seth, ancestor of
the existing human race.   We further learn that the serpent
who was cast down got under him the angels begotten upon
Eve by the planetary powers, and brought into existence six
sons who, with himself, form "the seven earthly demons."
These are the adversaries of mankind, because it was on account
of man that their father was cast down; and "this serpent
is called Michael and Sammael[3]."   Later Ialdabaoth sent the

---

[1] Irenaeus, Bk I. c. 28, pp. 232–234, Harvey.   This Adam is of course
not to be confused with Adamas.   Neither did he resemble the Adam of
Genesis, for he is described as being *immensum latitudine et longitudine*.
Harvey, *ubi cit.*, gives many parallels to this from the Talmud and Cabala,
which must be either taken directly from the Ophite author or borrowed from
a common source.   For Eve's creation, see n. 2, p. 58, *supra*.

[2] Cf. the vestures of light belonging to Jesus in the *Pistis Sophia*,
Chapter X, *infra*.   So Philo, *Quaest. et Sol. in Gen.* c. 53, explains that the
coats of skin made by God for Adam and Eve are a "figure of speech"
for a material body.   Origen, in like manner (*cont. Cels.* Bk IV. c. 40), says
that the clothing of the protoplasts in tunics of skin covers "a certain
secret and mystic doctrine far exceeding Plato's of the soul losing its wings
and being borne to earth."

[3] Irenaeus, Bk I. c. 28, pp. 234–236, Harvey.   The idea of the seven
evil demons is a very old one in the East.   See the Babylonian story of
the assault of the seven evil spirits on the Moon.   Sayce, *Gifford Lectures*,

Flood, sought out Abraham, and gave the Law to the Jews. In this, as in everything, he was opposed by his mother Sophia, who saved Noah, made the Prophets prophesy of Christ, and even arranged that John the Baptist and Jesus should be born, the one from Elizabeth and the other from the Virgin Mary[1]. In all this, it is difficult not to see a later interpolation introduced for the purpose of incorporating with the teaching of the earlier Ophites the Biblical narrative, of which they were perhaps only fully informed through Apostolic teaching[2]. It is quite possible that this interpolation may be taken from the doctrine of the Sethians, which Irenaeus expressly couples in this chapter with that of the Ophites, and which, as given by Hippolytus, contains many Jewish but no Christian features[3]. Many of the stories in this interpolation seem to have found their way into the Talmud and the later Cabala, as well as into some of the Manichaean books.

So far, then, the Ophites succeeded in accounting to their satisfaction for the origin of all things, the nature of the Deity, the origin of the universe, and for that of man's body. But they still had to account in detail for the existence of the soul or incorporeal part of man. Irenaeus, as we have seen, attributes it to Ophiomorphus, but although this may have been the belief of the Ophites of his time, the Naassenes assigned it a more complicated origin. They divided it, as Hippolytus tells us, into three parts which were nevertheless one, no doubt corresponding to the threefold division that we have before seen running through all nature into angelic, psychic, and earthly[4].

1902, p. 430, in which those who like to rationalize ancient myths can see a lunar eclipse. We meet again with Sammael and Michael as names of one of them in the diagram to be described later.

    [1] Irenaeus, Bk I. c. 28, p. 237, Harvey.

    [2] The LXX or Greek version of the Old Testament belongs to the Western Diaspora rather than to the Eastern. Perhaps this was why Paul and Barnabas in addressing the Phrygians were careful to give them a summary of Old Testament history. See Acts xiii. 16 *sqq.*

    [3] The Sethians had a book called the *Paraphrase of Seth* now lost, which from its name may easily have been a heretical version of the Book of Genesis. See Hippolytus, *op. cit.* Bk v. c. 21, p. 223, Cruice.

    [4] Hippolytus, *op. cit.* Bk v. c. 7, p. 145, Cruice, says that this was first taught by the " Assyrians," by which he evidently means the Syrians.

The angelic part is brought by Christos, who is, as we have seen, the angel or messenger of the triune Deity, into " the form of clay[1], " the psychic we may suppose to be fashioned with the body by the planetary powers, and the earthly is possibly thought to be the work of the earthly demons hostile to man[2]. Of these last two parts, however, we hear nothing directly, and their existence can only be gathered from the difference here strongly insisted upon between things " celestial earthly and infernal." But the conveyance of the angelic soul to the body Hippolytus' Ophite writer illustrates by a bold figure from what Homer in the *Odyssey* says concerning Hermes in his character of psychopomp or leader of souls[3]. As to the soul or animating principle of the world, Hippolytus tells us that the Ophites did not seek information concerning it and its nature from the Scriptures, where indeed they would have some difficulty in finding any, but from the mystic rites alike of the Greeks and the Barbarians[4]; and he takes us in turns through the mysteries of the Syrian worshippers of Adonis, of the Phrygians, the Egyptian (or rather Alexandrian) worshippers of Osiris, of the Cabiri of Samothrace, and finally those celebrated at Eleusis, pointing out many things which he considers as indicating the Ophites' own peculiar doctrine on this point[5]. That he considers the god worshipped in all these different mysteries to be one and the same divinity seems plain from a hymn which he quotes as a song of " the great Mysteries," and which the late Prof. Conington turned into English verse[6]. So far as any sense can be read into an

---

[1] πλάσμα τὸ πήλινον, Hippolytus, *op. cit.* Bk v. c. 7, p. 153, Cruice.

[2] This is certainly the opinion of the sect responsible for one of the later documents of the *Pistis Sophia*. See *Pistis Sophia*, pp. 346, 347, Copt. So Rossi's *Trattato gnostico*, before quoted, speaks throughout of Satan or the chief of the powers of evil as the ἀρχηπλασμα " originator of the form " ?

[3] Hippolytus, see n. 1, *supra*.

[4] Hippolytus, *op. cit.* Bk v. c. 7, p. 144, Cruice.

[5] *Ibid.* Bk v. c. 8, pp. 157–173, Cruice.

[6]   Son of Saturn, son of Jove
        Or born of mighty Rhea's love.
        Holy name, that sounds so dear
        To that ancient Rhea's ear.

[Thee

explanation made doubly hard for us by our ignorance of what really took place in the rites the Ophite writer describes, or of any clear account of his own tenets, he seems to say that the many apparently obscene and sensual scenes that he alludes to, cover the doctrine that man's soul is part of the universal soul diffused through Nature and eventually to be freed from all material contact and united to the Deity; whence it is only those who abstain from the practice of carnal generation who can hope to be admitted to the highest heaven[1].   All this is illustrated by many quotations not only from the heathen poets and philosophers, but also from the Pentateuch, the Psalms, the Jewish Prophets, and from the Canonical Gospels and St Paul's Epistles.

> Thee the old Assyrians [read Syrians] all
> The thrice-wept Adonis call.
> To thee for name has Egypt given
> The holy horned moon of heaven [Osiris].
> Thou the serpent-god of Greece
> The all reverenced Adam thou of Samothrace.
> Thee the Lydians, Phrygians thee,
> Invoke, the Corybantic deity.
> Thee Pappas now and now the dead,
> Now lifting up reborn the god-like head.
> Unfruitful now or barren desert brown,
> Now the rich golden harvest mowing down.
> Or whom the blossoming almond-tree
> Brought forth on the free hills the piper wild to be.

> > Attis, old Rhea's son I sing
> > Not with the wild bell's clashing ring
> > Nor Ida's fife, in whose shrill noise
> > The old Curetae still rejoice;
> > But with the mingling descant sweet
> > Of Phoebus' harp, so soft, so sweet,
> > Evan! Evan! Pan, I call!
> > Evan the wild Bacchanal:
> > Or that bright Shepherd that on high
> > Folds the white stars up in the silent sky.

Quarterly Review, June, 1851.

[1] πάνυ γὰρ πικρῶς καὶ πεφυλαγμένως παραγγέλλουσιν ἀπέχεσθαι ὡς ἀποκεκομμένοι τῆς πρὸς γυναῖκα ὁμιλίας. "For they very strictly enjoin that their followers should abstain, as if they were castrated, from companying with women," Hippolytus, *op. cit.* Bk v. c. 9, p. 177, Cruice.

The connection of such a system with orthodox Christianity seems at first sight remote enough, but it must be remembered that Hippolytus was not endeavouring to explain or record the Ophite beliefs as a historian would have done, but to hold them up to ridicule and, as he describes it, to " refute " them. Yet there can be no doubt that the Ophites were Christians or followers of Christ who accepted without question the Divine Mission of Jesus, and held that only through Him could they attain salvation. The difference between them and the orthodox in respect to this was that salvation was not, according to them, offered freely to all, but was on the contrary a magical result following automatically upon complete initiation and participation in the Mysteries[1]. Texts like " Strait is the way and narrow is the gate that leadeth into eternal life " and " Not every one that saith unto me Lord, Lord, shall enter into the kingdom of heaven " were laid hold of by them as showing that complete salvation was confined to a few highly instructed persons, who had had the sense to acquire the knowledge of the nature of the Deity and of the topography of the heavenly places which underlay the ceremonies of the Mysteries. Such an one, they said after his death would be born again not with a fleshly but with a spiritual body and passing through the gate of heaven would become a god[2]. It does not follow, however, that those who did not obtain this perfect *gnosis* would be left, as in some later creeds, to reprobation. The cry of " all things in heaven, on earth, and below the earth[3] " that the discord of this world[4] might be made to cease, which

---

[1] Τουτέστι, φησίν, οὐδεὶς τούτων τῶν μυστηρίων ἀκροατὴς γέγονεν εἰ μὴ μόνοι οἱ γνωστικοὶ τέλειοι. "This he (the Naassene writer) says signifies that none was a hearer of these mysteries save only the perfect Gnostics," Hippolytus, *op. cit.* Bk v. c. 8, p. 144, Cruice. The " this " refers to the text : " He that hath ears to hear, let him hear."

[2] ἐκ τῶν σωμάτων τῶν χοϊκῶν ἀναγεννηθέντες πνευματικοὶ οὐ σαρκικοί " being born again from the earthly body, not as fleshly but as spiritual men "......Οἱ δὲ αὐτοί, φησί, Φρύγες τὸν αὐτὸν πάλιν ἐκ μεταβολῆς λέγουσι θεόν. "For the Phrygians themselves declare, he says, that he who is ihus reborn is by reason of the change a god," Hippolytus, *op. cit.* Bk v. c. 8, pp. 165, 166, Cruice. Cf. Berger, *Études*, etc. p. 27.

[3] τῶν ἐπουρανίων καὶ ἐπιγείων καὶ καταχθονίων.

[4] τὴν ἀσυμφωνίαν τοῦ κόσμου.

the Naassene author quoted by Hippolytus daringly connects with the name of Pappas given by the Phrygians to Sabazius or Dionysos, would one day be heard, and the Apocatastasis or return of the world to the Deity would then take place[1]. If we may judge from the later developments of the Ophite teaching this was to be when the last spiritual man ($\pi\nu\epsilon\upsilon\mu\alpha\tau\iota\kappa\acute{o}s$) or perfect Gnostic had been withdrawn from it. In the meantime those less gifted would after death pass through the planetary worlds of Ialdabaoth until they arrived at his heaven or sphere, and would then be sent down to the earth to be reincarnated in other bodies. Whether those who had attained some knowledge of the Divine nature without arriving at perfect Gnosis would or would not be rewarded with some sort of modified beatitude or opportunity of better instruction is not distinctly stated, but it is probable that the Ophites thought that they would[2]. For just as those who have been admitted into the Lesser Mysteries at Eleusis ought to pause and then be admitted into the " great and heavenly ones," the progress of the Ophite towards the Deity must be progressive. They who participate in these heavenly mysteries, says the Naassene author, receive greater destinies than the others[3].

It might seem, therefore, that the Mysteries or secret rites of the heathens contained in themselves all that was necessary for redemption, and this was probably the Ophite view so far as the return of the universe to the bosom of the Deity and the consequent wiping out of the consequences of the unfortunate fall of Sophia or Prunicos were concerned. A tradition preserved by Irenaeus says that Sophia herself " when she had received a desire for the light above her, laid down the body she had received from matter—which was, as we have

---

[1] Hippolytus, *op. et loc. cit.* p. 165, Cruice.

[2] The Naassene writer says that the peace preached " to those that are afar off " of Ephesians ii. 17, refers to $\tau o\hat{\iota}s$ $\dot{\upsilon}\lambda\iota\kappa o\hat{\iota}s$ $\kappa a\grave{\iota}$ $\chi o\ddot{\iota}\kappa o\hat{\iota}s$ " to the material and earthly," and that " to those that are near " to $\tau o\hat{\iota}s$ $\pi\nu\epsilon\upsilon\mu\alpha\tau\iota$-$\kappa o\hat{\iota}s$ $\kappa a\grave{\iota}$ $\nu o\epsilon\rho o\hat{\iota}s$ $\tau\epsilon\lambda\epsilon\acute{\iota}o\iota s$ $\dot{a}\nu\theta\rho\acute{\omega}\pi o\iota s$ " to the spiritual and understanding perfect men." Hippolytus, *op. et loc. cit.*

[3] Hippolytus, *op. cit.* Bk v. c. 8, pp. 172, 173, Cruice.

seen, the visible heaven—and was freed from it[1]." But this
seems to be an addition which is not found in the Greek version,
and is probably taken from some later developments of the
Ophite creed. It is plain, however, that the whole scheme
of nature as set forth in the opinions summarized above is
represented as contrived for the winning-back of the light—
for which we may, if we like, read life—from matter, and this
is represented as the work of Sophia herself. The futile attempt
of the arrogant and jealous Ialdabaoth to prolong his rule by
the successive creation of world after world, of the archetypal
or rather protoplasmic Adam, and finally of Eve, whereby the
light is dispersed through matter more thoroughly but in ever-
diminishing portions[2], is turned against him by his mother
Sophia, the beneficent ruler of the planetary worlds, who even
converts acquaintance with the "carnal generation" which
he has invented into a necessary preparation for the higher
mysteries[3]. Thus Hippolytus tells us that the Naassenes

"frequent the so-called mysteries of the Great Mother, thinking
that through what is performed there, they see clearly the whole
mystery. For they have no complete advantage from the things
there performed except that they are not castrated. [Yet] they
fully accomplish the work of the castrated [*i.e.* the Galli]. For
they most strictly and carefully preach that one should abstain

---

[1] *Cum accepisset concupiscentiam superioris luminis, et virtutem sump-
sisset per omnia, deposuisse corpus et liberatam ab eo.* Irenaeus, Bk I. c. 28,
p. 229, Harvey. As he goes on to say: *Corpus autem hoc exuisse dicunt
eam, foeminam a foemina nominant,* it is plain that he is here referring to
the Third or Lower Sophia who was one of the personages in the Valentinian
drama and unknown, so far as we can tell, to the Ophites. The Latin
translator is no doubt responsible for this confusion.

[2] That this was the object of Ialdabaoth in creating Eve is plain from
Irenaeus' Latin text (Bk I. c. 28, p. 233, Harvey): *Zelantem autem Ialdabaoth voluisse excogitare evacuare hominem per foeminam, et de sua Enthy-
mesi eduxisse foeminam, quam illa Prunicos suscipiens invisibiliter evacuavit
a virtute.* He then goes on to relate the seduction of the archons which
plays so large a part in the Enochian literature, and which is made Sophia's
contrivance for nullifying the command to "Increase and multiply" in
Genesis.

[3] τὰ μικρὰ μυστήρια τὰ τῆς σαρκικῆς γενέσεως: Hippolytus, *op. cit.* Bk v.
c. 8, p. 172, Cruice.

from all companying with woman, as do the castrated. And the rest of the work, as we have said at length, they perform like the castrated[1]."

So far, then, as the general scheme of the redemption of light from matter is concerned, there seems to have been no fundamental necessity in the Ophite view for the Mission of Jesus. But they assigned to Him a great and predominant part in hastening the execution of the scheme, and thus bringing about the near approach of the kingdom of heaven. We have seen that Sophia provided in spite of Ialdabaoth for the birth of the man Jesus from the Virgin Mary, and the Naassene author said that

"into this body of Jesus there withdrew and descended things intellectual, and psychic, and earthly : and these three Men (*i.e.* the First Man, the Son of Man, and Christos) speak together through Him each from his proper substance unto those who belong to each[2]."

The Latin text of Irenaeus amplifies the statement considerably and says that Prunicus, as it calls Sophia, finding no rest in heaven or earth, invoked the aid of her mother the First Woman. This power, having pity on her repentance, implored the First Man to send Christos to her assistance. This prayer was granted, and Christos descended from the Pleroma to his sister Sophia, announced his coming through John the Baptist, prepared the baptism of repentance, and beforehand fashioned Jesus, so that when Christos came down he might find a pure vessel, and that by Ialdabaoth her own son, the " woman " might be announced by Christ. The author quoted by Irenaeus goes on to say that Christ descended through each of the seven heavens or planetary worlds in the likeness of its inhabitants, and thus took away much of their power. For the sprinkling of light scattered among them rushed to him, and when he came down into this world he clothed his sister Sophia with it, and they exulted over each other, which they (the Ophites) " describe as the [meeting of] the bridegroom and the bride."

---

[1] Hippolytus, *op. cit.* Bk v. c. 9, p. 177, Cruice.
[2] *Ibid.* Bk v. c. 6, p. 140, Cruice.

But "Jesus being begotten from the Virgin by the operation of God was wiser, purer, and juster than all men. Christos united to Sophia descended into Him [on His baptism] and so Jesus Christ was made[1]."

Jesus then began to heal the sick, to announce the unknown Father, and to reveal Himself as the Son of the first man. This angered the princes of the planetary worlds and their progenitor, Ialdabaoth, who contrived that He should be killed. As He was being led away for this purpose, Christos with Sophia left Him for the incorruptible aeon[2] or highest heaven. Jesus was crucified; but Christos did not forget Him and sent a certain power to Him, who raised Him in both a spiritual and psychic body, sending the worldly parts back into the world. After His Resurrection, Jesus remained upon earth eighteen months, and perception descending into Him taught what was clear. These things He imparted to a few of his disciples whom He knew to be capable of receiving such great mysteries, and He was then received into heaven. Christos sate down at the right hand of Ialdabaoth that he might, unknown to this last, take to himself the souls of those who have known these mysteries, after they have put off their worldly flesh. Thus Ialdabaoth cannot in future hold holy souls that he may send them down again into the age [*i.e.* this aeon]; but only those which are from his own substance, that is, which he has

---

[1] Irenaeus, Bk I. c. 28, § 6, p. 238, Harvey. The section is given almost word for word as in Irenaeus; but it is manifestly taken from some other source than that of the Greek text, and is inconsistent with the rest of the story. If the Lower Sophia or Prunicos (the Substitute) were born from the mere boiling over of the light shed upon her mother, of what had she to "repent"? In the *Pistis Sophia*, indeed, the heroine wins her way back to her former estate by repentance, but *her* fall has been occasioned by disobedience and ambition. So, too, the story about Jesus changing His form on His descent through the seven heavens is common to the story of Pistis Sophia and the legend of Simon Magus, which two it therefore connects (see Chapter VI, vol. I. p. 191, n. 4). It also appears in the *Ascension of Isaiah* which Mr Charles thinks may be dated about 150 A.D. (see Charles, *Ascension of Isaiah*, 1900, pp. xi and 62), but which is probably of much later date. There are other features to be noted in their place common to the *Pistis Sophia* and the last named work.

[2] That is to say, that which does not perish and return to the Deity.

himself breathed into bodies. When all the sprinkling of light is thus collected, it will be taken up into the incorruptible aeon. The return to Deity will then be complete, and matter will probably be destroyed. In any case, it will have lost the light which alone gives it life[1].

What rites or form of worship were practised by these Ophites we do not know, although Epiphanius preserves a story that they were in the habit of keeping a tame serpent in a chest which at the moment of the consecration of their Eucharist was released and twined itself round the consecrated bread[2]. Probably the very credulous Bishop of Constantia was misled by some picture or amulet depicting a serpent with his tail in its mouth surrounding an orb or globe which represents the mundane egg of the Orphics. In this case the serpent most likely represented the external ocean which the ancients thought surrounded the habitable world like a girdle. But the story, though probably untrue, is some evidence that the later Ophites used, like all post-Christian Gnostics, to practise a ceremony resembling the Eucharist, and certainly administered also the rite of baptism which is alluded to above in the tale of the descent of Christos. Hippolytus also tells us that they used to sing many hymns to the First Man; and he gives us a "psalm" composed by

---

[1] Irenaeus, Bk I. c. 28, § 7, pp. 238–241, Harvey. This again is given almost *verbatim*. The stay of Jesus on earth after His Resurrection, and His teaching His disciples "quod liquidum est," that is, without parable, is also told in the *Pistis Sophia*, but His post-Resurrection life is there put at 12 years. Irenaeus' Latin translator has, as has been said, evidently here got hold of some later developments of Ophitism not known to his author at the time that the Greek text was written. Yet some tradition of a long interval between the Resurrection and the Ascension was evidently current in the sub-Apostolic age. Irenaeus himself says on the authority of " those who met with John the Disciple of the Lord in Asia " that Jesus' ministry only lasted for one year from His Baptism, He being then 30 years old, and that He suffered on completing his 30th year; yet that He taught until He was 40 or 50 years old. See Irenaeus, Bk II. c. 33, § 3, p. 331, Harvey. Some part of this statement appears in the Greek text.

[2] Epiphanius, *Haer.* XXXVII. c. 5, p. 502, Oehler. Epiphanius, although generally untrustworthy, had been, as M. de Faye reminds us, a Nicolaitan in his youth. See de Faye, *Introd.* p. 116.

them which, as he thinks, "comprehends all the mysteries of their error[1]." Unfortunately in the one text of the *Philosophumena* which we have, it is given in so corrupt a form that the first German editor declared it to be incapable of restoration. It may perhaps be translated thus:

The generic law of the Whole was the first Intelligence of all
The second [creation?] was the poured-forth Chaos of the First-born
And the third and labouring soul obtains the law as her portion
Wherefore clothed in watery form [Behold]
The loved one subject to toil [and] death
Now, having lordship, she beholds the Light
Then cast forth to piteous state, she weeps.
Now she weeps and now rejoices
Now she weeps and now is judged
Now she is judged and now is dying
Now no outlet is found, the unhappy one
Into the labyrinth of woes has wandered.
But Jesus said: Father, behold!
A strife of woes upon earth
From thy spirit has fallen
But he [*i.e.* man?] seeks to fly the malignant chaos
And knows not how to break it up.
For his sake, send me, O Father;
Having the seals, I will go down
Through entire aeons I will pass,
All mysteries I will open
And the forms of the gods I will display,
The secrets of the holy Way
Called knowledge [Gnosis], I will hand down.

It is probable that this psalm really did once contain a summary of the essential parts of the Ophite teaching. In whatever way we may construe the first three lines, which were probably misunderstood by the scribe of the text before us, there can hardly be a doubt that they disclose a triad of three powers engaged in the work of salvation[2]. The fall of Sophia

---

[1] Hippolytus, *op. cit.* Bk v. c. 10, pp. 182–184, Cruice.

[2] Cruice, *op. et loc. cit.* p. 152, n. 3, remarks that the Supreme Triad here shown is τὸ νοερόν, τὸ χοϊκόν, τὸ ψυχικόν "the intellectual, the earthly, and the psychic or animal." This may be; but there is no

seems also to be alluded to in unmistakable terms, while the
Mission of Jesus concludes the poem. Jesus, not here distinguished from the Christos or Heavenly Messenger of the
Trinity, is described as sent to the earth for the purpose of
bringing hither certain " mysteries " which will put man on
the sacred path of Gnosis and thus bring about the redemption
of his heavenly part from the bonds of matter. These " mysteries " were, as appears in Hippolytus and elsewhere, sacraments comprising baptism, unction, and a ceremony at least
outwardly resembling the Christian Eucharist or Lord's Supper[1].
These had the magical effect, already attributed by the Orphics
to their own homophagous feast, of changing the recipient's
place in the scale of being and transforming him *ipso facto*
into something higher than man. That the celebration of
these mysteries was attended with the deepest secrecy accounts
at once for their being nowhere described in detail by Hippolytus' Ophite author, and also for the stories which were current
among all the heresiological writers of filthy and obscene rites[2].
Fortified by these mysteries, and by the abstinences and the
continence which they entailed—at all events theoretically,
and as a counsel of perfection—the Ophite could attend, as
we have seen, all the ceremonies of the still pagan Anatolians
or of the Christian Church indifferently, conscious that he alone
understood the inner meaning of either.

Another practice of the Ophites has accidentally come
down to us which deserves some mention. The division of
the universe into three parts, *i.e.* angelic, psychic, and earthly,
which we have already seen in germ in the system of Simon

---

proof that the Ophites ever gave Chaos or unformed Matter a place
in it, or made it the next principle to their Supreme Being. Probably
for the supposed "Chaos" in the second line of the Psalm should be
substituted some words like "the projected Thought" of the Father.
Miller has some curious remarks quoted in the same note on the metre of
the Psalm, which he points out is the same as in a poem of Lucian's, and in
the hymns of Synesius, Bishop of Ptolemais, already mentioned.

[1] Hippolytus, *op. cit.* Bk v. c. 7, p. 148 ; *ibid.* c. 9, p. 181, Cruice. They
probably resembled the ceremonies described at length in the *Pistis Sophia*
and the *Bruce Papyrus*. See Chapter X, *infra*.

[2] See p. 18 *supra*.

Magus, was by the Ophites carried so much further than by him that it extended through the whole of nature, and seriously affected their scheme of redemption. Father Giraud, as we have seen, goes so far as to say that in the opinion of Naassenes, matter hardly existed, and that they thought that not only did Adamas, or the first man, enter into all things, but that in their opinion all things were contained within him[1]. This pantheistic doctrine may have been current in Phrygia and traces of it may perhaps be found in the Anatolian worship of nature; but the words of the Naassene psalm quoted above show that the Naassenes, like all the post-Christian Gnostics of whom we know anything, thought that matter not only had an independent existence, but was essentially malignant and opposed to God. They divided, as we have seen, the universe which came forth from Him into three parts of which the angelic, noëtic, or pneumatic included, apparently, nothing but the Pleroma or Fulness of the Godhead consisting of the Trinity of Father, Son and Mother with their messenger Christos. Then followed the second, psychic, or planetary world, containing the heaven of Sophia with beneath it the holy hebdomad or seven worlds of Ialdabaoth and his descendants[2]. Below this came, indeed, the choïc, earthly, or terrestrial world, containing some sparks of the light bestowed upon it consciously by Sophia and unconsciously by Ialdabaoth, and inhabited by mortal men. But this world was the worst example of the " discord " (ἀσυμφωνία), or as it was called later, the "confusion" (κέρασμος), caused by the mingling of light with matter, and as such was doomed to extinction and to eternal separation from the Divine[3]. In like manner, the soul of man consisted of three

---

[1] Giraud, *op. cit.* p. 95.

[2] Sanctam autem hebdomadam septem stellas, quas dicunt planetas, esse volunt. Irenaeus, Bk I. c. 28, § 5, p. 236, Harvey.

[3] Hippolytus, *op. cit.* Bk v. c. 8, p. 159, Cruice, says that the " nothing " said in John i. 3, 4 to have been made without the Word is in fact this world. Τὸ δὲ "οὐδέν," ὃ χωρὶς αὐτοῦ γέγονεν, ὁ κόσμος ἰδικός ἐστιν · γέγονεν γὰρ χωρὶς αὐτοῦ ὑπὸ τρίτου καὶ τετάρτου. "But the 'nothing' which came into being without Him is the world of form ; for it came into being without Him by the Third and Fourth "—these last being evidently Sophia and Jaldabaoth respectively.

parts corresponding to the three worlds, that is to say, the pneumatic, psychic, and earthly ; and of these three, the last was doomed to extinction. Only by laying aside his earthly part as Jesus had done and becoming entirely pneumatic, could man attain to the light and become united with the Godhead. But to do so, his soul must first pass from choïc to psychic and thence to pneumatic, or, as the Naassene author quoted by Hippolytus puts it, must be born again and must enter in at the gate of heaven[1].

This rebirth or passage of the soul from the choïc to the psychic, and thence to the pneumatic, was, as has been said, the work of the mysteries, especially of those new ones which the Ophite Jesus or Christos had brought to earth with Him from above. The process by which these " changes of the soul " were brought about was, according to the Naassenes, " set forth in the Gospel according to the Egyptians[2]." The only quotation pertinent to the matter which we have from this lost work is one preserved for us by Clement of Alexandria which refers to the coming of a heavenly age " when the two shall be made one, and the male with the female neither male nor female[3] "—a saying which seems to refer to the time when all the light now scattered among the lower worlds shall return to the androgyne Adamas from whom it once issued. But it is probable that this gospel only described the upward passage of the soul in figures and parables probably conveyed in texts of the Canonical Gospel divorced from their context and their natural meaning, as in the Naassene author quoted by Hippolytus. Such a gospel might be a sufficient means of instruction

---

[1] Οὐ δύναται οὖν, φησι, σωθῆναι ὁ τέλειος ἄνθρωπος, ἐὰν μὴ ἀναγεννηθῇ διὰ ταύτης εἰσελθὼν τῆς πύλης. " The perfect [or initiated] man, he says, therefore cannot be saved unless he be born again, entering in through this gate." Hippolytus, *op. cit.* Bk v. c. 8, p. 165, Cruice.

[2] Hippolytus, *op. cit.* Bk v. c. 7, p. 144, Cruice.

[3] Clem. Alex. *Strom.* Bk III. c. 13, and n. 2, p. 196, Chapter VI, vol. I. The οὔτε ἄρρεν οὔτε θῆλυ of this passage and of Clement's Second Epistle to the Romans (Hilgenfeld, *N.T. extra canon.* pt I, p. 79) is compared by the Naassene author (Hipp. *op. cit.* Bk v. c. 7, p. 146, Cruice) with the emasculation of Attis, which is made a type of the soul " passing from the material parts of the lower creation to the eternal substance above."

for the living, who could puzzle out its meaning with the help
of their mystagogues or priests[1] ; but it must always have
been difficult for the best-instructed to remember the great
complications of worlds, planets, and celestial powers that lay
at the root of it.   How difficult then must it have been thought
for the disembodied soul to find its way through the celestial
places, and to confront the " guardians of the gate " of each
with proof of his exalted rank in the scale of being ?   What
was wanted was some guide or clue that the dead could take
with him like the *Book of the Dead* of the ancient Egyptians,
some memory or survival of which had evidently come down
to the Alexandrian worship[2], or like the gold plates which we
have seen fulfilling the same office among the worshippers of
the Orphic gods[3].

That the Ophites possessed such documents we have proof
from the remarks of the Epicurean Celsus, who may have
flourished in the reign of Hadrian (A.D. 117—138)[4].   In his
attack on Christianity called *The True Discourse*, he charges
the Christians generally with possessing a " diagram " in which
the passage of the soul after death through the seven heavens
is portrayed.   Origen, in refuting this Epicurean's arguments
more than a century later, denies that the Church knew anything
of such a diagram, and transfers the responsibility for it to
what he calls " a very insignificant sect called Ophites[5]."   He

---

[1] The Naassenes had priests.   Οἱ οὖν ἱερεῖς καὶ προστάται τοῦ δόγματος
γεγένηνται πρῶτοι οἱ ἐπικληθέντες Ναασσηνοί.   "The priests and chiefs of the
doctrine have been the first who were called Naassenes."   Hippolytus,
op. cit. Bk v. c. 6, p. 139, Cruice. Cf. also p. 77, *infra*.

[2] As we have seen, Aelius Aristides says the devotees of the Alexandrian
gods used to bury holy books in their tombs.   See Chapter II, vol. i.
p. 60, *supra*.

[3] See Chapter IV, *supra*.

[4] I have taken the earliest date for which there is any probability,
because it was in Hadrian's time that most of the great Gnostics taught,
and their speculations would therefore have been most likely to come to
heathen ears.   Keim, *Celsus Wahres Wort*, Zürich, 1873, however, makes
the date of the book 177–178 A.D., and this seems supported by the latest
critics.   See Patrick, *Apology of Origen*, 1892, p. 9, where the question is
thoroughly examined.

[5] Origen, *cont. Cels.* Bk VI. c. 24.

further says that he has himself seen this diagram and he
gives a detailed description of it sufficient to enable certain
modern writers to hazard a guess as to what it must have looked
like[1]. It seems to have been chiefly composed of circles, those
in the uppermost part—which Celsus says were those " above
the heavens "—being two sets of pairs. Each pair consisted
of two concentric circles, one pair being inscribed, according
to Origen, Father-and-Son, and according to Celsus, " a greater
and a less" which Origen declares means the same thing[2]. By
the side of this was the other pair, the outer circle here being
coloured yellow and the inner blue ; while between the two
pairs was a barrier drawn in the form of a double-bladed axe[3].

[1] See Matter, *Histoire du Gnosticisme*, Paris, 1843, Pl. III, and Giraud,
op. cit. Pl. facing p. 238.

[2] Origen, *cont. Cels.* Bk VI. c. 38. The fact is significant as showing
that the Ophites considered the Son as contained *within* the Father.

[3] ἐπιγεγραμμένον διάφραγμα πελεκοειδεῖ σχήματι, Origen, *op. et loc. cit.*
The πέλεκυς or double-bladed axe was the symbol of Zeus Labrandos
of Caria, and is often met with on the coins of Asia Minor, while it seems to
have played a prominent part in the worship of Minoan Crete and in
Mycenae. See Arthur Evans, *Mycenaean Tree and Pillar Cult*, 1901,
pp. 8–12. Ramsay, *Cities*, etc., I. c. 91, thinks that Savazos or Sabazios
was called in Phrygia Lairbenos, which may be connected with the word
Labrys said to be the name of the double axe. He found a god with this
weapon worshipped together with Demeter or Cybele in the Milyan country,
op. cit. pp. 263, 264, and he thinks the pair appear under the different
names of Leto, Artemis, Cybele, and Demeter on the one hand, and Apollo,
Lairbenos, Sabazios, Men, and Attis on the other throughout Asia Minor.
He points out, however, that they were only the male and female aspects of a
single divinity (*op. cit.* 93, 94). Is it possible that this is the explanation
of the double axe as a divine symbol ? The axe with one blade was the
ordinary Egyptian word-sign for a god (see *P.S.B.A.* 1899, pp. 310, 311)
and the double axe might easily mean a god with a double nature. If
this idea were at all prevalent in Anatolia at the beginning of our era, it
would explain Simon Magus' mysterious allusion to the flaming sword of
Genesis iii. 24, " which turns both ways to guard the Tree of Life," and is
somehow connected with the division of mankind into sexes. See Hippolytus, *op. cit.* Bk VI. c. 17; p. 260, Cruice. A very obscure Coptic text
which its discoverer, M. de Mély, calls " Le Livre des Cyranides " (*C. R. de
l'Acad. des Inscriptions*, Mai–Juin, 1904, p. 340) gives a hymn to the
vine said to be sung in the Mysteries of Bacchus in which the " mystery of
the axe " is mentioned.

"Above this last" Origen says "was a smaller circle inscribed 'Love,' and below it another touching it with the word 'Life.' And on the second circle, which was intertwined with and included two other circles, another figure like a rhomboid 'The Forethought of Sophia.' And within their (?) point of common section was 'the Nature of Sophia.' And above their point of common section was a circle, on which was inscribed 'Knowledge,' and lower down another on which was the inscription 'Comprehension[1].'"

There is also reference made by Origen to "The Gates of Paradise," and a flaming sword depicted as the diameter of a flaming circle and guarding the tree of knowledge and of life; but nothing is said of their respective places in the diagram.

Jacques Matter, whose *Histoire Critique du Gnosticisme* appeared in 1843, without its author having the benefit of becoming acquainted with Hippolytus' *Philosophumena*, which tells us so much as to the doctrines of the Naassenes or early Ophites, and Father Giraud, who has on the contrary drawn largely from it, and whose dissertation on the Ophites was published in 1884, have both given pictorial representations of the Ophite diagram. Although they differ somewhat in the arrangement of the circles, both are agreed that the blue and yellow circles signify the Holy Spirit and Christos. The Pleroma or Fulness of the Godhead consisting of Father, Son and Holy Spirit, with the Christos their messenger, therefore seems figured in these two pairs of circles. Both Matter and Father Giraud also arrange four other circles labelled respectively Knowledge, Nature, Wisdom, and Comprehension (Γνῶσις, Φύσις, Σοφία, and Σύνεσις) within one large one with a border of intertwined lines which they call the Forethought of Sophia (Πρόνοια Σοφίας). This may be the correct rendering, but it is hardly warranted by Origen's words given above, nor do we know of any powers, aeons, or other entities in the Ophite system called Gnosis or Physis[2]. In any event, however, it

[1] Origen, *op. et loc. cit.* The names of the circles, etc., in the original are from above downwards: Ἀγάπη, Ζωή, Πρόνοια Σοφίας, Γνῶσις, Σοφία, Φύσις, and Σύνεσις.

[2] Gnosis does appear in the Naassene Psalm given in this Chapter, but only as the name of the "Holy Way."

is fairly clear that this part of the diagram represents the
Sophia who fell from the Holy Spirit into matter, and that
her natural or first place should be the heaven stretched out
above the seven planetary worlds. Yet Irenaeus tells us that
the Ophites he describes thought that Sophia succeeded finally
in struggling free from the body of matter and that the super-
planetary firmament represented merely the lifeless shell she
had abandoned[1]. This is, perhaps, the view taken by the
framers of the diagram.

However that may be, Origen's discourse agrees with Celsus
in describing a " thick black line marked Gehenna or Tartarus "
which cuts, as he says, the diagram in two. This is specially
described by Celsus ; and if it surprises anyone to find it thus
placed above the planetary heavens, it can only be said that
later Gnostics, including those who are responsible for the
principal documents of the *Pistis Sophia* to be presently mentioned, put one of the places where souls were tortured in
" the Middle Way " which seems *above*, and not, like the
classical Tartarus, *below* the earth[2]. Below this again, come
the seven spheres of the planets dignified by the names of
Horaios, Ailoaios, Astaphaios, Sabaoth, Iao, Ialdabaoth and
Adonai respectively. These names are, indeed, those given
in Irenaeus as the names of the descendants of Sophia, although
the order there given is different. As to the meaning of them,
Origen declares that Ialdabaoth, Horaios, and Astaphaios are
taken from magic and that the others are (the Hebrew) names
of God[3]. But it should be noticed that Origen is in this place
silent as to their situation in the diagram, and that those assigned

---

[1] See n. 1, p. 58 *supra*.

[2] In this it is following strictly the tradition of the Enochian literature.
" And we ascended to the firmament, I and he, and there I saw Sammael
and his hosts, and there was great fighting therein and the angels of Satan
were envying one another." Charles, *Ascension of Isaiah*, c. VII. v. 9, p. 48,
and Editor's notes for other references.

[3] Origen, *cont. Cels.* Bk VI. c. 32. Horaios is probably connected with
the root אור " light " ; Astaphaios appears in the earliest texts as Astanpheus which may be an anagram for στέφανος " crown." Or it may be
חשטפה " inundation " which would agree with Origen's statement as
to this being the principle of water, for which see p. 73 *infra*.

to them in Matter's and Father Giraud's reconstructions are taken from the prayers or "defences" which will be given independently of it.

The division which Matter calls "Atmosphère terrestre" and Father Giraud "The Fence of Wickedness" (Φραγμὸς Κακίας) is also not to be found in Origen's description of the diagram, but is taken from another passage where he defines it as the gates leading to the aeon of the archons[1]. The remaining sphere, containing within itself ten circles in Matter's reconstruction and seven in Father Giraud's, is however fully described. The number ten is, as Matter himself admitted to be probable, a mistake of the copyist for seven[2], and there can be no doubt that the larger sphere is supposed to represent our world. The word "Leviathan" which in accordance with Origen's description is written both at the circumference and at the centre of the circle[3] is evidently Ophiomorphus or the serpent-formed son of Ialdabaoth whom we have seen cast down to earth by his father together with the protoplasts Adam and Eve[4]. He should according to the later Gnostics be represented in the shape of a "dragon" or serpent coiled round the world and having his tail in his mouth, while the seven circles within the ring thus formed are the seven Archons or ruling spirits created by him in imitation of Ialdabaoth. These are represented in beast-like form and are, as we have seen, hostile to man. The first four have the Hebrew angelic names of Michael, Suriel, Raphael, and Gabriel, perhaps because

---

[1] *Op. cit.* Bk VI. c. 31.

[2] Unless we take the ten circles as including the three gates of Horaios, Ailoaios, and Astaphaios. In this case, Jaldabaoth and his first three sons would alone form the higher part of the planetary world. This is unlikely, but if it were so, there would be an additional reason for calling Jaldabaoth, as does Irenaeus, a "fourth number." Theodore Bar Khôni, who wrote in the viiith century (see Chapter XIII, *infra*), in his notice of the Ophites gives the number of these heavens as ten. See Pognon, *Coupes de Khouabir*, Paris, 1898, p. 213.

[3] ἐπὶ τοῦ κύκλου καὶ τοῦ κέντρου αὐτοῦ κατέγραψε, Origen, *op. cit.* Bk VI. c. 25.

[4] Origen says, *loc. cit.*, that Leviathan is Hebrew for "Dragon." Cf. Ps. civ. 26.

the four planetary worlds to which they correspond bear also
Hebrew names of God[1]. The remaining three Thauthabaoth,
Erataoth, and Thartharaoth are probably taken from the peculiar corruption of Hebrew and Egyptian words to be found in
the Magic Papyri. Some of them, at any rate, we meet again
later. The word Behemoth which appears at the foot of the
diagram may be translated "animals[2]." It may either be a
further description of the seven Archons—as seems most likely—
or be taken in its etymological sense as the animal kingdom
which in the scale of being succeeds terrestrial man.

To this diagram, Origen adds the prayers or defences above
alluded to, which he draws from some source not mentioned.
He calls them the "instruction" which they (*i.e.* the Ophites)
receive after passing through the "fence of wickedness,—gates
which are subjected to the world of the Archons[3]"; but we
know from other sources that they are the speeches, "defences"
or passwords required to be uttered by the soul of the initiated
when, released from this world by death, she flies upwards
through the planetary spheres[4]. As they contain many in-
structive allusions, they can best be given in Origen's own
words, at the same time remarking that the reading is not in
all cases very well settled. The first power through whose
realm the soul had to pass is not here mentioned by name,

[1] That is to say: Jaldabaoth; Iao, which is probably one of the many
attempts to represent in Greek the Tetragrammaton יהוה called in English
Jehovah; Ailoaios or Eloaios, the singular of the well-known plural
name of God in Genesis אלהים "Elohim"; and Adonai, אדני, "the
Lord," which in many parts of the O.T. replaces the Tetragrammaton.
Harvey, however, *op. cit.* p. 33, n. 3, thinks Iao may simply represent the
initial of the name of Yahweh coupled with Alpha and Omega to show His
eternal nature. He connects this with "I am the first and the last" of
Isaiah xliv. 6, and Rev. i. 11. Yet the later Greeks called Dionysos Iao.
See the (probably spurious) oracle of Apollo Clarius quoted by Macrobius,
Saturnalia, Bk I. c. 18, II. 19 *sqq.*

[2] Giraud, *op. cit.* p. 230.

[3] πύλας ἀρχόντων αἰῶνι δεδεμένας: Origen, *cont. Cels.* Bk VI. c. 31.
Perhaps we should read διδομένας, "Gates which belong to the age of the
Archons," *i.e.* while their rule lasts.

[4] See the quotation from the Gospel of Philip later in this chapter,
p. 79, *infra.*

but by the process of exhaustion is plainly the one whom Irenaeus calls Adonaeus or Adonai.

To him the soul of the dead is to say :

" I salute the one-formed king, the bond of blindness, thoughtless oblivion, the first power preserved by the spirit of Pronoia and by Sophia; whence I am sent forth pure, being already part of the light of the Son and of the Father. Let grace be with me, O Father, yea let it be with me[1] ! "

In passing through the next mentioned, which is the realm of Ialdabaoth :

" Thou O First and Seventh, born to command with boldness, Ialdabaoth the Ruler (Archon) who hast the word of pure Mind (νοῦς), a perfect work to the Son and the Father, I bring the symbol of life in the impress of a type, and open the door to the world which in thy aeon thou didst close, and pass again free through thy realm. Let grace be with me, O Father, yea let it be with me[2] ! "

Arrived at Iao, he ought to say :

" Thou, O Second Iao and first lord of death, who dost rule over the hidden mysteries of the Son and the Father, who dost shine by night, part of the guiltless one.   I bear my own beard as a symbol and am ready to pass through thy rule, having been strengthened by that which was born from thee by the living word.   Let grace be with me, O Father, yea let it be with me[3] ! "

[1] This appears to be the sphere of the Sun to which the epithet μονό-τροπον " one-formed " is not inappropriate.   Why he should be called δεσμὸν ἀβλεψίας " bond of blindness," and λήθην ἀπερίσκεπτον " thought-less oblivion," does not appear.   πρώτην δύναμιν πνεύματι προνοίας καὶ σοφίᾳ τηρουμένην " the first power preserved," etc. coincides curiously with what is said in the *Pistis Sophia* as to the Ship of the Sun and the " Virgin of Light."

[2] This seems to be the sphere of Saturn, the furthest or 7th reckoning from the earth and therefore according to the astronomy of the time the nearest to the upper heavens.   Was the symbol of life the Egyptian ♀ or *ankh* ?   It was of course the jealous Jaldabaoth's or Ialdabaoth's wish that no human souls should penetrate beyond his realm.

[3] So the *Pistis Sophia* speaks repeatedly of the "Little Iao the Good." This should be the sphere of the Moon.   In the hymn to Attis given in this chapter, see n. 6, p. 54 *supra*, Attis-Dionysos-Osiris is identified with " the holy horned moon of heaven," and the name Iao may be connected

To Sabaoth :

" Ruler of the Fifth realm, King Sabaoth, advocate of the law of
thy creation. I am freed by grace of a mightier Pentad. Admit
me, when thou beholdest the blameless symbol of thy art preserved
by the likeness of a type, a body set free by a pentad. Let grace
be with me, O Father, yea let it be with me[1] ! "

To Astaphaios :

"O Astaphaios, Ruler of the third gate, overseer of the first
principle of water, behold me an initiate, admit me who have been
purified by the spirit of a virgin, thou who seest the substance of
the Cosmos. Let grace be with me, O Father, yea let it be with me[2] !"

To Ailoaios :

" O Ailoaios, ruler of the second gate, admit me who brings to thee
the symbol of thy mother, a grace hidden from the powers of the

---

with the Coptic ιος *ioh* or " moon." He may be called the πρῶτος
δεσπότης θανάτου " first lord of death," because Osiris, like Dionysos, was
the first to return to life after being torn in pieces. The φέρων ἤδη τὴν
ἰδίαν σύμβολον " bearing my own beard as a symbol " seems to refer to
the attitude of the Egyptian dead, who is represented as holding his beard
in his right hand when introduced into the presence of Osiris. See Budge,
Book of the Dead, 1898 (translation volume), frontispiece, or *Papyrus of
Ani, ibi cit.*

[1] This may be the sphere of Jupiter, who in one of the later documents
of the *Pistis Sophia* is made ruler of the *five* planets. Sabaoth is probably the Divine Name צבאות " [Lord of] Hosts " which the Greeks
took for a proper name. It, like Iao, appears often in the later documents.
The πεντὰς δυνατωτέρα " mightier Pentad " may refer to the Three
Men (Adamas, his son, and Christos), and the Two Women (the First
Woman and Sophia) placed at the head of the universe by the Ophites.

[2] This should be the sphere of Mercury, the messenger of the gods
and leader of souls, who, unlike the higher powers, sees the earth from
anigh and without veils. The παρθένου πνεῦμα " spirit of a Virgin " may
be the Virgin of Light of the *Pistis Sophia*, who plays such an important
part in the redemption of souls. Hippolytus' Naassene writer (Hipp.
op. cit. Bk v. c. 9, p. 181, Cruice) speaks of Jesus as the true gate and talks
in this connection of "Life-giving water" and of "we Christians celebrating
the mystery in the third gate "—an allusion which is unintelligible at
present, unless it refers to the waters of baptism.

authorities. Let grace be with me, O Father, yea let it be with me[1] ! "

and to Horaios :

" O Horaios, who didst fearlessly overleap the fence of fire receiving the rulership of the first gate, admit me when thou beholdest the symbol of thy power, engraved on the type of the Tree of Life, and formed by resemblance in the likeness of the Guiltless One. Let grace be with me, O Father, yea let it be with me[2] ! "

These defences have evidently got out of their proper order, and have probably been a good deal corrupted as well[3]. But their form and general purport are mostly intelligible and show undoubted signs of Egyptian origin. They were therefore probably not the work of the earlier Ophites or Naassenes, but were most likely introduced when the Ophite doctrines began to leave their primitive seat in Phrygia and to spread westward into North Africa and the south-east of Europe. The diagram itself seems to be fairly expressive of the more ancient teaching and in particular the division of all things

[1] The sphere of Venus ? The planet is said in one of the later documents of the *Pistis Sophia* to be ruled by a power from " Pistis Sophia, the daughter of Barbelo," another name for the material antitype of the heavenly Sophia or Mother of Life, whom we shall meet with later.

[2] The sphere of Mars ? No allusion is made elsewhere to the φραγμὸν πυρὸς " fence of fire " ; but we do of course often hear of an empyrean or heaven of fire stretching over the earth. The ζωῆς ξύλον is, according to both Origen and Celsus, the Cross ; Origen, *op. cit.* Bk VI. cc. 34, 37.

[3] The proper order would appear to be :

    (1) Horaios ♂ the guardian of the First Gate, *i.e.* that of Fire.
    (2) Ailoaios ♀ the guardian of the Second Gate, *i.e.* that of Air.
    (3) Astaphaios ☿ the guardian of the Third Gate, *i.e.* that of Water.

Above these we have (4) Adonai the ☉ the first power as distinguished from mere porters or guardians of gates, (5) Iao the ☽ called in the password the second, and (6) and (7) Sabaoth ♃ and Jaldabaoth ♄ above all. This would about correspond with the astronomy of the time, which tried to put the sun in the centre of our system. But the relative places of Sabaoth, Jaldabaoth, and Ailoaios are very uncertain, and Epiphanius in describing the Ophite sect whom he calls " Gnostics " says that some wished to make Ialdabaoth occupy the 6th heaven, and others Ailoaios, called by him Elilaios, while giving the 7th to Sabaoth. Epiph. *Haer.* XXVI. c. 10, p. 174, Oehler.

below the Godhead into three parts. Thus we find in it the
" middle space " or heaven of Sophia, itself perhaps the Paradise
whence the protoplasts and Ophiomorphus were hurled, then
the world of seven planets, and finally this earth under the
government of Ophiomorphus' seven angels. To judge from
Origen's remark that " they say there is a sympathy ($\sigma\upsilon\mu\pi\acute{a}\theta\epsilon\iota a$)
between the Star Phaenon (*i.e.* Saturn) and the lion-like power
(Michael)[1]," it is probable that the Ophites, like the Babylonian
astrologers, looked upon the system of " correspondences," as
it was afterwards called, as running through all nature in such
a way that every world and every power inhabiting it was a
reflection of the one above it[2]. That each world according
to the Naassenes contained a " Church " or assembly of souls[3]
is stated in the text quoted above, the " Captive " Church
there mentioned being evidently composed of the souls still
held in the grip of matter, the " Called " of those who had
passed into the planetary worlds, and the " Chosen " of those
who were purified enough to be admitted into the middle space
or Paradise of Sophia[4]. That these last were thought to be
eventually united with the Deity appears in some later developments of the Ophite faith, but the doctrine seems also to
have been known to the Naassenes, since the author quoted
by Hippolytus speaks of " the perfect gnostics " becoming

---

[1] Origen, *cont. Cels.* Bk VI. c. 31. If ♄ corresponds to Michael and also
to Jaldabaoth, ♃ ought to do the like to Suriel and Iao, ♂ to Sabaoth
(which would be appropriate enough) and to Raphael, the sun to Adonai
and Gabriel, and so on. No system of correspondences, however, can be
devised that does not break down on scrutiny. Sammael, which is here
Michael's other name, is used in the *Ascensio Isaiae* (see Charles, *Ascension
of Isaiah*, p. 6) as a name of Satan. But it may well be that good and bad
spirits occupying corresponding places in the universe were sometimes called
by the same names. So one of the documents of the *Pistis Sophia* speaks
of an angel cryptically named Zarazaz "who is called by the demons after
a strong demon of their own place, Maskelli ": *Pistis Sophia*, p. 370, Copt.

[2] Though Babylonian in origin it must early have found its way into
Egypt. See Maspero, *Ét. Égyptol.* II. p. 385 and Chapter VI, *supra*, vol. I.
p. 183 and n. 3.

[3] Soul, perhaps, does not here mean anything more than animating
principle, spark, or breath of life.

[4] See p. 42, *supra*.

" kingless " (that is, subject to no other being) and as appointed to " share in the Pleroma[1]."

Of the amount of success which the speculations of the Ophites enjoyed we know very little. Origen, as we have seen, speaks of them as being in his day " an insignificant sect " ; and we have no proof that their numbers were ever very large[2]. Father Giraud asserts on the faith of some of the smaller heresiologists and Conciliar Acts that they spread over the whole of Asia Minor, through Syria and Palestine into Egypt on the one hand, and, on the other, to Mesopotamia, Armenia, and even to India, and this is probably more or less correct[3]. But those who had actually read their writings, as Irenaeus and Hippolytus evidently had done, seem to have looked upon them more as the source of many later heresies than as formidable by their own numbers. Whether the Sethians with whom Irenaeus would identify them were really a subdivision of the Ophite sect may be doubted, because in Hippolytus' account of the Sethian doctrines, the existence of Jesus is never mentioned or referred to, and there is some reason for thinking them a non-Christian sect[4]. But the heresies of the Peratae

---

[1] ...τοὺς τελείους ἀβασιλεύτους γενέσθαι καὶ μετασχεῖν τοῦ πληρώματος, Hippolytus, *op. cit.* Bk v. c. 8, p. 168, Cruice. See also the same expression in n. 3, p. 41, *supra.*

[2] Origen's testimony on this point can be the better relied on, because his good faith, unlike that of writers like Epiphanius, is above suspicion. He and Clement of Alexandria are the only two writers on Gnosticism among the Fathers to whom M. de Faye (*Introd.* p. 1) will allow "intelligence " and " impartialité."

[3] He gives, *op. cit.* p. 79, a map showing their chief seats from the head of the Persian Gulf on the one hand to Crete and the Adriatic on the other.

[4] In the *Bruce Papyrus* mentioned in Chapter X, there is much said about a god called Sitheus, so that it is by no means certain that the Seth after whom they were named was the patriarch of Genesis. He might be the Egyptian Set, whose name is transliterated in the Magic Papyri as Σηϊθ. His appearance in Egypt first as the brother and then as the enemy of Osiris has never been fully accounted for. See "The Legend of Osiris," *P.S.B.A.* for 1911, pp. 145 *sqq.* Epiphanius' attempt in the *Panarion* (*Haer.* xxxix. c. 3, p. 524, Oehler) to connect the genealogy of Jesus with the Seth of Genesis is not even said to depend on the doctrines of the sect, and the whole chapter reads like an interpolation. Cf. Friedländer, *Vorchristliche jüdische Gnosticismus*, Göttingen, 1898, p. 25.

and of Justinus, which Hippolytus describes as not differing much from the Ophites, certainly resemble that which has been summarized above too closely for the resemblance to be accidental ; while the same remark applies to those of the Barbeliotae and Cainites described by Irenaeus, and to the Gnostics, Archontics, and others of whom we read in Epiphanius' *Panarion*. Most of these sects seem to have flourished on the Eastern or Asiatic outskirts of the Roman Empire, although some of them probably had settlements also in Egypt, Greece, Crete, and Cyrene. As the first Ophites had contrived to make an amalgam of the fervent and hysterical worship of nature in Anatolia with the Jewish and Christian tenets, so no doubt these daughter sects contrived to fit in with them the legends of the local cults among which they found themselves. But such compromises were not likely to last long when the Catholic Church began to define and enforce the orthodox faith, and the Ophites seem to have been one of the first to succumb. In the vth century A.D., there were still Ophite "colleges" to be found in the province of Bithynia ; for Theocritus and Evander, the bishops of Chalcedon and Nicomedia, "refuted" their leaders publicly with such effect, says Praedestinatus, that they afterwards broke into their "secret places" at the head of a furious mob, drove away their priests, killed the sacred serpents, and "delivered the people from that danger[1]." This is the last that we hear of them as an organized sect, and although Justinian in A.D. 530 thought right to include them by name in his law against heretics, it is probable that by then their opinions had long since passed into other forms[2].

Probably one of the first changes to take place in the Ophite faith was the withdrawal into the background of the serpent worship which respect for the ancient cults of Asia Minor had imposed upon the earlier members of the sect. In the diagram, Ophiomorphus does not seem to have been depicted in his proper shape, although he may perhaps be identified with the Leviathan there shown as surrounding the terrestrial world. Those Ophites who wished to obtain

---

[1] Praedestinatus, *de Haeresibus*, Bk I. c. 17, p. 237, Oehler.
[2] Matter, *Hist. du Gnost.* t. II. p. 176.

proselytes among Christian catechumens no doubt felt the advisability of not insisting upon this conception, inasmuch as " the serpent " was the figure under which the Oriental Christians loved to allude to the Pagan worships which still opposed them in Asia Minor[1]. Hence there arose much confusion among the Ophites themselves as to the character of the serpent, and while some, according to Irenaeus, asserted that Sophia the mother of Ialdabaoth herself became the serpent[2], Theodoret, a very late witness, thinks that the Ophites of his time held that Ophiomorphus, although originally the minister of Sophia, had gone over to the other side, and had become the enemy of mankind[3]. In this we may also, perhaps, see, if we will, the effect of Egyptian influence upon the earlier Ophite teaching ; for in Egypt, the serpent Apep was always looked upon as the enemy of Râ, the Sun-god, who was rightly considered the great benefactor of humanity. It is no doubt due to the same influence that in one of the documents of the *Pistis Sophia*—one part of which, as will be seen later, was probably written for the furtherance of a late form of the Ophite heresy —the serpent, while keeping his place in the Cosmos as the great ocean which surrounds the earth, is transformed into the outer darkness of the Canonical Gospels, and described as a huge torture-chamber for the punishment of souls[4]. The same document shows us how the Ophites, while adopting all the ideas of their predecessors the Orphics as to the respective states of the initiated and uninitiated after death,—including therein their reincarnation, the draught from the lake of memory and the like—contrived to mix with them the current astrological ideas of the time which made all these events happen in an order determined by the motions of the stars[5]. This tendency, already visible in Hippolytus' time in the Ophite

[1] See *Acta Philippi* before quoted *passim*.

[2] Irenaeus, Bk I. c. 28, § 8, p. 241, Harvey. King, *Gnostics*, etc. p. 101, quotes from Tertullian, *de Praescript.*, " Serpentem magnificant in tantum ut etiam Christo praeferant," which sounds like an Ophite doctrine ; but I have failed to verify the quotation.

[3] Theodoret, *Haer. Fab.* I. 24.

[4] *Pistis Sophia*, pp. 319, 320, Copt.

[5] *Ibid.* p. 384, Copt.

sect which he calls the Peratae[1], will, however, be better considered when we come to deal with the documents of the *Pistis Sophia* themselves.

There remains to be said that *the Gospel according to the Egyptians* mentioned above is the only apocryphal document that Hippolytus directly attributes to the earlier Ophites or Naassenes. The sects derived from them seem to have made use of a great number of others, among which we find a *Book of Baruch* otherwise unknown to us, *The Paraphrase of Seth*, the *Gospels of Nicodemus, Philip*, and *Thomas*, together with a *Gospel according to the Hebrews*, which may or may not have been identical with the one which Hippolytus calls that according to the Egyptians[2]. Of these, the first two are entirely lost, and the documents which we possess bearing the name of the Gospel of Nicodemus relate the events of the Crucifixion in much the same way as the Canonical Gospels, but add thereto the visit of Jesus to Hades. A *Gospel of Thomas*, which is also extant, contains only the account of miracles performed by Jesus in His infancy, and therefore goes to controvert the Ophite theory that Christos and Sophia only descended upon Him at His baptism, and that up to that period He was as other men. It is probable, however, that our copies of these Apocryphal Gospels have been severely edited so as to expunge everything which savoured of Gnostic teaching and may really have been partly or wholly the work of Ophites[3]. Of the *Gospel of Philip*, Epiphanius has preserved a short passage as follows :

"The Lord has revealed to me what the soul ought to say when she goes to heaven, and how she ought to answer each of the Powers on high. 'I have known myself,' she says, 'and I have collected myself from everywhere, and I have not begotten children for the Archon, but I have rooted out his roots, and I have collected the scattered members, and I know thee what thou art. For I, she

---

[1] Hippolytus, *op. cit.* Bk v. c. 13, pp. 188 *sqq.*, Cruice.

[2] See Giraud, *op. cit.* pp. 250 *sqq.* for references and editions. English translations of some of them have appeared in the "Apocryphal Acts" etc. of Clark's *Ante-Nicene Library*, and in *Cambridge Texts and Studies*.

[3] This is the opinion of Lipsius. See *Dict. Christian Biog. s.v.* Gospels, Apocryphal.

says, am from above[1].' And thus he [*i.e.* Philip] says, she is set free. But if, he says, she is found to have begotten a son, she is retained below, until she can receive again her own children, and draw them up to herself[2]."

Similar expressions are to be found in two of the documents of the *Pistis Sophia*, and the abstinence from sexual intercourse which they enjoin is direct and first-hand evidence rebutting the accusation of promiscuous immorality which Epiphanius brings against the Ophites or their related sects. Epiphanius attributes to the same sect of " Gnostici " the use of a *Gospel of Perfection* which " others "—the context shows that he means certain Ophites—" are not ashamed to call the Gospel of Eve." Of this he also preserves a single passage as follows :

"I stood upon a high mountain, and I saw a huge man and another who was mutilated [or perhaps only smaller, κολοβὸν] and I heard a voice of thunder, and I drew near to hearken and he spoke to me and said, ' I am thou and thou art I ; and where thou art, there am I, and I am scattered through all things. And whencesoever thou dost wish, collect me, and in collecting me, thou dost collect thyself[3].' "

Is the greater and lesser man here the Adamas or Father-and-Son of the Ophites, in which case the latter part of the passage doubtless refers to the scattering of the light through the world of matter and the necessity of its collection and return to the Godhead. The " I am thou and thou art I " phrase is repeated in the *Pistis Sophia* by the risen Jesus to His disciples[4], and seems to refer to the final union of the perfected human soul with the Deity.

---

[1] Cf. the similar expressions in the speech of the soul on the Orphic Gold Plates, Chapter IV, vol. I. pp. 131 *sqq.*

[2] Epiphanius, *Haer.* XXVI. c. 13, p. 190, Oehler.

[3] *Ibid.* p. 172, Oehler. Cf. the " Logia Jesu " published by the Egypt Exploration Fund in *Oxyrhynchus Papyri*, 1898, p. 3. " Wherever there are two, they are not without God, and wherever there is one alone, I say I am with him. Raise the stone, and there thou shalt find me, cleave the wood and there am I."

[4] *Pistis Sophia*, pp. 206, 230, Copt.

In addition to these books, the Ophites whom Irenaeus and Hippolytus describe quoted freely from the Canonical books of the Old Testament, from one of the apocryphal books of Ezra and from the Book of Tobit, as also from such books of the Canonical New Testament as the Gospels, including that of St John, and most of the Pauline Epistles, including that to the Hebrews[1]. But it would be going too far to say that they "accepted" these or attributed to them a Divine origin, or thought them inspired in the sense in which the word was used by the Catholic Church. On the contrary, Epiphanius complains that they thought many of the contents of the Old Testament Books at any rate were inspired only by Ialdabaoth and the creators of the world of matter for the purpose of misleading mankind[2]; and throughout they seem to have considered all the Canonical Scriptures that they quote as on an equality with the writings of Homer, Hesiod, the legendary Orpheus, and other heathen writers such as Herodotus. Without attempting to deny or question the historical truth of the facts or legends recorded by all these authors, they regarded them merely as figures having an allegorical or typical meaning, which they could interpret in any manner they pleased, so as to make them accord with their own preconceived theories. Thus the Naassenes when they found St Luke quoting from the Proverbs of Solomon that " the just will fall seven times and rise again," declared that this referred to the downward passage of man's soul through the planetary heavens[3]; and Justinus, one of the Ophite teachers, finding a story in Herodotus about Heracles and the serpent-tailed girl whom he met in Scythia, said that it was a type of the generation of the

---

[1] Grüber, *Die Ophiten*, Würzburg, 1864, pp. 173 *sqq.*, points out that the Ophites, like the Valentinians, seem to have used the Peshitto or Syriac version of the Canonical Books for their quotations. He says the fact had been already noticed by Harvey. It is, of course, another indication of the Anatolian or Syrian origin of the sect.

[2] Irenaeus, I. 28, c. 5, p. 237, Harvey, gives a list of the books which they assigned to each planetary power, Jaldabaoth taking the lion's share with the Hexateuch, Amos and Habbakuk.

[3] Hippolytus, *op. cit.* Bk v. c. 7, p. 150, Cruice. Proverbs xxiv. 16 seems the text referred to.

universe by the combination of the invisible and unforeseeing Demiurge and the female principle or Sophia[1]. The same dialectic had already been made use of by the Orphics, by Philo of Alexandria, and by Simon Magus; but the Ophites seem to have been the first to apply it to all literature. The full effect of this method of interpretation we shall see later.

Generally speaking, it may be said that the Ophites seem to have been the first to bring about any kind of amalgamation between the popular religions of the Near East and the rising faith of Christianity. By interpreting the "mysteries" or secret rites of Asia Minor and elsewhere in their own sense, they supplied Christianity with a mythology which it would otherwise have lacked and the absence of which must always have proved a bar to its propagation among other than Semitic peoples. At the same time they greatly exalted the figure of Christ, who in their system became much less the personal teacher and master of the Jewish-Christian communities[2] than the angel or messenger of the Supreme Being sent from above in pursuance of a vast scheme for the redemption of the human race. In this capacity it went some way towards identifying the historical Jesus with the great god of the Mysteries and towards giving the sacraments of the newly-founded Church the secular authority of the rites practised in them. The influence of the Ophite system or systems upon the sects which succeeded them is at present hard to define, but there can be little doubt that some of the documents, which have come down to us in the Coptic MSS. before mentioned and will be more fully described in Chapter X, can only be explained by reference to them.

---

[1] Hippolytus, *op. cit.* Bk v. c. 25, pp. 226, 227, Cruice. Sophia is evidently the serpent in this combination.

[2] The Ebionites, or whatever other Judaeo-Christian sect is responsible for the *Clementines*, make St Peter affirm that Jesus "did not proclaim Himself to be God," and that "that which is begotten cannot be compared with that which is unbegotten or self-begotten." See *Clem. Hom.* XVI. cc. 15, 16.

CHAPTER IX

POST-CHRISTIAN GNOSTICS : VALENTINUS

IT seems fairly plain that the originators of the Ophite teaching were uneducated men[1]. A few quotations from Homer and Pindar, probably familiar to anyone who listened to the Rhapsodists, are indeed to be found in the anonymous author whom Hippolytus quotes under the name of "the Naassene." But the reading of the learned of that day consisted not of poetry but of philosophy ; and there is no trace in his speculations of direct acquaintance with the works of any philosopher whatever. This is the more striking because Heraclitus of Ephesus, Zeno of Cyprus, and Cleanthes of Assos might have been brought into court in support of his cosmogonical ideas ; and the Stoic philosophy was especially an Asiatic one, having one of its principal homes in Tarsus, and therefore not very far from Phrygia proper. Its cosmology as taught in Rome at the period now under discussion[2], differed very little from that of the earlier Ophites, and its theory of "seminal reasons" ($\lambda\acute{o}\gamma o\iota\ \sigma\pi\epsilon\rho\mu\alpha\tau\iota\kappa o\acute{\iota}$) or particles of fiery matter descending from heaven to earth and there becoming formative principles, together with its belief in metensomatosis or transmigration has many resemblances with the Ophite

---

[1] The same may be said of practically all Christians of the Apostolic age. See Hatch, *H.L.* p. 124. It was the reproach which Celsus cast at the whole Christian community in the reign of Marcus Aurelius. See Origen, *cont. Cels.* Bk III. c. 44. Origen, *op. cit.* Bk III. c. 9, retorts that "now" (*i.e. circa* 230 A.D.) not only rich but highly-placed men and well-born ladies are to be found among the Christians. The change probably took place during the reign of Commodus ; Eusebius, *Hist. Eccl.* Bk v. c. 21. Origen and Eusebius agree that this entry of educated men into the Church brought heresy along with it. See Origen, *op. cit.* Bk III. c. 12.

[2] Bréhier, "La Cosmologie Stoicienne," *R.H.R.* t. LXIV. (1911), pp. 1–9.

scheme of redemption[1]. Yet the Naassene author in an age
when philosophy was most in fashion never appeals to the
authority of the founders of the Stoic school or of those followers
of theirs who must have been his contemporaries and countrymen; and Hippolytus, whose own acquaintance with Greek
philosophy was superficial and hardly first-hand, in his summary
of the Naassene doctrine draws no parallel between the two.
On the other hand, the Naassene author perpetually refers to
the Old Testament which he seems to have known in the Peshitto
or Syrian version, although, as will have been seen, he by no
means regards it from the Jewish standpoint as a divinely
inspired rule of life, and pushes down Yahweh, its God, into
a very inferior position in the scale of being. As the date of
the Peshitto has not yet been put further back than the second
century A.D.[2], this would lead one to suppose that it had only
recently come to the notice of the Naassene writer, who probably
welcomed it as a valuable source from which to draw materials
for spells and exorcisms. This excessive reverence for the
letter as apart from the spirit of a document is characteristic
of the magician of the early Christian centuries, and is further
exemplified in a magic papyrus of the IIIrd century A.D., now
in the British Museum, where " a number of single lines taken
without any regard to sense or on any discernible principle from
the Iliad and Odyssey " are arranged in a certain order for use
as a fortune-telling book, and appear in company with magical
recipes for obtaining dreams, compounding love philtres, and
all the usual paraphernalia of a wizard of the period[3]. Such a
use of writings venerable for their antiquity would never enter
into the head of anyone endowed with any literary sense, but
seems natural enough to persons of limited reading, to whom
they form their sole material for study. In reading into the
lives of the Jewish patriarchs hidden allusions to the theories

---

[1] A. W. Benn, *The Philosophy of Greece*, 1898, pp. 246, 255.

[2] Kenyon, *Handbook to the Textual Criticism of the N. T.*, 1901, p. 138,
says, " Mr Gwilliam, whose opinion, as editor of the Peshitto, is entitled to
all respect, believes it to be the original translation of the Scriptures into
Syriac," but thinks the question not yet decided.

[3] Kenyon, *Greek Papyri*, p. 83.

of the origin of the universe and the destiny of man then current over the whole Hellenistic world, the Naassenes did not behave differently from our own Puritans of Cromwell's time, who discovered in texts like "Take the prophets of Baal, Let not one of them escape[1]!" a justification for "knocking on the head out of hand," the clergy of the opposing party[2]. We may, if we please, picture to ourselves the earlier Ophites as a handful of merchants, artizans, freedmen, and slaves inclined by inherited custom to magical practices and to ecstatic or hysterical forms of religion, and, as it were, intoxicated by the new field of speculation which the translation of the Hebrew Scriptures into their own tongue had opened to them. At the same time, their anti-Semitic feeling, dating perhaps from the time of the Maccabaean resistance which had materially contributed to the downfall of the Syrian Empire, and considerably exacerbated by the atrocities committed by the Jewish rebels at the close of the ist century A.D., must have forced them into an attitude in every way opposed to Jewish national pretensions; while it is easy to understand that such persons must have caught eagerly at any *via media* which enabled them to reconcile the Jewish traditions, long familiar to them through spells and charms, with the legends of the Greek Mysteries, and at the same time protected them against the social and moral obloquy attaching to open adherence to the Jewish rites. Such considerations, perhaps, explain alike the immediate success of St Paul's preaching in Asia Minor, and the outburst of activity among the Gnostics which followed close upon it[3].

---

[1] 1 Kings xviii. 40.

[2] See the case of Dr Michael Hudson quoted by Sir Walter Scott from Peck's *Desiderata Curiosa* in his notes to *Woodstock*; and Cromwell's letter to the Houses on the siege of Drogheda.

[3] M. Cumont's theory, that the Jewish colonies in Phrygia had introduced the worship among the Pagans of Yahweh under the name of "Hypsistos" is not convincing; but it is probable that in religious matters these colonists gave more than they borrowed. The story of the king of Adiabene who wished to turn Jew (see Chapter XII, *infra*) is significant. Cf. the princes of the same kingdom who fell while fighting valiantly in the Jewish ranks in the Sunday battle of Gabao in which Cestius Gallus was defeated. See Josephus, *Bell.* Bk ii. c. 19, § 2.

The Gnostic speculations were, however, destined to pass out of the hands of unlearned men. Although it was hardly likely to have been noticed at the time, the day was past for national or particularist religions having for their object the well-being of one nation or city; and men's relations to the Divine world were coming to be looked upon as a matter concerning the individual rather than the State. Alexander's work in breaking down the barriers between people and people was beginning to bear fruit in the intellectual as it had already done in the political world, and the thoughtful were everywhere asking themselves, as Tertullian tells us, not only whence man and the world had come, but what was the meaning of the evil within the world[1]. Along with this, too, had come a general softening of manners which was extremely favourable to speculation on such subjects, and to which the vagaries of the Caesars of the Julian house have made us somewhat blind. A reign of terror might often exist among the great families in the capital under a jealous or suspicious Emperor, and the majority of the proletariat might there as in other large towns be entirely given up to the brutal or obscene amusements of the arena or the theatre. But in the provinces these things had little effect on the working of the system set up under the Empire; and the civilized world was for the first time, perhaps, in its history, beginning to feel the full benefits of good government and freedom from foreign invasion. It is quite true that the population were then, as at the present day, leaving the country and flocking into the towns, thereby acquiring new vices in addition to their old ones; but this also led, as town life must always do, to increased respect for the rights of their neighbours, and to the extension of the idea of law and order rather than of the right of the strongest as the governing principle of the universe. The Roman law, upon which the jurisprudence of every civilized country is still based, first took coherent shape in the reign of Hadrian; and Ulpian's fundamental maxim that before the law all men are free and equal was founded on a conception of the rights of the individual very different from the Oriental notion that all subjects high and low were the chattels of the king.

---

[1] Tertullian, *de Praescript.* c. VIII.

In these circumstances, new ethical ideals had arisen which affected all classes in the State.   As Sir Samuel Dill has said in his charming sketch of Roman manners under the Julian, Flavian and Antonine emperors, "It has perhaps been too little recognized that in the first and second centuries there was a great propaganda of pagan morality running parallel to the evangelism of the Church[1]."   But this ethical propaganda was an entirely lay affair, and the work not of the priests but of the philosophers[2]. It had, indeed, always been so in the Hellenic world, and while we find it exciting no surprise that a priest of the most sacred mysteries should be worse instead of better than other men[3], it was the philosophers to whom was committed what was later called the care of souls.   Thus Alexander had recourse, when prostrated by self-reproach after the killing of Clitus, to the ministrations of Anaxarchus, who endeavoured to console him with the sophism that kings are not to be judged like other men[4]. So, too, we hear of the Stoic philosopher, Musonius Rufus, when the army of Vespasian was besieging Rome, accompanying the Senate's embassy to the troops of Antonius, and preaching to them at the risk of his life upon the blessings of peace and the horrors of war[5].   Seneca, also, when about to die, endeavours to stay his friends' lamentations by reminding them of the " rules of conduct" by which alone they may expect consolation, and bequeaths to them the example of his life[6] ; while the " Stoic saint," Thrasea, when the sentence of death reaches him, is occupied in listening to a discourse of Demetrius the Cynic on the nature of the soul and its separation from the body[7]. This shows an attitude of mind very different from the merely magical or, as we should say, superstitious belief in the efficacy of spells and ceremonies ; and the example of Epictetus bears witness that it was that of slaves as well as of senators.

Gnosticism, therefore, was bound to become ethical as well as gnostical, or, in other words, to insist on the efficacy of conduct as well as of knowledge, so soon as it came into contact

[1] Dill, *Roman Society from Nero to Marcus Aurelius*, p. 346.
[2] *Ibid.* pp. 293, 294.
[3] Like Callias.   See Chapter II, vol. i. p. 76, *supra*.
[4] Arrian, *Anabasis*, Bk iv. c. 9.   [5] Tacitus, *Hist*. Bk iii. c. 81.
[6] Tacitus, *Annal.* Bk xv. c. 62.   [7] *Ibid.* Bk xvi. c. 34.

with thinkers trained in philosophy. Where it did so, in the first instance, cannot be told with any degree of certainty; but all probability points to Alexandria as one of the places where the post-Christian Gnosticism first made alliance with philosophic learning. Not only was Alexandria the natural meeting-place of Greeks and Orientals, but it was at the early part of the IInd century a great deal more the centre of the intellectual world than either Athens or Rome. Although Ptolemy IX Physcon is said to have expelled from it the philosophers and scholars of the Museum, they seem to have returned shortly afterwards, and in the meantime their dispersion in the neighbouring cities and islands, where most of them must have supported themselves by teaching, probably did a good deal towards diffusing the taste for philosophy over a wider area than before. In Philo's time, in particular, the Platonic philosophy had gained such a hold in the city that he, though a leader of the Jews, had had to assimilate it as best he might[1], and, as we have seen, to bring it more or less into harmony with the traditional beliefs of his own people. A century later we see the same thing occurring with the now rising sect of Christians; and a school of Christian philosophy was founded in Alexandria under the leadership of Pantaenus, the predecessor in office of the famous Clement of Alexandria[2]. If we may judge from the writings of this last, the expressed object of this school was to instil a knowledge of Greek literature and philosophy into Christian teachers, to bring about which it attempted to show that, while both philosophy and Christian theology alike aimed at the discovery of truth, the valuable parts of the philosophic doctrines were borrowed or derived from the writings held sacred by Jews and Christians[3]. Nor were the Alexandrians in the least likely to refuse a hearing to any new faith however wild. The leading place which Alexandria had gained among the markets of the world brought within its gates the adherents of every religion then known, and Jewish merchants and Christian artizans there mixed with Buddhist

[1] Matter, *Hist. du Gnost.* t. I. p. 398.

[2] Eusebius, *Eccl. Hist.* Bk IV. c. 6.

[3] Clem. Alex. *Strom.* Bk I. c. 15.

monks and fetish-worshippers from Central Asia, while the terms on which they met compelled a wide tolerance for one another's opinions, and predisposed its citizens to a practical amalgam of several apparently conflicting creeds[1].

It was into this atmosphere that Gnosticism entered at least as early as the reign of Hadrian. Who was answerable for its first introduction there we have no means of knowing, nor do we even know with any certainty what form Egyptian Gnosticism first took[2]. One would imagine that the Hellenizing tendency of the Samaritans might have brought to Alexandria the doctrines of Simon Magus, but there is no direct evidence to that effect. The case is different with Antioch, where one Saturninus or Satornilus—the name is spelt differently by Irenaeus and Hippolytus—seems to have put forth, at the period referred to, a *quasi*-Christian system having some likeness to that of the Ophites, its chief distinguishing feature being its hatred of Judaism and its God, for whose overthrow it declared Christ to have been sent[3]. Like the Ophites, Saturninus rigidly opposed the commerce of the sexes, declaring marriage and generation to be alike the work of Satan, the declared enemy of the world-creating angels, and of their leader the God of the Jews[4]. But the followers of this Saturninus seem to have been few in number, and although all the later heresiologists preserved the memory of his teaching, it is probable that the sect itself did not long survive its founder[5]. Basilides, whose name is associated with that of Saturninus by Irenaeus, Hippolytus, and Epiphanius, who all make him a fellow disciple with Saturninus of Menander, the continuator or successor of

---

[1] Cf. Hadrian's letter to Servian, Chapter II, vol. I. p. 86, *supra*.

[2] Amélineau, *Le Gnosticisme Égyptien*, p. 30. Its early shape was probably more magical and less ethical than its later developments, because, as the same author (*P.S.B.A.* 1888, p. 392) says, for several centuries it was only the lowest classes in Egypt that became Christians.

[3] Irenaeus, Bk I. c. 18, p. 197, Harvey. Hippolytus, *op. cit.* Bk VII. c. 28, p. 369, Cruice.

[4] So Hippolytus, *loc. cit.*, who copies Irenaeus' statement word for word. But something has evidently slipped out of the text. If Christ and Satan were both the enemies of Yahweh, we should have the συμφώνησις or fellowship declared impossible by St Paul in 2 Cor. vi. 15.

[5] Matter, *Hist. du Gnost.* t. I. p. 349.

Simon Magus[1], certainly flourished under the same reign at Alexandria, where he taught an extremely complicated doctrine, declaring that between the unknown Father of All and this world there was interposed a series of 365 heavens corresponding in number to the days of the year, the chief of them being called Abraxas, the letters of which word have that numerical value[2]. This is the account of Irenaeus, not materially varied by any of the other early writers on heresy, with the exception of Hippolytus, who gives us a long account of the doctrine of Basilides and his son Isidore, which according to their own account they derived from Matthias, the Apostle who replaced Judas and who received it secretly from Jesus Himself[3]. From Hippolytus, we learn that Basilides' complete or final teaching declared that there was a time when nothing existed—

"neither matter, nor substance, nor the Unsubstantial, nor simple, nor compound, nor the Intelligible, nor the Unintelligible, nor that which can be comprehended by the senses, nor that which cannot be so comprehended, nor man, nor angel, nor god, nor anything which can be named"—

and that this God-Who-Was-Not willed to make a world[4]. This act of volition, exercised in Hippolytus' words "without will or mind or consciousness[5]," produced the Seed of the World which contained within itself all the future universe, as the grain of mustard-seed contains the roots, stem, branches, leaves, and

---

[1] Irenaeus, Bk I. c. 18, p. 197, Harvey; Hippolytus, Bk VII. c. 28, p. 367, Cruice; Epiphanius, *Haer.* XXIII. c. 1, p. 135, Oehler.

[2] Irenaeus, Bk I. c. 19, § 1, p. 199, Harvey. For the name Abraxas see *ibid.* p. 203, and Hippolytus, *op. cit.* Bk VII. c. 26, p. 361, Cruice. As Harvey points out in his note, the passage containing it has evidently slipped out of Irenaeus' text and has been added at the foot of the roll.

[3] Hippolytus, *op. cit.* Bk VII. c. 20, p. 344, Cruice. The revelations in question must therefore have been made after the Resurrection. Clement of Alexandria says that Basilides was a disciple of Glaucias, the interpreter of Peter: *Strom.* Bk VII. c. 17.

[4] Hippolytus, *op. cit.* Bk VII. c. 21, pp. 345, 346, Cruice.

[5] ἀθελήτως καὶ ἀνοήτως καὶ ἀναισθήτως. Hippolytus, *loc. cit.* This στίγμα ἀμέριστον or "indivisible point" from which all things come is mentioned in Simon Magus' Apophasis (see Chapter VI, vol. I. p. 194, *supra*) as well as in the Bruce Papyrus of Chapter X, *infra*.

innumerable other seeds of the future plant[1]. In this Seed was
"a Sonhood, threefold in all things, of the same substance with
the God-Who-Was-Not and generated from non-existing things[2]."
Of this threefold Sonhood, one part was subtle or finely divided
like aether or air, one coarser, and one which needed purification ; and he goes on to describe how the finer part immediately
upon the projection of the Seed, burst forth and flew upwards
until it reached the Non-Existent-One, towards whom, Hippolytus says, "every nature strains," on account of "its beauty
and majesty[3]." The coarser part of the Sonhood attempted
to imitate the first, but failed to do so until helped by the Holy
Spirit who served it as the wing does the bird ; but although
the second Sonhood thereby attained beatitude, the Holy
Spirit could not enter into the Godhead along with him "because
it (or she) was of a different substance from him and had nothing
of his nature[4]." She was therefore left near it, purified and
sanctified by her contact with the Sonhood as a jar which has
once contained perfume still preserves its savour[5]. As for the
third Sonhood, it remained in the Seed of the World, which
thereafter gave birth to the Great Archon or Ruler, who is the
Demiurge or Architect of the Universe and fashions all cosmic
things. This Archon makes out of the things below him a Son
who by the arrangement of the God-Who-Was-Not is greater
and wiser than himself, whence the Archon causes him to sit
at his right hand[6]. This Son is in effect Christ, who reveals
to the Archon the existence of the worlds above him, and sends
the Gospel (here personified) into the world so that by it the
third Sonhood might be purified and thus raised to union with
the God-Who-Was-Not.

[1] Or like the Orphic egg from which Phanes came forth. See Chapter IV,
vol. I. p. 123, *supra*.

[2] Ἦν, φησίν, ἐν αὐτῷ τῷ σπέρματι Υἱότης, τριμερὴς κατὰ πάντα, τῷ οὐκ
ὄντι θεῷ ὁμοούσιος, γενητὴ ἐξ οὐκ ὄντων, Hippolytus, *op. cit.* Bk VII. c. 22,
p. 349, Cruice. If these are Basilides actual words, he would seem to
have been the first author to make use of the expression Homoousios.

[3] Hippolytus, *op. et loc. cit.* p. 350, Cruice.

[4] Ἔχειν μὲν αὐτὸ μετ' αὐτῆς οὐκ ἠδύνατο· ἦν γὰρ οὐχ ὁμοούσιον· οὐδὲ
φύσιν εἶχε μετὰ τῆς Υἱότητος. Hippolytus, *op. et loc. cit.* p. 351, Cruice.

[5] Had Basilides or Hippolytus read Horace ?

[6] Hippolytus, *op. cit.* Bk VII. c. 23, p. 353, Cruice.

There is no need to follow further the system of Basilides, nor to describe the extremely complicated tangle of worlds, principalities, powers, and rulers, including the 365 heavens and their Archon or ruler Abraxas, which Basilides interposes between this earth and the Godhead. M. Amélineau has endeavoured to show that, in this, Basilides was borrowing from the ancient Egyptian religion which he imagines to have been still flourishing in the Egypt of the second Christian century[1]. It may be so ; and, although M. Amélineau's proofs seem hardly strong enough to bear the weight of the conclusions he would draw from them, it may be conceded that in the Ogdoad and the Hebdomad of which we hear so much in Hippolytus' account of Basilides' teaching, we have a distinct echo of the extraordinary arithmetic of the Pharaonic or old Egyptian theology, wherein we are constantly meeting with an Ennead or " company " of nine gods which, as M. Maspero has shown, sometimes consists of eight, sometimes of ten, and sometimes of a still more discrepant number of individuals[2]. But Basilides' system was never intended for popular use ; for he himself said, according to Irenaeus, that only one out of a thousand or two out of ten thousand could understand it, and that his disciples should keep their adherence to it strictly secret, seeking to know all things, but themselves remaining unknown[3]. Its interest for us here lies in the fact that Valentinus who transformed post-

---

[1] Amélineau, *Le Gnosticisme Égyptien*, pp. 139–152. So Mallet, *Culte de Neith à Sais*, Paris, 1888, pp. 213, 214, says that both Basilides and Valentinus drew their doctrines from the late form of Egyptian religion which he describes.

[2] *Paut neteru.* Maspero, *Études Égyptol.*, II. pp. 244, 245. Cf. the whole of the luminous essay *Sur l'Ennéade* in the same volume and especially pp. 385, 386. Cf. Naville, *Old Egyptian Faith*, p. 117 ; Erman, *Hist. Egyptian Religion*, p. 78.

[3] *Tu enim, aiunt, omnes cognosce, te autem nemo cognoscat......Non autem multos scire posse haec, sed unum a mille, et duo a myriadibus.* Irenaeus, Bk I. c. 19, § 3, p. 202, Harvey. Epiphanius, *Haer.* XXIV. c. 5, p. 152, Oehler, while copying Irenaeus' account puts it rather differently, Ὑμεῖς πάντα γινώσκετε, ὑμᾶς δὲ μηδεὶς γινωσκέτω, which probably represents Irenaeus' own expression. One of the authors of the *Pistis Sophia* had evidently heard of Basilides' remark about 1 in 1000. Cf. *Pistis Sophia*, p. 354, Copt.

Christian Gnosticism, as will presently be seen, from an esoteric
or mystical explanation of Pagan beliefs[1] into a form of Christianity able to compete seriously with the Catholic Church, was
himself a native of Egypt, that he studied the Platonic philosophy
in Alexandria[2], and that he must have resided there at the same
time as Basilides, who was slightly older than he, and died
before Valentinus' doctrine was promulgated[3]. It is therefore
hardly possible that Valentinus should not have known of
Basilides' teaching and have borrowed from it, even without
the internal evidence of borrowing afforded by a comparison
of the two systems[4].   The almost total silence of the Fathers as
to Basilides' school after that of Valentinus became famous is
to be accounted for, as Matter points out, by supposing that
the hearers of Basilides, probably few in number, came over
to him in a body[5].

Basilides, therefore, forms a very important link between
Simon Magus and the pre-Christian Gnostics—with whom
Basilides was connected, as we have seen, through his master
and Simon Magus' successor Menander—on the one hand, and
Valentinus on the other.   But his teaching also explains to us
why so many of the features of the Ophite doctrines also re-
appear in the Valentinian heresy.   For the three Sonhoods of
Basilides, although described in a fantastic and almost unintelligible way by Hippolytus, seem to correspond in idea with

---

[1] So Irenaeus, *loc. cit.*, p. 203, Harvey, makes the Basilidians say that
they were neither Jews nor Christians : *Et Judaeos quidem jam non esse
dicunt, Christianos autem nondum*—or, as Epiphanius, *loc. cit.*, more strongly
puts it : Ἰουδαίους μὲν ἑαυτοὺς μηκέτι εἶναι φάσκουσι, Χριστιανοὺς δὲ μηκέτι
γεγενῆσθαι.

[2] Epiphanius, *Pan. Haer.* XXXI. c. 2, p. 306, Oehler. Amélineau,
Gnost. Ég. p. 168, defends Epiphanius' statement.

[3] Matter, *Hist. du Gnost.* t. II. p. 37, says that Basilides died about
135 A.D. and that Valentinus' teaching began to make itself heard about
the year following ; but he gives no authorities for the statement. Epiphanius, *loc. cit.*, does say, however, that Valentinus was later in time than
Basilides and "Satornilus" (Saturninus). There seems no authority for
Matter's statement that he was of Jewish origin.

[4] Amélineau, *Gnost. Ég.* p. 176, and Clement of Alexandria as there
quoted. Cf. King, *Gnostics*, p. 263.

[5] Matter, *Hist. du Gnost.* t. II. p. 36.

the First and Second Man and the Christos of the Naassene
writer; while the Holy Spirit, who is of inferior essence and
therefore remains below the Supreme Godhead, can hardly be
distinguished from the Sophia or Prunicos who in the Ophite
scheme plays so large a part in the work of the redemption of
the light. The power of the Great Archon or Ruler of this
World is also said in Hippolytus' account of the Basilidean
teaching, to rise no higher than the firmament, which was
placed between the hypercosmic spaces where soared the
Boundary Spirit, and the ordered universe[1],—a statement
which strictly corresponds to the limit placed on the power
and authority of the Ophite Ialdabaoth. The Archon of
Basilides who must, I think, be intended for Yahweh the God
of the Jews is, like Ialdabaoth, ignorant that there is anything
above him[2]; and although he differs from his prototype in
being better taught by his Son, this is easily explained by
the higher position occupied by both Jews and Christians in
Alexandria than in Phrygia. It is significant also that the
mystic and probably cryptogrammatic name Caulacau which
the Naassene writer uses for the Saviour of his system is applied
to the corresponding person in the system of Basilides[3].

[1] Ἐπεὶ οὖν γέγονε πρώτη καὶ δευτέρα ἀναδρομὴ τῆς Υἱότητος, καὶ μεμένηκεν
αὐτοῦ τὸ Πνεῦμα τὸ Ἅγιον τὸν εἰρημένον τρόπον, στερεωμάτων ὑπερκοσμίων
καὶ τοῦ κόσμου μεταξὺ τεταγμένον: Hippolytus, *op. cit.* Bk VII. c. 23, p. 353,
Cruice.

[2] Hippolytus, *loc. cit.* p. 354, Cruice.

[3] Hippolytus, *op. cit.* Bk v. c. 8, pp. 158, 159, Cruice, says simply in
speaking of the Naassene writer: οὗτοι εἰσὶν οἱ τρεῖς ὑπέρογκοι λόγοι
"Καυλακαῦ, Σαυλασαῦ, Ζεησάρ." "Καυλακαῦ" τοῦ ἄνω, τοῦ Ἀδάμαντος,
"Σαυλασαῦ," τοῦ κάτω θνητοῦ, "Ζεησάρ" τοῦ ἐπὶ τὰ ἄνω ῥεύσαντος Ἰορδάνου.
"These are the three weighty words: Caulacau [the name] of him who
is above, [*i.e.*] Adamas; Saulasau of the mortal one who is beneath;
Zeesar of the Jordan which flows on high." Epiphanius, *Haer.* xxv. c. 4,
pp. 162, 164, Oehler, says that they are taken from the words of Isaiah
xxviii. 10, צו לצו קו לקו זעיר שם translated in the A.V. "precept upon precept, line upon line, here a little"; but the resemblance is not very close,
and it is more probable that the barbarous words of the text cover some sort
of cryptogram. Irenaeus, Bk I. c. 19, § 3, p. 201, Harvey, says of the Basilidians: *Quemadmodum et mundus nomen esse, in quo dicunt descendisse et
ascendisse Salvatorem, esse Caulacau*, which Harvey says is unintelligible.
See Salmon, *s.h.v.* in *Dict. of Christian Biog.*, where he tries hard to explain

The popularity and success that attended Valentinus' own teaching may be judged from the pains that the Fathers took to oppose it. The five books *Against Heresies* so often quoted above were written by Irenaeus with the avowed intention of refuting Valentinus' disciples. Hippolytus, who aimed at a more encyclopaedic account of the heresies of his time, devotes more space to the Valentinian sect than to any other. Tertullian not only repeatedly gibes at them after his manner when treating of other matters, but composed a special book against them still extant, from which we learn of the existence of other treatises against them written by Justin Martyr, Miltiades a Christian sophist, and one Proculus, all which are now lost[1]. Those near to Valentinus in date seem hardly to have considered him an enemy of Christianity. Clement of Alexandria quotes several passages from the writings of him and his followers, and although it is always with the view of contradicting the statements of his fellow-countryman, he yet does so without any of the heat displayed by other controversialists[2]. On the other hand, the orthodox who wrote long after Valentinus was in his grave are most bitter against him. Epiphanius, who seldom had a good word for any one, calls him, with some justice, the chief of heretics[3]; Philaster of Brescia says he was more a follower of Pythagoras than of Christ, and that he led captive the souls of many[4]; Praedestinatus, that he and his followers throughout the East severely wounded the

the name and its use. Cheyne, *Prophecies of Isaiah*, 2nd ed. vol. i. p. 162, would make this Caulacau, however, equivalent to the " word of Jehovah " or Logos. Cf. Renan, *Hist. du Peuple d'Israel*, Eng. ed. 1897, ii. pp. 436, 437.

[1] Tertullian, *adv. Valentinianos*, c. 5.

[2] Clem. Alex. *Strom.* Bk ii. c. 20; Bk iv. cc. 9, 13; Bk vi. c. 6. So Origen, to whose frequent quotations from the Valentinian Heracleon we owe all that we know of that shrewd Biblical critic. See A. E. Brooke, *Fragments of Heracleon*, Cambridge Texts and Studies, vol. i. p. 4. De Faye's opinion that Clement and Origen were the only Fathers who treated Gnosticism with intelligence and sometimes judicially has been quoted above.

[3] Epiphanius, *Pan. Haer.* xxxi. c. 1, p. 306, Oehler.

[4] *Valentinus....Pythagoricus magis quam Christianus, vanam quandam ac perniciosam doctrinam eructans, et velut arithmeticam, id est numerositatis, novam fallaciam praedicans, multorumque animas ignorantium captivavit*, Philastrius, *de Haeresibus liber*, c. 38, p. 43, Oehler, vol. i.

Church of God[1]; while Eusebius in his *Life of Constantine* produces an Imperial edict against the Valentinians and other heretics, issued, according to him, some time before the baptism of its promulgator, and ordering that they shall no longer be allowed to assemble together and that their " houses of prayer " shall be confiscated to the use of the Catholic Church[2]. It was probably in pursuance of some such law, which also enjoined, as Eusebius tells us, the search for and destruction of their writings, that a conventicle of the Valentinians at Callinicum on the Eastern frontier of the Empire was burned by the Christian mob headed by their bishop and monks in A.D. 388[3]. The same scenes were no doubt enacted in other parts of the Empire; and we may, perhaps, see in the fury of the persecutors the measure of their fear.

Yet there is little in the Valentinian doctrine as described by the Fathers to account for the popularity that it evidently attained. Valentinus, like all the Gnostics, believed in one Supreme Source of all things; but he from the first threw over the extremely philosophical idea of Basilides, which some writers would derive from Buddhism[4], of a non-existent God as the pinnacle of his system. To fill the gap thus left, he returned to the older conception of the Ophites, and postulated a Bythos or Deep as the origin of all. But this " Unknowable Father " was by no means the mere abstraction without direct action upon the world or man that he was in the systems of the Ophites and of Basilides. As to the mode of his action, however, a schism—or rather, a difference of opinion—early manifested itself among his followers. Some of them gave to Bythos a female consort called, as Irenaeus, and, following him, Tertullian, tell us, Silence (Σιγή) and Grace (Χάρις), from whom all the subsequent aeons or manifestations of the Godhead descended[5].

---

[1] [*Valentiniani et Valentinus*] *Hi per orientem dispersi graviter dei ecclesiam vulnerarunt*, Praedestinatus, Bk I. c. 11, p. 235, Oehler, vol. I.

[2] Eusebius, *Vita Constantini*, Bk III. cc. 64, 65.

[3] Gibbon, *Decline and Fall*, vol. III. c. 27, p. 174, Bury.

[4] King, *Gnostics*, p. 13.

[5] Irenaeus, Bk I. c. 1, § 1, pp. 8, 9, Harvey; Tertullian, *adv. Val.* c. VII. Is this the "Grace" for whose presence the soul prays in the *apologiae* of the Ophites ? See last chapter.

Irenaeus partly explains away this by the statement that Bythos or the Perfect Aeon dwelt for boundless ages in rest and solitude (ἡσυχία), but that there existed with him Ennoia or Thought. Whether this last part of the statement was or was not thrown in so as to force a parallel between the system of Valentinus and that of Simon Magus from whom the orthodox insisted all later heresiarchs derived their teaching, cannot now be said. But Hippolytus, who, while not disputing this derivation, is just as anxious to show that Valentinus was also much indebted to the Pythagorean and Platonic philosophy learned by him at Alexandria, tells us that there were other Valentinians who insisted that the Father (or Bythos) was without spouse (ἄσυγος) not feminine (ἄθηλυς) and lacking nothing (ἀπροσδεής); and that Valentinus himself said that Bythos was " unbegotten (ἀγέννητος) not subject to conditions of space or time, having no counsellor, nor any substance that could be comprehended by any figure of speech[1]." Herein either Hippolytus or Valentinus seems to have been attracted by the ideas of the Neo-Pythagorean school of Alexandria, who indulged in many arithmetical theories about the Monad or Final Unity which went on producing male and female (*i.e.* odd and even) numbers alternately until it arrived at the perfect harmony of ten[2]. Yet those who study ancient religions by the comparative method will be more inclined to see in this diversity of opinion among the Valentinians a hesitation between the old idea current, as we have seen, in the Eastern Mediterranean, that a god may be bisexual and therefore capable of producing descendants without female assistance and the ancient Semitic view (due perhaps to the fact that Semitic languages know only two genders) which divided the Godhead like everything else into male and female[3].

---

[1] Ὅλως, φησί, γεννητὸν οὐδέν, Πατὴρ δὲ ἦν μόνος ἀγέννητος, οὐ τόπον ἔχων, οὐ χρόνον, οὐ σύμβουλον, οὐκ ἄλλην τινὰ κατ᾽ οὐδένα τῶν τρόπων νοηθῆναι δυναμένην οὐσίαν : Hippolytus, *op. cit.* Bk VI. c. 29, p. 280, Cruice.

[2] Diogenes Laertius, *Vit. Philosoph.* Bk VIII. c. 19.

[3] Philippe Berger, "Les Stèles Puniques de la Bibliothèque Nationale," *Gazette Archéologique*, 11me ann. Paris, 1876, p. 123, says that the Aryan genius sees atmospheric phenomena where the Semite imagines persons who unite and give birth (personnes qui s'unissent et s'engendrent les unes

However this may be, all the Valentinian schools seem to have agreed upon the emanation which immediately proceeded from the Deep or the Father of All. From Bythos, either alone or with the help of Sige[1], there proceeded Mind or Nous (Νοῦς), called also Monogenes[2] and the Father, the beginning of all subsequent things. This Nous is said to be " equal and like " to him from whom he had emanated, and by himself capable of comprehending the greatness of Bythos[3]. With Nous there also came forth a female Power named Aletheia or Truth (Ἀλήθεια), and this pair gave birth to a second syzygy, viz. Logos or the Word (Λόγος) and Zoe or Life (Ζωή), who in their turn produced a third pair, namely: Anthropos, Man (Ἄνθρωπος) and Ecclesia, the Church (Ἐκκλησία)[4]. The later Valentinians, from whom Irenaeus quotes, added to these six aeons, Bythos and his spouse Sige, thus making up the originating Ogdoad or eightfold Godhead again called the root and substance of all [subsequent] things[5]. Valentinus himself, however, probably did not give Bythos a spouse and held that he remained apart from and uplifted above his six principal emanations[6].

les autres). Renan, *Hist. du Peuple d'Israel*, Paris, 1887, t. i. p. 49, shows that all Semites are naturally euhemerists and therefore anthropomorphists.

[1] Amélineau, *Gnost. Ég.* pp. 198 *sqq.*, shows that Sige appears not only in the " Italic School " of Valentinus' followers, but also in the Oriental School which is more likely to represent the teaching of Valentinus himself. This may in fact be deduced from the words which Hippolytus puts into his mouth (*op. cit.* Bk vi. c. 29, p. 281, Cruice): Ἀγάπη, φησίν, ἦν ὅλος, ἡ δὲ ἀγάπη οὐκ ἔστιν ἀγάπη, ἐὰν μὴ ᾖ τὸ ἀγαπώμενον. " He, he says, is all Love, and Love is not Love, unless there is something to love." Thus the Orphics called their Phanes or firstborn god Eros.

[2] As has been many times said, not " Only-begotten," but " unique." See Badham in *Academy*, 5 Sept. 1896.

[3] ταύτην [Sige] δὲ ὑποδεξαμένην τὸ σπέρμα τοῦτο καὶ ἐγκύμονα γενομένην, ἀποκυῆσαι Νοῦν, ὅμοιόν τε καὶ ἴσον τῷ προβαλόντι, καὶ μόνον χωροῦντα τὸ μέγεθος τοῦ Πατρός: Irenaeus, Bk i. c. 1, § 1, p. 9, Harvey: " and she having received this seed and becoming pregnant, brought forth Nous, like and equal to him who had projected him, and alone containing the greatness of the Father."

[4] *Id.* Bk i. c. 1, § 1, pp. 9, 10, Harvey.

[5] *Ibid.* p. 10, Harvey.

[6] Hippolytus, *op. cit.* Bk vi. c. 29, p. 280, Cruice.

This subdivision of the Divine, resembling as it does the system of Simon Magus before described, may seem at first sight incredibly foolish and complicated, especially when it is considered that these "aeons," as Valentinus calls them, might be considered not only as powers but as worlds. So it did to the Fathers, who are never tired of pouring contempt upon it. Tertullian makes merry over the Valentinian conception of a universe with an endless series of heavens piled one over the other, as he says, like the " Lodgings to let " of a Roman *insula* or tenement house, or, had he ever seen one, of a New York skyscraper[1]. Irenaeus jokes cumbrously, comparing the Valentinian aeons to vegetables as if, he says, a gourd should bring forth a cucumber and this in its turn a melon[2]. Hippolytus, indeed, cannot indulge in such jeers because to do so would have stamped him in the opinion of all the learned of his time as an uneducated barbarian, his pet theory of Gnosticism being that all its doctrine was a plagiarism from the Greek philosophers and notably from Plato. Yet he never loses an opportunity of calling Valentinus' opinions " worthless " ; and goes out of his way to tack on to them the system of the Jewish magician Marcus, who, if we can believe the statements of the Fathers, exploited the rising sense of religion of the age for his own immoral or interested purpose[3].

Yet a statement that Tertullian lets drop, as if accidentally, may teach us to beware of taking Valentinus' supposed opinions on the nature of these hypostases or Persons of the Godhead more literally than he did himself. In his treatise against the Valentinians the " furious African barrister " is led away by the exigencies of his own rhetoric to tell us that there were some among them who looked upon all this elaborate description of the emanations of the Ogdoad as a figure of speech. All the aeons of the Ogdoad were according to them merely attributes or names of God. When, they said, God *thought* of producing offspring, He thereby acquired the name of *Father* ; and because his offspring was true, that of *Truth* ; and because He wished to appear in human form, he was called *Man* ; and because He

---

[1] Tertullian, *adv. Valentinianos*, c. 7.

[2] Irenaeus, Bk I. c. 5, § 2, p. 106, Harvey.   [3] See p. 128 *infra*.

assembled His attributes in His mind and selected from them
those most proper for His purpose, they were called the *Church*;
and as His only (or unique) Son was, as it were, uttered or sent
forth to mankind, He was called the *Word*; and from His powers
of salvation, *Life*; and so on[1].   As we have seen, Valentinus did
not invent *de novo* his conception of the Godhead, which bears
besides evident marks of having been adopted with slight modification from that of Simon Magus and the Ophites.   This statement of Tertullian gives us ground therefore for supposing that
he may really have held the same views respecting the Divine
Nature as the Catholic Church, merely giving an allegorical
explanation of the earlier opinions to convince his hearers that
the teaching of the Apostles was not so subversive of or inconsistent with the way of thinking of the ancient theologians and
philosophers as some of them thought.   Clement of Alexandria
shows similar comprehensiveness when he said that in the
Christian faith there are some mysteries more excellent than
others—or, in other words, degrees in knowledge and grace[2]
—, that the Hellenic philosophy fits him who studies it for the
reception of the truth[3], and that the Christian should rejoice
in the name of Gnostic, so long as he understands that the true
Gnostic is he who imitates God as far as possible[4].   He even
goes further, and himself uses the Gnostic method of personification of abstract qualities, as when he says that Reverence is the
daughter of Law[5], and Simplicity, Innocence, Decorum, and Love,
the daughters of Faith[6].   If Valentinus used similar metaphors,
it by no means follows that he was thereby advocating the
worship of many gods, which was the accusation most frequently
brought against him by the Catholic Church.   The same accusation might with equal propriety be made against John Bunyan
on account of his Interpreter and his Mr Greatheart.

But whatever Valentinus' own views with regard to the
Supreme Being may have been, he could no more escape than
did Philo or any other Platonist from the difficulty of explaining

---

[1] Tertullian, *adv. Valentinianos*, c. 36.
[2] Clem. Alex. *Strom.* Bk I. c. 1.
[3] *Ibid.* Bk I. cc. 7, 16.   [4] *Ibid.* Bk II. c. 19.
[5] *Ibid.* Bk II. c. 20.   [6] *Ibid.* Bk II. c. 12.

the connection of this Perfect God with imperfect matter[1], and this had to be the work in his system of an intermediate Power. This Power was that Nous or Monogenes whom we have seen was the first and unique being produced from the Unknowable Father, to whom he seems to have stood in much the same relation as the Dionysos of the Orphics did to the supreme Zeus[2]. Yet although it was through this lieutenant of the Unknown Father that all things were made, he also was too great to act directly upon matter. Seeing, says Hippolytus in this connection, that their own offspring, Logos and Zoe, had brought forth descendants capable of transmission, Nous and his partner Aletheia returned thanks to the Father of All and offered to him a perfect number in the shape of ten aeons[3]. These ten aeons were projected like the direct emanations of the Godhead in syzygies or pairs, their names being respectively Bythios or Deep (Βυθιὸς[4]) and Mixis or Mixture (Μίξις), Ageratos or Who Grows not Old (Ἀγήρατος) and Henosis or Oneness (Ἕνωσις), Autophyes or Self-Produced (Αὐτοφύης[5]) and Hedone or Pleasure (Ἡδονή), Akinetos or Who Cannot Be Moved (Ἀκίνητος) and Syncrasis or Blending (Σύγκρασις), Monogenes or the Unique (Μονογενὴς)[6] and Macaria or Bliss (Μακαρία). In like manner, Logos and Zoe wishing to give thanks to *their* progenitors Nous and Aletheia, put forth another set, this time an imperfect number, or twelve aeons, also arranged in syzygies and called Paraclete (Παράκλητος) and Faith (Πίστις), Fatherly (Πατρικὸς) and Hope (Ἐλπίς), Motherly (Μητρικὸς) and Love (Ἀγάπη), Ever-Thinking (Ἀείνους[7]) and Comprehension (Σύνεσις), Of the Church (Ἐκκλησιαστικὸς) and Blessedness (Μακαριότης), Longed-for (Θελητὸς) and Wisdom (Σοφία). It was through this last, as through her namesake in the system of the Ophites, that the Divine came to mingle with Matter.

---

[1] See Chapter VI, vol. I. p. 174, *supra*.
[2] Clem. Alex. *Strom.* Bk VII. c. 1.
[3] Hippolytus, *op. cit.* Bk VI. c. 29, p. 281, Cruice.   [4] *i.e.* Profound.
[5] Not " self-existent," but maker of his own φύσις or nature.
[6] See n. 2, p. 98 *supra*.
[7] Harvey reads here αἰώνιος " everlasting," which makes at least as good sense as the other.

Before coming to this, however, it will be well to say something here about the ideas that seem to lie behind the names of this series of aeons numbering, with the first six, twenty-eight in all, which thus made up what was known as the Pleroma or Fulness of the Godhead. If we arrange them in three families or groups according to their parentage, thus :

Children of Bythos (either alone or with Sige).

Nous—Aletheia.

Children of Nous and Aletheia.

Logos—Zoe.
Bythios—Mixis.
Ageratos—Henosis.
Autophyes—Syncrasis.
Monogenes—Macaria.

Children of Logos and Zoe.

Anthropos—Ecclesia.
Paracletos—Pistis.
Patricos—Elpis.
Metricos—Agape.
Ecclesiasticus—Macariotes.
Theletas—Sophia,

it will be seen that among the elder members of each group, that is, the three first syzygies, Nous-Aletheia, Logos-Zoe, and Anthropos-Ecclesia, the name of the male member of each syzygy is always that of an actual and concrete concept—the Mind, the Word, and Man,—showing perhaps how thought and speech all marked different stages in the evolution of the being called the Perfect Man[1] ; while the appellatives of the females of each syzygy—Truth, Life, and the Church—all connote

---

[1] Some memory of this seems to have enlivened the disputes between the Nominalists and Realists of the xiiith century. Cf. the wrangling of the Doctors at the School of Salerno in Longfellow's *Golden Legend*

I, with the Doctor Seraphic, maintain
That the word that's not spoken, but conceived in the brain,
Is the type of Eternal Generation,
The spoken word is the Incarnation.

abstract ideas[1]. With the Decad put forth by Nous and Aletheia, *i.e.* Bythios-Mixis, Ageratos-Henosis, Autophyes-Hedone, Acinetos-Syncrasis, and Monogenes-Macaria, every male aeon, as M. Amélineau has pointed out, has for name an adjective, while the females are all described by substantives[2]. But the names of the male aeons are all epithets or attributes peculiar to their father Nous, who is thus said to be the abysmal, never-ageing, creator of his own nature, immovable, and unique, and those of the female aeons are descriptive of different states or conditions arising from his action[3]. M. Amélineau thinks that the names of these last describe a successive degradation of the Divine Nature ; but this does not seem to have been Valentinus' intention, and it is hard to see for instance why Syncrasis or blending should be more unworthy than Mixis or simple mixture. Moreover, this group of aeons, unlike the six preceding them, are not reproductive and no direct descendants follow from their conjugation. Perhaps then we may best understand Valentinus' nomenclature as a statement that the coming together of Mind and Truth produced Profound Admixture, Never-ageing Union, Self-created Pleasure, Unshakeable Combination, and Unique Bliss. In like manner, the names of the members of the Dodecad or group of twelve aeons proceeding from Logos and Zoe may be read as describing the Comforting Faith, the Fatherly Hope, the Motherly Love[4], the Everlasting Comprehension, the Elect Blessedness, and the Longed-for Wisdom arising from the conjugation of the Word and Life or, in one word, from the Incarnation[5].

[1] They are also probably places or receptacles. In the *Pistis Sophia* we read repeatedly of the three χωρήματα and of the τόπος ἀληθείας.

[2] Amélineau, *Gnost. Égypt.* pp. 200 *sqq.*

[3] So Hope Moulton, *Early Zoroastrianism*, 1913, p. 114, points out that half of the Persian Amshaspands or archangels bear names expressing "what Mazda is" and the other half "what Mazda gives." There is much likeness, as has been said, between the Amshaspands and the "Roots" of Simon Magus.

[4] It is worth noticing that these are the three " theological " virtues, Faith, Hope, and Charity.

[5] Hippolytus, *op. cit.* Bk VI. c. 23, pp. 269–271, Cruice, wishes to make out that all this is derived from what he calls the " Pythagorean " system of numbers. Anyone wishing to pursue these " silly cabalisms " further is recommended to read Harvey's Introduction to Valentinus' system, *op. cit.* pp. cxv–cxvii.

To return now to the fall of Sophia which, in the system of Valentinus, as in that of the Ophites, brought about the creation of the universe. All the accounts of Valentinus' teaching that have reached us seem to agree that Sophia's lapse was caused, according to him, not by accident as with the Ophites, but by her own ignorance and emulation. Leaving the Dodecad, " this twelfth and youngest of the aeons," as Hippolytus describes her[1], soared on high to the Height of the Father, and perceived that he, the Unknowable Father, was alone able to bring forth without a partner[2]. Wishing to imitate him, she gave birth by herself and apart from her spouse, " being ignorant that only the Ungenerated Supreme Principle and Root and Height and Depth of the Universes can bring forth alone." " For," says he (*i.e.* Valentinus), " in the ungenerated (or unbegotten) all things exist together. But among generated (or begotten) things, it is the female who projects the substance, while the male gives form to the substance which the female has projected[3]." Hence the substance which Sophia put forth was without form and unshapen—an expression which Valentinus seems to have copied, after his manner, from the " without form and void " (ἄμορφος καὶ ἀκατασκεύαστος) of Genesis[4].

---

[1] Ἀπὸ δὲ τῶν δεκαδύο ὁ δωδέκατος καὶ νεώτατος πάντων τῶν εἰκοσιοκτὼ Αἰώνων, θῆλυς ὢν καὶ καλούμενος Σοφία, κατενόησε τὸ πλῆθος καὶ τὴν δύναμιν τῶν γεγεννηκότων Αἰώνων, καὶ ἀνέδραμεν εἰς τὸ βάθος τὸ τοῦ Πατρός. "But the twelfth of the twelve, and the youngest of all the eight and twenty aeons, who is a female and called Sophia, considered the number and power of those aeons who were begotten (?) and went on high to the height of the Father": Hippolytus, *op. cit.* Bk VI. c. 30, p. 283, Cruice. The "eight and twenty aeons" shows that Valentinus, according to Hippolytus, did *not* reckon Bythos and Sige in the first Ogdoad.

[2] A further proof that the primitive doctrine of Valentinus did not give a spouse to Bythos.

[3] Ἐν μὲν γὰρ τῷ ἀγεννήτῳ, φησίν, ἔστι πάντα ὁμοῦ· (ὁμοῦ seems here to mean "without distinction of time or place." Cf. the " None is afore or after other " of the Athanasian Creed) ἐν δὲ τοῖς γεννητοῖς, τὸ μὲν θῆλυ ἔστιν οὐσίας προβλητικόν, τὸ δὲ ἄρρεν μορφωτικὸν τῆς ὑπὸ τοῦ θήλεως προβαλλομένης οὐσίας. Hippolytus, *op. cit.* Bk VI. c. 30, p. 284, Cruice.

[4] Καὶ τοῦτο ἐστί, φησίν, ὁ λέγει Μωϋσῆς· "ἡ δὲ γῆ ἦν ἀόρατος καὶ ἀκατασκεύαστος." "And this, he says, is the saying of Moses. ' And the earth was *invisible* and unshapen ' "—a curious variant of the A.V., Hippolytus,

This Ectroma or abortion of Sophia, however, caused great alarm to the other members of the Pleroma, who feared that they might themselves be led into similar lapses, and thus bring about the destruction of the whole system. They accordingly importuned Bythos, who ordered that two new aeons, viz. Christos or Christ and the Holy Spirit, should be put forth by Nous and Aletheia to give form and direction to the Ectroma and to alleviate the distress of Sophia[1]. This was accordingly done, and this new pair of aeons separated Sophia from her Ectroma and drew her with them within the Pleroma, which was thereupon closed by the projection by Bythos of yet another aeon named the Cross ($\Sigma\tau\alpha\nu\rho\delta$s)[2], whose sole function was apparently to preserve the Pleroma or Divine World from all contamination from the imperfection which was outside[3]. This last aeon being, says Hippolytus, born great, as brought into existence by a great and perfect father, was put forth as a guard and circumvallation for the aeons, and became the boundary of the Pleroma, containing within him all the thirty

loc. cit. He goes on to say that this is "the good and heavenly Jerusalem," the land in which the children of Israel are promised milk and honey. It should be noticed, however, that even this unshapen being, like all the Sophias, was identified with the Earth.

[1] Hippolytus, op. cit. Bk VI. c. 31, pp. 284, 285. Irenaeus, Bk I. cc. 1, 4, p. 21, Harvey, says that Monogenes [Nous] put forth ($\pi\rho\delta\beta\alpha\lambda\epsilon$) the pair κατὰ προμήθειαν τοῦ Πατρὸς, apparently without the aid of his partner Aletheia. Hippolytus' account is the simpler, as making all the Pleroma thus descend from a single pair, and is therefore, probably, the earlier.

[2] Hippolytus, loc. cit., says that this new aeon was called Ὅρος "Horus," or "The Limit," because he separates the Pleroma or Fulness from the Hysterema or Deficiency (i.e. that which lacks God), which is one of those puns which will be familiar to all Egyptologists (see Erman, Life in Ancient Egypt, Eng. ed. p. 396, for other examples). He is also said to have been called Metocheus or the Partaker, because he shares in the Deficiency, doubtless as being partly outside the Pleroma. His name of Horus was probably suggested by that of the old Egyptian god whose figure must have been familiar to every Alexandrian. In the IInd century A.D., this last generally appears with hawk's head and human body dressed in the cuirass and boots of a Roman gendarme or stationarius, which would be appropriate enough for a sentinel or guard.

[2] Hippolytus, loc. cit. pp. 284, 285, Cruice.

aeons together. Outside this boundary remained Sophia's Ectroma, whom Christ and the Holy Spirit had fashioned into an aeon as perfect as any within the Pleroma; and she, like her mother, is now called Sophia, being generally distinguished from " the last and youngest of the aeons " as the Sophia Without[1].

This Sophia Without the Pleroma was by no means at peace within herself. She is represented as having been afflicted with great terror at the departure of Christos and the Holy Spirit from her, when they left her to take their places within the Pleroma, and as grieving over her solitude and " in great perplexity " as to the nature of the Holy Spirit. Hence she turned herself to prayers and supplications to Christos, the being who had given her form, and these prayers were heard. Meanwhile, the thirty aeons within the Pleroma had resolved, on finding themselves safe within the guard of Stauros, to glorify the Father or Bythos by offering to him one aeon who should partake of the nature of each, and was therefore called the " Joint Fruit of the Pleroma[2]." This was Jesus " the Great High Priest," who, on coming into existence was sent outside the Pleroma at the instance of Christos in order that he might be a spouse to the Sophia Without and deliver her from her afflictions[3]. This he did, but the four passions of

---

[1] Hippolytus, *loc. cit.* pp. 286, 287, Cruice. Christ and the Holy Spirit, having discharged the duty laid upon them, have retired with Sophia "the youngest of the aeons" within the Pleroma and cannot again issue forth.

[2] Hippolytus, *op. cit.* c. 32: ἔδοξεν αὐτοῖς μὴ μόνον κατὰ συζυγίαν δεδοξακέναι τὸν υἱόν, δοξάσαι [δὲ] καὶ διὰ προσφορᾶς καρπῶν πρεπόντων τῷ Πατρί. "It seemed good to them [the aeons of the Pleroma] not only to magnify the Son by conjunction, but also by an offering of pleasing fruits to the Father." So in the mysteries of Isis, Osiris is called the fruit of the vine Dionysos. See Athenagoras, *Legatid.* c. XXII. Plainly Bythos and Nous or Monogenes are here represented as Father and Son as in the Ophite myth. The new projection is necessary to accord with the text about the whole Pleroma dwelling together bodily in Jesus. Cf. Colossians i. 19.

[3] The expression ὁ ἀρχιερεὺς ὁ μέγας is repeated by Clement of Alexandria, *Protrept.* c. XII, possibly with reference to this passage. It may be noticed, however, that Jesus is here also made the Messenger or Ambassador of the Light as with the Ophites. It will be seen later that he occupies the same place with the Manichaeans. Cf. Chapter XIII, *infra.*

Sophia, namely, fear, grief, perplexity, and supplication, having once been created could not be destroyed, but became separate and independent beings. Thus it was that matter came into being, and was itself the creation of the Deity, instead of being, as in the earlier systems, of independent origin. For Jesus " changed her fear into the substance which is psychic or animal (οὐσία ψυχική), her grief into that which is hylic or material, and her perplexity into the substance of demons[1]." Of her supplication, however, Jesus made a path of repentance (ὁδὸν ἐπὶ μετάνοιαν) and gave it power over the psychic substance. This psychic substance is, says Valentinus, a " consuming fire " like the God of Moses, and the Demiurge or Architect of the Cosmos, and is called the " Place " (τόπος) and the Hebdomad or Sevenfold Power, and the Ancient of Days, and is, if Hippolytus has really grasped Valentinus' opinions on the point, the author of death[2]. He and his realm come immediately below that of Sophia Without, here somewhat unexpectedly called the Ogdoad, where Sophia dwells with her spouse Jesus[3]. His sevenfold realm is, it would seem, the seven astronomical heavens, of which perhaps the Paradise of Adam is the fourth[4]. Below this again comes this world, the

---

[1] Hippolytus, *op. cit.* Bk VI. c. 32, p. 289, Cruice.

[2] *Ibid.* p. 290, Cruice. Κατὰ τοῦτο τοίνυν τὸ μέρος, θνητή τις ἐστὶν ἡ ψυχή, μεσότης τις οὖσα· ἔστι γὰρ Ἑβδομὰς καὶ Κατάπαυσις. " According to this, therefore," [he has just said that fire has a twofold power, for there is a fire which devours everything and which cannot be extinguished] " part (of the Demiurge) is a certain soul which is subject to death, and a certain substance which occupies a middle place. For it is a Hebdomad and a laying to rest." ·The passage is not easy, but seems to mean that some of the souls made by the Demiurge are mortal, while others are susceptible of salvation. Cf. n. 1, p. 109, *infra*. The name Hebdomad evidently refers to the seven astronomical heavens under the rule of the Demiurge, and the title " Ancient of Days " identifies him, like the Jaldabaoth of the Ophites, with the God of the Jews.

[3] Called Ogdoadas or eighth, because it is next above the seven heavens ; but Sophia, the 28th, was the last of the aeons. We see, therefore, that Valentinus, like the Ophites of the diagram, is reckoning forwards and backwards in the most confusing way.

[4] So Irenaeus, Bk I. c. 1, § 9, pp. 44, 45, Harvey, says that they [the Valentinians] say that the seven heavens are endowed with intelligence (νοητούς) and that they suppose them to be angels, and that the Demiurge

Cosmos, ruled by a hylic or material Power called the Devil
(Διάβολος) or Cosmocrator, not further described by Valentinus
but apparently resembling the Satan of the New Testament[1].
Lowest of all is unformed and unarranged matter, inhabited by
the demons, of whom Beelzebub, as in the Gospels, is said to
be the chief[2]. We have then four " places " outside the Pleroma
or Godhead, arranged in a succession which reckoning from above
downwards may be thus summed up :

1. The Heaven of Sophia called the Ogdoad, wherein dwell
Sophia Without and her spouse Jesus[3].

is himself an angel like God. Also that Paradise is a heaven above the
third, and that a fourth angel rules (?) there, and that from him Adam
took somewhat while talking to him. Whatever this story may mean, it is
curious to see how readily the Gnostics identified in name a heavenly place
with its ruler, as in the titles of kings and peers.

[1] Irenaeus, Bk I. c. 1, § 10, pp. 47, 48, Harvey, says that the Devil or
Cosmocrator and all the spiritual things of evil (τὰ πνευματικὰ τῆς πονηρίας)
were made out of the pain (λύπη) of Sophia, and that he is the creation
of the Demiurge, but knows what is above him, because he is a spirit, while
his creator is ignorant that there is anything higher than himself, because
he is only ruler of animal things (ψυχικὰ ὑπάρχοντα). In this, which is
probably the teaching of Ptolemy, Valentinus' successor is seen to be
reverting to the Ophite ideas. Hippolytus, who here probably gives us
Valentinus' own doctrine, says on the other hand (*op. cit.* Bk VI. c. 33,
pp. 290, 291, Cruice): Ὥσπερ οὖν τῆς ψυχικῆς οὐσίας ἡ πρώτη καὶ μεγίστη
δύναμις γέγονεν εἰκὼν [the text is here restored by Cruice: τοῦ μονογενοῦς
υἱοῦ, οὕτω τῆς ὑλικῆς οὐσίας δύναμις] διάβολος, ὁ ἄρχων τοῦ κόσμου τούτου·
τῆς δὲ τῶν δαιμόνων οὐσίας, ἥτις ἐστὶν ἐκ τῆς ἀπορίας, ὁ Βεελζεβούδ.
"As therefore the first and greatest power of the animal substance (the
Demiurge) came into being as the image of the unique son (Nous), so the
power of the material substance is the Devil, the Ruler of this world ;
and Beelzebud [the power] of the substance of demons which came into
being from the perplexity " (of Sophia). It has been shown elsewhere
(*P.S.B.A.* 1901, pp. 48, 49) that this Beelzebud or Beelzebuth is written
in the Magic Papyri Jabezebuth or Yahweh Sabaoth, probably in pursuance
of the parallelism which gives every god or superior power his correspondent
personality in the inferior or evil world. In all magic, mediaeval or otherwise, Beelzebuth is carefully distinguished from Satan.

[2] Matthew x. 25, xii. 24, 27 ; Mark iii. 22 ; Luke xi. 15, have
βεελζεβούλ, while the Peshitto writes the more familiar Beelzebub.
See *P.S.B.A.* quoted in last note.

[3] Called also the Heavenly Jerusalem. Hippolytus, *op. cit.* Bk VI.
c. 32, p. 290, Cruice.

2.   The Sevenfold World called the Hebdomad created and ruled by the Demiurge or Ancient of Days.

3.   Our own ordered world or Cosmos created by the Demiurge but ruled by the Devil.

4.   Chaos or unarranged Matter ruled by Beelzebub, Prince of the Demons.

Much of this may be due to the desire apparently inborn in natives of Egypt to define with excessive minuteness the topography of the invisible world ; but the disposition of these different Rulers was by no means a matter of indifference to mankind.   The Demiurge, as in the Ophite system, was not, indeed, bad, but foolish and blind, not knowing what he did, nor why he created man.   Yet it is he who sends forth the souls of men which reach them at their birth and leave them at their death.   Hence, says Hippolytus, he is called Psyche or Soul as Sophia is called Pneuma or Spirit.   But this soul of man is little else than what we call the life, and here as in all else the Demiurge is controlled without knowing it by his mother Sophia, who from her place in the Heavenly Jerusalem directs his operations. The bodies of men the Demiurge makes from that hylic and diabolic substance which is matter[1], and the soul which comes

---

[1] Irenaeus, Bk I. c. 1, § 10, p. 49, Harvey: Δημιουργήσαντα δὴ τὸν κόσμον, πεποιηκέναι καὶ τὸν ἄνθρωπον τὸν χοϊκόν· οὐκ ἀπὸ ταύτης δὲ τῆς ξηρᾶς γῆς, ἀλλ' ἀπὸ τῆς ἀοράτου οὐσίας, ἀπὸ τοῦ κεχυμένου καὶ ῥευστοῦ τῆς ὕλης λαβόντα· καὶ εἰς τοῦτον ἐμφυσῆσαι τὸν ψυχικὸν διορίζονται. "Having indeed fashioned the world, he (the Demiurge) made material man ; not taking him out of this dry earth, but from the unseen substance, from the poured forth and liquid matter, and into him, they declare, he breathed that which is of the soul."   Although this might be taken for a Ptolemaic elaboration or embroidery of Valentinus' own doctrine, it is repeated in almost identical words in the *Excerpta Theodoti* of Clement of Alexandria, which represent the teaching of the Oriental School, and it is therefore possibly the statement of Valentinus himself.   Hippolytus, *op. cit.* Bk VI. c. 34, p. 293, Cruice, is quite in accord with this.   Irenaeus says later (Bk I. c. 1, § 11) with reference to the body of Jesus : καὶ ὑλικὸν δὲ οὐδ' ὁτιοῦν εἰληφέναι λέγουσιν αὐτόν· μὴ γὰρ εἶναι τὴν ὕλην δεκτικὴν σωτηρίας. "And they say that He took on Himself nothing whatever of matter ; for matter is not susceptible of salvation."   From which it is to be inferred that Valentinus rejected the resurrection of the body.

from him dwells within it as in an inn, into which all may enter.
Sometimes, says Valentinus—and in this instance at least we
know it is he, not one of his followers, who is speaking—the
soul dwells alone and sometimes with demons, but sometimes
with Logoi or " words," who are heavenly angels sent by Sophia
Without and her spouse the Joint Fruit of the Pleroma into
this world, and who dwell with the soul in the earthly body,
when it has no demons living with it[1].   After leaving the body
of matter, the soul will even be united with its especial angel in
a still more perfect manner, as is a bridegroom with his bride[2], a

---

[1] Irenaeus, Bk I. c. 1, § 4, p. 23, Harvey, says that when Jesus, the
Joint Fruit of the Pleroma, was projected, Angels of the same kind as
himself (ὁμογενεῖς) were projected with him as a guard of honour.   That
these are the spiritual spouses of the souls of men is confirmed by Hippolytus, *op. cit.* Bk VI. c. 34, p. 292, according to Cruice's emendation:
Ὑποδιήρηται δὲ καὶ τὰ ἐν τῇ Ὀγδοάδι, καὶ προβεβήκασιν ἡ Σοφία, ἥτις ἐστὶ
μήτηρ πάντων τῶν ζώντων κατ᾽ αὐτούς, καὶ ὁ κοινὸς τοῦ Πληρώματος καρπὸς ὁ
Λόγος, [καὶ] οἵτινες εἰσιν ἄγγελοι ἐπουράνιοι, πολιτευόμενοι ἐν Ἰερουσαλὴμ τῇ
ἄνω, τῇ ἐν οὐρανοῖς.   " The things which are in the Ogdoad also are sub-
divided, and there proceed (from it) Sophia who is, according to them, the
Mother of All Living, and the Joint Fruit of the Pleroma, the Logos, and
there are certain heavenly angels who are citizens of the Jerusalem which
is above, that which is in the heavens."   So later (*ibid.* p. 293, Cruice)...
οἵτινές εἰσι λόγοι ἄνωθεν κατεσπαρμένοι ἀπὸ τοῦ κοινοῦ τοῦ Πληρώματος
καρποῦ καὶ τῆς Σοφίας εἰς τοῦτον τὸν κόσμον, κατοικοῦντες ἐν [σώμα]τι
χοϊκῷ μετὰ ψυχῆς, ὅταν δαίμονες μὴ συνοικῶσι τῇ ψύχῃ.   " There are
certain Logoi sown from above in the world by the Joint Fruit of the
Pleroma and Sophia, which dwell in the material body with the soul, when
there are no demons dwelling with it."   Clement of Alexandria, in *Strom.*
Bk v. c. 14, points out that the notion of demons dwelling with the soul
is to be found in Plato, and quotes the passage from the Vision of Er (*Rep.*
Bk x. c. 15) about the souls of men between births each receiving from the
hand of Lachesis a demon as their guides through life.   It is more likely,
however, to have been derived from the Zoroastrian belief in the Fravashis
or Ferouers, celestial spirits who live with Ahura Mazda and the powers
of light, until they are sent on earth to be joined with the souls of men,
and to combat the powers of Ahriman (see L. C. Casartelli, *La Philosophie
Religieuse du Mazdéisme*, Paris, 1884, pp. 76–80, for references).   Cf.
Hope Moulton, *op. cit.* c. VIII. *passim.*

[2] Irenaeus, Bk I. c. 1, § 12, p. 59, Harvey: Τοὺς δὲ πνευματικοὺς ἀπο-
δυσαμένους τὰς ψυχὰς καὶ πνεύματα νοερὰ γενομένους, ἀκρατήτως καὶ ἀοράτως
ἐντὸς πληρώματος εἰσελθόντας νύμφας ἀποδοθήσεσθαι τοῖς περὶ τὸν Σωτῆρα

state which is sometimes spoken of as "the Banquet," and seems
connected with what has been said above about the meeting of
Jesus the Joint Fruit with the Sophia Without[1]. Yet this is
not a question of conduct or free will, but of predestination,
and seems to mark the chief practical difference between
Valentinus on the one hand and the Ophites and the pre-Christian
Gnostics on the other. The Ophites, as we have seen, believed
in the threefold nature of the soul, or its composition from the
pneumatic or spiritual, the psychical or animal, and the choic
or earthly, all which elements were thought to be present in
everyone. But they held, following their predecessors the
Orphici, that these divisions corresponded to what may be
called degrees of grace, and that it was possible for man to
pass from one category to the other, and become wholly pneumatic or psychic or earthly. Valentinus, however, introduces
a different idea and makes the distinction between the three

ἀγγέλοις. "And the Spirituals, or Pneumatis, doffing their souls and
becoming intelligent spirits, shall enter unperceived and unseen within the
Pleroma, and shall be given as brides to the angels about the Saviour."
This suggestion, which completely shocked the modesty of Tertullian, may
be connected with the Zoroastrian idea of the virgin who appears to the
believer as his conductor at the bridge Chinvat. See Chapter XII, *infra*.

[1] This appears in the *Excerpta Theodoti*, fr. 63, Migne's *Patrol. Graeci*,
t. IX. col. 689 : Ἡ μὲν οὖν πνευματικῶν ἀνάπαυσις ἐν Κυριακῇ ἐν Ὀγδοάδι ἡ
Κυριακὴ ὀνομάζεται· παρὰ τῇ μητρὶ ἔχοντα τὰς ψυχὰς τὰ ἐνδύματα ἄχρι
συντελείας· αἱ δὲ ἄλλαι πισταὶ ψυχαὶ παρὰ τῷ Δημιουργῷ· περὶ δὲ τὴν
συντέλειαν ἀναχωροῦσι καὶ αὐτοὶ εἰς Ὀγδοάδας. Εἶτα τὸ δεῖπνον τὸν γάμον
κοινὸν πάντων τῶν σωζωθέντων, ἄχρις ἂν ἀπισωθῇ πάντα καὶ ἄλληλα γνωρίσῃ.
"Therefore the repose of the Spirituals in [the dwelling] of the Lord,
that is, in the Ogdoad, is called the Lord's rest" (cf. Irenaeus, Bk I.
cc. 1, 9, p. 46, Harvey): "the garments [*i.e.* natures] containing the
souls [will remain] with the Mother until the Consummation. And the
other faithful souls (will remain) with the Demiurge ; and at the Consummation they will withdraw, and they also will go into the Ogdoad.
Then will be the Wedding Feast of all those who are saved until all things
shall be made equal and all things mutually made known." This heavenly
banquet, of which we may be quite sure Valentinus made the Marriage in
Cana a type, will be met with again in the worship of Mithras (Chapter XII,
infra). But it was also well known to the Orphics (see Abel's *Orphica*,
Frag. 227, etc.), and the question repeats itself : Did the Orphics borrow
the idea from the Persians, or the Mithraists from the Orphics ?

different categories of human souls one not of degree, but of essence[1]. Men have not a threefold soul, but belong to one of three classes, according to the source of their souls. Either they are pneumatic, *i.e.* spiritual, belonging wholly to Sophia, or psychic, that is animated by the Demiurge alone and therefore like him foolish and ignorant although capable of improvement, or hylic, that is formed wholly of matter and therefore subject to the power of the demons[2]. Nothing is said explicitly by Hippolytus as to how this division into classes is made ; but we know by other quotations from Valentinus himself that this is the work of Sophia who sends the Logoi or Words into such souls as she chooses, or rather into those which she has created specially and without the knowledge of the Demiurge[3].

The consequences of this division upon the future of mankind generally also differed materially from that of the Ophitic scheme. Only the pneumatics or spiritual men are by nature

[1] Valentinus may have found this doctrine in Egypt, where as Maspero points out (*Ét. Égyptol.* I. p. 398) only the rich and noble were thought to enjoy the life beyond the grave.

[2] Valentinus' remark about the Cosmocrator being superior in knowledge to the Demiurge because he is a *spirit* (see n. 1, p. 108 *supra*) much complicates the problem, and brings us pretty near to the Dualism of the Avesta. That all matter was in Valentinus' opinion transitory appears from Irenaeus, Bk I. c. 1, § 13, where it is said that when all the seed scattered by Sophia in the world, *i.e.* the souls of the Pneumatici, is gathered in, the fire which is within the Cosmos shall blaze forth and after destroying all matter shall be extinguished with it.

[3] Clem. Alex., *Strom.* Bk II. c. 8, quotes an epistle of Valentinus in which he speaks of the terror of the angels at the sight of man because of the things which he spoke: διὰ τὸν ἀοράτως ἐν αὐτῷ σπέρμα δεδωκότα τῆς ἄνωθεν οὐσίας, καὶ παρρησιαζόμενον "because of that within him which yielded a germ of the substance on high, and spoke freely." So Irenaeus, Bk I. c. 1, § 10, p. 51, Harvey : Ἔλαθεν οὖν, ὡς φασί, τὸν Δημιουργὸν ὁ συγκατασπαρεὶς τῷ ἐμφυσήματι αὐτοῦ ὑπὸ τῆς Σοφίας πνευματικὸς ἀνθρώπων [ἄνθρωπος] ἀρρήτῳ [adj. δυνάμει καὶ] προνοίᾳ. "It escaped the Demiurge, therefore, as they say, that the man whom he had formed by his breath was at the same time made spiritual by Sophia with unspeakable power and foresight." So that, as Irenaeus says a few lines later, man has his soul from the Demiurge, his body from Chaos, his fleshly part (τὸ σαρκικὸν) from matter, and his spiritual man from the Mother, Achamoth [*i.e.* חכמת "Wisdom "].

immortal or deathless, and when they leave the material body
go on high to the Ogdoad or Heaven of Sophia, where she sits
with Jesus the " Joint Fruit " of the Pleroma[1].   The hylics or
men who are wholly material perish utterly at death, because
their souls like their bodies are corruptible[2].   There remain the
psychic—the " natural men " of the New Testament[3]—who are
not so to speak " saved " ; but are yet capable of salvation.
How was this salvation to be brought about ?

Valentinus seems to have answered this by saying, as any
Catholic Christian would have done at the time, that it was
through the Divine Mission of Jesus.   Yet this Jesus, according
to Valentinus or the Valentinian author from whom Hippolytus
draws his account, was neither Jesus the Joint Fruit of the
Pleroma, who according to them remained with his spouse

---

[1] Clem. Alex. *Strom.* Bk iv. c. 13, quoting " a certain homily " (τις
ὁμιλία) of Valentinus : ᾽Απ᾽ ἀρχῆς ἀθανατοί ἐστε, καὶ τέκνα ζωῆς ἐστε αἰωνίας
καὶ τὸν θάνατον ἠθέλετε μερίσασθαι εἰς ἑαυτούς, ἵνα δαπανήσητε αὐτὸν καὶ
ἀναλώσητε καὶ ἀποθάνῃ ὁ θάνατος ἐν ὑμῖν καὶ δι᾽ ὑμῶν. ῞Οταν γὰρ τὸν μὲν
κόσμον λύητε, ὑμεῖς δὲ καταλύησθε, κυριεύετε τῆς κτίσεως καὶ τῆς φθορᾶς ἁπάσης.
"You were deathless from the beginning and the children of life everlasting,
and you wish to share out death among you, in order that you may dissipate
and destroy it and that death may die in and by you ; for when you put
an end to the world and are yourselves put an end to, you have rule over
creation and all corruption."   So one of the documents of the *Pistis
Sophia* speaks of this world being finally consumed by the fire " which
the perfect wield."   It was doubtless such predictions which gave colour
to the charge of incendiarism made by the Roman authorities against
the Christians generally.   For the translation of the pneumatics to the
Ogdoad see next note.

[2] Hippolytus, *op. cit.* Bk vi. c. 31, p. 290, Cruice : ᾽Εὰν ἐξομοιωθῇ τοῖς
ἄνω ἐν ᾽Ογδοάδι, ἀθάνατος ἐγένετο καὶ ἦλθεν εἰς τὴν ᾽Ογδοάδα ἥτις ἐστί, φησίν,
᾽Ιερουσαλὴμ ἐπουράνιος· ἐὰν δὲ ἐξομοιωθῇ τῇ ὕλῃ, τουτέστι τοῖς πάθεσι τοῖς
ὑλικοῖς, φθαρτή ἐστι καὶ ἀπώλετο.   " If [the soul] be of the likeness of those
on high in the Ogdoad, it is born deathless and goes to the Ogdoad which
is, he says, the heavenly Jerusalem ; but if it be of the likeness of matter,
that is, if it belongs to the material passions, it is corruptible and is utterly
destroyed."

[3] ψυχικὸς ἄνθρωπος translated in the A.V. by " natural man "
evidently means in the Valentinian sense those who are *animated* or have
had breathed into them the *breath* of life merely.   It has nothing to do with
soul as we understand the term.

Sophia in the Heavenly Jerusalem, nor Christos who with his consort the Holy Spirit was safe within the Pleroma. He was in effect a third saviour brought into being especially for the salvation of all that is worth saving in this devil-ruled and material world, in the same way that Christos and his consort had saved the first Sophia after she had given birth to the monstrous Ectroma, and as Jesus the Joint Fruit had saved this Ectroma itself. It is very probable, as M. Amélineau has shown with great attention to detail, that every system, perhaps every universe, had according to Valentinus its own saviour, the whole arrangement being part of one vast scheme for the ordering and purifying of all things[1]. Hence Valentinus explains, as the Ophites had failed to do, that salvation spreads from above downwards and that the redemption of this world was not undertaken until that of the universe of the Demiurge had been effected[2]. The Demiurge—and the statement has peculiar significance if we consider him the God of the Jews— had been taught by Sophia Without that he was not the sole God, as he had imagined, and had been instructed and " initiated into the great mystery of the Father and the Aeons[3]." Although

---

[1] Amélineau, *Gnost. Ég.* p. 225.

[2] Hippolytus, *op. cit.* Bk VI. c. 36, pp. 297, 298, Cruice: Ἔδει οὖν διορθωμένων τῶν ἄνω κατὰ τὴν αὐτὴν ἀκολουθίαν καὶ τὰ ἐνθάδε τυχεῖν διορθώσεως. " Wherefore when things on high had been put straight, it had to be according to the law of sequences that those here below should be put straight also."

[3] Hippolytus, *op. cit.* p. 297, Cruice: ἐδιδάχθη γὰρ ὑπὸ τῆς Σοφίας ὁ Δημιουργός, ὅτι οὐκ ἔστιν αὐτὸς Θεὸς μόνος ὡς ἐνόμιζε, καὶ πλὴν αὐτοῦ ἕτερος (οὐκ) ἔστιν· ἀλλ' ἔγνω διδαχθεὶς ὑπὸ τῆς Σοφίας τὸν κρείττονα· κατηχήθη γὰρ ὑπ' αὐτῆς, καὶ ἐμνήθη καὶ ἐδιδάχθη τὸ μέγα τοῦ Πατρὸς καὶ τῶν Αἰώνων μυστήριον, καὶ ἐξεῖπεν αὐτὸ οὐδενί, κ.τ.λ. " For the Demiurge had been taught by Sophia that he was not the only God and that beside him there was none other, as he had thought ; but through Sophia's teaching he knew better. For he had been instructed and initiated by Sophia, and had been taught the great mystery of the Father and of the Aeons, and had declared it to none "—in support of which the statement in Exodus (vi. 2, 3) about being the God of Abraham, Isaac, and Jacob, but " by my name Jehovah was I not known unto them " is quoted. The identification by Valentinus of the Demiurge with the God of the Jews is therefore complete.

it is nowhere distinctly stated, it seems a natural inference that the same lot will fall to the psychic men who are, like the Demiurge, "soul" rather than "spirit," and that they will receive further instruction in the Heaven of Sophia. Thus, he continues, the lapses[1] of the Demiurge had been set straight and it was necessary that those here below should go through the same process. Jesus was accordingly born of the Virgin Mary; He was entirely pneumatic, that is His body was endowed with a spiritual soul, for Sophia Without herself descended into Mary and the germ thus sown by her was formed into a visible shape by the operation of the Demiurge[2]. As for His Mission, it seems to have consisted in revealing to man the constitution of the worlds above him, the course to be pursued by him to attain immortality, and to sum up the whole matter in one word, the *Gnosis* or knowledge that was necessary to salvation[3].

Here the account of the teaching of Valentinus, which has been taken almost entirely from the *Philosophumena* or from quotations from his own words in trustworthy writers like

---

[1] σφάλματα "stumblings," Hippolytus, *loc. cit.*

[2] Hippolytus, *op. cit.* Bk VI. c. 35, p. 295, Cruice. I have taken what seems on comparison to be the original form of Valentinus' teaching. In the same chapter, Hippolytus tells us that his followers were divided on the question of the composition of the body of Jesus—the Italic School led by Heracleon and Ptolemy averring that it was psychic and that at His baptism only the πνεῦμα came upon Him as a dove, while the Oriental School of Axionicus and Bardesanes maintained that it was pneumatic from the first. Cf. n. 2, p. 116 *infra*.

[3] Amélineau, *Gnost. Ég.* p. 226. The *Excerpta Theodoti*, on which he relies, says (fr. 78): Μέχρι τοῦ βαπτίσματος οὖν ἡ εἱμαρμένη, φασίν, ἀληθής· μετὰ δὲ τοῦτο οὐκ ἔτι ἀληθεύουσιν οἱ ἀστρολόγοι. Ἔστι δὲ οὐ τὸ λουτρὸν μόνον τὸ ἐλευθεροῦν, ἀλλὰ καὶ ἡ γνῶσις τίνες ἦμεν, τί γεγόναμεν, ποῦ ἦμεν, ἢ ποῦ ἐνεβλήθημεν, ποῦ σπεύδομεν, πόθεν λυτρούμεθα, τί γέννησις τί ἀναγέννησις. "Until baptism then, they say the destiny [he is talking of that which is foretold by the stars] holds good; but thereafter the astrologers' predictions are no longer unerring. For the [baptismal] font not only sets us free, but is also the *Gnosis* which teaches us what we are, why we have come into being, where we are, or whither we have been cast up, whither we are hastening, from what we have been redeemed, why there is birth, and why re-birth." For baptism was to the Valentinian initiation, and a mystagogue of Eleusis would have expressed himself no differently.

Clement of Alexandria, abruptly ends, and we are left to conjecture.   We cannot therefore say directly what Valentinus himself taught about the Crucifixion.   Jesus, the historical Jesus
born of the Virgin Mary, though purely pneumatic or spiritual
at the outset, received according to one account some tincture
of the nature of all the worlds through which He had descended,
and must therefore, probably, have had to abandon successive
parts of His nature, as He reascended[1].   Probably, therefore,
Valentinus thought that the Spiritual or Divine part of Him
left Him before the Passion, and that it was only His material
body that suffered[2].   As we shall see later, this idea was much
elaborated by the later Gnostics, who thought that all those
redeemed from this world would in that respect have to imitate
their Great Exemplar.   If this be so, it is plain that it was
only that part of the soul of Jesus which He had received from
Sophia which returned to her, and was doubtless re-absorbed
in her being.   Yet there is nothing to make us believe that
Valentinus did not accept the narrative of the Canonical

[1] Irenaeus, Bk I. c. 1, § 13, pp. 60–62, Harvey; Amélineau, *Gnost.
Ég.* p. 226, and *Excerpta Theodoti* there quoted.

[2] Hippolytus, *op. cit.* Bk VI. c. 35, pp. 295, 296, Cruice: Ὁ δὲ Ἰησοῦς,
ὁ καινὸς ἄνθρωπος, ἀπὸ Πνεύματος Ἁγίου [καὶ τοῦ Ὑψίστου], τουτέστι τῆς
Σοφίας καὶ τοῦ Δημιουργοῦ, ἵνα τὴν μὲν πλάσιν καὶ κατασκευὴν τοῦ σώματος
αὐτοῦ ὁ Δημιουργὸς καταρτίσῃ, τὴν δὲ οὐσίαν αὐτοῦ τὸ Πνεῦμα παράσχῃ τὸ
Ἅγιον, καὶ γένηται Λόγος ἐπουράνιος ἀπὸ τῆς Ὀγδοάδος γεννηθεὶς διὰ Μαρίας.
"But Jesus, the new man, [has come into being] by the Holy Spirit and
by the Highest, that is by Sophia and the Demiurge, so that the Demiurge
might put together the mould and constitution of His body and that the
Holy Spirit might provide its substance; and that He might become the
Heavenly Logos....when born of Mary."   According to this, the body of
Jesus was a "psychic" or animal one; yet Hippolytus says immediately
afterwards (p. 296, Cruice), that it was on this that there was a division
between the Italic and the Oriental Schools of Valentinians, the former with ·
Heracleon and Ptolemy saying that the body of Jesus was an animal one,
the Holy Spirit coming on Him as a dove at His baptism, while the Orientals
with Axionicus and Bardesanes maintained that the body of the Saviour
was pneumatic or spiritual, "the Holy Spirit or Sophia and the power of
the Highest or Demiurgic art having come upon Mary, in order that what
was given to Mary might be put into form."   Apparently Valentinus was
willing to call the God of the Jews Ὕψιστος or "Highest," which M. Cumont
thinks was his name in Asia Minor.

Gospels in full[1], or to doubt that he taught that Jesus really suffered on the Cross, although he doubtless interpreted this in his usual fashion, by making it a symbol of the self-sacrifice of Jesus the Joint Fruit of the Pleroma, when He left that celestial abode to give form and salvation to the miserable Ectroma of Sophia[2]. Here again we can but gather Valentinus' opinions from those of his followers, who may have altered them materially to fit them to the exigencies of a situation of which we can form no very precise idea.

Of these followers we know rather more than in the case of any other of the early heresiarchs. According to Tertullian, Valentinus was brought up as a Christian, and expected to become a bishop of the Catholic Church, " because he was an able man both in genius and eloquence[3]." Finding, Tertullian goes on to say, that a confessor[4] was preferred to him, he broke with the Church and " finding the track of a certain old opinion " (doubtless, the Ophite) "marked out a path for himself." The same accusation of disappointed ambition was levelled against nearly every other heresiarch at the time, and may serve to show how greatly the place of bishop was coveted ; but we have

---

[1] With the exception of that of St John, since the part of the *Pistis Sophia* which it is suggested is by Valentinus does not quote it. His followers, however, knew of it, as in the *Excerpta Theodoti* the opening verse τὸ ἐν ἀρχῇ ἦν ὁ Λόγος καὶ ὁ Λόγος ἦν παρὰ τὸν Θεόν, καὶ Θεὸς ἦν ὁ λόγος is quoted with the comments of οἱ ἀπὸ τοῦ Οὐαλεντίνου on it. Cf. Amélineau, *Gnost. Ég.* p. 209, where the passage is given in n. 4.

[2] Irenaeus, Bk I. c. 1, § 13, pp. 60–62, Harvey : Εἰσὶ δὲ οἱ λέγοντες... Ἔπαθε δὲ λοιπὸν κατ' αὐτοὺς ὁ ψυχικὸς Χριστός, καὶ ὁ ἐκ τῆς οἰκονομίας κατεσκευασμένος μυστηριωδῶς, ἵν' ἐπιδείξῃ [δι'] αὐτοῦ ἡ μήτηρ τοῦ ἄνω Χριστοῦ, ἐκείνου τοῦ ἐπεκταθέντος τῷ Σταυρῷ, καὶ μορφώσαντος τὴν Ἀχαμὼθ μόρφωσιν τὴν κατ' οὐσίαν· πάντα γὰρ ταῦτα τύπους ἐκείνων εἶναι λέγουσι. " And there are some " (probably the Anatolic or Oriental School is meant) " who say.... And further the animal Christ, He who had been mysteriously formed by dispensation, suffered so that the Mother might show forth through Him the type of the Christ on high, of him who is extended by Stauros, and gave shape to Achamoth as regards substance : for they say that all things here are the types of others there."

[3] Tertullian, *adv. Valentinianos*, c. IV.

[4] That is, not a martyr, but one who had suffered for the faith without losing his life.

no means of judging its truth in this particular instance, and it
is repeated neither by Irenaeus, Hippolytus, nor Clement of
Alexandria who was in an exceptionally good position for knowing the truth of the case.   Irenaeus, however, says that Valentinus came to Rome during the papacy of Hyginus, flourished
(ἤκμασε) under that of Pius, and dwelt there until that of
Anicetus ; and this is confirmed by Eusebius, who connects
Valentinus' stay in Rome with the reign of Hadrian's successor,
Antoninus Pius[1]. Tertullian further declares that Valentinus did
not separate from the Church until the papacy of Eleutherus[2],
which did not commence until A.D. 174, and M. Amélineau
seems therefore well-founded in his inference that Valentinus
elaborated his system in Egypt while yet in the Church, and
that he went to Rome in order to impose it upon the rest of the
faithful[3].   If this be so, it would abundantly account for its
far closer approximation to the orthodox faith than that of
the Ophites, from which it appears to have been derived.
Epiphanius tells us further that after quitting Rome, Valentinus
died in Cyprus, where he made " a last shipwreck of his faith[4]."
Could we place implicit faith in Epiphanius' highly-coloured
statements, we might gather from this that Valentinus gave a
fresh turn to his doctrines after finding himself away from the
great cities in which he had hitherto spent his life.

However that may be, the time which, on the shortest
computation, Valentinus passed in Rome was quite sufficient
for him to set up a school there, and we are not surprised to hear
that thereafter there was a body of Valentinians in the West,
which was called the " Italic school."   Innovating, as Tertullian
said all heretics did, upon the system of their founder, they
taught, as before mentioned, that Sige or Silence was a real
spouse to the Ineffable Bythos or the Supreme Being and existed
side by side with Him from eternity[5].   They further said that

---

[1] Irenaeus, Bk III. c. 4, § 1, vol. II. p. 17, Harvey ; Eusebius, *Hist.
Eccl.* Bk IV. c. 11.   Cf. Amélineau, *Gnost. Ég.* p. 170.

[2] Tertullian, *de Praescpt.* c. xxx.   Amélineau, *Gnost. Ég.* p. 175, objects
to this.

[3] Amélineau, *Gnost. Ég.* p. 172, n. 1 ; *ibid.* p. 175.

[4] Epiphanius, *Pan., Haer.* xxxi. c. 2.

[5] Hippolytus, *op. cit.* Bk VI. c. 35, p. 296, Cruice.

the Dodecad or group of twelve aeons, of whom Sophia was the
last, emanated not from Logos and Zoe, but from the third
syzygy of Anthropos and Ecclesia[1]; and that the body of the
historical Jesus was not material but psychic or from the world
of the Demiurge[2], which seems to include the view held by other
Gnostics that it was a phantasm which only appeared to suffer
on the Cross, but did not do so in reality. We know the names of
several of the leaders of this Italic school, among whom were
Ptolemy, Secundus, and Heracleon. It was the doctrine of the
first of these apparently flourishing in Gaul in his time, which
spurred on Irenaeus to write against them[3]; while Heracleon
was called by Clement of Alexandria the most distinguished of
the school of Valentinus and taught in the last-named city[4].
Ptolemy's doctrine as described by Irenaeus seems to have
materially differed from that of his master only in the particulars
just given; while Secundus is said by the same heresiologist to
have divided the First Ogdoad into two tetrads, a right hand
and a left, one of which he called light and the other darkness[5].
Over against this, we hear from Hippolytus of an Eastern
school (Διδασκαλία ἀνατολική), which M. Amélineau shows
satisfactorily to have most closely represented the teaching of
Valentinus himself[6], and which was carried on after his death
by Axionicus and Bardesanes[7]. Of these, Axionicus is said to
have taught in his native city of Antioch; while Bardesanes was
evidently the same as the person called by the Syrians Bar
Daisan of Edessa, whose name was still great in the time of
Albiruni[8]. Theodotus, whose writings are quoted at some
length by Clement of Alexandria, and Alexander, whose arguments as to the body of Jesus are rebutted by Tertullian,
probably continued their teaching[9].

[1] Irenaeus, Bk I. c. 1, § 2, p. 13, Harvey.
[2] See n. 2, p. 116 *supra*.   [3] Irenaeus, *Prooem.* p. 4, Harvey.
[4] Clem. Alex. *Strom.* Bk IV. c. 9.
[5] Hippolytus, *op. cit.* Bk VI. c. 38, p. 302, Cruice. So Irenaeus, Bk I.
c. 5, § 2, p. 101, Harvey. This appears to be hyperbole rather than dualism.
[6] Amélineau, *Gnost. Ég.* p. 189.
[7] Hippolytus, *op. cit.* Bk VI. c. 35, p. 296, Cruice.
[8] Albîrûnî, *Chronology of Ancient Nations*, ed. Sachau, 1879, pp. 27, 189.
[9] De Faye, *Intro.* etc. p. 105, n. 1; Tertullian, *de Carne Christi*, c. XVI.

The life of Bar Daisan, of which some particulars have been preserved for us by Bar Hebraeus and other Eastern historians of the Church, throws considerable light upon the attitude towards Christianity of Valentinus and that Anatolic School which best represented his teachings. Bar Daisan was born some fifty years after Valentinus of rich and noble parents in the town of Edessa in Mesopotamia, where he seems to have been educated in the company of the future king of the country, Abgar Bar Manu[1]. He was probably a Christian from his infancy, early became a Christian teacher, and withstood Apollonius, a Pagan Sophist who visited Edessa in the train of the Emperor Caracalla, making avowal of his readiness to suffer martyrdom for the faith. According to Eusebius, he had the greatest abhorrence of the dualistic doctrine of Marcion and wrote books against him in his native Syriac which were afterwards translated into Greek[2]. He, or perhaps his son Harmonius[3], also composed a great number of hymns which were sung in the Catholic Churches of Mesopotamia and Syria; and it was not until a century and a half after his death that Ephrem Syrus, a doctor of the now triumphant and persecuting Church, found that these abounded in the errors of Valentinus, and deemed it necessary to substitute for them hymns of his own composition[4]. Valentinus seems in like manner to have lived in Rome as a Christian teacher, as we have seen, for at least sixteen years, and to have composed many psalms, some of which are quoted by Clement of Alexandria. If Tertullian is to be believed, he was qualified for the episcopate, which he must have had some chance of obtaining; and his want of orthodoxy cannot, therefore, have been manifest at the time or considered an objection to his candidature[5]. Moreover, Irenaeus says that Valentinus was the first who converted the so-called Gnostic

---

[1] See Hort, Bardaisan, in *Dict. Christian Biog.*

[2] Eusebius, *Hist. Eccl.* Bk IV. c. 30, says that Bar Daisan was first a Valentinian and afterwards recanted, " but did not entirely wipe away the filth of his old heresy."

[3] Rather a suspect name for a hymn writer.

[4] Ephrem Syrus' own date is given as 370 A.D., in *Dict. Christian Biog. s.h.n.*

[5] See n. 3, p. 117 *supra*.

heresy into the peculiar characteristics of his own school[1]; which agrees with Tertullian's statement that Valentinus was " at first a believer in the teaching of the Catholic Church in the Church of Rome under the episcopate of the Blessed Eleutherus[2]." It is evident, therefore, that long after his peculiar teaching was developed, he remained a member of the Church, and that it was not by his own wish that he left it, if indeed he ever did so.

One is therefore led to examine with some closeness the alleged differences between his teaching and that of the orthodox Christianity of his time ; and these, although they may have been vitally important, seem to have been very few. With regard to his views as to the nature of the Godhead, as given above, they do indeed seem to differ *toto coelo* from those shadowed forth in the Canonical Gospels and Epistles, and afterwards defined and emphasized by the many Œcumenical and other Councils called to regulate the Church's teaching on the matter. The long series of aeons constituting his Pleroma or Fulness of the Godhead seems at first sight to present the most marked contrast with the Trinity of Three Persons and One God in the Creeds which have come down to us from the early Church. But is there any reason to suppose that Valentinus regarded the members of these Tetrads, Decads, and Dodecads as possessing a separate and individual existence or as having any practical importance for the Christian ? We can hardly suppose so, when we consider the attitude of his immediate followers with regard to them. Some, as we have seen, were said to have put as the origin of all things, not a single principle but two principles of different sexes or, as Irenaeus says, a " dyad," thereby splitting the Supreme Being into two[3]. We can

---

[1] Irenaeus, Bk I. c. 5, § 1, p. 98, Harvey.

[2] See n. 2, p. 118 *supra*.

[3] This may have been due either to their Egyptian extraction, or to the necessity of putting the matter in a way that would be intelligible to their Egyptian disciples. Cf. Naville, *Old Egyptian Faith*, 1909, where he says that the Egyptian way of expressing abstract ideas is by metaphors. Their ancestors, the Egyptians of the early Dynasties, when they wanted to describe how gods of both sexes came forth from one single male deity, did so by means of a very coarse image. See Budge, Papyrus of Nesi-

imagine the outcry that this would have caused two centuries later when the different parties within the Christian Church were at each other's throats on the question whether the Son was of the same or only of like substance with the Father. Yet neither Valentinus, nor Ptolemy, nor Heracleon, nor any one of the Valentinian leaders seems to have borne the others any hostility on that account, to have dreamed of separating from them on such a pretext, or to have ceased to regard themselves both as Christians and followers of Valentinus. The only inference to be drawn from this is either that the account of their teaching has been grossly corrupted or that they considered such questions as matters of opinion merely, on which all might freely debate, but which were not to be taken as touchstones of the faith.

This view derives great support from the way in which Clement of Alexandria, Valentinus' countryman and the one among the Fathers who seems best fitted to understand him, regarded similar questions. M. Courdaveaux has shown with great clearness that Clement sometimes confounded the Third Person of the Trinity with the Second, and sometimes made Him His inferior. He also considered the Son as a simple creature of the Father, and, therefore, necessarily, of lower rank[1]. It was for such "heresies," as they were afterwards called, that Photius, who had Clement's now lost book of the *Hypotyposes* under his eyes, condemned him as a heretic, although his judgment in the matter has never been adopted by the Church. M. Courdaveaux also shows that Tertullian, even before he left the Church, looked upon both the Son and the Holy Spirit as only "members" of the Father, whom he considered to contain within Himself the complete divine sub-

Amsu, *Archaeologia*, vol. LII. (1890), pp. 440, 441. Cf. same author, *Hieratic Papyri in B.M.*

[1] Courdaveaux, *R.H.R.* Jan.–Fev. 1892, p. 293 and n. 7. Mgr Duchesne, *op. cit.* pp. 244, 245, agrees that Clement looked upon the Son as a creature only. Nor does there seem much difference between Valentinus' view of the relation between the Demiurge and the Unknown Father, and Clement's remarks about the Son whom he calls timeless and unbegotten and says that it is from Him that we must learn the "remote cause the Father of the Universe": *Strom.* Bk VII. c. 1. Cf. Justin Martyr, *c. Trypho.* c. 56.

stance ; and this was certainly none of the heresies for which his memory was arraigned[1]. It by no means follows that Valentinus' teaching was the same as that of the Church in all its details ; but it seems possible from these examples that he did not think it necessary to be more definite than the Church herself upon such points, and that he did not look upon them in any other light than as matters of opinion.

It should also be considered whether the language that Valentinus used regarding the nature and divisions of the Godhead is to be construed in the same sense and as implying the meaning that it would have done a few centuries later, when these points had been long discussed and the reasons for and against them marshalled and weighed. So far as can now be seen, he, like all Egyptians, never lost sight of allegory in dealing with matters transcending sense. Thus, when he speaks of the pretended union of Bythos and Sige, he is careful to say that there is nothing actually begotten, and that the whole story must be considered in a figurative sense :

"The Father [*i.e.* Bythos] alone," he says, "was unbegotten, not subject to conditions of place, nor time, taking no counsel, nor having any other being that can be comprehended by any recognized trope : but he was alone, and, as it is said, solitary, and resting in solitary repose within himself. And when he became fruitful, it seemed to him good at a certain time to engender and bring forth the most beautiful and perfect thing which he had within him : for he did not love solitude. For he was all love, but love is not love unless there is something to be loved[2]."

Between this and such Canonical texts as "God is love, and he that dwelleth in love dwelleth in God and God in him[3]," there may be a difference of application indeed, but none of language.

It seems, therefore, that in his theology Valentinus treated

---

[1] *R.H.R.* Jan.–Fev. 1891, p. 27. Tertullian's own heresy was of course Montanism. Harnack, *Hist. of Dogma*, Eng. ed., II. pp. 257, 258, says indeed that Hippolytus' own views of the Trinity coincide with those of Valentinus and are a relic of polytheism.

[2] Hippolytus, *op. cit.* Bk VI. c. 29, pp. 280, 281, Cruice.

[3] 2 John iv. 16. So Ἀγάπη "Love" is made the summit of the universe in the Ophite Diagram. See Chap. VIII *supra*.

the Ophitic ideas on which he worked very much as the Ophites had themselves treated the legends of Osiris and Attis. Dealing with their stories of aeons and powers as myths—that is to say as legends which whether true or not were only to be considered as symbols designed to show the way in which the world and man came forth from God—he thereby established his cosmology on a foundation which could be considered satisfactory by those half-heathen schools which had already contrived to reconcile the Pagan rites with the Jewish Scriptures and the Christian belief in the Mission of Jesus. But he went far beyond them in applying the same method of interpretation to all the acts of Jesus recorded in the Gospels. If Jesus were crucified upon the Cross, it was because its type the aeon Stauros had been set as a limit between that which is God and that which is not God but only godlike[1]. If He is said to go up to Jerusalem, it means that He went up from the world of matter to the Heaven of Sophia which is called Jerusalem[2]. If He were sent down to earth, it was because the higher worlds had already been put in the way of redemption by the gathering-in of Sophia into the Pleroma, the marriage of Sophia Without to Jesus the Joint Fruit, and the revelation to the Demiurge or God of the Jews that he was not the Supreme Being but only his reflection at several removes[3]. Every world is a copy of the one above it, every event must take place in every world in its turn, and all creation is like a chain which hung from the heavens is gradually drawn up to them, this creation of ours (κτίσις καθ᾽ ἡμᾶς) being its last link[4].

In all this, Valentinus wrote like a philosopher of the period, and, in fact, pretty much as Philo had done. But beyond this, he seems to have paid great attention to what is called the " pastoral " duty of a religious teacher or the care of souls, and to have busied himself to show how religion could be used to console and sustain the heart. All the fragments that we have left of the writings of himself and his followers are directed

---

[1] Neander, *Ch. Hist.* vol. II. p. 90.

[2] Heracleon, quoted by Origen in *Commentaries on St John*, Bk x. c. 19.

[3] Hippolytus, *op. cit.* Bk VI. c. 36, pp. 297, 298, Cruice.

[4] *Ibid. loc. cit.* p. 298, Cruice.

towards this end ; and would, from this point of view, do credit
to any doctor of the Church. This is especially the case with
the passage formerly quoted likening the human heart to an
inn, of which Clement of Alexandria gives the actual words as
follows :

"There is one good by whose coming is the manifestation, which
is by the Son, and by Him alone can the heart become pure, by
the expulsion of every evil spirit from the heart. For the multitude
of spirits dwelling in it do not suffer it to be pure ; but each of
them performs his own deeds, insulting it often with unseemly
lusts. And the heart seems to be treated somewhat like the court-
yard of an inn. For the latter has holes and ruts in it, and is often
filled with dung ; men living filthily in it, and taking no care for
the place because it belongs to others. So fares it with the heart
as long as no thought is taken for it, and it is unclean and many
demons dwell therein. But when the one good Father visits it,
it is sanctified and gleams with light. And he who possesses such
a heart is so blessed, that he shall see God[1]."

It is no wonder that M. Amélineau speaks in terms of admiration of the eloquence with which Valentinus applies himself to
the problem of the existence of evil, and that Neander should
say that he in great measure realized the idea of Christianity[2].

It seems indeed plain that Valentinus never intended to
break with the Catholic Church and that it is not likely that
he would have attempted during his life to found any organization that would have been in any way hostile to her[3]. Hence
it is in vain to search for any special rites belonging to the sect ;
and it is most probable that he and his immediate followers
continued to worship with the orthodox, and to resort to the
priests of the Church at large for the administration of the
Church's sacraments. Did they however demand any formal

[1] Clem. Alex. *Strom.* Bk II. c. 20.
[2] Amélineau, *Gnost. Ég.* p. 230 ; Neander, *Ch. Hist.* vol. II. p. 94.
[3] Neander, *op. et loc. cit.* p. 150 and note, says Clement of Alexandria
declares that while Marcion wished to found a Church, the other Gnostics
endeavoured to found schools (διατριβαί) only. Clem. Alex. *Strom.*
Bk VII. c. 15, seems to be the passage referred to ; but in the present state
of the text it may be doubted whether it will bear the construction Neander
puts upon it.

initiation into their own doctrines or, in other words, attempt to keep them in any sense secret ?   One can only say that there is no proof that they did so.   Clement of Alexandria and Origen both quote freely from the books written by Valentinus and his follower Heracleon in which their doctrines are openly set forth, and do not hint at any special difficulty they may have had in obtaining them.   Irenaeus, Tertullian, and Hippolytus do the same thing with regard to the writings of Valentinus and Ptolemy, and Irenaeus tells us that he has obtained his knowledge of their doctrines not only by reading their commentaries (on Scripture) but by personal conversation with their disciples[1].   It does not, therefore, look as if before the legal procedure of the State or the more summary methods of the Christian mob could be used by the Catholics for the suppression of opinion and discussion, the Valentinians ever tried to do what Basilides had recommended to his followers, and to found what was really a secret society either within or without the bosom of the Church[2].

It does not follow from this, however, that the Valentinians differed only in trifling points from the orthodox, or that the Fathers were wrong when they accused them of working grave injury to the nascent Church.   The compliances with heathenism which they allowed those who thought with them, such as attendance at the circus and the theatres, partaking of heathen sacrifices, and flight or even the denial of their faith in time of persecution[3], although justified by them with texts, such as : " That which is of the flesh is flesh ; and that which is of the Spirit is Spirit," must have aroused the most bitter hostility from those wise governors of the Church who saw clearly whither the struggle between the Church and the Roman Empire was tending.   The reward most constantly before the eyes of those about to obtain what was called "the crown" of martyrdom was that by thus giving their lives for the faith they would immediately after death become united with the Deity, instead

[1] Irenaeus, Bk I. Prooem. p. 4, Harvey.

[2] Cf. Renan, *L'Église Chrétienne*, p. 165.   The manner in which the Valentinians tried to make converts to their doctrines within the Church is described by Irenaeus, Bk III. c. 15, § 2, pp. 78, 80, Harvey, and Tertullian, *adv. Valentinianos*, c. 1.

[3] Renan, *L'Église Chrétienne*, pp. 152, 153, for references.

of waiting like other Christians for the Last Judgment[1].   Hence, intending martyrs were regarded even while yet alive with extraordinary reverence by the rest of the faithful, who, as we know from heathen as well as Christian writers, were in the habit of flocking into the prisons after them, weeping over them and kissing their fetters, and deeming it a privilege to minister in every way to the necessities of those who might by a sort of anticipation be regarded as already Divine[2].   It was on this veritable army of martyrs and on the enthusiasm which their triumphs excited that the Church mainly relied for victory in her warfare with the State.   But how was this army to be recruited if the ideas of Valentinus once gained the upper hand in the Christian community, and it came to be thought that the same reward could be gained by acquaintance with the relative positions of the heavens and their rulers, and an accurate knowledge of the constitution of the universe ?   It was in time of persecution that the Valentinians oftenest found adherents—" then the Gnostics break out, then the Valentinians creep forth, then all the opponents of martyrdom bubble up," as Tertullian describes it[3]; and it is easy to understand that those who had most to lose in position or ease of life would grasp eagerly at any intermediate course which would enable them to keep their faith in the religion recently revealed to them without going through the terrible trials to which their orthodox teachers sought to subject them.   Hence, the Valentinians probably in some sort justified Gibbon's remark that " the Gnostics were distinguished as the most polite, the most learned, and the most wealthy of the Christian name[4] " ; and this alone would probably account for the undying hostility which the Church always exhibited towards them.

It was also the case that the spread of the tenets of Valentinus and his followers was attended with some peculiar social dangers of its own.   Their division of mankind into the three

---

[1] Tertullian, *de Pudicitia*, and Pseudo Cyprian, *de Glor. Martyr. passim.*

[2] See Chap. VII, n. 1, p. 8 *supra.*

[3] Tertullian, *Scorpiace*, c. 1.

[4] Gibbon, *Decline and Fall*, Bury's ed. vol. II. p. 13. Cf. what Irenaeus, Bk I. c. 1, § 8, p. 36, Harvey, says as to the high price charged by the Valentinians for their teaching.

natural classes of spiritual, psychical, and hylic, if carried to
its logical conclusion, brought with it some strange results. As
the spiritual or pneumatics were saved in any event, and were,
already even in this life, as was expressly said, a kind of "gods,"
it was manifestly not for them to trouble themselves about
obedience to the moral law. The same conclusion applied to the
hylics who were doomed to annihilation in any case, and whose
struggles towards righteousness were bound to be inefficacious.
There remained the psychics or animal men, for whom indeed
a certain course of life was prescribed before they could attain
salvation. But with the excessive freedom of interpretation and
the licence of variation that Valentinus apparently allowed his
followers, the exact limits of this course must always have been
a matter of doubt ; and it was here that many corruptions and
debasements of his teaching began to show themselves. For it
was an age when religious impostors of all kinds found an easy
market in the credulity of their fellows, and charlatans everywhere abounded who were ready to support their claims to exclusive knowledge of holy things by false miracles and juggling
tricks. Hippolytus gives us a long list of such devices including the means of answering questions in sealed letters,
producing an apparition, and the like, which he declares the
heresiarchs learnt from the magicians and used as proof of their
own doctrines[1]. One knows at any rate from Lucian's evidence
that religious pretenders like Alexander of Abonoteichos were
not negligent of such practices, and charlatans of his kind were
perhaps especially likely to be attracted to the timid and wealthy
followers of Valentinus. A Valentinian impostor of this sort,
if the Fathers are to be believed, was the Jewish magician
Marcus, who taught a system corresponding in most points
with that given above, but made use of it in his own interest
as a means of moneymaking and for the corruption of women.
Irenaeus speaks of the doctrine of this Marcus as being an
especial snare to the Christians of Gaul, into which country
Marcus or some follower of his perhaps travelled while Irenaeus
was Bishop of Lyons[2]. By a mode of interpretation which was

---

[1] Hippolytus, *op. cit.* Bk IV. c. 4, §§ 1–15.
[2] Irenaeus, Bk I. cc. 7–8 *passim*, pp. 114–156, Harvey.

indeed a caricature of Valentinus' own, Marcus found proof of the existence and order of his aeons in the values of the letters composing Divine names and in words like Jesus and Christos[1]. He seems, too, to have himself administered baptism accompanied by exorcisms in the Hebrew language, and to have profaned the Eucharist with juggling tricks which made the cup to overflow and turned the water it contained into wine having the semblance of blood[2]. Thus, says Irenaeus, he contrived to draw away a great number from the Church and to seduce many of the faithful women. Valentinus, perhaps, is somewhat unfairly held responsible by the Fathers for such a perversion of his own teaching which he would, perhaps, have condemned as loudly as they. Scandals of the kind here hinted at were not unknown in the Catholic Church itself, and Christian ministers have been found in all ages, sects, and countries who have been willing to abuse for their own purposes the power which religion gives them over the opposite sex. It is true, too, that people, as has been well said, are seldom either as good or as bad as their creed, and the doctrine that "God sees no sin in His elect" has been preached in our own time without being followed by the "wretchlessness of most unclean living" which the 17th article of the Church of England declares to be one of the probable consequences of predestinarian teaching. The later Valentinians certainly did not forbid marriage, as is shown by the pathetic epitaph from a grave in the Via Nazionale quoted by Renan[3], and thus avoided some of the moral dangers with which the practice of celibacy is sometimes reproached.

Of the fortunes of the Valentinian sect after the death of

---

[1] Thus he says that the Dove signifies Alpha and Omega, the first and the last, because A and Ω, like περιστερά "dove," have the numerical value of 801.

[2] A similar miracle is performed by the risen Jesus in the Bruce Papyrus. See Chap. X *infra*.

[3]   *a.*

Φῶς πατρικὸν ποθέουσα, σύναιμε, σύνευνε, σοφή μου,
λούτροις χρεισαμένη Χ(ρειστο)ῦ μύρον ἄφθιτον, ἁγνὸν,
Αἰώνων ἔσπευσας ἀθρ[ῆ]σαι θεῖα πρόσωπα,
βουλῆς τῆς μεγάλης μέγαν ἄγγελον, υἱὸν ἀληθῆ,
[εἰς ν]υμφῶνα μολοῦσα καὶ εἰς [κόλπ]ους ἀνόρουσα[?]
[Αἰώνων πα]τρικοὺς κ[αὶ......

Valentinus, we have very little precise information. Tertullian speaks of it as being in his time the most numerous society of heretics (*frequentissimum plane collegium haereticorum*), and in the West it extended from Rome, as we have seen, into Gaul and even into Spain, where it existed at the end of the 4th century[1]. Probably, however, it here propagated itself sporadically, its opinions appearing now and then among isolated writers and teachers, who probably drew their disciples carefully from among the Christian community, and only disclosed their system to those who showed some aptitude for it. Of such was doubtless " my fair sister Flora " (ἀδελφή μου καλὴ Φλώρα),

b.

Οὐκ ἔσχεν κοινὸν βιότου [τ]έλος ἥδε θανοῦσα·
κάτθανε καὶ ζώει καὶ ὁρᾳ φάος ἄφθιτον ὄντως·
ζώει μὲν ζωοῖσι, θανὲν δὲ θανοῦσιν ἀληθῶς.
γαῖα, τί θαυμάζεις νέκυος γένος; ἢ πεφόβηται;

(Boeckh's) *C. I. G.* 9595a, t. I. and p. 594.

" Longing for the light of the Father, partner of my blood, partner of my bed, O my wise one !
Anointed at the font with the incorruptible and pure myrrh of Christ,
Thou hast hastened to behold the divine faces of the Aeons, [and]
The Great Angel of the Great Council, the true Son.
Thou hast gone to the nuptial couch and hast hurried to the fatherly bosoms of the Aeons
And......
Though dying, she has not suffered the common end of life,
She is dead, and yet lives and actually beholds the light incorruptible,
To the living she is alive, and dead only to those really dead.
O Earth, why dost thou wonder at this new kind of shade ? or dost thou fear it ? "

This was engraved on a *cippus* of white marble found about three miles from Rome in the Via Latina and is now in the Kircher Museum. Renan's translation is given in *Marc Aurèle*, p. 147. That the lady's name was Flavia seems evident from the acrostic contained in the first verse. She must also have been a pneumatic or spiritual from her husband's confident expectation that she would be raised to the Heavenly Jerusalem and by his assertion of her deathlessness. Hence it may be inferred that Valentinus' disciples even when of the highest spiritual rank were allowed to marry. Cf. Clem. Alex. *Strom.* Bk III. c. 17. The name " Angel of the Great Council " is applied to Christ by Justin Martyr (*c. Tryph.* c. 126) who says that He is so called by Ezekiel. The passage does not appear in the Canons.

[1] Matter, *Hist. du Gnosticisme*, t. II. p. 126, quoting St Jerome.

to whom Valentinus' successor Ptolemy wrote a letter setting out his tenets which Epiphanius has preserved for us[1]. As the quotations in it presuppose an acquaintance on her part with Old Testament history as well as with the Canonical Gospels and the Pauline Epistles, there can be little doubt that she was already a Christian convert.   This mode of propaganda was the more obnoxious to the episcopate that it was likely to escape for some time the observation of the overseers of the Church, and is quite sufficient to explain the pains which bishops like Irenaeus and Hippolytus took to expose and refute the doctrines of the Valentinians, as well as what they say with doubtful accuracy about the secrecy which was observed concerning them[2].   In the East, things were probably different, and Heracleon's Commentaries on the Gospels, from which Origen quotes freely, would on the face of it have been useless unless addressed to the Christian community at large, and make no attempt to conceal their heretical teaching.   In Egypt, however, the Gnostic teachers found a soil ready prepared for them.   Egyptian Christianity, whether founded, according to tradition, by St Mark or not, never seems to have gone through the intermediate stage of observing the prescriptions of the Jewish Law while preaching its abrogation, and, in Alexandria especially, so far appealed to those learned in the Hellenistic and other philosophies as to necessitate the founding of a Christian school there for their study.   The native Egyptians, too, had for millennia been given to mystic speculation about the nature of God and the destiny of the soul after death; and Valentinus, who must be presumed to have understood his own people, doubtless knew how to suit his teaching to their comprehension, even if he did not incorporate therein, as M. Amélineau has endeavoured to show, some of the more abstruse doctrines on these points of the old Egyptian religion[3]. Moreover, from the time of Hadrian onwards, the Egyptians were animated by a bitter and restless hatred against their

[1] Epiphanius, *Haer*. XXXIII. c. 3, pp. 401–413, Oehler. Cf. "the Elect Lady" to whom 2 John is addressed.

[2] It should be remembered that Valentinus had been dead some 50 years when Irenaeus and Hippolytus wrote.

[3] Amélineau, *Gnost. Ég.* Chap. v, pp. 281–320 *passim*.

Roman masters, and this feeling, which was by no means without justification, disposed them to embrace eagerly any ideas condemned by the bishops and clergy of Rome and of Constantinople. Hence the Valentinians had in Egypt their greatest chance of success, and the existence of documents like those described in the next chapter shows that Egyptian Christianity must have been largely permeated by their ideas perhaps up to Mohammedan times. Further East, the same causes produced similar effects, though in this case they were probably modified by the necessity of combating the remains of heathen religions which there lingered. The growing political power of the Catholic Church even before the conversion of Constantine probably drove the Valentinians to form separate communities wherever they were in sufficient numbers to do so, and thus is explained the possession by them of the " houses of prayer " of which the Constantinian Decree above quoted professes to deprive them. On the confines of the Empire and in provinces so far distant from the capital as Mesopotamia, these heretical communities probably lingered longer than in other places, and may have enjoyed, as in the case of Bardesanes, the protection and countenance of the native kinglets. Even here, however, the employment of the secular arm which its alliance with the State gave to the Church seems to have eventually forced them into an attitude of hostility towards it, as is shown by the " rabbling " of one of their conventicles in the way before mentioned. The accession of Julian brought them a temporary respite[1]; but on his death in the Persian campaign, the retreat of the Roman eagles probably gave them their quietus. Only in Egypt, it would seem, did their doctrines succeed in gaining anything like a permanent resting-place. Elsewhere, the ,rise of new heresies and especially of Manichaeism drove them out of their last strongholds.

Valentinianism, therefore, proved itself a stop-gap or temporary faith, which for two hundred years[2] acted as a half-

[1] Julian, *Ep.* 43, tells Hecebolius that the Arians of Edessa, "puffed up by their riches," have maltreated the Valentinians, and that he has therefore ordered the confiscation of the estates and treasure of the Church of Edessa. It is doubtful whether the edict can have been enforced before the emperor's death abrogated it.

[2] We get at a sort of minimum date for its persistence from the career

way house between heathenism and Christianity. In this
capacity, it was singularly efficient, and was one of the forces
which enabled, as Renan said, the ancient world to change
from Paganism to Christianity without knowing it. In particular, it seems to have attracted to itself the attention of the
learned and leisured class who were endeavouring, earnestly if
somewhat timidly, to work out a rule of faith and conduct from
the welter of creeds and philosophies with which the Empire
was swamped during the first Christian centuries. Such a class
is not that out of which martyrs are made, and is sure sooner
or later to acquiesce in the opinions of the majority ; but we
may be certain that the learned and polite Valentinians would
have listened with natural disgust to the simple and enthusiastic declamations of Jewish fishermen and artizans which had
for their chief theme the coming destruction and overthrow of
the social system in which they had grown up. The brilliant,
if baseless, speculations of Valentinus, which even now have
a certain attraction for the lovers of mysticism[1], gave them
exactly the kind of spiritual *pabulum* they craved for, and
enabled them to wait in hope and patience until Christianity,
forcing its way upward, as religions generally do, from the lowest
class of society, had become the faith of the governing ranks.
In this way, Valentinianism was probably one of the best
recruiting grounds for the Catholic Church, and Renan is
doubtless right when he says that no one who passed from
Paganism through the Gnosticism of Valentinus and his fellows
ever reverted to his former faith. Yet Valentinianism itself was
doomed to but a short life, and in its original form probably did
not survive its founder by much more than a century and a half.
One of its later developments we shall see in the next chapter.

of St Ambrose, who had been a Valentinian in his youth (see Eusebius,
Hist. Eccl. Bk VI. c. 18), and was made bishop of Milan in 374 A.D., he being
then 34 years old. The sect therefore had adherents in Italy about 360 A.D.

[1] It may be news to some that an attempt has lately been made to
revive in Paris the heresy of Valentinus. See the *Contemporary Review*
for May, 1897, or Jules Bois' *Les Petits Religions de Paris*, where a full
account of the services and hymns of " L'Église Gnostique " is given. Its
founder, Jules Doinel, was reconverted to Catholicism some time before
his death. Its present head is M. Fabre des Essarts.

CHAPTER X

THE SYSTEM OF THE PISTIS SOPHIA AND ITS RELATED TEXTS[1]

IN 1765, the British Museum purchased from the celebrated antiquarian, Dr Askew, a parchment MS. written in Coptic[2]. On palaeographic grounds it is said to be not earlier than the VIth century A.D., which agrees fairly with its state of preservation and the fact that it is written on both sides of the skins so as to present the appearance of a modern book[3]. Woide, then librarian of the Museum and pastor of the King's German Chapel at St James', published some extracts from it in his *Appendix to the Codex Alexandrinus* in 1799, and Dulaurier gave others in the *Journal Asiatique* in 1847[4]. It remained, however, untranslated until 1850, when Maurice Schwartze, a young German scholar who was sent over here to study our MSS. at the expense of the king of Prussia, turned it into Latin; and he having died soon after, his translation was published the following year by the learned Petermann. The British Museum text is written throughout in the Sahidic

---

[1] The chapter on Marcion and his doctrines should perhaps in strict chronological order follow on here, as Marcion's teaching was either contemporary with, or at most, but a few years later than, that of Valentinus. Cf. Salmon in *Dict. Christian Biog. s.v.* Marcion, Valentinus. But the earliest documents in the *Pistis Sophia* are, as will be seen, possibly by Valentinus himself, and, as all of them are closely connected with his doctrine, it seemed a pity to postpone their consideration.

[2] W. E. Crum, *Catalogue of the Coptic MS. in the Brit. Mus.*, 1905, p. 173, n. 2, says that it was bought at the sale of Askew's effects for £10. 10s. 0d., and that Askew himself bought it from a bookseller.

[3] H. Hyvernat, *Album de Paléographie Copte*, Paris, 1888.

[4] Matter, *Hist. du Gnost.* t. II. pp. 39–43, 347–348, and t. III. pp. 368–371.

dialect, and is the work of more than one scribe ; but it seems to be agreed by those who have studied it with knowledge that the documents it contains are neither continuous nor necessarily related ; and that it is in fact a series of extracts from earlier MSS.[1] Of these documents, the second commences with a heading, in a handwriting other than that of the scribe of this part, reading " the Second Book of Pistis Sophia " ; but as such a heading implies that the foregoing document was the First Book of Pistis Sophia, the whole MS. is generally known by that name[2].

The story presented in these two documents, although uncompleted, is, so far as it goes, perfectly consistent, and presupposes belief in a Gnostic system resembling at once those of the Ophites and of Valentinus. An introduction in narrative form informs us that Jesus, after rising from the dead, spent eleven years in teaching His disciples the arrangement of the heavenly places " only so far as the places " of a power whom He calls "the First Mystery," and declares to be " before all mysteries," and to be " within the veil," being " the father of the likeness of a dove[3]." The result of this

---

[1] See the present writer's article "Some Heretic Gospels" in the *Scottish Review* for July, 1893, where the MSS. treated of in this chapter and their divisions are described in detail. Schmidt, *Koptisch-gnostische Schriften*, Bd I. p. 14, speaks of this "Codex Askewianus" as "eine Miszellenhandschrift."

[2] Except where otherwise specified, subsequent references here to *Pistis Sophia* (in Italics) are to the first 253 pages of the Coptic MS. only.

[3] Cf. the ἐσώτερον τοῦ καταπετάσματος "within the veil" of Heb. vi. 19. For other instances of its use in this sense see Crum, *Cat. of the Coptic MSS. in the Brit. Mus.* p. 255, n. 1 ; and Clem. Alex. *Strom.* Bk v. c. 6. For the *dove*, Mr F. C. Conybeare, in a paper on the subject read before the Society of Historical Theology in Dec. 1892 (see *Academy* of 3rd Dec. 1892), said that the dove was " the recognised symbol of the Holy Spirit or Logos in the allegorizing theology of the Alexandrine Jews at the beginning of the 1st century A.D.," and quoted several passages from Philo in support. Cf. Origen, *cont. Cels.* Bk I. c. 31. But it was also the emblem, perhaps the totem-animal, of the great Asiatic goddess who, under the name of Astarte or Aphrodite, was worshipped as the *Mater viventium* or " Mother of all Living," with whose worship the serpent was also connected. It was doubtless to this that the text " Be ye wise as serpents, harmless as doves " refers. Both serpents and doves figure largely

limitation was, we are told, that the disciples were ignorant not only that any power existed higher than the First Mystery, but also of the origin of the "places" or worlds of those material and *quasi*-material powers who, here as in the earlier systems, are responsible for the governance of the world and the fate of mankind. While the disciples are sitting with Jesus on the Mount of Olives, however, He is carried away from them into Heaven by a great "power" or shape of light which descends upon Him. On His return, He tells them that this shape was "a vesture of light" or His heavenly nature which He had laid aside before being born into this world[1]. He also informs them that, when He first came into this world before His Incarnation, He brought with Him twelve powers which He took from "the Twelve Saviours of the Treasure house of Light[2]," and planted them in the mothers of the

in the Mycenaean and Cretan worship of the goddess. See Ronald Burrows, *Discoveries in Crete*, 1907, pp. 137, 138, and *Index* for references. In later Greek symbolism the dove was sacred to the infernal Aphrodite or Persephone whose name of Φερρεφάττα or Φερσεφάττα has been rendered "she who bears the dove." See de Chanot, "Statues Iconiques de Chypre" in *Gazette Archéologique*, 1878, p. 109.

[1] *Pistis Sophia*, p. 152, Copt. This metaphor is first met with in Philo, *Quaest. in Genesim*, Bk I. c. 53, who declares that the "coats of skin" of Gen. iii. 21 are the natural bodies with which the souls of the protoplasts were clothed. It was a favourite figure of speech with the Alexandrian Jewish writers. So in the *Ascensio Isaiae*, c. IV. 16, 17 : "But the saints will come with the Lord with their garments which are now stored up on high in the seventh heaven : with the Lord will they come, whose spirits are clothed....And afterwards they will turn themselves upward in their garments, and their body will be left in this world." Cf. Charles, *Ascension of Isaiah*, pp. 34, 35, and *Eschatology* (Jowett Lectures), pp. 399 *sqq.*, where he says that this was also the teaching of St Paul.

[2] The word Σωτήρ, which here as elsewhere in the book appears without any Coptic equivalent, evidently had a peculiar signification to the Valentinian Gnostics. Irenaeus, Bk I. c. 1, § 1, p. 12, Harvey, says that it was the name they gave to Jesus οὐδὲ γὰρ κύριον ὀνομάζειν αὐτὸν θέλουσι "for they do not choose to call Him Lord." In the later part of the book, the document called Μέρος τευχῶν Σωτῆρος (p. 253, Copt.) says that "he is saviour and ἀχώρητος (*i.e.* not to be confined in space), who finds the words of the mysteries and the words of the Third Receptacle which is within

twelve Apostles, so that when these last were born into the world they were given these powers instead of receiving, like other men, souls "from the archons (or rulers) of the aeons[1]." He also describes how He appeared among the archons of the Sphere in the likeness of the angel Gabriel, and found among them the soul of "Elijah the Prophet[2]." This He caused to be taken to "the Virgin of Light," that it might be planted in Elizabeth, the mother of John the Baptist[3], (*i.e.* the inmost of the three) and excelleth them all." From which it would appear that the chief qualification of a saviour in the eyes of the later Valentinians was that he was not restricted to his special place in the universe, but could visit at will the worlds below him. We seem therefore to be already getting near the Manichaean idea of *Burkhans* (messengers or Buddhas) who are sent into the world for its salvation. Cf. Chapter XIII *infra*.

[1] So that Judas Iscariot received a super-excellent soul as well as the other eleven, unless we are to suppose that his successor and substitute Matthias was one of those chosen from the beginning. It is curious that neither in this nor in any other Valentinian document is there any allusion to the treason of Judas. The phrase "Archons of the aeons" means, as will be seen later, the rulers of the twelve signs of the Zodiac.

[2] The "Sphere," here as elsewhere in the book, means the sphere of the visible firmament, which is below that of Heimarmene or Destiny.

[3] This παρθένος τοῦ φωτός or Virgin of Light appears here, I think, for the first time in any Gnostic document, although she may have been known to the Valentinians. See Irenaeus, Bk II. c. 47, § 2, p. 368, Harvey. She is, perhaps, a lower analogue of Sophia Without, and is represented as seated in or near the material sun which is said to give its light in its "true form" only in her τόπος or place, which is 10,000 times more luminous than that of the Great Propator or Forefather mentioned later (*Pistis Sophia*, p. 194, Copt.). Her function seems to be the "judging" of the souls of the dead, which does not apparently involve any weighing of evidence, but merely the examination of them to see what "mysteries" they have received in previous incarnations, which will determine the bodies in which they are reincarnated or their translation to higher spheres (*ibid.* pp. 239, 292). She also places in the soul a power which returns to her, according to the Μέρος τευχῶν Σωτῆρος, on the death of its possessor (*ibid.* p. 284, Copt.), thereby discharging the functions assigned in the last book of Plato's *Republic* to Lachesis. She is also on the same authority (*i.e.* the M. τ. Σ.) one of the rulers of the disk of the sun and of that of the moon (*ibid.* pp. 340–341, Copt.), and her place is one of the "places of the Middle" and is opposite to the kingdom of Adamas, which is called the "head of the aeons" (*ibid.* p. 236, Copt.). She reappears in Manichaeism

and He adds that He bound to it a power which He took from " the Little Iao the Good, who is in the middle." The object of this was, we are told, that John the Baptist might prepare the way of Jesus and baptize with water for the remission of sins.

Jesus then proceeds to describe His own Incarnation. When speaking, still in the shape of the angel Gabriel, with Mary His " mother after the body of matter," He planted in her the first power he had received from " Barbelo," which was the body He had worn " in the height[1] " ; and, in the

and it is said in the *Acta Archelai* that at the destruction of the world she will pass into " the ship " of the moon along with Jesus and other powers where she will remain until the whole earth is burnt up (c. XIII. p. 21 of *Hegemonius, Acta Archelai*, Beeson's ed., Leipzig, 1906, p. 21). In the Turfan texts (F. W. K. Müller, *Handschriften-Reste in Estrangelo Schrift aus Turfan*, III. Teil, Berlin, 1904, p. 77) appears a fragment of a prayer in which is invoked *yîšô kanîgrôšanâ* which Dr Müller translates Ἰησοῦς παρθένος τοῦ φωτός, " Jesus, Virgin of Light " ; but it is possible that there is some mistake in the reading.

[1] Barbelo is a name very frequently met with in the earlier heresiologists. Irenaeus, Bk I. c. 26, §§ 1, 2, pp. 221–226, Harvey, declares that there was a sect of Simonians called Barbeliotae " or Naassenes " who suppose " a certain indestructible (the Latin version says " never-ageing ") Aeon in a living virgin spirit whom they call Barbelo (masc.)," and gives an account of a string of other aeons issuing not from, but at the prayer of, this Barbelo, which is far from clear in the present state of the text. The sect appears, from what can be made out of his description, to have resembled the Ophites, of which it may have been a branch. Hippolytus, however, says nothing of them, and the account of Epiphanius (*Haer.* xxv. and xxvi., Vol. II, pt 1, pp. 160, 184, Oehler, is untrustworthy, inasmuch as he assigns the worship of Barbelo to two sects, one of which he calls Nicolaitans and the other Gnostics simply. To both of them he attributes after his manner unimaginably filthy rites, and it is plain from his making Barbelo the mother of Jaldabaoth and giving her a seat in the eighth heaven that he confuses her wilfully or otherwise with the Sophia of the Ophites. Her place in the system of the *Pistis Sophia* will be described in the text. The name is said by Harvey to be derived from the Syriac *Barba elo*, the Deity in Four or God in Tetrad, and the derivation is approved by Hort (*Dict. of Christian Biog. s.h.n.*). It appears more likely, however, that it is to be referred to the Hebrew root בבל " Babel " or confusion, a derivation which Hort also mentions. In Irenaeus' Greek text the name is spelt βαρβηλὼ, in the Latin " Barbelo " with an accusative " Barbelon," and in Epiphanius βαρβηλὼ and βαρβήρω. If we might alter this last into βαρβαριωθ, we might see

place of the soul, a power which He received from " the Great Sabaoth the Good, who is in the place of the right." After this digression, He resumes His account of what happened after His receiving the vesture of light on the Mount of Olives, and declares that He found written in this vesture five mysterious words " belonging [viz. in the language of] to the height[1]," which He interprets to His disciples thus :

"The mystery who is without the world, through whom all things exist, he is the giving forth and the lifting up of all and he has put forth all the emanations and the things which are in them all. And it is through him that all the mysteries exist and all their places. Come unto us, for we are thy fellows and thy members[2] ! We are one with thee, for thou and we are one. This is the First Mystery which existed since the beginning in the Ineffable One

it in a great number of magic spells of the period. Cf. Wessely, *Ephesia Grammata*, Wien, 1886, pp. 26, 28, 33, 34.

[1] *Pistis Sophia*, p. 16, Copt. The five words are *zama, zama, ôzza, rachama, ôzai.* Whatever they may mean, we may be quite sure that they can never contain with their few letters the three pages or so of text which are given as their interpretation. It is possible that the letters are used acrostically like the A G L A, *i.e.* ניבר לעולם אדני (? Ahih ? אהיה) אתה *Ate Gibor Lailam Adonai*, "The mighty Adonai for ever" (or "thou art the mighty and eternal Lord") commonly met with in mediaeval magic. Cf. Peter de Abano, *Heptameron, seu Elementa Magica*, Paris, 1567, p. 563 ; or, for other examples, F. Barrett, *The Magus*, 1801, Bk II. pp. 39, 40. The notable feature in these mysterious words is the quantity of Zetas or ζ's that they contain which points to the use of some sort of table like that called by Cabalists *ziruph*, or a cryptogram of the *aaaaa, aaaab*, kind. It should be noticed that Coptic scribes were often afflicted with what has been called Betacism or the avoidance of the letter Beta or β by every means, which frequently led to the substitution for it of ζ as in the case of Jaldabaoth = Ιαλδαζαω given above (Chap. VIII, n. 3, p. 46 *supra*).

[2] This idea of certain powers being the members or "limbs" of him from whom they issue recurs all through the *Pistis Sophia*. Cf. especially p. 224, Copt., where it is said that the χωρήματα or "receptacles" of the Ineffable go forth from his last limb. It is probably to be referred to the conception of the Supreme Being as the Man κατ' ἐξοχήν, which we have seen current among the Ophites. See Chap. VIII, n. 2, p. 38 *supra*. That the ancient Egyptians used the same expression concerning their own gods and especially Ra, see Moret, " Le Verbe créateur et révélateur," *R.H.R.*, Mai–Juin, 1909, p. 257. Cf. Amélineau, *Gnosticisme Égyptien*, p. 288. So Naville, *Old Egyptian Faith*, p. 227.

before he [*i.e.* the First Mystery] went forth, and we all are his name[1].

"Now therefore we all await thee at the last boundary which is the last mystery from within[2]. This also is part of us. Now therefore we have sent to thee thy vesture which is thine from the beginning, which thou didst place in the last boundary, which is the last boundary from within, until the time should be fulfilled according to the commandment of the First Mystery. And now that the time is fulfilled, clothe thyself in it! Come unto us, for we all stand near to thee that we may clothe thee with all the glory of the First Mystery by His command. Which glory is as two vestures, besides that which we have sent unto thee. For thou art worthy of them since thou art preferred before us and wast made before us. Wherefore the First Mystery has sent thee by us the mystery of all his glory, which is as two vestures. In the first is the glory of all the names of all the mysteries and of all the emanations which are in the ranks of the receptacles of the Ineffable One. And in the second vesture is the glory of the names of all the mysteries and of all the emanations which are in the ranks of the

---

[1] That is to say, their names make up his name as letters do a word. So in the system of Marcus referred to in Chap. IX *supra*, Irenaeus (Bk I. c. 8, § 11, p. 146, Harvey) explains that the name of Jesus ('Ιησοῦς) which might be uttered is composed of six letters, but His unutterable name of twenty-four, because the names of the first Tetrad of Ἄρρητος (Bythos), Σιγή, Πατήρ (Monogenes or Nous) and 'Αλήθεια contain that number of letters. See also § 5 of same chapter. Those who wish to understand the system are recommended to read the whole of the chapter quoted. As Irenaeus has the sense to see, there is no reason why the construction from one root of names founded on the principle given should not go on for ever.

[2] This is probably either the Horos or Stauros that we have seen brought into being in the teaching of Valentinus as a guard to the Pleroma, or, as is more probable, an antitype of the same power in the world immediately above ours. That there was more than one Horos according to the later Valentinians appears plain from the words of Irenaeus above quoted (see Chap. IX, n. 1, p. 105 *supra*). Probably each world had its Horos, or Limit, who acted as guard to it on its completion. That in this world, the Cross, personified and made pre-existent, fulfils this office seems evident from the Gospel of Peter, where it is described as coming forth from the Sepulchre with Jesus (*Mem. Miss. Archéol. du Caire*, 1892, t. IX. fasc. 1, v. 10). Cf. too, Clem. Alex. *Paedagogus*, Bk III. c. 12, and *Strom.* Bk II. c. 20.

two receptacles of the First Mystery. And in this vesture which
we have sent thee now, is the glory of the name of the Recorder
who is the First Precept[1], and the mystery of the Five Marks[2], and
the mystery of the great Legate of the Ineffable One who is the
same as that Great Light[3], and the mystery of the Five Prohegumeni
who are the same as the Five Parastatae[4]. And there is also in
that vesture the glory of the name of the mystery of all the ranks
of the emanations of the Treasure-house of Light, and of their
Saviours, and the ranks of those ranks which are the Seven Amen
and which are the Seven Sounds, and also the Five Trees [5] and also

---

[1] ʿO μηνευτος. The word is not known in classical Greek (but cf.
μηνυτής " a revealer "), and appears to have its root in μήν " the moon,"
as the *measure* of the month. From the Coptic word here translated
" Precept," we may guess it to be a personification of the Jewish Law or
Torah which, according to the Rabbis, before the creation of the world
existed in the heavens. Later in the book it is said that it is by command
of this power that Jeû places the aeons (p. 26, Copt.) ; that the souls of those
who receive the mysteries of the light (*i.e.* the psychics) will have pre-
cedence in beatitude over those who belong to the places of the First Precept
(p. 196, Copt.) ; that all the orders of beings of the Third χώρημα are
below him (p. 203, Copt.) ; and that he is " cut into seven mysteries,"
which may mean that his name is spelled with seven letters (p. 219, Copt.).

[2] Χάραγμαι. Are these the letters mentioned in last note ?

[3] Πρεσβευτής, properly, " ambassador " or " agent." Doubtless a
prototype of our sun. Elsewhere in the book, Jesus tells His disciples
that He brought forth from Himself " at the beginning " power (not *a*
power), which He cast into the First Precept, " and the First Precept cast
part of it into the Great Light, and the Great Light cast part of that which
he received into the Five Parastatae, the last of whom breathed part of that
which he received into the Kerasmos or Confusion " (p. 14, Copt.). The
Great Light is also called the Χάραγμα of the Light, and is said to have
remained without emanation (p. 219, Copt.).

[4] Παραστάται, " Comrades " or " witnesses " or " helpers." They
can here hardly be anything else but the Five Planets. It is said later
that it was the last Parastates who set Jeû and his five companions in
the " Place of the Right Hand " (p. 193, Copt.). When the world is destroyed, Jesus is to take the perfect souls into this last Parastates where
they are to reign with him (p. 230, Copt.) for 1000 years of light which are
365,000 of our years (p. 243, Copt.). Προηγούμενος " Forerunner " does
not seem to occur in classical Greek.

[5] We hear nothing more definite of these Five Trees, but they appear
again in Manichaeism, and are mentioned in the Chinese treatise from
Tun-huang, for which see Chap. XIII *infra*.

the Three Amen, and also the Saviour of the Twins who is the boy
of a boy[1], and the mystery of the Nine Guards of the Three Gates
of the Treasure-house of Light. And there is also within it the
glory of the name which is on the right, and of all those who are
in the middle. And there also is the glory of the name of the Great
Unseen One, who is the Great Forefather[2], and the mysteries of the

---

[1] This is a most puzzling expression and seems to have baffled the scribe,
as he speaks of them, when he comes to repeat the phrase (p. 216, Copt.),
as the " Twin Saviours," which is a classical epithet of the Dioscuri. In
Pharaonic Egypt, Shu and Tefnut the pair of gods who were first brought
into being by the Creator were sometimes called "The Twins." See
Naville, *Old Egyptian Faith*, p. 120. Cf. p. 171 *infra*.

[2] It is evident from the context that we here begin the enumeration
of the Powers of the Left, who are hylic or material and therefore the least
worthy of the inhabitants of the heavens. According to Irenaeus, the
Valentinians held that all of them were doomed to destruction. Τριῶν ὦν
ὄντων, τὸ μὲν ὑλικὸν, ὃ καὶ ἀριστερὸν καλοῦσι, κατὰ ἀνάγκην ἀπόλ-
λυσθαι λέγουσιν, ἅτε μηδεμίαν ἐπιδέξασθαι πνοὴν ἀφθαρσίας δυνάμενον
(Irenaeus, Bk I. c. 1, § 11, p. 51, Harvey). " There being three forms of
existences, they say that the hylic, which they call the left hand, must be
destroyed, inasmuch as it cannot receive any breath of incorruption."
So in the Bruce Papyrus to be presently mentioned, the " part of the left "
is called the land of Death. At their head stands " the Great Unseen
Propator," who throughout the *Pistis Sophia* proper is called by this title
only, and occupies the same place with regard to the left that Iao does in
respect of the middle, and Jeû of the right. In the Μέρος τευχῶν Σωτῆρος
(p. 359, Copt.) he is called by the name ἀγραμμαχαμαρεχ which
frequently appears in the Magic Papyri. It is there spelt indifferently
ακραμνικαμαρι, ακραμμαχαρι, ακραμμαχαμαρει, ακραμμαχαχαχαρι, and in a
Latin inscription on a gold plate, *acramihamari* (see Wessely, *Ephesia
Grammata*, p. 22, for references), which last may be taken to be the
more usual pronunciation. One is rather tempted to see in the name a
corruption of ἀγραμματέον in the sense of " which cannot be written,"
but I can find no authority for such a use of the word. As the ruler of the
material Cosmos he might be taken for the Cosmocrator who, as we have
seen, is called by Valentinus Diabolos or the Devil (but see n. 1, p. 152
infra). Yet he cannot be wholly evil like Beelzebuth for it is said in the
text (p. 41, Copt.) that he and his consort Barbelo sing praises to the Powers
of the Light. So in the Μέρος τευχῶν Σωτῆρος (p. 378, Copt.)
he is represented as begging for purification and holiness when the Great
Name of God is uttered. It is plain also from the statements in the text
(pp. 43, 44, Copt.) that in the *Pistis Sophia* he, Barbelo, and the Αὐθάδης
or Arrogant Power make up a triad called the great τριδυναμεῖς or

Three Triple Powers, and the mystery of all their places, and the mystery of all their unseen ones, and of all the dwellers in the Thirteenth Aeon, and the name of the Twelve Aeons with all their Archons, all their Archangels, all their Angels and all the dwellers in the Twelve Aeons, and all the mystery of the name of all the dwellers in Heimarmene[1], and all the heavens, and the whole mystery of the name of all the dwellers in the Sphere and their firmaments with all they contain and their places. Lo, then, we have sent unto thee this vesture, which none knoweth from the First Precept downward, because that the glory of its light was hidden within it, and the Spheres and all the places from the First Precept downward knew it not. Hasten, then, do on the vesture, and come unto us, for we have remained near thee to clothe thee with these two vestures by the command of the First Mystery until the time fixed by the Ineffable One should be fulfilled. Now, then, the time is fulfilled. Come unto us quickly, that we may clothe thee with them until thou hast accomplished the entire ministry of the completion of the First Mystery, the ministry which has been laid upon thee by the Ineffable One. Come then unto us quickly in order that we may clothe thee with them according to the command of the First Mystery. For yet a little while, a very little while, and thou wilt cease to be in the world. Come then quickly, that thou mayest receive all the glory which is the glory of the First Mystery."

This long address, in which the whole arrangement of the universe as the author supposes it to exist is set forth, is clearly the utterance of the heavenly powers belonging to the higher worlds whom Jesus has left on His descent to earth. Unintelligible as it seems at first sight, it can be explained to some extent by the tenets of the Ophites described in Chapter VIII, which formed, as we have seen, the basis on which Valentinus also constructed his system. The Ineffable

---

"Triple Powers" from whom are projected the powers called the "Twenty-four Invisibles." In another document of the same MS. (p. 361, Copt.) a power from him is said to be bound in the planet Saturn.

[1] This Εἱμαρμένη or "Destiny" is the sphere immediately above our firmament. It is evidently so called, because on passing through it the soul on its way to incarnation receives the Moira or impress of its own destiny, of which it cannot afterwards rid itself except by the grace of the mysteries or Valentinian sacraments. Cf. Chap. IX, n. 3, p. 115 *supra*.

One may be assumed to be the Bythos whom both the Ophites and Valentinus called by that epithet[1] and held to be the first and final source of all being. Although something is said here and elsewhere in the book of his " receptacles " and " places[2]," no particulars of them are given, they being apparently reserved for a future revelation[3]. The First Mystery, however, is spoken of later as a " Twin Mystery, looking inward and outward[4]," which seems to correspond to the Father-and-Son of the Ophite diagram. Later in the book, Jesus reveals to His disciples that He Himself is the First Mystery "looking outward[5]," and this seems to show that the author's conception of the relations between Him and the First Person of the Trinity did not differ much from that of the Catholic Church[6]. The world of this First Mystery extends downwards as far as what is here, as in the Epistle to the Hebrews[7], called " the veil," which is perhaps the veil of sense separating all things contaminated by mixture with matter from the Divine. This First Mystery is said to consist of twenty-four " mysteries " ; but these do not seem to be, as in the older systems, places or worlds, but rather attributes or aspects of the Deity which together go to make up His whole being, as a number of letters are required to make up a word or name[8]. But from some words of Jesus

---

[1] Ἄρρητος. Irenaeus, Bk I. c. 5, § 1, p. 99, Harvey. *Innominabilis*, Tertullian, *adv. Valentinianos*, c. 37. So Clem. Alex. *Strom.* Bk v. c. 10, says that God is ineffable, being incapable of being expressed even in His own power.

[2] Χωρήματα: τόποι.

[3] That [*i.e.* the First] mystery knoweth why there emanated all the places which are in the receptacle of the Ineffable One and also all which is in them, and why they went forth from the last limb of the Ineffable One....These things I will tell you in the emanation of the universe. *Pist. Soph.* p. 225, Copt.

[4] *Ibid.* p. 222, Copt.   [5] *Ibid.* p. 127, Copt.

[6] See Chap. IX, pp. 121, 122 *supra*.

[7] Heb. vi. 19.

[8] p. 203, Copt. Why there should be 24, when the dodecad or group of Aeons in the world above was only 12, it is difficult to say. But Hippolytus supplies a sort of explanation when he says (*op. cit.* Bk VI. c. 33, p. 292, Cruice) : Ταῦτά ἐστιν ἃ λέγουσιν · ἔτι [δὲ] πρὸς τούτοις, ἀριθμητικὴν ποιούμενοι

given later in the book, it would appear that its author did
not at all discard the view of the earlier Ophites that the
Supreme Being was to be figured as of human form, for we
find him remarking that the First Mystery himself proceeded
from the " last limb " or member of the Ineffable One[1]. For
the rest, it need only be pointed out here that the powers who
address Jesus in the quotation just given also speak of
themselves as His " members " ; but that notwithstanding
this, they must be looked upon as purely spiritual entities
having no direct connection with any material forms except
as paradigms or patterns[2]. Whatever the worlds which they

τὴν πᾶσαν αὐτῶν διδασκαλίαν, ὡς προεῖπον [τοὺς] ἐντὸς Πληρώματος Αἰῶνας
τριάκοντα πάλιν ἐπιπροβεβληκέναι αὐτοῖς κατὰ ἀναλογίαν Αἰῶνας ἄλλους, ἵν᾽
ᾗ τὸ Πλήρωμα ἐν ἀριθμῷ τελείῳ συνηθροισμένον. Ὡς γὰρ οἱ Πυθαγορικοὶ
διεῖλον εἰς δώδεκα καὶ τριάκοντα καὶ ἑξήκοντα, καὶ λεπτὰ λεπτῶν εἰσὶν ἐκείνοις,
δεδήλωται· οὕτως οὗ τοι τὰ ἐντὸς Πληρώματος ὑποδιαιροῦσιν. "This is
what they say. But besides this, they make their whole teaching
arithmetical, since they say that the thirty Aeons within the Pleroma again
projected by analogy other Aeons, so that thereby the Pleroma may be
gathered together in a perfect number. For the manner in which the
Pythagoreans divide [the cosmos] into 12, 30, and 60 parts, and each of
these into yet more minute ones, has been made plain " [see *op. cit.* Bk VI.
c. 28, p. 279, where Hippolytus tells us how Pythagoras divided each Sign
of the Zodiac into 30 parts " which are days of the month, these last into
60 λεπτὰ, and so on "]. " In this way do they [the Valentinians] divide
the things within the Pleroma." Cf. Μέρος τευχῶν Σωτῆρος p. 364,
Copt. In another book of the Philosophumena (Bk IV. c. 7 Περὶ τῆς
ἀριθμετικῆς τέχνης) he explains how the Pythagoreans derived infinity from
a single principle by a succession of odd and even or male and female numbers, in connection with which he quotes Simon Magus (*op. cit.* p. 132,
Cruice). The way this was applied to names he shows in the chapter
Περὶ μαθηματικῶν (*op. cit.* Bk IV. c. 11, pp. 77 *sqq.*, Cruice) which is in fact
a description of what in the Middle Ages was called Arithmomancy, or
divination by numbers.

   [1] p. 224, Copt. See also p. 241, Copt.—a very curious passage where
the Ineffable One is called " the God of Truth without foot " (cf. Osiris as
a mummy) and is said to live apart from his " members."

   [2] In the beginning of the Μέρος τευχῶν Σωτῆρος (p. 252, Copt.) it is
said of the Ineffable that " there are many members, but one body." But
this statement is immediately followed by another that this is only said
" as a pattern (παράδειγμα) and a likeness and a resemblance, but not
in truth of shape " (p. 253, Copt.).

inhabit may be thought to be like—and Jesus more than once tells His disciples that there is nothing on earth to which they can be compared—we can only say that they are two in number, and that it is the two " vestures of light " sent to Jesus on the Mount of Olives, or, in other words, His two natures, which give Him the means of ascending to the heavens of the Ineffable One and of the First Mystery respectively. If the author ever intended to discuss them further, he has certainly not done so in the *Pistis Sophia* properly so called[1].

On the other hand, the worlds and powers existing " below the veil," or within the comprehension of the senses, and symbolized by the third and inferior " vesture " sent to Jesus, are indicated even in the address given above with fair particularity. Their names and relative positions are not easy to identify ; but, thanks to some hints given in other parts of the book, the universe below " the veil " may be reconstructed thus[2] :—Its upper part contains the Treasure-house of light where, as its name implies, the light as it is redeemed from matter is stored up. There are below it five other worlds called the Parastatae or Helpers, in one of which Jesus is to reign during the millennium, and the ruler of the last of which arranges the pure spirits who dwell below it[3]. The highest

---

[1] What he does say is that the Ineffable One has two $\chi\omega\rho\dot\eta\mu\alpha\tau\alpha$ or receptacles and that the second of these is the $\chi\dot\omega\rho\eta\mu\alpha$ of the First Mystery. It is, I think, probable that an attempt to describe both these $\chi\omega\rho\dot\eta\mu\alpha\tau\alpha$ is made in one of the documents of the Bruce Papyrus. See pp. 191, 192 *infra*.

[2] In addition to the enumeration contained in the so-called interpretation of the mysterious " Five Words," there appears in the 2nd part of the *Pistis Sophia* (pp. 206 *sqq.* Copt.) a long rhapsody in which it is declared that a certain mystery knows why all the powers, stars, and heavenly " places " were made. These are here again set out *seriatim*, and as the order in the main corresponds with that in the five " words," translated in the text, it serves as a check upon this last. The order of the powers in the text was given in the article in the *Scottish Review* before referred to, and, although this was written 20 years ago, I see no occasion to alter it.

[3] It is the " last Parastates " who places Jeû and his companion in " the place of those who belong to the right hand according to the arrangement (*i.e.* οἰκονομία) of the Assembly of the Light which is in the Height of the Rulers of the Aeons and in the universes (κοσμοί) and every race which is therein " (p. 193, Copt.). A later revelation is promised as to these,

spirit in the Treasure-house is called the First Precept or the Recorder, and with him is associated the Great Light, who is said to be the "legate" of the Ineffable One[1]. In the Treasure-house there are also the orders of spirits set out in the address just quoted, the only two to which it is necessary to refer here being the Five Trees[2] and the Twelve Saviours. From the Five Trees emanated the great "Powers of the Right Hand" to be next mentioned ; while, as is before described, the Twelve Saviours furnished the spotless souls required for the Twelve Apostles[3]. The lower part of the same universe is called the Kerasmos or Confusion, because here the light, which in the upper part is pure, is mingled with matter. It is divided in the first instance into three parts, the Right-hand, the Middle, and the Left-hand[4]. Of these, the Right-hand contains the spirits who emanated from the Five Trees of the Treasure-house. At their head is Jeû, who has supreme authority over all the Confusion[5]. He is called the Overseer

but in the meantime it is said that Jeu emanated from the chosen or pure (εἰλικρινής) light of the first of the Five Trees (*loc. cit.*).

[1] See nn. 1 and 3, p. 141 *supra*. As has been said, it is difficult not to see in this "1st Precept" a personification of the Torah or Jewish Law.

[2] See n. 3, p. 146 *supra*.

[3] See n. 2, p. 136 *supra*.

[4] So Secundus, Valentinus' follower, taught according to Hippolytus (*v.* Chap. IX *supra*) "that there is a right and a left tetrad, *i.e.* light and darkness." This may be taken to mean that the constitution of the light-world was repeated point for point in the world of darkness. The middle world is of course that where light and darkness mingle.

[5] Jeû is generally called the ἐπίσκοπος or overseer of the Light He it is who has placed the Rulers of the Aeons so that they always "behold the left" (p. 26, Copt.). He is also said to have bound "in the beginning" the rulers of the Aeons and of Destiny and of the Sphere in their respective places (p. 34, Copt.), and that each and every of them will remain in the τάξις or order and walk in the δρόμος or course in which he placed them. We also hear in the *Pistis Sophia* proper of two "books of Jeû" "which Enoch wrote when the First Mystery spoke with him out of the Tree of Life and the Tree of Knowledge in the Paradise of Adam" (p. 246, Copt.). In the first part of the Μέρος τευχῶν Σωτῆρος, however Jeû is described as "the First Man, the ἐπίσκοπος of the Light, and the πρεσβευτής or Ambassador of the First Precept" (p. 322, Copt.) ; and it is further said in the same book that "the Book of Jeû (not books)

of the Light, and in his name we may possibly recognize a corruption of the Hebrew Yahweh. With him and of similar origin is Melchisedek[1], the Inheritor, Receiver or Purifier of the Light, whose office it is to take the portions of light as they are redeemed into the Treasure-house[2]. Another emanation from the Five Trees is an otherwise unnamed Guard of the Veil of the Treasure-house[3] which seems to be the veil dividing the

which Enoch wrote in Paradise when I (Jesus) spoke with him out of the Tree of Life and the Tree of Knowledge " was placed by His means in " the rock Ararad." Jesus goes on to say that He placed " Kalapataurôth the ruler who is over Skemmut in which is the foot of Jeû, and he surrounds all rulers and destinies—I placed that ruler to guard the books of Jeû from the Flood and lest any of the rulers should destroy them out of envy " (p. 354, Copt.).

[1] Melchizidek is very seldom mentioned in the *Pistis Sophia*, but when he is, it is always as the great παραλήμπτωρ or "inheritor" of the Light (p. 34, Copt.). Jesus describes how he comes among the Rulers of the Aeons at certain times and takes away their light, which he purifies (p. 35, Copt.). He is said to have emanated from the light of the 5th Tree of the Treasure House, as Jeû did from that of the 1st (p. 193, Copt.). In the Μέρος τευχῶν Σωτῆρος, he is called the great παραλημπτής or "receiver" of the Light (p. 292, Copt.). In the 2nd part of the last named document he is called Zorocothora Melchizidek, an epithet which C. W. King in *The Gnostics and their Remains* translates "light-gatherer." It is also said in the same 2nd part that "he and Jeû are the two great lights," and that he is the πρεσβευτής or "Legate " of all the lights which are purified in the Rulers of the Aeons (p. 365, Copt.). We may perhaps see in him and Jeû the antitypes of which the Great Light and the First Precept are the paradigms. Hippolytus, *op. cit.* Bk VII. c. 36, p. 391, Cruice, says that there was a sect, the followers of one Theodotus, a τραπεζίτης or money-changer, who said that there was " a greatest power named Melchizidek who was greater than Christ." Pseudo-Tertullian repeats the same story and adds that Melchizidek is " a celestial virtue of great grace," who does for heavenly angels and virtues what Christ does for men, having made himself " their intercessor and advocate." See *auct. cit.* (probably Victorinus of Pettau) *Against all Heresies*, c. XXIV. p. 279, Oehl. He doubtless founded his opinion on the passage in the Hebrews. The name seems to mean " Holy King " Cf. the " King of Glory " of the Manichaeans, see Chap. XIII *infra*.

[2] p. 35, Copt.

[3] He is said to have emanated from the 2nd Tree (p. 193, Copt.) and is nowhere distinctly named. But one may perhaps guess from the order in which he occurs in the 2nd part of the Μέρος τευχῶν Σωτῆρος that

Treasure-house from the Place of the Right-hand, and there are two others of equal rank who are called simply the two Prohegumeni or Forerunners[1]. Below these again is the Great Sabaoth the Good, who supplied, as we have seen, the soul which was in Jesus at His birth, and who is himself the emanation, not of any of the Five Trees, but of Jeû[2]. He seems to have a substitute or messenger called the little Sabaoth the Good, who communicates directly with the powers of matter. In the Middle come the powers who are set over the reincarnation of souls and the consequent redemption of mankind. Of these, the only two named are " the Great Iao the Good[3]," spoken of in one passage as the Great Hegumen (or Leader) of the Middle[4]. He, too, has a minister called "the Little Iao" who supplies the "power" which, with the soul of Elijah, animated the body of John the Baptist[5]. He also has twelve deacons or ministers under him[6]. The other

his name was Zarazaz, evidently a cryptogram like those mentioned in n. 1, p. 139 *supra*. It is also said that the Rulers call him " Maskelli after the name of a strong (*i.e.* male) ruler of their own place (p. 370, Copt.)." This name of Maskelli, sometimes written Maskelli-maskellô, is frequently met with in the Magic Papyri. Cf. Wessely, *Ephesia Grammata*, p. 28.

[1] They are said to have emanated from the 3rd and 4th Tree respectively (p. 193, Copt.).

[2] p. 193, Copt. He is evidently called *the Good* because there is a wicked Sabaoth sometimes called Sabaoth Adamas, and the Great because there is a Little Sabaoth the Good who seems to act as his messenger. It is this last who takes the power from the Great Sabaoth the Good which afterwards becomes the body of Jesus and " casts it into matter and Barbelo " (p 127, Copt.). He seems to be set over or in some way identified with what is called the Gate of Life (p. 215, Copt.) both in the *Pistis Sophia* and the Μέρος τευχῶν Σωτῆρος (p. 292, Copt.).

[3] p. 12, Copt., where he is oddly enough called the Little Iao the Good, I think by a clerical error. Later he is said to be " the great leader of the middle whom the Rulers call the Great Iao after the name of a great ruler in their own place " (p. 194, Copt.). He is described in the same way in the second part of the Μέρος τευχῶν Σωτῆρος (p. 371, Copt.).

[4] See last note.

[5] p. 12, Copt. This " power" is evidently the better part of man's soul like the Logoi who dwell therein in the passage quoted above from Valentinus, see Chap. IX, p. 112 *supra*.

[6] p. 194, Copt.

great Leader of the Middle is the Virgin of Light[1]. She it is who chooses the bodies into which the souls of men shall be put at conception, in discharge of which duty she sends the soul of Elijah into the body of John the Baptist, her colleague Iao's share in the work being apparently limited to providing the "power" accompanying it. She has among her assistants seven other virgins of light[2], after whose likeness Mary the Mother of Jesus and Mary Magdalene are said to have been made, and we also read of "receivers" who are under her orders[3]. The light of the Sun "in its true shape" is said to be in her place[4], and there is some reason for thinking that she is to be considered as the power which directs the material Sun, while her colleague Iao has the same office as regards the Moon[5].

We now come to the places of the left, the highest of which seems to be that which is called the Thirteenth Aeon. This is a part of the universe the existence of which Jesus conceals from His disciples until He receives his "vestures," and there is much mystery as to its origin. It seems to have been governed in the first instance by a triad consisting of an un-named power referred to as the Great Forefather or the Great Unseen One, a female power called Barbelo[6], and a second

[1] See n. 3, p. 137 *supra*.

[2] So the Μέρος τευχῶν Σωτῆρος (p. 327, Copt.).

[3] The likeness of Mary the Mother and Mary Magdalene to the seven Virgins appears in the translation of Amélineau (*Pistis Sophia*, Paris, 1895, p. 60). Schwartze (p. 75, Lat.) puts it rather differently. See also Schmidt, *K.-G.S.* bd. 1, p. 75. The "receivers" of the Virgin of Light are mentioned on p. 292, Copt.   [4] p. 184, Copt.

[5] pp. 340, 341, Copt. As ιο̣ϩ (ioh) is Coptic for the Moon, it is just possible that there may be a kind of pun here on this word and the name Iao. Osiris, whose name was often equated by the Alexandrian Jews with their own divine name Jaho or Jah, as in the Manethonian story of Osarsiph = Joseph, was also considered a Moon-god. Cf. the "Hymn of the Mysteries" given in Chap. VIII, where he is called "the holy horned moon of heaven."

[6] See note 1, p. 138 *supra*. The Bruce Papyrus (Amélineau, *Notice sur le Papyrus Gnostique Bruce*, Paris, 1882, p. 220) speaks of the "Thirteenth Aeon, where are the Great Unseen God and the Great Virgin of the Spirit (cf. the παρθενική πνεῦμα of Irenaeus) and the twenty-four emanations of the unseen God."

male called the Authades or Proud God[1] who plays a principal
part in the episode of Pistis Sophia which forms the ostensible
theme of the book. Of the Great Forefather, we are told
nothing of importance, but what is said of the female power
Barbelo bears out fully the remark which Hippolytus attributes to Valentinus that among the lesser powers or aeons
the female merely projects the substance, while it is the male
which gives form to it[2]. It is doubtless for this reason that
it is from her that the body of Jesus is said to have come—
i.e. that she provided the matter out of which it was formed
in the first instance, and which had, as He says later in the
present book, to be purged and cleansed by Himself[3]. She
is also spoken of throughout as the origin of all the matter
within the world of sense[4]. This triad, constantly referred
to throughout the book as the Three Tridynami or Triple
Powers, have put forth, before the story opens, twenty-four other
powers arranged in twelve syzygies or pairs who are spoken of as
the Twenty-four Unseen Ones, and who inhabit with them the
Thirteenth Aeon. Only one of these is named and this is the
inferior or female member of the last syzygy. She is named
Pistis Sophia, and gives, as we have seen, her name to the book[5].

We now pass from the unseen world, which can nevertheless be comprehended as being in part at least material, to
the starry world above us which is plainly within the reach

[1] See n. 2, p. 142 *supra*.

[2] See Chapter IX, p. 104 *supra*.

[3] p. 116, Copt.

[4] I suppose it is in view of this maternal aspect of her nature that she
is alluded to in the latter part of the Μέρος τευχῶν Σωτῆρος as
βαρβηλω βδελλη "Barbelo who gives suck"? Her place, according to
the Bruce Papyrus (Amélineau, p. 218), is said to be in the Twelfth Aeon.

[5] There have been many attempts to make this name mean something
else than merely "Faith-Wisdom." Dulaurier and Renan both tried to
read it "πιστὴ Σοφία" "the faithful Wisdom" or "La fidèle Sagesse."
If we had more documents of the style of Simon's *Apophasis*, we should
probably find that this apposition of two or more nouns in a name was
not infrequent, and the case of Ptah-Sokar-Osiris will occur to every
Egyptologist. The fact that the name includes the first and last female
member of the Dodecad of Valentinus (see p. 101 *supra*) is really its most
plausible explanation.

of our organs of sense. The controlling part in this is taken by the powers called the Twelve Aeons, who are ruled before the advent of Jesus by a power called, like the Supreme Being in the Ophite system, Adamas[1]. As they are called in one passage the 12 hours of the day, it may be concluded that they are the 12 zodiacal signs or, in other words, the Zodiac or 12 constellations of fixed stars through which the sun appears to pass in his yearly course[2]. Although nowhere expressly stated, it may be concluded that they emanated from the last member of the triad of the Left, *i.e.* the Authades, who is here said to have been disobedient in refusing " to give up the purity

---

[1] This Adamas seems to be an essentially evil power, who wages useless war against the Light on the entry of Jesus into his realm (p. 25, Copt.). His seat is plainly the Twelve Aeons or Zodiac (p. 157, Copt.), and it is said in the Μέρος τευχῶν Σωτῆρος that his "kingdom" is in the τοποι κεφαλης αἰώνων or Places of the head of the Aeons and is opposite the place of the Virgin of Light (p. 336, Copt.). In the second part of the same document (*i.e.* the μ. τ. σ.) it is said that the rulers of Adamas rebelled, persisting in the act of copulation (συνουσία) and begetting "Rulers and Archangels and Angels and Ministers (λειτουργοί) and Decans" (Δεκανοί), and that thereupon Jeû went forth from the Place of the Right and "bound them in Heimarmene and the Sphere." We further learn that half the Aeons headed by Jabraoth, who is also once mentioned in the *Pistis Sophia* proper (p. 128, Copt., and again in the Bruce Papyrus, Amélineau, p. 239), were consequently transferred to another place, while Adamas, now for the first time called Sabaoth Adamas, with the unrepentant rulers are confined in the Sphere to the number of 1800, over whom 360 other rulers bear sway, over whom again are set the five planets Saturn, Mars, Mercury, Venus, and Jupiter (pp. 360, 361, Copt.). All this seems to me to be later than the *Pistis Sophia* proper, to have been written at a time when belief in astrology was more rife than in Hadrian's reign, and to owe something to Manichaean influence. The original Adamas, the persecutor of Pistis Sophia herself, seems identifiable with the Diabolos or Cosmocrator of Valentinus, in which case we may perhaps see in the "Great Propator" a merely stupid and ignorant power like the Jaldabaoth of the Ophites and their successors. See p. 163 *infra*.

[2] p. 145, Copt. So Irenaeus in his account of the Valentinian doctrines, Bk I. c. 1, p. 12 *sqq.* I suppose there is an allusion to this in the remark of Jesus to Mary that a year is as a day (p. 243, Copt.). But all the astrology of the time seems to have divided the astronomical day not into 24, but into 12 hours. It was the same with the Manichaeans. See Chavannes and Pelliot, "Un Traité manichéen retrouvé en Chine," *Journal Asiatique*, série x, t. XVIII. (Nov.–Dec. 1911), p. 540, n. 4.

of his light," no doubt when the earth was made, and is accused
of ambition in wishing to rule the Thirteenth Aeon.   Through
his creature, Adamas their king, he induces the rulers of the
Twelve Aeons to delay the redemption of the light from matter.
It is from their matter that are made the souls, not only of
men, but of beasts, birds, and reptiles[1], and if they were allowed
to do as they pleased, the process would go on for ever, as it
is the habit of these Archons " to turn about and devour
their own *ejecta*, the breath of their mouths, the tears of their
eyes, and the sweat of their bodies," so that the same matter
is used over and over again[2].   Below the starry world comes
the Sphere of Heimarmene or Destiny, so called apparently
because both the earthly and heavenly lot of each soul is
determined on its downward passage through it, and below
that again the Sphere simply so called, which is the visible
firmament apparently stretched above us.   The Archons of
the Aeons, of whom Adamas is the chief, rule their own and
both these lower spheres, and the only hindrance to their
dilatory manoeuvres prior to the advent of Jesus was caused
by Melchizidek the Receiver of the Light[3], who came among
them at stated times, took away their light, and, after having
purified it, stored it up in the Treasure-house.   This was

[1] But curiously enough, not the "souls" of fish.   So in the Middle
Ages, the Manichaeans of Languedoc did not allow their "Perfects" to
partake of animal food nor even of eggs, but allowed them fish, because
they said these creatures were not begotten by copulation   See Schmidt,
Hist. des Cathares, Paris, 1843.   Is this one of the reasons why Jesus is
called Ἰχθύς ?

[2] This idea of man being made from the tears of the eyes of the heavenly
powers is an old one in Egypt.   So Maspero explains the well-known sign
of the *utchat* or Eye of Horus as that " qui exprime la matière, le corps du
soleil, d'où tous les êtres découlent sous forme de pleurs," " Les Hypogées
Royaux de Thébes," *Ét. Égyptol.* II. p. 130.   Moret, " Le verbe créateur et
révélateur en Égypte," *R. H. R.* Mai–Juin, 1909, p. 386, gives many instances
from hymns and other ritual documents.   It was known to Proclus who
transfers it after his manner to Orpheus and makes it into hexameters :

Thy tears are the much-enduring race of men,

By thy laugh thou hast raised up the sacred race of gods.

See Abel's *Orphica*, fr. 236.

[3] See n. 1, p. 148 *supra*.

apparently done through the medium of the sun and moon, who seem to have acted in the matter as the " receivers " of Melchizidek[1].

We can now resume the narrative of the book which has been interrupted in order that a description of the universe through which Jesus passes on His ascension might be given. He tells His disciples that clothing Himself in His third or least glorious " vesture," He flew up to the firmament, the gates of which opened spontaneously to give Him passage[2]. Entering in, the Archons there were all struck with terror at the light of His vesture, and wondered how the " Lord of the Universe[3] " passed through them unnoticed on his descent to earth[4]. The same scenes are repeated when He enters the Sphere of Destiny, and again when He reaches the Twelve Aeons or Zodiac of fixed stars. Before leaving the Twelve Aeons, Jesus takes away from its rulers a third part of their power, and alters their course, so that its direction is changed every six months. This He does, as He tells His disciples, for a double reason. He thereby prevents the Aeons from devouring their own matter, and so delaying the redemption of the light, and He further hinders their movements from being used by mankind in the divination and magic which the sinning angels taught when " they came down "—a clear reference to the story in Genesis of the fall of the angels as amplified in the *Book of Enoch*. This alteration, He declares,

---

[1] This is, perhaps, to be gathered from the *Pistis Sophia*, p. 36, Copt. Cf. Μέρος τευχῶν Σωτῆρος, pp. 337–338. In another part of the last-named document, the Moon-ship is described as steered by a male and female dragon (the caduceus of Hermes ?) who snatch away the light of the Rulers (p. 360, Copt.).

[2] This seems to be the passage referred to later by Origen. See n. 2, p. 159 *infra*.

[3] The usual epithet or appellation of Osiris *Neb-er-tcher*=Lord of Totality or the Universe. Cf. Budge, *Book of the Dead, passim*.

[4] So in the *Ascensio Isaiae*, of which Mr Charles says that " we cannot be sure that it existed earlier than the latter half of the 2nd century of our Era," it is said (Chap. IX, v. 15) " And thus His descent, as you will see, will be hidden even from the heavens, so that it will not be known who He is." Charles, *The Ascension of Isaiah*, p. 62. Cf. *ibid* pp. 67, 70, 73 and 79.

was foreshadowed by the text "I have shortened the times for my elect's sake[1]."

Passing upward to the Thirteenth Aeon, Jesus tells His disciples that he found Pistis Sophia dwelling alone in a place immediately below it, and He here makes a long digression to recount her history. She is, as has been said above, one of the twenty-four invisible but material emanations projected by the Great Unseen Forefather and his consort Barbelo, and formerly dwelt with her own partner, whose name is not mentioned, in the Thirteenth Aeon[2]. But one day happening to look forth from her place and beholding the light of the Treasure-house, she longed to ascend towards it and began to sing praises to it. This angered exceedingly the Authades or Proud God, the Third Triple Power or chief of the Thirteenth Aeon, who had already, as has been said, shown his disobedience in refusing to give up his light. Out of envy and jealousy of Pistis Sophia, he sends forth from himself a great power with a lion's face who is "half flame and half darkness" and bears the name of Jaldabaoth, which we have met with before among the Ophites[3]. This Jaldabaoth is sent below into the regions of Chaos, the unformed and shapeless darkness which is either below or surrounds the earth[4], and when Pistis Sophia sees him shining

---

[1] pp. 39, 40, Copt. The reference is apparently to the Book of Enoch, c. LXXX. (see Charles, *Book of Enoch*, pp. 212, 213, and the *Epistle of Barnabas*, N.T. extra can., c. IV. p. 9, Hilgenfeld). In the Latin version of the last-quoted book, it is assigned to Daniel, which shows perhaps the connection of Enoch with all this quasi-prophetic or apocalyptic iterature.

[2] According to the Valentinian system, his name was Θελητὸς or "the Beloved." See Chap. IX, p. 101 *supra*.

[3] See Chap. VIII *supra*. Here he occupies a far inferior position to that assigned him by the Ophites. In the Μέρος τευχῶν Σωτῆρος he sinks lower still and becomes merely one of the torturers in hell (p. 382, Copt., κ.τ.λ.). Thus, as is usual in matters of religion, the gods of one age become the fiends of the next. In the Bruce Papyrus (Amélineau, p. 212) he appears as one of the chiefs of the Third Aeon. It is curious, however, to observe how familiar the name must have been to what Origen calls "a certain secret theology," so that it was necessary to give him *some* place in every system of Gnosticism. His bipartite appearance may be taken from Ezekiel viii. 2.

[4] Probably the latter. See what is said about the Outer Darkness in the Μέρος τευχῶν Σωτῆρος, p. 319, Copt. where it is described as "a great

there, she mistakes his light for the light of the Treasure-house, and, leaving her consort, plunges downwards towards it. She is instantly seized by Jaldabaoth and other wicked powers sent forth by the Proud God, and grievously tormented with the object of taking from her her light, so that she may never again be able to return to her own place. In this plight, she sings several Metanoiae or hymns of penitence to the light, and after seven of these, Jesus, as He says, " from pity and without commandment," raises her to the uppermost parts of Chaos where she is slightly more at ease[1]. She continues here to sing hymns of penitence, but is tormented afresh until, after her ninth repentance, Jesus receives command from the First Mystery to succour her. This he does in a battle with fresh emanations from the Authades, including one in the shape of " a flying arrow[2]." Adamas, the king of the wicked Eons, also sends a power to the assistance of Jaldabaoth, and the other emanations of the Proud God turn into serpents, a basilisk with seven heads, and a dragon[3]. The powers of light sent by Jesus, however, defeat all her enemies, and the archangels Gabriel and Michael bear her aloft and establish her in the place below the Thirteenth Aeon, where Jesus finds her on His ascension as here recorded. But this is not the end. Jesus tells · her that when " three times " are fulfilled[4], she

dragon whose tail is in his mouth who is without the whole κόσμος and surrounds it."

[1] p. 83, Copt. So in the Manichaean legend, the First Man, on being taken captive by Satan, prays seven times to the Light and is delivered from the Darkness in which he is imprisoned. See Chap. XIII *infra*.

[2] This demon in the shape of a flying arrow seems to be well known in Rabbinic lore. Mr Whinfield in *J.R.A.S.*, April, 1910, pp. 485, 486, describes him as having a head like a calf, with one horn rising out of his forehead like a cruse or pitcher, while to look upon him is certain death to man or beast. His authority seems to be Rapaport's *Tales from the Midrash*.

[3] The basilisk with seven heads seems to be Death. See Gaster, "The Apocalypse of Abraham," *T.S.B.A.* vol. IX. pt 1, p. 222, where this is said to be the " true shape " of death. Cf. Kohler, " Pre-Talmudic Haggadah," *J.Q.R.*, 1895, p. 590. Death, as we have seen in Chap. IX, p. 107, was in the ideas of Valentinus the creature of the Demiurge. For the dragon, see Whinfield, *ubi cit.*

[4] These " three times " are not years. As the *Pistis Sophia* opens with the announcement that Jesus spent 12 years on earth after the Resurrection,

will be tormented again. This happens as predicted immediately before the descent of the "vesture" on Him on the Mount of Olives. Thereupon, He delivers her for the last time and restores her to her place in the 13th Aeon, where she sings to him a final hymn of thanksgiving.

This completes the episode of Pistis Sophia, and the rest of the book is filled with the questionings upon it of Mary Magdalene and the other disciples, among whom are prominent Mary the Mother of Jesus, Salome, Martha, St John the Divine, St Philip, St Thomas, and St Matthew, to which last-named three is said to be entrusted the recording of the words of Jesus, together with St Peter, St James and St Andrew. This has led some commentators to think that the work may possibly be the *Interrogations of Mary* ('Ερωτήσεις Μαρίας), concerning which Epiphanius says that two versions, a greater and a lesser, were used by several Gnostic sects[1]. These questionings and the answers of Jesus are extremely tedious, and include the comparison of the hymns of Pistis Sophia, fourteen in all, with certain named Psalms and Odes of David and Solomon of which they are said to be the "interpretation[2]." In the course of this, however, the purpose of the book is disclosed,

we may suppose that He was then—if the author accepted the traditional view that He suffered at 33—exactly 45 years old, and the "time" would then be a period of 15 years, as was probably the indiction. The descent of the "two vestures" upon Jesus is said (p. 4, Copt.) to have taken place "on the 15th day of the month Tybi" which is the day Clement of Alexandria (*Strom.* Bk I. c. 21) gives for the birth of Jesus. He says the followers of Basilides gave the same day as that of His baptism.

[1] Epiphanius, *Haer.* XXVI. t. II. pt 1, p. 181, Oehler.

[2] This doctrine of ἑρμηνεία occurs all through the book. The author is trying to make out that well-known passages of both the Old and New Testaments were in fact prophetic utterances showing forth in advance the marvels he narrates. While the Psalms of David quoted by him are Canonical, the Odes of Solomon are the Apocrypha known under that name and quoted by Lactantius (*Div. Inst.* Bk IV. c. 12). For some time the *Pistis Sophia* was the only authority for their contents, but in 1909 Dr Rendel Harris found nearly the whole collection in a Syriac MS. of the 16th century. A translation has since been published in *Cambridge Texts and Studies*, vol. VIII. No. 3, Cambridge, 1912, by the Bishop of Ossory, who shows, as it seems conclusively, that they were the hymns sung by the newly-baptized n the Primitive Church.

and appears as the revelation of the glories awaiting the believer in the world to come, the coming of the Millennium, and the announcement that Jesus has brought the "mysteries" to the earth for the salvation of men.   But before describing these, it may be as well to draw attention to the manifest likeness between the theology and cosmology of the *Pistis Sophia* proper and what has been said above of the tenets of the Ophites and of Valentinus.

At first sight, the *Pistis Sophia* in this respect seems to be almost entirely an Ophite book.   The Ineffable One, as has been said, is not to be distinguished from the Ophite Bythos, while "the First Mystery looking inward and outward" is a fairly close parallel to the First Man and the Son of Man of the Ophite system.   The names Sabaoth, Iao, and Jaldabaoth also appear both here and with the Ophites, although the last-named power now occupies a greatly inferior position to that assigned to him by them, and from a merely ignorant power has now become an actively malignant one.   The work assigned to Sophia Without in the older system is here taken in the Place of the Middle by the Virgin of Light, who is throughout the working agent in the salvation of mankind; but it should be noted that she here operates directly and not through a grosser power as with the Ophites.   The idea of a female divinity ordering the affairs of men for their good as a mother with her children had already gained possession of the heathen world in the character of (the Greek) Isis, and in the hint here given as to the resemblance between her delegates and the Virgin Mary, we may see, perhaps, the road by which the Christian world travelled towards that conception of the Theotokos or Mother of God which played such an important part in its later creed.   Among the powers inferior to her the names and places are changed, but the general arrangement remains nearly the same as with the Ophites, especially the Ophites of the diagram.   The starry world in particular here comes much into evidence, and is given more important functions than in any other Gnostic system except the Ophite[1].   The "Gates" of the firmaments are met

---

[1] Astrological doctrine first becomes prominent in Gnostic teaching

with both here and in the Ophite prayers or "defences" recorded by Origen[1], and an allusion put by this last into the mouth of Celsus and not otherwise explained. to "gates that open of their own accord," looks as if Origen's heathen adversary may himself have come across the story of the *Pistis Sophia*[2]. The general hostility of this starry world and its rulers towards mankind is a leading feature in both systems.

On the other hand, the parallels between the theology of the *Pistis Sophia* and that of Valentinus are even closer, and are too important to be merely accidental. The complete identification of Jesus with the First Mystery strongly recalls the statement of Valentinus, rather slurred over by the Fathers, that Jesus was Himself the Joint Fruit or summary of the perfections of the whole Pleroma or Godhead, and is a much more Christian conception than that of the earlier Ophites as to His nature[3]. So, too, the curious theory that each of

in the *Excerpta Theodoti* which we owe to Clement of Alexandria. We may therefore put their date about the year 200. This would be after the time of Valentinus himself, but agrees well with what M. Cumont (*Astrology and Religion*, pp. 96 *sqq.*) says as to the great vogue which astrology attained in Rome under the Severi. Its intrusion into the Valentinian doctrines is much more marked in the Μέρος τευχῶν Σωτῆρος than in the *Pistis Sophia*, and more in the Bruce Papyrus than in either.

[1] See Chap. VIII, pp. 73, 74 *supra*.

[2] Origen, *cont. Cels.* Bk VI. c. 34.

[3] Hippolytus (Chap. IX, p. 92), speaks of the Jesus of Valentinus as the Joint Fruit of the Pleroma simply. Irenaeus (Bk I. c. 1, p. 23, Harvey) goes into more detail: Καὶ ὑπὲρ τῆς εὐποιίας ταύτης βουλῇ μιᾷ καὶ γνώμῃ τὸ πᾶν Πλήρωμα τῶν Αἰώνων, συνευδοκοῦντος τοῦ Χριστοῦ καὶ τοῦ Πνεύματος, τοῦ δὲ Πατρὸς αὐτῶν συνεπισφραγιζομένου, ἕνα ἕκαστον τῶν Αἰώνων, ὅπερ εἶχεν ἐν ἑαυτῷ κάλλιστον καὶ ἀνθηρότατον συνενεγκαμένους καὶ ἐρανισαμένους, καὶ ταῦτα ἁρμοδίως πλέξαντας, καὶ ἐμμελῶς ἑνώσαντας, προβαλέσθαι προβλήματα εἰς τιμὴν καὶ δόξαν τοῦ Βυθοῦ, τελειότατον κάλλος τε καὶ ἄστρον τοῦ Πληρώματος, τέλειον καρπὸν τὸν Ἰησοῦν ὃν καὶ Σωτῆρα προσαγορευθῆναι, καὶ Χριστὸν, καὶ Λόγον πατρωνομικῶς καὶ κατὰ [καὶ τὰ] Πάντα, διὰ τὸ ἀπὸ πάντων εἶναι. "And because of this benefit, with one will and opinion, the whole Pleroma of the Aeons, with the consent of Christos and the Spirit, and their Father having set his seal upon the motion, brought together and combined what each of them had in him which was most beautiful and brightest, and wreathing these fittingly together and properly uniting them, they projected a projection to the honour and glory of Bythos, the most perfect beauty and star of the Pleroma, the perfect Fruit Jesus, who is also called Saviour

the lower worlds has its own "saviour" finds expression in both systems, as does the idea that Jesus received something from all the worlds through which He passed on His way to earth.   One may even find a vivid reminiscence of the Valentinian nomenclature in the name of Pistis Sophia herself, which combines the names of the feminine members of the first and last syzygies of the Valentinian Dodecad[1], Pistis there being the spouse of Paracletus or the Legate, and Sophia that of Theletus or the Beloved, while the cause of her fall in the present book is the same as that assigned in the system of Valentinus.   Hence it may appear that the author of the *Pistis Sophia*, whoever he may have been, was well acquainted with the Ophite and Valentinian theology, and that he continued it with modifications of his own after the innovating habit current among the Gnostics and noticed by Tertullian.

In the cosmology of the *Pistis Sophia*, again, the preference given to Valentinian rather than to the older Ophitic views is clearly marked.   The cause of the descent of the light into

and Christ, and after his Father Logos, and Pan, because He is from all."   Compare with these the words of Colossians ii. 9: ὅτι ἐν αὐτῷ κατοικεῖ πᾶν τὸ πλήρωμα τῆς θεότητος σωματικῶς.   "For in him dwelleth all the fulness of the Godhead bodily."

[1] That the Valentinians considered the Dodecad (and *a fortiori* the Decad) as having a collective entity, and as it were a corporate existence, seems plain from what Hippolytus says in narrating the opinions of Marcus: ταῦτα γὰρ δώδεκα ζῴδια φανερώτατα τὴν τοῦ ᾿Ανθρώπου καὶ τῆς ᾿Εκκλησίας θυγατέρα δωδεκάδα ἀποσκιάζειν λέγουσι.   "For they say that these 12 signs of the Zodiac most clearly shadow forth the Dodecad who is the daughter of Anthropos and Ecclesia" (Hipp. *op. cit.* Bk VI. c. 54, p. 329, Cruice). And again (*loc. cit.* p. 331, Cruice): ἔτι μὴν καὶ τὴν γῆν εἰς δώδεκα κλίματα διῃρῆσθαι φάσκοντες, καὶ καθ᾿ ἓν ἕκαστον κλίμα, ἀνὰ μίαν δύναμιν ἐκ τοῦ οὐρανῶν κατὰ κάθετον ὑποδεχομένην, καὶ ὁμοούσια τίκτουσαν τέκνα τῇ καταπεμπούσῃ κατὰ τὴν ἀπόρροιαν δυνάμει, τύπον εἶναι τῆς ἄνω δωδεκάδος.   "These are also they who assert that the earth is divided into twelve climates, and receives in each climate one special power from the heavens and produces children resembling the power thus sent down by emanation, being thus a type of the Dodecad above."   The doctrine of correspondences or, as it was called in the Middle Ages, of "signatures" is here most clearly stated. In all this the Valentinian teaching was doubtless under the influence of the ancient Egyptian ideas as to the *paut neteru* or "company of the gods," as to which see Maspero's essay *Sur L'Ennéade* quoted above.

matter in the first instance is no accident as with the Ophites, but is part of the large scheme for the evolution or, as the author calls it, the " emanation " of the universe which was devised and watched over in its smallest details by the First Mystery[1]. Whether the author accepted the wild story attributed to Valentinus by Irenaeus concerning the Fall of Sophia and her Ectroma, it is impossible to say, because, as we have seen, he omits all detailed description of the way in which the two higher worlds which we have called the heavens of the Ineffable One and the world of the First Mystery came into being[2]. But it is plain that both must have been made by or rather through Jesus, because it is stated in the mysterious five words written on the vesture of Jesus that it is through the First Mystery that all things exist, and that it was from him that all the emanations flowed forth[3]. As the *Pistis Sophia* also says that Jesus is Himself the First Mystery, this corresponds to the opening words of St John's Gospel, that " by Him all things were made[4]." Hence the author of

---

[1] It is said (p. 9, Copt.) that it is by him that the universe was created and that it is he who causes the sun to rise.

[2] As has before been said, this is attempted in one of the documents of the Bruce Papyrus. See pp. 191, 192 *infra*. In the present state of the text this attempt is only difficultly intelligible, and is doubtless both later in date than and the work of an author inferior to that of the *Pistis Sophia*.

[3] p. 16, Copt. Yet the First Mystery is not the creator of Matter which is evil, because Matter does not really exist. See Bruce Papyrus (Amélineau, p. 126) and n. 2, p. 190 *infra*.

[4] As mentioned in the *Scottish Review* article referred to in n. 1, p. 135 *supra*, there is no passage but one in the *Pistis Sophia* which affords any colour for supposing that the author was acquainted with St John's Gospel. All the quotations set forth by Harnack in his treatise *Über das gnostische Buch Pistis-Sophia*, Leipzig, 1891, p. 27, on which he relies to prove the converse of this proposition, turn out on analysis to appear also in one or other of the Synoptics, from which the author may well have taken them. The single exception is this (*Pistis Sophia*, p. 11, Copt.), "Wherefore I said unto you from the beginning, Ye are not from the Cosmos ; I likewise am not from it " ; John xvii. 14 : " (O Father) I have given them thy word ; and the world hath hated them, because they are not of the world, even as I am not of the world." The parallel does not seem so close as to make it certain that one document is copying from the other. Both may very possibly be taken from some collection of Logia now lost, but at one

the *Pistis Sophia*, if confronted with the story of the Ectroma, would doubtless have replied that this was merely a myth designed to teach the danger for the uninstructed of acting on one's own initiative instead of waiting for the commands of God, and that in his book he had told the same story in a slightly different way. This seems to be the only construction to be placed on the trials of Pistis Sophia herself, since her desire for light seems not to have been looked upon as in itself sinful, and the real cause of her downfall was the mistaking the light of Jaldabaoth for that of the Treasure-house. But her descent into Chaos, unlike the Fall of her prototype, apparently had nothing to do with the creation of the universe and its inhabitants, which in the *Pistis Sophia* seems to have taken place before the story opens. If they were supposed by the author to have originated in the passions of Sophia Without, as Hippolytus tells us Valentinus taught[1], they were none the less the direct work of Jesus, and the statement in Hippolytus, that in the Valentinian teaching Jesus made out of the supplication of Sophia Without a path of repentance, finds a sort of echo in the *Pistis Sophia*, where it is the " Metanoiae " or hymns of penitence many times repeated of Pistis Sophia, her antitype or copy, which bring Jesus to her succour. A further parallel may be found in Hippolytus' other statement from Valentinus that Jesus gave this " supplication " power over the psychic substance which is called the Demiurge[2]. In the *Pistis Sophia*, the heroine defeats the Authades with the assistance of Jesus ; and there does not seem much doubt that Pistis Sophia is eventually to receive her adversary the Authades' place, an event which is foreshadowed by the quotation of the text " His bishopric let another take " in one of her penitential psalms[3]. It would

time current in Alexandrian circles ; or from the *Gospel of the Egyptians*, from which the *Pistis Sophia* afterwards quotes.

[1] See Chap. IX, p. 107 *supra*.

[2] See last note. The *Authades* or Proud God of the *Pistis Sophia* seems to have all the characteristics with which Valentinus endows his Demiurge.

[3] So Pistis Sophia sings in her second hymn of praise after her deliverance from Chaos (p. 160, Copt.) " I am become pure light," which she certainly was not before that event. Jesus also promises her later (p. 168, Copt.)

also appear that Adamas, the wicked king of the Twelve Aeons, may be the Adversary or Diabolos described by the Valentinians[1] as the cosmocrator or ruler of this world, his rule being exercised in the *Pistis Sophia* through his servants, the Archons of " Heimarmene and the Sphere." The epithet of Adamas or ἀδαμαστὸς given in classical literature to Hades as the Lord of Hell would seem appropriate enough in his case. This would only leave Beelzebub, prince of the demons, unaccounted for ; but the author does not here give any detailed description of Chaos which may be supposed to be his seat. Although the omission was, as we shall see, amply repaired in other documents put forth by the sect, it may be here explained by the conviction of the nearness of the Parusia or Second Advent which marks the *Pistis Sophia*[2]. On the fulfilment of this hope, the Cosmos was, as we are informed, to be " caught up," and all matter to be destroyed[3]. What need then to elaborate the description of its most malignant ministers ?

The joys of the elect in the world to come, on the contrary, receive the fullest treatment. In the " completion of the Aeon, when the number of the assembly of perfect souls is made

that when the three times are fulfilled and the *Authades* is again wroth with her and tries to stir up Jaldabaoth and Adamas against her " I will take away their powers from them and give them to thee." That this promise was supposed to be fulfilled seems evident from the low positions which Jaldabaoth and Adamas occupy in the Μέρος τευχῶν Σωτῆρος, while Pistis Sophia is said to furnish the " power " for the planet Venus.

[1] See Chap. IX, p. 108 and n. 1 *supra.*

[2] All the revelations in the *Pistis Sophia* are in fact made in anticipation of the time " when the universe shall be caught up," and the disciples be set to reign with Jesus in the Last Parastates. Cf. especially pp. 193–206 Copt.

[3] The idea may not have been peculiar to Valentinus and his followers. So in the *Ascensio Isaiae* (x. 8–13) the " Most High the Father of my Lord " says to " my Lord Christ who will be called Jesus " : " And none of the angels of that world shall know that thou art Lord with Me of the seven heavens and of their angels. And they shall not know that Thou art with Me till with a loud voice I have called to the heavens, and their angels, and their lights, even unto the sixth heaven, in order that you may judge and destroy the princes and angels and gods of that world, and the world that is dominated by them." Charles, *Ascension of Isaiah*, pp. 70–71.

up[1]," or in other words when all pneumatic or spiritual men
have laid aside their material bodies, they will ascend through
all the firmaments and places of the lesser powers until they
come to the last Parastates, where they are to reign with
Jesus over all the worlds below it[2]. This is the place from
which the power, which the Great Light, the legate of the
Ineffable One, took from the First Precept and passed into
the Kerasmos or Confusion, originated ; and it was this world,
or rather its ruler, who arranged Jeû and the other Powers
of the Right Hand in their Places and thus set going the whole
machinery of salvation. Its "light" or glory is said to be
so tremendous that it can be compared to nothing in this
world, and here Jesus will reign with the disciples for 1000
"years of light" which are equal to 365,000 of our years[3].
Here the thrones of the twelve "disciples" ($\mu a\theta\eta\tau a i$) will
depend on His[4], "but Mary Magdalene and John the Virgin
shall be higher than all the disciples[5]." In the midst of these
beatitudes they will apparently receive further instruction or
further mysteries, the effect of which will be that they will
at the conclusion of the Millennium be united with Jesus in
so close a union that, as it is expressly said, they will become
one with Him, and finally they will become members of the
Godhead and, as it were, "the last limb of the Ineffable One[6]."
In the meantime they will be at liberty to visit any of the
worlds below them. All those who have received lesser
mysteries,—that is to say, who have received a lesser degree
of instruction and have not become wholly pneumatic or

[1] p. 194, Copt.

[2] p. 230, Copt.

[3] On the belief in the Millennium in the primitive Church, see Döllinger,
First Age of Christianity and the Church, Eng. ed. 1906, pp. 119, 123 and
268 and Ffoulkes, *s.v.* Chiliasts, in *Dict. Christian Biog.*

[4] p. 230, Copt. Cf. Luke xxii. 29, 30.

[5] p. 231, Copt. "disciples" not apostles. So the Manichaeans made
Manes to be attended by twelve disciples. See Chap. XIII *infra*.

[6] So Jesus says (p. 230, Copt.) of "the man who receives and accomplishes the Mystery of the Ineffable One " ; " he is a man in the Cosmos,
but he will reign with me in my kingdom ; he is a man in the Cosmos, but
he is a king in the light ; he is a man in the Cosmos, but he is not of the
Cosmos, and verily I say unto you, that man is I, and I am that man."

spiritual—will after death in this world go to the heaven of which they have received the mystery, or, in cases where their instruction has only just begun, be brought before the Virgin of Light, who will cause their souls to be sent back to earth in "righteous" bodies, which will of themselves seek after the mysteries, and, having obtained them, will, if time be allowed, achieve a more or less perfect salvation. Here, again, we meet with a close resemblance to the system of those later Ophites who possessed the diagram described by Origen ; for Jesus tells His disciples that those who have only taken these lower mysteries will have to exhibit a seal or token (σύμβολον) and to make an " announcement " (ἀπόφασις) and a defence (ἀπολογία) in the different regions through which they pass after death[1]. No such requirements, He says, will be made from those who have received the higher mysteries, whose souls on leaving the body will become great streams of light, which will pass through all the lower places " during the time that a man can shoot an arrow," the powers therein falling back terror-stricken from its light until the soul arrives at its appointed place. As, therefore, these seals and announcements and defences will be of no use to the disciples, the Jesus of the *Pistis Sophia* declares that He will not describe them in detail, they having been already set out in " the two great Books of Jeû[2]."

What now are these " mysteries " which have so tremendous an effect on their recipient as actually to unite him with the Deity after death ? The Greek word μυστήριον, which is that used in the Coptic MS., does not seem to mean etymologically more than *a secret*, in which sense it was applied to the ceremonies or secret dramas exhibited, as has been said, at Eleusis and elsewhere, and later, to the Christian Eucharist[3]. In the early part of the *Pistis Sophia* it is the word used to denote the First Mystery or first and greatest emanation of God, who is withdrawn from human contemplation and, as it were, concealed behind a veil impenetrable by the senses of man.

---

[1] p. 246, Copt.
[2] See last note and n. 5, p. 147 *supra*.
[3] Hatch, *op. cit.* p. 302 and note.

But in the part of the book with which we are now dealing it seems to refer not to hidden persons, but to secret things. These things seem to fall into two categories, one of which is spoken of as the Mystery of the Ineffable One, and the other as the Mysteries of the First Mystery. The Mystery of the Ineffable One is said to be one, but, with the provoking arithmetic peculiar to the book, it is immediately added that it " makes " three mysteries and also another five, while it is still one[1]. The Mysteries of the First Mystery on the other hand are said to be twelve in number, and these figures may possibly cover some allusion to the Ogdoad and the Dodecad of Valentinus[2]. It is also fairly clear that each of these Twelve Mysteries of the First Mystery must be some kind of ceremony, and a ceremony which can be performed without much pre-

---

[1] pp. 236, 237, Copt.

[2] *Loc. cit.* Or they may cover a kind of allegory, as we might say that Agape or Love makes Faith, Hope, and Charity. But I believe it to be more likely that the " 12 mysteries " are letters in a word. So in the Μέρος τευχῶν Σωτῆρος it is said of the "Dragon of the Outer Darkness," which is in fact the worst of all the hells described in that book : " And the Dragon of the Outer Darkness hath twelve true (αὐθέντη) names which are in his gates, a name according to each gate of the torture-chambers. And these names differ one from the other, but they belong to each of the twelve, so that he who saith one name, saith all the names. And these I will tell you in the Emanation of the Universe "—(p. 323, Copt.). If this be thought too trivial an explanation, Irenaeus tells us that the 18|Aeons remaining after deducting the Decad or Dodecad (as the case may be) from the rest of the Pleroma were, according to the Valentinians, signified by the two first letters of the name of Jesus : ἀλλὰ καὶ διὰ τῶν προηγουμένων τοῦ ὀνόματος αὐτοῦ δύο γραμμάτων, τοῦ τε ἰῶτα καὶ τοῦ ἦτα, τοὺς δεκαοκτὼ Αἰῶνας εὐσήμως μηνύεσθαι, Irenaeus, Bk I. c. 1, § 5, p. 26, Harvey. Equally absurd according to modern ideas are the words of the *Epistle of Barnabas* (c. x., pp. 23, 24, Hilgenfeld), where after quoting a verse in Genesis about Abraham circumcising 318 of his slaves (cf. Gen. xiv. 14), the author says "What then is the knowledge (γνῶσις) given therein ? Learn that the 18 were first, and then after a pause, he says 300. (In) the 18, I=10, H=8, thou hast Jesus ('Ιησοῦν). And because the Cross was meant to have grace in the T, he says also 300. He expresses therefore Jesus by two letters and the Cross by one. He knows who has placed in us the ungrafted gift of teaching. None has learned from me a more genuine word. But I know that ye are worthy."

paration or many participants. This we may deduce from
the following description of the merits of one of them :

"For the second mystery of the First Mystery, if it is duly accomplished in all its forms, and the man who accomplishes it shall speak
the mystery over the head of a man on the point of going forth from
the body, so that he throws it into his two ears :—even when the
man who is going forth from the body shall have received it aforetime,
and is a partaker of the word of Truth[1],—verily, I say unto you
that when that man shall go forth from the body of matter, his
soul will make a great flash of light, and will pass through every
Place until it come into the kingdom of that mystery.

" But and if that man has not [aforetime] received that mystery,
and is not a partaker of the word of Truth,—verily I say unto you
that man when he shall go forth from the body shall not be judged
in any Place whatever, nor shall he be tormented in any Place
whatever, and no fire shall touch him on account of that great
mystery of the Ineffable One which is in him ; and all shall make
haste to pass him from one hand to the other, and to guide him
into every Place and every order, until they shall lead him before
the Virgin of Light, all the Places being filled with fear before the
sign of the mystery of the kingdom of that Ineffable One which
shall be with him.

" And the Virgin of Light shall wonder and she shall try him,
but he will not be led towards the light until he shall have accomplished all the service of the light of that mystery, that is to say,
the purifications of the renunciation of the world and all the matter
that is therein[2]. But the Virgin of Light shall seal that soul with

---

[1] "The True Word" or the Word of the Place of Truth. The latter
expression is constantly used in other parts of the book, and seems to refer
to the χώρημα or "receptacle," that is the heaven, of the Aeon Ἀλήθεια,
that is the Decad. Cf. especially the Μέρος τευχῶν Σωτῆρος (pp. 377,
378, Copt.), where it is said that certain baptisms and a "spiritual chrism"
will lead the souls of the disciples "into the Places of Truth and Goodness,
to the Place of the Holy of all Holies, to the Place in which there is neither
female, nor male, nor shape in that Place, but there is Light, everlasting,
ineffable."

[2] These ἀποτάγματα are set out in detail in the Μέρος τευχῶν Σωτῆρος
(pp. 255 *sqq.* Copt.), where the disciples are ordered to "preach to the whole
world.....renounce (ἀποτασσετε) the whole world and all the matter
which is therein, and all its cares and all its sins, and in a word all its conversation (ὁμιλιαι) which is therein, that ye may be worthy of the

the excellent seal which is this****[1], and she shall have it cast in the same month in which it went forth from the body of matter into a righteous body which will find the God of Truth and the excellent mysteries in order that it may receive them by inheritance and also the light for eternity. Which is the gift of the second mystery of the First Mystery of that Ineffable One[2]."

The only ceremony to which such grace as is here set forth was likely to be attributed by any Christian in the early age of the Church was that of Baptism. It was called by writers like Gregory of Nazianza and Chrysostom a μυστήριον[3]; while we hear as early as St Paul's time of " those who are baptized over [or on behalf of] the dead " (βαπτιζόμενοι ὑπὲρ τῶν νεκρῶν)[4], the theory being, according to Döllinger, that those who had wished during their lives to receive baptism but had not done so, could thus obtain the benefit of the prayers of the Church, which could not be offered for an unbaptized person[5]. So much was this the case with some sects, that it was an offence charged by writers like Tertullian against the Valentinians that they were in the habit of delaying baptism as long as possible and even of putting it off till they were about to die[6], as in the case in the text. Baptism, too, was

mysteries of the Light, that ye may be preserved from all the punishments which are in the judgments " and so on. It should be noted that these are only required of the psychics or animal men.

[1] No doubt in the Greek original the actual seal was here figured. For examples, see the Bruce Papyrus, *passim*. The idea is typically Egyptian. As M. Maspero says in his essay on "La Table d'Offrandes," *R.H.R.* t. xxxv. No. 3 (1897), p. 325 : no spell was in the view of the ancient Egyptians efficacious unless accompanied by a talisman or amulet which acted as a material support to it, as the body to the soul.

[2] p. 238, Copt.

[3] Hatch, *op. cit.* p. 296, n. 1, for references.

[4] 1 Cor. xv. 29. The practice of " baptizing for the dead," as the A.V. has it, evidently continued into Tertullian's time. See Tertull. *de Resurrectione Carnis*, c. xlviii. p. 530, Oehler.

[5] Döllinger, *First Age*, p. 327.

[6] Hatch, *op. cit.* p. 307. The Emperor Constantine, who was baptized on his deathbed, was a case in point. The same story was told later about the Cathars or Manichaeans of Languedoc. The motive seems in all these cases to have been the same : as baptism washed away all sin, it was as well to delay it until the recipient could sin no more.

spoken of in sub-Apostolic times as the " seal " ($\sigma\phi\rho\alpha\gamma\iota\varsigma$)[1], or impress, which may be that which the soul has to exhibit, both in the Ophite system and in that of the *Pistis Sophia*, to the rulers of the next world. In any event, the rite was looked upon by Catholic and heretic alike as an initiation or commencement of the process by which man was united with Christ. The other eleven " mysteries of the First Mystery " are not specifically described in the *Pistis Sophia* ; but it is said that the receiving of any one of them will free its recipient's soul from all necessity to show seals or defences to the lesser powers and will exalt him after his death to the rank of a king in the kingdom of light, although it will not make him equal to those who have received the mystery of the Ineffable One[2]. It therefore seems probable that these " twelve mysteries of the First Mystery " all refer to the rite of baptism, and are called twelve instead of one only to accord with some trifling juggling with words and letters such as was common with the followers of Valentinus[3]. That baptism was held in the sub-Apostolic age to be, in the words of Döllinger, " not a mere sign, pledge, or symbol of grace, but an actual communication of it wrought by the risen and glorified Christ on the men He would convert and sanctify, and a bond to unite the body of the Church with its Head[4]," will perhaps be admitted. According to the same author, St Paul teaches that " by Baptism man is incorporated with Christ, and puts on Christ, so that the sacramental washing does away with all natural distinctions or race ;—Greek and Jew, slave and free, men and women, are one in Christ, members of His body, children of God and of the seed of Abraham[5]." He tells us also that the same Apostle " not only divides man into body and spirit, but distinguishes in the bodily nature, the gross, visible, bodily frame, and a hidden, inner, " spiritual " body not subject to limits of space or cognizable by the senses ;

[1] Hatch, *op. cit.* p. 295 and note, for references.
[2] p. 236, Copt.
[3] See n. 2, p. 166 *supra*.
[4] Döllinger, *First Age*, pp. 234, 235.
[5] *Ibid.* p. 235. Rom. vi. 4 ; Gal. iii. 27, 29, are quoted in support.

this last, which shall hereafter be raised, is alone fit for and capable of organic union with the glorified body of Christ, of substantial incorporation with it[1]." If Döllinger in the xixth century could thus interpret St Paul's words, is it extraordinary that the author of the *Pistis Sophia* should put the same construction on similar statements some sixteen centuries earlier? So the late Dr Hatch, writing of baptism in this connection, says: "The expressions which the more literary ages have tended to construe metaphorically were taken literally. It was a real washing away of sins; it was a real birth into a new life; it was a real adoption into a divine sonship[2]."

If this be so, it seems to follow that the Mystery of the Ineffable One must be the other and the greatest of the Christian sacraments. Jesus tells His disciples that it is the " One and unique word," and that the soul of one who has received it " after going forth from the body of matter of the Archons " will become " a great flood of light " and will fly into the height, no power being able to restrain it, nor even to know whither it goes. He continues:

" It shall pass through all the Places of the Archons and all the Places of the emanations of light, nor shall it make any announcement nor defence nor give in any symbol; for no Power of the Archons nor of the emanations of light can draw nigh to that soul. But all the Places of the Archons and of the emanations of light shall sing praises, being filled with fear at the flood of light which clothes that soul, until it shall have passed through them all, and have come into the Place of the inheritance of the mystery which it has received, which is the mystery of the sole Ineffable One, and shall have become united with his members[3]."

He goes on to explain that the recipient of this mystery shall be higher than angels, archangels, and than even all the Powers of the Treasure-house of Light and those which are below it:

---

[1] *Ibid.* p. 235. Rom. vii. 22; 1 Cor. vi. 14; Eph. iii. 16 and v. 30 are quoted in support.

[2] Hatch, *op. cit.* p. 342.

[3] p. 228, Copt.

"He is a man in the Cosmos; but he is a king in the light.   He is a man in the Cosmos, but he is not of the Cosmos, and verily I say unto you, that man is myself and I am that man.

" And, in the dissolution of the Cosmos, when the universe shall be caught up, and when the number of perfect souls shall be caught up, and when I am become king in the middle of the last Parastates, and when I am king over all the emanations of light, and over the Seven Amen, and the Five Trees, and the Three Amen, and the Nine Guards, and over the Boy of a Boy, that is to say the Twin Saviours, and when I am king over the Twelve Saviours and all the numbers of perfect souls who have received the mystery of light, then all the men who have received the mystery of that Ineffable One shall be kings with me, and shall sit on my right hand and on my left in my kingdom.   Verily I say unto you, Those men are I and I am those men.   Wherefore I said unto you aforetime : You shall sit upon thrones on my right hand and on my left in my kingdom and shall reign with me.   Wherefore I have not spared myself, nor have I been ashamed to call you my brethren and my companions, seeing that you will be fellow-kings with me in my kingdom.   These things, therefore, I said unto you, knowing that I should give unto you the mystery of that Ineffable One, and that mystery is I and I am that mystery[1]."

That this is the supreme revelation up to which the author of the *Pistis Sophia* has been leading all through the book, there can hardly be any doubt.   Its position shortly before the close of the book[2], the rhapsodic and almost rhythmical phrases with which the approach to it is obscured rather than guarded, and the way in which directly the revelation is made, the author falls off into merely pastoral matters relating to the lesser mysteries, all show that the author has here reached his climax.   But does this revelation mean anything else than that Jesus is Himself the victim which is to be received in the Sacrament or μυστήριον of the Altar ?   That the Christians of the first centuries really thought that in the Eucharist they united themselves to Christ by receiving His Body and Blood there can be no question, and the dogma can have come as no novelty to those who, like the Ophites, had combined with

[1] pp. 230, 231, Copt.

[2] The *Pistis Sophia* proper comes to an end twenty pages later.

Christianity the ideas which we have seen current among the
Orphics as to the sacramental efficacy of the homophagous
feast and the eating of the quivering flesh of the sacrifice
which represented Dionysos. Döllinger gives the views of
the primitive Church concisely when he says it is " because
we all eat of one Eucharistic bread, and so receive the Lord's
body, that we all become one body, or as St Paul says, we
become members of His body, of His flesh, and of His bones."
" We are nourished by communion," he continues, " with
the substance of His flesh and blood, and so bound to the
unity of His body, the Church ; and thus what was begun in
Baptism is continued and perfected in the Eucharist[1]." Thus,
Justin Martyr, who lived in the reign of Antoninus Pius, says
" the food which is blessed by the prayer of His word, and
from which our blood and flesh by transmutation are nourished,
is the flesh and blood of that Jesus who was made flesh[2]."
That the same idea was realized by the heretics may be gathered
from what has been said above as to the wonder-working
celebration of the Eucharist by Marcus, when the wine was
made to change visibly into blood before the eyes of the
recipient[3].

It is plain also that the *Pistis Sophia* does not look upon
this perfect union as within the reach of all. Basilides, the first
of the Egyptian Gnostics, had said that not one in a thousand
or two in ten thousand were fit to be admitted to the higher
mysteries, and the same phrase is repeated by Jesus Himself in
one of the later documents of the MS. of which the *Pistis Sophia*
forms part[4]. Those who were worthy of admission to the

---

[1] Döllinger, *First Age*, p. 239.   1 Cor. x. 16 *sqq.* ; Eph. v. 30, quoted in
support.

[2] Justin Martyr was probably born 114, and martyred 165 A.D.   For
the passage quoted in text, see his *First Apology*, c. LXVI., where he mentions
among other things that the devils set on the worshippers of Mithras to
imitate the Christian Eucharist by celebrating a ceremony with bread and
a cup of water.

[3] Hatch, *op. cit.* p. 308.   This visible change of the contents of the cup
of water to the semblance of blood is described in the Μέρος τευχῶν Σωτῆρος
(p. 377, Copt.), and with more detail in the Bruce Papyrus. Cf. p. 183 *infra*.

[4] Μέρος τευχῶν Σωτῆρος, p. 354, Copt.

mysteries of the Ineffable One and of the First Mystery were
the pneumatics or spiritual men predestined to them from
before their birth. For the others, the psychic or animal
men, there were the mysteries " of the light," which are, so
to speak, the first step on the ladder of salvation[1]. These
are nowhere described in the *Pistis Sophia* or first document
of the book, the hearer being therein always referred for their
details to the two great Books of Jeû mentioned above, " which
Enoch wrote when I (*i.e.* Jesus) spoke with him from the tree
of knowledge and from the tree of life, which were in the Paradise of Adam[2]." It is here expressly said that Jesus' own
disciples have no need of them ; but their effect is described
as purifying the body of matter, and transforming their
recipient into "light" of exceeding purity. On the death
of one who has taken them all, his soul traverses the different
heavens repeating the passwords, giving in the defences, and
exhibiting the symbols peculiar to each mystery until it reaches
the abode assigned to its particular degree of spiritual illumination. These mysteries of the light are open to the whole world
and there is some reason for thinking they are the sacraments
of the Catholic Church, the members of which body, Irenaeus
says, the " heretics " (Qy the Valentinians ?) held not to be saved
but to be only capable of salvation[3]. If the recipient of these

---

[1] Whether the author of the *Pistis Sophia* really intended to describe
them may be doubted ; but it is to be noted that the sacraments which
Jesus is represented as celebrating in the Μέρος τευχῶν Σωτῆρος can
hardly be they, although Jesus calls them in one place (p. 374, Copt.),
" the mysteries of the light which remit sins, which themselves are appel-
lations and names of light." These are administered to the twelve disciples
without distinction, and it is evident that the author of these books is quite
unacquainted with any division into pneumatic and psychic, and knows
nothing of the higher mysteries called in the *Pistis Sophia* proper " the
mysteries of the Ineffable One " and " the mysteries of the First Mystery."
We should get over many difficulties if we supposed the two later books to
be Marcosian in origin, but in any event they are later than the *Pistis
Sophia*.

[2] p. 246, Copt. So in the Manichaean text described in Chapter XIII,
Jesus is Himself called " the Tree of Knowledge."

[3] So Irenaeus, Bk I. c. 1, § 11, pp. 53, 54, Harvey : Ἐπαιδεύθησαν γὰρ
τὰ ψυχικὰ οἱ ψυχικοὶ ἄνθρωποι, οἱ δι᾽ ἔργων καὶ πίστεως ψιλῆς βεβαιούμενοι,

lesser mysteries dies before complete initiation, he has to undergo a long and painful series of reincarnations, his soul being sent back into the Sphere of Destiny and eventually into this world by the Virgin of Light, who will, however, take care that it is placed in a "righteous" body which shall strive after the mysteries until it finds them. But the way to these lower mysteries is the complete renunciation of this world. Man naturally and normally is entirely hylic or material, being, as Jesus tells His disciples in the *Pistis Sophia*, "the very dregs of the Treasure-house, of the Places of those on the Right Hand, in the Middle, and on the Left Hand, and the dregs of the Unseen Ones and of the Archons, and, in a word, the dregs of them all[1]." Hence it is only by the cleansing grace of the mysteries that he can hope to escape the fate which is coming upon the Kerasmos, and to obtain these, he must avoid further pollution.

"Wherefore preach you to the whole race of men, saying: Slacken not day and night until ye find the cleansing mysteries. Say unto them: Renounce the world and all the matter that is therein; for whoso buys and sells in the world and eats and drinks in its matter, and lives in all its cares and all its conversations, takes unto himself other matter as well as his own matter..... Wherefore I said unto you aforetime: Renounce the whole world and all the matter that is therein lest ye add other matter to your own matter. Wherefore preach ye to the whole race of men....cease not to seek day and night and stay not your hand until ye find the cleansing mysteries which will cleanse you so as to make you

---

καὶ μὴ τὴν τελείαν γνῶσιν ἔχοντες· εἶναι δὲ τούτους ἀπὸ τῆς Ἐκκλησίας ἡμᾶς λέγουσι· διὸ καὶ ἡμῖν μὲν ἀναγκαῖον εἶναι τὴν ἀγαθὴν πρᾶξιν ἀποφαίνονται· ἄλλως γὰρ ἀδύνατον σωθῆναι. Αὐτοὺς δὲ μὴ διὰ πράξεως, ἀλλὰ διὰ τὸ φύσει πνευματικοὺς εἶναι, πάντῃ τε καὶ πάντως σωθήσεσθαι δογματίζουσιν. "For the psychic (animal) men are taught psychic things, they being made safe by works and by mere faith, and not having perfect knowledge. And they say that we of the Church are these people. Wherefore they declare that good deeds are necessary for us: for otherwise we could not be saved. But they decree that they themselves are entirely and in every thing saved, not by works, but because they are pneumatic (spiritual) by nature."

[1] p. 249, Copt.

pure light, that ye may go into the heights and inherit the light of my kingdom[1]."

We see, then, that the author of the *Pistis Sophia* really contemplated the formation of a Church within a Church, where a group of persons claiming for themselves special illumination should rule over the great body of the faithful, these last being voluntarily set apart from all communion with their fellows[2]. This was so close a parallel to what actually occurred in Egypt in the IVth century, when the whole male population was said with some exaggeration to have embraced the monastic life[3], and submitted themselves to the rule of an ambitious and grasping episcopate, as to give us a valuable indication as to the authorship and date of the book. It may be said at the outset that the conception of the universe which appears throughout is so thoroughly Egyptian that it must have been written for Egyptian readers, who alone could have been expected to understand it without instruction. The idea of the Supreme Being as an unfathomable abyss was, as has been said in Chapter II, a very old one in Egypt, where one of the oldest cosmogonies current made Nu or the sea of waters the origin of both gods and men[4]. So was the peculiar theory that the lesser gods were the limbs or members of the Supreme[5]. An Ogdoad[6] or assembly of eight gods arranged in syzygies or

---

[1] p. 250, Copt. It is to be observed that these " cleansing mysteries " will only admit their recipients to the light of the Kingdom of Jesus—not to that of the First Mystery or of the Ineffable One.

[2] As did perhaps the Manichaeans afterwards. See *J.R.A.S.* for January, 1913, and Chap. XIII *infra*.

[3] So Charles Kingsley in *Hypatia*. Gibbon, *Decline and Fall*, vol. IV. c. 60, n. 15, quotes a statement of Rufinus that there were nearly as many monks living in the deserts as citizens in the towns.

[4] Mallet, *Le Culte de Neit à Saïs*, p. 200, points out that the God Nu described in the 18th Chapter of the *Book of the Dead* is "the infinite abyss, the Βυθός, the πατὴρ ἄγνωστος of the Gnostics." So Maspero in *Rev. Critique*, 30 Sept. 1909, p. 13, who declares that the author of the *Pistis Sophia* was influenced directly or indirectly by Osirian beliefs.

[5] Moret, *Le verbe créateur et révélateur*, p. 286, for references.

[6] Maspero, *Ét. Égyptol.* t. II. p. 187 : " L'ogdoade est une conception hermopolitaine qui s'est répandue plus tard sur toute l'Égypte à côté de l'ennéade d'Heliopolis. Les théologiens d'Hermopolis avaient adopté

couples was also well known in the time of the early dynasties, as was the Dodecad of twelve gods which Herodotus knew, and which M. Maspero refers on good evidence to the time of the Pyramid-Builders[1]. So was the view that men and other material things were made from the tears of the celestial powers[2], a notion well known to Proclus the Neo-Platonist, who attributed it to the legendary Orpheus[3]. Not less Egyptian —perhaps in its origin exclusively Egyptian—is the view that the knowledge of the places of the world after death and their rulers was indispensable to the happiness of the dead. "Whosoever," says M. Maspero in commenting upon some funerary texts of the Ramesside period, "knows the names of these (gods) while still on earth and is acquainted with their places in Amenti, will arrive at his own place in the other world and will be in all the places reserved for those who are justified[4]." The resemblance between the system of the *Pistis Sophia* and the doctrines of the Egyptian religion in the days of the Pharaohs has been pointed out in detail by the veteran Egyptologist the late Prof. Lieblein and has been approved by M. Maspero[5]. It extends to particular details as well as to general ideas, as we see from the ritual inscribed on the tombs at Thebes, where each "circle" or division of the next world is said to

le concept de la neuvaine, seulement ils avaient amoindri les huit dieux qui formaient le corps du dieu principal. Ils les avaient reduits à n'être plus que des êtres presque abstraits nommés d'après la fonction qu'on leur assignait, en agissant en masse sur l'ordre et d'après l'impulsion du dieu chef. Leur ennéade se composait donc d'un dieu tout-puissant et d'une ogdoade."

[1] "Son origine (l'ogdoade hermopolitaine subordonné à un corps monade) est fort ancienne : on trouve quelques-unes des divinités qui la composent mentionnées déjà dans les textes des Pyramides." Maspero, *op. cit.* t. II. p. 383. As he says later the actual number of gods in the Ennead or Ogdoad was a matter of indifference to the ancient Egyptian : "les dieux comptaient toujours pour neuf, quand même ils étaient treize ou quinze," *ibid.* p. 387. Cf. Amélineau, *Gnost. Ég.* pp. 294, 295.

[2] See n. 5, p. 175 *supra*, and Maspero, "Hypogées Royaux," *Ét. Égyptol.* II. p. 130, n. 2.

[3] See n. 2, p. 153 *supra*.

[4] Maspero, "Hypogées Royaux," t. II. p. 121.

[5] Maspero, *Rev. Crit.* 30 Sept. 1909, p. 13.

have its own song and its own " mystery," an idea often met with in the *Pistis Sophia*[1]. Even the doctrine in the *Pistis Sophia* that the dead had to exhibit a " seal " as well as a " defence " to the guardians of the heavenly places is explained by the Egyptian theory that no spell was effective without an amulet, which acted as a kind of material support to it[2]. The greater part of the allusions in the *Pistis Sophia* are in fact unintelligible, save to those with some acquaintance with the religious beliefs of the Pharaonic Egyptians.

At the same time it is evident that the MS. of the *Pistis Sophia* that has come down to us is not the original form of the book. All the scholars who have studied it are agreed that the Coptic version has been made from a Greek original by a scribe who had no very profound acquaintance with the first-named tongue[3]. This appears not only from the frequent appearance in it of Greek words following Coptic ones of as nearly as possible the same meaning; but from the fact that the scribe here and there gives us others declined according to the rules not of Coptic but of Greek accidence. We must therefore look for an author who, though an Egyptian and acquainted with the native Egyptian religion, would naturally have written in Greek; and on the whole there is no one who fulfils these requirements so well as Valentinus himself. The fact that the author never quotes from the Gospel according to St John indicates that it had not come to his knowledge; for the opening chapter of St John's Gospel contains many expressions that could easily on the Gnostic system of interpretation be made to accord with the Valentinian theology, and is in fact so used by later writers of the same school as the author of the *Pistis Sophia*[4]. Now the first direct and acknowledged quotation

---

[1] Maspero, "Hypogées Royaux," t. II. p. 118. Cf. *Pistis Sophia,* p. 84, Copt. and elsewhere.

[2] Maspero, "La Table d'Offrandes," *R.H.R.* t. xxxv. (1897) p. 325. As has been said, in the *Ascensio Isaiae,* anyone passing from one heaven to another has to give a password, but not to exhibit a seal.

[3] Amélineau, *Gnost. Ég.* p. 196 ; Schmidt, *Koptisch-Gnostische Schriften,* Bd I. p. xiii.

[4] It is so used in the *Excerpta Theodoti,* and in the Papyrus Bruce. See p. 190, *infra.*

from St John's Gospel that we have is that made by Theophilus,
who was made bishop of Antioch in A.D. 170, and the generally
received opinion is that this Gospel, whenever written, was
not widely known long before this date[1].   The only founders
of Gnostic sects of Egyptian birth prior to this were Basilides
and Valentinus, and of these two, Valentinus is the more likely
author, because he, unlike his predecessor, evidently taught
for general edification, and possessed, as the Fathers agree,
a numerically large following.   We have, moreover, some
reason for thinking that Valentinus actually did write a book
with some such title as the *Sophia*.   Tertullian, in his declama-
tion against the Valentinians, quotes a sentence from " the
Wisdom (Lat. Sophia) not of Valentinus but of Solomon[2]."   It
has been suggested that he is here referring to some saying of
the Valentinian aeon Sophia ; but no writings would in the
nature of things be attributed to her, and, as M. Amélineau
points out, it is more natural to think that he was here comparing a book with a book[3].   This figure of rhetoric was a
favourite one with Tertullian, for in his treatise *De Carne
Christi* we find him quoting in like manner the Psalms—
" not the Psalms of Valentinus, the apostate, heretic, and
Platonist, but the Psalms of David[4]."   The fact that the
story in the British Museum MS. is called *Pistis Sophia* instead
of *Sophia* only need not hinder us from identifying this
with the work presumably referred to by Tertullian, because
this title is, as has been said, the work of another scribe
than those who transcribed the original ; and Pistis Sophia

[1] Jean Reville, *Le Quatrième Évangile*, Paris, 1901, p. 321.   Mgr Duchesne,
Early Christian Church, pp. 102, 192, says in effect that St John's Gospel
appeared after the Apostle's death and was not accepted without opposition.   He thinks Tatian and Irenaeus the first writers who quoted from it
with acknowledgement of its authorship.   If we put the date of Tatian's
birth at 120 (see *Dict. Christian Biog. s.h.n.*) and allow a sufficient period for
the initiation into heathen mysteries which he mentions, for his conversion
and for his becoming a teacher, we do not get a much earlier date than 170
for his acceptance of the Fourth Gospel.   Irenaeus was, of course, later in
date than Tatian.

[2] Tertullian, *Adv. Valentinianos*, c. 2.

[3] Amélineau, *Gnost. Ég.* p. 180.

[4] Tertullian, *de Carne Christi*, c. 20.

is sometimes spoken of in the MS. itself as Sophia only[1].   Moreover, there is some reason for thinking that certain of the Fathers and even their Pagan adversaries had seen and read the story of *Pistis Sophia*.   The allusion quoted above from Origen to gates opening of their own accord seems to refer to one of its episodes, and Tertullian, in the treatise in which he says he is exposing the original tenets of the sect[2], uses many expressions that he can hardly have borrowed from any other source.   Thus, he speaks of Sophia " breaking away from her spouse[3] " which is the expression used by Pistis Sophia in her first Metanoia and is in no way applicable to the Valentinian Sophia of Irenaeus or Hippolytus.   He again speaks of the same Sophia as being all but swallowed up and dissolved in " the substance " evidently of Chaos, which is the fate which Pistis Sophia anticipates for herself in the MS.   Tertullian, like the *Pistis Sophia*, also assigns to the psychic substance the place of honour or right hand in the *quasi*-material world, while the hylic is relegated in both to the left hand[4].   The Paradise of Adam is said by him to be fixed by Valentinus " above the third heaven[5] " as it is in the *Pistis Sophia*, if, as we may suppose, the soul of the protoplast dwelt in the same place as that of Elijah.   The name of *Ecclesia* or the Church is given not only to a particular aeon in the Pleroma, but also to the divine power breathed into man from a higher world in both Tertullian and the *Pistis Sophia*[6], and, in the treatise *De Carne Christi*, Tertullian alludes contemptuously to an heretical doctrine that Christ possessed " any new kind of flesh miraculously obtained from the stars[7]," which seems to refer to the taking by Jesus in the opening of the *Pistis Sophia* of a body from " Barbelo " the goddess or Triple Power

---

[1] *E.g.* p. 47, Copt.   Cf. also *ibid.* pp. 147, 170, 176.

[2] Tertullian, *adv. Val.* c. v.

[3] *Op. cit.* c. 9.   [4] *Op. cit.* c. 18.

[5] *Op. cit.* c. 20.   [6] *Op. cit.* c. 25.

[7] Tertullian, *de Carne Christi*, c. 9.   Irenaeus, Bk II. c. 7, § 1, p. 270, Harvey, seems to have known both of Barbelo and of the Virgin of Light, since he speaks of *corpora sursum....spiritalia et lucida*, " spiritual and translucent bodies on high " casting a shadow below *in quam Matrem suam descendisse dicunt* " into which they allege their Mother descended."

set over matter and inspiring the benefic planet Venus. For
all which reasons it seems probable that in the *Pistis Sophia*
we have the translation of an authentic work by Valentinus.

The *Pistis Sophia*, however, is not the only work in the
British Museum MS. The first and second books of it, as
they are called by the annotator, come to an end, rather abrupt
but evidently intentional, on the 252nd page of the MS. There
then appears the heading in the hand of the annotator " Part
of the Texts of the Saviour[1]," and on this follow two pages
dealing with the " members " of the Ineffable One, as to which
it is expressly said that only a partial revelation is made[2].
These seem to have slipped out of their proper place, and are
followed by two discontinuous extracts from another treatise,
the second of which is also headed by the annotator " Part
of the Texts of the Saviour." This second part, which we
shall venture to take before the other, is evidently the introduction to or the commencement of a new treatise, for it
begins with the statement that " After they had crucified Our
Lord Jesus He rose from the dead on the third day," and
that His disciples gathered round Him, reminding Him that
they had left all to follow Him[3]. Jesus " standing on the
shore of the sea Ocean," then makes invocation to the "Father
of every Fatherhood, boundless light," in a prayer composed
of Egyptian and Hebrew words jumbled together after the
fashion of the spells in the Magic Papyri[4]. He then shows

---

[1] ΟΥ ΜΕΡΟC Ν̄ΤΕ Ν̄ ΤΕΥΧΟC Μ̄ ΝCⲰΤΗΡ, or (in Greek) Μέρος τευχῶν
Σωτῆρος.

[2] " This I say to you in paradigm, and likeness and similitude, but not
in truth of shape, nor have I revealed the word in truth," p. 253, Copt.
So in the next page (p. 254, Copt.), Jesus says of the perfect initiate that
" He also has found the words of the Mysteries, those which I have written
to you according to similitude—the same are the members of the Ineffable
One." From His mention of " writing," one would imagine that the
reference here is to documents such as the Bruce Papyrus which gives the
pictures of "seals" together with cryptographically written words.

[3] p. 357, Copt. This opening sentence could not have been written by
one of the Valentinians of Hadrian's time, who, as has been said above,
" did not choose to call Jesus, Lord," Irenaeus, Bk I. c. 1, I. p. 12, Harvey.

[4] In the address of Jesus beginning " O my Father, Father of every
Fatherhood, boundless light " with which this part of the M. τ. σ. opens, we

the disciples the " disk of the sun " as a great dragon with
his tail in his mouth drawn by four white horses and the disk
of the moon like a ship drawn by two white steers[1].   The two

can, with a little good will, identify nearly every word of the " galimatias "
which at first sight seems mere gibberish. Thus, the whole invocation reads:
αεηιουω, ϊαω, αωϊ, οϊαψινωθερ, θερ[ι]νοψ, νωψιθερ, ζαγουρη, παγουρη, νεθμομαωθ,
νεψιομαωθ, μαραχαχθα, θωβαρραβαυ, θαρναχαχαυ, ζοροκοθορα Ιεου Σαβαωθ.
The seven vowels to which many mystical interpretations have been
assigned, and which have even been taken for a primitive system of musical
notation (C. E. Ruelle, " Le Chant des Sept Voyelles Grecques," *Rev. des
Ét. Grecques*, Paris, 1889, t. II. p. 43, and pp. 393–395), probably express the
sound to Greek ears of the Jewish pronunciation of Yahweh or Jehovah.
The word Iao we have before met with many times both as a name of
Dionysos and otherwise, and is here written anagrammatically from the
difficulty which the Greeks found in dealing with Semitic languages written
the reverse way to their own.   The word ψινωθερ which follows and is also
written as an anagram is evidently an attempt to transcribe in Greek letters
the Egyptian words *P, Shai, neter* (*P* = Def. article, *Shai* = the Egyptian God
of Fate whose name Revillout, *Rev. Égyptol.* Paris, 1892, pp. 29–38, thinks
means " The Highest," and *neter* or *nuter* the determinative for " god "),
the whole reading " Most High God."   The words ζαγουρη παγουρη (better,
πατουρη) are from the Hebrew roots סגר פתר and seem to be the " he that
openeth and no man shutteth ; and shutteth and no man openeth " of
Rev. iii. 7. Νεθμομαωθ, which is often found in the Magic Papyri, is reminiscent of the Egyptian *neb maat* " Lord of Truth," the following νεψιομαωθ
being probably a variant by a scribe who was uncertain of the orthography.
Μαραχαχθα I can make nothing of, although as the phrase νεφθομαωθ
μαραχαχθα appears in the Magic Papyrus of Leyden generally called
W (Leemans, *Papyri Graeci*, etc. t. II. p. 154) in a spell there said to be written
by " Thphe the Hierogrammateus " for " Ochus the king," it is evidently
intended for Egyptian.   In the same spell appear the words θαρνμαχαχ
ζοροκοθορα and θωβαρραβαυ which are evidently the same as those
in the M. τ. σ., and of which I will only say that, while Mr King supposes
ζοροκοθορα to mean " light-gatherer," θωβαρραβαυ is in the leaden *tabula
devotionis* of Carthage (Molinier, " Imprecation gravée sur plomb," *Mem.
de la Soc. Nat. des Antiquaires de France*, série VI. t. VIII. Paris, 1897,
pp. 212–216) described as τον θεον του της παλινγενεσιας " the god of
rebirth."   The concluding words are of course merely " Yahweh of Hosts."

[1] The description of the moon-chariot drawn by two white oxen is
found in Claudian's *Proserpine*. According to Cumont (*Textes et Monuments relatifs aux Mystères de Mithra*, t. I. p. 126 and note) it was not until
Hadrian's time that this conception, which seems to have been Persian in
origin, became fixed in the West.

steering oars of this last are depicted as a male and a female dragon who take away the light from the rulers of the stars among whom they move. Jesus and His disciples are then translated to the place called the "Middle Way[1]." He there describes how the Archons of Adamas rebelled and persisted in engendering and bringing forth "rulers and archangels and angels and ministers and decans." We further hear, for the first time, that the Twelve Aeons, instead of being, as in the *Pistis Sophia*, all under the rule of Adamas, are divided into two classes, one Jabraoth ruling over six of them and Sabaoth Adamas over the other six; that Jabraoth and his subjects repented and practised "the mysteries of the light," including, as we have seen, abstinence from generation[2], whereupon they were taken up by Jeû to the light of the sun between the "places of the middle and those of the left." "Sabaoth Adamas," on the other hand, with his subjects to the number of 1800, were bound to the sphere, 360 powers being set over them, the 360 being controlled by the five planets Saturn, Mars, Mercury, Venus, and Jupiter. Jesus then describes in great detail the different tortures in the Middle Way and two other hells called Chaos and Amenti, wherein the souls of uninitiated men who commit sins are tormented between their incarnations[3], the final punishment being in the worst cases

[1] This "Middle Way" has nothing to do with the τόπος or "place" of the middle, where are set in the *Pistis Sophia* proper the powers who preside over incarnation. It is below the visible sphere (p. 364, Copt.) and is met with in Rabbinic lore. See Kohler, *op. cit.* p. 587.

[2] This division of the Twelve Aeons into two halves seems at first sight inconsistent with the description in the *Pistis Sophia* proper which always speaks of them as Twelve. Yet it is plain that the author of the *Pistis Sophia* knew the legend here given, as he makes John the Divine speak (p. 12, Copt.) of "the rulers who belong to the Aeon of Jabraoth" and had made peace with the mysteries of the light. These "rulers who repented" are again mentioned on p. 195, Copt. In the other part of the Μέρος τευχῶν Σωτῆρος (p. 356, Copt.), it is also said that the souls of Abraham, Isaac, and Jacob are to be placed in "the Place of Jabraoth and of all the rulers who repented" until Jesus can take them with Him to the light. So the Papyrus Bruce (Amélineau, p. 239).

[3] There are seven pages missing between the descriptions of the tortures of the Middle Way and those of Amenti and Chaos, the gap occurring at

annihilation. He then affords His disciples a vision of "fire and water and wine and blood" which He declares He brought with Him on His Incarnation, and celebrates a sacrament which He calls "the baptism of the First Oblation," but which seems to be a peculiar form of the Eucharist with invocations in the jargon alluded to above, and a thaumaturgic conversion of the wine used in it into water and *vice versâ*[1]. There are several *lacunae* in this part of the MS., and the tortures for certain specified sins are differently given in different places, so that it is probable that with the *Part of the Texts of the Saviour* has here been mixed extracts from another document whose title has been lost[2].

The remaining document of the British Museum MS., being the third in order of place, was probably taken from the same book as that last described, and was placed out of its natural order to satisfy the pedantry of the scribes, the rule in such cases being that the longer document should always come first. Like its successor, it deals largely with the "punishments" of the souls who have not received the mysteries of the light, and introduces a new and still more terrible hell in the shape of the "Dragon of Outer Darkness" which it declares to be a vast dragon surrounding the world, having his tail in his mouth, and containing twelve chambers, wherein the souls of the uninitiated dead are tortured after their transmigrations are ended until they reach the annihilation reserved for them at the last judgment[3]. There is also given here a

---

p. 379, Copt. It is possible that what follows after this is not from the Μέρος τευχῶν Σωτῆρος but an extract from yet another document.

[1] In the text of the M. τ. σ. (p. 377, Copt.), Jesus simply asks His father for a sign, and "the sign is made which Jesus had said." In the Papyrus Bruce where the same ceremony is described in almost identical words, it is said that the wine of the offering was turned into water which leaped forth of the vase which contained it so as to serve for baptism. Cf. Amélineau, *Gnost. Ég.* p. 253. That Marcus the magician by juggling produced similar prodigies, see Irenaeus, Bk I. c. 7, II. pp. 116, 117, Harvey.

[2] The name of Jaldabaoth, which in the whole of the rest of the MS. is spelt ϊαλλαβαωθ, appears on p. 380 immediately after the *lacuna* of seven pages as ϊαλταβαωθ, Ialtabaoth, which supports the theory of another author.

[3] This is also briefly mentioned in the part of the Μέρος τευχῶν Σωτῆρος just described. See pp. 386, *sqq.*, Copt.

very curious account of man's invisible part, which is said to be made up of the " Power " infused into it by the Virgin of Light which returns to its giver after death[1], and the Moira or Fate which it derives from the Sphere of Destiny and has as its sole function to lead the man it inhabits to the death he is predestined to die[2].   Then there is the Counterfeit of the Spirit, which is in effect a duplicate of the soul proper and is made out of the matter of the wicked Archons.   This not only incites the soul to sin, but follows it about after death, denouncing to the powers set over the punishments the sins it has induced the soul to commit[3].   All these punishments, to describe which is evidently the purpose of all the extracts from the *Texts of the Saviour* here given, are escaped by those who have received the mysteries.

The *Texts of the Saviour* therefore clearly belong to a later form of Gnosticism than the *Pistis Sophia* properly so called. The author's intention is evidently to frighten his readers with the fate reserved for those who do not accept the teaching of the sect.   For this purpose the division of mankind into pneumatic, psychic, and hylic is ignored[4], and this is especially

---

[1] This appears to contradict the *Pistis Sophia* proper, where it is said that the Virgin of Light gives the soul, and the Great Iao the Good the power.

[2] Cf. the speech of the crocodile in the tale of the *Predestined Prince*: " Ah; moi, je suis ton destin qui te poursuit ; quoi que tu fasses, tu seras ramené sur mon chemin."   Maspero, *Contes Populaires de l'Égypte Ancienne,* 3rd ed. Paris, n. d. p. 175.

[3] Evidently the Egyptian *ka* or double.   Cf. the " Heart Amulet " described by Erman, *Handbook of Egyptian Religion,* pp. 142, 143, where the dead says to his heart: " Oh heart that I have from my mother ! Oh heart that belongs to my spirit, do not appear against me as witness, provide no opposition against me before the judges, do not contradict me before him who governs the balance, thou art my spirit that is in my body....."   This seems to be a transcription of the 30th Chapter of the *Book of the Dead,* of which there are several variants, none of which however directly suggest that the heart is the accuser to be dreaded.   See Budge, *Book of the Dead,* 1909, vol. II. pp. 146–152.

[4] Thus the M. τ. σ. says (p. 355, Copt.) " For this I despoiled myself (*i.e.* laid aside my heavenly nature) to bring the mysteries into the Cosmos, for all are under [the yoke of] sin, and all lack the gifts of the mysteries.... Verily, verily I say unto you : until I came into the Cosmos, no soul entered

plain in certain passages where the torments after death of those who follow " the doctrines of error " are set forth. Magic, which has been spoken of with horror in the *Pistis Sophia*, is here made use of in the celebration of the rites described, and the miraculous power of healing the sick and raising the dead, though said to be of archontic, *i.e.* diabolic, origin is here recommended as a means to be employed under certain safeguards for the purpose of converting " the whole world[1]." Even the duration of the punishments and the different bodies into which the souls of the men are to be cast are made to depend upon the relative positions of the stars and planets which seem to be interpreted according to the rules of the astrology of the time,—a so-called science, which is spoken of scornfully in the *Pistis Sophia* itself[2]. Yet it is evident that the author or authors of the *Texts of the Saviour* are acquainted with the

into the light." Contrast this with the words of the *Pistis Sophia* proper (p. 250, Copt.) : " Those who are of the light have no need of the mysteries, because they are pure light," which are made the " interpretation " of the text : " They that are whole have no need of a physician, but they that are sick." See also the *Pistis Sophia*, p. 246, Copt., where it is said of the mysteries promised by Jesus that " they lead every race of men inwards into the highest places according to the χωρημα of the inheritance, so that ye have no need of the rest of the lower mysteries, but you will find them in the two books of Jeû which Enoch wrote etc."

[1] p. 280, Copt.

[2] M. τ. σ. p. 388, Copt., where it is said that the soul of the righteous but uninitiated man is after death taken into Amenti and afterwards into the Middle Way, being shown the tortures in each place, " but the breath of the flame of the punishments shall only afflict him a little." Afterwards he is taken to the Virgin of Light, who sets him before the Little Sabaoth the Good until the Sphere be turned round so that Zeus ($2+$) and Aphrodite ($♀$) come into aspect with the Virgin of Light and Kronos ($+z$) and Ares ($♂$) come after them. She then puts the soul into a righteous body, which she plainly could not do unless under the favourable influence of the " benefics " $2+$ and $♀$. This seems also to be the dominant idea of the *Excerpta Theodoti*, *q.v.* Compare this, however, with the words of the *Pistis Sophia* proper (pp. 27, 28, Copt.) where Mary Magdalene explains that the alteration made by Jesus in the course of the stars was effected in order to baffle those skilled in the mysteries taught by the angels " who came down " (as in the Book of Enoch), from predicting the future by astrology and magic arts learned from the sinning angels.

book which precedes it; for in a description of the powers which Jeû, who appears in both as the angelic arranger of the Kerasmos, " binds " in the five planets set to rule over it, we learn that he draws a power from " Pistis Sophia, the daughter of Barbelo " and binds it in the planet Venus or Aphrodite[1]. As this is the only reference to her, and receives no further explanation, it is plain that the writer assumed his readers to be well acquainted with Pistis Sophia's history, and Jeû, Melchisidek, Adamas, and Jaldabaoth, now one of the torturers in Chaos, appear, as we have seen, in both works. The author of the *Texts of the Saviour* also shows himself the avowed opponent of the Pagan deities still worshipped in the early Christian centuries, as is evidenced by his making not only the Egyptian Typhon, but Adonis, Persephone, and Hecate, fiends in hell. Oddly enough, however, he gives an explanation of the myth of the two springs of memory and oblivion that we have seen in the Orphic gold plates in the following passage, which may serve as an example of the style of the book :

" Jesus said : When the time set by the Sphere of Destiny[2] for a man that is a persistent slanderer to go forth from the body is fulfilled, there come unto him Abiuth and Charmon, the receivers of Ariel[3], and lead forth his soul from the body, that they may take it about with them for three days, showing it the creatures of the world. Thereafter they drag it into Amenti unto Ariel that he may torment it in his torments for eleven months and twenty-one days. Thereafter they lead it into Chaos unto Jaldabaoth and his forty-nine demons, that each of his demons may set upon it for eleven months and twenty-one days with whips of smoke.

---

[1] p. 361, Copt.

[2] That is the Sphere of Destiny acting through its emissary the Moira or Fate described above, p. 184 *supra*.

[3] It is a curious example of the fossilizing, so to speak, of ancient names in magic that Shakespeare should preserve for us in the *Tempest* and *Macbeth* the names of Ariel and Hecate which we find in the M. τ. σ. No doubt both were taken by him from mediaeval grimoires which themselves copied directly from the Graeco-Egyptian Magic Papyri mentioned in Chap. III *supra*. Cf. the use of Greek " names of God " like *ischiros* (sic !) *athanatos*, etc. in Reginald Scot's *Discovery of Witchcraft, passim*.

Thereafter they lead it into rivers of smoke and seas of fire that they may torment it therein eleven months and twenty-one days. Thereafter they lead it on high into the Middle Way that each of the Archons of the Middle Way may torment it with his own torments another eleven months and twenty-one days. And thereafter they lead it unto the Virgin of Light who judges the righteous and the sinners, and she shall judge it. And when the Sphere is turned round, she delivers it to her receivers that they may cast it forth among the Aeons of the Sphere. And the servants of the Sphere lead it into the water which is below the Sphere, that the boiling steam may eat into it, until it cleanse it thoroughly. Then Jaluha the receiver of Sabaoth Adamas, bearing the cup of oblivion delivers it to the soul, that it may drink therein and forget all the places and the things therein through which it has passed[1]. And it is placed in an afflicted body wherein it shall spend its appointed time[2]."

The object of the cup of oblivion is obviously that the wicked man may learn nothing from the torments he has endured. In the case of the righteous but uninitiated dead, the baleful effect of this cup will be annulled by " the Little Sabaoth the Good" who will administer to him another cup "of perception and understanding and wisdom " which will make the soul seek after the mysteries of light, on finding which it will inherit light eternal.

It would be easy to see in these features of the *Texts of the Saviour* the work of Marcus the magician who, as was said in a former chapter, taught, according to the Fathers, a corrupted form of the doctrine of Valentinus for his own interested purposes[3]. The distinguishing feature about his celebration of the Eucharist is the same as that given in the *Texts of the*

---

[1] So that it could not profit by the knowledge of the awful punishments prepared for sinners. I do not know that this idea occurs elsewhere.

[2] p. 380, Copt.

[3] The Marcosian authorship of the whole MS. is asserted by Bunsen, *Hippolytus and his Age*, vol. I. p. 47. Köstlin, *Über das gnostische System des Buch Pistis Sophia* in the Theologische Jahrbücher of Baur and Zeller, Tübingen, 1854, will have none of it, and declares the *Pistis Sophia* to be an Ophite work. In this, the first commentator on the book is followed by Grüber, *Der Ophiten*, Würzburg, 1864, p. 5, §§ 3, 4.

Saviour, and as Clement of Alexandria was acquainted with a sect in his day which substituted water for wine therein[1], it is probable that Marcosians were to be found during the latter part of the IInd century in Egypt. It is also to be noted that the annotator has written upon the blank leaf which separates the first and second books of the *Pistis Sophia* a cryptogram concealing, apparently, the names of the Ineffable One and the other higher powers worshipped by Valentinus, and this seems to be constructed in much the same way as the isopsephisms and other word-puzzles attributed by Irenaeus to Marcus[2]. The mixture of Hebrew names and words with Egyptian ones in the prayer of Jesus given in the *Texts of*

---

[1] Clem. Alex. *Strom.* Bk I. c. 19.

[2] Thus, according to Marcus (Irenaeus, Bk I. c. 8, § 11, pp. 145, 146, Harvey), " that name of the Saviour which may be pronounced, *i.e.* Jesus, is composed of six letters, but His ineffable name of 24." The cryptogram in the *Pistis Sophia* is in these words (p. 125, Copt.): "These are the names which I will give thee from the Boundless One downwards. Write them with a sign that the sons of God may show them forth of this place   This is the name of the Deathless One $\overline{aaa}$ $\overline{\omega\omega\omega}$, and this is the name of the word by which the Perfect Man is moved: *ιι*. These are the interpretations of the names of the mysteries. The first is *aaa*, the interpretation of which is $\phi\phi\phi$. The second which is *μμμ* or which is *ωωω*, its interpretation is *aaa*. The third is $\psi\psi\psi$, its interpretation is *ooo*. The fourth is $\phi\phi\phi$, its interpretation is *ννν*. The fifth is $\delta\delta\delta$, its interpretation is *aaa*, which above the throne is *aaa*. This is the interpretation of the second *aaaa*, *aaaa*, *aaaa*, which is the interpretation of the whole name." The line drawn above the three Alphas and Omegas is used in the body of the text to denote words in a foreign (*i.e.* non-Egyptian) language such as Hebrew; but in the Papyrus Bruce about to be described, the same letters without any line above are given as the name of " the Father of the Pleroma." See Amélineau's text, p. 113. The "moving" of the image ($\pi\lambda\acute{a}\sigma\mu a$) of the Perfect Man is referred to in Hippolytus (*op. cit.* p. 144, Cruice). That the Tetragrammaton was sometimes written by Jewish magicians with three Jods or *i.i.i.* see Gaster, *The Oldest Version of Midrash Megillah,* in Kohut's Semitic Studies, Berlin, 1897, p. 172. So on a magic cup in the Berlin Museum, conjuration is made " in the name of Jahve the God of Israel who is enthroned upon the cherubim...and in the name *A A A A* " (Stübe, *Judisch-Babylonische Zaubertexte,* Halle, 1895, pp. 23–27). For the meaning of the words "above the throne," see Franck, *La Kabbale,* p. 45, n. 2.

the Saviour would agree well with what the last-named Father says about Marcus being a Jew, and a prayer which he represents Marcus as making over the head of a convert baptized into his sect is couched in a jargon of the same character[1]. On the other hand, the opening sentence of the book calls Jesus " our Lord," which Irenaeus tells us the Valentinians carefully abstained from doing[2], and the long and detailed description of the different hells and their tortures is much more Egyptian than Jewish[3]. The remark attributed to Basilides as to one in a thousand and two in ten thousand being worthy to take the higher mysteries is here put into the mouth of Jesus, and perhaps it would be safer to attribute for the present the *Texts of the Saviour* not to Marcus himself, but to some later Gnostic who fused together his teaching with that of the earlier and more disinterested professors of Egyptian Gnosticism.

The same remarks apply with but little modification to some other fragments of Gnostic writings which have come down to us. In the Bodleian Library at Oxford is to be seen a MS. written on papyrus, which was brought to this country by the Abyssinian traveller, Bruce. This also is in the Sahidic dialect of Coptic, and although it has been badly damaged and the ink is rapidly disappearing in the damp climate of Oxford, yet a copy taken nearly a century ago by Woide makes its decipherment possible in most places. The Bruce Papyrus, like the British Museum parchment MS., contains more than one document. Unfortunately the arrangement of the leaves is by no means certain, and the two scholars who have studied it most thoroughly differ almost as widely as possible as to the order of its contents. M. Amélineau, a celebrated Egyptologist and Coptic scholar, who published in 1882 a copy of

---

[1] The opening words of the invocation βασεμὰ χαμοσσὴ βαιανορὰ μισταδία ῥουαδὰ κουστὰ βαβοφὸρ καλαχθεῖ which Irenaeus (Bk I. c. 14, § 2, pp. 183, 184, Harvey) quotes in this connection from Marcus certainly read, as Renan (*L'Église Chrétienne*, p. 154, n. 3) points out, " In the name of Achamoth " (*i.e.* Sophia).

[2] See n. 3, p. 180, *supra*. In the *Pistis Sophia* proper Jesus is never spoken of save as " the Saviour " or as " the First Mystery."

[3] Cf. Maspero, *Hypogées Royaux, passim*, esp. pp. 157 and 163.

the text with a French translation in the *Notices et Extraits* of the
Académie des Inscriptions, considers that the treatises contained
in it are only two in number, the first being called by the author
in what seems to be its heading *The Book of the Knowledge
of the Invisible God* and the second *The Book of the Great Word
in Every Mystery*. Dr Carl Schmidt, of the University of
Berlin, on the other hand, who, like M. Amélineau, has studied
the Papyrus at Oxford, thinks that he can distinguish in the
Bruce Papyrus no less than six documents, of which the first
two are according to him the two books of Jeû referred to
in the *Pistis Sophia*, two others, fragments of Gnostic prayers,
the fifth a fragment on the passage of the soul through the
Archons of the Middle Way, and the sixth, an extract from an
otherwise unknown Gnostic work which he does not venture
to identify further[1]. To enter into the controversy raised
by this diversity of opinion would take one outside the limits
of the present work ; but it may be said that at least one, and
that the most important, of the documents in question must
be later than the *Pistis Sophia*. Not only does this—which
M. Amélineau calls the *Book of the Knowledge of the Invisible God* and Dr Schmidt " Unbekanntes Altgnostisches
Werk "—quote the opening words of St John's Gospel : " In
the beginning was the Word and the Word was with God,
and the Word was God without whom nothing was made[2],"

---

[1] Schmidt's study of the Bruce Papyrus with a full text and translation
was published in the *Texte und Untersuchungen* of von Gebhardt and
Harnack under the title *Gnostische Schriften in Koptischer Sprache aus
dem Codex Brucianus*, Leipzig, 1892. He republished the translation of
this together with one of the *Pistis Sophia* in the series of early Greek
Christian literature undertaken by the Patristic Committee of the Royal
Prussian Academy of Sciences under the title *Koptisch-Gnostische Schriften*,
Bd I. Leipzig, 1905. His arrangement of the papyrus leaves makes much
better sense than that of Amélineau, but it is only arrived at by eliminating
all passages which seem to be inconsequent and attributing them to separate
works. The fragments which he distinguishes as A and B and describes
as " gnostischen Gebetes," certainly appear to form part of those which
he describes as the two " books of Jeû."

[2] Amélineau, "Notice sur le Papyrus gnostique Bruce," *Notices et Extraits
des MSS. de la Bibl. Nat.* etc. Paris, 1891, p. 106. This would seem to
make matter the creation of God, but the author gets out of the dilemma

which, as has been said, the author of the *Pistis Sophia* was unable
to do ; but it mentions in briefer form than this last the heavenly
origin of the souls of the Twelve Apostles[1]. There is also in
the same document a description of what appears to be the
" emanation of the universe," in which the following passage
occurs :

" And He [*i.e.* the Ineffable One] heard them [a prayer by the
lesser powers is referred to]. He sent them powers capable of
discernment, and knowing the arrangement of the hidden Eons.
He sent them according to the arrangement of those who are
hidden[2]. He established their Orders according to the orders of
the Height, and according to the hidden arrangement they began
from below upward in order that the building might unite
them. He created the aëry earth as a place of habitation for
those who had gone forth, in order that they might dwell thereon
until those which were below them should be made strong. Then
he created the true habitation within it[3], the Place of Repentance
(Metanoia) within it, the Place of Repentance within it, the antitype
of Aerodios[4]. Then [he created] the Place of Repentance within

by affirming (*op. cit.* p. 126) that " that which was not was the evil which
is manifested in matter " and that while that which exists is called αἰώνιος,
" everlasting," that which does not exist is called ὕλη, " matter."

[1] Amélineau, *op. cit.* p. 231.

[2] This word arrangement (οἰκονομία) occurs constantly in the *Pistis
Sophia*, as when we read (p. 193, Copt.) that the last παραστατης by the
command of the First Mystery placed Jeû, Melchisedek, and four other
powers in the τοπος of those who belong to the right hand προς οἰκονομιας
of the Assembly of the Light. There, as here, it doubtless means that
they were arranged in the same order as the powers above them in
pursuance of the principle that " that which is above is like that which
is below," or, in other words, of the doctrine of correspondences.
From the Gnostics the word found its way into Catholic theology, as when
Tertullian (*adv. Praxean*, c. 3) says that the majority of simple-minded
Christians " not understanding that though God be one, he must yet be
believed to exist with his οἰκονομία, were frightened." Cf. Hatch, *H.L.*
p. 324.

[3] Perhaps the House or Place of Ἀλήθεια or Truth many times
alluded to in the M. τ. σ.

[4] Aerôdios is shortly after spoken of as a person or power, so that here,
as elsewhere, in this literature, the *place* is called by the name of its ruler.

it, the antitype of Autogenes (Self-begotten or, perhaps, " of his
own kind "). In this Place is purification in the name of Autogenes
who is god over them and powers were set there over the source
of the waters which they make to go forth (?). Here are the names
of the powers who are set over the Water of Life : Michar and
Micheu, and they are purified in the name of Barpharanges[1].
Within these are the Aeons of Sophia. Within these is the true
Truth. And in this Place is found Pistis Sophia, as also the pre-
existent Jesus the Living, Aerodios, and his Twelve Aeons[2]."

What is intended to be conveyed by this it is difficult to say
in the absence of the context ; but the Pistis Sophia mentioned
is evidently the heroine of the book of that name, and the
abrupt mention of her name without explanation shows, as
in the *Texts of the Saviour*, that the author supposed his readers
to be acquainted with her story. While this part of the Papyrus
may possibly be an attempt by some later writer to fulfil the
promise to tell His disciples at some future time the "emanation
of the universe " frequently made by Jesus in the *Pistis Sophia*,
it cannot be earlier in date than this last-named document.

Another large fragment in the Bruce Papyrus is also connected with that which has been called above the *Texts of the
Saviour*, and helps to link up this with the system of the *Pistis
Sophia* proper. In the first part of the *Texts of the Saviour*
(*i.e.* the fourth document in the British Museum book), Jesus, as
has been mentioned, celebrates with prodigies a sacrament which
He calls the" Baptism of the first Oblation"; and He tells them
at the same time that there is also a baptism of perfumes,
another baptism of the Holy Spirit of Light, and a Spiritual
Chrism, besides which He promises them " the great mystery

---

[1] This word constantly occurs in the Magic Papyri, generally with another
word prefixed, as σεσενγεν βαρφαραγγης (Papyrus Mimaut, l. 12, Wessely's
Griechische Zauberpapyri, p. 116), which C. W. King (*Gnostics and their
Remains*, 2nd ed. p. 289) would translate " they who stand before the mount
of Paradise " or in other words the Angels of the Presence. Amélineau
(*Notices*, etc. p. 144, n. 2) will have Barpharanges to be " a hybrid word,
part Chaldean and part Greek " meaning " Son of the Abyss "—which is
as unlikely as the other interpretation.

[2] p. 143, Amélineau (*Notices*, etc.); p. 361, Schmidt, *K.-G.S.*

of the Treasure-house of Light and the way to call upon it so as to arrive thither," a "baptism of those who belong to the Right Hand," and of "those who belong to the Middle" and other matters. These promises are in some sort fulfilled in that part of the Bruce Papyrus which Dr Schmidt will have it is "the Second Book of Jeû[1]," where Jesus celebrates with accompanying prodigies three sacraments which He calls the Baptism of Fire of the Virgin of the Treasure-house of Light, the Baptism of the Holy Spirit, and a "mystery" which is said to take away from His disciples "the wickedness of the archons[2]." The details of these vary but very slightly from the "Baptism of the First Oblation" celebrated by Jesus in the *Texts of the Saviour*, and seem to have been written in continuation and as an amplification of it. But the *Texts of the Saviour*, as we have seen, also mention Pistis Sophia in such a way as to presuppose an acquaintance with her history; and the presumption that the author of the Bruce Papyrus had read the book bearing her name is confirmed by the repetition in it of the names of Jeû, here called "the Great Man, King of the great aeon of light," the Great Sabaoth the Good, the Great Iao the Good, Barbelo[3], the Great Light, and all the "Amens," "Twin Saviours," "Guardians of Veils" and the rest who are classed together in the *Pistis Sophia* as the great emanations of light, and mentioned in a connection which shows them to have the same functions in all these documents[4]. When we add to these the repetition of the tradition, formally stated for the first time in the *Pistis Sophia*, that Jesus spent twelve years with His disciples between His Resurrection and His

---

[1] According to Amélineau, *op. cit.*, "The Book of the Great Word in Every Mystery."

[2] pp. 188–199, Amélineau, *op. cit.*; Schmidt, *K.-G.S.* pp. 308–314.

[3] pp. 219, 220, Amélineau, *op. cit.*; Schmidt, *K.-G.S.* p. 226. She seems to be here called "the Great Virgin of the Spirit." Cf. the Ὑπέθεντο γὰρ Αἰῶνα τινὰ ἀνώλεθρον ἐν παρθενικῷ διάγοντι πνεύματι, ὁ βαρβηλὼθ ὀνομάζουσι, "For [some of them] suppose a certain indestructible Aeon continuing in a Virgin spirit whom they call Barbelo" of Irenaeus, Bk I. c. 27, § 1, p. 222, Harvey.

[4] The powers named are thus called in both the *Pistis Sophia* and the Bruce Papyrus. See *Pistis Sophia*, pp. 248, 252 Copt.; Amélineau, *op. cit.* p. 177.

Ascension[1], there can be little doubt that this part of the Papyrus Bruce also is subsequent to the *Pistis Sophia*. Similar arguments, which are only omitted here for the sake of greater clearness, apply to all the rest of Dr Schmidt's documents, and it follows that none of the contents of the Papyrus can be considered as any part of the " Books of Jeû " mentioned in the *Pistis Sophia*[2], which, therefore, remains the parent document on which all the others are based. As to their absolute date, it seems impossible to arrive at any useful conclusion. Both M. Amélineau and Dr Schmidt are agreed that the Coptic Papyrus is a translation from Greek originals ; and M. Amélineau does not put this too far forward when he suggests that it was made in the IInd and IIIrd century of our era[3]. Dr Schmidt is probably nearer the mark when he puts the actual transcription of the Papyrus as dating in the earliest instance from the vth century. His earliest date for any of the Greek originals is the first half of the IIIrd century[4].

If now we put these later documents—the *Texts of the Saviour* and those contained in the Bruce Papyrus—side by side, we notice a marked, if gradual, change of tendency from the comparatively orthodox Christianity of the *Pistis Sophia* proper. In the *Texts of the Saviour* notably, the fear of hell and its punishments is, as we have seen, present throughout, and seems to be the sanction on which the author relies to compel his readers to accept his teaching. In the documents of the Bruce Papyrus this is also to be found in more sporadic fashion, nearly the whole of the book being occupied by the means by which men are to escape the punishment of their

[1] According to the *Pistis Sophia* (p. 1, Copt.), 11 years elapsed between the Crucifixion and the descent of the " Vestures " upon Jesus on the Mount of Olives. We may imagine another year to have been consumed by the revelations made in the book.

[2] If the " Books of Jeû " were ever written we should expect them to bear the name of Enoch, who is said to have taken them down in Paradise at the dictation of Jesus. See p. 147, n. 5, *supra*. Very possibly the expression really does refer to some of the mass of literature once passing under the name of Enoch and now lost to us.

[3] Amélineau, *op. cit.* p. 72.

[4] Schmidt, *K.-G.S.* p. 26.

sins. These methods of salvation are all of them what we have earlier called gnostical or magical, and consist simply in the utterance of " names " given us in some sort of cryptogrammatic form, and the exhibition of " seals " or rather impressions (χαρακτῆρες) here portrayed with great attention to detail, which, however, remain utterly meaningless for us. Thus to quote again from what Dr Schmidt calls the Second Book of Jeû, Jesus imparts to His disciples the "mystery" of the Twelve Aeons in these words:

" When you have gone forth from the body and come into the First Aeon, the Archons of that Aeon will come before you. Then stamp upon yourselves this seal **, the name of which is zôzesê. Utter this once only. Take in your two hands this number, 1119. When you have stamped upon yourselves this seal and have uttered its name once only, speak these defences; ' Back! Protei Persomphôn Chous, O Archons of the First Aeon, for I invoke Êazazêôzazzôzeôz.' And when the Archons of the First Aeon shall hear that name, they will be filled with great fear, they will flee away to the West, to the Left Hand, and you will enter in[1] ":

and the same process with different names and seals is to be repeated with the other eleven aeons. This is, of course, not religion, such as we have seen in the writings of Valentinus, nor even the transcendental mysticism of the *Pistis Sophia*, but magic, and magic of a peculiarly Egyptian form. The ancient Egyptian had always an intense fear of the world after death, and from the first conceived a most gloomy view of it. The worshippers of Seker or Socharis, a god so ancient that we know him only as a component part of the triune or syncretic divinity of late dynastic times called Ptah-Seker-Osiris, depicted it as a subterranean place deprived of the light of the sun, hot and thirsty, and more dreary than even the Greek Hades or the Hebrew Sheol.

" The West is a land of sleep and darkness heavy, a place where those who settle in it, slumbering in their forms, never wake to see their brethren; they never look any more on their father and their mother, their heart leaves hold of their wives and children.

---

[1] Amélineau, *op. cit.* p. 211; Schmidt, *K.-G.S.* p. 322. The West or Amenti is the Egyptian name for Hades.

The living water which earth has for every one there, is foul here where I am; though it runs for every one who is on earth, foul is for me the water which is with me. I do not know any spot where I would like to be, since I reached this valley! Give me water which runs towards me, saying to me, 'Let thy jug never be without water'; bring to me the north wind, on the brink of water, that it may fan me, that my heart may cool from its pain. The god whose name is *Let Complete Death Come*, when he has summoned anybody to him, they come to him, their hearts disturbed by the fear of him; for there is nobody dares look up to him from amongst gods and men, the great are to him as the small and he spares not [those] who love him, but he tears the nursling from the mother as he does the old man, and everyone who meets him is filled with affright[1]."

The priests took care that such a picture did not fade from want of reproduction and, true to the genius of their nation, elaborated it until its main features are almost lost to us under the mass of details[2]. Especially was this the case with the religion of the Sun-God Ra, who after his fusion with Amon of Thebes at the establishment of the New Empire came to overshadow all the Egyptian cults save that of Osiris. The tombs of the kings at Thebes are full of pictures of the land of this Amenti or the West, in which horror is piled upon horror, and book after book was written that there should be no mistake about the fate lying in wait for the souls of men[3]. In these we see the dead wandering from one chamber to another, breathing a heavy and smoke-laden air[4], and confronted at every step by frightful fiends compounded from the human and bestial forms, whose office is to mutilate, to burn, and to torture the soul. The means of escape open to the dead was, under the xxth dynasty, neither the consciousness of a well-spent life nor the fatherly love of the gods, but the knowledge of passwords and mysterious names[5]. Every chamber had a guardian who demanded of the dead his own

---

[1] Maspero, "Egyptian Souls and their Worlds," *Ét. Égyptol.* I. p. 395.
[2] Maspero, "Hypogées Royaux," *Ét. Égyptol.* t. II. pp. 148, 165.
[3] *Ibid.* pp. 178, 179.
[4] *Ibid.* p. 31.
[5] *Ibid.* pp. 14–15.

name, without repeating which the soul was not allowed to enter[1]. Every fiend had to be repelled by a special exorcism and talisman[2], and every "circle" through which the dead passed had its own song and "mystery," which it behoved the dead to know[3]. Only thus could he hope to win through to the Land of Osiris, where he might enjoy a relative beatitude and be free to go about and visit the other heavenly places[4]. For this purpose, the map, so to speak, of the route was engraved on the walls of the tombs of those who could afford it, and the necessary words to be said written down. Those who were not so rich or so lucky were thought to be parcelled out, like the *fellahin* of that day, or the *villeins* of feudal times, in colonies among the different districts of the lower world, where they flourished or perished according to the number of talismans or "protections" that they possessed[5]. "If ever," says M. Maspero, "there were in Pharaonic Egypt mysteries and initiates, as there were in Greece and in Egypt under the Greeks, these books later than the *Book of the Other World* and the *Book of the Gates* are books of mystery and of initiates[6]." Thereafter, he goes on to say, the ancient popular religion disappeared more and more from Egypt, to give place to the overmastering sense of the terrors of death[7] and the magical means by which it was sought to lighten them.

It is to the survival of these ideas that books like the *Texts of the Saviour* and those in the Papyrus Bruce must be attributed. The Gnostic Christianity of Valentinus, direct descendant as it was of the amalgam of Christianity with pre-Christian faiths which the Ophites had compounded, no sooner reached the great mass of the Egyptian people than it found itself under their influence. In this later Gnostic literature we hear no more of the Supreme Father of Valentinus, "who alone"

[1] *Ibid.* p. 166. To make things more difficult, the guardian sometimes had a different name for every hour. Cf. *ibid.* p. 168.

[2] *Ibid.* pp. 124, n. 2, 163. For the talismans or amulets, see Maspero, "La Table d'Offrandes," *R.H.R.* t. xxxv. (1897), p. 325.

[3] Maspero, "Hyp. Roy." pp. 113, 118.

[4] *Ibid.* pp. 162, 163.   [5] *Ibid.* pp. 41, 163.

[6] *Ibid.* p. 178.   [7] *Ibid.* p. 179.

in his words, " is good " ; no more weight is laid upon the
Faith, Hope, and Love who were the first three members
of his Heavenly Man ; and the Jesus in whom were summed
up all the perfections of the Godhead becomes transformed
into a mere mystagogue or revealer of secret words and things.
All expectation of the immediate arrival of the Parusia or
Second Coming, when the world is to be caught up and all
wickedness to be destroyed, has passed into the background, as
has also the millennium in which the faithful were, in accordance with a very early belief in Egypt, to share the felicity
of those who had been kings on earth[1]. Instead we have only
appeals to the lowest motives of fear and the selfish desire to
obtain higher privileges than ordinary men. Even the avoidance of crime has no other sanction, and complete withdrawal
from the world is advocated on merely prudential grounds ;
while rejection of the mysteries is the unpardonable sin :

" When I have gone unto the light " (says the Jesus of the *Texts
of the Saviour* to His disciples) " preach unto the whole world,
saying : Renounce the whole world and the matter that is therein,
all its cares, its sins, and in a word all its conversation, that ye
may be worthy of the mysteries of the light, that ye may be saved
from all the torments which are in the judgments. Renounce
murmuring, that ye may be worthy of the mysteries of the light,
that ye may escape the judgment of that dog-faced one....
Renounce wrath, that ye may be worthy of the mysteries of the
light, that ye may be saved from the fire of the seas of the dragon-
faced one.... Renounce adultery, that ye may be worthy of
the mysteries of the kingdom of light, that ye may be saved from
the seas of sulphur and pitch of the lion-faced one..... Say unto
them that abandon the doctrines of truth of the First Mystery
' Woe unto you, for your torment shall be worse than that of all

---

[1] The kings, according to a belief which was evidently very old in the
time of the Pyramid-Builders, were supposed to possess immortality as
being gods even in their lifetime. Later, the gift was extended to rulers
of nomes and other rich men, and finally to all those who could purchase the
spells that would assure it. In Maspero's words " La vie d'au delà n'était
pas un droit pour l'Égyptien : il pouvait la gagner par la vertu des formules
et des pratiques, mais il pouvait aussi bien la perdre, et s'il était pauvre
ou isolé, les chances étaient qu'il la perdit à bref délai " (*op. cit.* p. 174).

men, for ye shall dwell in the great ice and frost and hail in the midst of the Dragon of the Outer Darkness, and ye shall escape no more from the world from that hour unto evermore, but ye shall be as stones therein, and in the dissolution of the universe ye shall be annihilated, so that ye exist no more for ever[1] '."

The priests who engraved the horrors of the next world on the walls of the royal tombs at Thebes would probably have written no differently.

Gnosticism then, in Egypt soon relapsed into the magic from which it was originally derived ; and we can no longer wonder that the Fathers of the Church strove as fiercely against it as they did. In the age when books like the *Texts of the Saviour* and the fragments in the Papyrus Bruce could be written, the methods of Clement of Alexandria, who treated Valentinus and his school as Christians bent on the truth though led into error by a misunderstanding of the purport of heathen philosophy, were clearly out of place. " Ravening wolves," " wild beasts," " serpents," and " lying rogues " are some of the terms the Fathers now bestow upon them[2], and as soon as the conversion of Constantine put the sword of the civil power into their hands, they used it to such effect that Gnosticism perished entirely in some places and in others dragged on a lingering existence under other forms. The compromise that had served for some time to reconcile the great mass of the unthinking people to the religion of Christ thus broke down[3] ; and Egypt again showed her power of

---

[1] p. 254, Copt.

[2] de Faye (*Intro.* etc. p. 110) shows clearly, not only that the aims and methods of the school of Valentinus changed materially after its founder's death, but that it was only then that the Catholic Church perceived the danger of them, and set to work to combat them systematically.

[3] To thinkers like Dean Inge (*Christian Mysticism*, 1899, p. 82) this was the natural and appointed end of Gnosticism, which according to him was " rotten before it was ripe." " It presents," he says, " all the features which we shall find to be characteristic of degenerate mysticism. Not to speak of its oscillations between fanatical austerities and scandalous licence, and its belief in magic and other absurdities, we seem, when we read Irenaeus' description of a Valentinian heretic, to hear the voice of Luther venting his contempt upon some *Geisterer* of the sixteenth century." It

resisting and transforming all ideas other than those which thousands of years had made sacred to her people.

Meanwhile, the bridge between Paganism and Christianity which Gnosticism afforded had been crossed by many. As the Ophites showed the inhabitants of Asia Minor how to combine the practice of their ancestral worships with the Christian revelation, so Valentinus and his successors allowed the rich man to enter the kingdom of heaven without the difficulties attendant on the passage of the camel through the needle's eye. The authors of the *Pistis Sophia* and the Bruce Papyrus went further and made it possible for the Egyptian *fellah*—then as now hating change, and most tenacious of his own beliefs—to accept the hope of salvation offered by the new faith while giving up none of his traditional lore upon the nature of the next world. In this way, doubtless, many thousands were converted to Christianity who would otherwise have kept aloof from it, and thus hastened its triumph over the State. But the law which seems to compel every religion to borrow the weapons of its adversaries leads sometimes to strange results, and this was never more plainly marked than in the case of Egypt. The history of Egyptian Christianity has yet to be written ; but it seems from the first to have been distinguished in many important particulars from that which conquered the West, and it is impossible to attribute these differences to any other source than Gnosticism. The Pharaonic Egyptian had always been fanatical, submissive like all Africans to priestly influence, and easily absorbed in concern for his own spiritual welfare. Given the passion for defining the undefinable and the love of useless detail which marked everything in the old faith, and in systems like those of the Coptic texts which form the subject of this chapter he had the religion to his mind. Nor were other and less abstract considerations wanting. The life of a scribe or temple servant, as the race began to lose the vigour which at one time had made them the conquerors of Asia, had come to be looked upon

---

may be so ; yet, after all, Gnosticism in its later developments lasted for a longer time than the doctrines of Luther have done, particularly in the land of their birth.

by the mass of the people as that which was most desirable on
earth[1] ; and here was a faith which called upon the Egyptian to
withdraw from the world and devote himself to the care of his
own soul. Hence the appeal of Gnosticism to those who would
escape hell to renounce all earthly cares fell upon good ground,
and Egypt was soon full of ignorant ascetics withdrawn from
the life of labour and spending their days in ecstasy or contemplation until roused to seditious or turbulent action at
the bidding of their crafty and ambitious leaders. For these
monks and hermits the Hellenistic civilization might as
well not have existed ; but they preserved their native superstitions without much modification, and the practices of magic,
alchemy, and divination were rife among them[2]. So, too,
was the constant desire to enquire into the nature and activities
of the Deity which they had brought with them from their
old faith, and which nearly rent Christianity in twain when
it found expression in the Arian, the Monophysite, and the
Monothelite controversies. In the meantime, the Catholic
Church had profoundly modified her own methods in the
directions which the experience of the Gnostics had shown
to be profitable. The fear of hell came to occupy a larger and
larger part in her exhortations, and apocalypse after apocalypse
was put forth in which its terrors were set out with abundant
detail. Ritual necessarily became of immense importance under
the pressure of converts who believed in the magical efficacy
of prayers and sacraments, in which every word and every
gesture was of mysterious import, and the rites of the Church
were regarded more and more as secrets on which only those
fully instructed might look. The use in them of pictures,
flowers, incense, music, and all the externals of the public
worship of heathen times, which according to Gibbon would
have shocked a Tertullian or a Lactantius could they have
returned to earth[3], must be attributed in the first instance

---

[1] Cf. Maspero, *Life in Ancient Egypt and Assyria*, Eng. ed. 1892, pp.
90–92, for the distaste of the Egyptians of Ramesside times for the life of
a soldier and their delight in that of a scribe.

[2] All these, especially alchemy, are illustrated in the Magic Papyrus
of Leyden known as W. See Leemans, *Pap. Gr.* t. II. pp. 83 *sqq.*

[3] Gibbon, *Decline and Fall*, vol. III. p. 214, Bury's ed.

to the influence of Gnostic converts. Renan is doubtless right when he says that it was over the bridge between Paganism and Christianity formed by Gnosticism that many Pagan practices poured into the Church[1].

Apart from these external matters, on the other hand, the outbreak of Gnosticism possibly rendered a real service to Christianity. To the simple chiliastic faith of Apostolic times, the Gnostics added the elements which transformed it into a world-religion, fitted to triumph over all the older creeds and worships; and their stealthy and in part secret opposition forced the Church to adopt the organization which has enabled her to survive in unimpaired strength to the present day. Jewish Christianity, the religion of the few pious and humble souls who thought they had nothing to do but to wait in prayer and hope for their Risen Lord, had proved itself unable to conquer the world, and its adherents under the name of Ebionites were already looked upon by the Gentile converts as heretics. Gnosticism, so long as it was unchecked, was a real danger to the Church, but without it Christendom would probably have broken up into hundreds of small independent communities, and would thus have dissipated the strength which she eventually found in unity. Threatened on the one hand by this danger, and on the other with the loss of popular favour which the attractions of Gnosticism made probable, the Church was forced to organize herself, to define her doctrines, to establish a regular and watchful hierarchy[2], and to strictly regulate the tendency to mystic speculation and arbitrary exegesis which she could not wholly suppress. Yet these measures could not come into operation without producing a reaction, the end of which we have yet to see.

[1] Renan, *L'Église Chrétienne*, pp. 154, 155, and authorities there quoted. Cf. Hatch, *H. L.* pp. 129, 130, 293, 307–309.

[2] Harnack, *What is Christianity?* p. 210; Duchesne, *Early Christian Church*, p. 32.

CHAPTER XI

MARCION

WE have seen that Valentinus left Alexandria to settle in Rome before promulgating his new doctrine[1], and the Eternal City seems at that time to have drawn to itself as with a magnet all those Oriental teachers of Christianity who wished to make innovation in religion. Rome in the IInd century had become a veritable sink into which poured men of all nations and creeds whether old or new. Besides the great flood of Isiacists, Mithraists, and worshippers of the Great Goddess and of the Syrian Baals, that now began to appear there, Alexander of Abonoteichos came thither under Marcus Aurelius to celebrate his newly-invented mysteries[2], and succeeded in gaining a foothold at the Imperial Court. Moreover in A.D. 140, the terrible war of extermination which Hadrian had been compelled much against his will to wage against the Jewish nation was at length over, and the effect of this was to transfer a great number of Asiatic and African Christians to the world's metropolis, while making it more than ever expedient for them to disclaim connection with the Jews. The slightly contemptuous toleration, too, which the statesmanlike Hadrian seems to have extended to the Christians[3], was not likely to be withdrawn without reason by his philosophic successor, Antoninus Pius; and it was doubtless the consciousness of this which led to the appearance of the various "apologies" for, or defences of, Christianity which Quadratus, Aristides, Justin Martyr, and other persons with some philosophic training now began to put forth. In such of these as have come down to us, the desire

---

[1] Chap. IX. p. 118 *supra*.

[2] Renan, *Marc Aurèle*, p. 49. Cf. Dill, *Nero to Marcus*, pp. 473–477.

[3] Renan, *L'Église Chrétienne*, pp. 31–33, and Hadrian's letter there quoted.

of their authors to dissociate themselves from the Jews, then at the nadir of their unpopularity, is plainly manifest, and no doubt gave the note to the innovators[1]. It is certainly very marked in the heresy of Marcion, which, unlike those of Valentinus and the other Gnostics, was to culminate in the setting-up of a schismatic Church in opposition to that founded on the Apostles.

Marcion was, according to the better account, a wealthy shipowner of Pontus and probably a convert to Christianity[2]. He seems to have been born at Sinope, at one time the most important of the Greek towns on the Southern shore of the Euxine or Black Sea. Mithridates the Great, who was also born there, had made Sinope his capital, and though it had no doubt declined in rank since his time, it must still have been, in the year 100 A.D. (the probable date of Marcion's birth), a flourishing and prosperous place[3]. As in all the cities of Asia Minor, the Stoic philosophy had there obtained a firm hold, and there is some reason for thinking that Marcion received lessons in this before his conversion[4]. Of the circumstances which led to this event we have no knowledge, and it was even said in later times that he was born a Christian, and that his father had been a bishop of the Church. A better founded story is that, on his conversion, he brought into the common fund of the Church a considerable sum of money, which is said to have been paid out to him on his expulsion[5]. When at the

[1] Of the defences mentioned in the text the Apology of Quadratus is the only one still lost to us. Justin Martyr's two Apologies are among the best known of patristic works. That of Aristides was found by Dr Rendel Harris in a Syriac MS. in 1889. For the identification of this by Dean Armitage Robinson with the story of Barlaam and Josaphat, see *Cambridge Texts and Studies*, vol. 1. No. 1.

[2] The account of Marcion's life given by Salmon (*s.v.* Marcion) in the *Dict. Christian Biog.* is here mostly followed. Abundant references to the Fathers and other sources are there given.

[3] Tertullian's talk (*adv. Marcion.* Bk I. c. 1) about its barbarism and the natives living in waggons is mere rhetoric. He probably knew nothing about the place.

[4] *Stoicae studiosus.* Tertullian, *de Praescript.* c. xxx.

[5] *Id. adv. Marc.* Bk IV. c. 4; and *de Praescript.* c. xxx., where the money is said to have been 200 sestertia or nearly £1800.

mature age of forty he went to Rome, it seems reasonable to
suppose that he accepted the orthodox teaching, as it is said
that there was some talk of his being made bishop of what was
even then the richest and highest in rank of all the Christian
Churches. At Rome, however, he fell in with one Cerdo, a
Syrian, who seems to have been already domiciled there and to
have taught in secret a pronouncedly dualistic system in which
God and Matter were set in sharp opposition to one another,
and in which it was held that a good God could not have been
the author of this wicked world[1]. This opinion Marcion
adopted and elaborated, with the result that he was expelled
from the Catholic Church, and thereupon set to work to found
another, having bishops, priests, deacons, and other officers in
close imitation of the community he had left[2]. It is said that
before his death he wished to be reconciled to the Church, but
was told that he could only be readmitted when he had restored
to the fold the flock that he had led away from it. This, on
the authority of Tertullian, he would have been willing to do ;
but his rival Church had by that time so enormously increased
in numbers, that he died, probably in 165 A.D., before he was
able to make the restitution required[3]. This story also can
only be accepted with a great deal of reserve[4].

It is abundantly plain, however, that Marcion was regarded
not only by the professed heresiologists of the succeeding age,
but also by teachers like Justin Martyr and the learned Clement
of Alexandria, as one of the most formidable enemies of the
Church, whose evil influence persisted even after his death[5].
By the reign of Gratian, his rival Church had spread over Italy,
Egypt, Palestine, Arabia, Syria, and Persia[6] ; and, although
the main authority for the increase is the always doubtful one

[1] Tertullian, *adv. Marc.* Bk I. c. 2. Cf. Pseudo Tertullianus, *adv. omn. Haer.* c. XVI.

[2] Neander, *Ch. Hist.* II. p. 150 ; cf. Tertullian, *de Praescript.* c. XLI.

[3] *Ibid. op. cit.* c. XXX. Salmon (*Dict. Christian Biog. s.v.* Marcion) wishes to transfer this story to Cerdo.

[4] Neander, *Church Hist.* II. p. 139, disbelieves it.

[5] Justin Martyr, *First Apol.* cc. XXVI., LVIII. He writes as Marcion's contemporary. Cf. Clem. Alex. *Strom.* Bk III. c. 3.

[6] Epiphanius, *Haer.* XLII. p. 553, Oehler.

of Epiphanius, this last was not likely to have unduly magnified
the success of the Church's rival, and his story has the confirmation of Tertullian that in his time the Marcionites made churches
" as wasps make nests[1]." Every Father of note seems to have
written against the heresiarch who had thus dared, as was said,
to turn away souls from Christ, and Polycarp, the saint and
martyr, when Marcion claimed acquaintance with him in Rome
on the strength of a former meeting in Smyrna, replied with
much heat, " Yes, I know thee! the first-born of Satan[2]."
So late as the Council in Trullo in the VIIth century, special
arrangements had to be made for the reception of Marcionites
who wished to be reconciled to the Church, and forms of abjuration of the sect are said to have lingered until the xth[3].

That this longevity was purchased by no willingness to
make the best of both worlds or to enjoy peace by compromising
with heathenism in the way we have seen prevalent among the
Alexandrian Gnostics, is at once evident. Alone among the
heretics of the sub-Apostolic Age, the Fathers declare, the
Marcionites held fast their faith in time of persecution, while
they refused to frequent the circus and the theatre and practised
an austerity of life putting to shame even the ascetics among
the orthodox[4]. Marcion himself underwent none of the slanders
on his personal morals which theologians generally heap upon
their opponents[5], and none of his tenets are said by either
Tertullian or Epiphanius, who took his refutation most seriously
in hand, to have been borrowed from those Pagan rites or
mysteries which they looked upon as forming the most shameful

---

[1] Tertullian, *adv. Marc.* Bk IV. c. 5.

[2] Eusebius, *Hist. Eccl.* Bk IV. c. 14.

[3] The council was held 692 A.D. See Salmon in *Dict. Christian Biog.*
s.v. Marcion.

[4] Tertullian, *adv. Marc.* Bk I. c. 27.

[5] The story that he seduced a virgin is now generally held to mean
merely that he corrupted the unsullied faith of the Church. Cf. Hegesippus
in Eusebius, *Hist. Eccl.* Bk v. c. 22. So Salmon, *art. cit. supra.* As Neander
points out (*Ch. Hist.* II. p. 136 note), Tertullian, had he known the story,
would certainly have published it. Yet he contrasts Marcion's chastity
with the real or supposed incontinence of his follower, Apelles (*de Praescript.*
c. XXX.).

source from which to contaminate the pure doctrine of the Church. Irenaeus, who was his junior by some twenty or thirty years, and may have known him personally, says indeed that he was a disciple of Simon Magus[1], but in this he may have alluded merely to his position as the founder of a rival Church. Hippolytus is silent about this; but, true to his system of attacking philosophy on account of its supposed connection with heresy, says that Marcion is a disciple, not of Christ, but of Empedocles[2]. There is much to be said for the view that Marcion's heresy was so well and firmly established before the end of the IInd century, that those who then denounced it really knew little of its beginnings[3]. They are, however, unanimous as to the more than Puritanical attitude adopted by its founders. The Marcionites were allowed neither to drink wine nor to eat flesh, and those believers in their tenets who were married had either to separate from their wives or to remain among the catechumens until about to die, it being unlawful for them to receive baptism save on their deathbeds[4].

Marcion's, indeed, seems to have been one of those ruggedly logical and uncompromising natures, not to be led away by reverence for authority or tradition, which appear once or twice in the history of most religions; and it is doubtless this quality which has led Prof. Harnack, as did Neander in the last century, to claim him as the first reformer of the Catholic Church[5]. Like another Luther, Marcion declared that the Church had become corrupted by the additions made by men to the pure teaching she had received from her Founder, and that only in return to her primitive faith was safety to be found. For this primitive faith, he appealed, like the makers of the German Reformation, to the words of Scripture, but he differed from them most widely in the limitations that he placed upon them. It was, he declared, impossible to find any attributes

[1] Irenaeus, Bk I. c. 25, p. 219, Harvey.

[2] Hippolytus, *op. cit.* Bk VII. c. 3, p. 370, Cruice.

[3] So Salmon, *art. cit.*, Renan, and others. This view, however, cannot apply to Justin Martyr who was, as we have seen, his contemporary. See n. 5. p. 205 *supra*.

[4] See Salmon (*Dict. Christian Biog. s.v.* Marcion) for authorities.

[5] See Harnack's article on *Marcion* in *Encyc. Brit.* (11th ed.).

in common between the God of the Old Testament and the Supreme (and benevolent) Being of whom Jesus announced Himself the Son, and he therefore rejected the Old Testament entirely. In the same way, he said that the Canonical Gospels then received among Christians had become overlaid with Jewish elements introduced by the Asiatic converts among whom they were first circulated ; and that the narrative in the Gospel according to Luke was alone trustworthy[1]. From this also, he removed the whole series of traditions concerning the Birth and Infancy of Jesus ; and made it begin in effect with the words of the fourth chapter in which is described the coming-down of Jesus to " Capernaum, a city of Galilee." These he combined with the opening words of Luke iii., so that the event was described as taking place in the " fifteenth year of the reign of Tiberius Caesar[2]." He also excised from the Gospel every-thing which could indicate any respect shown by the Founder of Christianity to the Torah or Law of the Jews, the allusions to the Jewish traditions concerning Jonah and the Queen of Sheba, the supposed fulfilment of the Jewish prophecies in the person and acts of Jesus, and the statement that He took part in the Paschal Feast. He further removed from it every passage which represents Jesus as drinking wine or taking part in any festivity, and in the Lord's Prayer he struck out the petition for delivery from evil, while modifying the " Hallowed be thy name ! " It has been suggested that in this last case he may have given us an older version than that of the Canon[3].

With the remainder of the New Testament, Marcion took similar liberties. He rejected entirely the *Acts of the Apostles*, The Apocalypse of St John, the *Epistle to the Hebrews*, and the Epistles generally called " Pastoral," as well as all those passing under the names of St John, St James, St Peter and St Jude.

---

[1] Tertullian, *adv. Marc.* Bk IV. c. 2. Marcion apparently knew nothing of St John's Gospel, which may not have become public till after his death. Had he done so, as Renan says (*L'Égl. Chrétienne*, p. 71), he would probably have preferred it to any other, because of its markedly anti-Jewish tendency.

[2] According to him, Jesus was not born of woman. Cf. Hippolytus, *op. cit.* Bk VII. c. 31, pp. 383–384, Cruice.

[3] The whole controversy is well summed up in Matter, *Hist. du Gnost.* t. II. pp. 238–242.

For the Apostle Paul, however, Marcion had a profound admiration, pronouncing him to be the only true follower of Jesus, and he accepted with some alterations the ten epistles which he thought could with confidence be attributed to him. These were the Epistles to the Galatians, the two to the Corinthians, the one to the Romans, both those to the Thessalonians, that to the Ephesians or, as he preferred to call it, to the Laodiceans, and those to the Colossians, to Philemon, and to the Philippians. From these ten epistles, he removed everything which described the fulfilment of the prophecies of the Jewish prophets, all allusions to the Parusia or Second Coming, and some expressions which seemed to him to militate against the asceticism that he himself favoured[1]. All these alterations seem to have been set down by Marcion in a book to which he gave the name of the *Antitheses*, and which contained his statement of the incongruities apparent between the Old and New Testaments. This book is now lost, and the details of Marcion's emendations have in consequence to be picked out from the treatise of Tertullian against him, the statements of Epiphanius, and the anonymous discourse *de Recta Fide* which is sometimes included in the works of Origen[2].

If these alterations of the Scriptures generally received depended on any independent tradition, or even upon a rational criticism, they would be of the greatest use to modern textual critics, who have in consequence hoped eagerly that some lucky chance might yet give us a copy of Marcion's Gospel[3]. But the Fathers make no allusion to any claim of the kind ; and in the absence of Marcion's own words, it seems likely that his alterations were merely dictated by the preoccupation regarding the Divine nature which seems with him to have amounted to a passion. Never, he said, could the jealous and irascible God

[1] See Matter, *op. cit.* t. II. pp. 246–260, where Marcion's emendations are given chapter by chapter and their sources cited.

[2] Hahn, in his *Antitheses Marcionis gnostici*, Königsberg, 1823, claimed to have restored this book, while Hilgenfeld has examined the extant remains of Marcion's Gospel in *Das Evangelium Marcions*. He attempted to restore Marcion's *Apostolicon* in the *Zeitschr. für hist. Theol.* 1855.

[3] The *Antitheses* seem to have been seen by Photius in the xth century, so that we need not despair.

of the Jews be identified with the loving and benevolent Spirit
whom Jesus called His Father. Hence there was not one God ;
but two Gods. One of these was the Supreme Being, perfect
in power as in goodness, whose name, as perhaps the Orphics
and the Ophites taught, was Love[1]. Too great to concern
Himself with sublunary things, and too pure, as Plato and
Philo had both said, to have any dealings with an impure and
sinful world, He remained seated apart in the third or highest
heaven, inaccessible to and unapproachable by man, like the
unknown Father of Valentinus and the other Gnostic sects[2].
Below Him was the Creator, or rather the Demiurge or Fashioner
of the World, in constant conflict with matter, which he is
always trying unsuccessfully to conquer and subdue in accordance with his own limited and imperfect ideas. Just, according
to Marcion, was the Demiurge, whom he identified with the
God of the Jews ; and it was this attribute of justice which
prevented him from being considered wholly evil in his nature,
as was Satan, the active agent of the matter with which the
Demiurge was always striving. Yet the Demiurge was the
creator of evil on his own showing[3], and as such is entitled to
no adoration from man, whom he has brought into a world full
of evil. Man's rescue from this is due to the Supreme God,
who sent His Son Jesus Christ on earth that He might reveal
to mankind His Heavenly Father, and thus put an end to the
sway of the Demiurge.

That Jesus on His coming was seized and slain by the Jews,
with at least the connivance of the Demiurge, Marcion admitted.
But as this might seem like a defeat of the Supreme Being by
His inferior, he was forced to accept the theory called Docetism
which was in favour with many other Gnostics. According to
this, the body of Jesus was not real flesh and blood, and had

---

[1] Like the Eros-Phanes of the Orphics and the Ophite Agape. So
Pausanias, Bk IX. c. 27, says the Lycomidae sang in the Mysteries hymns to
Eros, which he had read, thanks to a δαδοῦχος or torch-bearer at Eleusis.

[2] Tertullian, *adv. Marc.* Bk I. c. 2, says that Marcion is obliged to admit
the existence of a Creator, because his work is manifest ; but that he will
never be able to prove that of a higher God than he—a mode of reasoning
which might take him further than he intends.

[3] Isaiah, xlv. 7.

indeed no actual existence, but was a phantasm which only appeared to mankind in the likeness of a man[1]. Hence it mattered nothing that this body, which did not really exist, appeared to suffer, to be slain, and even to rise again. The Supreme God was not mocked, and the resurrection of the body was to Marcion a thing unthinkable.

In lesser matters, Marcion's dislike of the God of the Jews is, perhaps, more marked. Man's body, according to him, was made by the Demiurge out of matter[2], but without any spark from a higher world infused into it, as the Ophites and Valentinus had taught. Hence man was naturally inclined to evil, and the Law which the Demiurge delivered to him was more or less of a snare. Man was sure to give way to the evil desires inherent in matter, and on doing so became with all his race subject to the power of matter and the evil spirits inhabiting it. It is true that the Demiurge had devised a plan of salvation in the shape of the Law of the Jews delivered to them on Sinai. But this concerned one small people only, and it was but a fraction of that community which could hope to observe it in all its forms and ceremonies. Did they do so, the Demiurge would provide for them a modified felicity in that region of Hades called the Bosom of Abraham[3]. For those Gentiles, and even for those Jews who from weakness or obstinacy did not obey the Law, he had prepared punishment and, apparently, eternal tortures. It is true that he promised the Jews a Messiah who should lead them to the conquest of the earth, but this leader certainly was not Jesus[4]; and it is probable that Marcion thought that His Mission had put it out of the power of the Demiurge to fulfil any of these promises.

Possibly it was the same dislike of the Jews that led Marcion to consider St Paul as the only real apostle of Jesus. The others, he said, had overlaid the faith that they had received with Jewish traditions; but Paul, chosen by Jesus after His Ascension[5], had resisted their attempt to reintroduce the Law of the Jews, and was, in his own words, an apostle sent not

---

[1] Tertullian, *adv. Marc.* Bk III. c. 8.   [2] Neander, *Ch. Hist.* II. pp. 142 *sqq.*

[3] Tertullian, *adv. Marc.* Bk III. c. 24.

[4] *Op. cit.* Bk III. c. 4.   Cf. Neander, *Ch. Hist.* II. p. 144.

[5] Tertullian, *op. cit.* Bk v. c. 1.

from men, nor by man, but by Jesus Christ and God the Father
who raised Him from the dead[1]. Marcion also seems to have
laid stress upon St Paul's wonder that the Galatians were " so
soon removed from Him who hath called you to His grace to
another Gospel[2]," with the suggestion that this second gospel
was the contrivance of the Demiurge ; and generally to have
accentuated the controversy between St Peter and St Paul
mentioned in the Epistle bearing their name[3]. From the same
Epistle to the Galatians, Marcion appears to have erased the
name of Abraham where his blessing is said to have " come on
the Gentiles through Jesus Christ[4] " ; and in like manner, to
have read into the passage in the First Epistle to the Corinthians[5], where it is said that " the world by wisdom knew not
God," expressions implying that it was the " Lord of this
World," *i.e.* the Demiurge, who was ignorant of the Supreme
Being[6]. As this ignorance of the Demiurge was a favourite
theme of the Ophites and other Gnostics, it is possible that
Marcion was more indebted to these predecessors of his than
modern commentators on his teaching are inclined to allow ;
but he perhaps justified his reading by tacking it on to the
passage in the Second Epistle to the Corinthians which says
that " the God of this world hath blinded the minds of them
which believe not, lest the light of the glorious gospel of Christ,
who is the image of God, should shine upon them[7]." From the
Epistle to the Romans, in which he seems to have made very
large erasures[8], Marcion draws further arguments in favour of
his contention that the Jews were kept in ignorance of the
Supreme God, relying upon texts like :

" For they [*i.e.* Israel] being ignorant of God's righteousness and
going about to establish their own righteousness, have not submitted
themselves unto the righteousness of God[9]."

So, too, in the Second Epistle to the Thessalonians,
Marcion rejects the passage which declares that Jesus shall

---

[1] Gal. i. 1. Tertullian, *adv. Marc.* Bk v., contains most of Marcion's
dealings with the Pauline Epistles.

[2] Gal. i. 6, 7.   [3] Gal. ii. 11 *sqq.*   [4] Gal. iii. 14.

[5] 1 Cor. i. 21.   [6] Tertullian, *adv. Marc.* Bk v. c. 5.

[7] 2 Cor. iv. 4. Cf. Tertullian, *op. cit.* Bk v. c. 11.

[8] Tertullian, *op. cit.* Bk v. c. 14.   [9] Rom. x. 2, 3.

come "in flaming fire taking vengeance[1]," which he considered
inconsistent with the benevolence of Himself and His Father.
We do not know whom he considered to be the Antichrist there
predicted, as Epiphanius leaves us in doubt whether Marcion
accepted the verses which go by the name of the Little
Apocalypse, but Tertullian seems to imply that Marcion may
have assigned this part to the Messiah of the Demiurge[2]. In
like manner, he is said to have altered the passage in the Epistle
to the Ephesians which speaks of "the mystery which from
the beginning of the world hath been hid in God[3]," so as to
make it appear that the mystery was hid not *in* God, but *from*
the god who created all things, meaning thereby the Demiurge[4].

Until some lucky discovery gives us the text of Marcion's
Antitheses it is difficult to say whether he has been correctly
reported by his adversaries, or whether, which is probable
enough, they have suppressed evidence brought forward by
him in support of these erasures and interpolations. That in
putting them forward, he did so in such a way as to leave many
an opening to a skilled controversialist is easy to believe, and
there are many passages in Tertullian's refutation which show
that his forensically-trained adversary took advantage of these
with more eagerness than generosity. But the noteworthy thing
about the long drawn out dialectic of Tertullian's treatise
Against Marcion, is the way in which Marcion throughout
resolutely abstains from any of the allegorical or figurative
interpolations of Scripture which we have seen so prevalent
among all the Gnostic writers from Simon Magus down to the
authors of the *Pistis Sophia* and its connected texts. Everywhere, it would seem, he took the Biblical texts that he quotes
at their literal meaning and never seems to have attempted to
translate any of them by trope or figure. In like manner, we
find him, so far as his adversaries' account goes, entirely free
from that preoccupation concerning the divisions and order of
the spiritual world which plays so large a part in the speculations
of the systems hitherto described. Nor does he show any
tendency to the deification of abstract ideas which is really at

---

[1] 2 Thess. i. 8.   Cf. Tertullian, *op. cit.* Bk v. c. 16.
[2] Epiphanius, *Haer.* XLII. p. 676, Oehler; Tertullian, *loc. cit.*
[3] Ephes. iii. 8, 9.   [4] Tertullian, *op. cit.* Bk v. c. 18.

the root of all Gnostic systems whether before or after Christ. Nowhere does Marcion let fall an expression which could make us think of the Sophia or Wisdom of God as a separate entity or personified being, nor is the Logos of Plato and his Alexandrian admirers ever alluded to by him. Hence, he in no way contributes to the growth, so luxuriant in his time, of mythology and allegory[1]. In everything he exhibits the hard and unimaginative quality of the practical man.

These considerations have great bearing on the question of the source of his heresy. Had he busied himself, like the Gnostics, with elaborate descriptions of the invisible universe, one would have thought that he owed something to the ancient Egyptian theology, in which such speculations occupied nearly the whole care of its professors. Had he, on the other hand, studied to personify the attributes and qualities of the Supreme Being, one would have been able to connect his teaching with that of the Persian religion, in which, as will be seen in the next chapter, the idea of such personification took the principal place. This connection would have been natural enough, because the province of Pontus, whence Marcion came, had long been subject to the Persian power, and did not become Roman in name until the reign of Nero. Yet no trace of such a connection is even hinted at by adversaries perfectly well informed of the main tenets of the Persian religion[2]. The inference is therefore unavoidable that Marcion's views were original, and that they were formed, as was said by a critic of the last century, by a sort of centrifugal process, and after rejecting in turn all heathen and Jewish elements, as well as most of the traditions which had already grown up in the Catholic Church[3]. That Marcion

---

[1] But see n. 2, p. 217, *infra*.

[2] As is plain from the words of Plutarch quoting, as is generally thought, Theopompus of Chios. See *Is. et Os.* cc. XLVI., XLVII. Al-Bîrûnî, *Chronology*, p. 189, says indeed that both Bardesanes and Marcion borrowed from Zoroaster. But this was eight centuries after Marcion's death, and we have no evidence as to Al-Bîrûnî's means of knowledge of his tenets.

[3] Harvey's *Irenaeus*, I. p. cli. There is a curious resemblance to Marcion's Demiurge in the Clementine *Homilies*, XX. c. 2, where the king of this world who rules by law and rejoices in the destruction of sinners is mentioned. But the *Homilies* are probably Ebionite and certainly, in the form in which they have come down to us, later than Marcion.

was aware of this seems probable from the many efforts made
by him to be reconciled to the Church, or rather to convert the
whole Church to his way of thinking. In this, as in the em-
phasis which he laid on faith rather than knowledge as the
source of man's happiness in this world and the next, he again
anticipated in a most striking manner the views of the German
Reformers some fourteen centuries later[1].

A like analogy is to be seen in the practices of the Marcionite
churches, so far at any rate as we may trust to the reports of
their orthodox opponents. True, as it would seem, to his
conviction of the complete failure of the scheme of the Demiurge,
Marcion set his face even more sternly than our own Puritans
of Cromwell's time against anything that should look like
enjoyment of the things of this world[2]. His followers were
enjoined to eat no meat, to abstain from wine even in the
Eucharist, which in the Marcionite churches was celebrated with
water, and to observe perpetually the strictest continence[3].
The Sabbath was kept by them as a fast and, although this may
look like an obedience to Jewish custom, Epiphanius, who is our
sole authority for the observance, tells us that Marcion expressly
rejected this attribution[4]. Virginity was, according to him, the
only state of life for the true Christian; and although he
freely baptized unmarried men and eunuchs, he refused baptism
to married persons, as has been said, until they were divorced
or on the point of death[5]. To the enticements of the circus,
the gladiatorial shows, and the theatre, the Marcionites used,
according to Tertullian, to return the answer " God forbid ! ";
and they made the same reply, he tells us, when invited to save
their lives in time of persecution by sacrificing a few grains of

[1] Neander *Antignostikus*, Eng. ed. vol. II. p. 490, calls him the representative of the Protestant spirit. In modern times, it is perhaps sufficient
to notice Harnack's predilection, as shown in his *Dogmengeschichte*, for
Marcion and his works. Foakes-Jackson, *Some Christian Difficulties of the
Second and Twentieth Centuries* (Hulsean Lectures), Cambridge, 1903,
pp. 19 *sqq.*, thinks the study of the controversy between Marcion and
Tertullian should especially appeal to Modernists.

[2] Hippolytus, *op. cit.* Bk VII. c. 29, p. 378, Cruice.

[3] Epiphanius, *Haer.* XLII. p. 556, Oehler.　　　　[4] *Op. et loc. cit.*

[5] Tertullian, *adv. Marc.* Bk IV. c. 11　Cf. p. 207, *supra*.

incense to the genius of the Emperor[1]. The reason of all this austerity was apparently their contempt for the kingdom of the Demiurge and their resolve to do nothing to prolong his rule.

Of the spread of the Marcionite heresy we have very little more information than that given above. Prof. Harnack thinks 150–190 A.D. was the "golden age of the Marcionites[2]," but Tertullian evidently considered that some thirty years after the last of these dates they were nearly as numerous as the Valentinians, whom he speaks of as the largest sect of heretics[3]. An inscription found in a Syrian village refers to a "synagogue" of Marcionites occupying a site there in 318 A.D.[4], which is, as has been remarked, older than the earliest dated inscription of the Catholic Church. Theodoret, too, about 440 A.D., boasts of having converted more than a thousand of them, a statement which afterwards swells into eight villages and supposes that they were pretty thickly clustered together[5]. Yet they must have led a miserable existence, being persecuted by the Imperial authorities and their Christian brethren at once, and it is not to be wondered at that Marcion himself addresses some followers in a letter quoted by Tertullian as "my partners in hate and wretchedness[6]." It speaks volumes for their faith that they continued to hold it in spite of everything.

This was the more to their credit that they were by no means at one in matters of belief. In a passage quoted in a former chapter, Tertullian says that the Marcionites thought it fair to do what Marcion had done, that is, to innovate on the faith according to their own pleasure. This is a rhetorical way of putting it; for the successors of Marcion seem to have differed

---

[1] Tertullian, *op. cit.* Bk I. c. 27.

[2] Harnack in *Encyclopaedia Britannica* (11th ed.) *s.v.* "Marcion."

[3] He always couples Valentinus and Marcion together. Cf. *de Praescpt.* cc. XXIX., XXX. Justin Martyr, Marcion's contemporary, says (*First Apolog.* c. XXVI.) that "he is even now teaching men of every nation to speak blasphemies." Renan, *L'Égl. Chrétienne*, p. 363, thinks that the Marcionites were "much the most numerous sect before Arius."

[4] Foakes-Jackson, *Hulsean Lectures*, p. 108. Cf. Sanday, *The Gospels in the 2nd Cent.*, Oxford, 1876, p. 236.

[5] Theodoret, *Epp.* 113 and 145.

[6] συμμισούμενοι καὶ συνταλαίπωροι: Tertullian, *adv. Marc.* Bk IV. cc. 9, 30.

among themselves mainly upon one point, which was, in fact, the number of " principles " which lay at the beginning of things[1]. Thanks to his Stoical training, Marcion was forced to assign a large part in the formation of the cosmos to Matter, which he nevertheless thought to be essentially evil. But in that case, how did it come into existence ? It surely could not be the creation of the Supreme and benevolent Being whose name was Love ; and if not, how did it come to exist independently of Him ? To these questions it is possible that the essentially practical genius of Marcion saw no need to return any answer, and was content to regard them, like Epicurus before him, as insoluble problems. But his followers apparently refused to do so ; and hence there arose considerable diversity of opinion. According to an Armenian author of late date, Marcion himself taught that there were *three* principles, that is, the Supreme God, the Demiurge or Creator, and Matter, which he regarded as a sort of spouse to the Demiurge[2]. This, however,

[1] See Neander, *Ch. Hist.* vol. II. pp. 151 *sqq.* and Matter, *Hist. du Gnost.* t. II. pp. 298, 304.

[2] Eznig of Goghp, from whose History of the Armenian Church quotation has been made above. He says that Marcion taught that there were three heavens, in the highest of which dwelt the Good God, in the next the God of the (Jewish) Law, and in the third his angels. Below this lay Hyle or Matter who existed independently and was female. From the union of the God of the Law and Hyle, this earth was produced, after which its Father retired to his own heaven, leaving the earth to the rule of Hyle. When he desired to make man, Hyle supplied the dust of which he was formed, into which the God of the Law breathed his own spirit. Adam became the adorer of Hyle, upon which the God of the Law informed him that, if he worshipped any other God but him, he should die. On this Adam withdrew from Hyle, and this last, becoming jealous, made a number of gods and filled the world with them. Hence all men were cast into hell at death, until the Good God looked down from the highest heaven, had pity on them, and sent his Son to deliver the "spirits in prison," which He did directly He went down into hell after His own death. After Jesus had revealed Himself to the Creator and received his confession of ignorance, Jesus illuminated Paul and made him His apostle. It is extremely unlikely that this story should have formed part of Marcion's own teaching, although it may possibly have been told by some follower of his of Semitic blood, or, as Salmon suggests, by Cerdo. It is to be found in Neumann's translation of Eznig in the *Zeitschr. für hist. Theol.* vol. IV. and in the *Dict. Christian Biog. s.v.* Marcion.

is extremely unlikely in view of the unanimous assertion of the
Fathers nearer to him in point of time that he taught the
existence of two principles only ; and it is probable that the
theory of three principles, if seriously advanced, must have been
the work of one of his followers.   Tertullian, whose sophistry in
combating Marcion's teaching in this respect is here particularly
apparent, points out, indeed, that if the Creator be held to be
self-originated and not himself the creature of the Supreme
God, there must be nine gods instead of two[1]; but there is no
reason to suppose that Marcion ever troubled himself about such
dialectical subtleties.

The case was different with Apelles, who was certainly later
in date than Marcion and perhaps succeeded him in the headship of the sect, either immediately or at one remove[2].
According to Tertullian, Apelles left Rome for Alexandria
where he no doubt came in contact with the Gnostic opinions
there rife[3].   The slander that Tertullian sets on foot about him
to the effect that he forsook his master's continence and was
addicted to the company of women is unexpectedly refuted by
Tertullian's contemporary, Rhodo[4].   But Apelles must have
come in contact in Alexandria with the followers of Valentinus
and other Gnostic teachers, and their arguments no doubt
compelled him to modify the strict dualism of his master.
According to Rhodo, Apelles asserted that there was only one
principle of all things, which would imply that the Demiurge
was the creature of the Supreme God, and that Matter, instead
of being essentially evil and independent, must have been also
created by Him.   Hippolytus, who was possibly a little later than
Rhodo, amplifies this by the statement that Apelles held the
Demiurge to be the fashioner of things coming into being

---

[1] Tertullian, *adv. Marc.* Bk I. c. 16.

[2] Epiphanius, *Haer.* XLII. p. 688, Oehler, says Marcion was succeeded
by Lucian, whom Apelles followed.   Hippolytus, *op. cit.* Bk VII. cc. 37, 38,
p. 393, Cruice, is probably the source of Epiphanius' statement; but he does
not seem to have had any first-hand knowledge of the Marcionite heresy
or its chiefs, and is not here so good a witness as Tertullian, or Irenaeus,
who mentions neither Lucian nor Apelles.

[3] Tertullian, *de Praescript.* c. XXX.

[4] Eusebius, *Hist. Eccl.* Bk IV. c. 13.

(subsequent to him)[1], and that there was a third god or angel of
a fiery nature who inspired Moses, and even a fourth who was
the cause of evil. In this the Gnostic idea of correspondence
or reflection of one world in another is manifest; but it is evident
that it also approaches more nearly than does the uncompromising dualism of Marcion himself to the teaching of the Catholic
Church. The same tendency to compromise is evident in
Apelles' willingness to use the books of both the Old and the
New Testament, quoting with regard to them, if Epiphanius is
to be believed, the apocryphal saying of Jesus "Be ye wise
money-changers!" to be found in, among other works, the
Pistis Sophia[2]. Apelles seems also to have modified his master's
teaching with regard to the body of Jesus, which was, he said,
no phantasm, but a real body of flesh and blood assumed by
Him on His descent to the earth, and returned by Him piece by
piece on His Ascension to the different elements whence it was
drawn. His indebtedness in this to the sources from which the
author of the *Pistis Sophia* drew the same doctrine needs no
demonstration. Yet there is no reason to assert that Apelles
considered these "corrections" of Marcion's teaching in any
way essential or binding on his followers. He seems, too, to
have adopted one of the practices of the primitive Church in
paying attention to the ecstatical visions of "prophets" of
both sexes, his faith in the prophecies of a virgin named
Philumene being the foundation of Tertullian's slander on his
morals. There can be no doubt, however, that in spite of these
tendencies, he remained in essentials a true follower of Marcion,
and that like his master, he deprecated enquiry into insoluble
problems. "One ought not," he said, as Rhodo reports, "to
examine doctrine, but everyone should be steadfast in the faith.
Those who trust in Him that was crucified will be saved, if
only they do good works[3]." Herein he also, like Marcion

---

[1] ἐδημιούργησε τὰ γενόμενα. Hippolytus, *op. cit.* Bk VII. c. 37, p. 393,
Cruice.

[2] Epiphanius, *Haer.* XLII. p. 694, Oehler. The same Logion or saying
is also found in Clem. Alex. *Strom.* Bk I. c. 28, in the *Apostolical Constitutions*,
Bk II. c. 37, and in Clem. *Hom.* XVIII. c. 20.

[3] Eusebius, *Hist. Eccl.* Bk v. c. 13.

himself, seems to have anticipated by many centuries the teaching of the German Reformers.

Other followers of Marcion there were who, thanks to our lack of information concerning them, are to us merely names. Thus Tatian, who was according to tradition a disciple of Justin Martyr but fell away from orthodoxy after his teacher's death, seems to have held a kind of intermediate position between the two great schools of heresy. While teaching, according to Irenaeus, a system of aeons not unlike that of Valentinus, he adopted in full the notions of Marcion as to abstinence from marriage, from the eating of flesh, and from the use of wine, and may have been the founder of a separate sect called Encratites[1]. We hear, too, of one Prepon, "an Assyrian" or native of Syria, a follower of Marcion, whom Hippolytus represents as teaching that Jesus Himself was intermediate between the good and evil deities and came down to earth to be freed from all evil[2]. Rhodo also speaks[3] of Potitus and Basilicus, followers of Marcion, who held fast to his doctrine of two principles, while Syneros, as he affirms, led a school which asserted that there were three "natures." Lucian also, who, according to Hippolytus and Epiphanius, came in point of time between Marcion and Apelles[4], may have inclined to the same doctrine, and taught, unlike Marcion, that there would be a resurrection, not of the body nor of the soul, but of some part of man which he also defined as being of a "third nature[5]."

The conversion of Constantine put a violent end to any open propagation of the doctrines of Marcion or his successors. In the picturesque words of Eusebius "the lurking-places of the heretics were broken up by the Emperor's commands, and the savage beasts which they harboured were put to flight." Hence, he goes on to tell us, many of those who had been "deceived" crept secretly into the Church, and were ready to

[1] Irenaeus, Bk I. c. 26, § 1, p. 220, Harvey. According to Hippolytus, *op. cit.* Bk VIII. c. 16, p. 416, Cruice, he had been a disciple of Justin Martyr.

[2] Hippolytus, *op. cit.* Bk VII. c. 31, p. 382, Cruice.

[3] Eusebius, *op. et loc. cit. supra.*

[4] Hippolytus, *op. cit.* Bk VII. c. 37, p. 393, Cruice ; Epiphanius, *Haer* XLIII. p. 688, Oehler.

[5] Tertullian, *de Resurrectione*, c. II.

secure their own safety by every sort of dissimulation[1]. This practice, as we have seen, had always been popular among the Gnostics properly so called, whose religion consisted in part in the knowledge of the formulas secretly imparted and preserved with jealous care from all but the initiated. Although there is no distinct proof that the same course was now adopted by the Marcionites, there is some reason for thinking that this was the case. The postponement of baptism noticed above must have early divided the members of the Marcionite churches into grades of which the largest was in an inferior position to the others. It is unlikely that these catechumens, who might witness but not share in the sacraments celebrated for their higher-placed brethren, should have courted persecution on behalf of a faith with which they were not fully entrusted. The outbreak of the Arian controversy, which followed so closely on the conversion of Constantine, also carried within the Catholic Church those speculations about the Divine nature which had hitherto formed a fruitful source of dissension among the Marcionites themselves. With their synagogues and meeting-places taken away from them and handed over to the Catholics, many of them must have looked about for some tolerated community which they could join, and of all that thus offered themselves, the Catholic Church offered the greatest inducements to them.

Yet another way was open to the convinced Marcionite who could not bring himself to reject Marcion's view that the true purport of Jesus' teaching had been obscured by the additions of Judaizing apostles. The sect of the followers of Manes, who began to show themselves in the Western part of the Roman Empire shortly before Constantine's conversion, professed a dualism more uncompromising than any that Marcion had taught, and coupled with it an organization so skilful and effective that it was able for some ten centuries longer to defy the efforts of the rest of Christendom for its suppression. In its division of all Manichaeans into the two great classes of Perfect and Hearers it drew very close to Marcionite practice ; and the liberty which it allowed the Hearers of outwardly

---

[1] Eusebius, *Vita Constantini*, Bk III. cc. 64–66.

professing any faith they pleased must have enabled the
Marcionite who joined it to keep those articles of his former
creed most dear to him without coming into violent collision
with either Church or State. Hence the tradition seems well
founded which asserts that the majority of those Marcionites,
who did not become reconciled with the Catholic Church after
Constantine's alliance with it, joined the ranks of the Manichaeans, and so ceased to exist as a separate community[1].

The direct influence of Marcion's teaching upon that of the
Catholic Church was probably very small. In spite of the
efforts of recent writers to maintain the contrary[2], it is difficult
to see that this first attempt, honest and sincere as it undoubtedly was, at the reformation of Christianity ever bore
fruit of lasting value. Its main principle which, as we have
seen, was the rejection of the Jewish scriptures and their bearing
upon the Mission of Jesus, has been ignored, since Marcion's
death as in his lifetime, by every other Church and sect professing Christian doctrines. His common-sense view, that the
words of the Christian Bible must mean what their authors and
their contemporaries would have naturally taken them to mean,
and do not for the most part contain any deeply hidden or
allegorical significance, was in like manner repudiated by the
whole of Christendom, which, up to the latter part of the xixth
century, continued to construe the greater part of its sacred
books by trope and figure[3]. There remains then only the
asceticism and austerity that Marcion practised which the
orthodox could have borrowed from him. But, we have seen
that the religious abstinence from procreation, and from the
use of meat and wine, can be traced back to the appearance of
Orphism in Greece some five hundred years before the Birth of
Christ; and if the Christian Church adopted, as it partly did,

---

[1] So Salmon in *Dict. Christian Biog.* and Harnack in *Encyclopaedia
Britannica*, both *s.v.* Marcion.

[2] Hatch, *H.L.* p. 77, n. 1, quoting Harnack.

[3] Hatch, *op. cit.* pp. 75, 76, shows that the allegorical method introduced
by the Gnostics in order to avoid the difficulty of reconciling the Old
Testament with the New was at first scornfully rejected, but was soon
adopted by the orthodox, and was pursued by both Catholic and Protestant
writers up to a few years ago.

these practices in a modified form, it was by way of inheritance
from a source which was much nearer to it than Marcion's
heresy.   That many of Marcion's ideas have been revived in
our own day is likely enough, and this opinion has been put
forward with much skill and point by Dr Foakes-Jackson in
his Hulsean Lectures.   But this is a case of revival rather than
of descent, and a reformer who has to wait some eighteen
centuries before his ideas meet with acceptance, may well be
held to have failed to influence after ages.

Notwithstanding this, the heresy of Marcion will always have
great interest for the student of the History of Religions.   The
success—fugitive as such things go, but real enough for a
time—with which Marcion set up a Church over against that
tremendous polity which has been called without much exaggeration " the very master-piece of human wisdom," would be alone
sufficient to make it precious in the eyes of those who are not
blind to the romance of history.   To archaeologists it is the
more interesting that it is only in its direction that we are likely
to receive in future much additional light upon the struggles of
nascent Christianity with one category of its competitors.   The
very voluminous writings of the other Gnostics were destroyed
by the triumphant Church with such minute care that the Coptic
texts described in the last chapter form the only relics of this
once enormous literature that have survived to us.   The heathen
religions which for some time disputed the ground with the
Church have also left few traces partly for the same reason,
and partly because the secrecy to which they pledged their
votaries made it unlikely that many written documents of these
faiths would survive.   But the *Antitheses* of Marcion were in
the hands of Photius in the xth century ; and, although it is
dangerous to prophesy in such matters, it is by no means
impossible that some lucky discovery within the borders of the
Turkish Empire may yet give us a MS. that will enable us to
reconstruct them.   If that should ever be the case, we shall be
in a far better position than we are now to decide whether the
analogies between Marcionism and Protestantism that have been
detected of late years are essential or superficial.

CHAPTER XII

THE WORSHIP OF MITHRAS

FEW of us, perhaps, are inclined to recognize that, from its
first establishment down to the Mahommedan Invasion of the
viith century, the Roman Empire found itself constantly in the
presence of a bitter, determined, and often victorious enemy.
Alexander had conquered but had not destroyed the Persians ;
and, although the magic of the hero's personality held them
faithful to him during his too brief life, he was no sooner dead
than they hastened to prove that they had no intention of
tamely giving up their nationality.   Peucestas, the Royal body-
guard who received the satrapy of Persia itself on his master's
death, and was confirmed in it at the first shuffling of the cards
at Triparadisus, found it expedient to adopt the Persian
language and dress, with the result that his subjects conceived
for him an affection only equal to that which they afterwards
showed for Seleucus[1].   Later, when the rise of the Parthian
power under Arsaces brought about the defeat of Seleucus II
Callinicus, the opposition to European forms of government
found a centre further north[2], whence armies of lightly-equipped
horsemen were able to raid up to the Eastern shores of the
Mediterranean[3].   Thanks probably to the knowledge of this
support in reserve, when Western Asia found the military power
of the Greek kings becoming exhausted by internecine wars,
she began to throw off the alien civilization that she had in

[1] Droysen, *Hist. de l'Hellénisme*, t. II. pp. 33, 289.

[2] *Op. cit.* III. pp. 351, 352; 439, 450. As Droysen points out, in this
respect there was no practical difference between Parthian and Persian.

[3] As in B.C. 41, when the Parthians under Pacorus " rushed " Palestine.
See Morrison, *The Jews under the Romans*, p. 58, for authorities. Cf.
Chapter V. Vol. I. p. 101, n. 3, *supra*.

part acquired, and to return more and more to Persian ways[1]. When the Romans in their turn set to work to eat up the enfeebled Greek kingdoms, they quickly found themselves in presence of a revived nationality as firmly held and nearly as aggressive as their own, and henceforth Roman and Parthian were seldom at peace.   The long struggle with Mithridates, who gave himself out as a descendant of Darius[2], taught the Romans how strong was the reaction towards Persian nationality even in Asia Minor, and the overthrow of Crassus by the Parthians convinced his countrymen for a time of the folly of pushing their arms too far eastwards.

With the establishment of the Empire, the antagonism between Rome and Persia became still more strongly marked, and a struggle commenced which lasted with little intermission until the foundation of the Mahommedan Caliphate.   In this struggle the advantage was not always, as we should like to think, on the side of the Europeans.   While Augustus reigns, Horace boasts, there is no occasion to dread the " dreadful Parthians[3] " ; but Corbulo is perpetually fighting them, and when Nero commits suicide, the legend immediately springs up that the tyrant is not dead, but has only betaken himself beyond the Euphrates to return with an army of Rome's most dreaded enemies to lay waste his rebellious country[4].   Towards the close of the first Christian century, Trajan, fired, according to Gibbon, by the example of Alexander, led an army into the East and achieved successes which enabled him to add to his titles that of Parthicus[5] ; but the whole of his Oriental conquests were given back by the prudent Hadrian on his succession to the throne.   During the reign of Marcus Aurelius, Avidius Cassius

[1] This is shown by, among other things, the claims of the kings of Armenia, Cappadocia, and Pontus to be descended from the seven heroes who delivered Persia from the Magians after the death of Cambyses.   See Droysen, *op. cit.* II. p. 519 ; III. pp. 82, 83.

[2] Droysen, *op. cit.* III. p. 83.

[3] Horace, *Odes*, Bk IV. Ode 5.   Cf. his *Carmen Seculare*.

[4] Renan, *L'Antéchrist*, pp. 317, 318, for authorities.   A critical essay on the Neronic myth and its congeners is to be found in Dr Charles' *Ascension of Isaiah*, p. li *sqq.*

[5] Gibbon, *Decline and Fall* (Bury's ed.), vol. I. pp. 5, 205.

obtained some solid victories on the frontier ; but Macrinus is said to have bought off the Parthians with a bribe of nearly two millions of money. The rise of the Sassanian house and the retransfer of the leadership from the Parthians to their kinsmen in Persia proper brought about the reform of the Persian religion, and added another impulse to the increasing strength of Persian national feeling. Alexander Severus may have gained some successes in the field over Ardeshîr or Artaxerxes, the restorer of the Persian monarchy[1] ; but in the reign of the last named king's son and successor Sapor, the capture of the Emperor Valerian with his whole army, and the subsequent ravaging of the Roman provinces in Asia by the victors, showed the Republic how terrible was the might of the restored kingdom[2]. Aurelian, the conqueror of Palmyra, did much to restore the prestige of Roman arms in the East ; and although he was assassinated when on the march against Persia, the Emperor Carus shortly after led a successful expedition into the heart of the Persian kingdom[3]. In the reign of Diocletian, indeed, the Persians lost five provinces to the Romans[4] ; but under Constantine the Great the Romans were again vanquished in the field, and the Persians were only prevented by the heroic resistance of the fortified town of Nisibis and an incursion into their Eastern provinces of tribes from Central Asia from again overrunning the Asiatic possessions of Rome[5].

Henceforward, the history of the long contest between the two great empires—" the eyes," as the Persian ambassador told Galerius, " of the civilized world[6]," is the record of almost uninterrupted advance on the part of Persia and of continual retreat on the side of Rome. The patriotic enthusiasm of a Julian, and the military genius of a Belisarius, aided by the dynastic revolutions common among Oriental nations, might for

[1] Gibbon, *op. cit.* I. p. 209. Severus' victories are doubted by Gibbon ; and Prof. Bury apparently supports his author.

[2] *Op. cit.* I. pp. 269, 270. Prof. Bury in his Appendix 17 points out that the whole history of Valerian's capture is still very obscure.

[3] *Op. cit.* I. p. 340.

[4] *Op. cit.* I. p. 375. See Prof. Bury's note 83 on page cited.

[5] *Op. cit.* II. pp. 228–231.

[6] *Op. cit.* I. p. 373.

a time arrest the progress of the conquering Persians ; but, bit by bit, the Asiatic provinces slipped out of the grasp of the European masters of Constantinople.   In 603 A.D., it looked as if Persia were at length in the position to deliver the final blow in a war which had lasted for more than five centuries.   By the invasion of Chosroes and his successive captures of Antioch, Jerusalem, and Egypt, it seemed as if the Persians had restored the world-empire of Cambyses and Darius ; but the Persians then discovered, as Xerxes had done a millennium earlier, how dangerous it is for Orientals, even when flushed by conquest, to press Europeans too far.   The Roman Emperor Heraclius, who never before or afterwards gave much proof of military or political capacity, from his besieged capital of Constantinople collected an army with which he dashed into Persia in a manner worthy of Alexander himself.   After six brilliant campaigns he dictated to the Persians a triumphant peace in the very heart of their empire[1].   A few years later, and its shattered and disorganized remains fell an easy prey to the Mahommedan invaders.

The effect of this long rivalry might have been expected to produce in the Romans during its continuance a hearty dislike of the customs and institutions of the nation opposed to them ; but almost the exact contrary was the result.   It may be argued that Rome's proved skill in government was in no small measure due to her ready adoption of all that seemed to her admirable in the nations that she overcame.   Or it may be that the influence which the memory of Alexander exercised over all those who succeeded to his empire led them to imitate him in his assumption of Persian manners.   The fact remains that, long before the division of the Roman Empire into East and West, the Romans displayed a taste for Oriental luxury and magnificence which seems entirely at variance with the simplicity and austerity of the republican conquerors of Carthage.   It is hardly too much to say that while Alexander's conscious aim was to make Asia Greek, the Romans, on possessing themselves of his Asiatic conquests, allowed themselves to become to a

---

[1] Gibbon, *op. cit.* v. pp. 78 *sqq.*   Winwood Reade, *Martyrdom of Man*, pp. 249, 250, tells the story excellently and dramatically.

great extent " Medized," and showed an unexpected admiration for the habits and culture of Alexander's Persian subjects.

It may of course be said that this was in external matters only, and that the " Persian furniture " which excited Horace's wrath[1] might if it stood alone be looked upon as merely a passing fashion ; but the Court ceremonial introduced by Diocletian argues a steady tendency towards Persian customs and forms of government that must have been in operation for centuries. The household of a Julian Caesar was no differently arranged from that of a Roman noble of the period, and his title of Prince of the Senate showed that he was only looked upon as the first of his equals. But Diocletian was in all respects but language a Persian emperor or Shah, and his style of " Lord and God," his diadem, his silken state dress, the elaborate ritual of his court, and the long hierarchy of its officials, were all designed to compel his subjects to recognize the fact[2]. As usual, the official form of religion in the Roman Empire had for some time given indications of the coming change in the form of government. The sun had always been the principal natural object worshipped by the Persians, and a high-priest of the Sun-God had sat upon the Imperial throne of Rome in the form of the miserable Heliogabalus. Only 33 years before Diocletian, Aurelian, son of another Sun-God's priestess and as virile and rugged as his predecessor was soft and effeminate, had also made the Sun-God the object of his special devotion and of an official worship. Hence Diocletian and his colleague Galerius were assured in advance of the approval of a large part of their subjects when they took the final plunge in 307 A.D., and proclaimed Mithras, " the Unconquered Sun-God," the Protector of their Empire[3].

In spite of this, however, it is very difficult to say how

[1] Horace, *Odes*, Bk I. Ode 38.

[2] Gibbon, *op. cit.* I. p. 382. Cf. Cumont, *Religions Orientales*, p. 171. Lactantius, *de Mort. Persecutor.* c. XXI., says that this was the conscious aim of Galerius. Although his authority in such a matter is suspect, there can be little doubt of the fact.

[3] The actual decree of the emperors is given in Cumont, *Textes et Monuments*, t. II. Inscr. 367. The date should probably be 304 A.D. See n. on Table of Dates, Vol. I. *supra*.

Mithras originally became known to the Romans. Plutarch says indeed that his cult was first introduced by the Cilician pirates who were put down by Pompey[1]. This is not likely to be literally true ; for the summary methods adopted by these sea-robbers towards their Roman prisoners hardly gave much time for proselytism, while most of the pirates whom Pompey spared at the close of his successful operations he deported to Achaea, which was one of the few places within the Empire where the Mithraic faith did not afterwards show itself. What Plutarch's story probably means is that the worship of Mithras first came to Rome from Asia Minor, and there are many facts which go to confirm this. M. Cumont, the historian of Mithraism, has shown that, long before the Romans set foot in Asia, there were many colonies of emigrants from Persia who with their *magi* or priests had settled in Asia Minor, including in that phrase Galatia, Phrygia, Lydia, and probably Cilicia[2]. When Rome began to absorb these provinces, slaves, prisoners, and merchants from them would naturally find their way to Rome, and in time would no doubt draw together for the worship of their national deities in the way that we have seen pursued by the worshippers of the Alexandrian Isis and the Jewish exiles. The *magi* of Asia Minor were great supporters of Mithridates, and the Mithridatic wars were no doubt responsible for a large number of these immigrants.

Once introduced, however, the worship of Mithras spread like wild-fire. The legions from the first took kindly to it, and this is the less surprising when we find that many of them were recruited under the earliest emperors in Anatolian states like Commagene, where the cult was, if not indigenous, yet of very early growth[3]. Moreover the wars of the Romans against the Persians kept them constantly in the border provinces of the two empires, where the native populations not infrequently changed masters. The enemy's town that the legions besieged one year might therefore give them a friendly reception the next; and there was thus abundant opportunity for the acquaintance

[1] Plutarch, *Vit. Pomp.* c. XXIV.
[2] Cumont, *Rel. Or.* pp. 167, 168 ; 173, 174 ; *id. T. et M.* I. pp. 9, 10. Cf. *P.S.B.A.* 1912, pp. 127, 128.   [3] Cumont, *T. et M.* I. p. 247.

of both sides with each others' customs. When the Roman troops marched back to Europe, as was constantly the case during the civil wars which broke out on the downfall of the Julian house, they took back with them the worship of the new god whom they had adopted, and he thus became known through almost the whole of the Roman Empire[1]. "From the shores of the Euxine to the north of Brittany and to the fringe of the Sahara[2]," as M. Cumont says, its monuments abound, and, he might have added, they have been met with also in the Egyptian Delta, in Babylon, and on the northern frontiers of India. In our own barbarous country we have found them not only in London and York, but as far west as Gloucester and Chester and as far north as Carlisle and Newcastle[3]. The Balkan countries, like Italy, Germany, Southern France, and Spain, are full of them ; but there was one part of the Roman Empire into which they did not penetrate freely. This was Greece, where the memories of the Persian Wars long survived the independence of the country, and where the descendants of those who fought at Salamis, Marathon, and Thermopylae would have nothing to do with a god coming from the invaders' fatherland. It is only very lately that the remains of Mithras-worship have been discovered at the Piraeus and at Patras, in circumstances which show pretty clearly that it was there practised only by foreigners[4].

Notwithstanding this popularity, it is not easy to say exactly what god Mithras' European worshippers considered him to be. If length of ancestry went for anything in such matters, he might indeed claim a greater antiquity than any deity of the later Roman Pantheon, with the single exception of the Alexandrian gods. Mithras was certainly worshipped in Vedic India, where his name of Mitra constantly occurs in the sacred texts as the "shining one," meaning apparently the material sun[5]. He is there invoked in company with Varuna, generally con-

---

[1] Dill, *Roman Society from Nero to Marcus Aurelius*, pp. 593–597.

[2] Cumont, *T. et M.* I. p. 248.

[3] For the list see Cumont, *T. et M.* I. p. 258, n. 7. He thinks the worship was first introduced here by the legions from Germany.

[4] Avezou and Picard, "Bas-relief Mithriaque," *R.H.R.* t. LXIV. (Sept. Oct. 1911), pp. 179 *sqq.*

[5] Cumont, *T. et M.* I. p. 223, n. 2.

sidered the god of the sky, and therefore according to some, the prototype of the Greek Zeus and the Latin Jupiter[1]. His appearance in a similar connection in the sacred books of the Persians led the founders of the comparative study of religion to think that he must have been one of the primitive gods of their hypothetical Aryan race, and that his worship must go back to the imaginary time when Persians and Hindus dwelt side by side in the plains of Cashmere. But this theory is giving way before proof that the original home of the Indo-European race was Europe, and has been badly shaken by the discovery at Boghaz Keui of tablets showing that the gods Mithra and Varuna were gods of the Mitannians or Hittites[2] at some date earlier than 1500 B.C., and therefore long before the appearance of the Persians in history. If the worship of Mithras were not indigenous in Western Asia, it may therefore well have come there independently of the Persians[3].

There is no doubt, however, that the roots of Mithras-worship went very far down into the Persian religion. In the Yashts or hymns which are the earliest evidence of primitive Iranian beliefs, Mithra—to use the Avestic spelling of his name—frequently appears, not indeed as the material sun, but as the " genius of the heavenly light " which lightens the whole universe[4] and is the most beneficent among the powers of Nature. Mithras is not here, however, the Supreme Being, nor even the highest among the gods benevolent to man. This last place is occupied in the Zend Avesta by Ahura Mazda,

---

[1] Herodotus, Bk I. c. 131.   Cf. F. Max Müller, *Hibbert Lectures*, p. 276. The similarity of name between Varuna and the Greek Ouranos is fairly obvious.   Prof. Hope Moulton, *Early Zoroastrianism*, 1913, pp. 391, 392, n. 3, argues that the Persian god of the sky was called Dyaush or Zeus.

[2] Certainly of the Mitannians, who, according to Prof. Hugo Winckler, were one of the two main branches of the Hittites, and a Syrian people. See his report on Excavations at Boghaz Keui in the *Mitteilungen* of the Deutsche Orient-Gesellschaft for 1907.   The text is given in the *J.R.A.S.* for 1910, pp. 723 *sqq.*

[3] If we accept the latest theory which makes Russia the original home of the Aryan race (see Zaborowski, *Les Peuples Aryens d'Asie et d'Europe* Paris, 1908, p. 424) it may have even had a European origin.

[4] Cumont, *T. et M.* I. p. 225.

" the omniscient lord," who appears to be the Persian form of Varuna, the god of the sky whom we have seen associated with Mitra in the Vedas[1]. Nor is Mithras in the Zend Avesta one of the six Amshaspands, the deified abstractions or personified attributes of Ahura Mazda, who, in the later developments of the Persian religion, occupy towards him much the same position that the " Roots " of Simon Magus and the Aeons of the Pleroma among the Gnostics do towards the Boundless Power or the Ineffable Bythos[2]. In the later Avestic literature, he appears as the chief of the Izeds or Yazatas, a race of genii created by Ahura Mazda, who are the protectors of his universe and the helpers of mankind in their warfare against the powers of darkness[3]. In the latest as in the earliest Persian view of the personality of Mithras, therefore, it is plain that he occupies an intermediate position between the Creator and man.

It is not, however, in the religion associated with the name of Zoroaster that we must look for the origin of Mithraism. The date of the sacred books of Mazdeism and the historical existence of Zoroaster himself have recently been brought down to as late as the VIIth century B.C.[4] and the appearance in Asia of the Persian tribes as conquerors, whereas Mithras was, as we have seen, worshipped in Asia Minor nearly a millennium earlier. Moreover, the strict dualism which set Ahriman, the god of darkness and evil, in eternal and perhaps equal opposition to Ormuzd, the god of light and goodness, seems to have been unknown before the Sassanid reform in 226 A.D., by which time the worship of Mithras in Europe was at its apogee[5]. M. Cumont is, therefore, doubtless right when he thinks that Mithraism was derived not from Mazdeism, but from Magism

---

[1] James Darmesteter, *Essais Orientaux*, Paris, 1883, p. 113.

[2] Casartelli, *La Philosophie Religieuse du Mazdéisme sous les Sassanides*, pp. 17, 18.   [3] *Op. cit.* p. 73.

[4] 660–583 B.C. See A. V. Williams Jackson, *Zoroaster*, N.Y. 1901, p. 15 and Appx II. and III. Cf. D. Menant, "Parsis et Parsisme," *Conférences au Musée Guimet* (Bibl. de Vulgarisation), 1904, t. XVI. 1ère Ptie, p. 149.

[5] Darmesteter, *Le Zend Avesta* (Annales du Musée Guimet), Paris, 1892, p. xxvii, for dates. West, *Pahlavi Texts*, pt I. (Sacred Books of the East), pp. lxviii–lxix ; pt II. p. xxiv. Cf. Hope Moulton, *op. cit.* pp. 126, 127.

or the religion of the Magi, the tribe of Medes whose domination was put an end to by Darius the son of Hystaspes, and whose name was afterwards given to a priestly caste and has passed into our own language as the root of the word "magic."

That these Magi practised a religion different from that taught in the Avestic literature is plain enough. The romantic story told by Herodotus of the Magian who seized the throne of Persia during Cambyses' absence in Egypt on the pretence that he was the king's brother whom Cambyses had privily put to death[1], is fully confirmed by Darius' trilingual inscription on the Rock of Behistun, first copied and deciphered by Sir Henry Rawlinson and lately published in elaborate form by the British Museum[2]. Darius here narrates how " a certain man, a Magian, Gaumata by name...lied unto the people" (saying) 'I am Smerdis, the son of Cyrus, the brother of Cambyses.' Then all the people revolted from Cambyses and went over to him, even Persia and Media and the other provinces." Darius goes on to record that " thereupon Cambyses died by his own hand[3]," that the seven Persian nobles overthrew the pretender much in the way described by Herodotus, and that " I rebuilt the temples of the gods, which that Gaumata, the Magian, had destroyed. I restored that which had been taken away as it was in the days of old[4]." This he tells us he did " by the grace of Ahura Mazda," and that by this grace he always acted. The memory of these events was kept up by the festival of the Magophonia or Massacre of the Magi which was yearly cele- brated in Persia and during which no Magus dared show himself in the streets[5]. Darius' words show that there was a religious as well as a dynastic side to the Magian revolt, though whether the false Smerdis restored the old worship of the land, which he found in danger of being supplanted by Zoroastrianism or the worship of Ahura Mazda, may still be doubtful. In any event, the reformation or counter-reformation made by Darius

[1] Herodotus, Bk III. c. 61 *sqq.*

[2] *The Sculptures and Inscriptions of Darius the Great at Behistun*, British Museum Publications, 1907.

[3] *Op. cit.* pp. 8, 9.   [4] *Op. cit.* p. 14.

[5] Maspero, *Hist. Ancienne des Peuples de l'Orient Classique*, Paris, 1899, t. III. p. 674 ; Rawlinson, *History of Herodotus*, 1862, vol. II. p. 458.

did not succeed in entirely uprooting the old Magian faith, for Herodotus speaks of the Magi as still being in his time the priestly caste among the Persians, and as acting as diviners and sacrificers to the Achaemenian kings who ruled Persia up to Alexander's Conquest[1].

The Magian religion as it appears in Herodotus and other Greek authors, however, seems to have shown none of the hostility to the powers of darkness so apparent in the religious literature collected by the Sassanian kings. " The whole circuit of the firmament " was, according to Herodotus, their greatest god or Zeus ; and he says that they also " sacrifice to the sun and moon, to the earth, to fire and water, and to the winds " ; but that " they do not, like the Greeks, believe the gods to have the same nature as men[2]." He also tells us that later they borrowed from the Arabians and the Assyrians the worship of a goddess whom he calls Mitra, and although he is probably wrong as to the origin and sex of this deity, his evidence shows that Semitic admixture counted for something in the Magian worship. In other respects, the Magian seems to have been a primitive faith given up to the worship of the powers of nature or elements, which it did not personify in the anthropomorphic manner of either the Semites or the Greeks, and to have paid little attention to public ceremonies or ritual. It follows therefore that, like the religions of many uncivilized people of the present day, it would draw no very sharp distinction between good and evil gods, and would be as ready to propitiate or make use of the evil, that is those hostile to man, as the good or benevolent. Plutarch, who describes the religion of the Magi more than three centuries after Herodotus, when the name of Zoroaster the Persian prophet and the dualistic belief favoured by his teaching had long been popularly known in the West, says that the Magi of his time held Mithras to be the " Mediator " or intermediary between " Oromazes " or Light on the one hand, and " Areimanios " or Darkness and Ignorance on the other, and that they used to make bloody sacrifices to the last-named in a place where the sun never comes[3].

---

[1] Herodotus, Bk I. c. 140 ; VII. c. 113.　　[2] *Op. cit.* Bk I. c. 131.
[3] Plutarch, *de Is. et Os.* c. XLVI.

It is easy to see how such a cult, without the control of public
ceremonies and with its unabashed traffic with the powers of
evil, would be likely to degenerate into compulsion or magic.

There was, however, another popular superstition or belief
which, about the time when Mithraism made its appearance in
Europe, had spread itself over Western Asia. This was the
idea that the positions and changes of the heavenly bodies
exercise an influence over the affairs of the world and the lot
both of kingdoms and individual men. It probably began in
Babylonia, where the inhabitants had from Sumerian times
shown themselves great observers of the stars, and had been
accustomed to record the omens that they drew from their
motions for the guidance of the kings[1]. This kind of divination
—or astrology to call it by a familiar name—received a great
impulse after Alexander's Conquest, in the first place from the
break up of the Euphratean priestly colleges before referred to,
and the driving out of the lesser priests therein to get their own
living, and then from the fact that the scientific enquiry and
mathematical genius of the Greeks had made the calculation of
the positions of the heavenly bodies at any given date and hour
a fairly simple matter to be determined without direct observation[2]. It was probably no mere coincidence that the Chaldaei
and the Mathematici, as the astrologers called themselves,
should have swarmed at Rome under just those emperors in
whose reigns Mithraism began to push itself to the front[3].

While we may be sure that these factors, the religion of the
Magi, the practice of magic, and the astrological art, all counted
in the composition of the worship of Mithras, we yet know but
very little of its tenets. No work has come down to us from
any devotee of Mithras which will give us the same light on
the way his worshippers regarded him that the romance of

---

[1] As in the book called "The Illumination of Bel" found in Assur-
banipal's Library at Kuyunjik. See Sayce, "Astronomy and Astrology
of the ancient Babylonians and Assyrians," *T.S.B.A.* vol. III. pp. 146 *sqq.*
Cf. Chapter III, vol. I. p. 114 *supra* for examples.

[2] That tables were actually used for this purpose, was shown in the
Pall Mall Magazine for August, 1896 and with more detail in *Star-Lore*
for April, 1897.

[3] Dill, *Nero to Marcus Aurelius*, pp. 449, 450, for authorities.

Apuleius and the encomium of Aelius Aristides have cast on
the mental attitude of the devotees of the Alexandrian cult.
The extensive books of Eubulus and Pallas on Mithras and the
history of his worship, which Porphyry tells us were extant from
the reign of Hadrian down to his own time[1], are entirely lost,
and our only source of information, except a very few scattered
notices in the Fathers and in profane writers like the Emperor
Julian and Porphyry himself, are the sculptures and inscriptions
which have been found in his ruined chapels. These texts and
monuments the scholarly care of M. Cumont has gathered into
two large volumes, which will always remain the chief source
from which later enquirers must draw their materials[2]. From
their study he comes to the conclusion that, in the religion of
Mithras, there figured above him the Mazdean gods of good and
evil respectively called in the Zend Avesta Ahura Mazda and
Angro Mainyus, or in more familiar language, Ormuzd and Ahriman. Behind and above these again, he would place a Supreme
Being called Zervan Akerene or Boundless Time, who seems to
be without attributes or qualities, and to have acted only as the
progenitor of the opposing couple. This is at first sight very
probable, because the Orphic doctrine, which, as we have seen,
made Chronos or Time the progenitor of all the gods, was widely
spread in Asia Minor before Alexander's Conquest, and the
Persian colonies formed there under his successors must therefore have come in frequent contact with this most accommoda-
ting of schools[3]. Traditions of a sect of Zervanists in Western
Asia, who taught that all things came from Infinite Time, are
also to be found[4]. But most of these are recorded after
Mithraism had become extinct; and M. Cumont's proofs of the

---

[1] *Circa* 270 A.D. See Cumont, *T. et M.* I. p. 26.

[2] See Chap. III, Vol. I. p. 103, n. 4, *supra*.

[3] See Chap. IV, Vol. I. p. 123 *supra*.

[4] Cumont, *T. et M.* I. pp. 19–20, relies on a passage quoted by
Damascius from a certain Eudemos who may or may not be Eudemos of
Rhodes (Alexander's contemporary) that, " of the Magi and all the warrior
[or Medic: ἄρειον] race some call the intelligible " [*i.e.* that which can be
apprehended by the mind only and not by the senses] "and united
universe Topos (place), while others of them call it Chronos (Time), and
that from this universe are to be distinguished a good God and evil demon ;

existence of this dogma in the European religion of Mithras can be reduced on final analysis to a quotation from a treatise by Theodore, the Christian bishop of Mopsuestia who died in 428 A.D., directed, as it would seem, against the " Magi " of his time, in which he admits that their dogmas had never been written, and that the sectaries in question, whom he calls Magusaeans, said " sometimes one thing and deceived themselves, and sometimes another and deceived the ignorant[1]." M. Cumont's identification of the lion-headed statue often found in Mithraic chapels with the Supreme God of the system has been shown elsewhere to be open to serious question, and the figure itself to be susceptible of another interpretation than that which he would put upon it[2]. On the whole, therefore, while M. Cumont's mastery of his subject makes it very dangerous to differ from him, it seems that his theory of a Boundless Time as the pinnacle of the Mithraist pantheon cannot be considered as proved.

Whether Ormuzd and Ahriman played any important part in the Roman worship of Mithras is also doubtful. With regard to the first-named, both Greeks and Romans knew him well and identified him unhesitatingly with Zeus and Jupiter[3]. Hence we should expect to find him, if represented at all on the Mithraic sculptures, with the well-known features, the thunderbolt, and the eagle, which long before this time had become the conventional attributes of the Roman as well as of the Homeric father of gods and men. We are not entirely disappointed, for we find in a bas-relief formerly in a chapel of Mithras at Sissek

or as some say, prior to these, Light and Darkness." " Both the one and the other school therefore," Damascius goes on, " after the undivided Nature, make the double series of the higher powers distinct from one another, of one of which they make Oromasdes the leader, and of the other Arimanius." It seems evident from the above words, that only a certain sect of the Magi in the time of this Eudemos put Time at the head of their pantheon. Cf. Cory's *Ancient Fragments*, 1832, pp. 318, 319.

[1] Cumont, *T. et M.* I. p. 19.

[2] See " The Lion-headed God of the Mithraic Mysteries," *P.S.B.A.* 1912, pp. 125–142, and p. 251 *infra*.

[3] Darmesteter, *Ormuzd et Ahriman*, Paris, 1877, p. 1, quoting a lost book of Aristotle mentioned by Diogenes Laertius.

(the ancient Sissia in Pannonia) and now in the Museum at Agram, the bull-slaying scene in which Mithras figures and which will be presently described, surmounted by an arch on which is ranged Jupiter seated on his throne, grasping the thunderbolt, wielding the sceptre, and occupying the place of honour in a group of gods among whom we may distinguish Mars and Mercury[1]. In another bas-relief of the same scene, now at the Rudolfinum in Klagenfurt, he is depicted in a similar position in an assembly of the gods, which although much mutilated seems to show Zeus or Jupiter in the centre with Hera or Juno by his side[2]. But the most conclusive of these monuments is the great bas-relief found at Osterburken in the Odenwald, wherein the arch surmounting the usual bull-slaying scene contains an assembly of twelve gods with Zeus in the centre armed with thunderbolt and sceptre, while around him are grouped Apollo, Ares, Heracles, Hera, Athena, Aphrodite, Nike, Poseidon, Artemis, Hades, and perhaps Persephone[3]. When by the side of these we put the many inscriptions left by the legionaries to "the holy gods of the fatherland, to Jupiter best and greatest, and to the Unconquered One"; to "Jupiter best and greatest, and to the divine Sun, the Unconquered Sun," and other well-known names of Mithras, there can be no doubt that his worshippers used to adore him together with the head of the Roman Pantheon, and that they considered Mithras in some way the subordinate of or inferior to Jupiter[4]. Yet there

[1] Cumont, *T. et M.* II. p. 326 and Fig. 193.

[2] *Op. cit.* II. p. 336, reproduced in the article in the *P.S.B.A.* quoted in n. 2, p. 237 *supra*. In the collection of busts of the gods on the arch surrounding the Tauroctony at Bologna, the head of Zeus wearing the modius of Serapis appears with six others who, reading from left to right, are the Sun, Saturn, Venus, Jupiter, Mercury, Mars and the Moon. Although Jupiter here occupies the centre and place of honour, it is probable that both he and the other gods are here merely symbols of the planets. See Cumont, *op. cit.* II. p. 261 and Fig. 99.

[3] *Op. cit.* II. p. 349, and Pl. VI. So in the bas-relief of Sarrebourg, unfortunately much mutilated (*op. cit.* II. p. 514), a similar assembly of gods includes Neptune, Bacchus, and Vulcan, who are certainly not gods of the planets.

[4] For these inscriptions, see Cumont, *op. cit.* t. II., Inscriptions 80 (p. 107), 129 (p. 115), 318 (p. 140), 386 (p. 149), 522 (p. 167), and 470 (p. 160).

is nothing to show that the Mithraists as such identified in any way this Jupiter Optimus Maximus with the Persian Ahura Mazda, Oromasdes, or Ormuzd, or that they ever knew him by any of these outlandish names.

The case is different with Ormuzd's enemy Ahriman, who evidently was known by his Persian name to the Roman worshippers of Mithras. In the Vatican can be seen a triangular marble altar dedicated by a *clarissimus* named Agrestius who was a high-priest of Mithras, to " the god Arimanius[1]," and altars with similar inscriptions have been found at Buda-Pesth[2]. At a Mithraic chapel in York also, there was found a statue, now in the Museum of the Philosophical Society in that city, which bears an inscription to the same god Arimanius[3]. There is therefore fairly clear evidence that the Mithraists recognized Ahriman under his Persian name, and that they sacrificed to him, as Plutarch said the " magi " of his time did to the god whom he calls Hades[4], and this agrees with Herodotus' statement that the Persians used to do the same to " the god who is said to be beneath the earth[5]." Although this gave occasion to the Christian Fathers to accuse the Mithraists of worshipping the devil, we are not thereby bound to conclude that they looked upon Arimanius as an essentially evil being. It seems more probable that they considered him, as the Greeks did their Hades or Pluto, as a chthonian or subterranean power ruling over a place of darkness and discomfort, where there were punishments indeed, but not as a deity insusceptible of propitiation by sacrifice[6], or compulsion by other means such as magic arts[7]. It

[1] *Op. cit.* II. p. 98.   [2] *Op. cit.* II. p. 141.

[3] *Op. cit.* II. pp. 160, 392, 393, and article in *P.S.B.A.* quoted in n. 2, p. 237 *supra*.

[4] Plutarch, *de Is. et Os.* c. XLVI. Cf. Origen, *adv. Cels.* Bk I. c. 60.

[5] Herodotus, Bk VII. c. 114.

[6] Clem. Alex. *Strom.* Bk v. c. 11, says Zeus is the same as Hades. He quotes Euripides as authority for the statement, but I do not know the play in which it appears. He also, *op. cit.* Bk v. c. 14, quotes Xenocrates as saying that there is an " Upper and Lower " Zeus.

[7] Heracles, of course, applied compulsion to Hades. For the magic compulsion of the same power, see the Magic Papyrus of the Bibl. Nat. in Wessely's *Griech. Zauberpap.* p. 38.

has been shown elsewhere that his image in a form which fairly represents his attributes in this capacity appears with some frequency in the Mithraic chapels, where a certain amount of mystery attached to its exhibition[1]. It seems to follow from these considerations that the worshippers of Mithras attributed to their special god no inferiority to Ahriman as M. Cumont's argument supposes, and that the only power whom they acknowledged as higher than Mithras himself was the Roman equivalent of Ormuzd, the Jupiter Optimus Maximus adored throughout the Roman Empire of their time as the head of the Pantheon[2].

The connection of Mithras with the sun is also by no means easy to unravel. The Vedic Mitra was, as we have seen, originally the material sun itself, and the many hundreds of votive inscriptions left by the worshippers of Mithras to " the unconquered Sun Mithras[3]," to the unconquered solar divinity (*numen*) Mithras[4], to the unconquered Sun-God (*deus*) Mithra[5], and allusions in them to the priests (*sacerdotes*), worshippers (*cultores*), and temples (*templum*) of the same deity leave no doubt open that he was in Roman times a sun-god[6]. Yet this does not necessarily mean that he was actually the day-star visible to mankind, and the Greeks knew well enough how to distinguish between Apollo the god of light who was once at any rate a sun-god, and Helios the Sun itself[7]. On the Mithraic sculptures, we frequently see the unmistakable figure of Mithras riding in the chariot of the Sun-God driven by the divinity with long hair and a rayed nimbus, whom we know to be this Helios or his Roman equivalent, going through some ceremony of consecration with him, receiving messages from him, and seated side by side with him at a banquet which is evidently a ritual feast. M. Cumont explains this by the theory that Mithras, while in

---

[1] *P.S.B.A.* 1912, p. 137, for authorities.

[2] Jean Reville, *La Religion à Rome sous les Sevères*, Paris, 1886, p. 30.

[3] Cumont, *T. et M.* II. p. 91, no. 2 ; p. 99, nos. 30, 34 ; p. 102, no. 49; p. 103, no. 53.

[4] *Op. cit.* II. p. 99, no. 29.

[5] *Op. cit.* II. p. 105, no. 62 ; p. 116, no. 131.

[6] *Op. cit.* II. p. 96, nos. 17, 20 ; p. 117, no. 139 ; p. 145, no. 354.

[7] Pindar, *Isthm.* v. 1, where the Sun is said to be the son of Theia.

Persia and in the earliest Aryan traditions the genius of the
celestial light only[1], no sooner passed into Semitic countries
and became affected by the astrological theories of the Chaldaeans, than he was identified with their sun-god Shamash[2],
and this seems as reasonable a theory as can be devised. Another
way of accounting for what he calls the "at first sight contradictory proposition" that Mithras at once was and was not the
sun[3], is to suppose that while the Mithraists wished those who
did not belong to their faith to believe that they themselves
worshipped the visible luminary, they yet instructed their
votaries in private that he was a deity superior to it and in fact
the power behind it. As we shall see, the two theories are by
no means irreconcilable, although absolute proof of neither can
yet be offered.

One can speak with more certainty about the Legend or
mythical history of Mithras which M. Cumont has contrived
with rare acumen to reconstruct from the monuments found in
his chapels. It is comprised in eleven or twelve scenes or
tableaux which we will take in their order[4]. We first see the
birth of the god, not from the head of his father Zeus like Athena,
or from his thigh like Dionysos, but from a rock, which explains
his epithet of "Petrogenes" or rock-born. The god is represented
in this scene as struggling from the rock in which he is embedded
below the waist, and always uplifts in one hand a broad knife
of which we shall afterwards see him make use, and in the other
a lighted torch[5]. He is here represented as a boy, and wears the
Phrygian cap or so-called cap of liberty which is his distinctive
attribute, while the torch is doubtless, as M. Cumont surmises,
symbolical of the light which he is bringing into the world[6].
The rock is sometimes encircled by the folds of a large serpent,
probably here as elsewhere a symbol of the earth, and is in the

---

[1] Cumont, *T. et M.* I. p. 225, and n. 1 ; cf. Darmesteter, *Ormuzd et
Ahriman*, p. 65.

[2] Cumont, *T. et M.* I. p. 231.   [3] *Op. cit.* I. p. 200.

[4] *Op. cit.* I. pp. 304–306. The best and clearest example of these scenes
is perhaps that given in the bas-reliefs surrounding the Tauroctony in the
Mithraeum at Osterburken. See *op. cit.* II. p. 350 (Monument 246).

[5] *Op. cit.* II. Fig. 1 of Mon. 246 (p. 350).

[6] *Op. cit.* I. pp. 159 *sqq.*

Mithraic chapel discovered at Housesteads in Northumberland represented in the form of an egg, the upper part remaining on the head of the nascent god like an egg-shell on that of a newly-hatched chicken[1]. This is probably due to some confusion or identification with the Orphic legend of the First-born or Phanes who sprang from the cosmic egg; but the central idea of the rock-birth seems to be that of the spark, hidden as it were in the stone and leaping forth when struck. In one or two examples of the scene, the miraculous birth is watched by a shepherd or shepherds, which leads M. Cumont to draw a parallel between this and the Adoration of the Shepherds at the Birth of Christ.

The next two scenes are more difcult to interpret with anything approaching certainty. In one of them[2], Mithras is represented as standing upright before a tree from which he cuts or tears a large branch bearing leaves and fruit. He is here naked, save for the distinctive cap; but immediately after, he is seen emerging from the leafage fully clothed in Oriental dress. In the next scene—the relative order of the scenes seems settled by the places they most often occupy on different examples of the same sculptures[3]—Mithras in the Phrygian cap, Persian trousers, and flowing mantle generally worn by him, kneels on one knee drawing a bow, the arrows from which strike a rock in the distance and draw from it a stream of water which a kneeling man receives in his hands and lifts to his mouth[4]. Several variants of this scene exist, in one of which a suppliant is kneeling before the archer-god and raising his hands towards him as if in prayer; while in another, the rock may well be a cloud. M. Cumont can only suggest with regard to these scenes, that the first may be an allusion to the Fall of Man and his subsequently clothing himself with leaves as described in the Book of Genesis, and

[1] Cumont, *op. cit.* II. p. 395, and Fig. 315.

[2] *Op. cit.* II. p. 350, f (2) of Osterburken.

[3] It is not invariable, as the sculptor was sometimes evidently governed by considerations of space.

[4] *Op. cit.* II. p. 350, f (5) of Osterburken. Cf. Mon. 245, Pl. v (Neuenheim) and Mon. 251, Pl. VII (Heddernheim).

that the second scene may depict a prolonged drought upon earth, in which man prays to Mithras and is delivered by the god's miraculous production of rain. He admits, however, that this is pure conjecture, and that he knows no Indian, Persian, or Chaldaean legend or myth to which the scenes in question can be certainly attached. It seems therefore useless to discuss them further here.

Passing on, we come to a series of scenes, the meaning of which is more easily intelligible. In all of these a bull plays a principal part. It is abundantly clear that this bull is no terrestrial creature, but is the Goshurun or Heavenly Bull of the Zend Avesta, from whose death come forth not only man, but beasts, trees, and all the fruits of the earth[1]. In the Mithraic sculptures, we see the Bull first sailing over the waters in a cup-shaped boat[2] like the coracles still used on the Euphrates, or escaping from a burning stable to which Mithras and a companion have set fire[3]. Then he is depicted grazing peaceably or raising his head now and then as if alarmed by some sudden noise[4]. Next he is chased by Mithras, who seizes him by the horns, mounts him[5], and after a furious gallop casts him over his shoulders, generally holding him by the hind legs so that the horned head dangles to the ground[6]. In this position, he is taken into the cave which forms the chapel of Mithras.

Here, if the order in the most complete monuments be followed, we break off to enter upon another set of scenes which

[1] West, *Pahlavi Texts*, Pt 1, *S.B.E.* p. 20 (Bundahish); Porphyry, *de antro nympharum*, c. 18. Cf. Döllinger, *J. und H.* I. p. 419, and Tiele, *Religion of the Iranian Peoples* (Eng. ed.), Bombay, 1912, Pt 1, p. 113.

[2] Cumont, *T. et M.* II. p. 298, Fig. 154 (Sarmizegetusa); p. 309, Fig. 167 (Apulum); p. 326, Fig. 193 (Sissek). Döllinger, *J. und H.* I. p. 141, thinks this cup-shaped boat represents the Moon. But see against this Cumont, *op. cit.* I. pp. 167, 168.

[3] Cumont, *T. et M.* II. p. 515 and Pl. IX, Mon. 273 *ter* d (8) (Sarrebourg). Cf. *ibid.* II. p. 310, Fig. 168, Mon. 192 *bis* b (7), also I. p. 167 and n. 5.

[4] *Op. cit.* II. p. 346, e (1) and Pl. V (Neuenheim); II. p. 350, f (3) (Osterburken); II. p. 339, b (6) and Pl. IV (Mauls).

[5] *Op. cit.* II. p. 309, a (1) (Apulum); II. p. 326, b (3) and Fig. 193 (Sissek).

[6] *Op. cit.* II. p. 346, e (4) (Neuenheim); II. p. 309, a (2) (Apulum); II. p. 515, d (10) (Sarrebourg).

illustrate the relations between Mithras and the sun[1]. In what again seems to be the first in order, we see Mithras upright with a person kneeling before him who, from the rayed nimbus round his head, is evidently the god Helios or Sol[2]. In one representation of this scene, Mithras extends his left hand towards this nimbus as if to replace it on the head of its wearer[3] from which it has been displaced in yet another monument[4], while in the other, he displays an object not unlike a Phrygian cap which may, however, be, as M. Cumont suggests, something like a water-skin[5]. Generally, Mithras is represented as holding this object over the bared head of the kneeling Sun-God, as if to crown him with it[6]. Then we find Mithras with the ray-crowned Sun-God upright beside him, while he grasps his hand in token, as it would seem, of alliance or friendship[7]. If we accept the hint afforded by the theory that the rock yielding water on being split by the arrows of Mithras is really a cloud producing the fertilizing rain, we may imagine that we have here the unconquered god removing clouds which obscure the face of the great life-giving luminary and restoring to him the crown of rays which enables him to shed his kindly light upon the earth. The earth would thus be made fit for the creation of man and other animals which, as we shall see, follows ; but in any event, the meaning of the scene which shows the alliance is, as M. Cumont has pointed out, not doubtful[8]. In one monument, where Mithras grasps the hand of the person we have identified with the Sun-God before an altar, he at the same time draws his sword, as if to perform the exchange of blood or blood-covenant usual in the East on swearing alliance[9]. Possibly the crowning scene, as

---

[1] Cumont, *op. cit.* I. p. 304, puts these scenes in a slightly different order. That followed here is that adopted in the Mithraeum at Heddernheim, *op. cit.* II. Pl. VII, where the sequence is fairly plain.

[2] *Op. cit.* II. p. 365, d (7) (Heddernheim).

[3] *Op. cit.* II. p. 338, c (5) (Klagenfurt).

[4] *Op. cit.* II. p. 350, f (8) (Osterburken).

[5] *Op. cit.* I. p. 172.

[6] *Op. cit.* II. p. 272, c (2) (Serdica) ; II. pp. 303, 304, c (1) (Temesvar) ; II. p. 326, b (1) (Sissek).

[7] *Op. cit.* II. p. 337, c. (4) (Klagenfurt).

[8] *Op. cit.* I. p. 173.   [9] *Op. cit.* II. p. 201.

M. Cumont also suggests[1], is to be connected with Tertullian's statement that in the initiation of the Mithraist to the degree of *miles* or soldier, he was offered at the sword's point a crown, which he cast away from him saying that Mithras was his crown. If so, it would afford some proof that the initiate here, as in the mysteries of Isis, was made to impersonate the sun, which is on other grounds likely enough.

We return to the scenes with the Bull, which here reach their climax. This is the sacrifice of the Bull by Mithras, which forms the central point of the whole legend. Its representation, generally in bas-relief, was displayed in the most conspicuous position in the apse of the Mithraic chapel, where it occupied the place of the modern altar-piece, and such art as the Roman sculptors succeeded in displaying was employed to make it as impressive and as striking as possible[2]. It shows the god grasping with his left hand the nostrils of the beast, and kneeling with his left knee in the middle of the Bull's back, while with his right hand he plunges the broad-bladed dagger with which he was armed at his birth into the Bull's shoulder[3]. A dog leaps forward to lap the blood flowing from the wound, while at the same time a scorpion seizes the Bull by the genitals. A serpent also forms part of the group, but his position varies in the different monuments, while that of the other animals does not. Sometimes, he lifts his head towards the blood, as if to share it with the dog, sometimes he is extended along the ground beneath the Bull's belly in apparent indifference to the tragedy enacted above him[4]. Before the Bull stands generally a youth clothed like Mithras himself in Phrygian cap, tunic, and mantle, as well as the anaxyrides or tight trousers in which the Greeks depicted most Easterns, while another youth similarly attired stands behind the dying victim. These two human figures are alike in every particular save that one of them

---

[1] Cumont, *op. cit.* I. p. 173, and n. 3.

[2] Most of the monuments show the remains of colour.

[3] Like the thrust of the Spanish bull-fighter which is supposed to split the heart.

[4] Sometimes, though very rarely, the serpent is absent, as in the Mithraeum discovered at Krotzenburg near Hanau. *Op. cit.* II. p. 353.

bears a torch upright with the flame pointing upwards, while the other holds a similar torch reversed so that the flame juts towards the earth. We know from a Latin inscription that the torch-bearer with uplifted torch was called Cautes, he with the reversed one Cautopates, but of neither name has any satisfactory derivation or etymology yet been discovered[1].

The meaning of the group as a whole can, however, be explained by the documents of the later Persian religion. The *Bundahish* tells us that Ahura Mazda created before all things the Bull Goshurun, who was killed by Ahriman, the god of evil, and that from his side came forth Gayômort, first of men, while from his tail there issued useful seed-plants and trees, from his blood the vine, and from his seed the different kinds of beasts[2]. Save that the bull-slayer is here not the god of evil but the lord of light himself, the myth is evidently the same in the Mithraic bas-reliefs, for in some of the earliest monuments the Bull's tail is actually shown sprouting into ears of wheat, while in others the production of animals as a consequence of the Bull's death may be indicated, as well as the birth of the vine[3]. That the dog plays the part of the guardian of the Bull's soul is probable from what we know of later Persian beliefs[4], while the scorpion as the creature of Ahriman may be here represented as poisoning the seed of future life at its source[5]. That Mithras is not supposed to kill the Bull from enmity or other personal reasons, but in obedience to orders from some higher power, is shown by the listening pose of his head during the sacrifice. This is M. Cumont's opinion[6], as

[1] Cumont, *op. cit.* I. pp. 207, 208. Following the mention by Dionysius the Areopagite of a "threefold Mithras," M. Cumont thinks that the two torch-bearing figures are representations of Mithras himself. The theory is ingenious, but not very plausible. See *loc. cit.* pp. 208–213.

[2] *Op. cit.* I. p. 186, for authorities. Cf. Döllinger, *J. und H.* I. p. 420. Tiele, *Rel. of Iran. P.* pt 1, p. 113, says that "originally" the bull was slain not by Ahriman, but by its creator.

[3] *Op. cit.* I. p. 197. Cf. Porphyry, *de antro nymphar.* c. XVIII.

[4] D. Menant, "Les Rites Funéraires," *Conférences au Musée Guimet,* t. XXXV. pp. 181, 182.

[5] Cf. Plutarch, *de Is. et Os.* c. XLVII.

[6] So Cumont, *T. et M.* I. pp. 182, 305.

also that the serpent here takes no active part in the affair, but is merely a symbolic representation of the earth[1]. The whole drama is clearly shown as taking place in a cave or grotto, as appears from the arch of rocks which surmounts, and, as it were, acts as a frame to, the Tauroctony or bull-slaying scene in most Mithraic chapels. This cave, according to Porphyry, represents the universe.

The Legend, however, does not end with the death of the Bull. In the chapel at Heddernheim, the great slab on which the Tauroctony is sculptured in bas-relief is pivoted so as to swing round and display on its other face another scene which we find repeated in a slightly different form on many monuments[2]. Mithras and the Sun-God are here shown as partaking of a ritual feast or banquet in which grapes seem to figure. At Heddernheim, the grapes are tendered to the two gods over the body of the dead bull by the two torch-bearing figures Cautes and Cautopates, while on an arch above them various quadrupeds, dogs, a boar, a sheep, and a cow, are seen springing into life. In other monuments, the same scene generally appears as a banquet at which Mithras and Helios are seated side by side at a table sometimes alone, but at others in company with different persons who can hardly be any other than initiates or worshippers[3]. That this represents some sort of sacrament where a drink giving immortality was administered seems probable, and its likeness to representations of the Last Supper is sufficient to explain the complaint of Justin Martyr and other Fathers that the devil had set on the Mithraists to imitate in this and other respects the Church of Christ[4]. The final scene of all comes when we see Mithras arresting the glorious chariot of the Sun-God drawn by four white horses, and, mounting therein, being driven off by the ray-crowned Helios himself to the abode of light above the firmament[5]. In this

[1] *Op. cit.* I. p. 192.   [2] *Op. cit.* II. Pl. VIII.

[3] *Op. cit.* I. p. 175, Fig. 10, where some of the guests at the banquet wear the masks of crows and other animals corresponding to the Mithraic degrees.

[4] Justin Martyr, *First Apology*, c. LVI.

[5] Cumont, *T. et M.* II. Pl. VIII, shows this most clearly. Pl. v (Neuenheim), Fig 213, opposite p. 337 (Virunum), and p. 278, Fig. 121 (Orsova), leave no doubt possible.

also, it is easy to see a likeness between representations of the Ascension of Mithras and that of Elijah or even of Christ[1].

However this may be, the Legend of Mithras, as thus portrayed, shows with fair closeness the belief of his worshippers as to his place in the scheme of the universe. Mithras was certainly not the Supreme God, a rank in the system filled by Ahura Mazda, or his Latin counterpart, Jupiter Best and Greatest[2]. But this being, like the Platonic Zeus and the Gnostic Bythos, was considered too great and too remote to concern himself with the doings of the visible universe, in which Mithras acts as his vicegerent. Whether Mithras was or was not considered as in some sort the double or antitype of the Supreme Being cannot be said; but it is worth noticing that in the Vedas, as among the Hittites, Varuna and Mitra form an inseparable couple who are always invoked together, and that the same seems to have been the case with Ahura Mazda and Mithra in the oldest religious literature of the Persians[3]. It may therefore well be that the learned doctors of the Mithraic theology regarded their Supreme Being and Mithras as two aspects of the same god, an idea that, as we have seen, was current at about the same period among the Gnostics. It is, however, impossible to speak with certainty on such a point in the absence of any writings by persons professing the Mithraic faith, and it is highly improbable that the rugged soldiers who formed the majority of the god's worshippers ever troubled themselves much about such questions. For them, no doubt, and for all, perhaps, but a few carefully-chosen persons, Mithras was the Demiurge or Divine Artizan of the universe[4], which he governs in accordance with the laws of right and justice, protecting and defending alike man and those animals and plants useful to him which Mithras has himself created from his own spontaneous goodness. Hence he was the only god to whom they admitted allegiance, and although the existence

---

[1] Cumont, *op. cit.* I. p. 178, and Fig. 11.

[2] The Juppiter Optimus Maximus of the Palazzo Altieri. *Op. cit.* II. p. 104.

[3] Darmesteter, *Ormuzd et Ahriman*, p. 65.

[4] Porphyry, *de antro nympharum*, c. XXIV.

of other heavenly beings was not denied, it is probable that
most of them were looked upon as occupying at the best a
position less important to us than that of Mithras himself.

It is probable, moreover, that all the scenes in the Mithraic
sculptures in which we have seen the god taking part were
considered as being enacted before the creation of man and in
some heaven or world midway between the abode of Infinite
Light and this earth. That the grotto into which Mithras
drags the primordial Bull is no earthly cavern is plain from
Porphyry's remark that the Mithraic cave was an image of the
universe[1], as well as from the band of zodiacal figures or the
arch of rocks which sometimes encloses the bas-reliefs, the sky
being looked upon by the Babylonians as a rocky vault. The
sun and moon in their respective chariots also appear above
the principal scene ; and a further hint as to its whereabouts
may be found in the fact that the flowing mantle of Mithras is
sometimes depicted as spangled with stars, thereby indicating
that the scenes in which he appears are supposed to take place
in the starry firmament. Hence is explained the epithet of
μεσίτης or Mediator, which Plutarch gives him[2], and which
should be interpreted not as intercessor but as he who occupies
a position midway between two places[3]. That the higher of
these in this case was the Garôtman or abode of Infinite Light
of the Avestic literature, there can, it would seem, be no
question ; but what was the lower ?

Although the statement must be guarded with all the
reserves imposed upon us in all matters relating to the religion
of Mithras by the absence of written documents, it is probable
that this lower division of the universe was our earth. The
monuments give us with fair certainty the Mithraic ideas as to
how life was brought thither; but they tell us little or nothing
as to the condition in which the earth was at the time, nor
how it was supposed to have come into existence. Porphyry
tells us that the "elements" (στοιχεῖα) were represented in the
Mithraic chapel[4], and we find in some examples of the bull-
slaying scenes, the figures of a small lion and a crater or
mixing-bowl beneath the belly of the bull, which M. Cumont

---

[1] *Op. cit.* cc. v. vi.   [2] Plutarch, *de Is. et Os.* c. XLVI.
[3] Porphyry, *de antro nymph.* c. XXIV.   [4] *Op. cit.* cc. v. vi.

considers to be the symbols of fire and water respectively;
while the earth may be typified, as has been said above, by
the serpent, and the fourth element or air may be indicated by
the wind which is blowing Mithras' mantle away from his body
and to the left of the group[1]. If this be so, it is probable that
the Mithraist who thought about such matters looked upon the
four elements, of which the ancients believed the world to be
composed, as already in existence before the sacrifice of the
primordial bull brought life upon the earth; and that the work
of Mithras as Demiurge or Artizan was confined to arranging
and moulding them into the form of the cosmos or ordered
world. As to what was the ultimate origin of these elements,
and whether the Mithraists, like the Gnostics, held that Matter
had an existence independent of, and a nature opposed to,
the Supreme Being, we have no indication whatever.

Of Mithraic eschatology or the view that the worshippers
of Mithras held as to the end of the world, we know rather less
than we do of their ideas as to its beginning. The Persian
religion, after its reform under the Sassanid kings, taught that
it would be consumed by fire[2]; and, as this doctrine of the
Ecpyrosis, as the ancients called it, was also held by the Stoics,
whose physical doctrines were then fashionable at Rome, it is
probable enough that it entered into Mithraism also. But of
this there is no proof, and M. Cumont's attempt to show that
a similar conflagration was thought by the Mithraic priests to
have taken place before the Tauroctony, and as a kind of
paradigm or forecast of what was to come, is not very convincing[3]. Yet some glimpse of what was supposed to happen
between the creation of the world and its destruction seems to

[1] Cumont, *T. et M.* I. pp. 198 *sqq.* Damascius (in Cory's *Ancient
Fragments*, 1832, p. 319) attributes to the " Sidonians " a theogony which
would make "Otos," said by Cory to mean the Night Raven, the Νοῦς νοητός
born from Aer and Aura. Has this anything to do with the symbolism of
the crow, found always as the attendant of Mithras at the Tauroctony?

[2] Söderblom, *La Vie Future d'après le Mazdéisme*, Paris, 1901, pp. 265,
266, for authorities. Cf. Casartelli, *La Philosophie Religieuse du Mazdéisme*,
p. 186.

[3] Cumont, *T. et M.* I. p. 168. He relies on a fragment of Dion
Chrysostom which does not appear to have this meaning. See *ibid.* II.
p. 64.

be typified by a monstrous figure often found in the ruined chapels once used for the Mithraic worship, where it seems to have been carefully guarded from the eyes of the general body of worshippers. This monster had the body of a man[1] with the head of a lion, while round his body is twined a huge serpent, whose head either appears on the top of the lion's or rests on the human breast. On the monster's back appear sometimes two, but generally four wings, and in his hands he bears upright two large keys, for one of which a sceptre is sometimes substituted; while his feet are sometimes human, sometimes those of a crocodile or other reptile. On his body, between the folds of the serpent, there sometimes appear the signs of the four quarters of the year, *i.e.* Aries and Libra, Cancer and Capricorn[2], and in other examples a thunderbolt on the breast or on the right knee[3]. The figure is often mounted on a globe which bears in one instance the two crossed bands which show that it is intended for our earth, and in one curious instance he appears to bear a flaming torch in each hand, while his breath is kindling a flame which is seen rising from an altar beside him[4]. It is possible that in this last we have a symbolical representation of the Ecpyrosis. Lastly, in the Mithraic chapel at Heddernheim, which is the only one where the figure of the lion-headed monster was found *in situ*, it was concealed within a deep niche or cell so fashioned, says M. Cumont, that the statue could only be perceived through a little conical aperture or peep-hole made in the slab of basalt closing the niche[5].

M. Cumont's theory, as given in his magnificent work on

[1] M. Cumont, *op. cit.* I. p. 82, says that the sex is left undecided, so as to show that Infinite Time, the Supreme God according to him of the Mithraic pantheon, can produce by himself. This is certainly not the case with one of the statues given among his own monuments (*op. cit.* II. p. 213, Fig. 44), or that lately recovered from the Mithraeum at Sidon, for which see Pottier, "La Collection Louis de Clercq," *Conférences au Musée Guimet*, Bibl. de Vulg. t. XIX. 1906, Pl. opp. p. 236, or *P.S.B.A.* 1912, Pl. XIX, Fig. 18, or Cumont, *Les Mystères de Mithra*, Bruxelles, 1913, p. 235.

[2] Cumont, *T. et M.* II. p. 213, Figs. 43, 44.

[3] *Op. cit.* II. p. 216, Fig. 47 ; p. 238, Fig. 68; p. 259, Fig. 96.

[4] *Op. cit.* II. p. 196, Fig. 22. A hole in the back of the head, made apparently for "fire-breathing" purposes, was found in the Sidon statue also. See Cumont, *Les Mystères*, fig. 27.   [5] *T. et M.* II. p. 375.

the *Mystères de Mithra* and elsewhere, is that the figure represents that Zervan Akerene or Boundless Time whom he would put at the head of the Mithraic pantheon, and would make the father of both Ormuzd and Ahriman[1]. M. Cumont's opinion, on a subject of which he has made himself the master, must always command every respect, and it may be admitted that the notion of such a supreme Being, corresponding in many ways to the Ineffable Bythos of the Gnostics, did appear in the later developments of the Persian religion, and may even have been known during the time that the worship of Mithras flourished in the West[2]. It has been shown elsewhere, however, that this idea only came to the front long after the cult of Mithras had become extinct, that M. Cumont's view that the lion-headed monster was represented as without sex or passions has been shown to be baseless by later discoveries, and that the figure is connected in at least one example with an inscription to Arimanes or Ahriman[3]. M. Cumont has himself noted the confusion which a Christian, writing before the abolition of the Mithras worship, makes between the statues of Hecate, goddess of hell and patroness of sorcerers, and those of the lion-headed monster[4], and Hecate's epithet of Περσείη can only be explained by some similar association[5]. At the same time, M. Cumont makes it plain that the Mithraists did not regard these infernal powers Ahriman and Hecate with the horror and loathing which the reformed Zoroastrian religion afterwards heaped upon the antagonist of Ormuzd[6]. On the contrary the dedications of

---

[1] *Op. cit.* I. p. 78.

[2] The only evidence that he produces of this last fact is a quotation from Damascius, whose authority seems to be " Eudemus the Peripatetic," given in n. 4, p. 236 *supra*, that some of the Magi call the νοητὸν ἅπαν καὶ τὸ ἡνωμένον Topos and others Chronos. A good divinity and an evil demon according to the same author descend from this power, one of whom he says is called Oromasdes and the other Arimanius. It is not very clear how much of this is Eudemus and how much Damascius. No other author gives any hint that would allow us to attribute so early an age to Zervanism.

[3] *P.S.B.A.* 1912, pp. 139–142.

[4] Firmicus Maternus, *de errore*, c. IV. See Cumont, *T. et M.* I. p. 140, n. 7.

[5] They are mentioned together in the great Magical Papyrus of the Bibliothèque Nationale at Paris, Wessely, *Griechische Zauberp.* p. 73.

[6] Cumont, *T. et M.* I. p. 141.

several altars and statues show that they paid them worship
and offered them sacrifices, as the Greeks did to Hades and
Persephone, the lord and lady of hell, of whom the Mithraists
probably considered them the Persian equivalents.   From all
these facts, the conclusion seems inevitable that the lion-headed
monster represents Ahriman, the consort of Hecate[1].

If we now look at the religious literature of the time when
the worship of Mithras was coming into favour, we find a pretty
general consensus of opinion that the chthonian or infernal
god represented in the earlier Persian religion by this Ahriman,
was a power who might be the rival of, but was not necessarily
the mortal enemy of Zeus.   Whether Neander be right or not
in asserting that the prevailing tendency of the age was towards
Dualism[2], it is certain that most civilized nations had then come
to the conclusion that on this earth the bad is always mixed up
with the good.   Plutarch puts this clearly enough when he says
that nature here below comes not from one, but from two
opposed principles and contending powers, and this opinion, he
tells us, is a most ancient one which has come down from
expounders of myths ($\theta\epsilon o\lambda \acute{o}\gamma o\iota$) and legislators to poets and
philosophers, and is expressed " not in words and phrases, but
in mysteries and sacrifices, and has been found in many places
among both Barbarians and Greeks[3]."   The same idea of antagonistic powers is, of course, put in a much stronger form in
the reformed Persian religion, where the incursion of Ahriman
into the kingdom of Ormuzd brings upon the earth all evil in
the shape of winter, prolonged drought, storms, disease, and
beasts and plants hurtful to man[4].   But this does not seem to
have been the view of Ahriman's functions taken by the older
Magism, whence the worship of Mithras was probably derived[5].

[1] The absence of any corresponding statue of the goddess is perhaps
accounted for by the misogynic character of the Mithraic worship.   Yet
an empty niche corresponding to the one containing the lion-headed figure
appears in some Mithraea.

[2] Neander, *Ch. Hist.* II. p. 7 and note.

[3] Plutarch, *de Is. et Os.* c. XLV.

[4] Cumont, *T. et M.* I. p. 5, quoting West, *Pahlavi Texts*, Pt v. p. xxvi, 50.

[5] F. Rosenberg, *Le Livre de Zoroastre*, St Petersburg, I. p. 10, and n. 3,
says that the reform of Zoroaster was specially directed to the abolition
of the worship of Ahriman.

In Mithraism, it is not Ahriman, as in the *Bundahish*, but Mithras, the vicegerent of Ormuzd, who slays the mystic Bull, and by so doing he brings good and not evil to the earth. Nowhere do we find in the Mithraic sculptures any allusion to Ahriman as a god of evil pure and simple, or as one who is for ever opposed to the heavenly powers. We do, indeed, find in several Mithraea representations of a Titanomachia where the Titans, represented as men with serpent legs, are depicted as fleeing before a god like the Greek Zeus who strikes them with his thunderbolts[1]. But this is not more necessarily suggestive of two irreconcilable principles than the Greek story of the Titans, those sons of Earth who were persuaded by their mother to make war upon their father Uranos, who put their brother Kronos upon his throne, and who were in their turn hurled from heaven by Kronos' son Zeus. Even if we do not accept the later myth which reconciles Zeus to his adversaries[2], the story does not go further than to say that the Titans attempted to gain heaven and were thrust back to their own proper dwelling-place, the earth.

It is in this way, as it would seem, that the lion-headed monster of the Mithraic chapels must be explained. Ahriman, the god girt with the serpent which represents the earth, has rebelled against Ormuzd or Jupiter, and has been marked with the thunderbolt which has cast him down from heaven. But he remains none the less lord of his own domain, the earth, his sway over which is shown by the sceptre which he wields while standing upon it[3]. As for the keys which he bears, they are doubtless those of the gates behind which he keeps the souls and bodies of men, as the Orphics said, imprisoned, until he is compelled to release them by a higher power[4]. In all this,

[1] Cumont, *T. et M.* II. Monument 246, e (5) Osterburken, and others as in t. I. p. 157 and n. 3. Cf. also Pl. XVI, Fig. 7, in *P.S.B.A.* 1912.

[2] The Orphic invocation of the Titans referred to in Chap. IV, vol. I. p. 116, n. 3 *supra* can be thus explained.

[3] Cumont, *T. et M.* II. p. 215, Fig. 46 (Pl. XVIII, Fig. 13 of *P.S.B.A.* 1912); II. p. 238, Fig. 68 (Pl. XVIII, Fig. 15 of *P.S.B.A.* 1912).

[4] So in the leaden *dirae* from Cyprus now in the British Museum the Lord of Hell is invoked as "the god who is set over the gate of hell and the keys of heaven." *P.S.B.A.* t. XIII., 1891, p. 177.

his functions do not go beyond those of the Greek Hades, with whom Plutarch equates him.

It is however, possible that he was conceived by the Mithraists as occupying a slightly different place in the material universe from that of his Greek prototype. The true realm of Hades was generally placed by the Greeks below the earth, but that of the Mithraic Ahriman may possibly be just outside it. M. Cumont shows many reasons for supposing the lion-headed god to be connected with the idea of destiny[1], and in one of the very few contemporary writings which make distinct allusion to the Mithraic tenets, there is something which confirms this view. This occurs in a fragment embedded, as it were, in a Magic Payprus or sorcerer's handbook now in the Bibliothèque Nationale at Paris[2]. The document itself is probably not, as Prof. Albert Dieterich has too boldly asserted, a " Mithraic Liturgy " ; but it is evidently connected in some way with the Mithraic worship and begins with a statement that the writer is a priest who has received inspiration from " the great Sun-God Mithras." M. Georges Lafaye is of opinion that it narrates in apocalyptic fashion the adventures of the soul of a perfect Mithraist on its way to heaven, and this is probably correct, although it is here told for no purpose of edification but as a spell or charm[3]. The soul, if it be indeed she who is speaking, repeatedly complains to the gods whom she meets—including one in white tunic, crimson mantle and anaxyrides or Persian trousers who may be Mithras himself—of " the harsh and inexorable necessity " which has been compelling her so long as she remained in the " lower nature[4]." But the Sphere of Destiny or necessity, as we have seen in the *Pistis Sophia*, was thought to be the one immediately surrounding the earth, and although the document in which we have before met with this idea belongs to a different set of religious beliefs than those

---

[1] Cumont, *T. et M.* I. p. 294.

[2] Wessely, *Griechische Zauberp.* pp. 32 *sqq.*

[3] Georges Lafaye, "L'Initiation Mithriaque," *Conférences au Musée Guimet*, t. XVIII. 1906, pp. 98 *sqq.*

[4] Wessely, *Gr. Zauberp.* p. *cit.* in note 2 *supra*, and Lafaye, *op. cit. passim.*

here treated of, it is probable that both Gnostic and Mithraist drew it from the astrological theories current at the time which came into the Hellenistic world from Babylon. It is therefore extremely probable that the Mithraists figured Ahriman as ruling the earth from the sphere immediately outside it, and this would agree well with his position *upon* the globe in the monuments where he appears. It is some confirmation of this that, in another part of the Papyrus just quoted, the " World-ruler " (Cosmocrator) is invoked as " the Great Serpent, leader of these gods, who holds the source of Egypt [Qy, The Nile ?] and the end of the whole inhabited world [in his hands], who begets in Ocean Pshoi (*i.e.* Fate) the god of gods[1] " ; while the Great Dragon or Outer Darkness in the *Pistis Sophia* is said to surround the earth. That both orthodox Christians and Gnostics like the Valentinians looked upon the Devil, who, as lord of hell, was sometimes identified with Hades, as the Cosmocrator or World-Ruler requires no further demonstration[2], and in this particular as in others the Mithraists may have drawn from the same source as the Gnostic teachers[3].

That they did so in a related matter can be shown by direct evidence. Like the Ophites of the Diagram before described, the Mithraists thought that the soul descended to the body through seven spheres which were those of the " planets " Saturn, Venus, Jupiter, Mercury, Mars, the Moon, and the Sun in that order, which Origen, who mentions the fact, says that the Persian theology declared to be symbolized " by the names of the rest of matter," and also gave for it " musical reasons[4]." He further describes the different qualities which the soul in her passage receives from each sphere, and which it seems fair to conclude she gives back to them on her reascension. M. Cumont is no doubt right when he attributes the origin of

---

[1] Wessely, *op. cit.* p. 61.   [2] See Chapter IX, p. 108 *supra*.

[3] Lafaye, *L'In. Mith.* pp. 111, 112, goes further and says that both Gnostics and Manichaeans derived their doctrine from Mithraism, which formed a half-way house between Paganism and Christianity. But see Chapter XIII, *infra*.

[4] Origen, *adv. Cels.* Bk VI. c. 22. For " musical " there should probably be read mystical, the *r* being easily omitted by a copyist.

this tenet to the *mathematici* or astrologers and says that it too came originally from Chaldaea[1]. The seven heavens are also found in many Oriental documents of the time, including the *Book of the Secrets of Enoch*[2] and the *Apocalypse of Baruch*[3]. According to Origen, they were symbolized in the Mithraic chapels by a ladder of eight steps, the first seven being of the metals peculiar to the different planets, *i.e.* lead, tin, copper, iron, an alloy of several metals, silver, and gold, with the eighth step representing the heaven of the fixed stars[4]. The Stoics who held similar views, following therein perhaps the Platonic cosmogony, had already fixed the gate of the sky through which the souls left the heaven of the fixed stars on their descent to the earth in Cancer, and that by which they reascended in Capricorn[5], which probably accounts for the two keys borne by the lion-headed god on the Mithraic monuments, and for those two Zodiacal signs being displayed on his body. The other two signs, *viz.* Aries and Libra, may possibly refer to the places in a horoscope or genethliacal figure which the astrologers of the time called the *Porta laboris* and *Janua Ditis* respectively, as denoting the gate by which man " born to labour " enters life, and the " gate of Hades " by which he leaves it[6]. If, as Porphyry says, the doctrine of metempsychosis formed part of the Mithraic teaching, the keys would thus have a meaning analogous to the Orphic release from " the wheel[7]."

The other gods who appear on the Mithraic monuments are those known to us in classical mythology and are represented under the usual human forms made familiar by Greek and Roman art. By the side of, but in a subordinate position to Jupiter, we find, if M. Cumont be justified in his identifications,

[1] Cumont, *T. et M.* I. p. 38.

[2] Charles, *Bk of the Secrets of Enoch*, pp. xxx *sqq.*

[3] The Greek Apocalypse of Baruch, published by James in *Cambridge Texts and Studies*, vol. v. No. 1, p. 44.

[4] *adv. Cels.* Bk VI. c. 22. He has, however, got the order wrong, as copper is generally associated with the planet Venus, tin with Jupiter, iron with Mars, silver with the Moon, gold with the Sun, and lead with Saturn.

[5] Bouché Leclercq, *L'Astrologie Grecque*, p. 23, for authorities.

[6] *Op. cit.* p. 276. Cf. Cumont, *T. et M.* I. p. 40.

[7] Porphyry, *de Abstinentia*, Bk IV. c. 16.

nearly all the "great gods" of the Greco-Roman pantheon. Five of these, that is to say, Jupiter himself, Saturn, Mars, Venus, and Mercury may be intended as symbols of the planets which, then as now, bore these names. But there are others such as Juno, Neptune and Amphitrite, Pluto and Proserpine, Apollo, Vulcan, and Hercules who cannot by any possibility be considered as planetary signs[1]. M. Cumont's theory about these divinities is, if one understands him rightly, that these are really Persian or Avestic gods, such as Verethragna, represented under the classic forms of their Greek counterparts to make them attractive to their Roman worshippers[2]. This does not seem very probable, because the Persians did not figure their gods in human form[3]. Nor is there any reason to think that the Mithraists confined themselves to the *theocrasia* or the practice of discovering their own gods in the divinities of the peoples around them which we have seen so rife in Greece, Italy, and Egypt. But in the age when the worship of Mithras became popular in the Roman Empire, all paganism was groping its way towards a religion which should include and conciliate all others, and there is much evidence that the votaries of Mithras were especially determined that this religion should be their own. Isis, as we have seen, might proclaim herself as the one divinity whom under many names and in many forms the whole earth adored ; but the Mithraists apparently went further and tried to show that their religion contained within itself all the rest. They appear to have first gained access to Rome under an alliance with the priests of Cybele, whose image, with its emasculated attendants the Galli, was transported from Pergamum to the Eternal City during the critical moments of the Second Punic War[4]. Externally there were many analogies between the two cults, and Cybele's consort Attis, like Mithras, was always represented in a Phrygian cap and anaxyrides. One of the most

[1] Cumont, *T. et M.* I. p. 129, n. 6, for list of monuments.

[2] *Op. et loc. cit.* ; *id. Rel. Or.* p. 179.

[3] See p. 234, *supra.* The figure of the divine archer in the winged disk which figured on the coins called darics is, perhaps, the exception which proves the rule. Or is this meant for the Fravashi or genius of the king ? Cf. Hope Moulton, *Early Zoroastrianism*, p. 260.

[4] Somewhere about 204 B.C. See Cumont, *Rel. Or.* p. 58.

impressive, if most disgusting practices in the religion of Cybele
—the Taurobolium or blood-bath in which a bull was slaughtered
over a pit covered with planks pierced with holes through which
the blood of the victim dripped upon the naked votary below—
was borrowed by the Mithraists, and many of them boast on
their funereal inscriptions that they have undergone this ceremony and thereby, as they express it, have been " born again."
The *clarissimi* and high officials of the Empire who have left
records of the kind are careful to note that they are worshippers
of " the Great Mother " (Cybele) and Attis, as well as of Mithras[1],
and a similar statement occurs so frequently on the funereal and
other inscriptions of their wives as to lead to the hypothesis that
the ceremonies of the Phrygian Goddess were the natural refuge
of Mithras' female votaries[2]. So, too, the worship of the
Alexandrian divinities, which that of Mithras in some sort
supplanted, and which, as being as popular in the Greek world
as the last-named was in the Latin, might have been expected
to be hostile to it, yet had relations with it not very easy to be
understood.   In the assembly of the gods which in some of the
monuments crowns the arch set over the Tauroctony, the
central place is in one instance taken by Sarapis with the
distinctive *modius* on his head instead of Zeus or Jupiter[3], the
same priest often describes himself as serving the altars of both
gods, and " Zeus, Helios, Mithras, Sarapis, unconquered one ! "
is invoked in one of those spells in the Magic Papyri which
contain fragments of ritual prayers or hymns[4].   Possibly it is
for this reason, that the initiating priest in Apuleius' story whom
the grateful Lucius says he regards as his father, is named

---

[1] Orelli, *Inscpt. Latinar. selectar*. Turin, 1828, vol. I. pp. 406–412.

[2] See Cumont, *T. et M.* II. p. 95, inscr. 15, p. 98, inscr. 23 ; p. 100
inscr. 40 ; p. 101, inscr. 41.   The tomb of Vincentius in the Catacomb of
Praetextatus at Rome would show an instance of the joint worship of
Sabazius, the consort of the Great Mother, and of Mithras, if we could trust
Garrucci's restoration, for which see his *Les Mystères du Syncrétisme
Phrygien*, Paris, 1854.   It has been quoted in this sense by Hatch, *H.L.*
p. 290 ; but Cumont, *T. et M.* II. pp. 173 and 413, argues against this
construction.   For the pictures themselves, see Maass, *Orpheus*, München,
1895, pp. 221, 222.

[3] Cumont, *T. et M.* II. p. 261, Fig. 99.   [4] Kenyon, *Gk Papyri*, p. 65.

Mithras, as if the initiate had been led to the Mysteries of Isis through the worship of that god[1].

The same syncretistic tendency is particularly marked in the leaning of the Mithraists to the worship of the gods of Eleusis. " Consecrated to Liber [the Latin name of Dionysos] and the Eleusinian [goddesses]," " Mystes of Ceres," " priest " or " Chief Herdsman (*archibucolus*) of the god Liber," " hierophant of Father Liber and the Hecates," " Consecrated at Eleusis to the god Bacchus, Ceres, and Cora " are some of the distinctions which the devotees of Mithras vaunt on their tombstones[2]; while we learn that when the last survivors of the two sacred families who had for centuries furnished priests to the Eleusinian Mysteries died out, the Athenians sent for a priest of Mithras from one of the neighbouring islands, and handed over to him the care of the sacred rites[3]. It is even possible that the complaisance of the Mithraists for other religions went further than has hitherto been suspected. Not only does Justin Martyr after describing the celebration of the Christian Eucharist say,

"Wherefore also the evil demons in mimicry have handed down that the same thing should be done in the Mysteries of Mithras. For that bread and a cup of water are in these mysteries set before the initiate with certain speeches you either know or can learn[4] ";

but we know from Porphyry that the initiate into the rites of Mithras underwent a baptism by total immersion which was said to expiate his sins[5]. Among the worshippers of Mithras, on the same authority, were also virgins and others vowed to continence[6], and we hear that the Mithraists used, like the

---

[1] This is the more likely because his second initiator bears the name of Asinius, which, as he himself says (Apuleius, *Metamorph.* Bk XI. c. 27), was not unconnected with his own transformation into the shape of an ass. The Emperor Commodus was initiated into both religions (Lamprius, *Commodus*, c. IX.).

[2] See n. 1, p. 259, *supra*.

[3] Dill, *Nero to Marcus Aurelius*, p. 625, n. 3, quoting Gasquet, *Mithras*, p. 137. See also Gibbon, vol. III. p. 498, Bury (Appendix 15).

[4] Justin Martyr, *First Apology*, c. LXVI.

[5] Porphyry, *de antro nymph.* c. 15. Tertullian, *de Praescpt.* c. 40.

[6] Porphyry, *op. et loc. cit.*

Christians, to call each other "Brother" and address their priests as "Father[1]." St Augustine tells us that in his time the priests of Mithras were in the habit of saying, "That One in the Cap [*i.e.* Mithras] is a Christian too!" and it is not unlikely that the claim was seriously made[2]. During the reigns of the Second Flavian Emperors and before Constantine's pact with the Church, we hear of hymns sung by the legionaries which could be chanted in common by Christians, Mithraists, and the worshippers of that Sun-God the adoration of whom was hereditary or traditional in the Flavian House[3]. The Mithraists also observed Sunday and kept sacred the 25th of December as the birthday of the sun[4].

Of the other rites and ceremonies used in the worship of Mithras we know next to nothing. As appears from the authors last quoted, the whole of the worship was conducted in "mysteries" or secret ceremonies like the Eleusinian and the rites of the Alexandrian divinities, although on a more extended scale. The Mithraic mysteries always took place in a subterranean vault or "cave," lighted only by artificial light. The ruins of many of these have been found, and are generally so small as to be able to accommodate only a few worshippers[5], whence perhaps it followed that there were often several Mithraea in the same town or city[6]. The chief feature seems to have been always the scene of the Tauroctony or Bull-slaying which was displayed on the apse or further end of the chapel, and was generally carved in bas-relief although occasionally rendered in the round. The effect of this was sought to be

[1] See Cumont, *T. et M.* I. p. 339, for authorities.

[2] Augustine, *In Johann. evang. tractatus*, VII. or Cumont, *T. et M.* II. p. 59. This last thinks it more probable that the passage refers to Attis, as there is an allusion in it to redemption by blood. But this would hardly apply to the self-mutilation of the Galli, while it would to the blood-bath of the Taurobolium and Criobolium which so many high initiates of Mithras boast of undergoing.

[3] J. Maurice, "La Dynastie Solaire des Seconds Flaviens," *Rev. Archeol.* t. XVII. (1911), p. 397 and n. 1.

[4] Cumont, *T. et M.* I. p. 339, quoting Minucius Felix.

[5] *Op. cit.* I. p. 65.

[6] The remains of five Mithraea were found in Ostia alone.

heightened by brilliant colouring, perhaps made necessary by
the dim light, and there were certainly altars of the square or
triangular pedestal type, and a well or other source from which
water could be obtained. The benches for the worshippers
were of stone and ran at right angles to and on either side of
the Tauroctony, so as to resemble the choir stalls in the chancel
of a modern church[1]. We have seen that the lion-headed
figure was concealed from the eyes of the worshippers, and we
know that they used to kneel during at least part of the service,
which was not in accord with the practice of either the Greeks
or Romans, who were accustomed to stand with upturned palms
when praying to the gods[2]. Sacrifices of animals which, if we
may judge from the débris left in some of the chapels, were
generally birds[3], seem to have been made ; but there is no
reason to believe the accusation sometimes brought against the
Mithraists that they also slaughtered human victims in honour
of their god. Lampridius tells us, on the other hand, that the
Emperor Commodus on his initiation sullied the temple by
converting a feigned into a real murder[4], and we hear from
another and later source that in consequence of this only a
bloody sword was shown to the candidate[5]. It seems therefore
that somebody was supposed to suffer death during the ceremony, perhaps under the same circumstances as already
suggested in the kindred case of the Alexandrian Mysteries[6].

We are a little better informed as to the degrees of initiation,
which numbered seven. The initiate ascended from the degree
of Crow (*corax*), which was the first or lowest, to that of Father
(*Pater*), which was the seventh or highest, by passing successively

---

[1] Cumont, *T. et M.* II. p. 204, Fig. 30, and p. 493, Fig. 430 ; or
P.S.B.A. 1912, Pl. XIII. Figs. 1 and 2.

[2] Cumont, *T. et M.* I. p. 62.

[3] The story quoted from Pseudo-Augustine (Cumont, *op. cit.* I. p. 322)
about the hands of the initiates being bound with chickens'-guts which were
afterwards severed by a sword might account for the number of birds'
bones.

[4] Cumont, *op. cit.* II. p. 21, gives the passage from Lampridius mentioned
in n. 1, p. 260, *supra*.

[5] *Op. cit.* I. p. 322, quoting Zacharius rhetor.

[6] See Chapter II, Vol. I. p. 62, *supra*.

through the intermediate degrees of Man of the Secret (*Cryphius*), Soldier (*Miles*), Lion (*Leo*), Persian (*Perses*), and Courier of the Sun (*Heliodromus*)[1]. It would seem that either he, or the initiating priests, or perhaps the other assistants, had to assume disguises consisting of masks corresponding to the animals named in the first and fourth of these degrees, and to make noises like the croaking of birds and the roaring of lions[2]. These rightly recall to M. Cumont the names of animals borne by initiates or priests in other religions in Greece and Asia Minor and may be referred to totemistic times. We also know from a chance allusion of Tertullian that on being admitted to the degree of soldier, the initiate was offered a crown or garland at the point of a sword, which he put away from him with the speech, " Mithras is my crown ! ", and that never thereafter might he wear a garland even at a feast[3]. Porphyry, too, tells us that in the degree of Lion, the initiate's hands and lips were purified with honey. It has also been said by the Fathers that before or during initiation, the candidate had to undergo certain trials or tortures, to swim rivers, plunge through fire, and to jump from apparently vast heights[4] ; but it is evident from the small size of the Mithraea or chapels which have come down to us that these experiences would have demanded much more elaborate preparation than there was space for, and, if they were ever enacted, were probably as purely " make-believe " as the supposed murder just mentioned and some of the initiatory ceremonies in certain societies of the present day[5]. Lastly, there is no doubt that women were strictly excluded from all the ceremonies of the cult, thereby justifying in some

---

[1] Cumont, *T. et M.* II. p. 18, for the passage in St Jerome in which these degrees are enumerated. They all appear in the inscriptions given by Cumont, except that of Miles or Soldier. An inscription by two " soldiers " of Mithras has, however, lately been found at Patras and published by its discoverers, M. Charles Avezou and M. Charles Picard. See *R.H.R.* t. LXIV. (1911), pp. 179–183.

[2] Cumont, *T. et M.* I. pp. 315 *sqq.*   [3] Tertullian, *de Corona*, c. 15.

[4] Porphyry, *de antro nymph.* c. 15.

[5] Cumont, *T. et M.* I. p. 322. Gregory of Nazianza (A.D. 320–390) is the first authority for these tortures (κολάσεις) in point of time. Nonnus the Mythographer gives more details, but is three centuries later.

sort the remark of Renan that Mithraism was a " Pagan Freemasonry[1]."

It has also been said that the true inwardness and faith of the religion of Mithras was in these mysteries only gradually and with great caution revealed to the initiates, whose fitness for them was tested at every step[2]. It may be so, but it is plain that the Mithraist was informed at the outset of at least a good many of the tenets of the faith. The whole Legend of Mithras, so far as we know it, must have been known to the initiate soon after entering the Mithraic chapel, since we have ourselves gathered it mainly from the different scenes depicted on the borders of the great central group of the Tauroctony. So, too, the mystic banquet or Mithraic Sacrament which, if the Heddernheim monuments stood alone, we might consider was concealed from the eyes of the lower initiates until the proper moment came, also forms one of the subsidiary scenes of the great altar piece in the chapels at Sarmizegetusa, Bononia and many other places[3]. In a bas-relief at Sarrebourg, more-over, the two principal persons at the banquet, *i.e.* Mithras and the Sun, are shown surrounded by other figures wearing the masks of crows and perhaps lions[4], which looks as if initiates of all grades were admitted to the sacramental banquet. One can therefore make no profitable conjecture as to what particular doctrines were taught in the particular degrees, though there seems much likelihood in M. Cumont's statement that the initiates were thought to take rank in the next world according to the degree that they had received in this[5]. The belief that " those who have received humble mysteries shall have humble places and those that have received exalted mysteries exalted places " in the next world was, we may be sure, too profitable a one for the priests of Mithras to be neglected by them. It

---

[1] Renan, *Marc-Aurèle*, p. 577.　　　[2] Cumont, *T. et M.* I. p. 73.

[3] *Op. cit.* II. p. 294, Fig. 149 ; p. 298, Fig. 154 ; p. 300, Fig. 156 ; p. 304, Fig. 161 ; p. 488, Fig. 421.

[4] *Op. cit.* I. p. 175, Fig. 10.

[5] *Op. cit.* I. p. 39, n. 6, quoting the *Arda Viraf namak*. A quotation from Arnobius, *adv. gentes*, which follows, merely says that the Magi boast of their ability to smooth the believers' passage to heaven.

certainly explains the extraordinary order for the planetary spheres adopted by Origen[1], according to which the souls which had taken the lowest degree would go to the heaven of Saturn, slowest and most unlucky of the planets, while those perfected in the faith would enter the glorious house of the Sun.

Whether they were thought to go further still, we can only guess. It should be noticed that the mystic ladder of Mithras had *eight* steps, and we have seen that when the soul had climbed through the seven planetary spheres there was still before her the heaven of the fixed stars. The Sun seems in Origen's account of the Mithraic faith to have formed the last world to be traversed before this highest heaven could be reached; and it was through the disk of the Sun that the ancients thought the gods descended to and reascended from the earth. This idea appears plainly in the Papyrus quoted above, where the Mithraist is represented as an eagle who flies upwards " and alone " to heaven and there beholds all things[2]. He prays that he may, in spite of his mortal and corruptible nature, behold with immortal eyes after having been hallowed with holy hallowings, " the deathless aeon, lord of the fiery crowns," and that " the corruptible nature of mortals " which has been imposed upon him by " inexorable Necessity " may depart from him. " Then," says the author of the fragment— which, it will be remembered, claims to be a revelation given by the archangel of the great Sun-God Mithras—the initiate " will see the gods who rule each day and hour ascending to heaven and others descending, and the path of the visible gods through the disk of the god my father will appear." He describes the machinery of nature by which the winds are produced, which seems to be figured on some of the Mithraic monuments, and which reminds one of the physics supposed to be revealed in

---

[1] See Chap. VIII, p. 74, n. 3, *supra*.

[2] That those who had taken the degree of Pater were called ἀετοί or eagles appears from Porphyry, *de Abstinentia*, Bk IV. c. 16. Cumont doubts this; see *T. et M.* I. p. 314, n. 8. The idea probably had its origin in the belief common to classical antiquity that the eagle alone could fly to the sun, from which the Mithraist thought that the souls of men came, and to which those of perfect initiates would return. Cf. *op. cit.* I. p. 291.

the Enochian literature. Then, after certain spells have been recited, the initiate sees the disk of the Sun, which opens, disclosing " doors of fire and the world of the gods within them." Then follow more invocations to the gods of the seven planetary worlds who appear in due course, and presumably give him admission to their realms. After another invocation, in what may possibly be some Asianic or Anatolian language very much corrupted, the initiate beholds " a young god, beautiful, with fiery hair, in white tunic and purple mantle, and having on his head a crown of fire," who seems to be Helios or Sol, the driver of the sun's chariot on the Mithraic monuments. He is saluted as " Mighty in strength, mighty ruler, greatest king of gods ! O Sun, lord of heaven and earth, God of Gods ! " Next appear " seven virgins in linen robes having the heads of serpents," who are called " the seven Fortunes of heaven " and are, as M. Georges Lafaye surmises, the seven stars of the constellation of the Great Bear[1]. They are followed by seven male gods also dressed in linen robes and with golden crowns, but equipped with the heads of black bulls, who are called " the rulers of the Pole." These are they, we are told, who send upon the impious thunders and lightnings and earthquakes. And so we are led at last to the apparition of " a god of extraordinary stature, having a glance of fire, young and golden-haired, in white tunic and golden crown, clothed in anaxyrides, holding in his right hand the golden shoulder of a young bull." This, *i.e.* the shoulder, we are told, is called " Arctos, who moves the sky, making it to turn forwards and backwards according to the hour." But the god appears to be intended for Mithras, and the shoulder of the bull is probably an allusion to the bull-slaying scene which may serve to show that there were more interpretations than one placed upon the Tauroctony. The initiate hails this god as " Lord of water, consecrator of the earth, ruler of the air, shining-rayed One, of primeval rays ! " and the like, and continues :

" O Lord, having been born again, I die ! Having increased and again increasing, I come to an end by life-begotten birth, and coming into existence, and having been released unto death, I

[1] Lafaye, *L'Initiation Mithriaque*, p. 106.

pursue my way, as thou hast ordered from the beginning, as thou hast ordained. And having accomplished the mystery, I am *Pheroura miouri*."

Here the fragment abruptly breaks off, and plunges into directions for the manufacture of oracles and the other stuff common in Magic Papyri. One is not much inclined to believe with M. Cumont that the author of the galimatias knew nothing about Mithraism[1], and merely introduced Mithras' name into his opening to impress his readers with a sense of the value of his recipes. It seems more likely that the writer of the fragment had really got hold of some part of a Mithraic ritual, which he had read without understanding it, and that he was trying to work more or less meaningless extracts from it into his spells on the same principle that the sorcerers of the European Renaissance used when they took similar liberties with the words of the Mass. If this view be adopted, it follows that the concluding words given above confirm the view that the Mithraists, like the Orphics before them, taught the metempsychosis or reincarnation of souls[2]. Did the Mithraist think that his soul, when released from this "dread necessity," finally escaped from even the planetary spheres and, raising itself into the heaven of the fixed stars, became united with the Deity Himself? We can only ask the question without being able to suggest an answer supported by any evidence.

With regard to the priests who acted as celebrants in these strange mysteries, there are instances to be found in the inscriptions which make it plain that the priestly office was not confined or attached to any particular degree of initiation. *Pater Patrum* (Father of Fathers) is a designation which occurs too frequently on the monuments for it to mean anything but eldest or president of those who had taken the seventh or highest degree in one congregation[3]. But *Sacerdos* or *Antistes*

---

[1] Cumont, *T. et M.* II. p. 56.

[2] Porphyry, *de Abstinentia*, Bk IV. c. 16 says this was so.

[3] Cumont, *T. et M.* I. p. 318, n. 1, points out that an initiate might become Pater Patrum immediately after being made Pater or Pater sacrorum simply. This appears from the two monuments both dated the same year of Vettius Agorius Praetextatus, *op. cit.* II. p. 95.

indifferently is the name by which the priest of Mithras is
described by himself and others, and the holding of the office
seems not to have been inconsistent with the tenure at once
of other priesthoods and of high office in the State.   Thus
the *clarissimus* Vettius Agorius Praetextatus, who was Urban
Praetor, Proconsul of Achaea, Prefect of the City, Prefect of
the Praetorians of Italy and Illyricum, and Consul Designate
at the time of his death, was Father of Fathers in the religion
of Mithras besides being Pontiff of the Sun and Pontiff of Vesta[1].
This was at a very late date, when probably only a man of high
civil rank dared avow on his tombstone, as did Vettius, his
fidelity to the god ; but earlier, we find Lucius Septimius, a
freedman of Severus, Caracalla, and Geta, acting as " Father
and Priest of the Unconquered Mithras in the Augustan house"—
evidently a Court chaplain—, and a certain *clarissimus* Alfenius
Julianus Kamenius who is of consular rank, a quaestor and a
praetor, as a " father of the sacred things of the Highest Unconquered One Mithras[2]."   So, too, we find a veteran of the
IVth Flavian Legion acting as *pater sacrorum*, a decurion as
antistes and another as *sacerdos* of Mithras[3].   Evidently, the
cares of the priesthood did not occupy the priest's whole time,
and he never seems to have lived in the temple as did the clergy
of the Alexandrian divinities.   There was, on the faith of
Porphyry, a *summus pontifex* or Supreme Pontiff of Mithras,
who like the Christian bishop in the Epistle to Timothy was
forbidden to marry more than once[4] ; but this was probably
a high officer of State appointed directly by the Emperor.
No proof is forthcoming that a fire was kept perpetually burning
on the altar in the European chapels of Mithras, as perhaps was
the case with the temples of the faith in Asia Minor, or that
daily or any other regularly repeated services were held there,

---

[1] See Ammianus Marcellinus Bk XXII. c. 7, for his life under Julian.
His career is well described by Dill, *Roman Society in the Last Century of
the Western Empire*, 1899, pp. 17, 18, 30, 154, 155.

[2] Cumont, *T. et M.* II. p. 100, inscr. 35; p. 98, inscr. 24.

[3] *Op. cit.* II. p. 130, inscr. 225 ; p. 132, inscr. 239 ; p. 134, inscr. 257.
The two decurions may of course have been decurions of the rite only,
as to which see *op. cit.* I. p. 326.

[4] *Op. cit.* I. p. 324 : Tertullian, *Praescpt.* c. 40.

and such services moreover could seldom have been attended
by the soldiers with the colours, who seem to have made up
the majority of the god's worshippers. Prayers to the Sun-God
and other deities were no doubt offered by Mithraists, possibly
at sunrise and sunset, and perhaps special ones on the first day
of the week, which they very likely held sacred to their god.
But the small size of the Mithraea, and the scanty number of
the members of the associations supporting each[1], make it
extremely unlikely that there was anything like regular congregational worship, or that the faithful assembled there except
for initiations or meetings for conferring the different degrees.
The extremely poor execution of the bas-reliefs and other
sculptures found in the majority of these chapels all points the
same way. Most of these, together with the furniture and what
are nowadays called " articles de culte," were presented to the
chapel by private members of the association[2]. The fact that
the congregations of many chapels must have frequently
changed by the shifting of garrisons from one end of the Empire
to the other caused by the operations of war both external and
civil, also helps to account for their temporary and poverty-
stricken appearance when compared with the great and stately
temples reared to rival gods like Serapis.

Thus the truth of Renan's comparison of the Mithraic faith
with modern Freemasonry becomes more apparent, and we
may picture to ourselves the Mithraists as a vast society spread
over the whole of the Empire, consisting mainly of soldiers,
and entirely confined to the male sex. The example of the
Emperor Julian, himself a devotee of Mithras, but actively
concerned in the propagation of the worship of other divinities,
such as Apollo, Serapis, Mars, and Cybele[3], shows that its real
aim was not so much the conversion of individuals as the inclu-
sion of all other cults within itself. It was doubtless with this
view that Julian recalled from exile those heresiarchs who had
been banished by the Christian emperors and insisted on equal

---

[1] Cumont, *T. et M.* I. p. 65. Thirty-five seems to be the greatest
number belonging to any one chapel.

[2] *Op. cit.* I. p. 327.

[3] Amm. Marcell. *passim.*

toleration for all sects of Jews and Christians[1]. Themistius is
no doubt merely echoing the sentiments of the Mithraist
emperor when he writes to his Christian successor Jovian that
no lover of wisdom should bind himself to any exclusively
national worship, but should acquaint himself with all religions[2]. God, he says, requires no agreement on this subject
among men, and their rivalries in matters of faith are really
beneficial in leading their minds to the contemplation of other
than worldly things. But this highly philosophic temper was
not reached all at once ; and it is probable that the worship of
Mithras was, on its first importation into the West, but one
foreign superstition the more, as little enlightened and as
exclusively national as the Jewish, the Egyptian, or any of the
others. It was probably its rise to imperial favour under the
Antonines, when Commodus and many of the freedmen of
Caesar's House were initiated, that first suggested to its votaries
the possibility of using it as an instrument of government;
and henceforth its fortunes were bound up with those of
the still Pagan State. Its strictly monarchical doctrine, using
the adjective in its ancient rather than in its modern connotation, must have always endeared it to the emperors, who were
beginning to see clearly that in a *quasi*-Oriental despotism lay
the only chance of salvation for the Roman Empire. Its relations
with Mazdeism in the strict form which this last assumed after
the religious reforms of the Sassanian Shahs have never been
elucidated, and M. Cumont seems to rely too much upon the
later Avestic literature to explain everything that is obscure
in the religion of Mithras. If we imagine, as there is reason to
do, that Western Mithraism was looked upon by the Sassanian
reformers as a dangerous heresy[3], the Roman Emperors would
have an additional reason for supporting it ; and it is significant
that it was exactly those rulers whose wars against the Persians
were most successful who seem to have most favoured the

[1] Neander, *Ch. Hist.* III. p. 136.

[2] Marinus, *vita Procli*, pp. 67, 68 ; Neander, *op. cit.* III. p. 136.

[3] Witness the reduction of Mitra, who plays such an important part
in the religion of the Vedas, to the far lower position of chief of the Izeds
or Yazatas in the Sassanian reform.

worship of the Persian god. When Trajan conquered Dacia, the great province between the Carpathians and the Danube now represented by Hungary and Roumania, he colonized it by a great mass of settlers from every part of the Roman Empire, including therein many Orientals who brought with them into their new home the worship of their Syrian and Asianic gods[1]. It was hence an excellent field for the culture of a universal and syncretic religion such as that of Mithras, and the great number of Mithraea whose remains have been found in that province, show that this religion must have received hearty encouragement from the Imperial Court. From its geographical position, Dacia formed an effective counterpoise to the growing influence upon Roman policy of the Eastern provinces, and it might have proved a valuable outpost for a religion which was always looked upon with hostility by the Greek-speaking subjects of Rome. Unfortunately, however, a religion which allies itself with the State must suffer from its ally's reverses as well as profit by its good fortunes, and so the Mithraists found. When the Gothic invasion desolated Dacia, and especially when Valerian's disaster enabled the Goths to gain a footing there which not even the military genius of Claudius could loosen, Mithraism received a blow which was ultimately to prove fatal. The abandonment of Dacia to the Goths and Vandals by Aurelian in 255 A.D., led to its replanting by a race whose faces were turned more to Constantinople than to Rome, and who were before long to be converted to Christianity *en masse*[2]. Diocletian and his colleagues did what they could to restore the balance by proclaiming, as has been said above, the "unconquered" Mithras the protector of their empire at the great city which is now the capital of the Austrian Empire; but the accession of Constantine and his alliance with the Christian Church some twenty years later, definitely turned the scale against the last god of Paganism. Although the Mithraic worship may have revived for a moment under the philosophic Julian, who was, as has been said, peculiarly addicted to it, it possessed no real power of recuperation, and was perhaps

---

[1] Cumont, *T. et M.* I. p. 250, for authorities.
[2] Gibbon, *Decline and Fall* (Bury's ed.), I. p. 260 n. 106.

one of the first Pagan religions to be extinguished by the triumphant Christians[1]. In 377 A.D., Gracchus, the Urban Prefect of Rome, being desirous of baptism, carried into effect a promise made, as St Jerome boasts, some time before, and breaking into a chapel of Mithras, " overturned, broke in pieces and cast out " the sculptures which had seen the admission of so many initiates[2]. His example was followed in other parts of the Empire, and it is probable that some decree was obtained from the Emperor Gratian legalizing these acts of vandalism[3]. It is in this reign, M. Cumont finds, that most of the Mithraea were wrecked, and the very few which have come down to us in more complete state owe their preservation to the caution of their congregations, who blocked or built up the entrances to them in the vain hope that a fresh turn of the wheel might again bring their own cult to the top[4]. A conservative reaction towards the older faiths did indeed come for a moment under Eugenius ; but it was then too late. The masses had turned from Mithraism to Christianity, and the only adherents of the " Capped One " were to be found among the senators and high officials who had long connived at the evasion of the edicts prohibiting all forms of Pagan worship. The invasions of Alaric and Attila probably completed what the Christian mob had begun.

M. Cumont and Sir Samuel Dill are doubtless right when they attribute the downfall of Mithraism in great measure to its attitude towards women[5]. Mithraism was from the first essentially a virile faith, and had little need of the softer emotions. Hence we find in it none of the gorgeous public ritual, the long hours spent in mystic contemplation before the altar, or the filial devotion of the flock to the priest, that we see in the worship of the Alexandrian Gods. In spite of the great authority of M. Cumont, whose statements on the subject seem to have been accepted without much enquiry by later

[1] Reville, *Religion sous les Sevères*, p. 102.

[2] Cumont, *T. et M.* I. p. 347.

[3] Dill, *Last Century*, etc. p. 29, n. 2.

[4] Cumont, *T. et M.* I. p. 347.

[5] *Op. cit.* I. pp. 329, 330 ; Dill, *Nero to Marcus Aurelius*, p. 624.

writers, it will probably appear to the impartial student that
the priests of Mithras were more like the churchwardens or
elders of Protestant communities at the present day than the
active and highly organized hierarchy of the Alexandrian
divinities and of the Catholic Church. It is, as we have seen,
most probable that they never visited their chapels except in
company with the other devotees when an initiation into one
or other of the seven degrees of the cult was to be performed,
and, judging from the scanty numbers of the congregation, this
can only have been at fairly long intervals. Hence the daily
prayers and sacrifices of themselves and their congregations
were probably rendered elsewhere, either in the privacy of their
homes, or in the temples of other gods. In neither case would
they have much need for the assistance of women in their
propaganda, who would, moreover, have probably felt little
interest in a worship from the most solemn and distinctive
parts of which they were excluded. The Mithraists therefore
had to dispense with the support of a very large and important
fraction of the community which was easily won over to the
side of their rivals. Exceptional causes such as the perpetual
shifting of the legions from one end of the Empire to the other
at a time when communications between them were many times
more difficult than now, may have prevented such considerations
for some time from having their full weight. When once they
did so, the issue could not long be in doubt.

Nor was the very real, if somewhat vague, monotheism
which Mithraism taught, very likely to attract, at first sight,
the enthusiasm of a large and mixed population engaged in civil
pursuits. If the conjecture made above be correct, the Mithraist
in the ordinary way acknowledged no other god than Mithras,
although he would probably have admitted that he was but
the representative and antitype of the supreme Jupiter whom
he recognized as the official head of the State pantheon. As for
the other gods, he probably considered them as mere abstract
personifications of the powers of Nature, who were at the most
the creatures and subjects of Mithras " the friend," and whom
it might please him to propitiate by acts of worship which the
god would know how to appreciate. This is not very far from the

theories of the Stoics, always dear to the nobler spirits in the
Roman Empire, and coupled with the high Stoic ideal of duty,
forms one of the best working philosophies for the soldier ever
devised. But the soldier, removed as he is from care for his
daily necessities, and with instant and ready obedience to
another will than his own constantly required of him, has
always held different views on such subjects to the civilian ;
and such ideas were rather above the heads of the crowd, sunk
for the most part in abject poverty, utterly absorbed in the
struggle for daily bread, and only anxious to snatch some
passing enjoyment from a life of toil. What they, and even
more urgently, their womenfolk needed was a God, not towering
above them like the Eternal Sun, the eye of Mithras and his
earthly representative, shedding his radiance impartially upon
the just and the unjust ; but a God who had walked upon the
earth in human form, who had known like themselves pain and
affliction, and to whom they could therefore look for sympathy
and help. Such a god was not to be found in the Mithraic
Cave.

For these reasons, probably, Mithraism fell after a reign of
little more than two centuries. Yet for good or ill, few religions
have lived in vain ; and some of the ideas which it made
popular in Europe have hardly yet died out. The theory that
the emperor, king, or chief of the State is of a different nature
to other men, and is in a peculiar manner the care of the gods,
was first formulated in the West during the time that Mithraism
was in power and is a great deal more the creation of the Persian
religion than of the Egyptian, in which he was said to be the
incarnation of the Sun-God. This is fairly plain from the custom
to which M. Cumont has lately drawn attention of releasing
at the funeral or apotheosis of a Roman emperor a captive
eagle, representing the soul of the dead ruler, the upward flight
of the bird being held typical of the soul's ascension into heaven[1].
The connection of this practice with Mithraism is evident, since
" eagle " was one of the names given to the perfect Mithraist,
or he who had taken all the seven degrees of initiation, and had

[1] Cumont, "L'aigle funéraire des Syriens et l'apothéose des empereurs."
R.H.R., 1910, pt ii. pp. 159 *sqq.*

therefore earned the right to be called *pater sacrorum*[1].   The
Christian emperors of Rome continued probably the practice
and certainly the nomenclature associated with it, and Constantine and his successors were hailed by the Mithraic epithets
of " aeternus," " invictus," and " felix " as freely as his Pagan
predecessors.   From this period the notion of the " divinity
that doth hedge a king " descended to comparatively modern
times, and " Sacred Majesty " was an epithet of our own kings
down to the reign of the last Stuart.   Probably, too, it was the
custom of releasing an eagle at a royal funeral which so impressed the popular imagination that the metaphor became
transferred, as such things generally are sooner or later, to the
lower ranks of the community, and the figure of the soul being
borne aloft on wings took the place that it still occupies in
popular Christian literature.

The share that Mithraism had in diffusing the practices of
magic and astrology is by no means so clear.   That the Mithraists, like other pagans of the early centuries, were addicted to
magic is one of the most frequent accusations brought against
them by Christian writers, and the word magic itself, as has
been said above, is derived from those Magi from whom the
Mithraists were said to have derived their doctrine.   In support
of this, it can certainly be said that the worshippers of Mithras
by rendering a modified cult to Ahriman, whom the Christians
identified with Satan, laid themselves open to the suspicion of
trafficking with devils, and it is quite possible that they, like
the followers of many other religions at the time, looked with
favour upon the compulsion rather than the propitiation of the
lower powers.   Yet the strict monotheism of the faith which
practically looked to Mithras for the ultimate control and
regulation of all sublunary things, is certainly against this conclusion ;   and it should be noticed that the laws against the
practices of magic and astrology, then so intertwined that it is
difficult to separate them[2], were quite as severe under emperors
like Commodus and Diocletian who worshipped Mithras, as

---

[1] Cf. the "solitary eagle" of the Magic Papyrus quoted on p. 265 *supra*.
[2] Maury, *La Magie et L'Astrologie, passim*.   The Zend Avesta also
denounces magic as did the later Manichaeism.   See p. 342 *infra*.

under those of their successors who professed the faith of Christ. The rites of Hecate, however, were, as we have seen, closely connected with those of Mithras and were generally in the hands of Mithraists. These Hecatean rites seem to have been almost entirely magical in their character, and it is the name of Hecate that was handed down as that of the patroness of sorcerers through the Middle Ages and the Renaissance[1]. One of the priests of Mithras also goes out of his way to declare on his epitaph that he is *studiosus astrologiae*, and on the whole the Christian accusation was probably not without foundation.

[1] As in Shakespeare's *Macbeth*.

CHAPTER XIII

MANES AND THE MANICHAEANS

IT is generally said that the religion of Mithras ended and
was absorbed in Manichaeism, which may thus be supposed to
have inherited some, at least, of its doctrines[1]. This is one of
those statements which are copied by one author from another
until they acquire by mere repetition the force of an axiom;
but its truth is not obvious, nor does it appear to rest upon any
sound foundation. Except in the fact that both Mithraism and
Manichaeism came in the first instance from Persia, there is
little likeness between the two faiths, which are in all essential
respects diametrically opposed to each other. A strict dualism,
or the eternal antagonism of two equal principles, is the distinguishing feature of the religion of Manes, while the worship
of Mithras rested, as has been said in the last chapter, on an
equally uncompromising monotheism, which made the Supreme
Being, whether known as Jupiter or Ormuzd, at once the
creator and the governor of the universe. In this respect, it
drew near to Judaism, which it may have aimed at incorporating with itself, and was not ashamed to place on its
monuments scenes which can be referred to the Old Testament[2].

[1] So Cumont, *T. et M.* I. pp. 45, 349, 350. He seems to rely, however,
entirely on the passage in the *Acta Archelai* (as to which see n. 1, p. 280 *infra*),
wherein the supposed bishop Archelaus addresses the equally imaginary
Manes as "Savage priest and accomplice of Mithras!"—possibly a mere
term of abuse. See Hegemonius, *Acta Archelai*, ed. Beeson, Leipzig, 1906,
c. XL. p. 59.

[2] Cumont, *T. et M.* I. p. 41. He sees in the scenes which border the
Tauroctony references or parallels to the fig-leaves of Genesis, the striking
of the rock by Moses, and the ascension of Elijah. In the so-called Mithraic
Ritual of the Magic Papyrus of Paris, there are certain Hebrew words
introduced, such as πιπι (a well-known perversion of the Tetragrammaton),
σανχερωβ and σεμες ιλαμ (The "Eternal Sun").

Manichaeism, on the other hand, looked on Judaism with horror, rejected the Old Testament entirely, and was not improbably born in an outbreak of anti-Semitic fury[1]. But the discrepancy of doctrine is as nothing compared to the wide difference in those external matters which in a new religion most strike the imagination of the crowd, and have therefore much to do with its success or failure. The Mithraist was accustomed, as we have seen, to an allegorical and symbolical ritual in which the material image of his god was for ever before him; but the Manichaean, as we shall see later, forbade the use of images and his worship consisted merely of prayers and hymns. The Mithraists made frequent use in their ceremonies of the sacrifice of animals; but the Manichaeans looked with displeasure on the taking of the life even of plants. The worshipper of Mithras not only gloried in the outward profession of his religion, but by his avoidance of the wearing of garlands forced the notice of it on those of his fellows who were not of the faith. The follower of Manes, on the contrary, concealed his religion as carefully as Basilides wished his followers to conceal theirs, and even went to the length of outwardly adopting a creed different from his own. It is not therefore to be wondered at that the rulers of the Roman Empire, whose acquaintance with the worship of Mithras was a thousand times more profound than our own, should have favoured Mithraism and have made every effort to suppress Manichaeism. The very emperors who placed their reformed State under the protection of Mithras imposed the penalty of death upon those of their subjects who should venture to teach the religion of Manes[2].

[1] See the story which Josephus, *Antiq.* xx. cc. 2, 3, 4, tells about Izates, king of Adiabene, who wanted to turn Jew and thereby so offended his people that they called in against him Vologeses or Valkash, the first reforming Zoroastrian king and collector of the books of the Zend Avesta. Cf. Darmesteter, *The Zend Avesta* (Sacred Books of the East), Oxford, 1895, p. xl. Cf. Ém. de Stoop *La Diffusion du Manichéisme dans l'Empire romain*, Gand, 1909, p. 10.

[2] *Circa* 296, A.D. See Neander, *Ch. Hist.* II. p. 195, where the authenticity of the decree is defended. For the provocation given to the Empire by the anti-militarism of Manes see de Stoop, *op. cit.* pp. 36 37.

Not less different were the sanctions with which Mithraism and Manichaeism appeared in the West. The worship of Mithras came into the Roman world unobtrusively and without any claim to an exclusive revelation or special means of propaganda. But Manichaeism had at its back the personality of one of those wonderful men who appear at rare intervals in the world's history, to leave behind them a memorial of their empire over the minds of their fellows in the shape of a new creed. Manes was indeed, as the discoveries of the last decade have taught us, an innovator in religion entirely worthy to rank with Zoroaster, Buddha, and Muhammad, and when the difficulties in the way of his missionary activity are considered, his influence upon the religious ideas of those who came after him was at least as marked as that of any of them. Manes or Mânî—the first being the Greek form of the name—was born, according to his own deliberate statement, about the year 216 A.D., in a village of Babylonia called Mardînû situate on the Kutha canal to the south of Ctesiphon[1]. According to Christian tradition, his real name was Corbicius or Kubrik and he was a slave of unknown birth[2]; according to the Mahommedan writers his father was one Patecius or Fatak, while his mother is sometimes described as the "Lady Mary," sometimes as a Parthian princess, and is sometimes named Karossa[3]. Such legends grow up naturally round the birth of all founders of religions, and we should believe them the less in this case that they have been handed down to us by the professors of religions bitterly opposed to that of Manes. Yet the story about the Parthian princess seems confirmed by the free access that he seems to have always possessed to the court of the Persian monarchs of his time. Manes himself says, according

[1] Al-Bîrûnî, *Chronology of Ancient Nations*, p. 190. The date he gives is twelve years before the accession of Ardeshîr. E. Rochat, *Essai sur Mani et sa Doctrine*, Genève, 1897, p. 81, examines all the different accounts and makes the date from 214 to 218 A.D.

[2] Epiphanius, *Haer.* LXVI. c. 1, p. 399, Oehler; Socrates, *Hist. Eccl.* Bk I. c. 22; Hegemonius, *Acta Archelai*, c. LXIV.

[3] Muhammed ben Ishak, commonly called En-Nadîm, in the book known as the *Fihrist*, translated by Flügel, *Mani, seine Lehre und seine Schriften*, Leipzig, 1862, pp. 83, 116. 118, 119. Cf. Rochat, *op. cit.* p. 75.

to Al-Bîrûnî, that illumination came to him in his thirteenth year[1]; but this is contradicted by the *Fihrist*, which puts the age at which he received revelation as twenty-four[2]. The *Acta Archelai*, a Christian source obviously suspect in the state it has come down to us, would make him a priest of Mithras[3], a tradition which may have originated at a date when the Catholic Church recognized the danger to itself involved in the spread of the Mithraic religion. Another story would make him a Magus or one of the priestly caste entrusted by Ardeshîr with the propagation of the reformed religion of Zoroaster[4], which is discredited by the fact that it was the Magi who were from the outset his bitterest enemies[5]. A late Oriental writer says that he was a Christian priest having a cure of souls at Ahvâz[6], the capital city of the province of Huzitis, which again is negatived by the fact that he seems from his writings to have had little more than a hearsay knowledge of Catholic Christianity, although they show some acquaintance with the heresies of Bardesanes and Marcion[7]. He is said to have acquired great

[1] Al-Bîrûnî, *Chronology*, p. 190.

[2] Flügel, *op. cit.* p. 84; Rochat, *op. cit.* p. 83.

[3] Hegemonius, *Acta Arch.* c. XL., p. 59, Beeson. Rochat, *op. cit.* pp. 9–49, discusses the authenticity of the *Acta* chapter by chapter. He thinks the pretended discussion between Archelaus and Manes unhistorical, and the account of it possibly modelled on that between St Augustine and Faustus the Manichaean. The remainder of the *Acta* he considers fairly trustworthy as an account of Manes' own tenets. This may well be, as Epiphanius, *Haer.* LXVI. cc. 6–7, 25–31, transcribes the epistle to Marcellus, its answer, and the exposition of Turbo, and could scarcely have heard, as early as 375 A.D., about which time he wrote, of St Augustine's discussion. The *Acta* owe much to the care of the American scholar, Mr Beeson of Chicago, who has given us the careful edition of them mentioned in n. 1, p. 277 *supra*. It is a pity that he did not see his way to keep the old numeration of the chapters.

[4] Beausobre, *Hist. du Manichéisme*, Paris, 1734, Pt I. Bk II. cc. 1–4. Cf. Stokes in *Dict. Christian Biog. s.v.* Manes; Rochat, *op. cit.* p. 83.

[5] Rochat, *op. cit.* p. 89.

[6] Abulfarag in Kessler, *Forschungen über die Manichäische Religion*, Berlin, 1889, Bd I. p. 335; Rochat, *op. cit.* p. 84; Neander, *Ch. Hist.* II. p. 168.

[7] Flügel, *op. cit.* p. 85. Cf. Al-Bîrûnî, *India* (ed. Sachau), p. 55, where Manes quotes the opinion of Bardesanes' "partizans." There are many words put into the mouth of Manes in the work quoted which argue acquaintance with the *Pistis Sophia*.

skill in painting which he used to illustrate his teaching[1], and to have been a learned mathematician and astronomer. This is likely enough; but the only events of his life which seem well attested, are that he began at an early age to propagate his doctrine and that he succeeded in converting to it Peroz or Fîrûz the son of Ardeshîr, through whose means he obtained a formal hearing from Sapor or Shâpûr, the conqueror of Valerian and Ardeshîr's successor, shortly after this king's accession to the throne[2]. Sapor seems to have listened to Manes with respect and, according to an Oriental writer, to have even favoured his propaganda, until the Magi, to whom the revival of the Zoroastrian religion had been committed, convinced him of his error[3]. On this, Manes was exiled from Persia and retired, says Al-Bîrûnî, to India, China, and Thibet preaching his gospel[4]. On Sapor's death, he returned to Persia under Hormisdas or Ormuz, and again, it is said, succeeded in converting to his tenets the reigning monarch[5]. On Varanes' or Bahram's accession to the throne the following year, however, he was seized and put to death as a heretic after a disputation with the Chief of the Magi, in which he failed to support the test of an ordeal by molten metal proposed to him[6]. The most likely account of his death narrates that he was decapitated, and that his skin stuffed with straw was suspended at the gate of the town where the execution took place[7]. This was followed

[1] Abulmaali in Kessler, *op. cit.* p. 371; Firdaûsi, *ibid.* p. 375; Mirkhônd, *ibid.* p. 379. Cf. Rochat, *op. cit.* p. 81. He is said to have painted his pictures in a cave in Turkestan (Stokes in *Dict. Christian Biog. s.v.* Manes), which would agree well enough with the late German discoveries at Turfan, for which see A. von Le Coq in *J.R.A.S.* 1909, pp. 299 *sqq.*

[2] Flügel, *op. cit.* p. 85.

[3] Al-Jakûbi in Kessler, *op. cit.* pp. 328, 329; cf. Rochat, *op. cit.* p. 88.

[4] Al-Bîrûnî, *Chronology*, pp. 191, 192.

[5] Rochat, *op. cit.* p. 89. Al-Bîrûnî, whom he quotes, however, says merely that the Manichaeans increased under Ormuz, and also that Ormuz "killed a number of them." See last note.

[6] Al-Jakûbi in Kessler, *op. cit.* p. 330. But Darmesteter (see passage quoted in n. 2, p. 284 *infra*) puts this event as happening after Ormuz' death and under Shapur II.

[7] Al-Bîrûnî, *Chronology*, p. 191. The town is called Djundi-sâbur or Gundisabur.

by a great persecution of the Manichaeans throughout Persia, and it is fairly evident that this, like his own fate, was due to the hostility he had aroused in the Magi[1]. The date of his death is fixed with some accuracy at 275 A.D., so that he would then have reached the age of sixty years[2].

The causes underlying this sudden appearance of a new religion are doubtless to be looked for in the political and religious history of Persia at the time. Ardeshîr, as has been said above, gave new life to the feeling of Persian nationality which the Parthian Kings had kept alive during Greek supremacy in Asia, and succeeded in again founding a Persian Empire. Like Alexander, Antiochus Epiphanes, and again, Diocletian, he seems to have been thoroughly alive to the great effect that a faith common to the whole empire would have in uniting the peoples under his sway.

"Never forget," he says in the supposed testament that he is said to have left for the guidance of his son Sapor, "that as a king you are at once the protector of religion and of your country. Consider the altar and the throne as inseparable and that they must always sustain each other. A sovereign without religion is a tyrant, and a people which have no religion may be deemed the most monstrous of all societies. Religion may exist without a State, but a State cannot exist without religion; and it is by holy laws that a political association can alone be bound[3]."

Yet in spite of these sentiments, more pithily expressed perhaps in the "No bishop, no king" of our own James I, the task of founding a common religion for the whole of the new Persian empire must have presented some uncommon difficulties. Apart from the strong Semitic element dominant in their Babylonian province, the Parthians had always been eclectic in matters of faith, and Vonones, one of the last kings of Parthia, had shown himself to be a Philhellene of a type which must have been peculiarly offensive to a sovereign who was

[1] Al-Jakûbi, *ubi cit. supra*; Eutychius quoted by Stokes, *Dict. Christian Biog. s.v.* Manes.

[2] Rochat, *op. cit.* p. 93, examines all the evidence for this and comes to the conclusion given in the text.

[3] Malcolm, *History of Persia*, London, 1821, Vol. I. pp. 95, 96.

trying to revive the old Persian nationality[1]. The worship of
Mithras, the god most favoured by the legions with whom
Ardeshîr was soon to be at death-grips, must have been equally
out of the question; and the knowledge of this is probably to
be seen in the low place in the celestial hierarchy assigned to
the old Vedic god in the Avesta of Ardeshîr's day[2]. The
Jewish religion in Central Asia had lately given signs of proselytizing fervour, and it was the going-over of a Parthian kinglet
against the will of his people to the Jewish faith which first,
according to one account, gave the excuse for the intervention
of Vologeses or Valkhash and the subsequent reformation or
revival of the Zoroastrian religion[3]. At the same time, Christianity had already begun to share with Mithraism the devotion
of the legions stationed on the Roman frontier, and in the
Gnostic form favoured by the teaching of Marcion and
Bardesanes was pushing into Persia from Armenia and Edessa[4].
Nor can we doubt that Buddhism, already perhaps struck with
decay in its native country of India[5], but flourishing exceedingly
further East, was trying to obtain a foothold in that very
Bactria which was afterwards said to have been the historic
scene of Zoroaster's activity. Other small, but, as the event
was to show, highly vitalized faiths, were current in Western
Asia, and the power of the Magi when Ardeshîr overthrew the
Parthian power had declined so greatly that the statues of the
Parthian kings were placed in the temples of the gods and
adored equally with those of the divinities[6]. The Persians of
Herodotus' time, who did not believe in deities who had the
same nature as men, would have blushed at such a profanation.

[1] G. Rawlinson, *The 6th Oriental Monarchy*, 1873, p. 222; Rochat, *op. cit.* p. 53.

[2] See Chap. XII *supra*, p. 232.   [3] See n. 1, p. 278 *supra*.

[4] Al-Bîrûnî, *Chron.* p. 187, makes Manes the successor or continuator of
Bardesanes and Marcion. This was certainly not so; but it was probably
only from their followers that he derived any acquaintance with Christianity. See n. 7, p. 280 *supra*. So Muhammad or Mahommed, four centuries
later, drew his ideas of the same faith from the heretics of his day.

[5] Rhys Davids, *Buddhist India*, 1903, p. 318, says that after 300 A.D.
Buddhism was everywhere in decay in India.

[6] Rochat, *op. cit.* p. 58.

From this unpromising welter of creeds and cults, Ardeshîr delivered the State by restoring the worship of Ahura Mazda as the State religion. One of his first cares was to collect the fragments of the books which we now know as the Zend Avesta, in which the revelations of the national prophet Zoroaster were set down in a language not then understanded of the people. It was afterwards said that the MSS. of these books had purposely been destroyed or scattered by Alexander; but the fact seems to be that they had fallen into discredit through the turning-away of the Persians towards Hellenic and Semitic gods; and that a previous attempt to restore their authority by Valkhash or Vologeses I, the Parthian king who reigned from 50 to 75 A.D., had met with little encouragement from his subjects[1]. Most modern scholars are now agreed that the Avesta and the literature that grew up round it contain many doctrines not to be found in the Persian religion current in Achaemenian times, and evidently brought into it from foreign sources under the Hellenistic and Parthian kings. Such as it is, however, the Avesta formed the Sacred Book of Ardeshîr's reformation; while, in the order of the Magi, by him restored to more than their former power, the reformed Zoroastrian faith possessed an active, established, and persecuting Church, which reigned in Persia without a serious rival until the Mahommedan invasion.

Yet the first struggles of the reformation must have been sharp, and Darmesteter was doubtless justified when he saw in Manichaeism the first and possibly the strongest expression of the revulsion of Ardeshîr's subjects against the rigid orthodoxy which he sought to impose upon them[2]. That such a feeling persisted for some time is plain from the fact that Manes' "heresy" is said by Al-Bîrûnî to have been followed by that of Mazdak, who seems to have preached, like the Antinomian sects of Cromwell's time, a kind of Socialism including the community of women and of property[3]. There arose also about the same time or a little later the sect of Zervanists

---

[1] Darmesteter, *Zend Avesta*, pp. xl, xli.

[2] *Op. cit.* pp. xlvii *sqq.*

[3] Al-Bîrûnî, *Chron.* p. 192.

referred to in the chapter on Mithras, who taught that Boundless Time was the origin of all things and was superior to Ormuzd and Ahriman, to both of whom he was said to have given birth. They seemed to have gained great power in the reign of Yezdegerd II; and, if we may trust the Armenian authors, a proclamation commanding adherence to their doctrines was put forth by Yezdegerd's general Mihr Nerses on his invasion of Armenia in 450 A.D.[1] But the earliest and most enduring of these heresies or rebellions against the purified and restored religion of Ahura Mazda appears to have been that of Manes.

Were now the doctrines that Manes preached to his own undoing his invention, or did he draw them from some pre-existent source? It is said, in a Christian account which has come down to us, that they were the work of one Scythianus[2], a native, as his name implies, of "Scythia" (which here probably means Turkestan) and a contemporary of the Apostles, who married an Egyptian slave and learned from her all the wisdom of the Egyptians[3]. With the help of this and the tincture of dualism which he extracted from "the works of Pythagoras," the story goes on to say, Scythianus constructed a system which he taught to a disciple named Terebinthus, otherwise called Buddas or Buddha, before his own death in Judaea[4]. This

---

[1] Elisaeus Vartabed in Langlois' *Collection des Hist. de l'Arménie*, Paris, 1868, t. II. p. 190. The story is repeated almost word for word by Eznig of Goghp, *ibid.* p. 875. Cf. Neander, *Ch. Hist.* II. p. 171.

[2] Rochat, *op. cit.*, following Kessler, shows, it seems, conclusively, that this is another name for Manes' father, Fatak or Patecius.

[3] She was a courtezan at Hypselis in the Thebaid according to Epiphanius, *Haer.* LXVI. c. 11, p. 400, Oehler. As Baur, *Die Manichäische Religionssystem*, Tübingen, 1831, p. 468 *sqq.* has pointed out, this is probably an imitation of the story told about Simon Magus and his Helena (see Chap. VI *supra*). It seems to have arisen as an embroidery, quite in Epiphanius' manner, upon the story in the *Acta*, that Scythianus married a captive from the Upper Thebaid (Hegemonius, *op. cit.* c. LXII. p. 90, Beeson).

[4] Many guesses have been made as to the allusions concealed under these names, as to which see Rochat, *op. cit.* pp. 64–73. Neander (*Ch. Hist.* II. p. 16) quotes from Ritter the suggestion that Terebinthus may come from an epithet of Buddha, *Tere-hintu* "Lord of the Hindus." One wonders whether it might not have been as fitly given to a Jewish slave

Terebinthus gave out that he was born of a virgin and had been nursed by an angel on a mountain; and he also wrote four books in which the doctrines of Scythianus were set down[1]. These books he entrusted to an aged widow with whom he lived, and he was afterwards struck dead while performing a magical ceremony. On his death, she bought a boy of seven years old named Corbicius, whom she enfranchised, and to whom she left her property and Terebinthus' books some five years later. Thus equipped, Corbicius took the name of Manes, which may signify "Cup" or "Vessel[2]," and began to preach. This history has evidently been much corrupted and by no means agrees with the account before quoted from Oriental sources which bears greater marks of authenticity; but it is thought by some to be, like the 14th chapter of Genesis, a sort of allegory in which the names of peoples and systems are given as those of individual men[3]. If this be so, we should perhaps see in Scythianus the representative of those non-Aryan tribes of Medes of whom the Magi formed part, while in the name of Buddha we might find that of one of those Judaean communities holding a mixture of Magian and Buddhist tenets who according to one tradition were for long encamped near the Dead Sea[4]. Yet there is nothing specifically Buddhist or Egyptian about the doctrines of Manes as we know them[5], and if there were any likeness between the

sold at the Fair of the Terebinth with which Hadrian closed his war of extermination.

[1] These four books may have been intended for the *Shapurakhan*, the *Treasure*, the *Gospel* and the *Capitularies*, which Al-Bîrûnî, *Chron.* p. 1̄X̄l, attributes to Mani. Cf. Epiphanius, *Haer.* LXVI. c. 2, p. 402, Oehler, and the *Scholia* of Théodore bar Khôni in Pognon, *Inscriptions Mandaïtes des Coupes de Khouabir*, pp. 182, 183.

[2] Epiphanius, *op. cit.* c. 1, p. 398, Oehler.

[3] Colditz in Kessler, *op. cit.* pp. 15, 16. Cf. Rochat, *op. cit.* pp. 65, 66.

[4] Morrison, *Jews under Romans*, p. 325 for authorities. Philo, *de Vit. Contempl.* etc. c. III. says that similar communities existed in his time near the Mareotic lake in Egypt. But the date of the treatise and its attribution to Philo are alike uncertain. The first mention of Buddha in Greek literature is said to be that by Clem. Alex. *Strom.* Bk I. c. 15.

[5] Harnack in *Encyc. Britann.* 9th edition, *s.v.* Manichaeans, p. 48, says "There is not a single point in Manichaeism which demands for its

mythology and observances of the cult and those of its predecessors, it was probably introduced by Manes' followers rather
than by himself[1]. As to the doctrines of the Magi, Manes
certainly had no occasion to go to Judaea to find them; for
in the Persia of Ardeshîr and Sapor he must have heard quite
as much of them as he wished.

Probably, therefore, the Christian account of Manes' sources
is untrue, or rather, as M. Rochat suggests, it was composed at a
time and place in which Manichaeism had become a heresy or
alternative creed attached, so to speak, not to Zoroastrianism but
to Christianity, and had picked up from this and other faiths
many accretions[2]. The doctrine of Manes which has come
down to us from other sources is extremely simple, and seems
to accord better with the Puritanical simplicity of life and
ritual afterwards practised by his followers. Both the
Christian and the Mahommedan traditions agree that he believed
that there were two gods, uncreated and eternal, and ever-
lastingly opposed to each other[3]. One of these is the God of
Light and the other the God of Darkness; but he does not
seem to have given any specific or proper name to either[4].
It is possible that this last-named being may have been identified

---

explanation an appeal to Buddhism." This may be, but the discoveries
at Turfan and Tun-huang have made a connection between the two more
probable than appeared at the time he wrote. See also Kessler as quoted
by Rochat, *op. cit.* pp. 192, 193.

[1] This appears from the Chinese Treatise at Pekin mentioned later.
See p. 293, n. 2.

[2] Rochat, *op. cit.* p. 194. So Socrates, *Eccl. Hist.* Bk I. c. 22, calls
Manichaeism "a sort of heathen ('Ελληνίζων) Christianity."

[3] Hegemonius, *Acta*, c. VII. p. 91, Beeson; Flügel, *op. cit.*
p. 86.

[4] Certainly none is recorded in the Christian accounts, where Darkness
is called Hyle or Matter. En Nadîm (Flügel, *op. cit.* p. 86) makes Manes
call the good God "the King of the Paradise of Light" and (p. 90) the
Spirit of Darkness, Hummâma. Schahrastâni, as quoted in Flügel's note
(p. 240), makes this word mean "mirk" or "smoke" (*Qualm*). It would be
curious if Hummâma had any connection with the Elamite Khumbaba,
the opponent of the Babylonian hero Gilgamesh, because this personage
already figures in Ctesias' story about Nannaros, which has been recognized
as a myth relating to the Moon-god.

by him with Matter[1], although this would seem to be a remnant
of the Platonic philosophy of which there is no other trace in
his teaching. But it is certain that he regarded the God of
Darkness as entirely evil, that is to say, malevolent, and as
a power to propitiate whom man should make no attempt.
"I have considered it needful to despatch this letter to you"
says an epistle which there is much reason to consider expresses
the opinions, if not the actual words, of Manes himself[2]:

"first for the salvation of your soul and then to secure you against
dubious opinions, and especially against notions such as those teach
who lead astray the more simple (ἀπλούστεροι), alleging that both
good and evil come from the same Power, and introducing but one
principle, and neither distinguishing nor separating the darkness
from the light, and the good from the bad and the evil (φαῦλον),
and that which is without man from that which is within him, as
we have said formerly, so that they cease not to confuse and mingle
one thing with another. But do not thou, O my son, like most men,
unreasonably and foolishly join the two together nor ascribe them
both to the God of Goodness. For these teachers attribute to God
the beginning and the end, and make him the father of these ills *the
end of which is near a curse*[3]."

Although this epistle bears evident marks of having been
worked over and amplified by some writer of a later age than
that of the founder of Manichaeism, there cannot be much
doubt that it contains his teaching on the Two Principles of
all things. In the Christian account of Manes' doctrine which

---

[1] τὸ τῆς ὕλης δημιούργημα Hegemonius, *Acta*, c. VIII. p. 9, Beeson. Cf.
Alexander of Lycopolis, *adv. Manichaeos*, c. II.

[2] Epiph. *Haer.* LXVI. c. 6, p. 408, Oehler; Hegemonius, *Acta*, c. V.
pp. 5–7, Beeson. The authenticity of the letter is defended by Kessler,
op. cit. p. 166. Cf. Rochat, *op. cit.* p. 94 *contra*.

[3] τῶν κακῶν ἐπὶ τὸν θεὸν ἀναφέρουσιν, ὧν τὸ τέλος κατάρας ἐγγύς. It is
evidently intended for a quotation from Heb. vi. 8, which however puts
it rather differently as ἐκφέρουσα δὲ ἀκάνθας καὶ τριβόλους ἀδόκιμος καὶ
κατάρας ἐγγύς, ἧς τὸ τέλος εἰς καῦσιν. "But that which beareth thorns and
briers is to be rejected and is nigh unto cursing; whose end is to be
burned." The *Khuastuanift* or Manichaean confession mentioned later
repeats this phrase about God not being the creator of evil as well as of
good. See p. 335 *infra*.

M. Rochat thinks earlier than the epistle quoted above, Manes'
quondam follower Turbo says after recantation that his master
reverences two gods "unbegotten, self-existing (αὐτοφυεῖς),
eternal and set over against each other," and that "he represents one as good, the other as wicked, giving to the one the
name of Light and to the other that of Darkness[1]." So, too,
the Mahommedan writers who give what seems to be an independent account of Manes' opinions are agreed that he deduced
the origin of the world from "two Original Principles, one of
which is Light and the other Darkness, and which are separated
one from the other[2]." The absolute opposition from the outset
of good and evil therefore formed the pivot of Manes' whole
system, and was opposed quite as much to the Christian and
Jewish creeds as to the Mithraic and other modifications of
Persian religious ideas then or later in vogue, which held that
evil like good was the creation of the Supreme Being, and that
Ahriman or Pluto was a god having subordinate authority to,
but of the same nature as, Ormuzd or Zeus. This uncompro-
misingly dualistic theory gives an origin to evil independent
of that of good, and can only lead logically to the assertion of
its eternity. Whether Manes gave utterance to it for the first
time, or derived it from a theology then current in Persia, there
is little evidence to show[3]. The Zend Avesta itself in its
Sassanian recension does not seem to pronounce clearly on this
point, and has been thought by some high authorities to teach

---

[1] Hegemonius, *Acta*, c. VII. p. 9, Beeson.

[2] En Nadîm in Kessler, *op. cit.* pp. 386, *sqq.* Kessler's translation of
En Nadîm, which is given in the first Appendix to the work quoted,
differs slightly from that of Flügel and depends on a somewhat better text
than the last-named. It is therefore used when possible in the remaining
notes to this chapter. Flügel's book, however, has the advantage of a
commentary of some 300 pages marked with great erudition, and must
still be consulted by anyone wishing to be acquainted with its subject.

[3] Plutarch, *de Is. et Os.* c. XLV., says, however, that "evil must have a
principle of its own," so that it cannot be the work of a benevolent being.
As he is generally supposed to have taken his account of the Persian
teaching from Theopompos of Chios, who was at the Court of Ptolemy
about 305 B.C., his evidence is against those who, like M. Cumont, would
make the "Zervanist" opinion, which assumes a common principle for
good and evil, pre-Christian. Yet the point does not yet seem capable
of decision, as Plutarch *may* here be only giving us his own opinion.

the subordinate origin and ultimate extinction of evil[1], and by others exactly the reverse. It does, however, seem to be clear that unless Manes invented *de novo* the doctrine above quoted, it must have been from Persia that he obtained it. No other country with which he can have become acquainted has yet been shown to possess it[2].

Exclusively Oriental, too, in its origin must be the history of the conflict between these two Principles which follows. Each of them apparently dwelt in his own domain for countless ages untroubled by the existence of the other. The Light is the uppermost and is, according to the Mahommedan version of Manes' doctrine, without bounds in height and on each side. The Darkness lies below it, and is in like manner boundless in depth and in lateral extent[3]. Hence there is a long frontier at which they touch, and this spot was filled from the beginning by the celestial air and the celestial earth. If we may read into the tradition something which is not expressed there, but which seems to follow logically from it, this atmosphere and this earth were the heavier parts of the Divine substance, which sinking down formed a kind of sediment or deposit[4]. Each of these Two Principles has five "members" or components,

[1] Casartelli, *op. cit.* p. 44.

[2] This is really the *crux* of the whole question. If the idea could be traced back to the philosophers of Ionia (*e.g.* Heraclitus of Ephesus) and their theory of eternal strife and discord being the cause of all mundane phænomena, it is difficult to say whence the Ionians themselves derived it, save from Persia. We can, of course, suppose, if we please, that the Persians did not invent it *de novo*, but took it over from some of their subjects. Among these, the Babylonians, for instance, from the earliest times portrayed their demons as not only attempting to invade the heaven of the gods, but as being in perpetual warfare with one another. But the very little we know of Babylonian philosophy would lead us to think that it inclined towards pantheism of a materialistic kind rather than to dualism.

[3] En Nadîm, in Kessler, *op. cit.* p. 387; Flügel, *op. cit.* p. 86.

[4] The likeness of this to the cosmogony of the Ophites and their successor Valentinus is of course marked (cf. Chaps. VIII and IX *supra*). Manes may have borrowed it directly from Valentinus' follower Bardesanes, whose doctrines were powerful in Edessa and Mesopotamia in his time, or he may have taken it at first-hand from Persian or Babylonian tradition. That Manes was acquainted with Bardesanes' doctrines, see n. 7, p. 280 *supra*.

and this partition into five seems in the Manichaean teaching
to run through all things. Thus, the Mahommedan tradition
tells us that the "members" of the God of Light are Gentleness,
Knowledge, Intelligence, Discretion, and Discernment, those of
the Air the same five, of the (celestial) earth, the Breeze or
Ether, Wind, Light, Water, and Fire, and of the Darkness
Smoke, Flame, Hot Wind, Poison or Pestilence, and Gloom
or Fog[1]. In this, and especially in its deification of abstract
principles, we may see a reflection of Gnostic teaching which
may easily have reached Manes from Valentinus by way of
Bardesanes and the Oriental or Edessan School. On the other
hand, the borrowing may have been the other way, and Simon
Magus may have obtained these notions from the Persian Magi
and have handed them on to Valentinus and his successors.
This does not seem so likely as the other, but the point can
hardly be settled until we know more than we do at present
of the state of the Persian religion from the time of the
Achaemenian kings to the Sassanian reform.

However that may be, both the Christian and Mahommedan
traditions are agreed that the aggressor in the struggle between
the good God and the bad was the Evil One. The Mahommedan
source, here fuller than the Christian, tells us that the Darkness
remained in an unorganized condition for ages, although
consisting of the five members enumerated above. These parts,
however, seem to have sunk down and produced another
Earth called the Darker Earth, from which in course of time
came forth Satan. Satan was not, like the King of the Paradise
of Light, without beginning, but came into being from the
union of these five members of Darkness, having the head of
a lion, the body of a serpent, the wings of a bird, the tail of
a fish, and four feet like those of crawling animals[2], in which
figure we may see a kind of reflection of the Mithraic Ahriman[3].

---

[1] En Nadîm in Kessler, *op. cit.* p. 387; Flügel, *op. cit.* p. 86. Flügel's
text adds to these members other "souls" which he names Love, Belief,
Faith, Generosity, and Wisdom. Kessler substitutes Courage for
Generosity and seems to make these "souls" the members' derivatives.

[2] See last note.

[3] See Chapter XII, p. 251 *supra*. Here, again, the traditional and monstrous
figure of Satan may have been copied from the sculptured representations
of the composite demons of Babylonia (*e.g.* Rogers, *Religion of Babylonia*

Satan, on his emergence on the Darker Earth, perceived the rays of light from the upper world, piercing as we may suppose through the gloomy atmosphere of his own world, and conceived a hatred for them. Seeing, too, that these rays gained much in strength by their combination and mutual support, he withdrew within himself so as to unite himself more closely with his members[1]. Then again springing upwards, he invaded the realms of Light with the intention of there spreading calamity and destruction. The aeon—or world as the *Fihrist* calls it—of Discernment was the first to be aware of this invasion[2], and reported it to the aeon Knowledge, from whom it passed to the others in turn until it at last reached the ear of the Good God, here, as elsewhere in the *Fihrist*, called the King of the Paradise of Light. With the aid of the Spirit of his Right Hand, of his five worlds or members before mentioned, and of his twelve elements, of which we have before heard nothing[3], he made the First Man, clothing him by way of armour with the five "species" or powers of the celestial earth,

and Assyria, Frontispiece and Figs. 1 and 13). Yet if we take the Mithraic lion, as M. Cumont would have us do, as the symbol of fire and the serpent as that of the earth, we have in the five sorts of animals the five στοιχεῖα or elements of Aristotle. Cf. Aetius, *de Placitis Philosophorum*, ed. Didot, Bk I. c. iii. § 38 (Plutarch, *Moralia*, II.), p. 1069. Yet the nearest source from which Manes could have borrowed the idea is certainly Bardesanes, who, according to Bar Khôni and another Syriac author, taught that the world was made from five substances, *i.e.* fire, air, water, light and darkness. See Pognon, *op. cit.* p. 178; Cumont, *La Cosmogonie Manichéenne d'après Théodore bar Khôni*, Bruxelles, 1908, p. 13, n. 2.

[1] En Nadîm in Kessler, *op. cit.* p. 388; Flügel, *op. cit.* p. 87. As the ancients were unacquainted with the properties of gases, it is singular that they should have formed such a conception as that of the compressibility and expansibility of spirits. Yet the idea is a very old one, and the Arabian Nights story of the Genius imprisoned in a brass bottle has its parallel in the bowls with magical inscriptions left by the Jews on the site of Babylon (Layard, *Nineveh and Babylon*, 1853, pp. 509 *sqq.*), between pairs of which demons were thought to be imprisoned. Cf. Pognon, *op. cit.* p. 3. Something of the kind seems indicated in the "Little Point," from which all material powers spring, referred to by Hippolytus and the Bruce Papyrus.

[2] So in the *Pistis Sophia*, it is the "last Parastates" or assistant world who breathes light into the Kerasmos, and thus sets on foot the scheme of redemption. Cf. Chapter X, p. 146 *supra*.

[3] Yet the Fundamental Epistle speaks of the twelve "members" of God, which seem to convey the same idea. See *Aug. c. Ep. Fund.* c. 13.

the Breeze, Wind, Light, Water and Fire as before enumerated[1].
With these He despatched him to fight Satan, who in his turn
did on his armour in the shape of *his* five "species," Smoke,
Flame, Poison, Hot Wind, and Gloom[2]. The fight lasted

---

[1] Thus En Nadîm in Kessler, *op. cit.* pp. 388, 389; Flügel, *op. cit.* p. 87.
But here the Christian tradition gives more details than the Mahommedan.
Hegemonius, *Acta*, c. VII., p. 10, Beeson, and Bar Khôni (Pognon, p. 185),
are in accord that the God of Light produced from himself a new Power
called the Μήτηρ τῆς Ζωῆς or Mother of Life, that this Mother of Life projected the First Man, and that the First Man produced the five elements
called also his "sons," to wit, wind, light, water, fire and air, with which
he clothed himself as with armour. See Cumont, *Cosmog. Manich.* p. 16,
n. 4, for the harmonizing of the texts [N.B. the omission of πῦρ from his
quotation from the *Acta* is doubtless a clerical error]. The identification
of the Mother of Life with the "Spirit of the Right [Hand]" is accepted by
Bousset, *Hauptprobleme*, pp. 177, 178, and may be accounted for by the
crude figure by which the Egyptians explained the coming-forth of the
universe from a single male power. See Budge, *Hieratic Papyri in the
Brit. Mus.* p. 17.

[2] These were also the "sons" of Darkness or Satan. See Bar Khôni
(Pognon, p. 186). The reason that led the God of Light to send a champion
into the lists was, according to Bar Khôni (Pognon, p. 185), that the five
worlds of his creation were made for peace and tranquillity and could
therefore not help him directly in the matter. Cf. St Augustine, *de Natura
Boni*, c. XLII. But Manes doubtless found it necessary to work into his
system the figure of the First Man which we have already seen prominent
in the Ophite system. Cumont, *Cosmog. Manich.* p. 16, says few conceptions were more widely spread throughout the East. It is fully examined
by Bousset, *Hauptprobleme*, in his IVth chapter, "Der Urmensch." The
First Man is, in the Chinese treatise lately found at Tun-huang in circumstances to be presently mentioned, identified with the Persian Ormuzd
and the five elements are there declared to be his sons. See Chavannes
and Pelliot, *Un Traité Manichéen retrouvé en Chine*, pt 1, *Journal Asiatique*,
série X., t. XVIII. (1911), pp. 512, 513. The 12 elements which helped in
his formation seem to be mentioned by no other author than En Nadîm.
St Augustine, however, *Contra Epistulam Fundamenti*, c. 13, speaks of
the "12 members of light." The Tun-huang treatise also mentions "the
12 great kings of victorious form" whom it seems to liken to the 12 hours
of the day. As the *Pistis Sophia* does the same with the "12 Aeons"
who are apparently the signs of the Zodiac, it is possible that we here have
a sort of super-celestial Zodiac belonging to the Paradise of Light, of which
that in our sky is a copy. It should be remembered that in the Asiatic

long, but in the end Satan triumphed, and dragged the First
Man down into the Realm of Darkness, where he took from him
his light[1]. During the fight, too, the elements had become
mingled, so that the Ether henceforth was mixed with the
Smoke, the Fire with the Flame, the Light with the Darkness,
the Wind with the Hot Wind, and the Cloud with the Water.
This it is which brings about the confusion or mixture seen in
the present world, wherein everything which is beautiful, pure,
or useful, such as gold and silver, comes from the armour of
the First Man, and everything foul, impure, and gross, from
that of his infernal opponent[2]. After the fight, the King of
the Paradise of Light descended with another Power called the
Friend of the Lights, who overthrew Satan, and the Spirit of
the Right Hand or Mother of Life recalled, either by her voice
or by another power called the Living Spirit, the First Man from
his prison in the lowest Darkness. The First Man, on his
deliverance, in this account mounts again to the Realms of
Light, but before doing so "cuts the roots" of the Five Infernal

cosmogonies the fixed stars belong to the realm of good as the representatives of order, while the planets or "wanderers" are generally evil.

[1] En Nadîm in Kessler, *op. cit.* p. 389; Flügel, *op. cit.* pp. 87, 88.
According to the Christian tradition, the Powers of Darkness devoured
only the soul of the First Man which was left below when his body, as will
presently be seen, returned to the upper world. See Hegemonius, *Acta*,
c. VII., p. 10, Beeson.

[2] Both the Christian and the Mahommedan traditions agree as to this
result of the fight, which is paralleled not only by the more or less successful attempt of Jaldabaoth and his powers to *eat* the light of Pistis Sophia,
but also by a similar case in orthodox Zoroastrianism. For all these see
Cumont, *Cosmog. Manich.* p. 18, n. 4. Bar Khôni (Pognon, p. 186), goes
further and describes the surrender of the First Man as a tactical effort
on his part, "as a man who having an enemy puts poison in a cake and
gives it to him." Alexander of Lycopolis (*adv. Manich.* c. III.), on the other
hand declares that God could not avenge himself upon matter (as he calls
Darkness) as he wished, because he had no evil at hand to help him, "since
evil does not exist in the house and abode of God"; that he therefore
sent the soul into matter which will eventually permeate it and be the death
of it; but that in the meantime the soul is changed for the worse and
participates in the evil of matter, "as in a dirty vessel the contents suffer
change." These, however, are more likely to be the ideas of the Christian
accusers than the defences of the Manichaean teachers.

Elements so that they can no more increase[1].   Then the King
of the Paradise of Light orders an angel to draw the Confusion
or Mixture of the Elements to that part of the Realm of Darkness which touches the Realm of Light, and to create out of
it the present world, so as to deliver the imprisoned elements
of Light from the Darkness with which they are contaminated.
This is done, and a Universe having six heavens and eight
earths is formed, each heaven having twelve gates, together with
terraces, corridors, and places in such profusion as to point to
some confusion in the translation into the Syriac which has come
down to us.   The only thing that concerns us in this, perhaps, is
that the visible world, presumably the lowest of the eight, has
a ditch dug round it in which is thrown the Matter of Darkness
as it is separated from the Light, and outside this a wall so that
it cannot escape.   This is in view of the End of the World[2].

[1] En Nadîm in Kessler, *op. cit.* pp. 389, 390; Flügel, *op. cit.* p. 87.   As
Kessler points out, En Nadîm gives two accounts doubtless taken from
different Manichaean sources.   In one, he says simply that the King of
the Paradise of Light followed with other gods and delivered the First
Man, the actual victor over Darkness being called "the Friend" of the
Lights (like Mithras).   He then goes on to say that Joy (*i.e.* the Mother
of Life) and the Spirit of Life went to the frontier, looked into the abyss
of hell and saw the First Man and his powers were held enlaced by Satan,
"the Presumptuous Oppressor and the Life of Darkness"; then she called
him in a loud and clear voice, and he became a god, after which he returned
and " cut the roots of the Dark Powers."   For Bar Khôni's amplification
of this story see p. 302, n. 1, and p. 324 *infra*.   The whole of this, together
with the cutting of the roots, is strongly reminiscent of the *Pistis Sophia*.

[2] En Nadîm in Kessler, *op. cit.* pp. 391, 392; Flügel, *op. cit.* p. 98.
The *Acta* (Hegemonius, *op. cit.* c. VIII., p. 11, Beeson) say that the "Living
Spirit" before mentioned "created the Cosmos, descended clothed with
three other powers, drew forth the rulers (οἱ ἄρχοντες) and crucified them
in the firmament which is their body the Sphere."   "Then he created the
lights (φωστῆρες) which are the remnants of the soul, caused the firmament
to encompass them, and again created the earth [not the Cosmos] with
its eight aspects."   The Latin version after "earth" adds "they (*sic !*) are
eight," which if it refers to the aspects would agree with En Nadîm.   Alexander of Lycopolis (*adv. Manich.* c. III.), who had been a follower of Manes
and was a Christian bishop some 25 years after Manes' death, says that
"God sent forth another power which we call the Demiurge or creator
of all things; that this Demiurge in creating the Cosmos separated from
matter as much power as was unstained, and from it made the Sun and

So far there is no great difference—at all events, no irre-concilable difference—between the Christian and the Mahom-medan accounts of Manes' doctrines. The machinery set up for the process of the redemption of the light, however, differs somewhat conspicuously in the two traditions. The Mahom-medan writers declare that in Manes' teaching the Sun and Moon were created for the purification of the Light, the Sun drawing to itself those light-elements which had become contaminated by the demons of heat and flame and the Moon exercising a like attraction on those which had suffered from the embrace of Satan's other powers. Both luminaries bear these elements into the Column of Praises or Glory which is perpetually mounting from the Sun to the World of Light, bearing with it the praises of men, their hymns of gratitude, and their pure words and good works[1]. This will continue until

Moon; and that the slightly stained matter became the stars and the expanse of heaven." "The matter from which the Sun and Moon were taken," he goes on to say, "was cast out of the Cosmos and resembles night" [Qy the Outer Darkness?], while the rest of the "elements" consists of light and matter unequally mingled. Bar Khôni (Pognon, *op. cit.* p. 188), as will presently be seen, says that the Living Spirit with the Mother of Life and two other powers called the Appellant and Respondent [evi-dently the "three other powers" of the *Acta*] descended to earth, caused the Rulers or Princes to be killed and flayed, and that out of their skins the Mother of Life made 11 heavens, while their bodies were cast on to the earth of darkness and made 8 earths. The Living Spirit then made the Sun, the Moon, and "thousands of Lights" (*i.e.* Stars) out of the light he took from the Rulers. That this last story is an elaboration of the earlier ones seems likely, and the flaying of the Rulers seems to be reminis-cent of the Babylonian legend of Bel and Tiamat, an echo of which is also to be found in the later Avestic literature. See West, *Pahlavi Texts* (S.B.E.), pt iii. p. 243. Cf. Cumont, *Cosmog. Manich.* p. 27, n. 2.

[1] En Nadîm in Kessler, *op. cit.* p. 392; Flügel, *op. cit.* pp. 89–90. This would agree perfectly with the system of the *Pistis Sophia*, where it is said that the "receivers of the Sun and Moon" give the particles of the light as it is won from matter to Melchizedek, the purifier, who purifies it before taking it into the Treasure-house (pp. 36, 37, Copt.). The idea that the Sun's rays had a purifying effect shows shrewd observation of nature before his bactericidal power was discovered by science. So does the association of the Moon with water, which doubtless came from the phenomenon of the tides. Is the Column of Glory the Milky Way?

none but a feeble fragment of the Light remains in this world, when the angels charged with its maintenance will abandon their task, and return to the World of Light. A fire will then break out, which will burn for 1468 years and will set free the remainder of the Light imprisoned in matter by consuming its envelope. Satan or Hummâma, the Spirit of Darkness, will then acknowledge his defeat, and will be driven into the tomb prepared for him, the entrance to which will be closed with a stone the size of the world[1]. In the Christian tradition these matters are more complicated, and Manes is said to have taught that there exists a great wheel bearing twelve vases or buckets after the fashion of an Egyptian *sakiyeh*, which raise the redeemed portions of Light to the Sun, who gives them to the Moon, who in her turn delivers them to the Aeons of the Light, who place them in the Column of Glory here called the Perfect Air[2]. The Christian account is also more detailed with regard to the functions of the angels charged with the conduct of the world, making out that one of them supports this earth on his shoulders and is therefore called Omophorus, great earthquakes and commotions taking place when from weariness he shifts his burthen from one shoulder to the other, while another, called

---

[1] The Ecpyrosis or final conflagration is always present in orthodox Mazdeism, where it inspires its Apocalypses, and is in effect the necessary conclusion to the drama which begins with the assault on the world of light by Ahriman. For references, see Söderblom, *op. cit.* chap. IV. From the Persians it probably passed to the Stoics and thus reached the Western world slightly in advance of Christianity. "The day when the Great Dragon shall be judged" is continually on the lips of the authors of the *Pistis Sophia* and the Μέρος τευχῶν Σωτῆρος, and the conception may therefore have reached Manes from two sources at once. The angels maintaining the world as mentioned in the text are of course the Splenditenens and Omophorus about to be described.

[2] Hegemonius, *Acta*, c. VIII. p. 12, Beeson. St Augustine (*contra Faustum*, Bk xx. c. 10) mentions the Wheel briefly and rather obscurely. It seems to have fallen out of the account of Bar Khôni. But see the Tun-huang treatise (Chavannes et Pelliot, *op. cit.* 1ère partie, pp. 515, n. 2, 516, 517, n. 3). There can be little doubt that it is to be referred to the Zodiac. The Aeons of the Light seem to be the five worlds who here play the part of the Parastatae in the *Pistis Sophia*.

Splenditenens, holds the heavens by their backs[1]. The stars
are also in the Christian tradition fashioned out of the purer
part of the Light which was *not* captured by the Satanic powers,
whereas the Mahommedan tradition says nothing about their
origin[2]. The Christian writers also make the Manichaeans tell
a story about the appearance of a beautiful virgin who appears
to the male and female devils who were crucified or fixed in
this world on the deliverance of the First Man. She appears
to the male fiends as a beautiful woman and to the female as
a desirable young man; and when they covet and pursue her,
she flies from them and disappears. The anger of the Great
Archon or Satan on this causes the appearance of clouds in

[1] Hegemonius, *Acta*, c. VIII. pp. 11, 12, Beeson, mentions Omophorus,
but not Splenditenens. Splenditenens is, however, well known to St
Augustine, who describes him (*contra Faustum*, Bk XV. c. 7) as *Splenditenentem magnum, sex vultus et ora ferentem, micantemque lumine*, "Great
Splenditenens, bearing six faces and mouths, and glittering with light."
So later (*op. cit.* Bk XX. c. 9) he says, *Splenditenentem, reliquias eorumdem
membrorum Dei vestri in manu habentem, et cetera omnia capta, oppressa,
inquinata plangentem, et Atlantem maximum subter humeris suis cum eo
ferentem, ne totum ille fatigatus abjiciat.* "Splenditenens, who has in his
hand the remains of these members of your God [*i.e.* the five elements or
"sons" of the First Man] and who mourns the capture and oppression and
defilement of all the rest; and huge Atlas, who bears everything with him on
his shoulders, lest he should be wearied and cast it away." Bar Khôni
(Pognon, pp. 188, 189) describes them both, and calls Splenditenens "the
Ornament of Splendour," while he makes the pair two of the five sons of
the Living Spirit, as more clearly appears in the Tunhuang treatise (Chavannes et Pelliot, *op. cit.* p. 549, and notes 2 and 5). Where Manes found
the figure of Splenditenens is not apparent, but the world-bearing angel is
an old conception in Western Asia, as M. Cumont has shown in his before-
quoted *Cosmogonie Manichéenne*, App. II. He appears prominently on the
Mithraic monuments and was no doubt the original of the Greek Atlas.

[2] Alexander of Lycopolis, *op. cit.* c. III., says plainly that the Sun and
Moon were formed out of that part of the light (here called δύναμις
"power"), which, although it had been captured by the powers of matter,
had not been contaminated, while that which had suffered some slight
and moderate stain became the stars and sky. The *Acta* (Hegemonius,
op. cit. c. VIII. p. 11, Beeson), as we have seen, says that the Living Spirit
created the lights (φωστῆρες, luminaria), which are the remnants of the soul
(*i.e.* the armour of the First Man) and caused the firmament to surround
them. The author here evidently refers to the Sun and Moon only.

this world and thereby obscures the Sun's light, whilst his sweat becomes rain[1].

On the origin of terrestrial man, there is also considerable discrepancy between the two streams of tradition. The Mahommedan tells us that Adam was born from the conjunction of one of "these Archons" or Princes, and a star. Nothing is said to tell us what is meant by "these" princes, but as the phrase is used in other passages by the same writer to denote the Satanic hierarchy one can but suppose that it is one of the rulers of darkness who is here indicated[2]. The same writer goes on to say that the conjunction was "beheld" [or aided?] by a pair of Archons, one male and the other female, and that a second similar conjunction resulted in the birth of Eve. There is evidently a reference here to some legend of which we have lost the trace[3], and the Christian tradition assigns to Adam an entirely different origin and declares that he was made by all the "princes" or archons on the advice of one of their number, who persuaded the others to give up some of the light they had received which they knew would otherwise be taken from them and to make from it man in their own image and after the form of the "First Man" against whom they had fought with temporary success[4]. This story is clearly the same as that which we have already seen current among the Ophites, and it now seems most probable that it here appears not—as was once

---

[1] The whole of this story, which is the reverse of edifying, is studied by M. Cumont, with the fullest references to the authorities, in his *Cosmogonie Manichéenne* before quoted, to which it forms Appendix I, under the heading "La Séduction des Archontes." To this I must refer the reader, only remarking that, while I fully agree that the goddess in question is probably derived from the Mother of the Gods who under the name (*inter alia*) of Atargatis was worshipped throughout Asia Minor, I do not see that she had any connection with the "Virgin of Light" of the *Pistis Sophia*. This Virgin of Light did, indeed, pass into Manichaeism, but she had there a very different name and attributes from the Mother of the Gods. See p. 323, n. 4 *infra*.

[2] En Nadîm in Kessler, *op. cit.* p. 393; Flügel, *op. cit.* pp. 90, 91.

[3] Kessler, *op. et pag. cit.* n. 1, says it has dropped out of the text, which seems likely.

[4] Hegemonius, *Acta*, c. XII. pp. 19, 20, Beeson. The story is given *verbatim* later, p. 306 *infra*.

thought—as an interpolation foisted into the teaching of Manes by the Christian writer, but because both Ophite and Manichaean derived the story independently of each other from legends current in Western Asia[1].

The Mahommedan writer then plunges into a long and elaborate account of how the "Five Angels," meaning thereby apparently the "members" Gentleness, Knowledge, Intelligence, Discretion and Discernment, on beholding Adam and Eve, prayed to certain powers which seem to be those which descended with the King of the Paradise of Light after the defeat of the First Man properly so called. These Powers include the First Man himself and the Mother of Life[2], and the

---

[1] The Mandaeans or Disciples of St John described on p. 305 seem a likely source, as they have many traditions about the protoplasts, some of which clearly go back to before the Christian Era. None of those mentioned by Brandt, *Die Mandäische Religion*, Leipzig, 1889, pp. 34–39, however, seem to be exactly similar to the story in the text.

[2] This Mother of Life is one of the most prominent, though not one of the most active figures in the Manichaean pantheon. Her identification with the Spirit of the Right Hand or first Power created by the Supreme God of Light has been mentioned above (note 1, p. 293 *supra*). She doubtless has her immediate origin in the great mother goddess worshipped throughout Western Asia, whose most familiar name is Cybele, but whom we have seen (Chap. II *supra*) identified with Isis, Demeter, and all the goddesses of the Hellenistic pantheon. See as to this, Bousset, *Hauptprobleme*, pp. 58 *sqq.*, although he, too, falls into the error of identifying with her the Virgin of Light of the *Pistis Sophia*. That the name "Mother of Life" at least passed to all these goddesses is certain; but it also found its way into Egyptian Christianity; for in the Coptic spell or amulet known as the *Prayer of the Virgin in Bartos* (*i.e.* Parthia), studied by Mr W. E. Crum (*P.S.B.A.* vol. XIX. 1897, p. 216), the Virgin Mary is represented as saying "I am Mariham (Μαριάμ), I am Maria, I am the Mother of the Life of the whole World!", and the popularity of the "Prayer" is shown by its frequent appearance in Ethiopic and Arabic versions (*op. cit.* p. 211). So, too, in the evidently Christian *Trattato Gnostico* of F. Rossi (*Memorie della Reale Accademia di Torino*, ser. II. t. xliii. p. 16) the magician says "I entreat thee, O God, by the great revered Virgin (παρθένος) in whom the Father was concealed from the beginning before He had created anything." Bar Khôni, again (Pognon, pp. 209–211), speaks of the Kukeans, who seem to have been a semi-Christian sect, and who taught that the coming of Jesus to earth had for its object the redemption of His bride, the Mother of Life, who was detained here below, like the Helena of Simon Magus.

The Mother of Life is mentioned in all the Mahommedan and Christian writers who have treated of Manichaeism (for the references, see Chavannes et Pelliot, *op. cit.* 1ère partie, p. 511, n. 1), in the Pahlavi MS. discovered by the Germans at Turfan (F. W. K. Muller, *Handschriften-Reste in Estrangelo-Schrift*, pp. 47, 55), and in the Chinese treatise from Tun-huang (Chavannes et Pelliot, *op. cit.* p. 511 *et al.*). In this last, she is called Chan-mou, which is translated "the Excellent Mother," and En Nadîm in one passage (Kessler, *op. cit.* p. 399; Flügel, *op. cit.* p. 100) calls her Nahnaha, which Flügel would translate "The Aversion of the Evil Ones." It should be noticed, however, that her part in the cosmogony is small, and that she acts upon the world, like all these supercelestial powers, only through her descendants or "sons." These are treated of later (see p. 323 and n. 1, p. 302 *infra*). Titus of Bostra as quoted by Flügel, *op. cit.* p. 210, speaks of her as δύναμις τοῦ ἀγαθοῦ οὐκέτι φῶς αἰσθητὸν ἀλλ' ὡς ἂν φαίη προβολὴ τοῦ θεοῦ. "[The] Power of the Good One, no longer a perceptible light, but as if one should say, an emanation of God." Some years ago, we could hardly have looked for her prototype or first appearance in the history of religions in any other direction than Babylonia, where the worship of Ishtar, her Babylonian counterpart, goes back as far as we can trace Babylonian religion. Now, however, it is plain that other races than the Babylonians may have been concerned in the spread of the worship of the Great Mother throughout Western Asia. In the Zoroastrian faith, she seems to appear as Spenta Armaiti, the one certainly female power among the seven Amshaspands, who in the Pahlavi texts is set over the earth, as Vohu Mano is made protector of the beasts, Asha Vahishta of the fire, and Khshathra Vairya is set over metals. But besides this, she is identified in the Gâthâs with the Wisdom of God (for references see pp. 136–137 of M. Carnoy's article in the *Muséon* mentioned below), an identification which Plutarch (*de Is. et Os.* c. XLVII.) admits by translating her name as σοφία, and like the Sophia of the Gnostics is given as a spouse to her creator Ahura Mazda, to whom she bears the First Man Gayômort (Darmesteter, *Le Zend-Avesta*, t. I. pp. 128–129). Yet we now know that this figure may have come into the Zoroastrian pantheon neither from Semitic sources nor, as Darmesteter thought, from Plato. M. A. Carnoy in a study called *Armaiti-Ârmatay* (*Muséon*, n.s. vol. XIII. (1912), pp. 127–146) shows the identity of the Persian Amshaspand with the Vedic goddess Aramati. We have already seen that the Vedic gods Varuna and Mitra were worshipped by Hittites in Asia Minor before the XIIth century B.C., and Prof. Garstang believes that the Earth-Mother was the great goddess of the Hittites, and was the one worshipped in Roman times at Hierapolis or Mabug as the *Dea Syria* or Atargatis, a name that he equates with Derceto, the mother of Semiramis in classic legend, and declares to be compounded of Ishtar or Astarte and the Aramaic "Athar or Athe." See Strong and Garstang, *The Syrian Goddess*, pp. 1–8, and notes 24, 25, and 30, on pp. 52, 53 and 30 *op.*

Living Spirit[1], and were besought by the Five to send to earth
a Saviour who should give Adam and Eve Knowledge and

cit. Zoroaster and Manes may therefore have taken their mother goddess
from an Aryan rather than from a Semitic original.

[1] This Living Spirit is the most active agent of the Light in the Manichaean system, and seems to have held his place unaltered through all the
changes of Manichaean teaching.　Alexander of Lycopolis (*contra Manich.*
c. III.) speaks of him as the Δημιουργός or Architect of the Universe.　The
earliest part of the *Acta* (Hegemonius, c. VII. p. 10, Beeson) says that he was
put forth from the Father (or Supreme God of Light) in consequence of
the prayers of the First Man after his defeat, that he delivered this last,
crucified or bound the Archons in the firmament (as Jeû is said to have
done in the *Pistis Sophia*), made the Sun and Moon and appointed their
courses, and further made the eight earths.　St Augustine, *contra Faustum*,
Bk xx. c. 1, makes the Manichaean Faustus call him the "Third Majesty
whom we acknowledge to have his seat and his lodging-place in the whole
circle of the atmosphere.　From whose powers and spiritual inpouring
also, the earth conceived and brought forth the suffering Jesus who is the
life and salvation of men and is hanging on every tree."　St Augustine
further speaks (*op. cit.* Bk xx. c. 9) of "your mighty (*potentem* for *viventem*)
Spirit, who constructs the world from the captive bodies of the race of
darkness or rather from the members of your God held in subjection and
bondage."　St Augustine (see *contra Faustum*, Bk xv. c. 6) also knows
that the Living Spirit has, like the First Man, five sons, to whom we shall
return later.　The Mahommedan writers have much less to say on the
subject.　En Nadîm (Kessler, *op. cit.* p. 390; Flügel, *op. cit.* p. 88) says
abruptly that "Joy [*i.e.* the Mother of Life] and the Spirit of Life went to
the frontier, looked into the abyss of hell and saw there the First Man and
his angels," whereupon the Spirit of Life called the First Man with a voice
of thunder and the latter "became a god."　This story is so without
connection with the context that Kessler is probably right in attributing
it to another source from that from which the *Fihrist* has drawn up to
this point.　The source in question was probably a late one; for Bar
Khôni (*op. cit.* pp. 186–188) supplies many more details which will be given
in the text.　Bar Khôni also amplifies the story in the *Fihrist* into a
descriptio of how the Living Spirit, on seeing the First Man in the Darkness, spoke "a word which took the appearance of a pointed sword" (cf.
Revelation i. 16), and how this word caused to appear the image of the
First Man.　A dialogue then ensues between apparently the sword and
the image, which appear to be here identified with the Appellant and
Respondent of later Manichaeism, and the pair are drawn up out of hell.
See Cumont, *Cosmog. Manich.* p. 24, and note 5.　Al Bîrûnî, *Chronology*,
p. 190, also knows of the Spirit of Life and says that Manes "preached"
of him.　In the Turfan texts there is occasional mention of the "Spirit"

Goodness and deliver them from the devils. Their prayer was heard, and Jesus was sent upon earth "accompanied by a god," with whose aid the Archons were again overthrown and imprisoned, while Adam and Eve were set free[1]. Jesus then addressed Adam and revealed to him the whole secret of the cosmogony, enlightening him upon the origin and functions of the different heavenly worlds or paradises, of the gods, of hell, of the devils, of the earth and sky, and of the sun and moon. He then showed him, continues the Mahommedan tradition, the seductive power of Eve, put him on his guard against it, and breathed into him the fear of yielding to it. Adam, it is said, listened to these commands obediently.

The result of this abstinence on Adam's part—we are still pursuing the Mahommedan account of the Manichaean teaching —was seen in the sequel. The Archon or Demon who was practically the father of the present race of mankind became enamoured of Eve, and engendering with her begot a son "ugly and of a reddish colour," who was named Cain. Cain in turn had relations with his mother Eve, and from this incest was born a son of white colour who was named Abel. From the further intercourse of Cain and Eve were born two daughters, one called "the Wisdom of the World," and the other "the Daughter of Pleasure." Cain took the last-named to wife and gave the other in marriage to Abel; but he did not know that

together with the Father and the Son (Müller, *Handschriften-Reste*, pp. 26, 28), and also of the "commands" of the Holy Spirit to the Hearers, which are plainly allusions to the Living Spirit or Ζῶν Πνεῦμα of the Christian Fathers. In the Tun-huang treatise (Chavannes et Pelliot, *op. cit.* pp. 510, 556) he is repeatedly mentioned, and although nothing is said of his demiurgic or world-creating powers, the part which he and the Mother of Life play in the rescue of the First Man after his defeat is recognized, and he is spoken of as forming the third person of a Trinity of which the two other members are the Father or highest God of Light and the "Son of the Light." Finally (*op. cit.* p. 557), he is said to be "a white dove," whereby his likeness to the Holy Spirit of the Christian Trinity already noted by Faustus is emphasized (see Augustine, *ubi cit. supra* and Bk xx. c. 6).

[1] This conception of Jesus as a warrior has already been seen in the *Pistis Sophia*, see p. 156 *supra*. So we read of "Jesus the victorious" in the Tun-huang treatise, p. 566, n. 3.

the Wisdom of the World was filled with Light and divine wisdom, while the Daughter of Pleasure possessed nothing of the kind.   In the sequel, one of the Angels had relations with the Wisdom of the World and begot two daughters, called Help (Farjâd) and Bringer of Help (Barfarjâd).   Abel accused Cain of being the father of these girls, whereupon Cain killed him and took the "Wisdom of the World" as his own second wife.   The Rulers of Darkness were annoyed at this, and the "Great Devil," here called Sindîd, taught Eve magical formulas by the aid of which she again enticed Adam to intercourse. The result was a son "beautiful and of an agreeable countenance," whom Eve wished to kill as having nothing of the Archons in him.   Adam arranged to have the child fed exclusively on milk and fruits, and drew three magic circles round him bearing the names of the King of the Paradise of Light, the First Man, and the Spirit of Life respectively, to protect him against the devils.   He then went to a high place and entreated God for him, whereupon one of the Three Powers last named appeared and gave him a Crown of Glory, at the sight of which Sindîd and the Archons fled away.   Then a tree appeared to Adam called the Lotus, from which he drew milk with which to nourish his son whom he called first after the tree, and then Seth (Schâthîl).   Eve, on the instigation of Sindîd, again persuaded Adam to intercourse, which so disgusted Seth that he took with him the Wisdom of the World, her two daughters Help and Bringer of Help, and "Siddikût," which seems to be the community of the elect or Perfect Manichaeans, and journeyed to the East in search of the Divine Light and Wisdom.   At their death all these entered into Paradise, while Eve, Cain, and the daughters of Desire went to hell[1].

---

[1] En Nadîm in Kessler, *op. cit.* pp. 393 *sqq.*; Flügel, *op. cit.* pp. 90 *sqq.* Theodore bar Khôni (Pognon, *op. cit.* pp. 189 *sqq.*), gives a much more elaborate account of the creation of man and the other animals, for which and for its explanation the reader must be referred to the elaborate analysis of M. Cumont (*Cosmog. Manich.* pp. 34–49, and App. II., "La Séduction des Archontes").   It should be noted, however, that some part of this story was known to St Augustine.   See especially *contra Faustum*, Bk VI. c. 8.

The story about the protoplasts of the Book of Genesis has been given in more detail than it perhaps deserves because of its manifest connection with the doctrines of the extant sect of Mandaites, Hemerobaptists, or Disciples of St John still to be found in certain villages near the Shât-el-Arab and even in considerable towns like Bussora. These sectaries declare themselves to have inherited the faith of John the Baptist, and have a sacred book called the Sidra Rabba, which has been known to Europeans since the xviith century, and contains, among other things, many stories like those given above. The Mandaites are a violently anti-Christian sect, and say that the historical Jesus was a fiend who obtained baptism from St John the Baptist by means of a trick, and they display a similar hatred of the religions of both the Jews and the Mahommedans. Nevertheless, most modern writers consider them related to, and perhaps the modern representatives of, the Mughtasilah or "Washers[1]." This last sect is certainly very ancient, and its history can in fact be traced as far back as the beginning of the reign of Trajan[2], while the Mahommedan author, from whom the traditional account of Manes' doctrines has been quoted above, says that Manes was in his youth one of the Mughtasilah. From this Prof. Kessler, who perhaps devoted more attention to the Manichaean religion than any living scholar, built up the theory that the doctrines of the Mughtasilah were one of the principal sources from which Manes formed his system. He even says that the Fatak or Patecius whom tradition gives as a father to Manes must be identified with that Scythianus or Terebinthus whom the Christian tradition makes Fatak's predecessor, was one of the Mughtasilah, and helped Manes both in the construction of his system and in its propagation[3]. This may be so, but very little evidence is available in support of the theory; and the points which the Mandaites and the Manichaeans undoubtedly possess in common do not seem to

---

[1] So Rochat, *op. cit.* pp. 157, 158.

[2] Kessler, *op. cit.* pp. 72, 80; Brandt, *Mandäische Religion*, p. 178.

[3] Rochat, *op. cit.* pp. 156–178, has carefully examined the resemblances between the system of Manes and that of the Mandaites and declares that it is at present impossible to say which of them has borrowed from the other.

be more than can be explained by the contact which must necessarily have taken place between two neighbouring sects both
persecuted successively by Persian Shahs, Christian Emperors,
and Mahommedan Caliphs.   The Christian tradition of Manes'
teaching concerning the protoplasts says merely that "he who
said 'Let us make man in our own image'" was the same Prince
of Darkness who thereby counselled the other Archons to give
up their light in order to make man in the likeness

"of the form that we have seen, that is to say, of the First Man.
And in that manner," it continues, "he created the man. They
created Eve also after the like fashion, imparting to her of their
own lust, with a view to the deceiving of Adam. And by these
means the construction of the world proceeded from the operations
of the Prince[1]."

The teaching of Manes with regard to Jesus is not very
clear in the Christian tradition, no doubt because the writers
who recorded it were careful to remove from it as much as
possible everything which in their view savoured of blasphemy.
Yet the Christian author before quoted makes Manes say that
the God of Light whom he calls "the Good Father" sent his
well-beloved son upon earth for the salvation of man's soul
and "because of Omophorus" or the world-sustaining angel.
This son, by whom he can hardly mean any other than the historical Jesus, "came and transformed himself into the semblance of
a man and showed himself to men as a man, although he was
not a man, and men imagined that he had been begotten[2]."
It is also to Him that is attributed the construction of the
wonderful wheel before alluded to as equipped with twelve vases
which the sphere causes to revolve, and which thus scoops up,
as it were, the souls of the dying[3].   The Christian account also
narrates that in

"the Paradise which is called the Cosmos [Qy the "heavenly"
earth or the Sun?], there are trees such as Desire and other deceits,

[1] Hegemonius, *Acta*, c. XII., pp. 19, 20, Beeson.

[2] *Op. cit.* c. VIII., p. 12, Beeson.

[3] Chavannes et Pelliot (*op. cit.* p. 517, n. 3) make this the work of the
Living Spirit, but they are clearly wrong. The text of the *Acta* referred
to in the last note leaves no doubt that it is that of the "Son."

whereby the minds of those men [those who reach it?] are corrupted. But the tree in Paradise, whereby they know the good, is Jesus and the knowledge of Him which is in the Cosmos. And whoso receives it, distinguishes between good and evil. Yet the Cosmos itself is not of God, but it was made from portions of matter, and therefore all things in it will disappear[1]."

There is not really any very great difference between this and the Mahommedan tradition quoted above which makes Jesus the messenger sent from above to give knowledge to Adam, especially if we consider that Manes probably, like most of the Gnostics, placed Paradise not upon the earth but in one of the heavens intermediate between us and the abode of the Supreme Being[2]. That Manes supposed Jesus to have descended to this earth also is plain from his own words quoted by Al Bîrûnî from the *Shapurakan* or book written by Manes for King Sapor:

"Wisdom and deeds have always from time to time been brought to mankind by the messenger of God. So in one age they have been brought by the messenger called Buddha to India, in another by Zaradusht [*i.e.* Zoroaster] to Persia, in another by Jesus to the West. Thereupon this revelation has come down, this prophecy in this last age through me, Mânî, the messenger of the God of Truth to Babylonia[3]."

Manes' ideas as to the salvation of man's soul again differ little in the two streams of tradition. The Christian, here perhaps the fuller of the two, describes him as teaching that the soul of man, as also that of beasts, birds, other animals, and plants, is part of the light which was won by the demons from the First Man, while all bodies are of that matter which is the same as darkness. Man's body, we are told, is called a cosmos by parallelism with the great Cosmos, and all men have roots

---

[1] Hegemonius, *Acta*, c. XI., p. 18, Beeson.

[2] This is the tradition evidently known to the author of the Μέρος τευχῶν Σωτῆρος when he makes Jesus say "When I spoke with Enoch out of the Tree of Knowledge in the Paradise of Adam." (See Chap. X, p. 173 *supra*.)

[3] Al Bîrûnî, *Chronology*, p. 190.

here below bound to things which are above[1]. It is the cutting
of these roots by the demons which causes death. On the death
of a man who has attained the knowledge of the truth during
this life, his soul is taken up in the wheel to the Sun, by whom
after it has been purified it is passed over to the Moon, the two
luminaries being represented as ships or ferry-boats sailing to-
and-fro in the upper air. When the Moon is full, she ferries
the souls with which she is filled towards the East, and then
delivers them to the Aeons of Light who place them in the
Pillar of Glory before described. She then returns for a fresh
supply greatly reduced in circumference, whereby her waxing
and waning is explained[2]. In the case of a man who has not
attained the knowledge of the truth, a small portion of the
soul only is purified and is then reincarnated in the body of
a dog, a camel, or some other animal, according to the sins
which it has committed. Thus, if he has killed a mouse, he will
become a mouse, if a chicken a chicken, and so on, while those
who have been employed in the reaping of corn will themselves
become corn or some other kind of plant in order that they may
be reaped and cut in turn. The soul of the homicide will, it
is said, go to inhabit the body of a leper[3]. There will, apparently,
be five of these reincarnations[4], and between them the soul which
has not found knowledge of the truth is given over to the demons
in order that they may subdue it in the "Gehennas" of fire.
This, like its transference into other bodies, is for the sake of
teaching it better; but if it still remains without knowledge,

---

[1] Hegemonius, *Acta*, c. IX., p. 14, Beeson. This idea of the macrocosm
and microcosm according to which the body of man is a *replica* of the
universe is found in nearly all later mysticism—also in the Cabala and in
the later Zoroastrian treatises. In the Tun-huang treatise it forms the
chief theme of the homiletic part of the work.

[2] *Op. cit.* c. VIII., pp. 12, 13, Beeson. The Latin version has *vir* "man"
for *aer* "air" in its description of the Column of Glory. Probably a
clerical error.

[3] *Op. cit.* c. X., pp. 15, 16, Beeson. The word used is κέλεφος; but
the Latin texts all read "elephant."

[4] Ἐρῶ......πῶς μεταγγίζεται ἡ ψυχὴ εἰς πέντε σώματα, *op. et cap. cit.* p. 15,
Beeson.

it is cast into the great fire until the Consummation of the World[1].

The Mahommedan tradition as to what occurs at death goes into more details, and it is here that we catch the first glimpse of that doctrine of predestination which plays so prominent a part in the later teaching of the Manichaean Church. When a just or perfect or "true" Manichaean is on the point of death, the First Man sends to him a "shining god of light" in the form of "the Wise Guide" accompanied by three other gods and with them "the bowl of water, the garment, the fillet for the head, the circlet and the crown of light[2]." With them comes the virgin who is like to the soul of the just one. There also appear to him the devil of greed, that of pleasure, and others with them. Directly the just one who is dying sees them, he calls to his help the goddess[3] who has taken the form of the Wise Guide and the three gods her companions. They draw near to him, and at the sight of them the devils turn and flee. Then the gods take the just one, do on him the crowns and the garment, put in his hand the bowl of water, and mount with him to the Column of Praises in the sphere of the Moon, to the First Man and to Nahnaha the Mother of Life, until they reach the place in the Paradise of Light he occupied in the beginning[4].

---

[1] The soul of the rich man is in the same chapter said to pass into the body of a beggar and thereafter εἰς κόλασιν αἰώνιον "to everlasting punishment." Is it from this source that the Calvinists took their doctrine of eternal damnation? The reprobation of the rich as such and without regard to the use they might make of their wealth perhaps accounts for the levelling and republican politics of the mediaeval sectaries.

[2] The Bowl of water reminds one of the cup of soberness and reflection administered to just souls by the little Sabaoth the Good in the Μέρος τευχῶν Σωτῆρος. See Chap. X, p. 187 *supra*. The garment was probably the "heavenly nature" with which the soul had to be clothed before it could ascend to the upper spheres of light (cf. the *Pistis Sophia*). That the crown was designed as a protection against the spirits of evil, there are many indications in the last-mentioned document.

[3] Kessler would here read "gods" for "goddess."

[4] That is to say, the particular world of light, whether Gentleness, Knowledge, Intelligence, Discretion, or Discernment, from which the soul descended. As the "armour" of the First Man, from which the souls of men are formed, was made with the aid of these five worlds, it is reasonable

His body remains stretched (upon the earth) in order that the Sun, the Moon, and the Gods of Light may take from it its powers, *i.e.* the Water, the Fire, the gentle Breeze, which are then borne upwards to the Sun and become a god. The rest of the body, which is all darkness, is cast into hell[1].

This description of the lot of the blessed after death is certainly taken from no other source than that from which the Zoroastrian books put forth by the Sassanian kings are drawn.

"At the end of the third night," says the Hatoxt Nask[2], one of the earliest Zoroastrian documents that have come down to us, "at the dawn of day, the soul of the faithful thinks that it is in a garden and smells its perfumes. Towards it a wind seems to blow from the region of the South perfumed, more perfumed than any other wind. Then the soul of the faithful thinks that he breathes this wind with his nostrils. 'Whence blows this wind, the most perfumed that I have breathed with my nostrils?' While encountering this breeze, his religion (conscience, *daena*, spiritual life), appears to him in the form of a beautiful young girl, shining, with white arms, robust, of fair growth, of fair aspect, tall, high-bosomed, of fair body, noble, of shining race, with the figure of one who is 15 years old, as fair in form as the fairest creatures that exist. Then the soul of the faithful speaks to her, and asks 'What virgin art thou, thou the most beautiful in form of the virgins that I have ever seen?' Then she who is his religion answers: 'O youth of good mind, of good words, of good deeds, of good religion, I am thine own religion incarnate[3].'"

So, too, the Vendidad, which may be a little later in date than the document just quoted, represents Ahura Mazda as saying in answer to Zarathustra himself:

to suppose that one or other predominates in the soul of everyone. Hence probably the degree in the Manichaean hierarchy to which any hearer might attain was thought to be decided for him before his birth, and governed his destination after death. Thus it is said in the *Pistis Sophia*: "Those who have received exalted mysteries shall be in exalted places, and those who have received humble mysteries in humble places in the light of my kingdom." Cf. Chavannes et Pelliot, *op. cit.* 1ère partie, p. 533, n. 1 and St Augustine as there quoted.

[1] The words given in the text are almost *verbatim* from En Nadîm. See Kessler, *op. cit.* pp. 398–399; Flügel, *op. cit.* p. 100.

[2] One of the 21 Nasks of the Sassanian Avesta.

[3] Söderblom, *op. cit.* p. 83.

"After a man has disappeared, after a man dies, the impious and malevolent demons make their attack. When the dawn of the third night shines forth and the day begins to lighten, the well-armed Mithra arrives at the mountains giving forth holy radiance and the Sun rises. Then, O Spitama Zarathustra...she comes, the beautiful, the well-made, the strong, of fair growth, with her dogs, full of discernment, rich in children [*i.e.* fruitful], the longed-for, virtuous one. She leads the souls of the faithful above the Hara Berezaiti; she sustains them across the bridge Chinvat in the road of the spiritual divinities. Vohu Mano rises from his golden throne. Vohu Mano says, 'O faithful one, how hast thou come hither from the perishable world to the imperishable?' Rejoicing, the faithful pass before Ahura Mazda, before the beneficent Immortals, before golden thrones, before the house of hymns, the dwelling of Ahura Mazda, the dwelling of the beneficent Immortals, the dwelling of the other faithful ones. When the faithful is purified, the wicked and malevolent demons tremble by reason of the perfume after his departure as a sheep pursued by a wolf trembles at the [scent of the?] wolf[1]."

To return, however, to the Mahommedan account of Manes' doctrine. This last by no means confined his survey of the state of man's soul after death to the single case of the justified dead.

"When death draws nigh to a man who has fought for religion and justice, [he is represented as saying,] and who has protected them by protecting the Just, the gods whom I have mentioned appear and the devils are there also. Then he calls the gods to his help and seeks to win them by showing to them his works of piety, and that which he has done to protect the religion and the Just. The gods deliver him from the devils, while leaving him in the condition of a man in this world, who sees fearful shapes in his dreams, and who is plunged in dirt and mud[2]. He remains in this state until his Light and his Spirit are freed [evidently by transmigration] when he arrives at the meeting-place of the Just. Then, after having wandered for long, he dons their vesture. But when death appears to the sinful man, to him who has been ruled by greed

---

[1] *Op. cit.* pp. 89 *sqq.*

[2] See the Orphic belief about the uninitiated being plunged in mud, Vol. I. chap. IV. p. 131 *supra.*

and desire, the devils draw near to him, they seize him, torment him, and put fearful shapes before his eyes. The gods are there also with the vesture, so that the sinful one thinks they have come to deliver him. But they have only appeared to him to reproach him, to remind him of his actions, and to convince him of his guilt in having neglected the support of the Just. He wanders unceasingly throughout the world, and is tortured until the coming of the End of the World, when he will be thrown into hell. Thus, Manes teaches," continues the tradition, "that there are three paths for the soul of man. One leads to Paradise, which is the path of the Just. Another leads back to the world and its terrors, which is the path of the protectors of the faith and the helpers of the Just. The third leads to hell, which is the path of the sinful man[1]."

Yet there is nothing to show that the sins which thus doom a man to hell are within his choice to commit or to leave alone as he chooses. Rather does it appear that his freedom from sin depends on the admixture of light which enters into his composition at his birth. Of all this the Christian tradition says nothing.

It is, nevertheless, in the division here set forth of the adherents of the religion into the Just and the protectors of the Just, that the great distinction between the Manichaean religion and all its contemporaries appears. Both traditions are agreed that those who listen to the teaching of Manes are to be divided into five classes, viz. the Masters who are the sons of Gentleness; those who are enlightened by the Sun, who are the sons of Knowledge or the Priests; the Elders who are the sons of Intelligence; the Just who are the sons of Discretion; and the Hearers who are the sons of Discernment[2]. The first three classes we may safely neglect for the present, as they evidently correspond to the three superior or directing orders of the Manichaean Church to which we shall have to return

---

[1] Kessler, *op. cit.* pp. 399–400; Flügel, pp. 100–101.

[2] This is, I think, the only construction to be put on the words of the *Acta*: τῆς δὲ ψυχῆς ἐστι τὰ ὀνόματα ταῦτα, νοῦς, ἔννοια, φρόνησις, ἐνθύμησις, λογισμός. Hegemonius, *Acta*, c. x., p. 15, Beeson. For the Mahommedan tradition, see En Nadîm in Flügel, *op. cit.* p. 95. The whole question of the organization of the Manichaean Church is elaborately discussed by Flügel in n. 225 on this passage, *op. cit.* pp. 293–299.

later; but the last two, the Just and the Hearers, give us the
key to the organization of the sect, and explain how it was
able to maintain itself for so long against its numerous enemies.
He who would enter into the religion, says the Mahommedan
tradition, must examine himself that he may see whether he
is strong enough to conquer desire and greed, to abstain from
meats, from wine, and from marriage, to avoid all that can be
hurtful in (to?) water or fire, and to shun magic and hypocrisy[1].
These abstinences are those that are demanded of the perfect
Manichaeans, who have been called above the Just or the
Sons of Discretion, and who with their superiors constitute the
Manichaean Church. These are they whom the Christian tradition speaks of as the Elect, and for whom, as we have seen, there
is reserved after death a glorious ascension and an immediate
return to the Paradise of Light. So Valentinus, like many other
Gnostics, divided Christians into the two classes of pneumatics
and psychics, the first-named of whom were to occupy a more
distinguished position in the world to come than the other.
There is nothing to show, however, that Valentinus or any other
Gnostic ever imposed any discipline on the pneumatics than that
prescribed for the psychics, or that he thought that those who
were going to take a higher rank in the next world should
observe a stricter mode of life in this. The Catholics, indeed,
had already adopted the view that the celibate member of the
Church possessed "a higher calling" than his married brethren;
but there is no reason to suppose that they therefore assigned
to them a higher place in the next world, or thought that those
who had not the gift of continence were to be permitted any
relaxation of the moral law imposed upon celibate and married
alike. It is therefore probable that it was from Buddhism,
with which Manes must have made himself well acquainted
during his journeys into India, that he borrowed the scheme
by which those who believed in the truth of his teaching could
delay subjecting themselves to the austerities necessary for
salvation until their next incarnation.

However this may be, there can be little doubt that this is
the meaning of the position he assigned to the Hearers.

[1] Kessler, *op. cit.* p. 398; Flügel, *op. cit.* pp. 94, 95.

"If," he says according to the Mahommedan author, "he who would enter into the religion does *not* feel strong enough to practise the abstinences before enumerated, let him renounce the attempt. If, however, he is filled with love for the faith, yet cannot conquer desire and greed, let him seek to progress by protecting the faith and the Just, and let him fight against evil actions on the occasions when he can give himself to labour[1], piety, vigilance, prayer 'and humility. This will fill him with contentment both in this ephemeral world, and in the eternal world to come, and he will put on the body of the second degree in the state which follows after death[2]."

Unless they are greatly belied, some of his later followers looked upon this as a licence to the Hearers to commit such sins as they chose[3] in this life, yet it is evident that this formed no part of Manes' original teaching. He imposed upon the Hearers, says the Mahommedan tradition, ten commandments, which were: to abstain from prayers offered to idols, from lying, from avarice, from murder, from adultery, from false teaching, from magic, from double dealing, from doubt in religion and from slackness and want of energy in action. They also had to recite certain prayers which will be mentioned in their place, and to fast two days when the Moon is new as when she is full, as also when the Sun enters the sign of Sagittary. A three days' fast was also obligatory on the first appearance of the Moon after the entry of the Sun into the signs of Capricorn and of Libra. But they were to feast on Sunday, a day which the Perfect, according to the Mahommedans, kept as a fast, their own weekly feast being held on Monday[4].

The attitude of Manes to other religions was also without

---

[1] This is perhaps the first instance in antiquity of the Gospel of Work. That these virtues of the believer are made five in number, so as to accord with the five worlds of light, needs no demonstration.

[2] See passages from Kessler and Flügel quoted in n. 1, p. 313 *supra*.

[3] Rainerio Saccone, a Manichaean Perfect in Languedoc, who afterwards turned Inquisitor, said that he had often heard the Elect lamenting that they had not taken the opportunity of committing more sins before receiving the "Baptism of the Spirit" which was thought to wash them away. See H. C. Lea, *History of the Inquisition*, vol. I., p. 94.

[4] Flügel, *op. cit.* pp. 95–97. See, however, n. 4, p. 349 *infra*.

precedent or parallel. Of the Jews and of their religion he seems to have had a detestation so strong and so deeply rooted that it is difficult not to see in it some connection with political events of which we have lost the record. The war of extermination which Hadrian had been forced to wage against the Jews of Palestine must have been over nearly a century before Manes began to teach; but the Babylonian Jews can hardly have been affected by this, and the story of the king of Adiabene quoted above shows that shortly before the time of Ardeshîr they actively pursued the proselytizing policy which their countrymen in the West had been forced to abandon.

Doing so, they doubtless brought |down, upon themselves the wrath of the national prejudices of their hosts, who looked upon proselytizing as a bid for political power[1]. This probably provoked reprisals, and it is quite possible that Manes' teaching derived some of its strength from the revulsion felt by Ardeshîr's Aryan subjects to the borrowings from Judaism to be found both in Mithraism and the Avestic literature. But whatever its cause, there can be no doubt about the hatred felt by Manes for the Jewish religion, which is prominent in every tradition of his teaching. The earlier Gnostics, like Marcion, had made the God of the Old Testament a harsh but just and well-meaning tyrant; but Manes would have none of this, and declared that he was a fiend.

"It is the Prince of Darkness," the Christian tradition makes him say, "who spoke with Moses, the Jews, and their priests. Thus the Christians, the Jews, and the Pagans are involved in the same error when they worship this God. For he led them astray in the lusts that he taught them, since he was not the God of Truth.

[1] Josephus, *Antiquities*, Bk xx. cc. 2–4, breaks off his history at the critical point. The Book of Esther is, perhaps, sufficient proof of the experience of the Oriental Jews in enduring periodical *pogroms* at least as often as their co-religionists in modern Russia. Johnson (Oriental Religions), *Persia*, 1885, p. 410, quotes, apparently from Firdûsi, that the "old Persian nobles" were driven by Ardeshîr's reforms into Seistan, where they were the ancestors of the present Afghan clans. As some of these clans call themselves the Beni Israel, it is possible that the Jews rather than the nobles were expelled on this occasion, as happened before under Cyrus.

Whence those who put their hope in that God who spoke with Moses and the Prophets will be bound with him, because they have not put their trust in the God of Truth. For he, the God of the Jews, spoke with them according to their lusts[1]."

In a very different spirit, however, Manes dealt with all the other religions that he knew. He acknowledged the Divine origin of the teachings of Zoroaster, of Buddha, and of Jesus alike, with the reservation that he should himself be regarded as the Paraclete, which here seems to mean nothing more than the Legate or Ambassador, sent by the Good God to complete their teaching. "Mânî, the messenger of the God of Truth to Babylonia[2]" is the title which, as we have seen, he gives himself in the most authentic record of his teaching. He aimed, in short, at establishing a universal religion which should include within its scope the three faiths that between them commanded the allegiance of the whole civilized world, and should acknowledge him as its founder and chief. Had his plans come to fruition in his lifetime, he would have attained an empire over the minds of men far greater and wider than any ever claimed or dreamed of by the most ambitious of the Roman pontiffs.

The full details of the way in which he proposed to establish this new faith we shall probably never know; but discoveries made during the last decade have shown us that his plans were well fitted to their purpose. The successive expeditions of Drs Grünwedel and von Le Coq to Turfan have shown that up to as late as the XIth century A.D., there was still a strong body of Manichaeans probably belonging to the Ouigur nation in Chinese Turkestan, living apparently in complete amity with their Buddhist countrymen[3]. The writings that were there discovered, to which we shall have to refer more in detail later,

---

[1] Hegemonius, *Acta*, c. XII. pp. 20–21, Beeson; Ephraem Syrus in Kessler, *op. cit.* p. 302. For Mahommedan confirmation, see Schahrastâni in *op. cit.* p. 339.

[2] Al Bîrûnî, *Chronology*, p. 190.

[3] See Le Coq's *Short Account* in *J.R.A.S.* 1909, pp. 299–322. Another and more popularly written one by the same author appeared in the *Conférences au Musée Guimet*, Paris, 1910 (Bibl. de Vulgarisation, t. XXXV.).

are mostly written in a script resembling the Estranghelo or
Syriac but with an alphabet peculiar to the Manichaean
religious documents, and which cannot, one would think, have
been adopted by those who used it for any other purpose than
that of concealment[1].   Judging from this and the practice of
the sect in Europe from the time of Diocletian onward, it
seems highly probable that among Buddhists, the Manichaean
hearers professed Buddhism, and among Zoroastrians, Zoroastrianism, hoping that thus they might be able to turn their
fellows to their way of thinking without openly dissenting from
the reigning religion.   The persecution that Bahram I instituted against them immediately upon Manes' execution was
perhaps less a reason than a pretext for this.

This is certainly borne out by their proceedings when they
found themselves among Christians.

"You ask me if I believe the gospel," said the Manichaean Perfect,
Faustus, in his dispute with St Augustine (himself for nine years
before his conversion a Manichaean Hearer).   "My obedience to its
commands shows that I do.   I should rather ask you if you believe
it, since you give no proof of your belief.   I have left my father,
brother, wife and children and all else that the gospel requires; and
you ask me if I believe the gospel.   Perhaps you do not know what
is called the gospel.   The gospel is nothing else than the teaching
and the precept of Christ.   I have parted with all gold and silver.
I have left off carrying money in my purse; content with food
obtained from day to day; without anxiety for the morrow and
without care as to how I shall be fed or wherewithal I shall be
clothed; and you ask if I believe the gospel?   You see in me the
blessings of the gospel; and yet you ask if I believe the gospel.
You see me poor, meek, a peacemaker, pure in heart, mourning,
hungering, thirsting, bearing persecutions and hatred for righteousness' sake; and do you doubt if I believe in the gospel[2]?"

So, too, Manes in the epistle to Marcellus which, although much
altered and corrupted by its Catholic transcribers, is probably
a genuine document, is careful to begin in language which seems
imitated from the Epistles of St Paul:

---

[1] The Marcionites, another much hated sect, also used a secret script.
[2] St Augustine, *contra Faustum*, Bk v. c. 1.

"Manes, an apostle of Jesus Christ, and all the saints who are with me, and the virgins, to Marcellus, my beloved son; Grace, mercy, and peace be with you from God the Father, and from our Lord Jesus Christ; and may the right hand of light preserve you from the present evil world and from its calamities, and from the snares of the wicked one, Amen[1]."

While in the Disputation which follows and which is certainly a later interpolation, or possibly a concoction of some later author, he is represented as saying "My brother, I am indeed a disciple of Christ, and, moreover, an apostle of Jesus." Yet in spite of this and a few other passages of the same kind, it is plain that neither Manes, nor any of those who believed on his teaching, were Christians in any sense in which the term could not be applied to the followers of Mahommed or many another professedly anti-Christian teacher. Manes entirely rejected the account of the Incarnation given in the Gospels, alleging, as a modern critic might do, that it was not the account of eyewitnesses, but a mass of fables which had grown up after the memory of the events recorded had faded away[2]. Jesus, he said, was not born of woman, but came forth from the Father or First Man, and descended from heaven in the form of a man about thirty years of age[3]. But the body in which He appeared was an illusion only and was no more that of a real man than the dove which descended upon Him at the baptism in Jordan was a real dove, and it was not true to say that He was put to death by the Romans and suffered on the cross[4]. So far from that being the case, he declared that Jesus, the mortal or suffering Jesus, was nothing but the universal soul diffused throughout Nature and thus tormented by its association with matter. Thus, he said, the Jesus *patibilis* may be said to be hanging from every tree[5].

To say that such teaching was likely to alter in the course of a generation or two is merely to assert that it followed the

---

[1] Hegemonius, *Acta*, c. v., pp. 5, 6.
[2] Augustine, *contra Faust.* Bk VII. c. 1.
[3] *Op. cit.* Bk XXIII. c. 2; *ibid.* Bk XXXII. c. 7.
[4] *Op. cit.* Bk XXVI. cc. 6, 8; *ibid.* Bk XXIX. c. 1.
[5] *Op. cit.* Bk XX. c. 2.

course of evolution which can be traced in all religions, and it is possible that in what has been said in the last paragraph concerning Jesus, we have rather the opinions of the Manichaeans of the fourth century than those of Manes himself. Yet even in this we see exemplified the chameleon-like habit peculiar to the Manichaeans of modifying their tenets in outward appearance so as to make them coincide as nearly as possible with the views of those whom they wished to win over to them. Thus when the Catholic doctrine of the Trinity, the Three Persons and One God, began to take shape under the pressure of the Arian controversy, the Manichaeans were not long in matching it with a Trinity of their own[1]:

"We worship," said Faustus the Manichaean Perfect, "under the triple appellation of Almighty God, the Father and His Son Christ and the Holy Spirit. While these are one and the same, we believe also that the Father properly dwells in the highest or chief light, which Paul calls "light inaccessible," and the Son in the second or visible light. And as the Son is himself two-fold according to the apostle, who speaks of Christ as the power of God and the wisdom of God, so we believe that His power dwells in the Sun and His wisdom in the Moon[2]. We also believe that the Holy Spirit, the third majesty,

---

[1] Cumont, *Cosmog. Manich.* p. 15, points out that the Manichaeans had already figured to themselves their King of the Paradise of Light as existing in the three Persons of Father, Mother, and Son in the shape of the Light, the Mother of Life and the First Man. This Trinity corresponds in every particular with that worshipped in Asia Minor under the names of Zeus (or Hadad), Cybele, and Atys, at Eleusis as Dionysos, Demeter, and Iacchos, in Greek Egypt as Osiris, Isis, and Horus, and in Persia, according to M. Cumont, as Ormuzd, Spenta Armaiti, and Gayômort. Cf. Bousset, *Hauptprobleme*, pp. 333–337. That its origin can be traced, as the last-named author seems to think, to the Babylonian Triad, Ea, Damkina, and Marduk, is more doubtful. The Manichaeans really acknowledged, as they were never tired of affirming, only two gods, Light and Darkness, and considered all the lesser powers of Light, including man's soul, as formed from God's "substance." When, therefore, they spoke of trinities, tetrads, and so on, it was in all probability for the purpose of producing that show of outward conformity with other religions which was one of the most marked features of their system.

[2] This is a reversal of the position in the *Pistis Sophia*, where the female power or Virgin of Light is placed in the Sun and the male Iao in the Moon.

has His seat and His home in the whole circle of the atmosphere[1] By His influence and inpouring of the spirit, the Earth conceives and brings forth the suffering Jesus, who, as hanging from every tree, is the life and salvation of man[2]."

In like manner, while not denying them in terms, the Manichaeans attempted to refine away all the significance of the Crucifixion and the Atonement, by representing them as merely symbolical. In one Apocryphal book called the *Wanderings of the Apostles*, which seems to be of Manichaean origin, Jesus appears to St John, who is sunk in grief at the supposed sufferings of his Master, and tells him that His Crucifixion was a mere phantasmagoria or miracle-play performed to impress the plebeian crowd at Jerusalem. Then He vanishes and in His stead appears a cross of pure light, surrounded by a multitude of other forms representing the same shape and image. From this cross comes a Divine voice saying sweetly:

"The cross of light is, for your sakes, sometimes called the Word, sometimes Christ; sometimes the Door, sometimes the Way; sometimes the Bread, sometimes the Sun; sometimes the Resurrection, sometimes Jesus; sometimes the Father, sometimes the Spirit; sometimes the Life, sometimes the Truth; sometimes Faith and sometimes Grace[3]."

As will presently be seen, now that we have under our hands the writings of Manichaean communities domiciled in Persian and Chinese territory, we find in them similar compromises with the faiths of Zoroaster and Buddha.

Yet after the Mahommedan conquest of Asia, and in regions where they were free, as it would seem, from the pressure of their Zoroastrian and Christian competitors, the Manichaeans appear to have evolved a theology as formal and as detailed as any of the Gnostic systems which we have examined. This

[1] Compare the statement of Herodotus (Bk I. c. 131) that Zeus (or Ormuzd) in the opinion of the ancient Persians was the name of "the whole circle of air."

[2] Augustine, *contra Faust.* Bk xx. c. 2.

[3] This is to be found in Harduin's *Acta Consilii*. The quotation in the text is taken from Matter, *Hist. de Gnost.* t. III. p. 89, and Neander, *Ch. Hist.* II. p. 187.

is in the main set out by Theodore Bar Khôni, the Nestorian
Bishop of Kashgar, in his *Book of Scholia* written in Syriac and
Mandaean which has been in part translated by the scholarly
care of M. Pognon, late Consul of France at Aleppo, and has lately
been commentated by M. Cumont. M. Pognon at first identified
Bar Khôni with the nephew of the Nestorian Patriarch Iwannis
(Johannes or John), whose reign began in 893 A.D., and he
quoted Assemani's *Bibliotheca Orientalis* in his support[1].
Later, however, he withdrew this, and put him a century
earlier[2]. M. Cumont, on the other hand, thinks that Bar
Khôni lived at the end of the vith century or the beginning
of the viith, and therefore before the Mahommedan invasion[3].
In any event, the *Scholia* describe a body of Manichaean
doctrine considerably later in date than any of the Christian
sources hitherto referred to, and probably formed in an atmosphere where the necessity for outward conformity to either the
Zoroastrian or the Christian faith was a good deal less cogent
than it was further west. Its agreement with the Mahommedan
tradition drawn from above is also well marked, and it derives
much support from the Manichaean MSS. lately recovered from
the oasis of Turfan in Turkestan, and in that of Tun-huang in
China. It is possible, although no proofs are yet forthcoming,
that it was this Neo-Manichaeism, as it has been called, that
inspired the Manichaean sectaries who were imported in the
ixth and xth centuries into Bulgaria, whence their missionaries
found their way later into Italy, France, and other countries of
Southern Europe.

The system disclosed in these documents begins, as does
nearly every Manichaean writing, with the assertion of the
existence of two gods, that is to say, the God of Light and the
God of Darkness. As the Kingdom of Darkness, whenever and
wherever described, is the exact opposite and counterpart of

[1] Pognon, *op. cit.* p. 5; Assemani, *Bibl. Orient.* t. III. p. 198 *cit.*

[2] Cumont, *Cosmog. Manich.* p. 106. It seems probable that the Kashgar in question is the country in Chinese Turkestan still called by that
name. M. Pelliot, however, will have none of this and insists that Bar
Khôni's Kashgar was Al Wasit near Bagdad. For the controversy, see
J.R.A.S. 1913, pp. 434 *sqq.*, 696 *sqq.* and 1914, pp. 421–427.

[3] Cumont, *Cosmog. Manich.* p. 1, n. 2, and authorities there quoted.

that of the Light, we shall not return to it again, but assume that in describing the one we are *mutatis mutandis* describing the other. The God of Light has one substance of which all the powers of light were made, but three forms or hypostases, called in the Greek Formula of abjuration "faces" or persons, which added to his own personality make a supreme tetrad. These three hypostases are his wisdom, power, and goodness, by which is probably meant that he operates in the lower powers through these qualities, while remaining himself remote in the "inaccessible light[1]." He possesses also five houses or dwellings, which are also called his worlds and even his members. Their names according to Bar Khôni are Intelligence, Knowledge, Thought, Reflexion, and Feeling[2]. These seem to be

---

[1] Ἀναθεματίζω πάντας οὓς ὁ Μάνης ἀνέπλασε θεούς, ἤτοι τὸν τετραπρόσωπον Πατέρα τοῦ Μεγέθους καὶ τὸν λεγόμενον Πρῶτον Ἄνθρωπον......καὶ τὸν ὀνομαζόμενον Παρθένον τοῦ φωτὸς κ.τ.λ. "I anathematize all those whom Manes lyingly makes gods, to wit, the Father of Greatness in four Persons, and the so-called First Man...and the famous Virgin of Light," etc., Kessler, *op. cit.* p. 403. His quotation of the Formula is from the works of the Apostolic Fathers edited by Cotelerius in 1724 (Amsterdam). It seems to have been administered to converts from Manichaeism to Catholicism down to a very late date. See Beausobre, *Hist. du Manichéisme*, t. I. pp. 66–67.

[2] Pognon, *op. cit.* p. 184. Cumont, *Cosmog. Manich.* pp. 9, 10, would substitute Reason for Knowledge and Will for Feeling. The Greek names as given in the *Acta* (Hegemonius, *op. cit.* c. x. p. 15, Beeson) are νοῦς, ἔννοια, φρόνησις, ἐνθύμησις, λογισμός which the Latin translator makes into *mens, sensus, prudentia, intellectus, cogitatio.* The first of these may pass as correct, since Nous appears as the first emanation of the Highest God in all the systems which preceded that of Manes and from which he is likely to have copied. Of the rest, it can only be said that they are the translations by scribes of Syriac or Mandaite words which were ill calculated to express metaphysical abstractions, and that their copyists were seldom well acquainted with the etymology of any of the three languages. Hence they generally made use of what they thought were the corresponding expressions in the works of great heresiologists like Irenaeus and Hippolytus without troubling themselves much as to their appropriateness. In the passage from the *Acta* above quoted, the five qualities named are said to be the "names of the soul," which is explained by what is said later (*op. cit.* c. x. p. 17, Beeson) that "the air (ἀήρ) is the soul of men and beasts and birds and fish and creeping things." En Nadîm (Kessler, *op. cit.* p. 387; Flügel, p. 86), as has been said on p. 291 *supra*, gives the "members of the air" as Gentleness, Knowledge, Intelli-

ranged in this order below the dwelling of the inaccessible light, so as to cut off all approach to it by a fivefold wall. On the attack of the powers of darkness before mentioned, the God of Light, called by Bar Khôni the Father of Greatness, that is to say, the Very Great or Greatest[1], creates by his word the Mother of Life, who in her turn evokes the First Man as already described. Thus is constituted, if M. Cumont be right, the First Triad of Father, Mother, and Son[2]. From the Turfan documents, we know that the Father was called, in Turkestan at any rate, by the name of Azrua or Zervan, and the Son Khormizta or Ormuzd[3]. As for the appellation of the Mother we are still in ignorance[4].

gence, Discretion and Discernment, which are the same as those which he has just attributed to the King of the Paradise of Light. St Augustine (c. *Faust.* Bk xx. c. 15) says in like manner that the Manichaeans thought their souls "members of God," which seems to refer to the same belief. Bar Khôni (Pognon, *op. cit.* p. 186), as has been said, not only assigns the five dwellings of Intelligence, Knowledge, Thought, Reflexion and Feeling to the Living Spirit, but makes him draw his five sons from them, and M. Cumont (*Cosmog. Manich.* p. 10, n. 3) quotes the *Acta Thomae* as saying that the Third Legate or Srôsh is "the Legate of the five members, Nous, Ennoia, Phronesis, Enthymesis and Logismos." From all which we may gather that the Supreme God of Light and his "Second" and "Third" creations were each alike thought to have the same five dwellings or hypostases consisting of abstract qualities, although the exact significance of the names given to them for the present escapes us.

[1] This is the usual Oriental and Semitic figure of speech which leads Arabs at the present day to nickname any European with a large beard "the Father of Hair," and makes the Sphinx of Ghizeh the "Father of Terrors." In the same way, the Mother of Life means doubtless the Very Great Life or Source of Life.

[2] Cumont, *Cosmog. Manich.* p. 15.

[3] See the *Khuastuanift*, pp. 335, 342 *infra*, and the Tun-huang treatise (Chavannes et Pelliot, *op. cit.* p. 513, and n. 1). Cf. also Müller, *Handschriften-Reste*, p. 102.

[4] She cannot possibly be the Virgin of Light, as in the *Acta* she is said to retire at the Ecpyrosis into the Moon-ship along with that personage. See Hegemonius, *op. cit.* c. XIII. p. 21, Beeson. The name "Virgin of Light" also appears in the Turfan texts as an epithet of Jesus, if the words are not wrongly translated. See Müller, *Handschriften-Reste*, pp. 75, 77. The name Nahnaha given her by En Nadîm has been referred to in n. 2, p. 300 *supra*.

When the First Man or Ormuzd marched against his enemy, he also evoked five elements called sometimes his sons and sometimes his members. These are the Ether, the Wind, the Light, the Water, and the Fire before mentioned, which together compose the soul of the world, and hence of man, who is in every respect its image. When he was conquered by Satan and dragged down to the lowest pit of hell, he prayed, says Bar Khôni, seven times to the Very Great Father, and he in compassion created, again by his word, the Friend of the Lights[1], who evoked the Great Ban[2], who evoked the Living Spirit. Here we have the second triad or "second creation," of which, as has been said, only the last member takes any active part in what follows. As we have already seen, the Living Spirit speaks a word like a sharp sword, and the image of the First Man answers[3] and is drawn up out of hell. These two, the sword or Appellant and the image or Respondent, together mount towards the Mother of Life and the Living Spirit, and the Mother of Life "clothes" the Image—no doubt with a form or "nature,"—while the Living Spirit does the same with the compelling word[4]. Then they return to the earth of darkness where remains the soul of the First Man in the shape of his five sons.

[1] Probably Mithras, who is in the Vedas and elsewhere called "Mithra the Friend." Mithras is invoked under his own name in the Turfan texts (Müller, *Handschriften-Reste*, p. 77), but the fragment is too mutilated to be able to deduce from it his place in the pantheon.

[2] This name, to be found nowhere but in Bar Khôni, cannot be explained. Pognon says it may be written the Great Laban, which gets us no nearer to its meaning.

[3] The image is probably his body or substance, which is of the substance of the Very Great Father. So Satan is in the Coptic *Trattato gnostico* of Rossi quoted in n. 2, p. 300 *supra* described as the ἀρχηπλάσμα, probably as being the very substance of darkness as the Very Great Father is of the Light.

[4] This is the conjecture of M. Cumont (*Cosmog. Manich.* pp. 24, 25). As he says in note 5 on the first-mentioned page, the passage as it stands is inconsistent. The Appellant and Respondent under the names of Kroshtag and Padwakhtag appear in the *Khuastuanift* and also in the Tun-huang treatise (pp. 521 *sqq.*) without the part they play in the world being immediately apparent. The former document, however (see p. 343

In the meantime, the Living Spirit has also given birth to five sons.   He, like the Very Great Father of whom he is perhaps the reflexion, has five worlds named like those of his paradigm from which he draws certain other powers.   From his Intelligence, says Bar Khôni, he produces The Ornament of Splendour, who is none other than the Splenditenens we have seen drawing the heavens after him; from his Reason, the Great King of Honour, who is described as sitting in the midst of the celestial armies; from his Thought, Adamas of the Light armed with shield and spear; from his Reflexion the King of Glory whose function is to set in motion the three wheels of the fire, the water, and the wind, which apparently raise to the upper spheres the portions of those elements still left below; and finally from his Feeling the great Omophorus or Atlas who bears the earths on his shoulders[1].   Immediately on evocation, three of these powers were set to work to kill and flay the rulers of darkness, and to carry their skins to the Mother of Life.   She stretches out the skins to make the sky, thereby fashioning ten or eleven or even twelve heavens.   She throws their bodies on to the Earth of Darkness, thereby forming eight earths[2].   Thus the soul or sons of the First Man are rescued from the Powers of Darkness, and the machinery of the redemption of the Light is set on foot.

There is, however, a third act to the drama.   Again, the lesser Powers of Light, this time the Mother of Life, the First Man, and the Living Spirit, cry to the Very Great Father.

infra), speaks of them as being concerned in the purification of the Light. MM. Chavannes and Pelliot (*op. cit.* p. 521, n. 1) think it possible that they may represent the portions of the "armour" of the First Man which were not sullied by contact with matter, and compare them to the last two Amshaspands, Haurvetât and Ameretât. See also their *Traité Manicheen*, etc. 2ᵐᵉ ptie, in the *Journal Asiatique*, XI série, t. I. (1913), p. 101. One might liken them to the Cautes and Cautopates appearing in the Mithraic monuments, as to which see Chapter XII, p. 246 *supra*.

[1] All these subordinate deities were known to St Augustine. Cf. *id. c. Faust.* Bk xv. c. 6.

[2] Evidently Manes accepted the dictum of Valentinus quoted above (Chap. IX, p. 104 *supra*), that with celestial powers it is always the female who gives the form.

Satan, or, as the Mahommedan tradition calls him, Hummâma, is still in existence, although his "sons," the Rulers of Darkness, the Hot Wind, the Smoke, and the others have been crucified or fixed in the firmament, and he is still actively working with his remaining powers against the Light. The Light-Powers feel themselves contaminated and oppressed by the contact, and perhaps even in some fear lest they should again have the worst in a renewal of the conflict. Again, the Very Great Father hears them and sends to their assistance a third creation, called this time simply the Messenger.

Who this Messenger is, is the main puzzle of the new documents. The author of the *Acta* knew something of him, for he speaks of a "Third Legate," who, when the world is burning in the great conflagration which will mark the redemption of the last particles of light, will be found in the Ship of the Moon with Jesus, the Mother of Life, the Virgin of Light and the twelve other powers to be presently mentioned[1]. M. Cumont, in his able analysis of Bar Khôni's system, thinks that this "Third Legate" resembles the Neryôsang of the Persians, who in the later Mazdean literature is made the

---

[1] Hegemonius, *Acta*, c. XIII, p. 21, Beeson. Αἱ δὲ προβολαὶ πᾶσαι, ὁ Ἰησοῦς ὁ ἐν τῷ μικρῷ πλοίῳ, καὶ ἡ μήτηρ τῆς ζωῆς, καὶ οἱ δώδεκα κυβερνῆται, καὶ ἡ παρθένος τοῦ φωτὸς καὶ ὁ πρεσβύτης ὁ τρίτος ὁ ἐν τῷ μεγάλῳ πλοίῳ, καὶ τὸ ζῶν πνεῦμα καὶ τὸ τεῖχος τοῦ μεγάλου πυρὸς καὶ τὸ τεῖχος τοῦ ἀνέμου, καὶ τοῦ ἀέρος, καὶ τοῦ ὕδατος, καὶ τοῦ ἔσωθεν πυρὸς τοῦ ζῶντος πρὸς τὸν μικρὸν φωστῆρα οἰκοῦσιν, ἄχρις ἂν τὸ πῦρ καταναλώσῃ τὸν κόσμον ὅλον· ἐν ποσοῖς ποτε ἔτεσιν, ὧν οὐκ ἔμαθον τὴν ποσότητα. "But all the emanations [*i.e.*], Jesus who is in the small ship, and the Mother of Life and the 12 pilots, and the Virgin of Light, and the Third Legate who is in the large ship, and the Living Spirit and the wall [it should be "guardian," as MM. Chavannes and Pelliot explain] of the great fire, and the guardian of the Ether, and of the air, and of the water, and of the inner living fire, abide near the lesser light until the fire has consumed the whole Cosmos. But for how many years I have not learned." The Latin version runs: *Prolationes autem omnes Jesus in modica navi, et mater vitae et duodecim gubernatores et virgo lucis et senior tertius. Unde et majori in navi vivens spiritus adhibetur, et murus ignis illius magni, et murus venti et aeris et aquae et interioris ignis vivi, quae omnia in luna habitabunt usquequo totum mundum ignis absumat ; in quot autem annis numerum non didici :*—which appears to be nonsense. The number of years which Turbo, who is here speaking, had not learned, is said by En Nadîm to be 1468.

herald of Ormuzd, and has also features in common with
Gayômort the First Man, and Mithras[1]. But it is plain from
the Tun-huang treatise lately discovered, as well as from the
fragments found at Turfan, that the Third Legate corresponds
most closely to the Mazdean genius or divinity Sraôsha, the
angel of Obedience[2]. Sraôsha is described in the Srôsh Yashts
as the "Holy and Strong Srôsh," "the Incarnate Word, a
mighty-speared and lordly god." He it is who is called the
"fiend-smiter," who is said to watch over the world and to
defend it from the demons, especially at night, to fight for the
souls of the good after death, and, in the older Mazdean traditions, to judge the dead with Mithra and Rashnu as his
assessors, like Rhadamanthos, Minos, and Eacus among the
Greeks[3]. In the Turfan texts he is called the mighty, and in
the Tun-huang treatise is likened to a judge, while in both sets
of documents he has his proper appellation of Srôsh[4].

This third creation was no more content than his two
predecessors to enter upon the task allotted to him without
further help. His first act upon arriving hither, according to
Bar Khôni, was to evoke or call into existence twelve virgins

[1] Cumont, *Cosmog. Manich.* pp. 58 *sqq.* and Appendix I.

[2] Chavannes et Pelliot, *op. cit.* (1ère ptie), p. 522, and n. 1. For the
part played by him in the Chinese treatise see *op. cit.* p. 536, and n. 2.
He is called "Mighty Srôsh" in the Turfan texts (Müller, *Handschriften-
Reste*, p. 75).

[3] J. Darmesteter, *The Zend Avesta*, part I. (S. B. E. vol. 4, pp. 87, 99)
and part II. (S. B. E. vol. 23, pp. 159–167). All the passages in which he is
referred to come from the Vendidad, but he is also mentioned in the
Bundahish. See West, *Pahlavi Texts*, part I. (S. B. E. vol. 5, p. 128).

[4] See n. 2 *supra.* M. Cumont (*Cosmog. Manich.* p. 34) thinks that
this Messenger was added to the two triads (of Father, Mother, and Son,
and the Friend of the Lights, Great Ban, and Living Spirit, respectively) in
order to make up "the sacred number of seven." But seven is a number
singularly neglected by the Manichaeans, who paid the greatest reverence
to five, and preferred to seven the three and the twelve. Nor do I think
that there is any real parallel in Manichaeism to the Seven Amshaspands
of Zoroastrianism. The actual word *amshaspand* is used in the Tun-huang
treatise (Chavannes et Pelliot, *op. cit.* 1ère ptie, p. 544), but with an entirely
different signification from that of archangel or divinity. It seems there
to mean simply "element." Cf. Chavannes et Pelliot, *op. cit.* 2me partie,
p. 101.

with their vestures, their crowns, and their guards. The Turfan texts give us the names of these powers, four of whom seem to be attributes of sovereignty, and eight of them virtues. Their names in the order of the new texts are respectively, Dominion, Wisdom, Victory, Persuasion, Purity, Truth, Faith, Patience, Uprightness, Goodness, Justice and Light, and they are probably the twelve "pilots" whom the *Acta* describe as being at the Ecpyrosis in the Moon-ship with their father, with Jesus, and with the other powers[1]. But there is much plausibility in M. Cumont's theory that this Third Legate or Srôsh is supposed until that event to inhabit the Sun, and that his 12 "daughters" are the signs of the Zodiac among whom he moves[2]. According to Bar Khôni, it is the same Legate who is ordered by the Great Ban to create a new earth and to set the whole celestial machinery—the Sun and Moon-ships and the three wheels of fire, air, and water—in motion[3]. Yet we hear nothing in any other document of any addition to the number of eight earths already created, and we can only therefore suppose that Bar Khoni's phrase refers to the gradual purification of this world of ours by Srôsh.

Bar Khôni also makes the appearance of this last Legate responsible for the appearance of man upon the earth, as to which he recites a story which seems at first sight to be an elaboration of the Gnostic and Manichaean tradition preserved by the Christians and mentioned above. The Legate, he makes

---

[1] I can find no parallel to these powers in any other system, save that of the *Pistis Sophia*, where appear twelve Saviours of the Treasure-house of Light, from whom the souls of the Twelve Apostles of Jesus were said to be drawn. If, therefore, they are not the signs of the Zodiac, they may be an invention of the Manichaeans to accord with the *magistri* or highest order of their Church (see p. 330 *infra*).

[2] Cumont, *Cosmog. Manich.* p. 36.

[3] Pognon, *op. cit.* pp. 189, 190. He says it was the Messenger (or Srôsh) who ordered the Great Ban to create a new world. M. Kugener, however (Cumont, *Cosmog. Manich.* p. 37, n. 4), says that the passage can be read as in the text, and this avoids the improbability of the younger power or Third Legate giving orders to one of the "second creation." The three wheels, fire, water, and earth, may possibly have been conceived as surrounding the earth, as with the Ophites of the Diagram. Cf. Chap. VIII, n. 3, p. 74 *supra*.

Manes say, was of both sexes, and on his appearance in the
Sun-ship, both the male and female rulers of Darkness became
so filled with desire that they began to give up the light which
they had taken from the sons of the First Man. With this was
mingled their own sin, half of which fell into the sea and there
gave birth to a horrible monster like the King of Darkness.
This was conquered and slain by Adamas of the Light, but that
which fell upon the land fructified as the five kinds of trees[1].
Moreover, the female demons, who were pregnant at the time,
miscarried and their untimely births ate of the buds of the
trees. Yet these females remembered the beauty of the Legate
whom they had seen, and Asaqlun or Saclas[2], son of the King
of Darkness, persuaded them to give him their sons and
daughters, in order that he might make from them an image of
the Legate. This they did, when he ate the male children and
his wife Namraël consumed the female. In consequence
Namraël gave birth to a son and a daughter who were called
Adam and Eve. Jesus was sent to Adam and found him sleeping a sleep of death, but awoke him, made him stand upright,
and gave him to eat of the Tree of Life, while he separated him
from his too seductive companion. This story is not confirmed
by any of the new documents; and in the present state of our
knowledge it is impossible to say whether it contains an old
Asiatic tradition, of which the Biblical accounts of the protoplasts and of the Sons of God making love to the daughters of
men are the only remnants which have till now come down to
us, or whether—as is at least as likely—the whole story is a
blend by the Manichaeans of Jewish, Mandaite, and Pagan
legends. The main point in it for our consideration is its
introduction of a Jesus who is certainly not the same as the

---

[1] I read this, perhaps wrongly, thus instead of Five Trees as does Pognon
(*op. cit.* p. 191). The five kinds of trees are often referred to in the Tun-huang
treatise and in the *Khuastuanift*.

[2] This Saclas, who appears many times in Greek heresiology with his
wife Nebrod, called in the text Namraël (for references, see Cumont,
Cosmog. Manich. p. 73, and notes 3, 4, and 5), was known to Hippolytus,
who uses both names in his description of the tenets of the Peratae, a name
which may be equivalent to that of the Medes. See Hipp. *Philosoph.* Bk
v. c. 14, pp. 194, 195, Cruice.

Jesus *patibilis* whom St Augustine and the other Christian Fathers make Manes describe as born of the Living Spirit and the Earth, and as hanging on every tree. This other Jesus, who came to the earth in the time of Adam, is a fourth emissary or Saviour put forth by the second and third creations according to the *Fihrist* and called by Bar Khôni "Jesus the shining one." In the Turfan texts he is, as has been said, perhaps equated with the Virgin of Light, and in the Tun-huang treatise he is spoken of as "Jesus the Victorious[1]." Evidently he is conceived as one of the Burkhans or Buddhas who fight against the Powers of Darkness, and the Jesus *patibilis* is but another name for the fragments of light or "armour" of the First Man left on this earth. The borrowing of the name revered among Christians is but one of the compromises by which the Manichaeans hoped to draw those of other faiths into their net.

A like plasticity is shown in the organization of the Manichaean Church. The first disciples of Manes, to whom he gave special commandments, were, according to Christian tradition, only seven in number, in which if anywhere in the system we may see a reflexion of the seven Amshaspands of the Avesta[2]. But later there seems to have been instituted a band of twelve Apostles in manifest imitation of the Apostles of Jesus, who perhaps corresponded to the Masters or highest degree that we have seen called the Sons of Gentleness. These were presided over by a Manichaean Pope who figured as the representative and Vicegerent of Manes himself. There were also seventy-two bishops answering to the seventy-two disciples of Christ, who are perhaps to be identified with the Sons of Knowledge. Then came the Presbyters or Sons of Intelligence whose functions were chiefly those of missionaries and who were perpetually, like Faustus, travelling for the propagation of the faith[3]. This seems

---

[1] Chavannes et Pelliot, *op. cit.* 1ère ptie, p. 566, and n. 3.

[2] Hegemonius, *Acta*, c. xi. p. 18, Beeson.

[3] Augustine, *de Haeresibus*, c. 46, p. 210, Oehler. See also Chavannes et Pelliot, *op. cit.* 1ère ptie, p. 569, and n. 2; p. 572, and nn. 2, 3; and p. 581, and n. 4. MM. Chavannes and Pelliot discuss the question of the organization of the Manichaean Church in the second part of their memoir. See *op. cit.* 2me ptie, pp. 193, 196 and n. 2. They also give a dissertation on

to have been the organization generally adopted for Christian countries, and we meet with it there up to a very late date. Yet there is no reason to suppose that it was necessarily copied by the Manichaeans of Central Asia or India, or that the Manichaeans always obeyed some central authority. What organization they did adopt outside Europe and Africa we shall probably have to wait to discover when more of the documents coming from Turkestan have been deciphered.

The extreme simplicity of the Manichaean ritual also made easy to them all such adaptations to the ways of their neighbours. Hating images with as much energy, perhaps, as Zoroaster himself, they had neither statues nor lights nor incense in their meeting-places, which must in the West have been as bare and as unadorned as a Scottish conventicle. The whole service seems to have consisted of hymns and prayers, in the first of which the mythology of the sect doubtless found expression, while the second mainly consisted of those praises of the Powers of Light, which praises were thought, as has been said, to have an actual and objective existence and thus to fulfil a considerable part in the scheme of redemption. Up to the present we have very few examples of the hymns. The *Hymn of the Soul*, of which Prof. Bevan has published an English translation, is probably Manichaean in origin[1], and St Augustine tells of a "love song" in which the Father, meaning thereby probably Srôsh, the third legate[2], is represented as presiding at a banquet crowned with flowers and bearing a sceptre, while twelve gods, three from each quarter of the globe, are grouped round him "clothed in flowers" singing praises and laying flowers at his feet. These are said to represent the seasons[3]; and we hear also of myths doubtless expressed in song describing

the common life of the Elect. It remains to be seen whether this was anything more than a copy of the monastic institutions of the Buddhists. For obvious reasons, such an organization was not adopted in lands where they had outwardly to conform to other religions.

[1] So Professor Harnack and Mr Conybeare in the *Encyc. Brit.* (XIth ed.), vol. XVII. p. 576, *s.v.* Manichaeism.

[2] "*Beatus pater*" is the name given to the *Tertius legatus* by Evodius, *de recta fide, passim.*

[3] Augustine, *c. Faust.* Bk XV. c. 5.

the great angel Splenditenens, whose care is the portions of
Light still imprisoned in matter and who is always bewailing
their captivity[1]; and of his fellow angel Omophorus who, as
has been said, bears the world on his shoulders like the classical
Atlas[2]. Doubtless, too, some of these hymns described that
last conflagration, which seems to have occupied so great
a place in the speculations of the early Manichaeans, when the
justified faithful, secure in the two great ships which sail about
on the ocean of the upper air, shall behold the world in flames
and the last portion of the imprisoned Light mounting in the
Column of Praises, while Satan and his hosts are confined for
ever in the gross and dark matter which is henceforth to be
their portion[3]. Possibly the Turfan discoveries may yet recover
for us some important fragments of this lost literature.

With regard to the prayers, we are a little better informed.
"Free us by thy skill, for we suffer here oppression and torture
and pollution, only that thou (the First Man?) mayest mourn
unmolested in thy kingdom," is one of those which St Augustine
has preserved for us[4]. So, too, the Mahommedan tradition has
handed down a series of six doxologies or hymns of praise out
of a total of twelve which seem to have been obligatory, perhaps
on all Manichaeans, but certainly on the Perfect. The suppliant
is, we are told, to stand upright, to wash in running water or
something else, in which we may perhaps see either the origin
or an imitation of the ceremonial ablutions of the Mussulman,
then to turn towards the Great Light, to prostrate himself and
to say:

"Blessed be our guide, the Paraclete, the Messenger of the

[1] *Op. cit.* Bk xx. c. 9.

[2] Cumont, *Cosmog. Manich.* App. 2, "L'Omophore." He shows that
this belief in an angel who supports the world on his shoulders goes back
to the Assyrian cylinder-seals, where is found a world-bearing divinity in
exactly the same pose as that reproduced in the Mithraic bas-reliefs.

[3] One of the silk banners obtained by the German expedition seems to
have depicted this scene. See A. von Le Coq, *Chotscho*: Facsimile-Wiedergaben der Wichtigerer Funde der Ersten Kgl. Preuss. Expedition nach
Turfan, Berlin, 1913, Bd 1, p. 1 and Pl. IV. 6.

[4] Augustine, *c. Faust.* Bk xx. c. 17. Is the prayer addressed to the
First Man or to Splenditenens, whom St Augustine represents as mourning
over the pollution of the Light?

Light. Blessed be his angels, his guards, and highly praised his shining troops."

Then he is to rise and, prostrating himself again, to say:

"Thou highly-esteemed one, O thou shining Mânî our guide, thou the root of illumination, branch of uprightness, thou the great tree, thou who art the sovereign Remedy."

A third prostration, and the praise runs:

"I prostrate myself and praise with a pure heart and a sincere tongue, the Great God, the Father of the Lights and of their elements, the most highly praised, the glorified, thee and all thy Majesty and thy blessed worlds that thou hast called forth! To praise thee is to praise equally thy troops, thy justified ones, thy word, thy majesty, thy good pleasure. For thou art the God who is all Truth, all Life, and all Justice."

Then comes a fourth prostration and the sentence:

"I praise all the gods, all the shining angels, all the lights, and all the troops who are from the Great God, and I prostrate myself before them."

The speech after the fifth prostration is:

"I prostrate myself and I praise the great troops, and the shining gods who, with their Wisdom spread over the Darkness, pursue it and conquer it."

While the sixth, and last given in full, is simply:

"I prostrate myself and I praise the Father of Majesty, the eminent one, the shining one who has come forth from the two sciences[1]."

It seems fairly plain that these praises are addressed not so much to the "King of the Paradise of Light" or Highest God of Goodness as to the lesser Powers of Light. The recent expeditions of European scholars to Central Asia have succeeded in recovering for us almost in full the Confession-Prayer repeated

---

[1] The praises in the text are all given by En Nadîm. See Flügel, *op. cit.* p. 96. Are "the two sciences" the Living Spirit and his Intelligence or Reason? If so the "Father of Majesty" probably means the *Beatus Pater* of note 2, p. 331 *supra*.

ritually by the Manichaean Hearers or laymen which, besides confirming the Christian and Mahommedan accounts of Manes' teaching summarized above, shows a greater belief in the efficacy of repentance and the enforcement of a stricter morality upon all classes of Manichaeans than we should have imagined from the accounts of their adversaries[1].   We are fortunate in possessing more than one text of this Confession-Prayer, that found by the energy of our English emissary, Dr (now Sir Marc Aurel) Stein, in the "Cave of the Thousand Buddhas" at Tun-huang, proving almost identical with the one discovered in Turfan by the Russian Expedition and now in St Petersburg, while both can be checked and supplemented by fragments also found at Turfan by Profs. Grünwedel's and von Le Coq's expeditions to the same place and taken to Berlin[2].   The title and first few lines of this prayer have been lost, owing to the fact that the Chinese plan of writing on a continuous sheet of paper many yards in length, which was then rolled up with the last lines innermost, was adopted by its transcribers.   All the specimens yet found are in Turkish, the Russian MS. being in the dialect called after the nation using it, Ouigour or Uighur, and like that found by Dr Stein and the Berlin fragments, in the Manichaean modification of the Estranghelo or Syriac script.   The prayer or litany is in 15 sections or classes, the number having doubtless a mystical reference[3], and is followed in the Russian and English examples by a recapitulation which is not without value.   The version which follows is a compound

---

[1] The Mediaeval Inquisitors were in especial never tired of denouncing the immorality of the Manichaean Hearers.   See H. C. Lea, *History of the Inquisition*, index.

[2] The original documents are described by Prof. A. von Le Coq in "Turkish Khuastuanift from Tun-huang," *J.R.A.S.* 1911, pp. 277–279.

[3] There are many allusions in Manichaean literature to three worlds of light, which seem to be (1) the light inaccessible, or heaven of God; (2) the light intelligible, *i.e.* that can be comprehended by the mind only, which is inhabited by the First Man; and (3) the perceptible light, of which the Sun and Moon are the rulers.   See especially Chavannes et Pelliot, *op. cit.* 1ère ptie, pp. 564 and 586, and 2me ptie, p. 102, n. 2. The Manichaeans' addiction to the number five needs no insistence. Fifteen, *i.e.* 3×5, is therefore a number which came naturally to them.

of all the three sources mentioned above, and has been here divided into three parts, although it is not so in the original, for convenience of commentary.

KHUASTUANIFT

Sect. I. "[The Son of ?] the God Khormuzta even the Fivefold God descended from the heavens with the purity of all the gods, to war against the Demon; he (the Fivefold God) battled against the Shimnus[1] of evil deeds, and against the five species of the Kingdom of the Demons. God and the Devil, Light and Darkness then intermingled. The youth of the Divine Khormuzta even the Fivefold God, and our souls, joined battle with Sin and the Demon-world and became ensnared and entangled with it. All the princes of the Demons came with the insatiable and shameless Demon of Envy and a hundred and forty myriads of demons banded together in evil intent, ignorance, and folly. He himself, the Born and Created (*i.e.* the Fivefold God or son of Khormuzta) forgot the eternal heaven of the Gods and became separated from the Gods of Light. Hence, O my God! if the Shimnu (Great Devil) of evil intent has led astray our thoughts and inclined us to devilish deeds.—If, becoming thereby foolish and without understanding, we have sinned and erred against the foundation and root of all bright spirits, even against the pure and bright Azrua the Lord[2].—If thereby Light and Darkness, God and the Devil have intermingled...

here follows a lacuna of several pages which Prof. von Le Coq suggests was filled with "an explanation of the allegorical story of the combat" and its practical application.

" ...If we have said...is its foundation and root.—If we have said if anyone animates a body it is God; or that if anyone kills, it is God.—If we have said Good and Evil have alike been created by God. If we have said it is He [God] who has created the eternal

---

[1] Shimnu seems to be the Buddhist word for "devil." Cf. Neander, *Ch. Hist.* vol. ii. p. 181. Prof. von Le Coq (*J.R.A.S.* 1911, p. 300) says it is of Soghdian origin. Chavannes et Pelliot, *op. cit.* 1ère ptie, p. 523, n. 3, seek to show that it is the equivalent of Ahriman.

[2] On this word see p. 323 *supra*; cf. Chavannes et Pelliot, *op. cit.* 1ère ptie, p. 542, n. 2, which seems to summarize all that there is to be said about it, and p. 342 *infra*.

Gods. If we have said the Divine Khormuzta and the Shimnu (Great Devil) are brethren[1]. O my God, if in our sin we have spoken such awful blasphemies, having unwittingly become false to God. If we have thus committed this unpardonable sin. O my God, I N.N.[2] now repent. To cleanse myself from sin, I pray : *Manâstâr hîrzâ !* (My sin remit!) "

Sect. II. "When because of the God of the Sun and Moon and of the Gods enthroned in the two resplendent Palaces, the foundation and root of the light of all the Burkhans[3] of Earth and Water go to the heaven prepared for their assembly (foundation and root), the first gate they reach is the God of the Sun and Moon. In order to deliver the Fivefold God and to sever the Light from the Darkness he rolls along the lower part of the heavens in fulness and lights up the four corners of the earth. O my God, if in our sin we have unwittingly sinned against the God of the Sun and Moon, the Gods enthroned in the two resplendent Palaces. If, although calling him the True, Mighty, and Powerful God, we have not believed in him. If we have uttered many spoken blasphemies. If we have said the God of the Sun and Moon dies, and his rise and setting comes [?] not by [his own?] strength, and that should he [trust to his?] own strength, he will not rise [?]. If we have said, our own bodies were created before the Sun and Moon. To cleanse ourselves from this unwitting sin also, we pray : *Manâstâr hîrzâ* (Our sin remit)."

Sect. III. "Since, in defence of the Fivefold God, even the youth of the Divine Khormuzta, his five members, that is to say, First, the God of the Ether ; Secondly, the God of the Wind ; Thirdly, the God of the Light ; Fourthly, the God of the Water ; Fifthly, the God of the Fire, having battled against Sin and the

---

[1] This was of course the exact statement of Zervanism, which the *Khuastuanift* implicitly condemns. Cf. Mihr Nerses' proclamation in 450 A.D. quoted on p. 285 *supra*.

[2] This was the name of the owner, which was *Raimast Parzind* in the Tun-huang text of Sir Marc Stein.

[3] This was the name given to the incarnate, as distinguished from the spiritual, messengers of the God of Light to man. Thus Zoroaster is always spoken of in Manichaean literature as a Burkhan, and doubtless the historical Buddha and Jesus were included in the same category. Cf. Chavannes et Pelliot, *op. cit.* 1ère ptie, p. 572, n. 2.

Demon-world were ensnared and entangled[1], and have intermingled with the Darkness. Since they were unable to go to the heaven of God and are now upon the earth. Since the ten heavens above, the eight earths beneath, exist on account of the Fivefold God. Since of everything that is upon the earth the Fivefold God is the Majesty, the Radiance [?], the Likeness, the Body, the Soul, the Strength, the Light, the Foundation and the Root. O my God, if in our sin we have unwittingly offended against or caused grief to the Fivefold God by an evil and wicked mind. If we have allowed our fourteen members to gain domination over us. If by taking animated beings with our ten snake-headed fingers and our thirty-two teeth, we have fed upon them and have thus angered and grieved the Gods [?][2]. If we have in any way sinned against the dry and wet earth, against the five kinds of animals, and against the five kinds of herbs and trees. O my God, to cleanse ourselves from sin, so pray we now: *Manâstâr hîrzâ!* (Our sin remit!)"

Sect. IV. "If we have unwittingly sinned against the divine Burkhans of the hosts (of the Messenger God[3]) and against the merit-attaining pure Elect. If although we have called them the true and divine Burkhans and the well-doing and pure Elect, we have not believed on them. If although we have uttered the word of God, we have through folly acted against it and not performed it [?]. If instead of spreading the decrees and commandments, we have impeded them. O my God, we now repent and to cleanse ourselves from sin, we pray: *Manâstâr hîrzâ!* (Our sin remit!)"

Sect. V. "If we have wandered into sin against the five kinds of animated beings, that is to say, First, against two-footed man; Secondly, against the four-footed animals; Thirdly, against the flying animals; Fourthly, against the animals in the water; Fifthly, against the animals upon earth which creep on their bellies. O my God, if in our sin against these five kinds of animated and moving

---

[1] Obviously the authors of the *Khuastuanift* knew nothing of the doctrine put forth by the Manichaeans in Christian lands that the First Man offered himself as a sacrifice to destroy the sons of Darkness.   Cf. n. 2, p. 294 *supra*.

[2] Because by so doing the existence of the diabolic creation would be prolonged.

[3] The words "of the Messenger" [God] are not in Prof. von Le Coq's version.

beings from the great to the small, we have beaten and wounded, abused, and injured, and pained, or even put them to death. If thus we have become the tormentors of so many animated and moving beings. O my God, to cleanse ourselves from sin, so pray we now: *Manâstâr hîrzâ!* (Our sin remit!)"

It will be seen that in these first five sections or clauses of the Confession, we have a confirmation in all essential points of the version of the faith taught by Manes as it has been preserved for us by the Mahommedan authors quoted above. It is even possible that it was from this source that the author of the *Fihrist* and Al-Bîrûnî derived some of their information concerning the Manichaeans, and although it is impossible as yet to fix any date for the Confession except within very wide limits, it may be said that it is probably earlier than either of the Mahommedan writers. It is certainly earlier than 1035 A.D., the date at which the grotto at Tun-huang in which one of the copies was bricked up[1]. But it seems plain that it must have long before been used in the Manichaean worship from the fact that copies differing little, if at all, from each other have been found in two different scripts. As two of these are in the Turkish language, it seems likely that they were translated for proselytizing purposes into this from the earlier Syriac version shortly after the conquest of the Tou-kiue or Turks by the Ouigours, which some authors put as far back as the viith century A.D.[2] The tenets of the Manichaeans must have been well settled for this to be possible, and we have here, therefore, an account at first hand of Manichaean teaching at a date much earlier than the Mahommedan authors quoted above, and first reduced to writing between the earliest promulgation of Manes' own teaching and the Mahommedan conquest of Persia. It is, therefore, contemporary, or nearly so, with the period of activity

[1] Cf. Chavannes et Pelliot, *op. cit.* 1ère ptie, pp. 503, n. 1. On this being mentioned in a paper in the *J.R.A.S.* 1913, Dr F. Denison Ross said that he thought the date should be put 300 years later, *J. cit.* p. 81. He has since withdrawn this (*J.R.A.S.* 1913, pp. 434–436).

[2] See the luminous historical study by M. Henri Cordier, "Les Fouilles en Asie Centrale," *Journal des Savans*, Paris, 1910, pp. 219 *sqq.*, especially pp. 249, 250.

of the Zoroastrianism revived by the Sassanides, and it is interesting to find how much nearer in appearance to the cosmology and theology of the Avesta are those of the *Khuas-tuanift* than is the Christianized form of Manichaeism introduced into Europe and Africa and combated by St Augustine. Khormuzta, the First Man, is certainly Ahura Mazda, Oromazes, or Ormuzd, while the Fivefold God here spoken of as the "youth" is clearly to be identified with his five sons or the armour left below on his defeat[1]. Hence it is probable that the Manichaeans in Upper Asia did not wish to appear as the worshippers of any other deities than those of the Persian nation[2], although where Christianity was the religion of the State, they were willing to call these deities by other names[3]. Yet the dualism which is the real characteristic of the faith of Manes here as elsewhere admits of no compromise, and the sin against which the Section II is directed is plainly that Zervanist heresy which would make *Zervan akerene* or Boundless Time the author of all things, and Ormuzd and Ahriman alike his sons. The part played by the Sun and Moon in the redemption of the Light is here the same as that assigned to them in both the Christian and the Mahommedan accounts of Manes' own teaching, but nothing is here said of the wheel which appears in the former[4]. The Divine "Burkhans" mentioned in Section III are, as we shall see later, the Divine Messengers sent from time to time into the present world to assist in the redemption of the Light. The sinfulness of feeding upon, injuring, or even angering the lower animals is here much more strongly insisted upon than in the other documents and

---

[1] Chavannes et Pelliot, *op. cit.* 1ère ptie, p. 513, n. 1. Müller, *Handschriften-Reste*, pp. 20, 22. Von Le Coq, *J.R.A.S.* 1911, p. 301.

[2] Ormuzd, "the whole circuit of the sky," although he calls him, *more Graecorum*, Zeus, "the sun and moon, the earth, fire, water and the winds," were "the only gods whose worship had come down to the Persians from ancient times" in the days of Herodotus. Cf. Herodotus, Bk I. c. 131.

[3] Faustus (Aug. *v. Faust.* Bk II. c. 4) distinctly says "Jesus Christ is the son of the First Man." Cf. also c. 5.

[4] It is very doubtful whether it is referred to or not in the Tun-huang treatise. Cf. Chavannes et Pelliot, *op. cit.* 1ère ptie, pp. 515, n. 2, and p. 516, n. 3.

demands repentance even in the case of the Hearers, and this points directly to a closer connection with Buddhism than hitherto has been thought possible. It is plainly opposed to the later Zoroastrian teaching, which makes the killing of certain animals belonging to the creation of Ahriman a religious duty; and may therefore have only been adopted by the Manichaeans when they found themselves in contact with a large community of professed Buddhists.

The next five sections of the *Khuastuanift* run thus:

Sect. VI. "If, O my God, we have wandered into sin, and have committed the ten kinds of sin in thoughts, words, and deeds. If we have made up fraudulent lies; if we have sworn false oaths; if we have borne false witness; if we have treated as guilty guiltless men; if by fetching and carrying tales we have set men at variance, and thereby have perverted their minds; if we have practised magic; if we have killed many animated and moving beings; if we have given way to wanton pleasures; if we have wasted the hard-earned gains of industrious men; if we have sinned against the God of the Sun and Moon[1]. If in our past and present lives since we have become Manichaeans [*i.e.* Hearers] we have sinned and gone astray, thereby bringing confusion and discord upon so many animated beings, O my God, to cleanse ourselves from sin, so pray we now, *Manâstâr hîrzâ!* (Our sin remit!)"

Sect. VII. "Who is he who wandering in sin comes to the entry of the two poison-laden ways, and to the road which leads astray to the Gate of Hell? The first is he who holds to false doctrines; the second is he who invokes the Demon as God and falls down before him. O my God, if wandering in sin, we have failed to recognize and understand the true God and his pure faith, and have not believed what the Burkhans and the pure Elect have preached[2], and have instead believed on those who preach falsely, saying 'I preach the true God, and I expound the faith rightly.' If we have accepted the words of such a one and have unwittingly kept wrongful fasts, and have unwittingly bowed ourselves wrongfully, and wrongfully

[1] The Power whom Faustus (Aug. *c. Faust.* Bk xx. c. 2) calls "God the Son."

[2] Evidently the incarnate or human messengers, Zoroaster, Buddha, Jesus, and Manes. The heavenly "legates" are never depicted as "preaching" to men.

given alms; or if we have said 'We will acquire merit' and thereby have unwittingly committed evil deeds; or if, invoking the Demon and the Fiend as God, we have sacrificed to them animated and moving beings; or if, saying, 'this is the precept of the Burkhan,' we have put ourselves under a false law and have bowed ourselves, blessing it. If, thus sinning against God, we have prayed to the Demon. O my God, to cleanse ourselves from sin, so pray we now: *Manâstâr hîrzâ!* (Our sin remit!)"

Sect. VIII. "When we came to the knowledge of the true God and the pure Law, we knew the Two Principles and the Law of the Three Ages[1]. The Light Principle we knew to be the Paradise of God and the Dark Principle to be the Land of Hell. We knew what existed before Heaven and Earth, the Earth of God, was. We knew how God and the Demon fought with one another, and how Light and Darkness became mingled together, and how Heaven and Earth were created. We knew how the Earth of the Rulers and its Heaven will disappear, and how the Light will be freed from the Darkness, and what will then happen to all things. We believed in and put our faith in the God Azrua, in the God of the Sun and Moon, in the Mighty God[2], and in the Burkhans, and thus we became Hearers. Four bright seals have we carved upon our hearts. One is Love which is the seal of the God Azrua[3]; the second is Faith, which is the seal of the God of the Sun and Moon; the third is the Fear of God which is the seal of the Fivefold God; and the fourth is the wise Wisdom, which is the seal of the Burkhans. If, O my God, we have turned away our spirits and minds from these four (categories of) Gods; if we have spurned them from their rightful place, and the Divine Seals have thus been broken, O my God, to cleanse ourselves from sin, so pray we now: *Manâstâr hîrzâ!* (Our sin remit!)"

Sect. IX. "In the Ten Commandments, we have been ordered to keep three with the mouth, three with the heart, three with the hand, and one with the whole self. If, O my God, we have wittingly or unwittingly by cleaving to the love of the body, or by listening

[1] The Past, Present and Future, called the "Three Moments" in the Tun-huang treatise. See Chavannes et Pelliot, *op. cit.* 11me ptie, pp. 114, 116.

[2] Probably the strong or mighty Srôsh or *Tertius Legatus*.

[3] This may be compared to the Ophite Diagram in which Agape or Love is made the summit of the Pantheon. See Chap. VIII p. 68 *supra*. See also the same dogma in Valentinus, Chap. IX p. 123 *supra*.

to the words of wicked companions and friends, of associates and fellows; or by reason of our having much cattle and other possessions; or by our foolish attachment to the things of this world, we have broken these ten commandments, and have been found wanting and of no avail: O my God, to cleanse ourselves from sin, so pray we now: *Manâstâr hîrzâ!* (Our sin remit!)"

Sect. X. "We have been ordered to render every day, with a whole mind and a pure heart, four praises to the God Azrua, to the God of the Sun and Moon, to the Mighty God, and to the Burkhans. If from lack of the fear of God or from slackness our praises have been offered unseemly, or if in offering them we have not turned our hearts and minds towards God, so that our praises and prayers have not reached God in pure wise, but have remained in another place: O my God, to cleanse ourselves from sin, so pray we now: *Manâstâr hîrzâ!* (Our sin remit!)"

This second part of the Confession, perhaps, deals with errors of conduct as the first does with errors of belief. The ten sins given in the VIth Section do not agree exactly with the list given in the *Fihrist* which says that the Manichaean Hearers were enjoined to abstain from prayers offered to idols, from lying, from greed, from murder, adultery, theft, from false teaching, from magic, from doubt in religion, and from slackness in action[1]; but perhaps all these prohibitions could be read into the list in the *Khuastuanift*. The VIIth Section seems to be directed not so much against other religions as against schisms within the Manichaean Church[2], and it is evident that its authors knew of bloody sacrifices offered to the Powers of Darkness as described by Plutarch apart from the magic or sorcery condemned in the preceding section. In the VIIIth Section, we have also for the second time a new name for God in the word Azrua, which Prof. von Le Coq leaves unexplained; but which M. Gauthiot considers to be the same as, or rather the equivalent in Soghdian of Zervan[3]. Zervan, however, can hardly be here the Supreme God worshipped by Yezdegerd, especially as the *Khuastuanift* has just, as we have

---

[1] Flügel, *op. cit.* pp. 95, 96.

[2] As to these, see En Nadîm in Flügel, *op. cit.* pp. 97–100.

[3] Chavannes et Pelliot, *op. cit.* 1ère ptie, p. 543, n. 2.

seen, formally condemned as blasphemers those who say that
Ormuzd and Ahriman are brethren, and therefore by implication
those who give both Powers Zervan for a father. It seems
more likely that the name is either a corruption of Ahura Mazda
or perhaps of the Sanskrit Asura; but in any event, there can
be no doubt that it denotes the King of the Paradise of Light,
as the Highest Good God is called in the *Fihrist*. The division
of the Ten Commandments of Manes into three of the mouth,
three of the hand, three of the heart, and one of the whole
being recalls St Augustine's description of the threes eals,
the *signaculum oris*, *signaculum manus*, and *signaculum sinus*,
observed by the Manichaeans[1]; while the description in Section
X of the four praises (or hymns) to be rendered daily bears
out what is said above as to the praises of man being of
importance for the actual redemption of the Light.

The remaining sections of the *Khuastuanift* are:

Sect. XI. "We have been ordered to give reverently seven kinds
of alms for the sake of the pure Law. It has also been ordered that
when the angels of the Light of the Five Gods and the two Appellant
and Respondent Gods bring to us the Light of the Five Gods which
is to go to the Gods to be purified, we should in all things order
ourselves [or, "dress ourselves," according to Le Coq] according to
the Law. If, through necessity or because of our foolishness, we
have not given the seven kinds of alms according to the Law, but
have bound the Light of the Five Gods, which should go to the Gods
to be purified, in our houses and dwellings, or if we should have
given it to evil men or to evil animals, and have thereby wasted it
and sent it to the Land of Evil, O my God, to cleanse ourselves from
sin, so pray we now: *Manâstâr hîrzâ!* (Our sin remit!)"

Sect. XII. "We have been ordered to keep every year 50 days
of *Vusanti*[2] after the manner of the pure Elect, and thereon [?] to

---

[1] Augustine, *de Moribus Manichaeorum*, c. x. Cf. Baur, *Die Manichäische Religionssystem*, pp. 248 *sqq*. Chavannes et Pelliot, *op. cit.* 1ère ptie,
p. 547, n. 1, examine the question whether these are borrowed from
Buddhism as F. W. K. Müller and Cumont assert, and incline to the view
that Manes took them from Zoroastrianism.

[2] The word *vusanti* does not seem to be explained by Prof. von Le Coq.
Has it any connection with the Sanskrit *vasanta* "spring"? In that case,

please God by observing pure fasts. If, by reason of the care of our houses and dwellings or of our cattle and other possessions; or by reason of our need and poverty [foolish attachments, *apud* Le Coq]; or because of the greedy and shameless Demon of Envy; or of our irreverent hearts, we have broken the fast, either wittingly or by foolishness; or having begun it have not fasted according to the Rite and the Law. O my God, to cleanse ourselves from sin, so pray we now: *Manâstâr hîrzâ!* (Our sin remit!)"

Sect. XIII. "We have been ordered to pray every Full Moon [literally, every day of the Moon-God], to acknowledge before God, the Law, and the pure Elect, our sins and transgressions in prayer for the cleansing of ourselves from sin. If now wittingly, or by feebleness of mind, or from idleness of body, or because our minds were set on the cares and business of this world, we have not thus gone to prayer for the cleansing of ourselves from sin. O my God, to cleanse ourselves from sin, so pray we now: *Manâstâr hîrzâ!* (Our sin remit!)"

Sect. XIV. "We have been ordered to keep each year seven *Yimki*[1] [Days of Atonement?] and one month's rigid fast [?]. We have also been ordered when meeting together in the House of Prayer to keep the *Yimki* and to observe the fast, to acknowledge in prayer with a whole mind to the Divine Burkhans the sins which we have committed during the year and which we know through our senses. O my God, if we have not kept the *Yimki* seemly; if we have not observed the month's rigid fast perfectly and seemly; if we have failed to acknowledge in prayer the sins of the year which we know through our senses, and have thus failed in so many of our duties.

the 50 days fast may have been continuous like the Christian Lent and the Mahommedan Ramadan. But it seems more likely that it refers to the weekly fast on Sunday which, the *Fihrist* notwithstanding, seems to have been incumbent on all the Manichaeans, Elect and Hearers alike. So Chavannes et Pelliot, *op. cit.* 2me ptie, p. 111, n. 2. See n. 4, p. 349 *infra*.

[1] Prof. von Le Coq says (*J.R.A.S.* 1911, p. 307) that this word is as yet unexplained and may belong to another language than Turkish. One is almost tempted to see in it a corruption of the Yom Kippur or Day of Atonement of the Jews. Judaism is the last religion from which the Manichaeans would have consciously borrowed; it may well be that both Jews and Manichaeans were here drawing from a common source.

O my God, to cleanse ourselves from sin, so pray we now: *Manâstâr hîrzâ!* (Our sins remit!)"

Sect. XV. "How many evil thoughts do we not think every day! How many deceitful and unseemly words do we not speak! How many unseemly deeds do we not do! Thus do we prepare torments for ourselves by crimes and frauds. Since we have walked body and soul in the love of the greedy and shameless Demon of Envy, and the Light of the Five Gods which we absorb in our food every day thereby goes to the Land of Evil. Wherefore, O my God, to cleanse ourselves from sin, so pray we now: *Manâstâr hîrzâ!* (Our sins remit!)"

Here follows a lacuna of four lines, after which the Confession resumes:

"O my God. We are full of defects and sins! We are thine adversaries and grieve thee by thoughts, words and deeds, for the sake of the greedy and shameless Demon of Envy. Gazing with our eyes, hearing with our ears, seizing with our hands, and trampling with our feet, we ever torture and impede the Light of the Five Gods, the dry and wet earth, the five kinds of animals, and the five kinds of plants and trees. So full are we of defects and sins! On account of the Ten Commandments, the seven kinds of Alms, the three seals, we are called Hearers; yet we cannot perform what these claim of us. If, wandering in sin, we have sinned against the Gods of Light, against the pure Law, against the Herald God[1] and the Preacher, the Men of God [the Preachers, according to Le Coq], against the pure Elect. If we have not walked according to the letter and spirit of the spoken words of God. If we have grieved the hearts of the Gods. If we have been unable to keep the Days of Atonement, the rigid fast, to offer the Praises and the Blessings according to the Law and the Rite. If we have been found lacking and unprofitable, and have day by day and month by month committed sins and trespasses—to the Gods of Light, to the Majesty of the Law, to the pure Elect, to cleanse ourselves from sin, so pray we now: *Manâstâr hîrzâ!* (Our sin remit!)"

These last five sections of the *Khuastuanift* give us a glimpse of the religious observances of the Manichaeans which alters somewhat the picture of them which we should have formed from

---

[1] Is this the *Tertius Legatus* or another?

the account of St Augustine and other Christian writers. The seven kinds of alms referred to in Section XI, are not, as might be thought, the gifts to necessitous or helpless persons prescribed alike by the Christian and the Mahommedan religions. It is apparent both from the context and from other sources of information that they are the offerings of food made by the lay or lowest members of the Manichaean community to the Elect or Perfect, who are spoken of in the subsequent sections as being already a species of Gods. This practice was certainly known to St Augustine, and was not likely to sink into oblivion in a community in contact with Buddhists, among whom monks living upon food given in alms by the faithful were a common sight. But the reason assigned by St Augustine for the practice, which was before obscure, here receives full explanation. The particles of light diffused through matter, and therefore inhabiting the bodies of animals and plants, could only, in Manichaean opinion, be set free by passing into the bodies of the semi-divine Elect. Thus says St Augustine in his treatise against the Manichaean Perfect, Faustus[1]:

"This foolish notion of making your disciples bring you food, that your teeth and stomach may be the means of relieving Christ who is bound up in it, is a consequence of your profane fancies. You declare that Christ is liberated in this way—not, however, entirely; for you hold that some tiny particles of no value still remain in the excrement, to be mixed up and compounded again in various material forms, and to be released and purified at any rate by the fire in which the world will be burned up, if not before."

With the substitution of the "Light of the Fivefold God" for Christ—the use of this last name being probably either the gloss of St Augustine himself, or else the concession made by the Manichaean missionaries after their manner to the religious prepossessions of those among whom they hoped to gain converts—we have here the doctrine more plainly stated in the *Khuastuanift*. The Hearers are to labour perpetually, idleness being one of the Manichaean deadly sins, and to present

---

[1] Augustine, *c. Faust.* Bk II. c. 5. Cf. Chavannes et Pelliot, *op. cit.* 1ère ptie, p. 539, and n. 1.

the fruits of their labour in the shape of food to the Perfect. Not only will the particles of Light imprisoned in this last thus be conveyed to the Land of the Gods; but it will be prevented from going to the Land of Evil, which it would do if it were consumed by the bodies of the Hearers or, *a fortiori*, of those profane persons who belonged to other faiths than the Manichaean. Thus is explained the inhumanity of which many writers accuse the Manichaean community, which led them to refuse food to their neighbours in time of famine, alleging that all that they produced must be reserved for those of the Faith[1].

This explains also the merit assigned to the observance of the many fasts enjoined in the concluding sections of the *Khuastuanift*. The fifty *Vusanti* fasts together with the month's rigid fast to be kept by the Hearers would all have the effect of diminishing their consumption of food in the shape of animals and plants, which hinders the liberation of the particles of Light imprisoned therein. In the choice of the days set apart for these fasts we see another instance of the Manichaean practice as assimilating the outward observances of other religions. The fifty *Vusanti* fasts would give an average of very nearly one a week, and were probably kept on Sunday, the distinction between the Elect and the Hearers in this respect noted by the Mahommedan writer being probably due to some misconception. The month's rigid fast possibly accorded with the Arab Ramadan and must have been very useful in preventing the Hearers from appearing singular when among Mahommedans; and the seven *Yimki* or Days of Atonement seem to have been copied from the observances of the Jews. So possibly was the ritual practice alluded to in the XIVth section of meeting together at certain times to confess their sins, and as this is here said to take place in the House of Prayer, it entirely disposes of the theory set up by earlier writers that the Manichaeans had no temples, synagogues, or churches of their own[2]. The confession and prayer enjoined in Section XIII were doubtless to be repeated privately and in whatever place the

---

[1] Chavannes et Pelliot, *op. cit.* 1ère ptie, p. 573, n. 3.

[2] So Baur, *op. cit.* This was doubtless true in the West and in lands where they were exposed to severe persecution.

Hearer found himself at the fortnightly periods there specified, and this Litany was very probably the *Khuastuanift* itself[1].

What other ritual was performed in these Manichaean meeting-places is still doubtful. The Christian writers declare that the Manichaeans celebrated a sacrament resembling the Eucharist with the horrible accompaniments before alluded to in the case of the followers of Simon Magus[2]. The same accusation was made, as has been many times said above, by nearly all the sects of the period against each other, and we have no means of determining its truth. It is however fairly certain from the silence observed on the subject by the *Khuastuanift* that no sacramental feast of any kind was either celebrated by or in the presence of the Hearers or general body of Manichaeans. If the Perfect or Elect partook of any such meal among themselves, it possibly consisted of bread and water only and was probably a survival of some custom traditional in Western Asia of which we have already seen the traces in the Mysteries of Mithras[3]. The pronounced Docetism which led the Manichaeans to regard the body of the historical Jesus as a phantom shows that they could not have attributed to this meal any sacramental efficacy like that involved in the doctrines either of the Real Presence or of the Atonement.

The case is different with regard to pictures. The Manichaeans forbade the use of statues or probably of any representations of the higher spiritual powers, no doubt in recollection of the idea current among the Persians even in Herodotus' time,

---

[1] This explains its translation from its original Pahlavi into the language of the converts and each copy bearing the name of the owner.

[2] See Cumont, *Cosmog. Manich.* p. 56, for authorities. Cf. also de Stoop, *op. cit.* p. 22. As has been many times said above, every religion and sect at the time accused the others of these filthy practices, without our being able to discern any proof of the justice of the accusation in one case more than in another. In any case, St Augustine, here the chief authority, could not have known of it at first hand, as he had never been more than a Hearer, and he himself says (*contra Fortunatum*, Bk I. App.) that while he had heard that the Elect celebrated the Eucharist, he knew nothing of the mode of celebration. Cf. Neander, *Ch. Hist.* II. p. 193.

[3] All contemporary authorities are agreed that they were forbidden to drink wine.

that the gods had not the nature of men. Yet the Jewish and later the Mahommedan prohibition against making likenesses of anything had evidently no weight with them, and even before the recent discoveries there was a tradition that Manes himself was in the habit of using symbolical pictures called Ertenki-Mani as a means of propaganda[1]. The truth of this is now amply confirmed by the German discoveries at Turfan, where Prof. von Le Coq found frescoes representing possibly Manes himself, together with paintings on silk showing the souls of the faithful dead in the Moon-ship[2]. Sir Marc Stein seems to have secured similar relics at Tun-huang, and when these are more thoroughly examined it is possible that they may throw light upon many points of Manichaean symbolism yet obscure to us. The fact that the Manichaean meeting-houses were decorated with symbolical pictures seems thereby already established.

Of their fasts, the principal ones have been already indicated in the *Khuastuanift*, and their feasts seem to have been few, almost the only one of which any mention has come down to us being that which was called the Festival of the Bema or pulpit, when an empty chair on five steps was placed in a conspicuous position in the meeting-house and adored by all present. This was said to have been done in commemoration of Manes as their founder and on the date preserved as the anniversary of his death[3]. If it be really true that any Manichaeans whether Hearers or otherwise kept Sunday as a holiday, it must have been, as Neander suggests, not because it was the day of the Resurrection, in which their Docetic doctrines prevented them from believing, but as the day of the Sun. In like manner they probably observed Christmas as the birthday not of Jesus, but of the Sun-god in accordance with the traditions preserved by the worshippers of Mithras[4].

---

[1] Neander, *op. cit.* II. p. 170.

[2] Le Coq, *Chotscho*, Vol. I. Pl. I. and IV.

[3] Aug. *c. Ep. Fundamenti*, c. 8.

[4] Augustine, *c. Faust.* Bk XVIII. c. 5, whom he quotes, does not say however that they kept Sunday as a festival, but merely that they then worshipped the Sun: *Vos in die, quem dicunt solis, solem colitis.*

St Augustine speaks, too, of their keeping Easter[1]. It seems possible that this was only done in Christian countries, in accordance with their usual custom of conforming in outward matters, and we have no evidence of their doing anything of the sort in Turkestan.

Of the sacred books of the Manichaeans we hear much, although only one has survived to us in anything like completeness. Thus we hear from Al-Bîrûnî that the Manichaeans have a gospel of their own "the contents of which from the first to the last are opposed to the doctrine of the Christians," and this he says was called "the Gospel of the Seventy[2]." He also tells us of a book written by Manes himself called *Shaburkan* or Shapurakhan which was doubtless written for the edification of King Shâpûr or Sapor, the son of Ardeshîr, whose name it bears[3]. In this Manes seems to have described his own birth and his assumption of the office of heavenly messenger or "Burkhan," besides the saying as to the Burkhans before him, Zoroaster, Buddha, and Jesus, as described above[4]. We also hear from Al-Bîrûnî that he wrote a gospel arranged according to the 22 letters of the alphabet, which does not seem to be the same as the Gospel of the Seventy[5], and we hear from other sources of a Book of the Giants, a Book of Secrets, a Book of Precepts, a Book of Lifegiving, and others, together with many letters or epistles all supposed to be by Manes' own hand[6]. As has been said, he and his followers rejected the Old Testament entirely, not indeed denying its inspiration, but declaring this to have come from the Evil Principle. Of the New Testament, Faustus, the Manichaean Perfect who disputed with St Augustine, puts the matter very clearly when he says:

"We receive only so much of the New Testament as says anything to the honour of the Son of Glory, either by Himself or by His apostles; and by the latter only after they had become perfect and

---

[1] Aug. *c. Ep. Fundamenti*, c. 8 and de Stoop, *op. cit.* p. 27.

[2] Al-Bîrûnî, *Chronology*, p. 27.　　　　[3] *Ib.* pp. 121, 190.

[4] A few other undoubted extracts from the Shapurakhan are to be found in Müller, *Handschriften-Reste, passim,* and others quoted at second hand from Mahommedan writers in Kessler, *op. cit.,* as to which see *ib.* pp. 180–191.

[5] Al-Bîrûnî, *op. cit.* p. 225.　　　　[6] See Kessler, *op. cit.* p. 191 *sqq.*

believers. As for the rest, anything that was said by them either in their simplicity and ignorance, while they were yet inexperienced in the truth, or with malicious design was inserted by the enemy among the statements of truth, or was incautiously asserted by other writers and thus handed down to later generations—of all this we desire to know nothing. I mean all such statements as these—that He was shamefully born of a woman; that as a Jew He was circumcised; that He offered sacrifices like a heathen; that He was meanly baptized, led into the wilderness, and miserably tempted[1]."

Thus it seems that the Manichaeans accepted only such facts of the Gospel narrative as did not conflict with their own doctrines, and although they are said to have had an especial veneration for St Paul, there is no reason to think that this extended to the writings of the Apostle to the Gentiles, or had any other motive than that of external conformity with the religion of those whom they were endeavouring to convert. As himself the Paraclete announced in the New Testament, Manes claimed for himself an authority superior to that of all apostles, and if he made use of any of the writings attributed to them, it was probably only in the shape of isolated passages divorced from their context. On the other hand, his followers seem to have made free use of apocryphal or pseudepigraphical books written in the names of the apostles and containing statements which could be explained as confirming Manes' teaching. A great number of these had as their common authors the names of St Thomas and St Andrew, and the Fathers declare that they were for the most part the work of one Leucius, whom they assert was a Manichaean[2]. It may be so; but, as all the copies of these works which have come down to us have been expurgated or, in the language of the time, "made orthodox," by the removal of heretical matter, there is little proof of the fact.

More authentic, however, than these pseudepigrapha and much fuller than the extracts preserved by Christian or Mahom-

---

[1] Aug. *c. Faust.* Bk XXXII. c. 7.

[2] See Albert Dufourcq, *De Manichaeismo apud Latinos*, Paris, 1900, where all these apocrypha are carefully examined. The *Quo vadis* story appears on p. 40.

medan writers is a treatise found in the cave of the Thousand
Buddhas at Tun-huang which has been published only last
year. It seems by an extraordinary chance to have nearly
escaped us, having been apparently missed by all the European
expeditions because it was written in Chinese characters.
Hence it was removed to Pekin by orders of the Chinese
Government under the impression that it was Buddhist in its
nature, and has since been published in a Chinese publication
founded for the purpose of preserving the Tun-huang MSS. by
Mr Lo Tchen-yu, a Chinese scholar of great philosophical and
archaeological attainments[1]. It is written on a continuous roll
of paper over six metres in length, which has led unfortunately
to the disappearance of the title and the first few words of the
treatise. The remainder shows, however, that it purports to
be a sort of allocution addressed by Manes, here as in the
Khuastuanift called the "Legate of the Light," to Adda or
Addas, whom we know from the Christian documents before
quoted to have been one of the three great missionaries said to
have been dispatched by Manes into foreign countries to
propagate his doctrine[2]. Of these three, Thomas, Hermas, and
Addas, the last-named is said to have been allotted "Scythia,"
which here as elsewhere doubtless means Turkestan, and his
name therefore gives a reasonable air of authenticity to the
text. The whole document is written in the form of a Buddhist
sutra, and has been translated with an excellent commentary
by the French Sinologist, M. Edouard Chavannes, with the help
of M. Paul Pelliot, the leader of the French Expedition to
Turkestan which probably first discovered it[3]. It entirely
confirms the Mahommedan account of the teaching of Manes
given above as well as that appearing in the *Khuastuanift*, and
shows that St Augustine, alike in his authentic writings and in
the tract *de Haeresibus* generally, although perhaps wrongfully,
attributed to him, was drawing from well-informed sources.
There are many grounds for thinking that it may originally
have been written in Pahlavi, in which case it may have been

---

[1] Chavannes et Pelliot, *op. cit.* p. 508, and n. 1.
[2] Hegemonius, *Acta*, c. XIII. p. 22, Beeson.
[3] Chavannes et Pelliot, *op. cit.* 1ère ptie, pp. 399, 400.

contemporary with Manes himself; but it frequently makes use
of Buddhist phrases often derived from the Sanskrit[1]. If the
view here taken of the date of the original treatise is well
founded, these may have been introduced by Manes during the
time that the tradition mentioned above says that he spent in
Turkestan for the elaboration of his doctrine. At all events
they show that the practice of adapting his religion, as far as
might be, to accord with that previously held by those among
whom he was trying to make proselytes, goes back to the very
origin of the sect.

This treatise was evidently written for edification rather than
for instruction, and gives us a curious idea of the imagery by
which the Manichaean teachers sought to enforce their teaching.
The theory of the macrocosm and the microcosm, which teaches
that the body of man is in itself a copy of the great world or
universe, is here carried to excess[2], and we hear much of the
"trees" which certain demons, previously sticking to the
elements, says the treatise, "like a fly to honey, a bird to bird-
lime, or a fish to the hook[3]," plant in the soul to the corruption
and ultimate death of the better desires there implanted by
the Light. The combat waged against the diabolic vices by
the virtues is also described with great minuteness, but in
language in which it is sometimes difficult to discover whether
the author is consciously using allegory or not. Thus he says
that the Devil, to whom he attributes the formation of the
body of man, "shut up the Pure Ether" (one of the five light
elements)

"in the city of the bones. He established (there) the dark thought
in which he planted a tree of death. Then he shut up the Excellent

---

[1] *Op. cit.* 1ère ptie, pp. 509, n. 5, 510, n. 2, 533, nn. 2 and 4.

[2] Nowhere is this curious theory, which forms the base of most Mediaeval
Cabala and magic, more clearly stated. Thus the Tun-huang treatise says
in describing the fashioning of the body of man by the devils (as in the
Μέρος τευχῶν Σωτῆρος), "there is not a single formation of the universe
(or cosmos) which they did not imitate in the carnal body" (Chavannes
et Pelliot, *op. cit.* 1ère ptie, p. 527); and in the next page "The demon...
shut up the five natures of Light in the carnal body of which he made a
little universe (microcosm)."

[3] Chavannes et Pelliot, *op. cit.* 1ère ptie, p. 514.

Wind in the city of the nerves. He established (there) the dark feeling in which he planted a tree of death. Then he shut up the strength of the Light in the city of the veins. He established (there) the dark reflection in which he planted a tree of death. Then he shut up the Excellent Water in the city of the flesh. He established there the dark intellect, in which he planted a tree of death. Then he shut up the Excellent Fire in the city of the skin. He established there the dark reasoning in which he planted a tree of death. The Demon of Envy [the name generally used in the treatise for the Devil] planted these five poisonous trees of death in the five kinds of ruined places. He made them on every occasion deceive and trouble the original luminous nature, to draw in from without the nature which is stranger to it, and to produce poisonous fruit. Thus the tree of the dark thought grows within the city of the bones; its fruit is hatred: the tree of the dark feeling grows within the city of the nerves; its fruit is irritation: the tree of the dark reflection grows within the city of the veins; its fruit is luxury [wantonness]: the tree of the dark intellect grows within the city of the flesh; its fruit is anger: the tree of the dark reasoning grows within the city of the skin; its fruit is folly. It is thus then that of the five kinds of things which are the bones, the nerves, the veins, the flesh, and the skin, he made a prison and shut up there the five divisions of the First Principle of Light....[1]"

and so on. One might sometimes think one was reading John Bunyan and his Holy War with its defence of the town of Mansoul.

Most of the information contained in this Pekin Treatise has been dealt with in its place, but there are one or two matters concerning the cosmology of Manes which are of importance as showing the connection of his system with that of his predecessors. One regards the two great angels, here called Khrostag and Padvaktag[2] or the Appellant and Respondent, who are mentioned in the *Khuastuanift* (p. 343 *supra*) as bringing the

---

[1] *Op. cit.* pp. 528, 529.

[2] Their Chinese names are discussed by MM. Chavannes and Pelliot (*op. cit.* 1ᵉʳᵉ ptie, pp. 521, n. 1, 542, n. 1, 543, nn. 1, 2, and 544, n. 1), wherein are gathered nearly all that can be said about them. The learned commentators decide that their functions still remain mysterious. But see next note *infra*.

light to be purified[1]. As has been said above, they show a great
likeness to the two last Amshaspands of Zoroastrianism called
Haurvetât and Ameretât; and like them are never mentioned
separately, but always together[2]. Another point, already
referred to, is that the Zoroastrian Sraôsha, the strong archangel
who guards the world at night from the demons, is here mentioned several times by name[3]. Yet another point is that the
two sexes are here said to have been formed by the devil out of
jealousy and rage at beholding the sun and moon, and in
imitation of the two luminaries. This is an entirely different
story not only from those given above as Manichaean but from
that given in the *Great Announcement* attributed to Simon
Magus, and both differ from that told in the *Pistis Sophia*.
It seems plain therefore that in attributing these various origins
to the division of mankind into sexes, none of the three teachers
was drawing upon tradition, but was merely inventing *ad hoc*.

There remains to be considered the history of the sect, as
to which we have become better informed during the last few
decades than at one time seemed possible[4]. Prohibited in the
Roman Empire from the outset, they nevertheless made their
way along both shores of the Mediterranean, and all the efforts
of the Imperial authorities proved powerless to suppress them.
Constantine directed an enquiry into their tenets, it is said,
with some idea of making them into the religion of the State,

[1] W. Radloff, *Chuastuanift, das Bussgebet der Manichäer*, St Petersburg,
1909, pt I. pp. 19, 20. Von Le Coq, *J.R.A.S.* 1911, p. 294: "when the
Gods Kroshtag and Padwakhtag, the Appellant and Respondent, should
have brought to us that part of the light of the Fivefold God that, going
to God, is there to be purified."   One is inclined to compare this with Jeû
and Melchizidek receiving and purifying the light won from this world, or
with Gabriel and Michael in the *Pistis Sophia* bearing the heroine upward
out of Chaos; but the parallel may be accidental and is easily pushed too
far.

[2] Like the "Twin Saviours" of the *Pistis Sophia*, whose functions are
never even alluded to in that document.

[3] See notes 2 and 3, p. 327 *supra*.

[4] M. de Stoop's *Essai sur la Diffusion du Manichéisme* is most in-
forming on this head. See also A. Dufourcq's Thesis quoted in n. 2, p. 351
supra. A very brief summary of the history of the sect was given by the
present writer in *J.R.A.S.* 1913, pp. 69–94.

and although he found this impracticable or unsafe, he seems to have been at first inclined to extend to them toleration[1]. His successors, however, quickly reverted to the earlier policy of Diocletian, and law after law of gradually increasing severity was passed until adherence to Manichaeism was finally punished with death and confiscation[2]. Pagans like the Emperor Julian and his friend and teacher Libanius were able occasionally to intervene in their favour; but no sect was ever more relentlessly persecuted, and the institution of the Dominican Inquisition can be traced back to the *Quaestiones* set up by Justinian and Theodora for their routing out and suppression[3]. In the case of what was practically a secret society, it would be difficult to say whether the Imperial measures would have availed to entirely destroy their propaganda, and it is possible that the Manichaean Church always maintained a sporadic existence in Europe[4] until events to be presently mentioned led to its revival in the xth century. Meanwhile in the East, they remained on the confines of what was, up to the Mahommedan conquest in 642 A.D., the Persian Empire, and no doubt after their manner professed outward adherence to the Zoroastrian faith, while at the same time propagating their own doctrines in secret[5]. It

---

[1] For the enquiry by Strategius, afterwards called Musonianus, and Prefect of the East under Constantius, see Ammianus Marcellinus, Bk xv. c. 13. Cf. Neander, *Ch. Hist.* IV. 488 *sqq.* That the persecution instituted against them by Diocletian slackened under Constantine and Constantius, see de Stoop, *op. cit.* pp. 40, 41.

[2] See the Laws of Theodosius and Valentinian II, quoted by de Stoop, *op. cit.* pp. 41, 42.

[3] Gibbon, *Decline and Fall*, III. p. 153. Justinian put to death not only convicted Manichaeans, but those who being acquainted with members of the sect, did not denounce them. See de Stoop, *op. cit.* p. 43.

[4] The Manichaeans seem always to have been favoured by the better classes and high officials of the Empire who maintained for some time a secret leaning towards Paganism. See de Stoop, *op. cit.* p. 84. The case of Barsymès, the banker or money-changer whom Theodora made Praetorian Prefect, and who was allowed according to Procopius (*Anecdota*, c. XXII. 7) to profess Manichaeism openly, was doubtless only one of many. It is apparently this Barsymès who is invoked in the Turfan texts as "the Lord Bar Simus," see Müller, *Handschriften-Reste*, pp. 45, 59.

[5] That this was the professed policy of the sect seems plain from the words they attributed to Manes himself: "I am not inhuman like Christ

was probably the Arab conquest which drove them to make their headquarters on the very borders of the civilized world as known to the ancients and in what is now Turkestan. Here a large part of the population seems to have been Buddhist, doubtless by reason of its dealings with China, and in the presence of that gentle faith—whose adherents boast that they have never yet shed blood to make a convert—the Manichaeans enjoyed complete toleration for perhaps the first time in their history[1]. They made use of it, as always, to send out missionaries into the neighbouring countries, and certainly obtained a foothold in China, where the Chinese seem to have confused them with the Christians. Their hatred of images doubtless caused the iconoclastic Emperors of the East to enter into relation with them, and we hear that Leo the Isaurian induced many of them to enter the Imperial armies. It was possibly these last whom the Emperor John Tzimiskes settled in what is now Bulgaria, whence, under the names of Paulicians, Bogomiles, and other aliases, they promoted that movement against the Catholic Church which provoked the Albigensian Crusades and the establishment of the Dominican Inquisition in the West[2]. To follow them there would be to travel beyond the scope of this book; and it need only be said in conclusion that they formed the bitterest and the most dangerous enemies that the Catholic Church in Europe ever had to face. It was possibly this which has led the rulers of the Church of Rome to brand nearly all later heresy with the name of Manichaean; yet it may be doubted whether some of their doctrines did not survive in Europe until the German Reformation, when they may have helped to inspire some of the wilder Protestant sects of the xvith and xviith centuries. With the suppression of the Albigenses, however, the existence of Manichaeism as an organized faith comes to an end.

who said: Whoso denieth me, him will I deny. I say unto you: Whoso denieth me before man and saves himself by this falsehood, him will I receive with joy, as if he had not denied me." Cf. de Stoop, *op. cit.* p. 46, quoting Cedrenus; Al Bîrûnî, *Chronology*, p. 191.

[1] Von Le Coq, *Exploration Archéologique à Tourfan*, Confces au Musée Guimet (Bibl. de Vulg. t. xxxv.), 1910, p. 278.

[2] de Stoop, *op. cit.* pp. 86, 144.

CONCLUSION

CONSTANTINE'S accession proved to be, like the coming of
Alexander, a turning-point in the history of the world. His
so-called conversion put into the hands of the Catholic Church
a weapon for the suppression of all rivalry, of which she was
not slow to make use. Already in his reign many of the
heathen temples were torn down[1], and under the rule of his
morose and gloomy successor, Constantius, the work of demolition went on apace[2]. The accession of the philosophic Julian
gave the worshippers of other gods than Christ a short respite,
and even allowed some of the temples destroyed in the former
reigns to be restored by or at the expense of the Christians[3].
Julian's heroic death in Persia again threw the crown into the
hands of a Christian emperor, whose reign of seven months
gave him little time, as he perhaps had small inclination, for
persecution[4]; but under his successors Valentinian and Valens,
heathen sacrifices were forbidden under severe penalties. The
end came under Gratian, when the temple estates were confiscated, the priests and vestals deprived of the stipends which
they had hitherto received from the public treasury, and the
heathen confraternities or colleges were declared incapable of
receiving legacies[5]. Only a few rich men like the Vettius
Agorius Praetextatus whom we have seen among the worshippers
of Mithras, or the Quintus Aurelius Symmachus, whose learned

---

[1] Neander, *Ch. Hist.* III. pp. 34, 35.

[2] *Op. cit.* III. p. 46.

[3] Sozomen, *Hist. Eccl.* Bk v. c. 5, for instances. Cf. Neander, *op. cit.*
III. pp. 66, 67.

[4] Neander, *op. cit.* III. p. 96.

[5] *Op. cit.* III. p. 100.

and patriotic life has been so well described by Sir Samuel Dill[1], could henceforth venture to practise, even with maimed rites, the faiths condemned by the Court and the Church.

As for the Gnostic sects, which since Hadrian's time had striven with such success as we have seen to combine magic and other ancient beliefs with Christianity, they found but short shrift at the hands of the triumphant Church. By an edict issued by Constantine before his own reception into the Church, all their "houses of prayer" were confiscated for the benefit of the Catholic Church, their meeting even in private forbidden, and their books seized and burned[2].

"Thus," says Eusebius, "were the lurking places of the heretics broken up by the emperor's command, and the savage beasts they have harboured (I mean the chief authors of their impious doctrines) driven to flight. Of those whom they had deceived, some, intimidated by the emperor's threats, disguising their real feelings, crept secretly into the Church. For since the law directed that search should be made for their books, those of them who practised evil and forbidden arts were detected, and these were ready to secure their own safety by dissimulation of every kind[3]."

Throughout the length and breadth of the Roman Empire all but a very few Roman nobles thus professed the faith of Christ. In the words of the dying Julian, the Galilaean had conquered.

From this time until our own, Christianity has reigned in the West with no serious rival. In the VIIth century, when Mahommed's Arabs, flushed with the enthusiasm of a new faith which owed something at least to the relics of Gnosticism, poured in upon an Empire wearied out alike by perpetual war against the barbarians and by its own civil and religious dissensions, the Church was compelled to abandon to them her conquests in Africa and the East. In Europe, however, she continued in unchecked supremacy, gathering to herself and

---

[1] S. Dill, *Roman Society in the Last Century of the Western Empire*, pp. 143–166.

[2] Eusebius, *Vita Constantini*, Bk III. cc. 64, 65.

[3] *Op. cit.* c. 66.

assimilating the barbarians who at one time seemed likely to extinguish all civilization; and she thus became a bond uniting many nations and languages in one community of faith and thought. She even succeeded in keeping alive the remains of that Greek art and learning which still form our best and proudest intellectual possession, and if during her reign many of the precious monuments of antiquity perished, the fault was not entirely hers. In every respect, her rule was supreme; and such enemies as she had in Europe were those of her own household. The Manichaeans who, as has been said, once bid fair to deprive her of some of her fairest provinces, never dared to make open war upon her, and their secret defection was punished by an unsparing use of the secular arm. The German Reformation of the xvith century has probably left her stronger than before, and the few losses that she has suffered in the Old World have been more than compensated by the number of lieges she has succeeded in attaching to herself in the New.

In the days of her infancy, and before she thus came into her inheritance, Christianity borrowed much from the rivals over which she was in the long run to reign supreme. Her outward observances, her ritual, and the organization of her hierarchy, are perhaps all due to the associations that she finally overcame. The form of her sacraments, the periods of her fasts and festivals, and institutions like monachism, cannot be explained without reference to those religions from whose rivalry she so long suffered. That, in such matters, the Church should take what was useful to her was, as said above, part of her consciously expressed policy, and doubtless had much to do with her speedy triumph. To show that her dogmas also took many things from the same source would involve an invasion into the domain of professional theology, for which I have neither authority nor desire. But if, at some future time, investigation should show that in this respect also Christianity owes something to her forerunners and rivals, the argument against her Divine origin would not thereby be necessarily strengthened. That, in the course of her development, she acquired characteristics which fitted her to her environment would be in strict conformity with the laws which appear to govern the evolution of all institutions; and if the Power ruling the universe chooses to work by law rather than by what seems to us like caprice, such a choice does not show Him to be lacking either in wisdom or benevolence.

As was said at the outset, everyone must be left to place his own interpretation on the facts here attempted to be set forth. But if, *per impossibile*, we could approach the study of the origins of Christianity with the same mental detachment and freedom from prejudice with which we might examine the worship of the Syrian Jupiter Dolichenus or the Scandinavian Odin, we should probably find that the Primitive Church had no need of the miraculous powers which were once assigned as the reason for her gradual and steady advance to all but universal dominion. On the contrary, it may be that Christianity would then appear as a link—although a most important and necessary link—in a regular chain of events which began more than three centuries before she emerged from her birthplace in Palestine into that Roman world which in three centuries more was to be hers of right. No sooner had Alexander's conquests made a world-religion possible, than there sprang up, as we have seen, in his own city of Alexandria, a faith with a far higher and purer idea of Divinity than any that had until then been known in the West. Then the germs already present in small fraternities like those of the Orphics and the Essenes blossomed forth into the fantastic and unwholesome growths, as we must needs think them, of that Gnosticism which marked the transition of the ancient world from Paganism to Christianity. Lastly there came in from the countries under the influence of Rome's secular enemy, Persia, the heresy of Marcion, the religion of Mithras, and the syncretistic policy of Manes and his continuators. Against all these in turn, Christianity had to struggle in a contest where the victory was not always on her side: and if in time she overthrew them all, it can only be because she was better fitted to the needs of the world than any of her predecessors or contemporaries.

TABLE OF DATES

N.B. The dates which follow are only approximate, no attempt having here been made to harmonize the system of chronology lately adopted by the professors of the Berlin school with those formerly in use. For the dates of the reigns of the Egyptian and Asiatic Successors of Alexander, I have mainly relied upon the excellent work of M. Bouché-Leclercq as given in his French version of Droysen's *Hellenismus*, his *Histoire des Lagides* and (especially) his *Histoire des Séleucides*, the second volume of which, containing the chronological tables, maps, and indexes, has appeared at the close of this year (1914). The dates of the Parthian and Bactrian kings are given with all reserve and are in effect conjectures based on the slipshod statements of compilers like Justin, Quintus Curtius, and Trogus Pompeius. For the Parthian dates I have followed, though without any confidence in its accuracy, the chronology of Prof. Eduard Meyer, and for the Bactrian, those given in Mr H. C. Rawlinson's *Bactria*.

The dates in Vol. II, which deals with the centuries after Christ, are for the most part fairly well ascertained, and those given in Prof. Bury's edition of Gibbon have been used wherever possible. For matters not mentioned in Gibbon, such as the lives of the obscurer Christian Fathers and leaders of sects, recourse has generally been had to Smith and Wace's *Dictionary of Christian Biography* and other books of the kind. The only serious discrepancy here noticeable arises from the habit still prevalent among certain Continental writers of beginning the Christian Era four years earlier than others, so as to increase all subsequent dates by 4. Thus M. Cumont, in his *Mystères de Mithra* and elsewhere, invariably gives the date of the Carnuntum inscription proclaiming Mithras the Protector of the Roman Empire, as 307 A.D., although he asserts that the *Iovii et Herculi religiosissimi Augusti* responsible for the inscription are Diocletian and Galerius. Diocletian, however, resigned the purple, and retired into private life in the year 305 A.D., by the reckoning of Prof. Bury and others, and it is plain therefore that M. Cumont puts the date too far forward according to our ideas. To bring it into line, I have therefore ventured to alter the date of the inscription quoted by him to 304 A.D., which would moreover coincide with the persecution of the Christians, which he thinks may have owed some of its severity to the rivalry of the Mithraic faith. The same procedure has been followed in one or two other cases.

B.C.

336. Accession of Alexander.

340 to 260. Zeno of Citium (founder of Stoic school) flourished.

340 to 288. Pyrrho of Elis flourished.

334 to 322. Aristotle and first Peripatetic School flourished.

331. Foundation of Alexandria.

Alexander transports many Jews to Alexandria and gives them equal rights with Macedonians.

330. Death of Darius.

326. Alexander conquers Punjab.

324. Alexander at Susa celebrates marriage of Europe and Asia.

323. Death of Alexander and first division of Empire.

Ptolemy, son of Lagos, made satrap of Egypt.

321. Second division of Alexander's Empire at Triparadisus.

320. Ptolemy captures Jerusalem and transports many Jews to Alexandria.

Circa 316. Euhemerus of Messene flourished.

312. Ptolemy and Seleucus defeat Demetrius Poliorcetes at Gaza.

Ptolemy seizes Syria, but evacuates it when defeated by Demetrius near Myontes.

Many Jews voluntarily emigrate to Egypt.

312. Seleucus conquers Media and Persia, and enters Babylon in triumph.
Beginning of Seleucid Era.

310. Antigonus Monopthalmos by treaty abandons Eastern Provinces to Seleucus.

307. Demetrius Poliorcetes at Athens.

Demetrius of Phalerum leaves Athens for Alexandria.

Probable foundation of Museum.

306 to 270. Epicurus flourished.

306. Ptolemy I Soter proclaims himself King of Egypt.

302. Coalition against Antigonus. Ptolemy invades Syria, and Lysimachus Asia Minor.

301. Battle of Ipsus, and further division of Empire between Seleucus, Lysimachus, and Cassander.

300 to 220. Cleanthus of Assos (Stoic philosopher) flourished.

298. Cession of Valley of Indus by Seleucus to Chandragupta.

297. Destruction of Samaria by Demetrius Poliorcetes.

294. Seleucus transports many Jews from Babylon to Antioch and other Syrian cities.

293. Many Jewish colonies founded in Cyrene and Libya.

292. Seleucus gives his wife Stratonice and the Eastern Provinces to his son Antiochus.

288. Coalition against Demetrius Poliorcetes.

Accession of Bindusara (Amitrochates) to Chandragupta's Indian Kingdom.

283. Accession of Ptolemy II Philadelphus.

B.C.

283. Demetrius Poliorcetes dies a prisoner in the hands of Seleucus.

282. Seleucus conquers Asia Minor from Lysimachus.

281. Lysimachus defeated and slain at Corupedion.
Accession of Antiochus I Soter on assassination of Seleucus.

280.? Establishment of Greek worship of Serapis, Isis, and Horus at Alexandria.

280 to 207. Chrysippus of Soli (Stoic philosopher) flourished.

280. Pyrrhus invades Italy.
Invasion of Thrace by Celtic tribes.

278. Pyrrhus' campaign in Italy.

277. Settlement of Celtic tribes (Galatae) in Asia.

276. Translation of Pentateuch into Greek by order of Ptolemy Philadelphus.

274. First Syrian War. Ptolemy Philadelphus against Antiochus Soter and Magas of Cyrene.

273. Ptolemy Philadelphus sends embassy to Rome to conclude alliance.

265. Accession of Asoka, grandson of Chandragupta.

264. Asoka's missions to Greek Kings.
First Punic War.

261. Accession of Antiochus II Theos.

258. Second Syrian War. Ptolemy Philadelphus against Antiochus Theos.

252. Diodotus revolts against Antiochus Theos and founds Kingdom of Bactria.

250. Association of Greek Sarapiasts at Athens.

249. Arsaces revolts against Antiochus Theos and founds Arsacid Kingdom of Parthia.

248. Accession of Tiridates on death of his brother, Arsaces of Parthia.

247. Accession of Seleucus II Callinicus on death of his father, Antiochus Theos.

246. Accession of Ptolemy III Euergetes.
Third Syrian War. Ptolemy Euergetes against Seleucus Callinicus.

245.? Accession of Diodotus II on death of his father, Diodotus of Bactria.

244. Ptolemy Euergetes overruns Upper Asia as far as Susa.

241. War between Seleucus Callinicus and his brother Antiochus Hierax.
Accession of Attalus as dynast of Pergamum.

238. Ptolemy Euergetes and his wife Berenice II deified. Decree of Canopus.
Attalus defeats Galatae and proclaims himself King of Pergamum.

230. Euthydemus of Magnesia seizes throne of Bactria on death of Diodotus II.

229. Rome first intervenes in affairs of Greece on behalf of Acarnanians.

226. Accession of Seleucus III Soter on death of his father, Seleucus Callinicus.

B.C.

225. Attalus of Pergamum, "Friend of Rome," defeats Seleucus Soter and seizes Syrian Asia Minor.

222. Accession of Antiochus III the Great, on assassination of his father, Seleucus Soter.

221. Accession of Ptolemy IV Philopator on death of his father, Ptolemy Euergetes.

219. Antiochus the Great reconquers Asia Minor.
Antiochus the Great captures Jerusalem from Ptolemy Philopator.

217. Antiochus the Great transports 2,000 Jewish families from Babylon to Phrygia and Lydia.
Ptolemy Philopator defeats Antiochus the Great at Raphia and recaptures Jerusalem and Samaria.
Second Punic War.

216. Worship of Greek Sarapis and Isis established in Boeotia.

211. Accession of Artabanus I to throne of Parthia on death of his father Tiridates.

210. Artabanus of Parthia attacked by Antiochus the Great, who besieges his capital, but finally makes alliance with him.
First Macedonian War. Romans and Aetolians against Philip.

205. Accession of Ptolemy V Epiphanes.
Antiochus the Great seizes Palestine.

204. Statue of Great Mother brought from Pessinus to Rome.
Scopas reconquers Palestine for Ptolemy Epiphanes and Jews revolt to latter.

200. Second Macedonian War.

198. Antiochus the Great defeats Scopas at Panion and reoccupies Jerusalem and Samaria.

197. Accession of Eumenes II on death of his father, Attalus of Pergamum.
Philip defeated by Romans at Cynoscephalae.

196. Coronation of Ptolemy Epiphanes at Memphis. Rosetta Stone set up.

191. Ptolemy Epiphanes sends embassy to Rome to offer alliance.

190. Romans defeat Antiochus the Great at Magnesia.
Accession of Demetrius on death of Euthydemus of Bactria.
Accession of Priapatius on death of Artabanus of Parthia.

187. Accession of Seleucus IV Philopator on death of his father, Antiochus the Great.

182. Accession of Ptolemy VI Eupator.

181. Accession of Ptolemy VII Philometor.

180. Serapeum at Delos in existence.

175. Demetrius of Bactria annexes Cabul and Punjab.
Accession of Antiochus IV Epiphanes on death of his brother, Seleucus Philopator.

B.C.

175. Eucratides rebels against Demetrius of Bactria and seizes throne.

173. Antiochus Epiphanes seizes Judaea and Coele-Syria.

172. Third Macedonian War.

171. Antiochus Epiphanes invades Egypt and defeats Ptolemy Philometor at Pelusium.

170. Antiochus Epiphanes plunders Temple of Jerusalem.
Ptolemy Philometor and Ptolemy Euergetes II made joint kings by Romans.
Accession of Mithridates I to throne of Parthia.

168. Antiochus Epiphanes' second invasion of Egypt stopped by Romans. Circle of Popilius Laena.

166. Antiochus Epiphanes again pillages Temple and persecutes Jewish religion.
Samaritans make peace with Antiochus Epiphanes and accept Hellenization.
Revolt of Maccabees against Syria.

164. Accession of Antiochus V Eupator on death of his father, Antiochus Epiphanes.

162. Judas Maccabaeus besieged in Jerusalem by Lysias for Antiochus Eupator. Peace made on Philip's attempt to seize regency.
Romans send embassy to Antiochus Eupator which compels him to burn his ships and kill his elephants.
Demetrius escapes from Rome and invades Syria.

161. Romans recognize Demetrius as King of Syria with title of Demetrius I Soter.
Judas Maccabaeus sends embassy to Rome, is attacked by Demetrius Soter, and slain. Judaea, under his brother Jonathan, submits to Syria.
Timarchos, Satrap of Media, and Ptolemy, dynast of Commagene, proclaim themselves Kings, and are recognized by Romans.

160. Ptolemy Philometor expelled from Egypt by Euergetes II, but restored by Romans.
Ptolemy, son of Glaucias, a recluse in Serapeum of Memphis.

159. Accession of Attalus II Philadelphus on death of his brother, Eumenes of Pergamum.

154. Ptolemy Euergetes II made King of Cyrene.
Foundation of Jewish Temple or Oneion at Leontopolis in Egypt.

152. Alexander Bala, pretender to throne of Syria, recognized by Romans as son of Antiochus Epiphanes.

151. Coalition of Egyptian and Asiatic Kings with Romans against Demetrius Soter of Syria.

150. Demetrius Soter defeated and slain by coalition of Egyptian and Asiatic kings. Alexander Bala succeeds to throne of Syria, and marries Cleopatra Thea, daughter of Ptolemy Philometor.

B.C.

149. Third Punic War.
145. Ptolemy Philometor invades Syria and defeats Alexander Bala at Oenoparas. Ptolemy killed in battle and Alexander by Nabathaeans.

Accession of Ptolemy IX (Euergetes II) Physcon as sole king of Egypt.

Accession of Demetrius II Nicator to throne of Syria. Civil war between Demetrius and Diodotus (Trypho) as regent for infant Antiochus VI Epiphanes Dionysos.

144. Ptolemy Physcon expels philosophers from Museum.
142. Simon Maccabaeus succeeds as High Priest Jonathan slain by Trypho.

Simon Maccabaeus proclaims independence of Judaea.

141. Simon Maccabaeus sends embassy to Romans who receive Jews as "Friends of Rome."
140. Mithridates I of Parthia seizes part of Bactria, Media, Susiana, and Persia.
139. Demetrius Nicator invades Parthia and is taken prisoner by Mithridates.

Beginning of Era of Arsacides.

Antiochus VI Epiphanes Dionysos murdered by Trypho, who is made King by army.

138. Accession of Attalus III Philometor on death of his father, Attalus II of Pergamum.

Accession of Phraates II to throne of Parthia.

137. Antiochus VII Sidetes, brother of Demetrius Nicator, takes throne of Syria.
135. Antiochus Sidetes defeats Trypho, who commits suicide, at Apamea.

John and Judas Maccabaeus, sons of Simon, defeat, at Modein, army of Antiochus Sidetes.

Simon Maccabaeus assassinated by his son-in-law Ptolemy.

John Hyrcanus succeeds his father Simon as High Priest.

Hierocles, last Greek King of Bactria, after invasion of Sacae, transfers his capital to Sialkôt.

Attalus of Pergamum bequeaths his kingdom to Romans.

134. Siege of Jerusalem by Antiochus Sidetes. Jews made tributaries to Syria.
130. Antiochus Sidetes invades Parthia and reconquers Babylonia and Media.

Menander (the Milinda of Buddhists) King of Cabul and Punjab.

129. John Hyrcanus sends embassy to Rome for help against Syria.

Medes rebel against Antiochus Sidetes, who is defeated by Phraates II of Parthia and commits suicide.

Restoration of Demetrius Nicator to throne of Syria. Phraates II of Parthia slain in battle against Scythians.

B.C.

129. Accession of Artabanus II of Parthia.

126. Demetrius Nicator defeated and slain by pretender, Alexander Zabina.

125. Destruction of Samaria by John Hyrcanus.

124. Accession of Mithridates II the Great on death of Artabanus II in battle against Tocharians.

122. Accession of Antiochus VIII Grypus, son of Demetrius Nicator, who with the help of Egypt defeats and slays Alexander Zabina.

120. Accession of Mithridates Eupator as King of Pontus.

117. Accession of Cleopatra III and Ptolemy X Lathyrus.
   Civil war in Syria between Antiochus Grypus and Antiochus IX Cyzicenus, son of Antiochus Sidetes. Division of Syria between them.

113. Antiochus Cyzicenus invades Judaea, and is ordered by Romans to withdraw.

106. Accession of Ptolemy XI Alexander.
   Aristobulus succeeds his father, John Hyrcanus, as High Priest, and proclaims himself King.

105. Municipality of Puteoli builds Serapeum.
   Aristobulus of Judaea annexes Iturea.
   Alexander Jannaeus succeeds, as King, his brother Aristobulus.

98. Alexander Jannaeus, trying to annex Ptolemais and Gaza, is defeated by Ptolemy Lathyrus, then King of Cyprus.
   Alexander Jannaeus makes league with Cleopatra III, who compels Ptolemy to withdraw.

96. Alexander Jannaeus captures Gaza and massacres inhabitants.
   Accession of Seleucus VI Epiphanes Nicator on assassination of his father, Antiochus Grypus.

95. Antiochus X Pius, son of Antiochus Cyzicenus, defeats and slays Seleucus Epiphanes near Mopsuestia.

94. Division of Syria. Antiochus Pius reigns in Upper Syria, Philip I and Demetrius III Eucaerus, sons of Antiochus Grypus, in Coele-Syria.

93. Antiochus Pius slain in battle against the Parthians in Commagene.
   Ariobarzanes, King of Cappadocia, expelled by Mithridates Eupator of Pontus, but reinstated by Romans under Sulla.

89. Alexander Jannaeus crucifies 800 Pharisees at Bethome and restores peace in Judaea.

88. Demetrius Eucaerus invades Judaea and defeats Alexander Jannaeus at Sichem, but is taken prisoner by Parthians and dies in captivity.
   Interregnum in Parthia.
   First Mithridatic War.

B.C.

87. Antiochus XII Dionysos, son of Antiochus Grypus, crowned King of Syria at Damascus.

84. Sulla makes peace with Mithridates.

Antiochus Dionysos defeated and slain at Motho by Aretas the Philhellene, King of Nabathaeans.

83. Tigranes, King of Armenia, becomes King of Syria.

82. Sulla dictator.

81. Accession of Ptolemy XII Alexander II.

Accession of Ptolemy XIII Auletes.

Circa 80. College of Pastophori of Greek Isis at Rome founded.

79. Death of Alexander Jannaeus, and accession of his widow, Salome Alexandra.

78. Death of Sulla.

77. Tigranes builds Tigranocerta, and transports thither many peoples of different race.

76. The Arsacid Sinatroces, captive among the Scyths, released by them to become King of Parthia.

75. Second Mithridatic War.

74. Nicomedes of Bithynia bequeaths his kingdom to Mithridate Eupator of Pontus.

Third Mithridatic War.

72. Mithridates, defeated by Lucullus, takes refuge with his son-in-law Tigranes.

70. Accession of Phraates III of Parthia.

69. Tigranes invades Palestine, but is bought off by Salome Alexandra.

Tigranes defeated and Tigranocerta taken by Lucullus.

Antiochus XIII Asiaticus, son of Antiochus Pius, made King of Syria.

Death of Salome Alexandra, and accession of her son Aristobulus as King, with John Hyrcanus II as High Priest.

67. Pompey suppresses the Cilician pirates. Reported introduction of Mysteries of Mithras into Italy.

66. Phraates III of Parthia, Friend of Rome, invades Armenia.

Tigranes submits to Pompey, and is allowed to retain Great Armenia.

Civil war in Palestine between Aristobulus and John Hyrcanus II.

65. Siege of Jerusalem by Nabathaeans and Pharisees, raised by command of Pompey's lieutenant Scaurus.

64. Ariarathes, King of Cappadocia, receives from Romans Lesser Armenia, Gordyene, and Sophene.

Osrhoene and Edessa made into separate kingdom under Arab prince Ariamne.

Syria becomes Roman province.

63. Death of Mithridates Eupator.

Death of Antiochus Asiaticus.

B.C.

61. Pompey captures Jerusalem, and puts an end to Maccabaean Kingdom. Aristobulus sent captive to Rome.

    Samaria and all forcibly Judaized communities regain their autonomy.

58. Ptolemy Auletes, expelled from Egypt, flies to Rome.

    Statues of Isis at Rome thrown down by order of Consul, A. Gabinius.

57. Alexander, son of Aristobulus of Judaea, rebels, and is defeated by Gabinius, Proconsul of Syria.

56. Aristobulus escapes from Rome and heads new revolt in Judaea.

55. Accession of Orodes I to throne of Parthia.

    Fresh revolt of Jews under Alexander suppressed by Gabinius, who makes Antipater the Idumean ruler of Judaea.

    Ptolemy Auletes restored to throne of Egypt by Gabinius.

53. Crassus and Roman army defeated by Parthians at Carrhae.

52. Fresh revolt of Jews suppressed by Cassius.

51. Accession of Cleopatra VI and Ptolemy XIV.

50. Temple of Isis at Rome destroyed by Consul, L. Aemilius Paulus.

48. Julius Caesar and Cleopatra besieged in Alexandria by Egyptian rebels. Death of Ptolemy XIV.

    Temples of Isis near Capitol thrown down at bidding of augurs.

47. Cleopatra made queen jointly with Ptolemy XV.

    Antipater and Jewish troops take part in raising of siege of Alexandria.

    Julius Caesar repeals Jewish tribute and liability to military service, and gives Jews religious liberty and self-government.

    John Hyrcanus II made hereditary ethnarch of Judaea.

46. Herod, son of Antipater, enters Roman army and is made military governor of Coele-Syria.

45. Death of Ptolemy XV. Cleopatra makes her son Caesarion co-regent with her as Ptolemy XVI.

    Hermaeus last Greek ruler in India.

44. Assassination of Julius Caesar.

    Fresh revolt of Jews on Caesar's death suppressed by Cassius, who makes Herod Procurator of Coele-Syria.

43. Triumvirs Antony, Octavian, and Lepidus decree temple to Isis and Serapis.

42. Battle of Philippi and division of Roman world between Mark Antony and Octavian.

41. Death of Antipater of Judaea. Mark Antony makes Herod and his brother Phasael joint tetrarchs under John Hyrcanus II.

40. Pacorus, prince of Parthia, invades Palestine, and takes John Hyrcanus II and Phasael away captive.

39. Parthians driven out of Palestine by P. Ventidius Bassus.

    Herod proclaimed King of Judaea by Romans.

B.C.

38. Caius Sossius, Legate of Syria, captures Jerusalem, and puts Herod on throne.

31. Battle of Actium. Herod deserts Mark Antony.

30. Herod makes submission to Octavian, and receives increase of territory.

    Death of Cleopatra and Caesarion. Egypt becomes Roman province.

    Octavian becomes Emperor with title of Augustus.

28. Augustus orders all temples of Alexandrian gods outside *Pomoerium*.

21. M. Vipsanius Agrippa, the consul, forbids celebration of Egyptian rites within 1 mile of Rome.

20. Phraates IV of Parthia sends Augustus his four sons as hostages, and returns Roman standards captured with Crassus.

    Herod rebuilds Temple of Jerusalem.

4. Death of Herod. Fresh revolt of Jews suppressed by Varus.

   Augustus divides Herod's Kingdom between the tetrarchs Archelaus, Antipas, and Philip.

A.D.

2. Accession of Phraates V or Phraataces on murder of his father, Phraates IV of Parthia.

5. Accession of Orodes II of Parthia.

6. Archelaus deposed and banished. Judaea becomes a Roman province.

8. Accession of Vonones I of Parthia.

14. Accession of Tiberius.

16. Vonones expelled from Parthia by Artabanus, King of Media.

    Artabanus makes war on Rome, and is in turn expelled.

19. Expulsion of Jewish colony from Rome.

    Tiberius destroys Temple of Isis and throws statues into the Tiber.

24. Death of Philip, Jewish tetrarch.

26. Pontius Pilate appointed Procurator of Judaea.

36.? John the Baptist put to death by Antipas.

    Interregnum in Parthia. Struggle between pretenders, Tiridates II, Cumianus, and Bardanes I.

37. Accession of Caligula.

    Antipas defeated by Aretas, King of Nabathaeans.

    Agrippa receives Philip's tetrarchy with title of King.

39. Antipas deposed and banished. His tetrarchy added to Agrippa's kingdom.

41. Judaea added to Agrippa's kingdom.

    Accession of Claudius.

44. Death of Agrippa. Cuspius Fadus made Procurator of Judaea.

47. Tiberius Alexander (nephew of Philo) succeeds Cuspius as Procurator.

A.D.

47. Gotarzes, son of Artabanus of Media, having been expelled from Parthia by his brother Bardanes, retakes crown on Bardanes' death.

48. Revolt of Jews. Tiberius Alexander replaced by Cumanus.

Circa 50. Clement of Rome born: died about 95 A.D.

51. Accession of Vonones II to throne of Parthia followed immediately by that of Vologeses I.
    War between Rome and Parthia.
    Temple of Isis at Rome rebuilt.

52. Ummidius Quadratus, Legate of Syria, deposes Cumanus, and appoints Felix Procurator of Judaea.

54. Accession of Nero.

55. Nero makes worship of Greek Isis *religio licita*.

60. Porcius Festus succeeds Felix as Procurator of Judaea.

62. Death of Porcius. Albinus succeeds him.
    Persecution of Christians by Ananus, the High Priest.
    Martyrdom of James the Just.

63. Vologeses I of Parthia, defeated by Corbulo, signs treaty of peace.

64. Gessius Florus succeeds Albinus as Procurator of Judaea.

66. Tiridates invested King of Armenia by Nero.
    Revolt of the Jews. Roman garrison of Jerusalem massacred after surrender. Cestius Gallus, Legate of Syria, attacks Jerusalem, but is beaten off.

67. First Jewish War. Vespasian replaces Cestius as Legate.

68. Accession of Galba.

69. Accession of Otho.
    Otho appears in public in dress of priest of Isis.
    Domitian escapes from Capitol in similar dress.
    Accession of Vitellius.
    Vespasian consults oracle, and works miraculous cures, in Temple of Isis at Alexandria.

70. Accession of Vespasian.
    Siege and sack of Jerusalem by Titus. Burning of Herod's Temple.

70–107. St Ignatius flourished.

72. Vespasian deposes Antiochus IV of Commagene, last of Seleucides.

77. Accession of Vologeses II of Parthia. Many pretenders, some of whom reign concurrently with him till his death.

79. Accession of Titus.

80. Domitian rebuilds Temple of Isis which had been burned.
    Statius mentions Mithraic Tauroctony in his *Thebaid*

81. Accession of Domitian.

Circa 83. Earliest Mithraic Inscription known.

96. Accession of Nerva.

98. Accession of Trajan.

A.D.

Circa 100. Marcion born; died about 165.

Menander, Simon Magus's successor, flourished.

102. Earliest dated Mithraic Inscription by T. Claudius Livianus, Praetorian Prefect.

113–117. War between Rome and Parthia.

116. Revolt of Jews throughout East suppressed by Lucius Quietus.

117. Accession of Hadrian.

117–138. Basilides the Egyptian flourished.

Circa 120. Hadrian places in his *lararium* images of Greek Serapis and Isis.

120–160. Tatian flourished.

121. Justin Martyr born: martyred about 151.

Circa 125. Saturninus of Antioch flourished.

130. Hadrian rebuilds Jerusalem and names it Aelia Capitolina.

Circa 130. Apelles the Marcionite born: died about 180.

132. Revolt of Jews, under the Messiah Bar Cochba, and War of Extermination.

138. Accession of Antoninus Pius.

138–160. Valentinus the Gnostic flourished.

Circa 140. Cerdo the Syrian flourished.

147. Irenaeus of Lyons born: died about 202.

Vologeses III restores Parthian Kingdom, and collects books of Avesta.

150. Tertullian born: died about 220 A.D.

Circa 150. Marcus the magician flourished.

Hermas Pastor appears.

155. Clement of Alexandria born: died about 211.

Bardesanes or Ibn Daisan born: died about 223.

162. War between Rome and Parthia. Parthian Kings substitute Aramaic for Greek on their coins.

164. Destruction of Parthian capital, Seleucia on the Tigris, by Avidius Cassius.

170. Heracleon the Valentinian born: died about 210.

Circa 170. Lucian the Marcionite flourished.

Ptolemy the Valentinian flourished.

170–183. Theophilus of Antioch flourished.

179. Pantaenus founds Christian school at Alexandria.

180. Accession of Commodus.

185. Origen of Alexandria born: died about 253.

191. Accession of Vologeses IV to throne of Parthia.

193. Accession of Pertinax. Murder of Pertinax, and sale of Empire by Praetorians to Didius Julianus.

Accession of Septimius Severus.

195. War between Rome and Parthia.

Circa 200. Axionicus the Valentinian flourished.

A.D.

209. Accession of Artabanus IV of Parthia.
211. Accession of Caracalla and Geta.
216. Birth of Manes: died 275.
     War between Rome and Parthia.
217. Accession of Macrinus.
219. Accession of Heliogabalus.
221. Alexander Severus proclaimed Caesar.
222. Accession of Alexander Severus.
     War between Rome and Parthia.
Circa 222. Hippolytus of Porta Romana flourished.
226. Ardeshîr, son of Sassan, conquers Artabanus IV of Parthia, and
     founds Sassanid dynasty of Persia.
230. War between Rome and Persia.
235. Accession of Maximin.
     Persecution of Christians.
238. Accession and death of the two Gordians.
     Maximus and Balbinus proclaimed Emperors with Gordian III as
     Caesar, but are murdered by Praetorians.
     Accession of Gordian III.
     Manes begins to teach.
241. Accession of Sapor (Shapûr) I of Persia on death of his father Ardeshîr.
242. War between Rome and Persia.
244. Accession of Philip the Arabian.
246. M. Julius Philippus proclaimed Augustus jointly with his father,
     Philip the Arabian.
249. Accession of Decius.
     Persecution of Christians.
251. Accession of Gallus.
253. Accession of Valerian.
     Gallienus proclaimed Augustus jointly with his father Valerian.
254. First appearance of Franks, who attack Rhine and invade Spain and
     Africa.
260. War between Rome and Persia.
     Valerian taken prisoner by Sapor, and dies in captivity.
260–268. Reign of Gallienus and the Thirty Tyrants.
     Right of Church to hold property recognized.
268. Accession of Claudius.
270. Accession of Aurelian.
     St Anthony introduces monachism into Church.
272. Accession of Hormisdas (Ormuz) I of Persia.
273. Aurelian captures Palmyra, and puts an end to Zenobia's Kingdom.
     Aurelian decides case of Paul of Samosata, and affirms primacy of
     Roman Church.
273. Accession of Varanes (Bahram) I of Persia.

A.D.

275. Manes put to death by Varanes I.
  Accession of Tacitus.
276. Accession of Varanes II of Persia.
  Accession of Probus.
282. Accession of Carus.
283. Carinus proclaimed Augustus jointly with his father Carus.
284. Numerian proclaimed Augustus jointly with his brother Carinus on death of Carus.
  Accession of Diocletian.
286. Maximian proclaimed Augustus jointly with Diocletian.
287. Edict of Diocletian against Manichaeans. Teachers to be burned: Hearers' goods to be confiscated.
292. Constantius Chlorus and Galerius proclaimed Caesars under the two Augusti.
293. Accession of Varanes III of Persia followed by that of Narses.
296. War between Rome and Persia.
Circa 300. Alexander of Lycopolis flourished.
302. Accession of Hormisdas II of Persia.
303. Persecution of Christians. Era of Martyrs.
304. Mithras declared at Carnuntum Protector of Roman Empire.
305. Abdication of Diocletian and Maximian.
  Constantius Chlorus and Galerius become Augusti.
  Maximin and Severus proclaimed Caesars.
306. Death of Constantius Chlorus. Constantine proclaimed Augustus by army, but allowed title of Caesar only by Galerius.
  Severus proclaimed Augustus in place of Constantius Chlorus.
  Maximian and Maxentius, his son, rebel.
307. Severus, besieged in Ravenna by Maximian, surrenders and commits suicide.
  Maximian gives his daughter Fausta to Constantine, and proclaims him Augustus jointly with himself.
  War of Augusti, Maximian, Maxentius, and Constantine, against Galerius, who proclaims Licinius and Maximin Augusti jointly with himself.
308. Maximian plots against Constantine, who puts him to death.
  Ephrem Syrus born: died 373.
310. Accession of Sapor II of Persia.
311. Death of Galerius; Licinius and Maximin divide Eastern provinces between them.
312. War between Constantine and Maxentius, who is defeated at Turin, Verona, and Saxa Rubra, and slain.
  Edict of Toleration by Constantine and Licinius.
313. Maximin declares war against Licinius, but is defeated at Heraclea and slain.

A.D.

314. War between Constantine and Licinius, who is defeated and makes peace.

315. Pachomius groups monks together in monasteries and institutes common life.

316 ?. Death of Diocletian.

320. Epiphanius of Constantia born: died about 400 A.D.

323. War between Constantine and Licinius, who is defeated and put to death.

Constantine becomes sole Emperor.

Constantine issues renewed edict of toleration.

324 ?. Constantine directs enquiry into Manichaean doctrines by Musonianus (Strategius), Praetorian Prefect of the East.

325. Constantine summons Council of Nicaea.

327. Foundation of Constantinople and transfer of capital of Empire thither.

337. Baptism and death of Constantine.

BOOKS AND ARTICLES REFERRED TO
IN TEXT OR NOTES

N.B.—The works of the better-known classical writers (e.g. Livy) and of Fathers of the Church (e.g. St Augustine) have been omitted from the following list. Authors included in the first category are quoted either from the collection Müller-Didot or from Teubner's series; those in the second, from Migne's *Patrologia*. The place of publication, when not specially mentioned, is London, and the edition quoted is, subject to the same reservation, the last published. In the body of the book, the full title, date, and other particulars of the work referred to are given the first time of mention only, abbreviations being used in subsequent references.

ABANO, PETER DE. Heptameron, seu Elementa Magica. Paris, 1567.

ABEL, EUGENIUS. Orphica. Lipsiae, 1885.

ABU RAIHÂN, called AL BÎRÛNÎ. Chronology of Ancient Nations. Translated from the Arabic by Dr C. Edward Sachau. 1879. See also AL-BÎRÛNÎ, *infra*.

Académie des Inscriptions et Belles Lettres. Comptes-Rendus des Séances. 4e Série. Paris, 1873, etc. In progress.

The Academy. 1869, etc. In progress.

Ägyptische Sprache, Zeitschrift für. See *Zeitschrift, infra.*

AL-BÎRÛNÎ. Alberuni's India. An English Edition with Notes and Indices by Dr Edward C. Sachau. 2 vols. 1910.

ALLINE, M. See *Xenia.*

AMÉLINEAU, E. Essai sur le Gnosticisme Égyptien. Paris, 1887. (*Annales du Musée Guimet*, t. XIV.)

—— Les Actes Coptes du martyre de St Polycarpe. 1888. See *Proceedings of Society of Biblical Archaeology*, vol. X.

—— Notice sur le Papyrus Gnostique Bruce. Paris, 1891. (Notices et Extraits des MSS. de la Bibliothèque Nationale et autres Bibliothèques, t. XXIX, 1ère ptle.)

AMELUNG, W. Le Sarapis de Bryaxis. 1903. See *Revue Archéologique*, 4o série, t. II, ptle ii.

Anon. Cerinthus and the Gnostics. 1886. See the *London Quarterly Review* for October, 1886.

Ante-Nicene Christian Library. Edited by Alexander Roberts and James Donaldson. 24 vols. and 1 additional volume. Edinburgh, 1868 to 1897.

Antiquaires de France, see Société Nationale des A. de F.

Archaeologia : Miscellaneous Tracts relating to Antiquity. See Society of Antiquaries of London.

ARCHELAUS, Bishop of Caschar. Acta (wrongly attributed to). See HEGEMONIUS.

Archiv für wissenschaftliche Erforschung des alten Testaments. Halle, 1869–1872.

Asiatic Society. See Royal Asiatic Society of Great Britain, etc.

Association pour l'encouragement des Études grecques. See *Revue des Études grecques.*

AVEZOU, CH., et PICARD, CH. Bas-relief Mithriaque. 1911. See *Revue de l'Histoire des Religions,* t. LXIV.

AURELIUS AUGUSTINUS. Augustini librum de Haeresibus ad Quod-vultdeum. See Oehler, Corpus Haereseologicum, vol. I.

BADHAM, F. B. The Word Monogenes. See *The Academy,* 5 Sept., 1896.

BARRETT, FRANCIS. The Magus or Celestial Intelligencer, being a Complete System of Occult Philosophy, 1801.

BAUR, FERDINAND CHRISTIAN. Das Manichäische Religionssystem. Tübingen, 1831.

BEAUSOBRE, ISAAC DE. Histoire critique de Manichée et du Manichéisme. Amsterdam, 1734–9. 2 vols.

BENN, ALFRED WILLIAM. The Philosophy of Greece. 1898.

BERGER, PHILIPPE, Membre de l'Institut. Études des Documents nouveaux fournis sur les Ophites par les Philosophoumena. Nancy, 1873.

—— Les Stèles Puniques de la Bibliothèque Nationale. See *Gazette Archéologique,* 11ᵉ année (1876).

BERNARD, J. H., Bishop of Ossory. The Odes of Solomon. Translated from the Syriac Text. Cambridge, 1912. (Cambridge Texts and Studies, vol. III.)

Biblical Archaeology. See Society of Biblical Archaeology.

BISSING, Freiherr F. W. von. Cult of Isis in Pompeian Paintings. Oxford, 1908. See *Transactions of 3rd International Congress of Religions.*

BÖHMER, HEINRICH. Les Jésuites. Traduit de l'Allemand par Gabriel Monod. Paris, 1910.

BOUCHÉ-LECLERCQ, AUGUSTE. Histoire de la Divination. Paris, 1879–1882. 4 vols.

—— L'Astrologie grecque. Paris, 1899.

—— La Politique religieuse de Ptolémée Soter et le culte de Serapis. See *Revue de l'Histoire des Religions,* t. XLVI, 1902.

—— Les Reclus du Serapéum de Memphis. Paris, 1903. See PERROT, Mélanges.

—— Histoire des Lagides. Paris, 1903–1907. 4 vols.

—— L'Intolérance Religieux et Politique. Paris, 1912. (Bibliothèque de Philosophie Scientifique.)

BOURIANT, U. L'Évangile de St Pierre (Fragments Grecs du livre d'Énoch). See Mémoires de la Mission Archéologique Française du Caire, t. IX, fasc. 1 (1892).

BOUSSET, WILHELM. Hauptprobleme des Gnosis. Göttingen, 1907. (Forschungen zur Religion und Litteratur des Alten und Neuen Testaments. Herausg. von Dr Bousset und Dr Hermann Gunkel.)

BRANDT, A. J. H. WILHELM. Die Mandäische Religion, ihre Entwickelung und geschichtliche Bedeutung. Leipzig, 1889.

BREASTED, JAMES HENRY, Ph.D. Ancient Records. Chicago, 1906. 4 vols.

—— The History of Egypt. New York, 1909.

BRÉHIER, ÉMILE. La Cosmologie Stoicienne à la Fin du Paganisme. See *Revue de l'Histoire des Religions*, t. LXIV, 1911.

BROOKE, ALAN ENGLAND. Fragments of Heracleon. Cambridge, 1891. (Cambridge Texts and Studies, vol. I.)

BRUNET DE PRESLE, CHARLES MARIE WLADIMIR. Le Serapéum de Memphis. Paris, 1865. (Mémoires de l'Académie des Inscriptions. Mémoires présentés par divers savants. Série I, t. 2.)

—— Les Papyrus grecs du Musée du Louvre. Paris, 1865. (Notices et Extraits des MSS. de la Bibliothèque Nationale et des autres Bibliothèques, publiés par l'Institut de France, t. XVIII, Pt. 2.)

BUDGE, ERNEST ALFRED THOMPSON WALLIS, Litt.D., etc. The Papyrus of Nesi-Amsu. See *Archaeologia*, vol. LXII, Pt 2 (1890).

—— The Book of the Dead. 1898. 3 vols.

—— The History of Egypt. 1902. 8 vols.

—— The Gods of the Egyptians. 1904. 2 vols.

—— Egyptian Hieratic Papyri in the British Museum. 1910.

—— Osiris and the Egyptian Resurrection. 1911. 2 vols.

BUDGE, E. A. T. WALLIS, KING, L. W., and THOMPSON, R. CAMPBELL. The Sculptures and Inscriptions of Darius the Great at Behistun. 1907.

BUNSEN, CHRISTIAN CARL JOSIAS (Baron). Hippolytus and his Age. 1852. 4 vols.

BURROWS, RONALD. Discoveries in Crete. 1907.

CALLISTHENES, Pseudo-. The History of Alexander the Great. Translated from the Syriac by E. A. Wallis Budge. Cambridge, 1887.

CARNOY, A. Armaiti-Ârmatay. Louvain, 1912. See *Le Muséon*, n.s. t. XIII (1912).

CASARTELLI, LOUIS CHARLES, Bishop of Salford. La Philosophie Religieuse de Mazdéisme. Paris, 1884.

CHABAS, JEAN MARIE FRANÇOIS. Le Papyrus Magique Harris. Traduction et commentaire d'un MS. Égyptien. Chalon-sur-Saône, 1860.

CHANOT, E. DE. Statues Iconiques de Chypre. Paris, 1878. See *Gazette Archéologique*, 1878.

CHARLES, R. H., D.D., etc. Apocalyptical Literature. See Hastings, Dictionary of the Bible, *s.h.v.*

—— Apocalyptical Literature, 1899. See Cheyne's Encyclopaedia Biblica, *s.h.v.*

—— The Book of Enoch. Translated from the Ethiopic. Oxford, 1893.

—— The Apocalypse of Baruch. Translated from the Syriac. 1896.

—— The Assumption of Moses. Translated from the Latin. 1897.

—— A Critical History of the Doctrine of a Future Life in Israel, in Judaism, and in Christianity. 1899. (The Jowett Lectures.)

—— The Ascension of Isaiah. Translated from the Ethiopic. 1900.

—— The Book of Jubilees. Translated from the Ethiopic. 1902.

—— The Testaments of the XII Patriarchs. Translated from the Greek. 1908.

—— The Apocrypha and Pseudepigrapha of the Old Testament. Edited by R. H. Charles. Oxford, 1913. 2 vols.

CHAVANNES, EDOUARD, et PELLIOT, PAUL. Un Traité Manichéen retrouvé en Chine. Paris, 1913. (Extrait du *Journal Asiatique*, 1911–1913. Pagination of Journal given in Extrait and used in notes *infra*.)

CHEYNE, THOMAS KELLY, D.D., etc. Prophecies of Isaiah. A new translation. 1889. 2 vols.

—— Jewish Religious Life after the Exile. New York, 1898. (American Lectures on the History of Religions.)

CHEYNE, T. K., and BLACK, J. SUTHERLAND. See Encyclopaedia Biblica.

CLEMENT OF ALEXANDRIA. Clemens Alexandrinus. Edidit Otto Stählin, Leipzig, 1905. (Die Griechischen Schriftsteller der ersten Drei Jahrhunderte. Kirchenväter-Commission der Kgl. Preuss. Akad. der Wissenschaften.)

[CONINGTON, JOHN, Prof.] Origen's Philosophoumena. 1851. See *Quarterly Review* for 1851.

Contemporary Review, The. 1886, etc. In progress.

CONYBEARE, FREDERICK CORNWALLIS. The Holy Spirit as a Dove. 1892. See *The Academy*, 3 Dec., 1902 (Paper read at meeting of Society of Historical Theology).

—— The Apology of Apollonius. 1894.

COOK, ARTHUR BERNARD. The Bee in Greek Mythology. 1895. See *Journal of Hellenic Studies*, vol. xv. 1895.

COOK, STANLEY A. David. 1899. See Cheyne's Encyclopaedia Biblica, *s.h.v.*

CORDIER, HENRI, Memb. de l'Institut, etc. Les Fouilles en Asie Centrale. Paris, 1910. See *Journal des Savans*, 1910.

CORY, ISAAC PRESTON. Ancient Fragments of the Phoenician, Chaldaean, Egyptian, Tyrian, Carthaginian, Indian, and Persian writers. First edition. 1832.

COURDAVEAUX, V. Tertullien. See *Revue de l'Histoire des Religions*, t. XXIII (1891).

COURDAVEAUX, V. Clément d'Alexandrie. Paris, 1892. See *Revue de l'Hist. des Religions*, t. XXII (1892).

COWLEY, A. E. Samaritans. 1903. See Cheyne's Encyclopaedia Biblica, *s.h.v.*

CROOKE, W. The Popular Religion and Folklore of Northern India. Westminster, 1896. 2 vols.

CRUM, W. E. Prayer of the Virgin in Bartos. 1897. See *Proceedings of Society of Biblical Archaeology*, vol. XIX (1897).

—— Catalogue of the Coptic MSS. in the British Museum. 1905.

CUMONT, FRANZ. Textes et Monuments relatifs aux Mystères de Mithra. Bruxelles, 1896, 1899. 2 vols.

—— Hypsistos. See *Revue de l'Instruction Publique en Belgique*, 1897.

—— Catalogus Codicum Astrologorum. Bruxelles, 1898, etc. In progress.

—— Les Religions Orientales dans le Paganisme Romain. Paris, 1906. (*Annales du Musée Guimet*. Bibliothèque de Vulgarisation, t. XXIV.)

—— Recherches sur le Manichéisme. Bruxelles, 1908, etc. In progress.

—— L'Aigle funéraire des Syriens et l'apothéose des Empereurs. Paris, 1910. See *Revue de l'Histoire des Religions*, t. LXII (1910).

—— Astrology and Religion among the Greeks and Romans. Translated from the French by J. B. Baker. New York, 1912. (American Lectures on the History of Religions.)

—— Les Mystères de Mithra. Bruxelles, 1913.

DAMASCIUS. De Primis principiis. See Cory's Ancient Fragments.

DARESSY, GEORGES, Secrétaire du Musée du Caire. Un Décret de l'An XXIII de Ptolémée Epiphane. See Recueil de Travaux, t. XXXIII (1911).

DAREMBERG, CHARLES VICTOR, et SAGLIO, EDMOND. Dictionnaire des Antiquités grecques et romaines. Paris, 1873, etc. In progress.

DARMESTETER, JAMES. Ormuzd et Ahriman. Paris, 1877. (Bibliothèque de l'École des Hautes Études, fasc. XXIX.)

—— The Zend Avesta. Oxford, 1880–1887. 3 parts. (Sacred Books of the East.)

—— Essais Orientaux. Paris, 1883.

—— Le Zend Avesta. Paris, 1893. 3 vols. (*Annales du Musée Guimet*, tt. XXI, XXII, XXIV.)

DAVIDS, T. W. RHYS. Buddhist India. 1903. (Story of the Nations Series.)

DECHARME, P. Cybele. See DAREMBERG et SAGLIO, Dictionnaire des Antiquités, *s.h.v.*

DEISSMANN, ADOLF, D.D. New Light on the New Testament from records of the Graeco-Roman Period. Translated from the German by Lionel R. M. Strachan. Edinburgh, 1907.

DELAGE, YVES, et GOLDSMITH, M. Les Théories de l'Évolution. Paris, 1909. (Bibliothèque de Philosophie scientifique.)

DEUBNER, LUDWIG. De Incubatione capita quatuor. Lipsiae, 1900.

Deutsche Orient. Gesellschaft. *Mitteilungen*. Berlin, 1898, etc. In progress.

DIETERICH, ALBRECHT, Prof. Abraxas: Studien zur Religionsgeschichte. Leipzig, 1891. (Festschrift Usener.)

—— De Hymnis Orphicis. Marburg, 1891.

DILL, Sir SAMUEL. Roman Society in the Last Century of the Western Empire. 1899.

—— Roman Society from Nero to Marcus Aurelius. 1904.

DÖLLINGER, JOHANN JOSEPH IGNAZ, D.D., etc. The Gentile and the Jew in the Courts of Christ. Translated from the German by N. Darnell. 1902. 2 vols. (German title: Judenthum und Heidenthum.)

—— First Age of Christianity and the Church. Translated from the German by H. N. Oxenham, 1906. (German title: Christentum und Kirche in der Zeit der Grundlegung.)

DREXLER, A. Isis. See Roscher's Lexikon der Mythologie, *s.h.v.*

DROYSEN, JOHANN GUSTAV. Histoire de l'Hellénisme. Paris, 1883. 3 vols. Traduite de l'Allemande sous la direction de A. Bouché-Leclercq. (German titles: Geschichte des Alexanders des Grossen; Geschichte des Hellenismus.)

DUCHESNE, Monsignor LOUIS, Membre de l'Institut, etc. Early History of the Christian Church from its Foundation to the end of the third century. Translated from the French. 1909, etc. In progress. (French title: Histoire ancienne de l'Église.)

DUFOURCQ, ALBERT. De Manichaeismo apud Latinos. Paris. 1900.

DUSSAUD, RENÉ. Les Papyrus judéo-araméens d'Elephantine. See *Revue de l'Histoire des Religions*, t. LXIV (1911).

DYER, LOUIS. The Gods in Greece. 1891. (Lowell Lectures.)

Egypt Exploration Fund. The Oxyrhynchus Papyri. 1898, etc. In progress.

—— *The Journal of Egyptian Archaeology*, 1914, etc. In progress.

Encyclopédie, La Grande. Paris, 1887, etc. In progress.

Encyclopaedia Biblica. Edited by T. K. Cheyne and J. Sutherland Black. 1899, etc. 4 vols.

Encyclopaedia Britannica, 9th edition, Edinburgh, 1875–1889.

—— 11th edition, Cambridge, 1910–1911.

EPIPHANIUS OF CONSTANTIA (or Salamis). S. Epiphanii episcopi Constantiensis Panaria eorumque Anacephalaeosis. See Oehler, Corpus Haereseologicum, tt. 2, 3.

ERMAN, ADOLF, Ph.D., etc. Die Ägyptischen Beschwörungen. See *Ägyptische Zeitschrift*, 1883.

—— Life in Ancient Egypt. Translated from the German by H. M. Tirard. 1894.

—— Handbook of the Egyptian Religion. Translated from the German. 1905. (Handbücher des Kgl. Museums zu Berlin.)

Etymologicum Magnum. Oxon. 1848.

EVANS, Sir ARTHUR, P.S.A., etc. The Mycenaean Tree and Pillar Cult and its Mediterranean Relations. 1901.

The Expositor, series 5. 1895, etc. In progress.

FAYE, EUGÈNE DE. Introduction à l'Étude du Gnosticisme au IIᵉ et au IIIᵉ Siècle. Paris, 1903. (Also in *Rev. de l'Histoire des Religions*, tt. XLV and XLVI.)

—— Formation d'une Doctrine de Dieu au IIᵉ Siècle. See *Revue de l'Histoire des Religions*, t. LXIV (1911).

—— Gnostiques et Gnosticisme, Étude critique des documents du Gnosticisme Chrétien aux IIᵉ et IIIᵉ siècles. Paris, 1913. (Bibliothèque de l'École des Hautes Études: Sciences Religieuses, t. XXVII.)

FFOULKES, EDMUND SALUSBURY. Chiliasts. See Smith's Dictionary of Christian Biography, *s.h.v.*

FIVEL, LÉON. Le Dieu Glycon à Nicomédie. Paris, 1879. See *Gazette Archéologique*, 1879.

FLEET, J. F., Ph.D., etc. The Day on which Buddha died. 1909. See *Journal of the Royal Asiatic Society*, 1909.

FLÜGEL, GUSTAV, Ph.D., etc. Mani, seine Lehre und seine Schriften. Leipzig, 1862.

FOAKES-JACKSON, F. J., B.D., etc. Some Christian Difficulties in the Second and Twentieth Centuries. Cambridge, 1903. (Hulsean Lectures.)

FORSHALL, JOSIAH. Description of the Greek Papyri in the British Museum. 1839.

FOSSEY, CHARLES. Les Fouilles Allemandes à Boghaz-Keui. Paris, 1909. See *Journal des Savans*, 1909.

FOUCART, GEORGE. Histoire des Religions et Méthode Comparative. Paris, 1912.

FOUCART, PAUL, Membre de l'Institut, etc. Les Associations Religieuses chez les Grecs. Paris, 1873.

—— Recherches sur l'origine et la nature des Mystères d'Éleusis. Paris, 1895. (*Id.*, t. XXXV.)

—— Les Grands Mystères d'Éleusis. Paris, 1900. (Extrait des Mémoires de l'Académie des Inscriptions et Belles Lettres, t. XXXVII.)

—— Le Culte de Dionysos en Attique. Paris, 1904. (*Id.*, t. XXXVII.)

FRANCK, ADOLPHE. La Kabbale. Paris, 1843.

—— Le Gnosticisme Égyptien. See *Journal des Savans*, Avril, 1888.

FRAZER, Sir J. G., D.C.L., etc. The Golden Bough. 1913–1915. 12 vols.

FREEMAN, EDWARD AUGUSTUS, D.C.L., etc. Historical Essays. 1871–1892. 4 vols.

FRIEDLÄNDER, M. Der vorchristliche jüdische Gnosticismus. Göttingen, 1898.

FULLER, JOHN MEE. Ebionites. See Smith's Dictionary of Christian Biography, *s.h.v.*

FULLER, JOHN MEE. Tatianus. See *ibid. s.h.v.*

GARDNER, PERCY, Litt.D., etc. The Coins of the Greek and Scythic kings of Bactria and India in the British Museum. 1884.

GARRUCCI, RAFFAELE. Les Mystères du syncrétisme Phrygien dans les catacombes Romaines de Prétextat. Paris, 1854.

GASTER, MOSES, Ph.D., etc. The Apocalypse of Abraham. 1893. See *Transactions of Society of Biblical Archaeology*, vol. IX. pt 1 (1893).

—— The Oldest Version of Midrash Megillah. Berlin, 1897. See Kohut's Semitic Studies.

Gazette Archéologique. Paris. 1875–1887.

GIBBON, EDWARD. The Decline and Fall of the Roman Empire. Edited by J. B. Bury, Litt.D., etc. 1897–1900. 7 vols.

GIRAUD, FRANÇOIS, M.S.T., etc. Ophitae. Dissertatio historica theologica de eorum origine, placitis, ac fatis. Paris, 1884.

GLEICHEN, ALFRED EDWARD WILFRID, Count. The Anglo-Egyptian Soudan. 1905.

GOBLET D'ALVIELLA, Le Comte. Ce que l'Inde doit à la Grèce. Paris, 1897.

GRAUX, CH. Mélanges: Recueil dedié à la mémoire de C. G. Paris. 1884.

GRIFFITH, F. LL., M.A., etc. Stories of the High Priests of Memphis. Oxford, 1900.

—— The old Coptic Magical Texts of Paris. Leipzig, 1900. (Extract from *Ägyptische Zeitschrift*, Bd XXXVIII. 1900.)

GRIFFITH, F. LL., and THOMPSON, Sir HERBERT, Bart. The Demotic Magical Papyrus of London and Leiden. 1904.

GROTE, GEORGE. A History of Greece. 1888. 10 vols.

GRÜBER, JOHANN NEPOMUC. Die Ophiten. Würzburg, 1864. 2 vols.

GUIGNEBERT, CHARLES. L'Évolution des Dogmes. Paris, 1910. (Bibliothèque de Philosophie Scientifique.)

GUIGNIAUT, JOSEPH DANIEL. Les Religions de l'Antiquité. Traduit de l'Allemand par L. F. A. Maury et E. Vinet. Paris, 1825, etc. tt. 4. (German title: Symbolik, von A. F. Creuzer.)

HAHN, AUGUST. Antitheses Marcionis gnostici. Königsberg, 1823.

—— Evangelium Marcionis ex auctoritate veterum monumentorum descripsit Augustus Hahn. Lipsiae, 1832. (Thilo's Codex Apocryphus Novi Testamenti, t. I.)

HALÉVY, JOSEPH. Recherches Bibliques, Pt 1. Le Tétragramme. Paris, 1884. See *Revue des Études juives*, t. IX. 1884.

HARNACK, ADOLF, D.D., etc. Über das gnostische Buch Pistis Sophia. Leipzig, 1891. (Texte und Untersuchungen zur Geschichte der Altchristlichen Literatur von Oscar von Gebhardt und Adolf Harnack.)

—— Outlines of the History of Dogma. Translated from the German by Neil Buchanan. 1894. 7 vols. (German title: Dogmengeschichte.)

HARNACK, ADOLF, D.D., etc. What is Christianity? Translated from the German by T. B. Saunders. 1904. (German title: Das Wesen des Christentums.)

—— The Expansion of Christianity in the First Three Centuries. Translated from the German by James Moffatt. 1908. 2 vols. (German title: Die Mission und Ausbreitung des Christentums in den ersten Drei Jahrhunderten.)

—— Marcion. See Encyclopaedia Britannica, 11th ed. *s.h.v.*

HARNACK, A., and CONYBEARE, F. C. Manichaeans. See *ibid. s.h.v.*

HARRISON, Miss JANE. Prolegomena to History of Greek Religion. 1903.

HARTLAND, EDWIN SIDNEY, F.S.A., etc. Ritual and Belief: Studies in the History of Religion. 1914.

HASTINGS, JAMES, D.D., etc. A Dictionary of the Bible. Edinburgh, 1900–1904. 5 vols.

HATCH, EDWIN, D.D., etc. The Influence of Greek Ideas and Usages upon the Christian Church. 1890. (Hibbert Lectures.)

HAUSRATH, ADOLF. A History of New Testament Times. Translated from the German by C. T. Poynting and P. Quenzer. 1878, etc. In progress. (German title: Neutestamentliche Zeitgeschichte.)

HEGEMONIUS. Acta Archelai. Edited by Charles Henry Beeson of Chicago. Leipzig, 1906. (Die Griechischen Schriftsteller der ersten Drei Jahrhunderte. Kirchenväter-Commission der Kgl. Preuss. Akad. der Wissenschaften.)

Hellenic Studies, Journal of. See Society for Promotion of Hellenic Studies, *infra.*

HERMATHENA. A series of Papers on Literature, Science, and Philosophy, by members of Trinity College, Dublin. Dublin, 1873, etc. In progress.

HIERONYMUS, Pseudo-. Indiculus de Haeresibus. See Oehler, Corpus Haereseologicum, vol. I.

HILD, J. A. Étude sur les Démons dans la littérature et la religion des Grecs. Paris, 1881.

HILGENFELD, ADOLF. Kritische Untersuchungen über die Evangelien Justins, der Clementinischen Homilien und Marcions. Halle, 1850.

—— Das Apostolikon Marcions. Gotha, 1855. See *Zeitschrift für hist. Theol.*, Bd 25 (1855).

—— Novum Testamentum extra canonem receptum. Lipsiae, 1884. 4 vols.

—— Die Ketzergeschichte des Urchristentums. Leipzig, 1884.

HIPPOLYTUS, Bishop of Porte Romana. Philosophoumena, sive Haeresium omnium confutatio. E codice Parisino productum recensuit Latine vertit, etc. Patricius Cruice. Paris, 1860.

HOGARTH, DAVID G. Philip and Alexander of Macedon. 1897.

HOLDICH, Sir THOMAS, K.C.M.G. The Gates of India. 1910.

HORT, FENTON JOHN ANTHONY, D.D., etc. Colarbasus. See Smith's Dictionary of Christian Biography, *s.h.v.*

HORT, FENTON JOHN ANTHONY, D.D., etc. Bardaisan. *Ibid., s.h.v.*
—— Barbelo. *Ibid. s.h.v.*

HOWERTH, IRA W. What is Religion? See *International Journal of Ethics.* 1903.

HUBERT, H., et MAUSS, M. Esquisse d'une théorie générale de la Magie. Paris, 1904. (Published as *L'Année Psychologique*, 7ᵉ année.)

HUTTON, FREDERICK WOLLASTON, F.R.S. Darwinism and Lamarckism. 1899.

HYVERNAT, H. Album de Paléographie Copte. Paris, 1868.

INGE, WILLIAM RALPH, D.D., Dean of St Paul's. Christian Mysticism, 1899. (Bampton Lectures.)

Institut Français d'Archéologie orientale. *Mémoires publiés par les membres de l'Institut.* Le Caire, 1902, etc. In progress.

International Congress of Religions, Third. *Transactions.* Oxford, 1908. 2 vols.

International Journal of Ethics. Philadelphia, 1890, etc. In progress.

IRENAEUS, Bishop of Lyons. Sancti Irenaei episcopi Lugdunensis libros quinque adversus Haereses. Edidit W. Wigan Harvey, S.T.B., etc. Cambridge, 1857. 2 vols.

ISIDORE OF SPAIN. Isidorus Hispalensis de Haeresibus. See Oehler, Corpus Haereseologicum, vol. I.

JACOBI, H. G. The Antiquity of Vedic Culture. 1909–1910. See *Journal of the Royal Asiatic Society*, 1909, 1910.

JAMES, MONTAGUE RHODES, Litt.D., etc. The Greek Apocalypse of Baruch. Cambridge, 1897. See (Apocrypha Anecdota) Cambridge Texts and Studies, vol. V.

JANET, PIERRE, Membre de l'Institut. L'Automatisme Psychologique. Paris, 1899.

JASTROW, MORRIS, Ph.D., etc. The Religion of Babylonia and Assyria. Boston, U.S.A., 1898.

JELLINEK, ADOLF, Ph.D., etc. Über das Buch der Jubiläen und das Noah-Buch. Leipzig, 1855.

JENSEN, P., Ph.D., etc. Die Kosmologie der Babylonien. Strassburg, 1890.

JÉQUIER, GUSTAVE. Le Livre de ce qu'il y a dans l'Hadès. Paris, 1894.

JEVONS, FRANK BYRON, Litt.D. Introduction to the Study of Comparative Religion. New York, 1908. (Hartford-Lamson Lectures on the Religions of the World.)

Jewish Quarterly Review. London, 1888, etc. In progress.

JOHNSON, SAMUEL. Oriental Religions and their relation to universal religion: Persia. 1885.

JOHNSON, WALTER. Byways of British Archaeology. 1912.

Journal des Savans. Paris, 1816 etc. In progress.

Journal of Egyptian Archaeology. See Egypt Exploration Fund.

Journal of Hellenic Studies. See Society for the Promotion of Hellenic Studies.

Journal of the Royal Asiatic Society. See Royal Asiatic Society of Great Britain and Ireland.

JULICHER, A., D.D., etc. Essenes. See Cheyne's Encyclopaedia Biblica, *s.h.v.*
—— Gnosis. *Ibid., s.h.v.*

KEIM, CARL THEODOR. Celsus' Wahren Wort. Zurich, 1873.

KENYON, Sir FREDERIC GEORGE, K.C.B. Greek Papyri in the British Museum. Catalogue with Texts. 1893.
—— Handbook to the Textual Criticism of the New Testament. 1912.

KERN, OTTO, Ph.D., etc. De Orphei, Epimenidis, Pherecydis, Theogoniis Quaestiones criticae. Berlin, 1888.
—— Die Herkunft des orphischen Hymnenbuchs. 1910. See Carl, Robert, Genethliakon.

KESSLER, KONRAD, Ph.D., etc. Forschungen über die Manichäische Religion. Berlin, 1889. Bd I (all published).

KHÔNI, THEODORE BAR, Bishop of Kashgar. Scholia. 1898. See Pognon, Inscriptions Mandaïtes.

KING, C. W. The Gnostics and their Remains. 1887.

KING, LEONARD WILLIAM, Litt.D. The Seven Tablets of Creation. 1902. 2 vols.
—— Chronicles of Early Babylonian Kings. 1907. 2 vols.

KOHLER, KAUFMANN. Pre-Talmudic Haggadah. 1895. See *Jewish Quarterly Review*, 1895.

KOHUT, GEORGE ALEXANDER. Semitic Studies by various authors in memory of Rev. Dr Alexander Kohut. Berlin, 1897.

KÖSTLIN, K. R., D.D., etc. Über das gnostische System des Buchs Pistis Sophia. Tübingen, 1854. (*Theologische Jahrbücher*, ed. Baur and Zeller.)

KRALL, JAKOB, Ph.D., etc. Tacitus und der Orient. Wien, 1880. 4 vols. (Untersuchungen aus der Alten Geschichte, Erster Heft.)

KRÜGER, T. HERMANN. Gnosticismus. See La Grande Encyclopédie, *s.h.v.*

KUENEN, ABRAHAM, D.D., etc. The Religion of Israel. Translated from the Dutch by A. H. May. 1874. 3 vols. (Dutch title: De Godsdienst van Israel tot den ondergang van den Joodschen staat.)

LAFAYE, GEORGES. Isis. See Daremberg et Saglio, Dict. des Antiquités, *s.h.v.*
—— Histoire du Culte des Divinités d'Alexandrie hors de l'Égypte. Paris, 1884. (Bibliothèque des Écoles Françaises d'Athènes et de Rome. Fasc. 33e.)
—— L'Initiation Mithriaque. Paris, 1906. (Conférences au Musée Guimet. Bibl. de Vulgarisation, t. XVIII (1906).)

LANE, EDWARD WILLIAM. Manners and Customs of the Modern Egyptians. Paisley, 1896.

LANGDON, STEPHEN, Ph.D., etc. A Preliminary Account of a Sumerian Legend of the Flood and the Fall of Man. 1914. See *Proceedings of the Society of Biblical Archaeology*, vol. XXXVI (1914).

LANGLOIS, VICTOR. Collection des Historiens anciens et modernes de l'Arménie. Paris, 1868, etc. 2 vols.

LAYARD, Sir AUSTIN HENRY. Discoveries in the Ruins of Nineveh and Babylon. 1853.

LEA, HENRY CHARLES. A History of the Inquisition of the Middle Ages. 1887–1888. 3 vols.

LE COQ, A. von. A Short Account of...the First Royal Prussian (Second German) Expedition to Turfan in Chinese Turkestan. 1909. See *Journal of the Royal Asiatic Society*, 1909.

—— Exploration Archéologique à Tourfan. Paris, 1910. (Conférences au Musée Guimet. Bibl. de Vulgarisation, t. XXXV (1910).)

—— Turkish Khuastuanift from Tun-huang, 1911. See *Journal of the Royal Asiatic Society* for 1911.

—— Chôtscho. Facsimile-Wiedergaben der wichtigeren Funde der Ersten Kgl. Preussen Expedition nach Turfan. Berlin, 1913. Bd 4.

LEEMANS, CONRAD, Litt.Hum.D., etc. Papyri Graeci Musei Antiquarii Publici Lugduni Batavi. Lugduni Batavorum, 1883–1885. 2 vols.

LEFÉBURE, EUGÈNE. L'Importance du Nom chez les Égyptiens. See *Sphinx*, vol. I (1897).

LEGGE, F. Witchcraft in Scotland. Paisley, 1891. See *Scottish Review*, vol. XX (1891).

—— Some Heretic Gospels. 1893. *Ibid.* vol. XXII (1893).

—— Devil Worship and Freemasonry. 1896. See *The Contemporary Review*, 1896.

—— The Sign Nutir or Neter. 1899. See *Proceedings of Society of Biblical Archaeology*, vol. XXI (1899).

—— Divination in the XVIIth Century. 1899. See *National Review* for 1899.

—— The Names of Demons in the Magic Papyri. 1900. See *Proceedings of Society of Biblical Archaeology*, vol. XXII (1900).

—— The Titles of the Thinite Kings. 1908. See *Proceedings of Society of Biblical Archaeology*, vol. XXX (1908).

—— The Legend of Osiris. 1911. *Ibid.*, vol. XXXIII (1911).

—— The Lion-headed God of the Mithraic Mysteries. 1912. *Ibid.*, vol. XXXIV (1912).

—— Western Manichaeism and the Turfan Discoveries. 1913. See *Journal of the Royal Asiatic Society* for 1913.

—— The Greek Worship of Serapis and Isis. 1914. See *Proceedings of Society of Biblical Archaeology*, vol. XXXVI (1914).

LENORMANT, FRANÇOIS. Dionysos Zagreus. Paris, 1879. See *Gazette Archéologique*, 1879.

—— Baubo. See Daremberg et Saglio, Dict. des Antiq., *s.h.v.*

—— Eleusinia. *Ibid.*, *s.h.v.*

LÉVI, SYLVAIN. Bouddhisme et les Grecs. Paris, 1891. See *Revue de l'Histoire des Religions*, t. XXIII (1891).

Lévy, Isidore, Directeur ancᴺ à l'École des Hautes Études. Sarapis. Paris, 1913. Extrait de la *Revue de l'Histoire des Religions* (1911, 1913).

Lightfoot, Joseph Barber, Bishop of Durham. Epistles to Colossians and Philemon. 1876.

—— The Apostolic Fathers: revised texts with Introductions and English translations. 1891.

Lillie, Arthur. Buddhism in Christendom, or Jesus the Essene. 1887.

—— Buddha and Buddhism. Edinburgh, 1900.

Lipsius, Richard Adalbert, D.D., etc. Gospels Apocryphal. 1880. See Smith's Dictionary of Christian Biography, *s.h.v.*

Literature, see Royal Society of, *infra.*

Lobeck, Christian August. Aglaophamus, sive de Theologiae mysticae Graecorum causis. Königsberg, 1829. 2 vols.

Loeb, Isidore. La Cabbale juive. See La Grande Encyclopédie, *s.h.v.*

London *Quarterly Review*, New series. 1899, etc. In progress.

Loret, Victor. Les Enseignes Militaires des Tribus et les Symboles Hiéroglyphiques des Divinités. Paris, 1902. See *Revue Égyptologique* for 1902.

—— Quelques idées sur la forme primitive de certaines Religions Égyptiennes. Paris, 1904. See *idem* for 1904.

—— L'Égypte en Temps du Totemisme. Paris, 1906. (Conférences au Musée Guimet. Bibl. de Vulgarisation, t. xix (1906).)

Lovatelli, A. Caetani. Il Culto d'Iside in Roma. Roma, 1891. (Miscellanea Archeologica.)

Lubbock, Sir John, afterwards Lord Avebury. Origin of Civilization. 1889.

Luebbert, Edward, Ph.D., etc. Commentatio de Pindaro dogmatis de migratione animarum cultore. Bonn, 1887.

Lupton, Joseph Hart. Dionysius pseudo-Areopagitica. See Smith's Dictionary of Christian Biography, *s.h.v.*

Lyall, Sir Alfred, K.C.S.I., etc. Asiatic Studies. 1882.

Maass, Ernst, Ph.D., etc. Orpheus: Untersuchungen zur Griechischen Römischen Altchristlichen Jenseitsdichtung und Religion. München, 1895.

McCrindle, J. W. The Invasion of India by Alexander the Great. Westminster, 1893.

Macdonald, Miss L. Inscriptions relating to Sorcery in Cyprus. 1891. See *Proceedings of Society of Biblical Archaeology*, t. xiii (1891).

MacGiffert, A. C. Prolegomena to the Church History of Eusebius. Oxford, 1890. (Schaff and Wace, Nicene Library.)

Mackay, Charles, LL.D., etc. Memoirs of Extraordinary Popular Delusions. 1869.

Mahaffy, John Pentland, D.D., etc. Alexander's Empire. 1887. (Story of the Nations Series.)

—— Greek Life and Thought. 1887.

—— The Greek World under Roman Sway. 1890.

MAHAFFY, JOHN PENTLAND, D.D., etc.   The Empire of the Ptolemies. 1895.

MALCOLM, Sir JOHN.   A History of Persia.   1820. 2 vols.

MALLET, D.   Le Culte de Neit à Sais.   Paris, 1888.

MARIETTE, FRANÇOIS AUGUSTE FERDINAND, Pasha.   Dendérah: description générale du grand temple de cette ville.   Paris. 1875.

—— Le Serapéum de Memphis.   Publié après le MS. de l'auteur par M. G. Maspero.   Paris, 1882, etc. 2 vols.

MARSHALL, J. T.   Pre-existence of Souls.   See Hastings, Dictionary of the Bible, *s.h.v.*

MASPERO, Sir GASTON, Membre de l'Institut, K.C.M.G., etc.   Études de Mythologie et d'Archéologie Égyptiennes.   Paris, 1893, etc.   In progress. Tt. 7. (Quoted *infra* as "Ét. Égyptol.")

—— Egyptian Souls and their Worlds.   See Ét. Égyptol. t. 1.

—— Les Hypogées Royaux de Thèbes. See *id.*, t. 2.

—— Sur l'Ennéade.   See *id.*, t. 2.

—— The Dawn of Civilization.   1894.   (A translation of t. I of Histoire Ancienne des Peuples de l'Orient Classique *infra*.)

—— Les Inscriptions des Pyramides de Saqqarah.   Paris, 1894.

—— Histoire Ancienne des Peuples de l'Orient Classique.   Paris, 1895–1897. Tt. III.   (An English translation of these three volumes was published by the S.P.C.K. in 1894–1900 under the titles of: The Dawn of Civilization, The Struggle of the Empires, and The Passing of the Empires.)

—— Comment Alexandre devenait Dieu.   Paris, 1896.   (Annuaire de l'École des Hautes Études. 1897.)

—— La Table des Offrandes.   Paris, 1897.   See *Revue de l'Histoire des Religions*, t. XXXV (1897).

—— Histoire ancienne des Peuples de l'Orient.   Paris, 1904.

—— Contes Populaires de l'Ancienne Égypte.   Paris (1905).

—— La Fille du Prince de Bakhtan.   See last-named.

—— Review of J. Lieblein's Pistis Sophia, les conceptions Égyptiennes dans le Gnosticisme.   Paris, 1909.   See *Revue Critique*, 30 Sept., 1909.

MATTER, JACQUES.   Histoire critique du Gnosticisme.   Paris, 1843, 1844. Tt. 3.

MAURICE, JULES.   La Dynastie Solaire des Seconds Flaviens.   Paris, 1911.   See *Revue Archéologique*, 4e série, t. XVIII (1911).

MAURY, LOUIS FERDINAND ALFRED.   Histoire des Religions de la Grèce Antique.   Paris, 1857. Tt. 3.

—— La Magie et l'Astrologie dans l'Antiquité et en Moyen Age.   Paris, 1860.

—— Découvertes sur l'Égypte.   Paris, 1885.   See *Revue des Deux Mondes* for September, 1885.

MAX MÜLLER, FERDINAND, P.C., etc.   Lectures on the Original Growth of Religion as illustrated by the Religions of India.   1880.   (Hibbert Lectures.)

DE MÉLY, F. Le Livre des Cyranides. Paris, 1904. See *Compte-Rendu de l'Académie des Inscriptions*, Mai-Juin, 1904.

MENANT (Mdlle) D. Parsis et Parsisme. Paris, 1904. (Conférences au Musée Guimet. Bibl. de Vulgarisation, t. XVI (1904).)

—— Les Rites Funéraires. Paris, 1910. See *id.*, t. XXXV (1910).

MOLINIER, R. P. Imprécation gravée sur plomb. Paris, 1897. See *Mémoires de la Société Nationale des Antiquaires de France*, série VI, t. VIII (1897).

MONCEAUX, PAUL. Orpheus. See Daremberg et Saglio, Dict. des Antiquités, *s.h.v.*

—— Orphici. See *ibid.*, *s.h.v.*

—— Sabazios. See *ibid.*, *s.h.v.*

MORET, ALEXANDRE. Le Rituel du Culte Divin Journalier en Égypte. Paris, 1902. (*Annales du Musée Guimet*. Bibliothèque des Études, t. XIV.)

—— Le Verbe créateur et révélateur. See *Revue de l'Histoire des Religions*, t. LXVII (1909).

MORFILL, W. R. The Book of the Secrets of Enoch. Edited by R. H. Charles. Oxford, 1896.

MORRISON, W. D. The Jews under Roman Rule. 1890. (Story of the Nations Series.)

MOULTON, JAMES HOPE, D.Lit., etc. Early Zoroastrianism. 1913. (Hibbert Lectures, Second Series.)

MOZLEY, JOHN RICKARDS. Lucianus. See Smith, Dictionary of Christian Biography, *s.h.v.*

MÜLLER, CARL OTTFRIED. Introduction to a Scientific System of Mythology. Translated from the German by John Leitch. 1844. 2 vols. (German title: Prolegomena zu einer wissenschaftlichen Mythologie.)

—— History of the Literature of Ancient Greece. Translated from the German by John Wm Donaldson. 1858. 2 vols. (German title: Geschichte der griechischen Literatur bis auf das Zeitalter Alexanders.)

MÜLLER, F. W. K. Handschriften-Reste in Estrangelo-Schrift aus Turfan. Berlin, 1904. (Extract from *Abhandlungen des Kgl. Preuss. Akad. der Wissenschaften*, 1904.)

Muséon, Le. Études philosophiques, historiques, et religieuses. Louvain, 1900, etc. In progress.

National Review, The. Edited by Sir Alfred Austin and W. J. Courthope. 1883, etc. In progress.

NAVILLE, EDOUARD, D.C.L., etc. The Old Egyptian Faith. Translated from the French by Colin Campbell. 1909. (Conférences au Collège de France. Fondation Michonis.)

NEANDER, JOHANN AUGUST WILHELM, D.D. Antignostikus, or the Spirit of Tertullian. Translated from the German by J. E. Rylands. 1851. (German title: Antignostikus: Geist des Tertullianus.)

NEANDER, JOHANN AUGUST WILHELM, D.D. General History of the Christian Religion and Church. Translated from the German by Joseph Torrey. 1853. 9 vols. (German title: Allgemeine Geschichte der christlichen Religion und Kirche.)

NEUMANN, CARL FRIEDRICH. Marcions Glaubenssystem. 1866. See *Zeitschrift für die Hist. Theol.*, Bd IV.

OEHLER, FRANCISCUS. Corpus Haereseologicum. Berolini, 1856–1861. 3 vols.

OPPERT, JULIUS. Le Peuple et la Langue des Mèdes. Paris, 1879.

ORELLI, JOHANN CASPAR von. Inscriptionum Latinarum selectarum amplissima collectio. Turin, 1828. 2 vols.

PARISOTTI, A. Ricerche sul culto di Iside e Serapide. Roma, 1888. (Studi e Documenti di Storia e Diritto.)

PARTHEY, GUSTAV. Zwei griechische Zauberpapyri des Berliner Museums. Berlin, 1866. (Extract from *Abhandlungen der Kgl. Preuss. Akad. der Wissenschaften*, 1865.)

PATER, WALTER. Plato and Platonism. 1901.

PATRICK, JOHN, D.D. The Apology of Origen in reply to Celsus. 1892.

PERROT, G. Mélanges présentées à, etc. Paris, 1903.

PHILASTER OF BRESCIA. Philastrii Episcopi Brixiensis Haereseon Catalogus. See Oehler, Corpus Haereseologicum, vol. I.)

PINCHES, THEOPHILUS GOLDRIDGE, LL.D. The Religious Ideas of the Babylonians. 1893. See *Victoria Institute Transactions*.

Pistis Sophia, see VALENTINUS, *infra*.

PLUTARCH OF CHAERONEA. Über Isis und Osiris, nach neuverglichenen Handschriften mit Übersetzung und Erläuterungen herausgegeben. Von Gustav Parthey. Berlin, 1850.

POGNON, H., Membre de l'Institut. Inscriptions Mandaïtes des Coupes de Khouabir. Paris, 1898.

PORTER, FRANK C. Apocrypha. See Hastings, Dict. of Bible, *s.h.v.*

POTTIER, E. La Collection Louis de Clercq. Paris, 1906. (Conférences au Musée Guimet. Bibl. de Vulgarisation, t. XIX (1906).)

PRAEDESTINATUS. De Haeresibus Liber. See Oehler, Corpus Haereseologicum, vol. I.

PURSER, LOUIS CLAUDE, etc. Orphica. See Smith's Dictionary of Greek and Roman Antiquities, *s.h.v.*

Quarterly Review, The. 1890, etc. In progress.

RADLOFF, W. Chuastuanift, das Bussgebet der Manichäer. St Petersburg, 1909.

RAMSAY, Sir WILLIAM MITCHELL. The Church in the Roman Empire. 1893.
—— The Cities and Bishoprics of Phrygia. Oxford, 1895. 2 vols.
—— St Paul, the Traveller and the Roman Citizen. 1897.
—— A Historical Commentary on St Paul's Epistle to the Galatians. 1899.

RAWLINSON, GEORGE, Canon, etc. History of Herodotus. New Edition. 1862. 4 vols.

—— The Sixth Oriental Monarchy. 1873.

RAWLINSON, Sir HENRY CRESWICKE, K.C.B., etc. The Cuneiform Inscriptions of Western Asia. 1861, etc. In progress.

RAYET, OCTAVE. Inscriptions du Musée de l'École Évangélique à Smyrne. Paris, 1877. See *Revue Archéologique*, nouv. sér. t. XXIII (1877).

READE, WILLIAM WINWOOD. The Martyrdom of Man. 1910.

Recueil de Travaux relatifs à la Philologie et à l'Archéologie Égyptiennes et Assyriennes. Publié sous la direction de G. Maspero. Paris, 1870, etc. In progress.

REINACH, ADOLPHE. Review of Em. Schmidt's Kultübertragungen. See *Revue de l'Histoire des Religions*, t. LXVIII (1913).

REINACH, SALOMON. Cultes, Mythes, et Religions. Paris, 1909–1912. 4 vols.

Religions, International Congress of. *Transactions*. Oxford, 1908.

RENAN, JOSEPH ERNEST. Les Apôtres. Paris, 1866. (Les Origines du Christianisme.)

—— L'Antéchrist. Paris, 1873 (*id.*).

—— Les Évangiles. Paris, 1877 (*id.*).

—— L'Église Chrétienne. Paris, 1879 (*id.*).

—— Marc Aurèle. Paris, 1882 (*id.*).

—— The Influence of the Institutions, Thought and Culture of Rome on Christianity. Translated by Charles Beard. 1884. (Hibbert Lectures.)

—— Histoire du Peuple d'Israel. Paris, 1887. 5 vols.

RÉVILLE, ALBERT. Les Religions des Peuples Non-civilisés. Paris, 1883. 2 vols.

RÉVILLE, JEAN. La Religion à Rome sous les Sévères. Paris, 1886.

—— Le Quatrième Évangile. Paris, 1901.

REVILLOUT, EUGÈNE. Les Décrets de Rosette et de Canope. Paris, 1877. See *Revue Archéologique* for 1877.

—— Les Arts Égyptiens. Paris, 1880. See *Revue Égyptologique* for 1880.

—— Le Livre d'Incantation du Nome de Pandje (Oxyrinque). Planchettes Bilingues. See *Revue Égyptologique* for 1882 and 1892.

Revue Archéologique, IIIᵉ série. Paris, 1883, etc. In progress.

Revue Critique d'Histoire et de Littérature. Paris, 1866, etc. In progress.

Revue des Deux Mondes, IIIᵉ période. Paris, 1874, etc. In progress.

Revue Égyptologique. Paris, 1880, etc. In progress.

Revue des Études anciennes. Bordeaux, 1899, etc. In progress.

Revue des Études grecques. Paris, 1888, etc. In progress. (Published by L'Association pour l'encouragement des Études grecques.)

Revue des Études juives. Paris, 1881, etc. In progress. (Published by la Société des Études juives.)

Revue de l'Histoire des Religions. Paris, 1880, etc. In progress. (*Annales du Musée Guimet*. Quoted *infra* as R.H.R.)

Revue d'Histoire et Littérature Religieuses. Paris, 1910, etc. In progress.

Revue de l'Instruction publique en Belgique. Mons, 1865, etc. In progress.

ROBERT, CARL. Genethliakon. Berlin, 1910. (*Festschrift* on 60th birthday.)

ROBINSON, J. ARMITAGE, D.D., etc. Appendix to the Apology of Aristides (by J. Rendel Harris). Cambridge, 1891. (Cambridge Texts and Studies, vol. I, No. 1.)

ROBIOU, FÉLIX. De quelques MSS. Gréco-Égyptiens du Louvre. Paris, 1884. See Graux, Mélanges.

ROCHAT, E. Essai sur Mani et sa Doctrine. Genève, 1897.

ROGERS, ROBERT WM, LL.D., etc. The Religion of Babylonia and Assyria. 1908. 2 vols.

ROSCHER, WILHELM HEINRICH. Lexikon der Mythologie. Leipzig, 1889, etc. In progress.

ROSENBERG, FRÉDÉRIC. Le Livre de Zoroastre. St Petersburg. 1904.

ROSSI, FRANCISCO. Di alcuni MSS. Copti nella Biblioteca Nazionale di Torino. Turin, 1883. (*Memorie della Reale Accademia delle Scienze di Torino*, 2ᵃ serie, t. XLIII.)

Royal Asiatic Society of Great Britain and Ireland. Journal. 1839, etc. In progress. (Quoted *infra* as *J.R.A.S.*)

Royal Society of Literature. *Transactions.* 2nd series. 1843, etc. In progress.

RUELLE, G. E. Le Chant des Sept Voyelles Grecques. See *Revue des Études Grecques*, 1889.

RZACH, ALOIS. Sibyllina Oracula. Prague, 1891.

SALMON, GEORGE, D.D., etc. Caulacau. See Smith, Dictionary of Christian Biography, *s.h.v.*

—— Clementines. See *idem, s.h.v.*

—— Gnosticism. See *idem, s.h.v.*

—— Hippolytus Romanus. See *idem, s.h.v.*

—— Jaldabaoth. See *idem, s.h.v.*

—— Marcion. See *idem, s.h.v.*

—— Saturninus. See *idem, s.h.v.*

—— Simon Magus. See *idem, s.h.v.*

—— Valentinus. See *idem, s.h.v.*

—— The Cross References in the Philosophumena. Dublin, 1885. See *Hermathena*, No. XI (1885).

SANDAY, WILLIAM, D.D., etc. The Gospels in the Second Century. Oxford, 1876.

Savans, Journal des. See *Journal des Savans.*

SAYCE, ARCHBALD HENRY, D.D. The Ancient Empires of the East. 1884.

—— The Astronomy and Astrology of the Babylonians. 1874. See *T.S.B.A.*, vol. III (1874).

—— The Religions of Ancient Egypt and Babylonia. Edinburgh, 1902. (Gifford Lectures.)

SCHMIDT, CARL, Lic.D., etc. (of Berlin University). Gnostische Schriften in Koptischer Sprache aus dem Codex Brucianus. Leipzig, 1892. (Texte und Untersuchungen of Gebhardt and Harnack.)

—— Koptisch-gnostisch Schriften. Erster Bd. Leipzig, 1905. (Die Griechischen Christlicher Schriftsteller der ersten Drei Jahrhunderte. Herausg. von der Kirchenväter-Commission der Kgl. Preuss. Akad. der Wissenschaften.)

SCHMIDT, CHARLES GUILLAUME ADOLPHE (of Strasburg). Histoire et Doctrine de la Secte des Cathares ou Albigeois. Paris, 1849. 2 vols.

SCHMIDT, MORIZ, and MERX, A. Die Assumptio Mosis. Halle, 1868. See *Archiv für wissenschaftliche Erforschung des Alten Testaments.* 1868.

SCHMIEDEL, PAUL W., D.D. Simon Magus. See Cheyne's Encyclopaedia Biblica, *s.h.v.*

—— Community of Goods. See *idem, s.h.v.*

SCHÜRER, EMIL. History of the Jewish People in the times of Jesus Christ. Translated from the German by Sophia Taylor and P. Christie. Edinburgh, 1865. 8 vols. (German title: Geschichte des jüdischen Volkes im Zeitalter Jesu Christi.)

SCOT, REGINALD. The Discoverie of Witchcraft. 1651.

Scottish Review, The. 1883, etc. In progress.

SKEAT, WALTER WILLIAM. Malay Magic: an Introduction to the Folklore and Popular Religion of the Malay Peninsula. 1900.

SMITH, Sir CECIL HARCOURT, LL.D. Orphic Myths on Attic Vases. 1890. See *Journal of Hellenic Studies*, 1890.

SMITH, R. TRAVERS. Ephraim the Syrian. See Smith's Dictionary of Christian Biography, *s.h.v.*

SMITH, Sir WILLIAM, D.C.L. A Dictionary of Greek and Roman Antiquities. 1890.

SMITH, Sir WILLIAM, and WACE, HENRY, D.D., etc. A Dictionary of Christian Biography, Literature, Sects, and Doctrines. 1877–1887. 4 vols.

Société Nationale des Antiquaires de France. *Mémoires,* 6ᵉ série. Paris, 1891, etc. In progress.

Society of Antiquaries of London. *Archaeologia :* Miscellaneous Tracts relating to Antiquity. 1770, etc. In progress.

Society of Biblical Archaeology. *Transactions.* 1872–1893. 9 vols. (Quoted as *T.S.B.A.*)

—— *Proceedings.* 1879, etc. In progress. (Quoted *infra* as *P.S.B.A.*)

Society for the Promotion of Hellenic Studies. The *Journal of Hellenic Studies.* 1880, etc. In progress. (Quoted *infra* as *J.H.S.*)

SÖDERBLOM, NATHAN. La Vie Future d'après le Mazdéisme. Paris, 1901. (*Annales du Musée Guimet.* Bibl. d'Études, t. IX.)

Sphinx : Revue critique embrassant le domaine entier de l'Égyptologie. Upsala (1896, etc.). In progress.

STÄHELIN, H. Die Gnostischen Quellen Hippolyts. Leipzig, 1890.

STANLEY, ARTHUR PENRHYN, D.D., etc. Lectures on the History of the Jewish Church. 1883. 3 vols.

STEINDORFF, GEORGE, Ph.D. Religion of the Ancient Egyptians. New York, 1905. (American Lectures on the History of Religions.)

STEPHANI, LUDOLPH. Compte-rendu de la Commission Impériale Archéologique. St Petersburg, 1850.

STEPHEN OF BYZANTIUM. Ἄγραι. See Etymologicum Magnum, *s.h.v.*

STOCK, ST GEORGE. Simon Magus. See Encyclopaedia Britannica, *s.h.v.*

STOKES, G. T., B.D. Manes. See Smith's Dictionary of Christian Biography, *s.h.v.*

STOOP, EM. DE, Ph.D., etc. La Diffusion du Manichéisme dans l'Empire romain. Gand, 1909.

STRACK, HERMANN L. Le Sang et la fausse accusation du Meurtre Rituel. Traduite de l'allemande par Salomon Reinach. Paris, n.d. [1892?]. (German title: Blutaberglauber in der Menschheit.)

STRONG, HERBERT A., LL.D. The Syrian Goddess, being a translation of Lucian's *de Dea Syria*. Edited by John Garstang, D.Sc. 1913.

STÜBE, R., Ph.D. Jüdisch-Babylonische Zaubertexte. Halle, 1895.

SYKES, PHILIP M., C.M.G., etc. Historical Notes on Khurassan. 1910. See *Journal of the Royal Asiatic Society* for 1910.

TALBOT, H. Fox. On Ineffable Names. 1865. See *Transactions of the Royal Society of Literature*, 2nd ser., vol. VIII (1866).

TARN, WILLIAM WOODTHORPE. Antigonos Gonatas. Oxford, 1913.

TAYLOR, C. Pirke Aboth. Cambridge, 1877.

TERTULLIAN. Quinti Septimii Florentis Tertulliani quae supersunt omnia. Edidit Franciscus Oehler. Lipsiae, 1853–1861. 3 vols.

TERTULLIAN, Pseudo- (Victorinus of Pettau?). Liber adversus omnes Haereses. See Oehler, Corpus Haereseologicum, vol. I.

THEON ALEXANDRINUS. Commentaire sur le premier livre de l'Almagest de Ptolémée. Par l'Abbé Halma. Paris, 1821. 2 vols.

THOMPSON, M. S. The Asiatic or Winged Artemis. 1909. See *Journal of Hellenic Studies*, vol. XXIX (1909).

TIELE, CORNELIUS PETRUS, Theol.D., etc. Elements of the Science of Religion. 1897. 2 vols. (Gifford Lectures.)

—— The Religion of the Iranian Peoples. Part I (all published). Translated from the German by G. K. Nariman. Bombay, 1912. (German title: Geschichte der Religion im Altertum bis auf Alexander den Grossen. Bd II. Die Religion bei den iranischen Völkern.)

TURMEL, J. L'Angélologie depuis le faux Denys l'Aréopagite. Paris, 1898. See *Revue d'histoire et littérature religieuses*, t. IV (1898).

TYLOR, Sir EDWARD BURNETT, D.C.L., etc. Primitive Culture. 1871. 2 vols.

VALENTINUS. Pistis Sophia. Opus gnosticum Valentino adjudicatur e codice M. S. Coptico Londinensi. Descripsit et Latine vertit M. G. Schwartze. Edidit J. H. Petermann. Berlin, 1851.

VELLAY, CHARLES.   Le Culte et les Fêtes d'Adonis-Thammuz.   Paris,
1904.   (*Annales du Musée Guimet.*   Bibl. d'Études, t. XVI.)

VETTIUS VALENS.   Vettii Valentis Anthologiarum libri.   Primum edidit
Gulielmus Kroll.   Berolini.   1908.

Victoria Institute.   *Journal of the Transactions.*   1866, etc.   In progress.

VITEAU, J., et MARTIN, FRANÇOIS.   Les Psaumes de Salomon.   Paris,
1911.

WESSELY, KARL, Ph.D., etc.   On the Spread of Judaeo-Christian Religious
Ideas among the Egyptians.   1886.   See *The Expositor,* ser. III,
vol. IV (1886).

—— Ephesia Grammata.   Wien, 1886.   (Zwölfter Jahresbericht über
das K.K. Franz-Joseph Gymnasium.)

—— Griechische Zauberpapyrus von Paris und London.   Wien, 1888.

—— Neue Griechische Zauberpapyri.   Wien, 1893.   (Denkschriften der
Kaiserlichen Akademie der Wissenschaften in Wien.   Philosophisch-
Historische Classe, Bd XLII.)

WEST, EDWARD WILLIAM.   Pahlavi Texts, Pts I–IV.   Oxford, 1880.
(Sacred Books of the East.   Vols. 5, 18, 24 and 37.)

WHINFIELD, E. H.   The Seven-headed Dragon.   1910.   See *Journal of
the Royal Asiatic Society.*

WIEDEMANN, ALFRED, Ph.D., etc.   The Ancient Egyptian Doctrine of
the Immortality of the Soul.   Translated from the German.   1895.
(German title: Die Unsterblichkeit der Seele nach altägyptischer
Lehre.)

—— The Religion of the Ancient Egyptians.   Translated from the German.   1897.   (German title: Die Religion der alter Ägypter.)

WILLIAMS-JACKSON, ABRAHAM VALENTINE, Prof., etc.   Zoroaster, the
Prophet of Ancient Iran.   New York, 1901.

WOODS, F. H., B.D.   The Hope of Israel.   Edinburgh, 1896.

Xenia.   Athens, 1912.

YUNG, ÉMILE, M.D.   Hypnotisme et Spiritisme: les faits positifs et les
faits présumés.   Genève, 1890.   (Conférences publiques prononcées
dans l'Aula de l'Université de Genève.)

ZABOROWSKI, M. S.   Les Peuples Aryens d'Asie et d'Europe.   Paris,
1908.

Zeitschrift für Ägyptische Sprache und Alterthumskunde.   Leipzig, 1863, etc.
In progress.   (Quoted *infra* as *Ä.Z.*)

Zeitschrift für historische Theologie.   Leipzig, 1852, etc.   In progress.

INDEX

Abel, Ophite story of, ii. 52; and Manichaean, ii. 304

Aberamenthôu, name used in Magic Papyri and *Pistis Sophia*, i. 102. *See* Jesus, *Texts of Saviour*

Abiuth, receiver of Ariel in *Texts of Saviour*, ii. 186

Abraham, named in Mag. Pap., i. 106 *n*. 6; ii. 34; an astrologer *apud* Artapanus, i. 173; inspired by Ialdabaoth, ii. 53; Bosom of, in Marcion's system, ii. 211

Abraxas, in system of Basilides, ii. 90, 92

Abydos, gods of, i. 33 *n*. 1; excavations at, i. 36

Achaea, worship of Goddesses Twain in, i. 135; Cilician pirates deported to, ii. 229

Achaemenides, Persian religion under, i. 122; ii. 234

Achamoth, Sophia of Ophites, ii. 45 *n*. 1; called the Mother by Valentinus, ii. 112 *n*. 3; the Sophia Without of Valentinus, ii. 117 *n*. 2; baptism in name of, by Marcus, ii. 189 *n*. 1. *See* Sophia (2)

Acheron, Isis shining in, i. 60

Achilles, his horror of Hades, i. 59, 150; his flattery of Zeus, i. 95; his purification by Ulysses, i. 121 *n*. 4

Achrammachamari, name of Great Propator in *Texts of Saviour* and Mag. Pap., ii. 142 *n*. 2

Acropolis, sacred things of Eleusis lodged in, i. 39; Serapeum built opposite, i. 52

Acrostics, use of, in Jewish, Greek and Christian literature, i. 169 *n*. 1; in Valentinian epitaph, ii. 129 *n*. 3

Adam, the protoplast, Ophite story of, ii. 52, 58, 70; and Manichaean, ii. 299; and neo-Manichaean, ii. 329

Adam or Adamos, god of Samothrace, i. 139 *n*. 1; ii. 54 *n*. 6

Adamas, the Ophite, the First Man or Great Light, ii. 38; gives birth to Second Man or Son, *ibid.*; called Father-and-Son, ii. 39; androgyne, ii. 40; forms triad with Holy Spirit, ii. 41 *nn*. 2, 3; all things except matter contained in, ii. 44 *n*. 2, 64; all light returns to, ii. 65, 80; called Caulacau, ii. 94 *n*. 3. *See* First Man, Caulacau, Hades

Adamas, king of the Twelve Aeons in *Pistis Sophia*, his rebellion, ii. 48 *n*. 4, 152 *n*. 1; place of, ii. 137 *n*. 3; ruler of Zodiac, ii. 152; delays redemption of souls, ii. 153; sends demon in shape of flying arrow, ii. 156; probably Diabolos or Cosmocrator of Valentinus, ii. 163. *See* Sabaoth Adamas

Adamas of the Light, in neo-Manichaeism, ii. 325; slayer of monster, ii. 329

Adonai, epithet of Zeus in Mag. Pap., i. 106; in Coptic, ii. 46 *n*. 3; son of Ophite Sophia, ii. 47; ruler of planetary sphere in Diagram, ii. 69; meaning of name of, ii. 71 *n*. 1; address of soul to, ii. 72

Adonis, wailed for in Athens, *temp.* Alcibiades, i. 16; Dying God of Mediterranean, i. 37; Asiatic form of Dionysos, i. 47; identified with Osiris, i. 55; identified with Dionysos by Orphics, i. 137, 145; identified with Dionysos at Eleusis, i. 139 *n*. 1; androgyne, i. 185; Ophites attend mysteries of, ii. 21, 54; identified with Phrygian god, ii. 31; fiend in hell in *Texts of Saviour*, ii. 186

Advent, the. *See* Parusia

Aegean, islands of, birthplace of gods, i. 16, 52; early worship of Alexandrian gods in, i. 52; and of Eleusinian, ii. 135

of, ii. 347, 349; Apocrypha of, ii. 351; Imperial laws against, ii. 356

Manichaeism, prominence of First Man in, i. lxi; and of Sophia, ii. 45 *n.* 1; Virgin of Light in, ii. 137 *n.* 3; like Avesta, condemns magic, ii. 275 *n.* 2; contrasted with Mithraism, ii. 277, 278; opposed to Judaism, ii. 278; first rebellion against Ardeshîr's religious reform, ii. 284, 285; owes little to Egypt or Buddhism, ii. 286; simplicity of teaching of, ii. 287; its quinary system, ii. 290, 291, 330; its cosmology like that of *Pistis Sophia*, ii. 295 *n.* 1, 296 *n.* 1; its androgyne virgin, ii. 298, 299 *n.* 1, 328, 329; its system of transmigration, ii. 308; teaches eternal punishment, ii. 309; its Ten Commandments, ii. 314, 341, 342; its *Burkhans* or Messengers, ii. 336; its fasts and alms, ii. 314, 344–347; Constantine's enquiry into, ii. 356; favoured by Julian and the philosophers, *ibid.*; ends with Albigenses, ii. 357

Marathon, Iacchos-song heard before Battle of, i. 65 *n.* 6. *See* Callias

Marcion, the heresiarch, groundless accusations of immorality against, i. 179 *n.* 2; ii. 206; differs from other Gnostics as to aeons, i. 187 *n.* 2; accusation of ambition against, ii. 8 *n.* 3; native of Pontus, ii. 9, 204; his followers alter his doctrines (Tertullian), ii. 27, 216, 217; ignores Sophia, ii. 45 *n.* 1, 214; contemporary of Valentinus, ii. 134 *n.* 1; his life and date, ii. 204, 205; his relations with Stoics, *ibid.*; wide-spread and longevity of heresy of, ii. 205, 206, 216; compared to Luther, ii. 207, 208; his alterations of Scripture, ii. 208, 209; his *Antitheses*, ii. 209, 213, 223; his Supreme Being, ii. 210; his Docetism, ii. 210, 211; his Demiurge the God of the Jews, ii. 211; his dislike of Judaism, 211, 212; his rejection of allegory, ii. 213; original nature of his teaching, ii. 214; anticipation of Protestant doctrines and practices, ii. 215, 216; his views as to matter, ii. 217; his influence on Church slight, ii. 222; Manes acquainted with his tenets, ii. 280, 283

Marcionites, the, endure till xth cent., ii. 206; their practices, ii. 207;

golden age of, last half of iind cent., ii. 216; their divisions, ii. 216, 217; their relations with Manichaeism, ii. 221, 222

Marcus, the heresiarch, his Cabalisms, i. 171 *n.* 1; ii. 9 *n.* 1, 129; accusations of immorality against, i. 179 *n.* 2; ii. 9 *n.* 1, 99, 128; his conjuring tricks, i. 202; ii. 129, 183 *n.* 1; a Jew, ii. 9 *n.* 1; his supposed companion Colarbasus, ii. 20 *n.* 1; a Valentinian (Irenaeus), ii. 99, 128; his life and practices, ii. 128, 129; possible connection of, with *Texts of Saviour*, ii. 187–189; and with Bruce Papyrus, ii. 193

Marcus Aurelius, the Emperor, Alexander of Abonoteichos at Court of, i. 24; ii. 202; his generals' victories over Persians, ii. 225, 226. *See* Avidius Cassius

Marcus Volusius, the aedile, his escape in dress of priest of Isis, i. 53

Marduk, the god, called by number 50, ii. 35 *n.* 4; name of, ineffable, ii. 37 *n.* 1. *See* Bel, Merodach

Mariamne, sister of Philip the Apostle, source of Ophite tradition (Hippolytus), ii. 26; mentioned in *Acta Philippi*, ii. 26 *n.* 2; a sect named after her, *ibid.*

Marks, the Five, the mystery of, in *Pistis Sophia*, ii. 141

Marriage, rejected by Orphics, i. 128; and by Essenes, i. 152; admitted by Simon Magus, i. 196, 202; rejected by Ophites, ii. 79, 80; and by Saturninus, ii. 89; admitted by Valentinus. ii. 129; rejected by *Texts of Saviour*, ii. 174; by Marcion, ii. 207, 215; by certain Mithraists, ii. 260; by Manichaean Elect, ii. 313

Mars, the god, why identified with Ares, i. 17; on Mithraic monuments, ii. 238; devotion of Julian to, ii. 269. *See* Ares

Mars, the planet, presides over a seventh part of terrestrial things, i. 116; a malefic in astrology, i. 118 *n.* 1; one of the seven heavens of Ophites, ii. 48, 74 *n.* 2; a ruler of the sidereal world in *Texts of Saviour*, ii. 182. *See* Correspondences

Martha, the sister of Mary, interlocutor of Jesus in *Pistis Sophia*, ii. 157

Martial, the poet, quoted, i. 54, 66, 67

Phrygia, home of Ophites, i. lx; ii. 28; birthplace of most legends of Dying God, i. 38; worship of Orphic Sabazius comes from, i. 137; ii. 28; "Mysteries of the Mother" in, i. 143; Simonians scattered through (Theodoret), i. 199; meeting-place of different creeds, ii. 28; its government by priest-kings, ii. 29; worship of androgyne deity in, ii. 30, 67 *n.* 3; defection from Judaism of Ten Tribes in, ii. 32; prevalence of Jewish magicians in, *temp.* Apostles, ii. 33; is Jewish tradition responsible for Phrygian cosmogony? ii. 34, 35; mother of gods called Cybele in, ii. 40; great goddess of, perhaps derived from Ishtar, ii. 45 *n.* 1; traces of pantheism in, ii. 64; double axe used by gods of (Ramsay), ii. 67 *n.* 3; Ophites spread southward from, ii. 74; Stoic philosophy has a seat in, ii. 83

Phrygians, the, "first-born of men" (Apuleius), i. 56; why St Paul gives them summary of O.T. history, ii. 53 *n.* 2; Ophite interpretation of their mysteries, ii. 54; their belief in deification of man, ii. 56 *n.* 2; call Dionysos or Sabazius, Pappas, ii. 57

Phryne, belongs to Greek confraternity for foreign worship, i. 22

Piankhi, King of Egypt, abandons Egypt for Ethiopia after conquest, i. 31

Pindar, knows identification of Dionysos with Apollo, i. 48; describes blessedness of initiates into Mysteries, i. 59; supporter of Orphism, i. 122; his doctrine of transmigration, i. 129; his poems recited at games, i. 135; quoted, i. 48, 59, 123 *n.* 1, 129 *n.* 3, 134 *n.* 2

Piraeus, the, confraternities for foreign worships cluster in, i. 21; early confraternity of Serapiasts in, i. 52; courtezans principal members of confraternities in, i. 137; Mithraic monuments at, ii. 230

Pisistratids, the, date of flight of, and reform of Mysteries, i. 43 *n.* 2; Onomacritos flees with them to Persia, i. 121; some Orphic elements come into Greece, *temp.*, i. 122

Pistis or Faith, member of Valentinian Dodecad, ii. 101

Pistis Sophia, probable origin of name

of, ii. 151 *n.* 5, 160; found by Jesus alone in place below 13th Aeon, ii. 155; her history, ii. 155–157; meaning of allegory of, ii. 162; receives her adversary's place, *ibid.*; sometimes called Sophia only, ii. 179; reappears in *Texts of Saviour* as "the daughter of Barbelo," ii. 186; and in Bruce Papyrus, ii. 192

Pistis Sophia (the book), Jeû the First Man appears in, i. lxi; written in Greek, translated into Coptic, i. lxii, ii. 177; as in other apocrypha, Jesus changes his shape according to heavens he traverses, i. 191 *n.* 4, ii. 60 *n.* 1, 154; texts, translations, and summaries of, ii. 13; principal document of, Valentinian, ii. 17, 159–163; like Babylonians, makes heavens formed from powers of evil, ii. 44 *n.* 3; Ialdabaoth in, projection of ruler of material world, ii. 46 *n.* 3; features in common with *Ascensio Isaiae*, ii. 60 *n.* 1; puts stay of Jesus on earth after Resurrection at 12 years, ii. 61 *n.* 1; Eucharistic ceremony of, ii. 63 *n.* 1, 192; powers mentioned in Diagram and in, ii. 72 *nn.* 1, 3, 73 *n.* 2, 74 *n.* 1; "Receptacles" and Place of Truth in, ii. 103 *n.* 1; Valentinian document in, does not quote Fourth Gospel, ii. 117 *n.* 1, 177; MS. of, and its provenance, ii. 134, 135; heavens of Ineffable One and First Mystery not described in, ii. 146; Melchizidek seldom mentioned in, ii. 148 *n.* 1; thought by some the *Interrogations of Mary*, ii. 157; doctrine of interpretation in, ii. 157 *n.* 2; appears at first sight entirely Ophite, ii. 158; but more clearly Valentinian, ii. 159, 160, 161; Authades of, compared to Valentinus' Demiurge, ii. 162 *n.* 2; Adamas of, compared to Valentinus' Diabolos, ii. 163; nearness of Parusia dominant in part of, *ibid.*; description of Millennium in, ii. 164; lesser initiates must give passwords and seals, ii. 165, 169; mystery of the First Mystery is Baptism, ii. 168–170; mystery of the Ineffable One is the Eucharist, ii. 170–171; supreme revelation of book union with Jesus, ii. 171; "Mysteries of Light" not described in *P.S.*

the great goddess of, called Atargatis and other names, ii. 45 *n.* 1; Ophites spread throughout, ii. 76

Syria Dea. See Atargatis

Tacitus, the historian, on foundation of Alexandrian religion, i. 44 *n.* 1; describes bringing of Bryaxis' statue to Alexandria, i. 48 *n.* 3; calls Jews enemies of the human race, i. 167. *See* Manetho, Timotheos

Talmud, the, calls Babylonian Jews the Ten Tribes, ii. 32; existence of Cabala indicated in (Kuenen), ii. 35 *n.* 2; Yahweh's Council or *familia* (Taylor), ii. 43 *n.* 2; First Man in (Harvey), ii. 52 *n.* 1; Ophite stories find their way into, ii. 53

Tammuz, analogy of Dionysos with, i. 122 *n.* 3; women weeping for, in Temple of Jerusalem, ii. 32

Tarentum, unnamed poet of, author of "serpent father of bull" verse, ii. 39 *n.* 4

Tarn, Mr W. W., attributes story of Antigonos' deification to Antigonos Gonatas, i. 19 *n.* 1

Tarsus, a centre of Stoic teaching, ii. 83

Tartarus. *See* Gehenna

Tatian, the heresiarch, a disciple of Justin Martyr, becomes heretic from ambition, ii. 8 *n.* 3; his opinions and connection with Marcion, ii. 220

Taurobolium, the (or blood bath), adopted by Mithraists from worship of Cybele, ii. 259; allusion to, in St Augustine, ii. 261 *n.* 2

Taxo, mystic name of Antiochus Epiphanes' opponent in *Assumption of Moses*, i. 170

Taylor, Thomas, the Platonist, first translator of Orphic hymns, i. 141 *n.* 2

Telesterion, the, Hall of Initiations at Eleusis used for torchlight meeting, i. 39; no entry into, for uninitiated, i. 41; could not have held more than 3000, i. 65

Tenedos, temple of Alexandrian gods at, i. 53

Terebinthus, name of Manes' teacher, ii. 285, 286; also called Buddha, ii. 285; suggested meaning of name, ii. 285 *n.* 4

Termessus, worship of Alexandrian gods at, i. 53

Tertullian, interest of heathen in early centuries in ethical questions, i. xlix *n.* 1; ii. 86; supposed astonishment of, at *post*-Constantinian ritual (Gibbon), i. 85; first to formulate doctrine of Trinity (Harnack), i. 89 *n.* 2; accuses Gnostics of magic and astrology, i. 109 *n.* 1; says Valentinians give heavens reason and make angels of them, i. 187 *n.* 2; tract *Adversus omnes Haereses* wrongly ascribed to, ii. 10 *n.* 1, 25; accuses Gnostics of concealing their opinions, ii. 18 *n.* 1; the like of innovating on doctrines of their leaders, ii. 27, 28; makes Valentinus give a consort to Bythos, ii. 96; his jests on piled-up heavens of Valentinians, ii. 99; his explanation of names of Valentinian Ogdoad, ii. 99, 100; says Valentinus becomes heretic because not made bishop, ii. 117; date of Valentinus' separation from Church, ii. 118; his own heretical views on Trinity, ii. 122; his formal heresy Montanism, ii. 123 *n.* 1; describes respect paid by primitive Church to martyrs, ii. 127; says Gnostics make adherents in time of persecution, *ibid.*; refers to baptism for dead, ii. 168 *n.* 4; "the Sophia not of Valentinus, but of Solomon," ii. 178; had probably read the *Pistis Sophia*, ii. 179; his account of Marcion's life, ii. 204; of Marcion's repentance and death, ii. 205; "Marcionites make Churches as wasps make nests," ii. 206; his testimony to good morals of Marcion and Marcionites, *ibid.*; on Marcion's rejection of all Gospels but Luke's, ii. 208; *Antitheses* of Marcion can be reconstructed from refutation of, ii. 209; his *dictum* that Marcion can never prove existence of highest God, ii. 210 *n.* 2; on Marcion's anti-Jewish views, ii. 211; on Marcion's dealings with Pauline Epistles, ii. 212; controversy between Marcion and T. recommended to Modernists (Foakes-Jackson), ii. 215 *n.* 1; says Marcionites sect largest but one, ii. 216; his sophistry in refutation of Marcion, ii. 218; quotes Lucian the Marcionite's doctrine on resurrection, ii. 220; "Mithras is my crown," ii. 245, 253 *n.* 3; says initiate into Mithraic mys-